The Illustrated
WORLD
ATLAS

The Illustrated

WORLD

ATLAS

CRESCENT BOOKS

NEW YORK

Edited by
B. M. Willett
Cartographic Editor

Contents

The World Today

Contributors
John Chesshire, Science Policy Research Unit, Sussex University;
Dr Richard Crockett, Institute of Geological Sciences; Arthur Kilgore,
Gordon MacKerron, Science Policy Research Unit, Sussex University;
Pauline Marstrand, Science Policy Research Unit, Sussex University;
Professor J.H. Paterson, Department of Geography, Leicester University;
John Rowley, Editor of *People*, the journal of the International Planned
Parenthood Federation; Howard Rush, Science Policy Research Unit,
Sussex University; Robert Stewart.

Illustration Acknowledgements
The publishers would like to thank the following individuals and
organizations for their kind permission to reproduce the photographs in this
section; Ardea, London; Paul Brierley; Camera Press Ltd.; Bruce Coleman
Ltd.; *The Daily Telegraph*; Susan Griggs Agency Ltd; Maldwyn Glover;
The John Hillelson Agency Ltd.; Alan Hutchison Library; Picturepoint Ltd.;
Rex Features Ltd.; John Topham Picture Library; Transworld Feature
Syndicate; Zefa Picture Library.

Library of Congress Cataloging-in-Publication Data

The Illustrated world atlas.
  Includes index.
  1. Atlases
G1021.14 1987 912 86-675542
ISBN 0-517-63607-7

Printed and bound in Hong Kong

Foreword

This World Atlas presents the reader with two complementary views of the world. The maps and index are a detailed source of reference on the world as it is today while the introductory essays describe many of the important aspects of life on this planet at the end of the twentieth century, and consider what the future may bring in a world where changes take place at an accelerating pace.

The maps are designed to show where places are and to make available a large quantity of information about them.

The Idea of Location There are two related but really quite different kinds of location – absolute and relative. By absolute location is meant the identification of a point on the surface of the earth by reference to a network of lines composed of parallels of latitude and meridians of longitude. The numbering of parallels begins at the Equator and continues as degrees of a quarter circle to the Poles (90°), both North and South. The meridians are numbered from the Prime Meridian, which passes through Greenwich, England, to 180° either East or West.

Relative location means the identification of a place in relation not to the network just described, but to other places or areas. For example, Greenwich is (relatively) located in Great Britain, in England, near the mouth of the River Thames, about 10 miles East of London. If you ask where Greenwich is, any of these answers could be appropriate.

Regional Maps There are 65 pages of regional maps in the atlas, containing a wealth of detail. Information given includes landforms and drainage features and selected aspects of human occupation such as settlements, railways, highways, canals, pipelines, and political boundaries. Surface relief is brought out by combining contours with layer-colouring and relief-shading.

Layer-colouring serves to mark off one range of elevation from the next, and each map contains in its margins an altitude scale which indicates in metres the values of the contours employed. The layer-colouring also extends below sea-level, and shows the continental shelf.

Relief-shading serves to emphasize changes in elevation, and, in addition, contributes a three-dimensional quality to the land surface.

Other natural features such as drainage – rivers, lakes, reservoirs and canals – are shown in conventional blue, and transportation is shown in black for railways, in red for major highways.

The settlements shown on the maps have been classified into nine categories, reflecting size of population and importance.

The regional maps are both physical and political in character. All international boundaries are reinforced with red for clarity and emphasis, and provincial and other sub-national boundaries are shown for a number of major countries.

World and Continental Maps Physical and political maps of the world introduce the atlas and each continental section similarly begins with summary physical and political maps.

Scale The importance of scale, and of distinguishing between maps at different scales, cannot be overestimated. Thus, the map of the continent of Africa (page 48) is shown at a scale of 1:40,000,000 whereas the map of East Africa (page 52) is drawn at a scale of 1:7,500,000. A larger-scale map means that very much more can be shown of terrain, of settlement, of transportation and other features and such scales are used for parts of the world where the users' interests are likely to require them.

The Spelling of Place Names In this atlas, the principle followed is that, for settlements at least, and where the Roman alphabet is employed, the indigenous spellings are used, except for a relatively few places which are so well known that the indigenous spelling would be confusing to the reader. For many of the names in this latter group alternative spellings are also given.

In cases where the Roman alphabet is not employed in the native language, transliteration and romanization are required. In these cases, the recommendations of the U.S. Board on Geographic Names and the U.K. Permanent Committee on Geographical Names are followed wherever possible.

Index The index at the back of the atlas contains over 30,000 place names. Reference is given to the largest-scale map on which the place appears, and this is followed by a description of the absolute location of the place in terms of latitude and longitude.

The World Today

The planet earth

THE earth was formed approximately four-and-a-half billion years ago, although some of the materials that form its surface today may have been laid in place, by the action of rivers for example, only yesterday. By contrast to the age of the planet, the history of man on earth dates back only one million years, and the period of man's occupance of which we have any direct knowledge represents only a minute fraction of this shorter span of time.

During this short period of time, nevertheless, human beings have developed a remarkable variety of races, languages and cultures. Since the earth is a sphere, natural conditions of temperature, landscape and fertility range widely between polar and tropical, and some of the variety of mankind's development is clearly due to this variety in nature. Man has adapted to living in both hot and cold climates, and not only his lifestyle but some of his institutions, such as religion, reflect this adaptation. Yet there is a much greater variety in human life-forms and customs than can be accounted for by environment alone. For one thing, members of the same race, or language group, may be bitterly opposed to one another on political or religious grounds. For another, a sense of belonging draws people together in national or tribal groupings, which develop their own particular means of cultural expression.

Basic resources
Man's primary need is his own life support. Alone among the planets, as far as we know, the earth provides the conditions necessary to sustain life. These conditions we know as resources. Fundamental to the resource structure of the earth is the energy of the sun: it is the power plant that drives all other systems. At a secondary level are the mineral deposits, soils and water on the earth; and thirdly, there are the plants that support animal life, and those animals which exist by preying, species upon species. All these can be classed as the earth's natural resources.

At the highest level, where man exists in total isolation from the natural world, there is a further resource component: what is normally referred to as human resources. These are represented by the ability of man to think, work, invent and find uses for natural materials; to apply skill or power to these materials and transform them. Many animals can build them-

selves a home in ways that display great engineering skill. Most creatures, however, can only build one kind of structure. Man can build a whole range of structures and design new forms to suit his needs as he anticipates them.

Unequal distribution
The distribution of natural resources over the earth's surface is far from even. The whereabouts of mineral deposits depend on random events in a remote geological past; patches of fertile soil depend on events more recent but, to man, equally capricious — the flow of rivers or the movement of ice. When it comes to agriculture, the activity that has been basic to the survival of man and his increase in numbers, we find that, in round figures, 20 per cent of the earth's surface is barred to him by ice or perennially frozen soil; 20 per cent is composed of highlands too cold, rugged or barren for the cultivation of crops; 20 per cent is arid or desert, and between five and 10 per cent of the remainder has no soil, either because it has been scraped by ice or because it is permanently wet or flooded. This leaves only 30-35 per cent of the land surface where food production is possible, together with the oceans and whatever resources may be obtained from that source.

We can think of these natural resources as forming a cover, or coating, of varying thickness over the earth's surface: in some places it is deep and rich; in others it is for all practical purposes non-existent. In the same way, observation shows that human resources vary in quality from place to place. What, in fact, we are observing are different levels of technical ability and equipment among different peoples. Whereas, however, we can accept that natural resource distribution is either random or climatically determined, and therefore unchangeable, the explanation for different development levels of human resources is a much more complex matter.

Why have some nations or groups advanced more rapidly than others in technology? Why have some lost the lead they once had? A number of explanations have been offered in order to answer these questions. One of these is climatic — that some environments are more stimulating to effort and inventiveness than others. Some are racial — and may, in due course, become racist — arguing that one race is more gifted than another. Yet others

▲**The earth in space** *was an unfamiliar view we obtained when* *man first ventured beyond his natural environment: a small, rocky*

Pluto: diameter approx. 3,000km; 5,900 million km from sun

Neptune: diameter 49,500km; 4,496.6 million km from sun

focus on the structure of society, and the opportunities it affords for the use of individual talents and the freedom to innovate.

The key to exploitation
Each of these theories in isolation can be disproved, simply by pointing out the exceptions to it. Whatever the explanation, however, the fact is clear: that the ability to make use of what nature has provided in the way of resources varies critically from society to society, and that a high level of human resource input can provide a good living for people in areas, such as Scandinavia, where the natural endowment is meagre, while people may live on top of a veritable treasure chest of natural riches, as, it would appear, the Brazilians do, without necessarily obtaining the benefit of

them. It is, after all, only a few years since the oil states of the Middle East were among the world's poorest nations. If we think of the earth as a storehouse of natural wealth, then it is human ingenuity — the human resources represented by technical skills — which provides the key to open it.

Fortunately, no nation today possesses a monopoly of these skills, or is, for that matter, debarred from acquiring them. It is a slow process to do so, but one that can be speeded up if those societies which are relatively advanced will help those that are only at the beginning. Human resources have transformed parts of this planet once judged to be too cold, or too dry, or too poor to support the dense populations, either on the land or in the great cities, that now occupy them.

planet with much surface water and a dense atmosphere.

Plate Tectonics

The migration of the continents is a feature unique to Planet Earth. The complementary, almost jigsaw-puzzle fit of the coastlines on each side of the Atlantic Ocean inspired Alfred Wegener's theory of continental drift at the beginning of the twentieth century. The theory suggested that an ancient supercontinent, which Wegener named Pangaea, incorporated all of the earth's land masses and gradually split up to form the continents we see today. The modern theory of plate tectonics attributes continental drift to movements in crustal plates underlying the oceans as well as the continents. These movements are caused by the slow but continuous welling-up of material from deep within the earth along a series of mid-ocean ridges. Geological evidence that the continents once formed a single land mass is provided by distinctive rock formations that can be assembled into continuous belts when Africa and South America are lined up next to each other. Distribution of some plants and animals in the past, as well as ancient climatic zones, can only be explained by the theory of plate tectonics.

200 million years ago

135 million years ago

Present day

150 million years' time

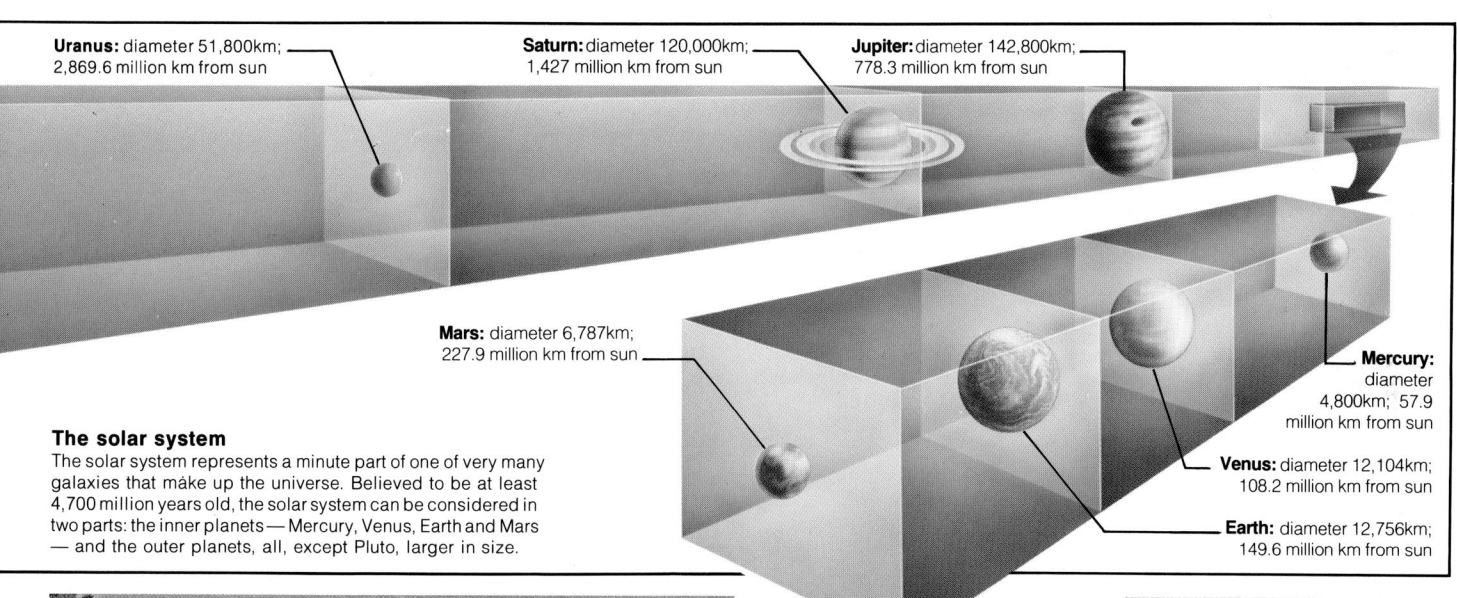

Uranus: diameter 51,800km; 2,869.6 million km from sun

Saturn: diameter 120,000km; 1,427 million km from sun

Jupiter: diameter 142,800km; 778.3 million km from sun

Mars: diameter 6,787km; 227.9 million km from sun

Mercury: diameter 4,800km; 57.9 million km from sun

Venus: diameter 12,104km; 108.2 million km from sun

Earth: diameter 12,756km; 149.6 million km from sun

The solar system

The solar system represents a minute part of one of very many galaxies that make up the universe. Believed to be at least 4,700 million years old, the solar system can be considered in two parts: the inner planets — Mercury, Venus, Earth and Mars — and the outer planets, all, except Pluto, larger in size.

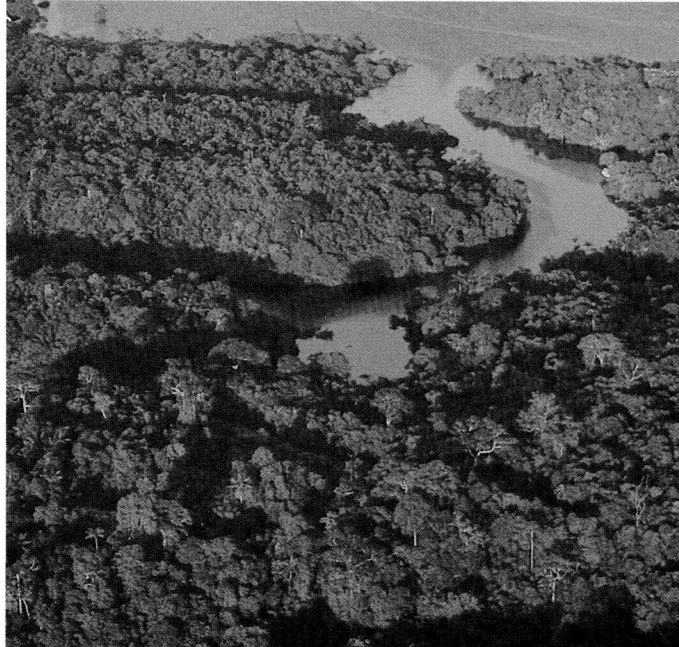

▶ **The evolution of man** *as a unique social and cultural animal has produced a variety of races, languages, religious and social systems. A political rally in China illustrates one aspect of culture.*

◀ **The Amazon basin** *is one of the few remaining wildernesses on earth. Such vast areas of forest play a vital role in global ecology — by helping to maintain the balance of oxygen in the atmosphere.*

▶ **Throughout history** *man has found various ways of expressing his beliefs in supernatural powers. Here, monks follow the teachings of the Dalai Lama in a temple in Tibet — one facet of religion today.*

3

A crowded planet

FROM man's earliest ancestors on the planet earth, more than one million years ago, until the beginnings of settled agriculture some 10,000 years ago, the number of human beings alive at any one time did not exceed five million. By 1800 the world was home to one billion people. The second billion was reached by 1930, the third by 1960 and the fourth billion by 1970. The likelihood is that the fifth billion will be reached by 1987 and that a sixth billion will be added by the end of the century, when United Nations demographers estimate that the earth will "carry" 6,127,000,000 human beings.

The key to population growth
What happens after that depends on the speed at which the rate of population growth slows down over the coming decade. The annual growth rate is believed to have peaked at about two per cent in 1970, declining to between 1.6 and 1.7 per cent today. This deceptively small statistic is adding some 80 million people to the world's population each year and, because the world's total population includes such a high proportion of young people who have yet to grow up and have children, it is going to take a long time for the population to stabilize at somewhere between eight and 15 billion, some time in the twenty-first century.

The cause of this extraordinary explosion in human numbers over the past 200 years lies essentially in declining death rates rather than in increasing birth rates. Medical advances and improved conditions of life first cut death rates in Europe. The subsequent explosion in the numbers surviving was partly masked by the massive exodus to new countries, with some 60 million migrants travelling to the Americas and elsewhere before World War II. An even greater and faster increase in numbers began in the developing countries of Asia, Africa and Latin America before World War II as a much more rapid drop in death rates followed the spread of scientific technology to prevent and control disease and improvements in the availability of food.

As death rates declined in Europe birth rates also slowly came down, and today population growth in all modern industrialized countries is low or non-existent. In a few cases, such as West Germany and Austria, the population has even begun to decrease. But less than one-third of the world's population lives in these developed regions, and it is among the two-thirds in the developing countries that population is growing fast. Although the rates of growth have begun to fall in many countries, the proportion of the world's population in the developing countries of Asia, Africa and Latin America will continue to rise until the year 2000.

The distribution of people
At the moment Europe remains the most densely populated area of the globe, with an average of 100 people per square kilometre. The vast territories of southern and eastern Asia are, however, not far behind, and within the next 100 years they are likely to have three times the density of present-day Europe, according to United Nations estimates. In Asia as a whole, population is likely to increase from 2.8 billion to 3.6 billion in the next 20 years. Africa, by contrast, is relatively lightly populated at present, though individual countries such as Egypt, Rwanda and Lesotho have high populations in relation to productive land. The African continent is likely to add another 400 million people to its 1979 population of 455 million by the turn of the century, while Latin America's population will grow from 360 million to some 600 million in the same period.

Of more concern to many governments than overall density of population is the distribution within national boundaries. The growth of cities is one of the most striking features of our time. At the beginning of this century there were only 250 million city dwellers in the world. Today 1,500 million people live in urban areas and by the year 2000, it is believed, more than half the world's population, or some 3,000 million people, will be living in towns and cities.

The call of the city
The growth of cities is partly the result of natural increase, but more significantly the result of migration from the countryside, where population growth often coincides with rural stagnation and a shortage of work. Unlike the situation in the nineteenth century, there are few unused fertile areas left in the world. And the only job opportunities are those which appear to beckon from the growing cities. Already one-third of the urban inhabitants in less-developed countries are squatters living on the fringes of cities such as Djakarta, Bombay, Calcutta, Rio de Janeiro, Manila and Mexico City. These are among the fastest growing settlements in the world today.

Taking both rural and urban areas of the developing world together, more than 40 per cent of the population is either unemployed or underemployed, two billion are continually undernourished and some 1,400 million are illiterate. The causes of such problems are complex, but rapid population growth makes all of them more difficult to solve. As a result, four-fifths of the developing world's population now live in countries which have adopted policies aimed at slowing down the rate of population growth.

Since the world conference on population in Bucharest in 1974, governments have increasingly come to realize that such policies stand the best chance of success if they involve social and development policies which create a wish for smaller families, as well as access to family planning information and services. The motivation for small families involves the reduction of infant and child mortality, the expansion of basic education, especially for girls, an increase in the income of the rural poor, a more equal distribution of wealth and — of particular importance — the improvement of the status of women in society. Where such measures have been taken along with the provision of family planning services, including access to early abortion and a range of fertility control methods, rapid declines in fertility have taken place. The most spectacular example in recent years has been China.

Millions of people in the developing world, however, have no access to modern birth control methods and, indeed, some governments, on religious grounds or for strategic reasons, actively discourage family planning programmes. With greater pressures being put upon the earth's limited resources, from agricultural land to mineral wealth, and the ever-increasing impact of man's activities on the environment, the prospect of further population growth poses many and varied problems.

▲ **Most of the world's poor** *live in appalling conditions. Having migrated to the cities in the hope of greater opportunities, many people find themselves in even worse surroundings. Shanty towns, such as this one in Sao Paulo, are home to a large proportion of the inhabitants of the world's fastest-growing cities.*

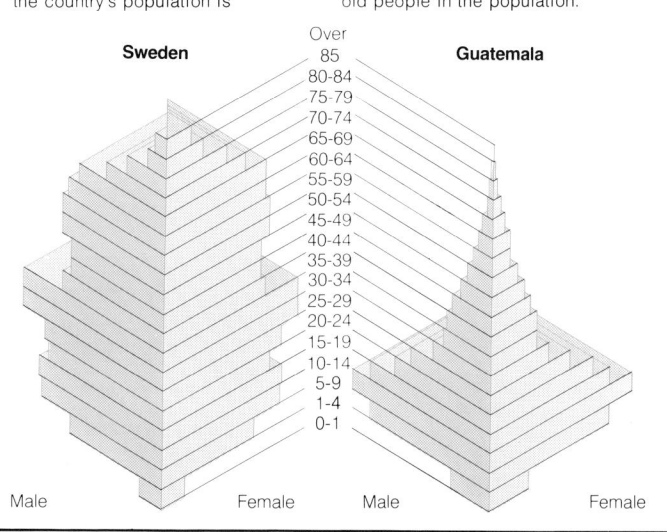

Age/sex structure

Age pyramids illustrate the differences in population structure between developed and developing countries. The broad base of the pyramid for Guatemala shows that the country's population is increasing rapidly. In general, as birth and death rates decline, such a diagram loses its pyramid shape and becomes barrel-shaped. This indicates an increasing number of old people in the population.

Sweden   **Guatemala**

Over 85
80-84
75-79
70-74
65-69
60-64
55-59
50-54
45-49
40-44
35-39
30-34
25-29
20-24
15-19
10-14
5-9
1-4
0-1

Male   Female   Male   Female

▲ **India,** *with the second-largest population in the world, has introduced many birth control methods. At this sterilization clinic many vasectomies are carried out at one session.*

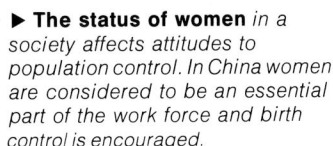

▶ **The status of women** *in a society affects attitudes to population control. In China women are considered to be an essential part of the work force and birth control is encouraged.*

▲ **Birth rates remain high** *in many of the less-developed countries. Large numbers of children are very often encouraged by the societies, for religious, economic and political reasons.*

World population in 1500

two million people

10 million

Present day population and projected population for the year 2000

20 million people

100 million

100 million (estimate for the year 2000)

By about 8000 BC there were approximately five million people on earth. From then on, numbers increased by between 0.04 and 0.06 per cent a year until about 1650. The "doubling time" of human numbers had been reduced from 1,500 to 200 years by 1800, by which time world population had reached one billion.

Environment in danger

ALL life on our planet is confined to a thin skin of earth, air and water that is no more than 10 kilometres thick. It depends for its healthy existence on green vegetation which turns sunlight into chemical energy and maintains the balance of oxygen and carbon dioxide in the atmosphere. On this process are based the complex food chains made up of many thousands of plant and animal species, all of which are vulnerable to the activities of man.

The mounting impact of man on the environment is partly the result of his increased numbers. It is also due to the enormous increase in industrial activity and consumption of the earth's resources, particularly in the countries of the northern hemisphere. A two per cent annual increase in population since the middle of this century has been accompanied by a four per cent annual increase in consumption, a rate of growth which, if maintained for a century, will increase consumption 50 times and create an even greater impact on the biological environment.

The impact of man

The oceans, grasslands, croplands and forests have all felt the impact of man's rapidly increasing exploitation of these resources for food, fuel and living space. Forests play a vital role in maintaining the ecological status quo, preserving watersheds, preventing soil erosion and the silting of dams, moderating climate and providing fuel, building materials and paper. But the destruction of trees for farmland and firewood has a long history, and by the middle of this century between one-third and one-half of the earth's original forest cover had gone.

Forest management in western Europe, the Soviet Union and North America now shows an awareness of the need to conserve existing woodland, while China is striving to undo the destruction of past generations. Almost everywhere in the developing world, however, the remaining tree cover is under pressure as the growing population increases the demand for firewood supplies and farmland. Serious deforestation is occurring in the Himalayas, causing erosion and flooding in the plains below, and similar problems are reported from eastern India, Pakistan, Thailand, the Philippines, Malaysia, Tanzania and elsewhere. The tropical forests

of southeast Asia, central and west Africa and Amazonia are also severely threatened, and with them the earth's richest store of rare plants and animals.

The loss of farmland

Arable land, which makes up one-tenth of the earth's land surface, is also under great pressure. The area of cropland is being reduced by serious erosion and conversion to non-agricultural use at a faster rate than new land is brought under the plough. Japan, for example, lost six per cent of cropland in the 1960s.

The oceans, too, have recently been exploited more intensively than ever before: the fish catch trebled from 21 to 72 million tonnes between 1950 and 1980. As a result, many areas have been overfished, particularly in the North Atlantic, where there have been sudden declines in catches of cod, haddock, sole and herring. The Peruvian anchovy has been grossly overfished and several species of whale have been hunted almost to the point of extinction.

The oceans are suffering also from another consequence of man's escalating consumption: the generation of excessive and dangerous wastes. The seas, which cover two-thirds of the earth's surface, have become a dustbin for oil, chemicals, radioactive materials, sewage, junk metal, pesticides and detergents, among many other products. Approximately one million tonnes of oil seep into the sea from ships and drilling rigs each year, and many inland seas and estuaries are now so heavily polluted that fish, if they survive at all, are not safe to eat. Pollution is also having its effect on human health through the air we breathe and the food and water we consume. Some 600,000 different chemicals are in daily use and every year several thousand new ones enter into significant use. Among the illnesses they have produced are parasitic infections, emphysema, heart disease and some cancers. With polluted rivers running across national frontiers and acid rain falling over a wide area of Europe, pollution can now be considered an international problem.

A growing concern

The long-term effects of some of man's activities are uncertain. There is considerable concern about the fluorocarbons contained

Environmental pollution

The possibility that the earth's climate may be changing has been a subject much discussed in recent years. Untypical, "freak" weather during the 1970s may well be the result of natural trends of cooling and warming that the earth has experienced throughout its history, but there are suggestions that the activities of man may fundamentally alter the world's climatic patterns. A manifestation of this is what is known as the "greenhouse effect". Carbon dioxide in the atmosphere is transparent to the shortwave infra-red heat radiation from the sun, but opaque to longwave infra-red radiation emitted from warm objects on earth. What this means, in effect, is that heat can get in but it cannot get out as easily. Measurements show that the level of carbon dioxide in the air has increased significantly during this century, possibly by as much as 15 per cent. The combustion of fossil fuels produces carbon dioxide and is the chief culprit, but ploughing land also releases large amounts of soil-held gas into the atmosphere.

Industrial effluent and untreated sewage are the most common pollutants of water, but the increasing use of fertilizers in food production means that larger amounts of nitrates and phosphates are leached into river systems. The over-abundance of chemicals such as phosphates in lakes and coastal waters produces an increase in algae on the surface, which blots out the light necessary for plant life. This, in turn, reduces the oxygen content and, ultimately, marine life. More and more water systems are "dying" as a result.

in aerosol cans. Half a million tonnes of these chemicals are released into the atmosphere each year, and it is thought they may be destroying the ozone layer which filters out the harmful ultraviolet radiation from the sun. The result of this could be an increase in the incidence of skin cancer, damage to crops and even a change in climate. The ozone layer may be threatened also by the release of nitrous oxides from nitrogen fertilizers, on which man depends for greater crop yields.

Of more immediate concern is the environmental stress caused by rapid urbanization. By the end of the century more than half the world's six billion people will be city dwellers if present trends continue. The lack of basic services in many cities and the crowding and stress suffered by the majority of urban dwellers in the less-developed countries pose a great environmental problem, albeit local in effect.

There is a rapidly increasing awareness of the environmental impact of man's activities. It is, however, often difficult to put a price on the conservation of nature and the protection of our vulnerable environment.

▲ **The world is in danger** of losing some of its rarest fauna as a result of man's activities. Such animals are either hunted into extinction or their habitats are ruined by human encroachment.

▼ **Road vehicles** consume vast amounts of oil and other raw materials, pollute the air and eat up land space for roads and car parks.

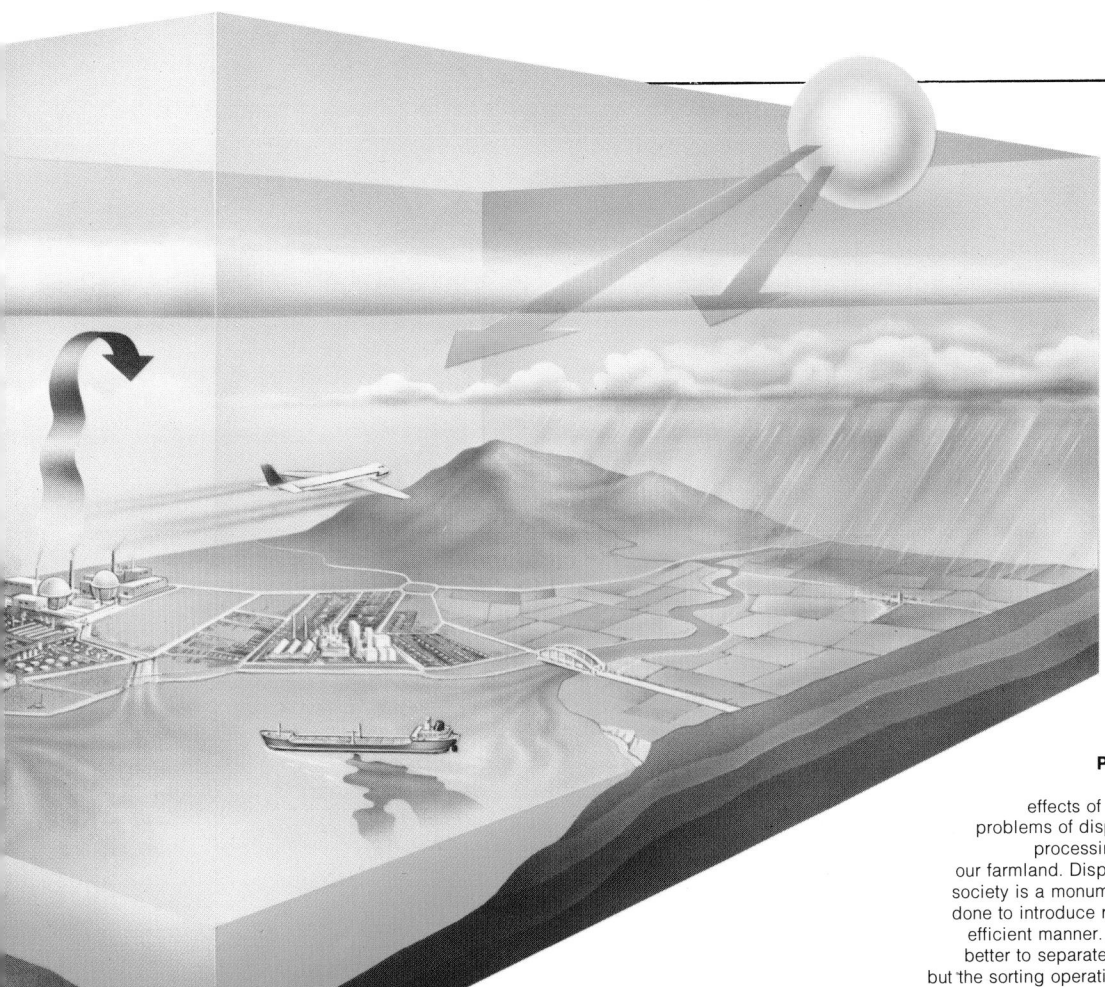

Pollution of the air can take the form of smogs — for which London was notorious before the 1950s — produced by the accumulation in the air of sulphur dioxide, sulphuric acid and smoke from industry, and the photochemical hazes produced largely by car exhaust fumes. Ironically, clean air acts that have reduced the smoke content of the air have furthered the photochemical reactions which are initiated by the sun's energy. It is argued by some experts that pollution of the air increases the cloud cover — particles provide a nucleus around which cloud droplets can condense — which reflects solar radiation back into space and which would therefore lower temperatures on earth. The problem of pollution is certainly not a localized one: as a result of air currents and winds, "acid rain" now falls over parts of western Europe that are not themselves industrialized regions, inhibiting forest growth.

Pollution of the land in its most obvious form is all too familiar: the devastating effects of open-cast mining on the landscape; the problems of disposing of waste products from industrial processing; and the scattering of chemicals over our farmland. Disposing of the waste produced by modern society is a monumental problem and so far little has been done to introduce recycling on a large scale or in the most efficient manner. Before burning refuse, for example, it is better to separate the glass, metal or plastic constituents, but the sorting operation is a costly one. Noise is increasingly a problem, also. To stand within a few metres of a heavy lorry, for example, can cause stress and, after a time, damage to the hearing of human beings. And visual pollution, especially for urban dwellers, in the form of hoardings or advertisements has become a common feature of society.

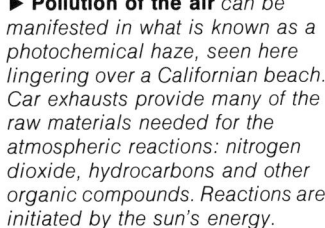

▶ **Pollution of the air** can be manifested in what is known as a photochemical haze, seen here lingering over a Californian beach. Car exhausts provide many of the raw materials needed for the atmospheric reactions: nitrogen dioxide, hydrocarbons and other organic compounds. Reactions are initiated by the sun's energy.

▼ **The destruction of tree cover,** overgrazing and overcropping contribute to the spread of deserts. The Sahara has crept both north and south – as in the Sahel region shown here – at a rate of almost 100 kilometres in the last 17 years, with the recent loss of 650,000 sq kilometres of productive land.

▲ **The air is still clear** and the land unscarred in regions of the earth that are apparently remote from the industrialized world. Studies of tissues from certain animals in the far northern and southern latitudes, however, shows evidence of pollution in the form of insecticides and other man-made chemicals that are carried to all parts of the globe by the earth's wind and water systems.

Feeding the world

WORLD food supplies have been increasing steadily and, in spite of predictions of impending disaster, have not yet been outstripped by population growth. Although current methods for determining accurately either world population or global food production figures are woefully inadequate, official United Nations statistics estimate that the earth's population has been increasing at less than two per cent annually while food production is growing at 2.9 per cent. While these figures are encouraging they do mask a high level of malnutrition, which is thought to affect between 60 and 400 million people. The cause of this problem is poverty created by an unequal distribution of land, wealth and opportunity rather than actual food shortages.

Nutritional requirements
Over the past two decades, as the young science of nutrition gathered more information, our understanding of nutritional requirements has become more exact. Figures on how many people were inadequately fed were previously based on the assumption that each person needed at least 3,000 kilocalories, including 90 grams of protein, a day. More recent findings have had the effect of revising these figures downwards to 1,990 kilocalories a day for developing countries and 2,320 kilocalories a day for developed countries. These figures are still only an average. Individual nutritional requirements vary, depending on age, sex, level of physical activity and even the climate of the region in which one lives. For example, the range extends from 820 kilocalories for a female child of less than one year to 3,100 kilocalories for a teenage boy.

The new recommended kilocalorie requirements mean that, on average, every individual needs the equivalent of 250 kilograms of grain a year. If the marketed supplies of food could have been equally distributed, then during the early 1970s, when concern about the amount of food available was so high, every person could have had 2,240 kilocalories a day, which is more than enough to engage in a healthy and active life. By the end of the 1970s approximately 1,300 million tonnes of food were reaching the market each year. That would have been enough to feed almost 5,200 million people, more than 1,000 million more than are on earth at the present time.

How much land is available?
During the same period in which nutritional requirements have been revised, our knowledge of how much food can be produced has also improved. Findings based on detailed studies of soil conditions, water availability, climate and crop characteristics indicate that there is the physical capability to produce enough food for even the highest estimate of population in the next 100 years. Studies show that a great deal more land is suitable for agricultural use than was previously believed. In southeast Asia, for example, only about 75 per cent of land which could be put under production is presently farmed.

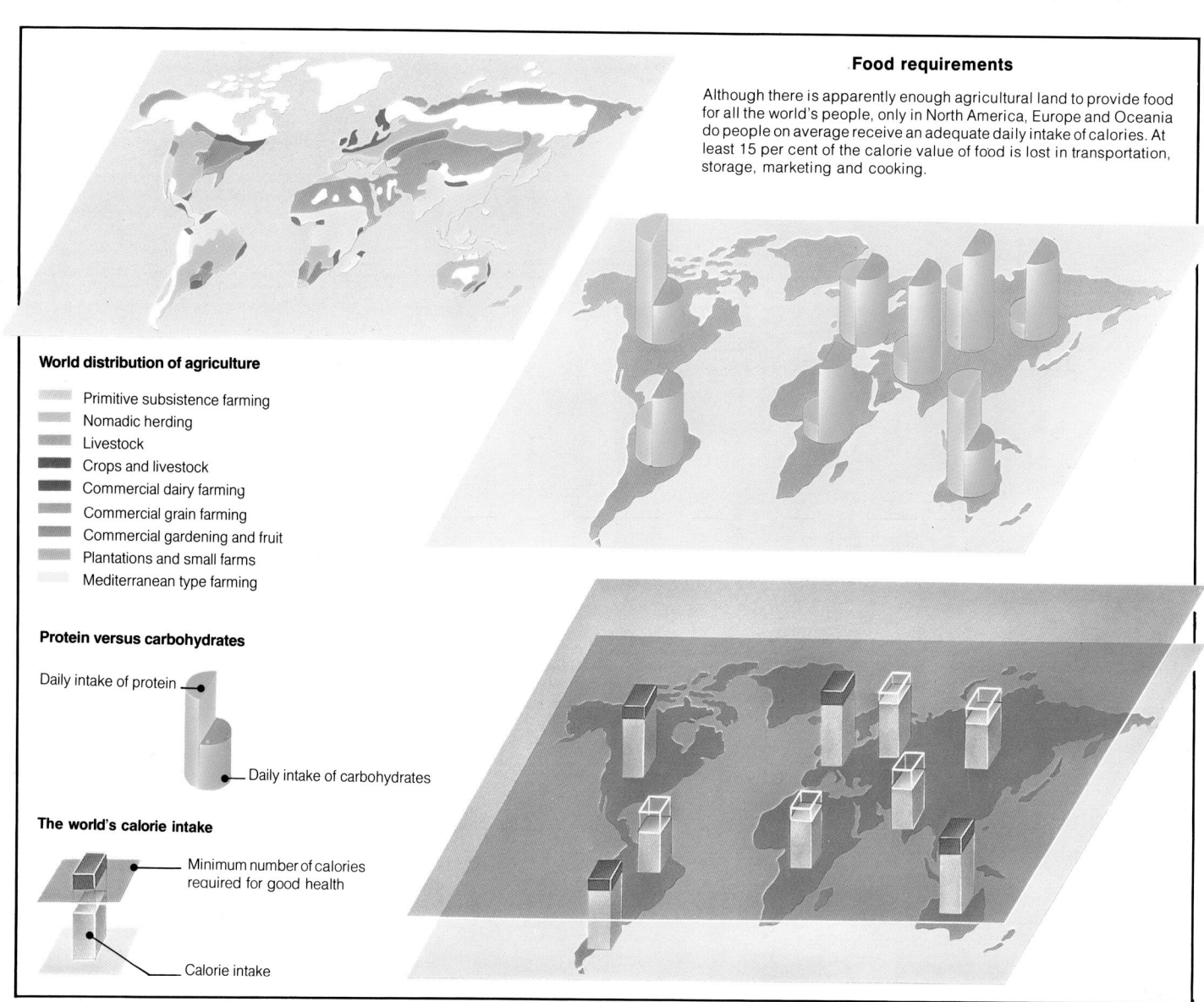

Food requirements

Although there is apparently enough agricultural land to provide food for all the world's people, only in North America, Europe and Oceania do people on average receive an adequate daily intake of calories. At least 15 per cent of the calorie value of food is lost in transportation, storage, marketing and cooking.

World distribution of agriculture

- Primitive subsistence farming
- Nomadic herding
- Livestock
- Crops and livestock
- Commercial dairy farming
- Commercial grain farming
- Commercial gardening and fruit
- Plantations and small farms
- Mediterranean type farming

Protein versus carbohydrates

Daily intake of protein

Daily intake of carbohydrates

The world's calorie intake

Minimum number of calories required for good health

Calorie intake

From the use of United Nations soil maps and studies of crops by the International Biological Programme it is estimated that there are 3,714 million hectares of land suitable for farming. Of these, 1,900 million have the potential for irrigation, a technique which can improve crop yields dramatically. Of course, competing uses for this land and the inability, for social and economic reasons, to gain access to "best-practice" techniques will mean that not all of this area is used to the fullest of its potential. If, however, only 1,208 million hectares were to be irrigated and crop yields were to reach 65 per cent of their potential, then 32,390 million tonnes of grain could be produced each year. That would be enough to feed 30 times the number of people on earth today.

Animal and plant resources
In addition to availability and productivity of land, food production depends on effective utilization of animals and plants. Plant-eating mammals and birds are all potentially edible. There are also numerous other animals, fish, insects and crustaceans which are eaten in some parts of the world but not in others. Many of these are in serious danger of elimination if industrial development takes place without consideration for the environmental requirements of these creatures. We need a world inventory of edible species so that these food sources are not lost by accident and not reduced without replacement.

Many of the hoofed animals thrive better in their home countries than imported sheep and cattle. They can be managed as wild herds by culling a calculated proportion each year for food. A further development would be domestication, as was performed on the original wild cattle of Europe. With modern knowledge of genetics animal breeding programmes could achieve targets in shorter periods than were necessary for the familiar breeds, and such animals as the eland and saiga antelope could be improved to meet the desired characteristics of meat, milk and hides that have been developed successfully in familiar domestic breeds.

More plants to eat
Just as the animal resources of most of the world are hardly yet developed, so too are indigenous plants in many regions where it is urgent that more food is produced locally. The International Biological Programme of 1963-74 identified several hundreds of plants which can fix nitrogen and, therefore, do not need nitrogen fertilizers. Many of these plants produce edible parts and could be improved by selection to become crops. Social anthropological studies show that people eat a much wider variety of plants and parts of plants than is generally supposed. An inventory of these would indicate which have the widest degree of acceptance and these could then be the subject of deliberate programmes of improvement to increase production.

The third factor in food production is technology, and its suitability to the societies that adopt it. So far, wherever a new technology has been introduced into a society where land and other resources are unequally distributed, the effect has been to increase the gap between rich and poor. Even when more food has been produced, poor people seldom get more of it, and there are many documented instances when they have got less.

The future of food production raises many issues, but the overriding aim should be to increase the food supplies available to the millions of people who still go hungry. The problem is to try to ensure that technical advance will for the present keep pace with population growth, and will in the long run overtake it so that those millions can have an adequate diet in the future. The question is what kind of food production is most suitable.

▲ **Nomadic pastoralism** is practised on marginal lands where extremes of temperature or lack of water make cultivation virtually impossible. Subsistence farming makes no impact on world food markets, but half the world's population lives off the land and produces little or no surplus.

▲ **The rolling plains** of the North American continent have made the United States the granary of the world, on which millions of hungry mouths depend. (The USSR is actually the largest grain producer, but also the greatest consumer.) A series of bad harvests in the 1970s reduced world grain reserves to a few days' supply.

▶ **The dire conditions** of most of the world's poor — here typified by a mother and her children in the slums of an Indian city — do not offer much opportunity for an adequate diet.

▼ **It is claimed** that half the food bought in the United States ends up in the waste bin. We are constantly encouraged to buy more even though obesity is an extensive problem in the western world.

▲ **Commercial livestock ranching** is big business, especially in North America. It is often argued that we do not need as much meat as we eat and that cattle consume too much grain.

What kind of food production?

WITH the world's population increasing by 70 or 80 million each year, and with many of the present population living off a totally inadequate diet, there can be little doubt about the urgency of increasing available food supplies. Nor is there any question about the two principal ways of doing so. They are to increase the area at present cultivated or grazed by farmers, and to obtain higher production per unit area from the existing farmlands.

In certain respects, these two objectives overlap. The effective area of cultivation will be doubled, for example, if a single, annual crop can be replaced by double-cropping. To obtain two crops in place of one, however, will probably require either a new breed of plant, which will mature faster, or an addition to the water supply, probably by irrigation, to provide enough water for double-cropping.

Extending the farming frontier

The principal methods by which the cultivated or pastured area can be extended are by clearance of forest, by irrigation, by drainage, by breeding hardier stocks and by removing the barriers presented by disease. The first three date back to antiquity. Irrigation was the basis of the Egyptian, Mesopotamian and some Central American civilizations, while in Europe, where nearly 90 per cent of the potentially arable land is cultivated, forest clearance has historically been the main method of extending the farming frontier, just as it has been for the past three centuries in eastern North America. Forest clearance assumes that the need for, or value of, land under agriculture is greater than the value of land under trees, an assumption that could realistically be made in medieval Europe, but that has ceased to hold good, for example, along the Canadian margins of agriculture. It is probable, in fact, that worldwide at present the forest is advancing on the farmland rather than the reverse. The potential for extra cropland, however, does exist in many areas of the world.

Irrigation and drainage both involve re-directing natural water supplies, and together they have already transformed great areas of Asia (the continent with by far the largest irrigated area, and where the Chinese have been using valley and delta drainage for millennia), the Middle East and North America. The Mississippi Valley and the Central Valley of California are today two of the world's most productive farming regions, yet a century ago one was a tangle of swamps and trees, and the other an area of desert and salt pans. Irrigation and drainage hold out good prospects for further increasing the area of farmland, but the capital costs are enormous, and the more irregular the water supply, the higher those costs become.

The breeding of hardy and quick-maturing plants has already served to push back frontiers by permitting the use of land formerly unsuitable for cultivation because of low temperatures or a short growing season. It is by this means that the great cereal areas of the Canadian prairies and the Soviet steppes have been enlarged still further.

The removal of barriers raised by disease would open up other great areas to the food producer. Africa, one of the most seriously food-deficient regions of the world, would be the principal target in this respect: only 22 per cent of its potentially arable land is cultivated, and much of it is unproductive because of diseases such as sleeping sickness.

A green revolution

The other main method of producing more food is by increasing yields per hectare. If yields world-wide were at the level of those in northwest Europe or the American Midwest, then every hectare of the world's farmland could support between 15 and 20 people on average, instead of the present global figure of between 2.8 and 3.0. The problems are not those of technology, but of supply, economics and education.

On the technical side, the major contribution so far has been made by the plant breeders. The heart of the so-called green revolution of the past four decades has been the scientific creation of high-yielding strains of corn, wheat, rice and other crops, together with improved breeds of livestock. A series of international institutes, most of them located in less-developed countries, now provide a focus for this work. Sometimes the development concerns the period necessary for the plant to mature: a rice that matures in 120 days instead of 160 may permit two crops to be grown each year instead of one. Sometimes it is a case of altering the density of planting: it is possible by scientific breeding to double the number of plants per square metre without overcrowding or loss of growth. Alternatively, the actual structure of the plant may be involved: it must have a shorter stem, for instance, in order to be able to support a heavier head.

Other areas of technical innovation are in the use of chemical fertilizers and pesticides, and in educating the farmer in a wider range of expertise, thus encouraging him to make more innovations. There is, however, the limitation imposed on adopting the new farming techniques by economics. Not only are supplies of seed for the new "wonder crops" limited at present, but the additional fertilizer input and the equipment to harvest and store larger crops have to be paid for. And this cost is not purely financial. Chemical fertilizer production involves far greater energy inputs than the additional food energy yielded by their use. It is necessary, therefore, to possess the raw materials, whose price has been soaring, and to consume other resources, before the farmer can produce more food. It is small wonder that many farmers cling to traditional methods.

Certainly, improvements in food supply can be made: by cutting down losses due to pests and disease; by mariculture, or farming the sea for food; by organizing the marketing of products through co-operatives and re-organizing the tenure of land; and in the future, perhaps, by the development of synthetic food stuffs. Most of these, however, are long-term projects and, like the cross-breeding of plants, cannot be hurried.

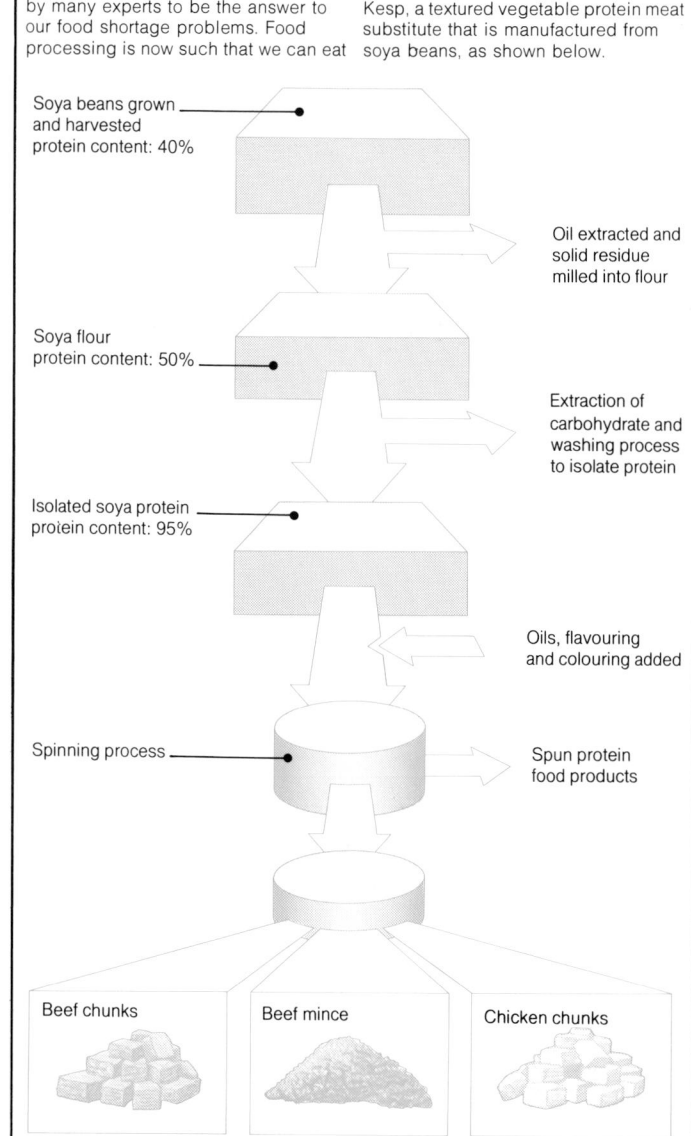

Textured vegetable protein

Textured vegetable protein is thought by many experts to be the answer to our food shortage problems. Food processing is now such that we can eat what appears to be meat but is in fact Kesp, a textured vegetable protein meat substitute that is manufactured from soya beans, as shown below.

Soya beans grown and harvested
protein content: 40%

Oil extracted and solid residue milled into flour

Soya flour
protein content: 50%

Extraction of carbohydrate and washing process to isolate protein

Isolated soya protein
protein content: 95%

Oils, flavouring and colouring added

Spinning process

Spun protein food products

Beef chunks

Beef mince

Chicken chunks

▲ **Deserts** are not necessarily infertile regions and, once water is supplied, they can be transformed into highly productive areas, as in the Algerian Sahara. Water can be pumped from underground reservoirs, or basins can be dug so that the root systems of crops can reach groundwater supplies. Fences protect crops from sand.

▼ **The world fish catch** reached more than 60 million tonnes a year in the 1970s as a result of greater efficiency and better technology. Some species have been seriously overfished. Attention is now being paid to aquaculture — the artificial culturing of fish — and fish farming, which increases natural stocks in the open sea or seawater tanks.

▲ **Terracing** is the traditional method of cultivation on the densely populated island of Bali in Indonesia and is being usefully employed in other regions where land is in short supply. In contrast to the terraces shown here, however, modern schemes often involve mechanized excavations and produce non-irrigated crops.

▶ **Sorghum** could be grown as an energy crop as well as for food. It has a high concentration of carbon dioxide around its green pigment and can convert solar energy 10 times as efficiently as other crops.

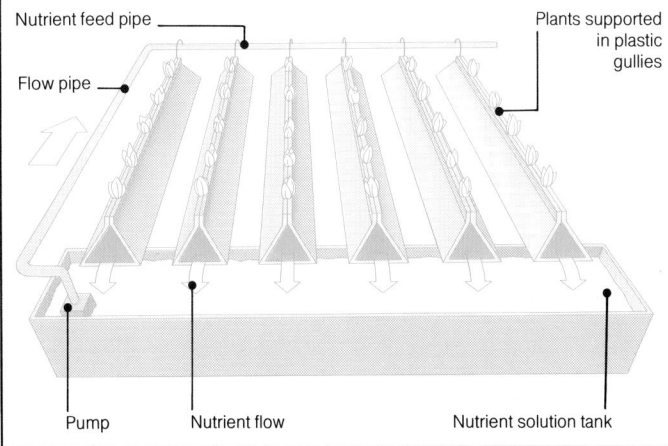

Nutrient film technique

Technology has come to play an increasingly important role in modern agriculture and one new method — the nutrient film technique — means that the farmer can actually grow crops without any soil. This is done with the aid of the device shown here, whereby crops are planted, either outdoors or in greenhouses, in plastic trays. A solution containing all the vital nutrients the plant needs is constantly circulated through the trays. This method — first developed by the Glasshouse Crops Research Institute in England — has proved highly successful and is used in many parts of the world.

Nutrient feed pipe

Plants supported in plastic gullies

Flow pipe

Pump   Nutrient flow   Nutrient solution tank

Man's quest for energy

SINCE the Industrial Revolution there has been a close relationship between economic activity and world energy use. For many years a one per cent increase in economic growth has been matched by a similar increase in energy demands. Because of this close, historic relationship, and given fears of impending resource scarcity, energy is very much at the centre of the debate about man's future. Energy underlies everyday life: it heats and lights homes, offices and factories, drives machinery and raises steam for industrial processes, fuels trans-port systems, and is a key require-ment for food production — directly for tractors and food processing and indirectly for the production of fertilizers and pesticides.

Since man learnt to utilize fire, the quest for energy has been a key feature of every civilization. Humans, animals, wood, wind and water were harnessed and the availability of such sources of energy set the limits to economic activity within societies.

First use of fossil fuels

Since the process of industrializa-tion and urbanization began, man has increasingly supplemented the use of renewable sources of energy by exploiting the depletable fossil fuels. At first coal was mined at or near the surface, but as demand grew and technology improved, underground mining complexes were developed. Coal was used in boilers, steam engines and locomo-tives and in open fires to heat homes; converted to coke it fuelled a breakthrough in iron and steel production, and as gas it supplied street lighting and domestic heat-ing; some was used to make chemi-cals, dyes and explosives.

Coal dominated world energy supplies until the 1950s, although oil and natural gas were by then widely used in the United States. In 1900, coal accounted for 94 per cent of the world's use of commer-cial fuels, oil four per cent and natural gas one per cent, and wood and hydroelectric power for the remainder. By 1950, these percen-tages had changed to 62, 25 and nine respectively, and in 1974, the year after the oil crisis, to 32, 45 and 21. Today oil and natural gas account for more than two-thirds of world fossil fuel supplies.

The other dramatic development since the beginning of this century has been a change in the scale of demand for energy. World con-sumption of fossil fuels increased ten-fold between 1900 and 1980 from 760 million tons of coal equi-valent (tce) to 8,500 million tce. The western industrialized economies, mainly North America, Western Europe and Japan, consumed 60 per cent of the total, the USSR and Eastern Europe 23 per cent, and the poorer, less-developed countries (including those with large popula-tions such as India and China) only 17 per cent of the total.

World energy supplies

Coal production reached 4,125 mil-lion tonnes in 1984 and is forecast by the World Energy Conference to double by the year 2000. The main producers are the USSR, USA,

World energy consumption

Per capita consumption in kilograms of coal equivalent

More than 2,500
1,000-2,500
250-1,000
100-250
Less than 100

A continuation of current trends of energy consumption for 75 years would lead to an annual world consumption of about 80,000 million tce in the year 2050: today's poor countries, with 75 per cent of the world's people, would still account for only one-third of total energy consumption.

▶ **Large pipelines** — *used here to carry oil across the desert in Qatar — have higher capital costs but lower running costs than other forms of transport. They also raise international political issues.*

◀ **Modern, industrialized society** *— epitomized by the New York skyline — is dependent upon vast supplies of energy. In 1981 the total amount of energy produced commercially was the equivalent of 2.1 tonnes of coal per person.*

China, Poland, the UK and West Germany. Amongst developing countries, India is the major producer. Ultimately recoverable resources are vast — more than one million, million tonnes.

Oil production rose to 4,000 million tce in 1980, the major producers being the USSR, USA, Saudi Arabia, Iran, Venezuela and Iraq. A major recent development has been the exploitation of offshore oil resources. Ultimate crude oil reserves are estimated at between 250 and 300 thousand million tonnes, with a similar quantity in unconventional forms such as oil shales, tar sands and synthetic oils, exploitable at higher costs. Natural gas has become a major world fuel only relatively recently. Proved reserves are estimated at between 70 and 90 thousand million tce, but this is thought to be conservative.

Nuclear power is based on the fission (or splitting) of uranium atoms in a range of reactor types, the dominant categories being water-cooled (mainly in the USA, France, West Germany and Japan) and gas-cooled (mainly in the UK). Future reactor types include fast breeders based on a mixture of uranium and plutonium fuel and the high temperature reactor. Nuclear power at present provides about 11 per cent of world electricity requirements but a substantial increase is planned by 2000. The extent of uranium reserves is subject to considerable uncertainty and this also applies to thorium, which may prove a suitable alternative fuel, although no commerical thorium reactors have been put into operation yet.

Only about 14 per cent of world hydroelectric potential is exploited at present, mainly at sites in industrialized countries. The capital costs of major hydro schemes are often beyond the reach of developing countries unless aided by massive financial assistance.

Industry is the largest consumer of energy in the developed world, accounting for 35-40 per cent of total demand. Those industries concerned with processing of materials — iron and steel, chemicals, aluminium, bricks — account for two-thirds of this total. Technical changes in industrial processes have led to improved energy efficiency and recent fuel price increases will encourage this further. Increased recycling of materials will also reduce the energy demand per unit of output. Public and private services account for 10-15 per cent of energy demands in the developed countries, mainly for heating and lighting.

Energy use in the home
Domestic use accounts for 20-25 per cent of energy demand. Of this about 60 per cent is used for space heating and air conditioning; 20-25 per cent for water heating; 10 per cent for cooking and between five and 10 per cent (almost entirely as electricity) for appliances such as washing machines, televisions and so on. Many appliances, for example hi-fi, use little electricity, but others such as tumble driers and dishwashers may be key future growth areas. Improved insulation of buildings could reduce domestic energy demands.

Transport accounts for 25 per cent of energy demand in the USA and 20 per cent in Western Europe. The largest proportion is used by road transport, especially the private car. A range of new technologies might reduce fuel consumption per mile by 20-40 per cent in the coming decades and there is scope for improving the efficiency of public transport systems.

Over the next 20-30 years, the world will experience a transition from a dependence on oil and gas towards greater use of coal, nuclear power and renewable energy sources. Major technical changes will be necessary and will require a considerable developmental period before widespread application is possible.

How one nuclear reactor works

Certain atoms of uranium break into fragments when a neutron is added to the nucleus. If this occurs, the uranium atom is split into two and energy is released in the form of heat. At the same time neutrons are given off and they continue the process of splitting other nuclei. This is called a chain reaction and it forms the basis of the generation of nuclear power. In a nuclear reactor the chain reaction is kept going at a steady rate and the heat is used to produce steam to drive electricity generators. In order to maintain a steady rate the number of neutrons that continue the reaction has to be controlled. This is done by absorbing excess neutrons in control rods made of boron. If neutrons produced by the reaction are slowed down they can split the nuclei more easily. The slowing down is achieved by surrounding the fuel with a moderator — so-called because it moderates the speed of the neutrons. The reactor is protected by a concrete shield to prevent the escape of dangerous radiation. In a gas-cooled reactor, such as the one shown here, the heat produced by the reaction is removed by circulating carbon dioxide gas. Alternatively, the heat can be removed by circulating water through the system. The heat is used to convert water to steam.

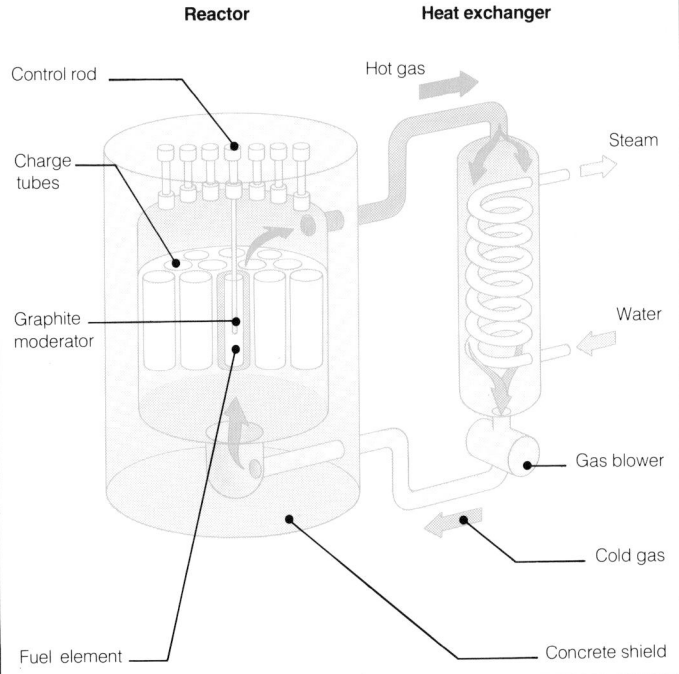

Reactor — Heat exchanger

Control rod
Charge tubes
Graphite moderator
Fuel element
Hot gas
Steam
Water
Gas blower
Cold gas
Concrete shield

▲ **Natural gas** was once considered to be a useless by-product of drilling for oil and was burnt off. Today, however, technical developments, such as liquefied natural gas tankers and large pipeline networks, have enabled a rapid growth in its use. Deposits are found in association with oil or on their own, as in this Iranian field.

▶ **Millions of people** in the less-developed countries are dependent for energy on what nature supplies, mainly firewood and dung. Non-commercial consumption of energy is difficult to assess accurately, but is probably in the region of 1,500 tce. Such energy sources are steadily being replaced by fossil fuels, however.

▶ **Recoverable coal reserves** are vast enough to last for almost 3,000 years at current rates of consumption. Greater concern for the environment may affect production techniques, however. Open-cast mining — seen here in West Virginia — is one of the most economical mining methods but it usually has a devastating effect on the landscape.

Energy alternatives

AT PRESENT the world depends almost entirely on non-renewable sources for its energy. Nearly 90 per cent of our energy is derived from the major non-renewable fossil fuels: coal, oil and natural gas. A high proportion of the rest, especially in countries of the Third World, comes from wood which, although renewable in principle, is being rapidly depleted. We are never likely to run out of any of these resources completely, but we are already experiencing large increases in the cost of obtaining each unit of fossil fuel. This trend will continue and will impose an ever-increasing strain on the world's systems of production and the societies built on them.

We are at the moment ill-equipped to deal with this eventuality: none of the possible renewable sources of energy are anywhere near ready to start replacing fossil fuels. Moreover, the processes of developing and commercializing major new technologies are extremely difficult and lengthy. Nuclear power, for instance, has been under intensive and massively funded development for more than 30 years, and yet it is still far from being a mature technology and supplies only one per cent of the world's energy demand. Renewable energy, by which we mean direct solar, geothermal, hydroelectric, wind, wave and tidal power, biomass fuels and nuclear breeding and fusion, will require a similar, if not greater, volume and intensity of effort if it is to make a substantial impact on world energy supplies in 50 years' time.

Renewable energy and lifestyles
Renewable energy sources (with the exception of nuclear) are often called "alternative" energy. Alternative energy tends to be linked with the idea of alternative culture — implying a radical change in lifestyle both at an individual level and in the political, economic and social spheres. It is perhaps unfortunate that practitioners of 'alternative culture' in the West are rarely good advertisements for the advantages of their lifestyle but it is certainly true that at their existing (mainly rudimentary) stage of development, most renewable energy sources are most compatible with a low energy-using, rural society with limited industrialization. This is because the majority of renewables provide only diffuse, low-grade energy, which is subject to considerable variability in supply.

Much of the development effort in renewable energy must, therefore, be concentrated on making it as compatible as possible with urban, industrial society. The difficulties of achieving this (through effective storage and the up-grading of low-grade heat, for instance) are what makes the development of renewable energy sources so expensive. In the long term, therefore, widespread reliance on renewable energy will probably not require major and fundamental changes to existing lifestyles. Renewable nuclear sources (breeders and fusion), on the other hand, are specifically designed to fit existing industrial societies and their development in the future may well be compatible only with even more centralized and interdependent societies than exist at present.

Sources of renewable energy
Direct solar energy is the most obviously attractive source because of its abundance. The major problems in its development (common to a number of renewables) concern its low efficiency and its variability, which requires the development of storage technologies. High yields of useful energy from the sun are therefore likely to need heavy capital investment. Domestic space heating technology is reasonably well developed and electricity production from direct solar sources has been demonstrated, but enormous problems remain to be solved.

Hydroelectricity is the only renewable source in significant commercial use, and it provides more than one-fifth of the world's electricity. Its main problems are that it is not a genuinely renewable source in the long term (because of reservoir silting) and that most sites suitable for large-scale development have already been used in

▲ **Wind power** was used traditionally for pumping water or grinding corn and modern wind power generators have been built in some areas, such as the Orkneys. Wind is an attractive energy source since its use produces no extra heat load on the environment.

◀ **The world's largest solar furnace,** at Odeillo in the French Pyrenees, uses a large concave mirror to focus the sun's rays. In regions where there is strong sunshine during the day, solar energy can be used for space heating or to supply hot water to homes or larger buildings that have a low requirement for hot water.

many industrialized countries. Geothermal sources make use of the earth's internal heat to supply either heat or electricity. Limited commercial development has already taken place. Diffuseness is again a major developmental problem.

Wind power has improved significantly since the heyday of traditional windmills. It may well prove extremely suitable for rural use (pumping and electricity) where climatic conditions are suitable. Wave power could in principle supply large amounts of electricity, but has not yet been substantially demonstrated, and its development faces major technical and economic problems. Tidal power has already been demonstrated on a fairly large scale, but there are few suitable sites in the world.

Biological sources of energy (wood, dung, wastes and crops) are already of vital importance to the Third World, though there are major problems of depletion. The main long-term problem for biomass fuels is competition with food production for the use of land.

The future of nuclear power
Fast breeder nuclear reactors — which "breed" their own fuel in the form of plutonium — and fusion reactors — in which common light

elements fuse and release energy — can be considered as renewable sources. Breeders are being built on a commercial scale, but technical, safety and environmental problems remain to be solved. They are, nevertheless, a long-term possibility for electricity production and have massive government backing in both capitalist and communist countries as the main "technical fix" for fossil fuel scarcities. Nuclear fusion is an attempt to reproduce on earth the fusion reaction of the sun, and it would mean an end to the world's energy problems. Fusion occurs, however, at temperatures of about 100 million degrees and the problems of holding the resulting "plasma" stable and then safely extracting energy are currently well beyond our technical capabilities.

The obvious and enormous difficulties that still need to be overcome before renewable energy can by widely used, together with the ever-rising costs of non-renewable sources, lead to two main conclusions: that there is a critical need to promote energy conservation as a way of reducing demand and buying time; and that we will almost certainly need to rely on a combination of a large number of renewable energy sources.

▲ **A considerable number** of sites suitable for hydroelectric power schemes remain unexploited in less-developed countries, but constructing a dam such as the Kariba poses enormous financial, technical and political problems for the developing nations.

Solar power
Solar collectors operate in much the same way as a greenhouse. Air inside a metal-backed box with a transparent lid of either glass or plastic is heated by the sun. The glass traps the infra-red radiation and so the box becomes a collector for the heat. Another version has copper pipes in which water is heated instead of air. A solar system can only be effective if the heat can be stored for release when the house needs warming. This is done by means of the heating of a rock store, usually placed beneath the house, or by heating water in a storage tank.

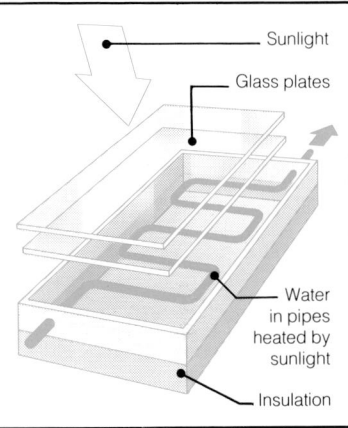

Sunlight
Glass plates
Water in pipes heated by sunlight
Insulation

▲ **Power from geothermal sources** makes use of heat stored in the earth in volcanic regions or deep sedimentary basins. Electricity can be generated from turbines driven by the pressure of underground streams of hot water and steam. Geothermal power is produced commercially in Iceland, the USA, Italy and New Zealand.

Power from the sea

One wave power converter consists of a "duck" that rocks backwards and forwards on a spindle and can extract up to 90 per cent of the energy contained in a wave that it intercepts. No commercial wave power station has yet been built, but to produce power in quantity a long series of ducks in concrete rafts would be needed. They would drive a generator within the axle linking them. It is agreed that, for greatest efficiency, wave power stations should be designed to extract energy not from the biggest waves that occur only a few times a year but from the average-sized waves that flow all the time. The stations will still have to withstand powerful storm waves, however. The average Atlantic wave can produce a power equivalent of about 70 kilowatts per metre. That is enough to heat seven medium-sized houses in a temperate climate for an hour. In a tidal power scheme a basin reservoir is created by constructing a barrage across a tidal estuary. Seawater enters and leaves the basin through ducts containing turbines that power generators. Such schemes are restricted to estuaries whose tidal range between high and low water is extremely large, such as the Rance estuary in northwestern France. The Severn estuary in England is a possible site for the future development of tidal power.

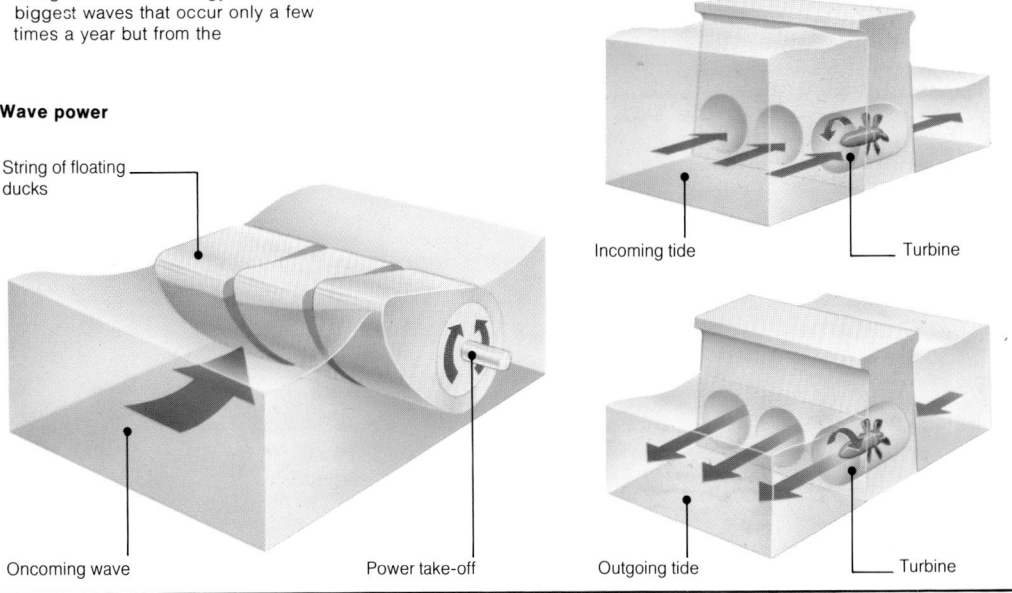

Wave power

String of floating ducks

Oncoming wave

Power take-off

Tidal power

Incoming tide

Turbine

Outgoing tide

Turbine

The earth's mineral wealth

MODERN industrial society is dependent upon an assured supply of a wide variety of mineral commodities besides those that are used as a source of energy. Very few countries are totally devoid of all non-fuel minerals but, conversely, even the few exceptionally mineral-rich nations, such as Australia, Canada and South Africa, usually need to import at least one critically important commodity.

Bulk minerals used for construction purposes, for example crushed stone, sand, gravel, cement and clay, are widely distributed geographically and are therefore unimportant in terms of international trade. Moreover, although they are consumed in large quantities, they have a low intrinsic value and can rarely be transported economically for any great distance even within their countries of origin.

Of other important mineral commodities, some, such as iron ore and bauxite (the raw material of the aluminium industry), are mined and consumed in vast quantities, but because of an unequal global distribution of resources, the considerable cost of transportation has to be borne by the many consumer nations. At the other extreme, minerals such as the various precious metals, diamonds, cobalt, chromium and many others have a high intrinsic value, are not consumed in vast tonnages and, in their case, transportation costs have relatively little significance.

Three categories

When considered in terms of their end-use, the minerals entering international trade fall broadly into three categories. Minerals required as raw materials for the iron and steel industry include, in addition to the iron ore itself, the ores of the alloying metals such as tungsten, nickel, manganese and chromium and sometimes special grades of limestone for smelting purposes.

Non-ferrous metals used in their own right and not mainly as an adjunct to the iron and steel industry form a distinct category of their own. These include the base metals such as copper, lead, tin and zinc and also the precious metals.

A third category includes those substances that are loosely termed industrial minerals, and embraces those which are not utilized as a source of metal. Some, like phosphate rock, fluorspar and potash, are essential raw materials in the large-scale manufacture of important chemicals. Others, like ceramic and refractory clays, asbestos, talc and mica, are sought because of certain distinctive physical and chemical properties.

The growth and survival of the world's mineral industry demands considerable expertise at all levels of exploitation, including prospecting, mining, processing and utilization. The widespread search for minerals on and beyond continental limits requires much investment in geological, geophysical and geochemical exploration methods, and reflects the reality that mineral resources are far from being randomly or equally distributed.

A geological revolution

An intellectual revolution in the earth sciences in the last two decades has led to a better understanding of how continental segments or "plates" have evolved and moved relative to each other through more than three billion years of planetary history. In turn, this wider understanding of geological processes has encouraged a broader insight into the mechanism of formation and the reasons for the distribution of many key mineral commodities. For example, the presence of many large copper-bearing ore bodies of the so-called porphyry type along the geologically active western margins of both North and South America can be related to the present-day seismic and volcanic activity in those regions. This kind of correlation provides guidelines for the location of analogous ore bodies in much more ancient terrains.

Other major mineral resources, well exemplified by the major iron ore deposits of Australia, Brazil and South Africa and bauxite in several tropical countries, have a distribution related not so much to deep-seated crustal processes as to climatic or other physical conditions that were prevalent at specific periods in the earth's history. The recognition of the role that such palaeo-environmental factors have had on the formation of these ores serves to focus the search for further mineral deposits.

Exploration for new mineral deposits is also assisted by increasingly refined methods of detection. Discovery of such deposits is now rarely dependent upon the recognition of visible traces of ore but instead requires detection of the subtle physical and chemical effects which may be the only tangible manifestation of important ore bodies concealed beneath considerable thicknesses of barren rock. Such improvement in prospecting techniques owes much to modern methods of rapid chemical analysis, complex electronic circuitry in geophysical instruments, automatic data processing and remote sensing, using both aircraft and satellite-borne detection devices.

A success story so far

In the fields of mining, handling and milling of ore, economies resulting from the increasingly larger scale of operation have enabled the mining industry to keep pace with ever increasing demand for most commodities. The development of large and highly mechanized open-cast mining operations at the expense of labour-intensive underground methods has resulted in a significant reduction of the economic ore cut-off grade. Further developments in the processing of low-grade ores, for example by chemical and bacterial leaching, suggest that the process of technical improvement may continue. Mining of sub-sea mineral resources can also be expected to commence in the near future, although there the barriers are of a political nature.

Despite the continuing success of the mining industry, demand for most commodities continues to rise. Investigation of the potential resources that, it is hoped, will provide the necessary margin of reserves ahead of production must therefore be pursued vigorously. Although this search has so far proved successful, some alarm has been expressed that shortages may soon appear in the supply of some key mineral commodities.

Where economic minerals occur

The distribution and concentration of minerals of economic significance is controlled by the major geological processes of magmatism (the melting, movement and solidification of volcanic and other igneous rocks), metamorphism (chemical and physical changes to rocks brought about by heat and pressure below the zone of weathering) and sedimentation (the transport and deposition of material derived from the weathering of other rocks).

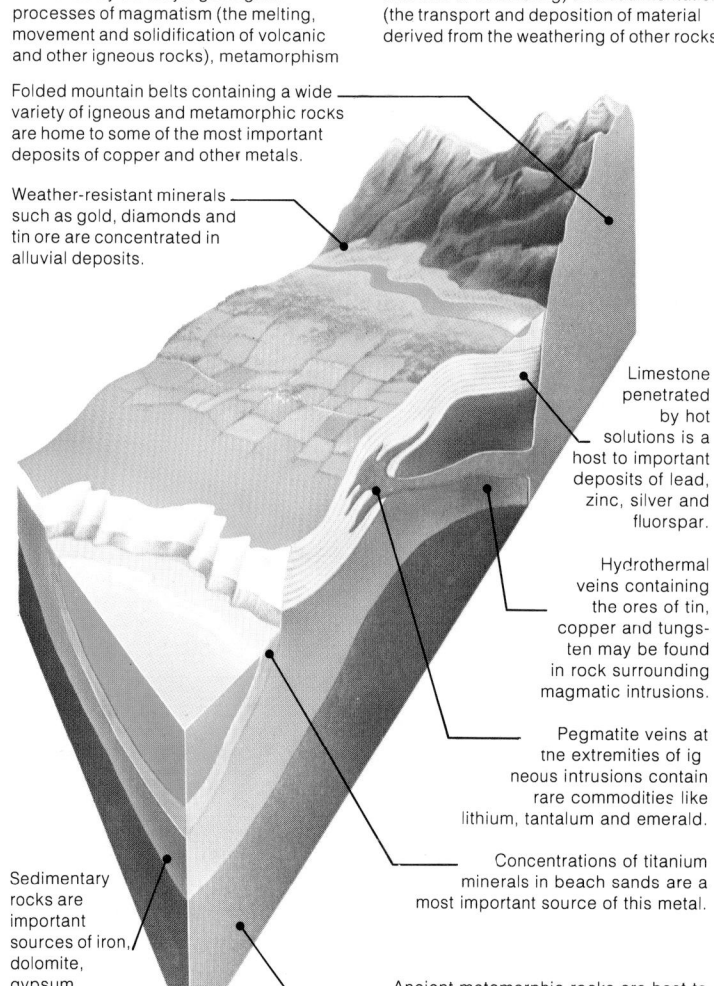

Folded mountain belts containing a wide variety of igneous and metamorphic rocks are home to some of the most important deposits of copper and other metals.

Weather-resistant minerals such as gold, diamonds and tin ore are concentrated in alluvial deposits.

Limestone penetrated by hot solutions is a host to important deposits of lead, zinc, silver and fluorspar.

Hydrothermal veins containing the ores of tin, copper and tungsten may be found in rock surrounding magmatic intrusions.

Pegmatite veins at the extremities of igneous intrusions contain rare commodities like lithium, tantalum and emerald.

Concentrations of titanium minerals in beach sands are a most important source of this metal.

Sedimentary rocks are important sources of iron, dolomite, gypsum, potash and others.

Ancient metamorphic rocks are host to many economic minerals; for example, gold, nickel, iron, asbestos.

▲ **More than two-thirds** of the world's metallic mineral output is produced by open-cast methods which are cheaper and easier now that technology is available to remove thick overburden.

▲ **Satellite surveying** includes taking photographs that emphasize certain bands of the light spectrum and reveal many large-scale geological features that would be unrecognizable from the ground. Satellite-borne detection devices have reduced the time and increased the efficiency of mineral prospecting on the ground.

▶ **The precious metals,** long valued as a store of wealth, are of increasing importance to industries such as electronics, dentistry, photography and aerospace.

Major mineral deposits

Relatively few mineral deposits are of economic value, and of those the metals are the most important. Iron, the fourth most abundant element in the earth's crust, occurs widely and 480 million tonnes are produced annually. Aluminium is the most common metal, but only 17 million tonnes are produced a year. Tin deposits are restricted to a few areas which makes it an expensive metal (production: 210,000 tonnes). Other major metals include copper (8.5 million tonnes), gold (less than 950 tonnes), silver (about 12,000 tonnes), uranium (41,000 tonnes) and lead and zinc, which usually occur together (4.7 & 6.2 million tonnes respectively). The distribution of major deposits of the world's most valuable minerals is shown on the map below.

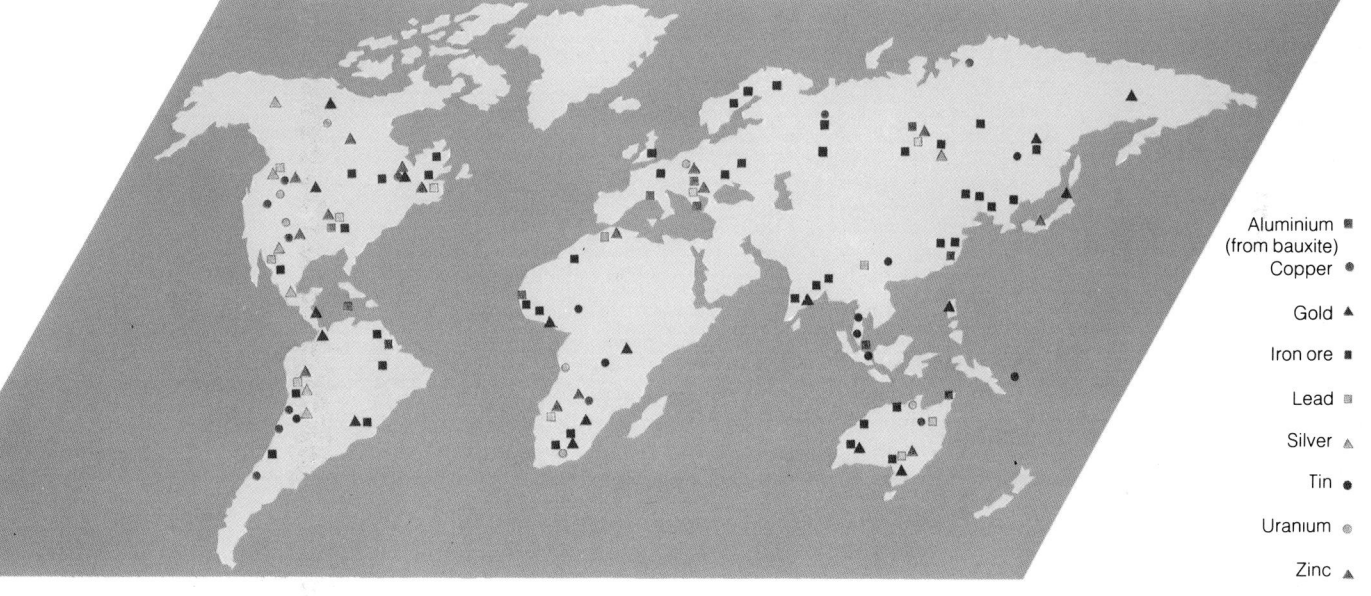

Aluminium ▪
(from bauxite)
Copper ●

Gold ▲

Iron ore ▪

Lead ▫

Silver ▵

Tin •

Uranium ◉

Zinc ▴

Asbestos (chrysotile)

Mercury (cinnabar)

Uranium (autunite)

Iron (haematite)

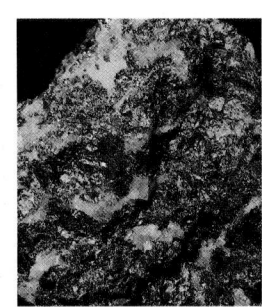

Copper (bornite)

A conserving future

IN THE context of an ever-increasing world population and the consequent rise in demand for living space, food and raw materials, it has been predicted by some economic forecasters that a crisis in the supply of our most important mineral resources is imminent. Although the mining industry has been successful in continuing to discover new resources ahead of demand, it is suggested that the number of new discoveries of ore yet to be made must be finite and that sooner or later mankind will be faced with an absolute shortage of many key commodities which are essential to an industrial society.

The question of conservation

At the simplest level of argument, conservation of minerals is proposed as a desirable object of international co-operation simply to delay for as long as possible the point at which society can no longer rely on supplies. A diametrically opposed view is, however, often supported, not least by the mining industry itself. This argues that the efficient utilization of all resources that are available and can be extracted economically at the present time, far from being discouraged, should be vigorously pursued. Only this will give an innovative society the economic encouragement that it needs to discover

technical solutions to the problems of raw material shortages that may occur in the near future.

Expressed in this way, arguments for and against mineral conservation appear to be somewhat academic. However, recent history has shown that for two reasons, political and environmental, conservation or, more accurately, the efficient utilization of mineral resources is a desirable end. In the political sphere, the growth of producer cartels such as OPEC (petroleum), CIPEC (copper) and the IBA (bauxite) may well have the effect of encouraging countries which are net importers of the commodities concerned to examine more closely the efficiency with which those commodities are utilized.

The growing pressure of mining on the environment is partly the result of increased demand requiring bigger mines, but it can also be attributed to the exhaustion of high-grade ore deposits, resulting in a shift of emphasis towards large-scale extractive operations that are able to work vast low-grade deposits at a profit.

Political and environmental pressures, although fundamental in encouraging the efficient use of non-renewable resources, can often act indirectly. For example, the increases imposed for political reasons upon the price of crude

petroleum not only encourage less wasteful use of the refinery products themselves but also, at second hand, the efficient use of, say, metals produced in smelters dependent upon oil-based energy.

How to improve efficiency

The efficient use and therefore, ultimately, the conservation of mineral resources involves a critical examination of the way in which they are utilized at all stages from their removal from the ground, through processing, fabrication, usage and recovery as scrap.

At the point at which minerals are mined there is often scope for improvement in recovery ratios. Open-cast mining often permits the recovery of almost 100 per cent of the ore available, but such favourable recoveries are rarely attainable with underground mining. And it must be admitted that in some cases the installation of mechanization to improve the economic performance of underground mining results in a concomitant reduction in the attainable reserves available. Mechanical cutters on longwall faces, for example, can only work on seams that are more than a minimum thickness.

The processing and fabrication stages in the conversion of raw material to finished product offer the opportunity for resource conservation in the way in which energy is used and also in terms of the way in which the final products are designed. Nevertheless, scrutiny of the energy input of manufacturing processes demands a sophisticated degree of analysis. For example, the use of the light metals aluminium and magnesium in automobile components can only be justified if the amount of fuel

saved during the lifetime of the vehicle more than offsets the higher energy cost of smelting these substitute metals.

Substitution of many important commodities to meet specific shortages can be envisaged. A good example is aluminium which can substitute for copper as an electrical conductor or for steel in the construction industry. But the physical properties of substitutes are never identical, and in some cases substitution does not appear to be a realistic possibility. Silver, for example, is probably irreplaceable for photographic purposes.

Recycling

It is probable that in the short term recycling of scrap and waste will create more impact than substitution on resource conservation. Once again, however, the trade-offs have to be considered. While little energy input is involved in collecting high-quality process scrap from the floor of a machine shop, the same is not necessarily true if useful materials have to be separated at great expense from general industrial waste. There also tend to be restrictions on the uses to which recovered material can be put. Scrap aluminium usually contains some silicon and can therefore be used for making castings but not for many fabrication purposes. The total efficiency of scrap recovery is closely related to the purpose to which the material is put.

The technical aspects of mineral conservation appear to be fairly well understood. Encouragement for their implementation requires social and political initiative although the operation of the simple law of supply and demand will be effective in time.

The life-span of minerals

World demand for the 20 minerals most vital to modern society is expected to double by 1988 and treble by 2000. This will greatly reduce the life-span of world reserves of the major minerals.

Shortages of minerals in the future will inevitably raise market prices. This will mean that deposits uneconomical at present will become workable which will, in turn, encourage exploration. A

price rise will also encourage the further use of scrap metal. Scrap materials containing scarce minerals will also rise in price and the recycling market will increase.

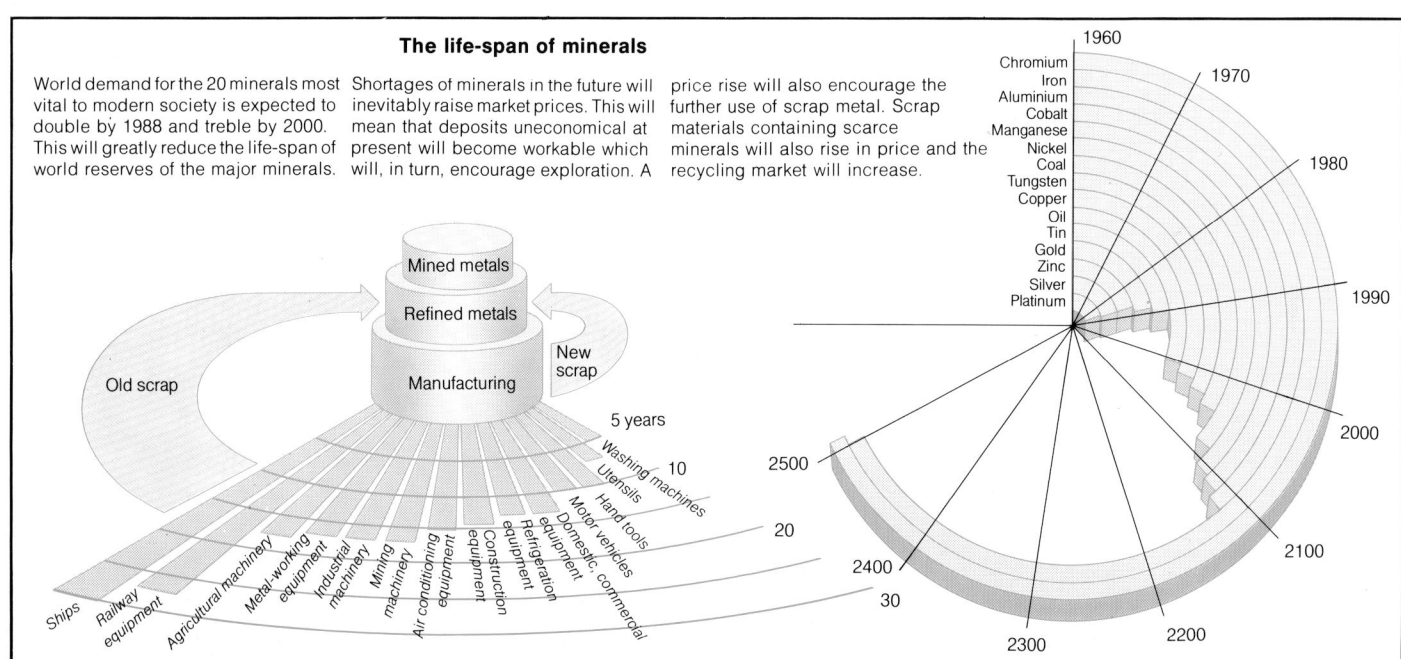

▲ **Iron,** and its principal alloy, steel, are the most important and widely used metals. Iron and steel mills, consuming vast quantities of energy and water as well as raw materials, and the steel-consuming industries such as ship-building represent more than anything else the road to industrialization for the less-developed world.

▶ **More and more** food and drink is sold in non-returnable containers, especially bottles and cans, which create mountains of litter. Aluminium cans, for instance, are no good for composting, they do not degrade and therefore have to be removed. They can be recycled but separation is a costly process.

▲ **Millions of cars** are dumped each year when they could be recycled. Since they contain plastic, rubber and other metals as well as steel the end-product from crushing has to be refined before it can be re-used.

▲ **If more motor vehicles** could be produced economically from substitute materials such as glass reinforced plastic, a significant saving of metals would be made.

◀ **Bridges** constructed from reinforced concrete as opposed to metal are another step towards the conservation of minerals.

▼ **Manganese nodules,** found beyond depths of about three kilometres below the surface of the oceans, may be commercially dredged in the future. The origin of these nodules is uncertain, but they may prove an invaluable source of heavy metals as land deposits become increasingly depleted.

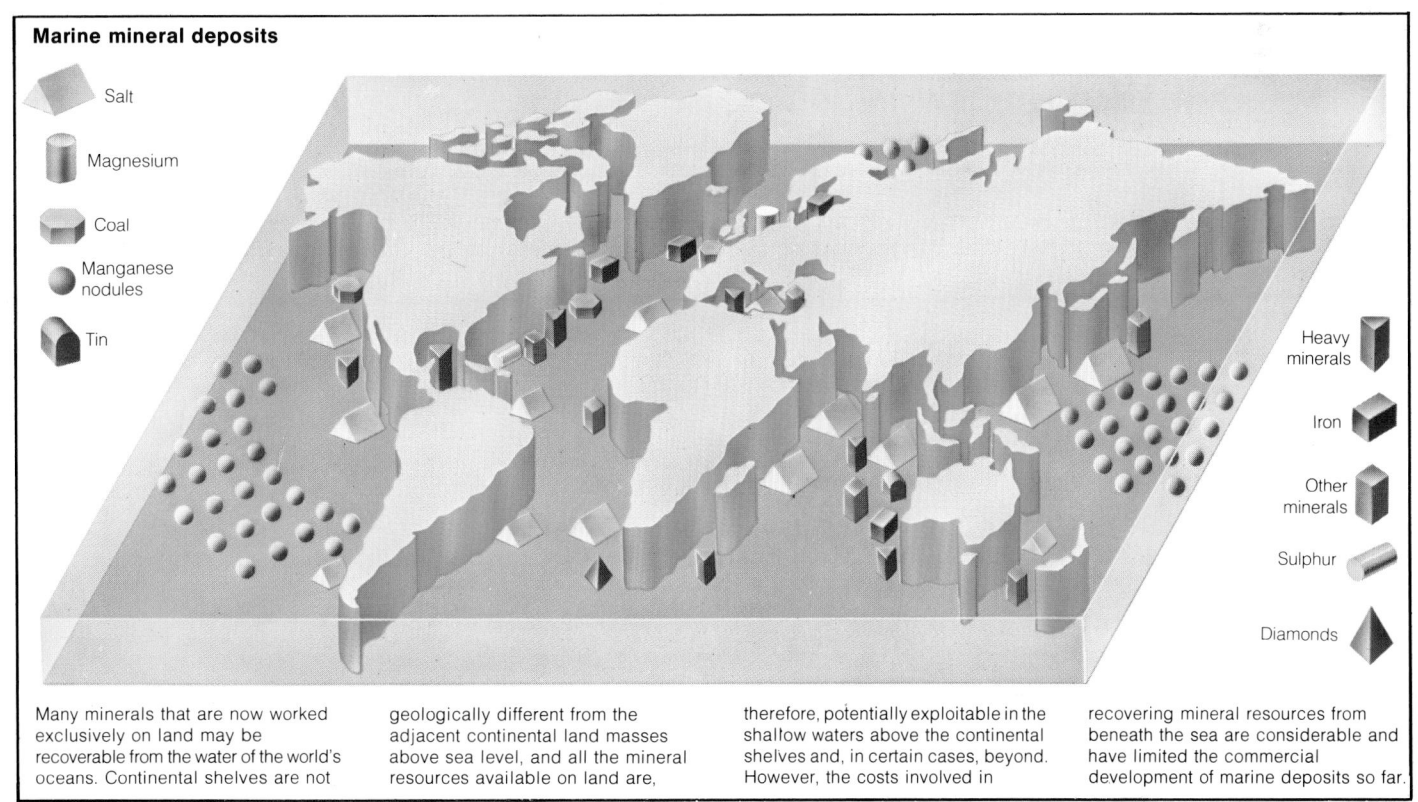

Marine mineral deposits

Salt

Magnesium

Coal

Manganese nodules

Tin

Heavy minerals

Iron

Other minerals

Sulphur

Diamonds

Many minerals that are now worked exclusively on land may be recoverable from the water of the world's oceans. Continental shelves are not geologically different from the adjacent continental land masses above sea level, and all the mineral resources available on land are, therefore, potentially exploitable in the shallow waters above the continental shelves and, in certain cases, beyond. However, the costs involved in recovering mineral resources from beneath the sea are considerable and have limited the commercial development of marine deposits so far.

Economic trends

THE object and function of international trade is to make the world as a whole richer in the supply of material goods, whether they be raw materials (including food) or manufactured products. Two countries will engage in trade only if each of them gains by it, except in circumstances which allow one country to exercise compulsion over the other.

Growth of world trade
In the last 20 years the value of world trade has increased about twenty-fold (although inflation magnifies the real extent of this expansion). In 1948 the value of imports stood at US $62,700 million and exports were valued at $57,000 million. In 1982 the corresponding totals (in millions) were $1,955,000 and $1,885,000. Nevertheless, the continuing growth of international trade has done little to bring about a more equal distribution of wealth among the nations of the world. With a few exceptions, such as Australia, New Zealand and Denmark, those countries that have concentrated in the last 100 years or more on developing their manufactures have come to appropriate a disproportionate share of the world's wealth.

In the nineteenth century, the influential German economist Friedrich List argued strongly that only when a country had developed its own national industries could it share in the profits that were the reward of the international division of labour. He went even further and gave his opinion that only a country that exported manufactured products and imported food could rise in the international wealth tables. His influence is still felt today. Most leaders of Third World countries are engaged in an effort to industrialize their economies. Yet it may well be that many of them would profit more from international trade if they ceased to identify prosperity and national pride with steel mills and oil refineries.

A Third World
About 140 countries comprise what has come to be called the Third World. These countries are variously described as "less-developed", "under-developed" or "developing", names that assume Western patterns of development and industrial growth as norms, and desirable norms at that. The people of the Third World, comprising some two-thirds of the world's population, live, for the most part, in dire poverty. National per capita income figures

for the seven major regions of the globe show how marked is the divide between the standard of living enjoyed by those living in developed countries and that of the rest of the world. In 1984 annual per capita income was about $14,000 in North America, $9,000 in Europe and Oceania. In stark contrast were the average figures for Africa ($300), Asia excluding Japan ($800) and Latin America ($1,000). In the 1970s the national income of some oil-producing countries of the Third World has risen dramatically, but there is no guarantee that their present prosperity will survive the depletion of their oil resources.

It is rare for more than 10 per cent of the gross national product of a Third World country to consist of manufactures. Most developing economies lack the required capital and trained skills for large-scale industry. Their chief preoccupation is with providing enough food for their people. As a result they contribute only a small part of the total volume of world trade. Again, 1980 import/export figures (in millions of US dollars) reveal large discrepancies between North America (319,359/238,879) or Europe (1,014,128/895,062) and, for instance, Africa (85,513/95,875) or Central and South America (113,824/105,099). The same point is made by comparing the figures for Australia and New Zealand (27,864/27,308) with those for less-developed Oceania (3,539/2,439).

Patterns of trade
A breakdown of world trade figures reveals a number of trends that have become apparent in recent years. Although the developed market economies of the West retain the lion's share of world trade, the volume of their international trade has been growing at a slower rate than that of the Third World and the centrally planned economies (the Soviet bloc members of COMECON and China). Between 1970 and 1976 the volume of world trade rose by 21.2 per cent. The rate of growth in the developed market economies was only 16.7% in the second half of the decade but increased to 22.9% in 1978–9. The comparative figures for the Third World countries were 18.5% and 39.1%.

This dramatic shift in trading patterns reflects, of course, the oil boom enjoyed by those members of OPEC, whose exports rose by 48.2 per cent between 1973 and 1976. That rise is almost entirely explained by exports of oil and was

GNP and world trade

Gross national product and patterns of export trade reveal much about the world economy. The nations with the largest GNPs are those which dominate international trade, and have done so for at least a century. The most apparent feature of patterns of international trade is the fact that approximately 75 per cent of it flows between developed, capitalist countries. Since the distribution of resources is uneven across the globe, the production of goods varies from one region to another and gives some a "comparative advantage". Such differences in the cost of production of goods leads, through the development of trade, to specialized areas of production. Some experts argue, however, that this is the result of relationships between developed and under-developed economies. Wealth is extracted from less-developed countries and accumulated in the economic capitals of the developed world. This reflects the free trade philosophy of the nineteenth century when what we now know as the Third World supplied primary products for industrial centres in the Western world. Resource-rich countries, however, have come to command rather more respect in trading agreements today.

Exports _____

Gross national product _____

not shared by the rest of the Third World. It does not, therefore, represent a permanent shift in the patterns of international trade.

More important, in the long run, may be the perceptible rise in the Third World's share of the trade in manufactured goods. World exports of machinery and transport equipment, for example, rose by 19.3 per cent between 1970 and 1979. The developing economies increased their exports of these goods by 35.2 per cent in the same period. Their exports of primary materials and food, on the other hand, moved at exactly the same rate as those of the world as a whole — increasing by about 16 per cent. In time, if this trend continues, the relative wealth of the industrialized West and its partners may decline.

The cry for a new international economic order is an attempt by developing countries to strengthen and realize the potential of their resources and at the same time mitigate the relations of dependency that have characterized their integration into the international economic order. Moves have already been made to stabilize export earnings, increase the flow of aid and technology from the developed to the developing world, and gain favourable trading privileges. But such developments have yet to make a truly significant mark on patterns of international trade and the overwhelming dominance of the Western world in the global economic system.

▲ **The London stock exchange** *epitomizes the sophistication and the dominance of developed countries in the world of finance and trade. Bidding and counter-bidding in stock and commodity markets reflect the economic climate of the world.*

▼ **In many parts** *of the developing world, goods are traded in relatively primitive market conditions, such as here in Morocco. For most people economic activity does not extend beyond the local market place.*

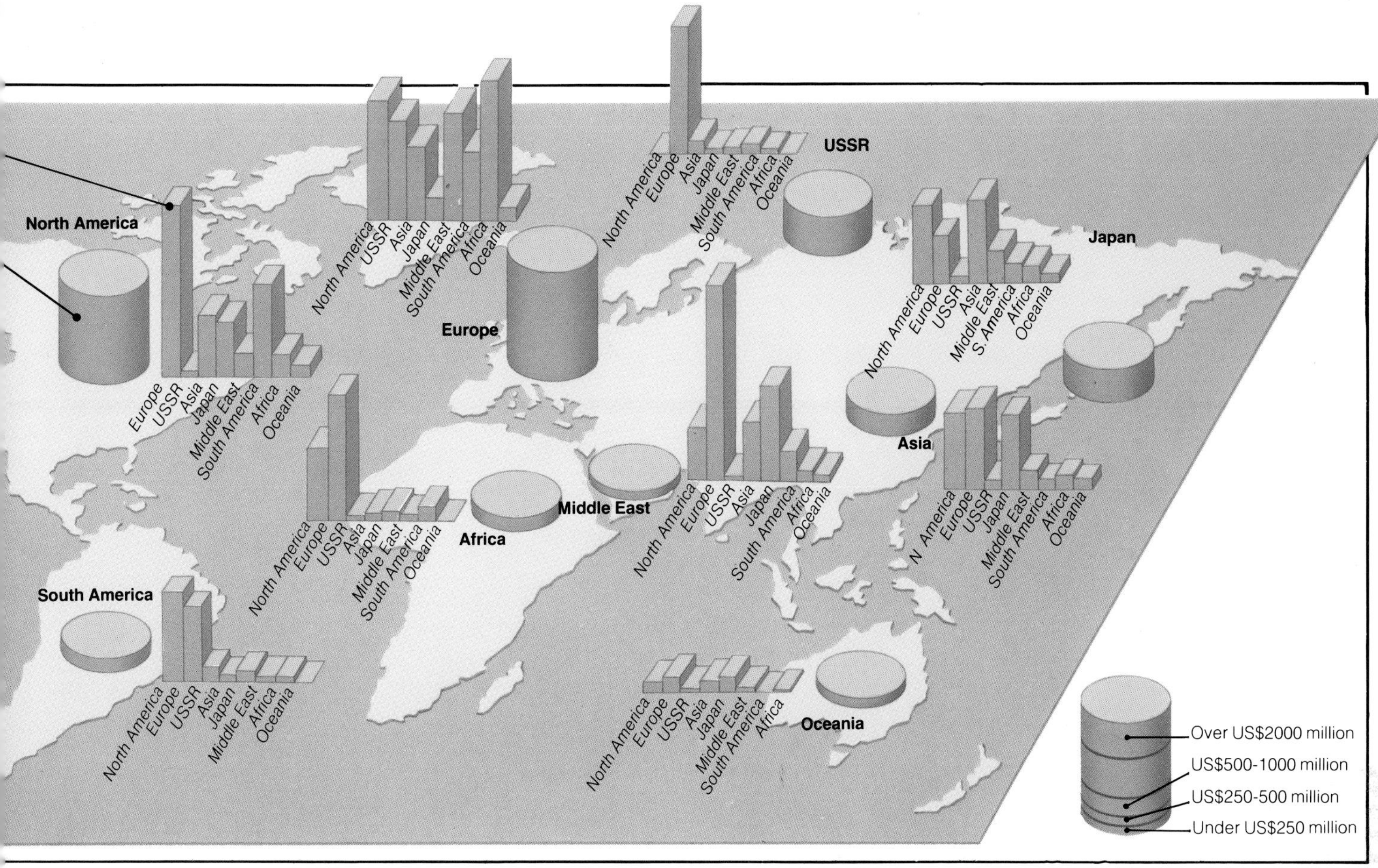

North America

Europe USSR Japan Middle East South America Africa Oceania

North America USSR Asia Japan Middle East South America Africa Oceania

Europe

USSR

North America Europe Asia Japan Middle East South America Africa Oceania

North America Europe USSR Asia Japan Middle East S. America Africa Oceania

Japan

North America Europe USSR Asia Japan Middle East South America Africa Oceania

Asia

North America Europe USSR Japan Middle East South America Africa Oceania

Africa

North America Europe USSR Asia Japan Middle East South America Africa Oceania

Middle East

N. America Europe USSR Japan Middle East South America Africa Oceania

South America

North America Europe USSR Asia Japan Middle East Africa Oceania

North America Europe USSR Asia Japan Middle East South America Africa

Oceania

Over US$2000 million
US$500-1000 million
US$250-500 million
Under US$250 million

The multinationals

The emergence of vast multinational companies is of more than economic and industrial significance. The activities of such organizations affect governmental policy and the relationships between nations. The operations of multinationals span the earth and represent a startling example of international co-operation. Many have annual sales exceeding the gross national product of a small nation.

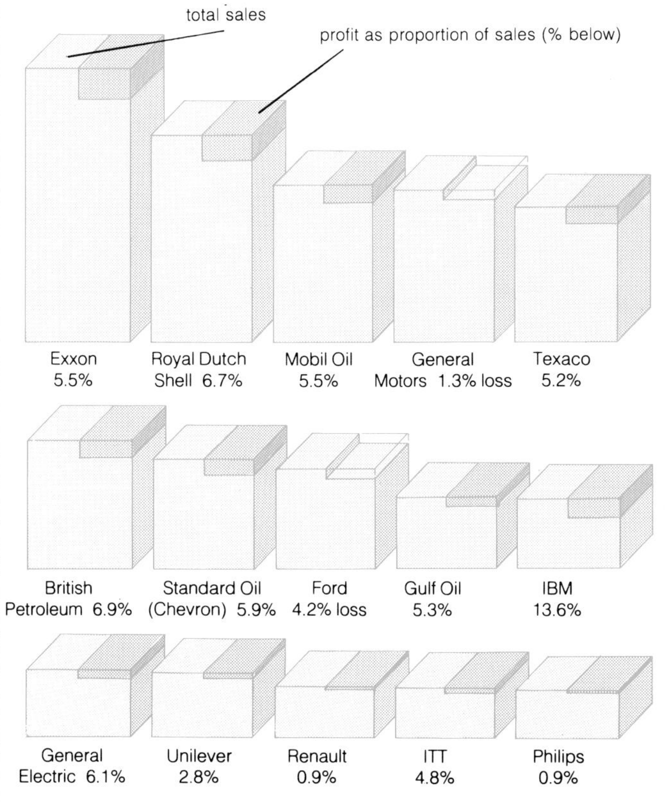

total sales

profit as proportion of sales (% below)

| Exxon 5.5% | Royal Dutch Shell 6.7% | Mobil Oil 5.5% | General Motors 1.3% loss | Texaco 5.2% |

| British Petroleum 6.9% | Standard Oil (Chevron) 5.9% | Ford 4.2% loss | Gulf Oil 5.3% | IBM 13.6% |

| General Electric 6.1% | Unilever 2.8% | Renault 0.9% | ITT 4.8% | Philips 0.9% |

▲ **The export of luxury goods** *such as motor cars is obviously important for a healthy balance of payments. Another characteristic of developed economies is the export of what is known as "capital" goods — equipment and machinery used in the production of other items, such as farm implements.*

▶ **Regional trading groups** *are formed to stimulate production and trade, but can produce economic anomalies. Certain products can be over-priced because prices are maintained by government subsidies. This leads to wastage. Here French farmers protest against Common Market policies.*

The politics of possession

WHEN the various resource categories — people, land, minerals and energy — are examined in relation to one another, we discover their full political significance. The resources possessed by a nation combine to form the resource structure on which economic and military strength are based. Agriculture, for instance, is essential for a healthy and productive labour force, while substantial energy inputs are required to exploit and develop mineral resources and increase agricultural production.

Resources and power

The power base that is formed by the multifarious links between resources defies the temptation to make a direct correlation between the possession of a single resource and political power. In the case of population, for example, what are regarded as the three most powerful countries in the world — the USA, the USSR and the People's Republic of China — are among the four most populous countries in the world. When one looks to India and Bangladesh, however, with the second- and eighth-largest populations respectively, any direct correlation between power and the size of population breaks down. Quite clearly, the population in these latter countries is out of all proportion to the possession and development of other resources. The access that a population has to other resources, including capital and knowledge, will determine how much it will add to or detract from the political power of the state.

In isolation one can observe the political importance assigned to the categories of resources as links in the power base of a state. In a pariah state such as Israel, self-sufficiency in agriculture is of strategic importance, enabling the country to resist external pressures.

Energy is an increasingly important component of the resource structure, driving countries such as the United Kingdom, France, Brazil and India to develop politically unpopular nuclear power programmes. Industrialized countries such as the United States hold strategic stockpiles of the most important minerals to mitigate any interruption in supply that could arise during political conflicts.

It is bordering on a truism to state that an optimal mix of resources enhances the power of a state while the greater the sum total of that mix, the stronger will be the base from which a state exercises power. The USA and the USSR, as superpowers, derive much of their power from the possession of large amounts of all categories of resources. Saudi Arabia, a country with a sparse population and few agricultural and mineral resources, stands as an

▲ **International conventions,** whether they be conferences on population or desertification, or political gatherings such as this International Socialist Convention, are a feature of the modern world.

◄ **Rockets on display** in Moscow's Red Square during May Day celebrations in fact, through the media, show off the Soviet Union's military might to the world.

The Arab-Israeli conflict is a serious threat to world peace. This picture was taken when Israeli-occupied territory extended to the Suez canal.

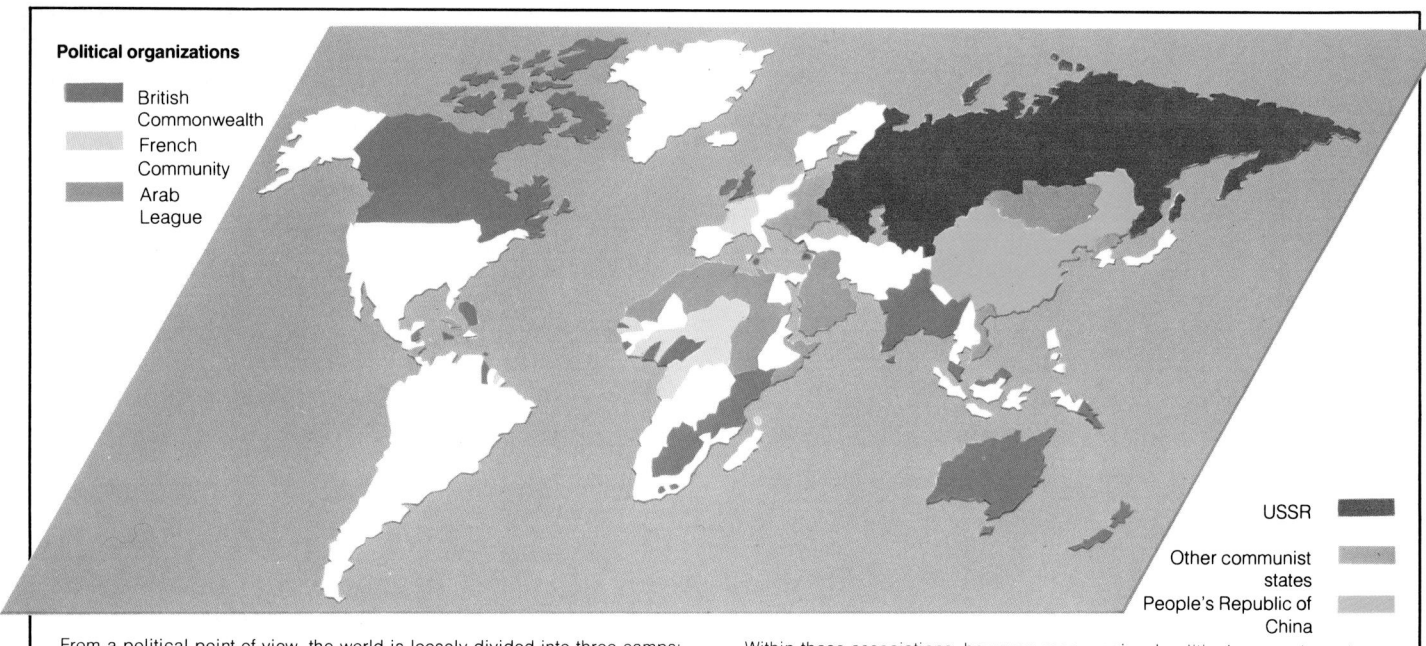

Political organizations

- British Commonwealth
- French Community
- Arab League

- USSR
- Other communist states
- People's Republic of China

From a political point of view, the world is loosely divided into three camps: the capitalist, Western bloc, the socialist states and the so-called "Group of 77". Within these associations, however, many regional political groups have been formed since World War II.

aberration to this pattern. As the world's largest exporter of oil, Saudi Arabia is able to exercise power in world politics far beyond the capability of other single resource states — a power that belies the country's scarcity of resources.

Dependency and power

An abundance or lack of resources is also critical to the dependency structure. A country that is deficient in certain resources often becomes reliant upon external sources. This dependence on external sources for resources is reinforced when a country depends on foreign exchange to finance development and when that foreign exchange is earned primarily by the export of a few commodities. Such nations are forced to look to external sources for aid in financing development and in turn become politically vulnerable as aid is tied to exports

from the donor country or preconditions set by lending institutions.

It is contended by some observers that today's world is one of interdependence, where even the most self-reliant countries such as the USSR and China depend on imports of wheat and high technology from the West, while the West's own power is diminished because of its dependence on developing countries for raw materials.

The lessons of World War II altered the utility of war as a political tool by which a state could seize resources. Total war had become exceptionally costly in terms of the drain on resources and the destruction wrought by modern warfare. What emerged from the War was a bipolar political world characterized by two distinct blocs, with two resource-rich superpowers, the USA and the USSR, serving as respective leaders of each bloc.

The West sought to reduce competition over resources and institutions such as the General Agreement on Tariffs and Trade (GATT) and the International Monetary Fund (IMF) were founded to encourage free trade and stable monetary relations at an international level. The socialist bloc sought a system in which states were to be as self-reliant as possible, with centrally planned economies.

Recent political trends

Two apparent trends have led some to believe that the rift between East and West is diminishing. The first is the disintegration of both political blocs. In 1971 the USA ceased to exchange gold for dollars, marking an end to the post-war monetary system and America's unchallenged leadership of the West. And the socialist bloc has developed rifts within itself. The second trend

is that of convergence between East and West. Western countries such as the UK and Denmark often include a high degree of central planning in their economies, while socialist countries rely on trade with the West to obtain many products.

The rise of a new political bloc of developing countries, otherwise known as the Group of 77, has recently given prominence to a new confrontation over the allocation of resources — the "North-South dialogue". In the mid-1970s the United Nations General Assembly adopted resolutions calling for the transfer of real resources from developed (both capitalist and socialist) to developing countries.

The preoccupation of all countries with political self-interest where ownership and control of resources is concerned shows that resources remain inseparable from the achievement of political ends.

▲ **The education gap** *between developed and less-developed countries is of great significance in a world where an educated population is considered to be a vital resource. Practical training rather than theoretical learning is perhaps the most crucial element of education in the Third World.*

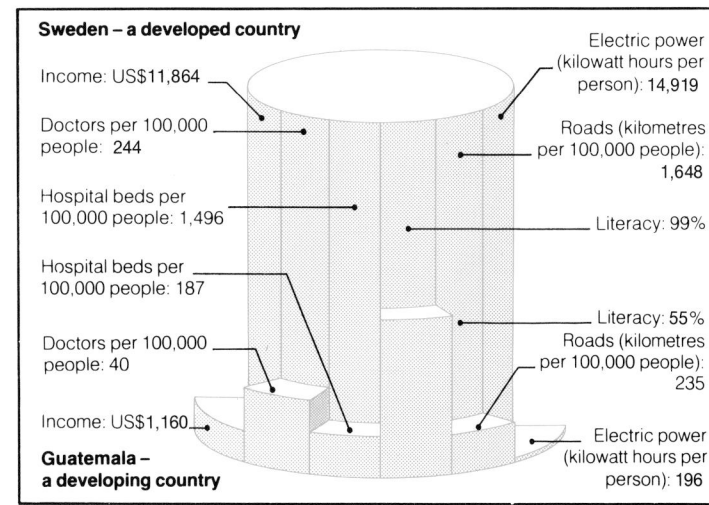

Sweden – a developed country

Income: US$11,864

Doctors per 100,000 people: 244

Hospital beds per 100,000 people: 1,496

Hospital beds per 100,000 people: 187

Doctors per 100,000 people: 40

Income: US$1,160

Guatemala – a developing country

Electric power (kilowatt hours per person): 14,919

Roads (kilometres per 100,000 people): 1,648

Literacy: 99%

Literacy: 55%

Roads (kilometres per 100,000 people): 235

Electric power (kilowatt hours per person): 196

The North/South dialogue

The "haves" versus "have-nots" debate concerning the differences in standards of living or opportunities between the developed and Third worlds has become polarized in what is known as the "North-South dialogue". This is what amounts to a confrontation over the allocation of resources and is an attempt on the part of developing countries to take full advantage of the resources they possess and, at the same time, do away with their dependence on the developed countries which has been a feature of their integration into the international economic system so far. Their goal can only be reached when they have true economic as well as political independence.

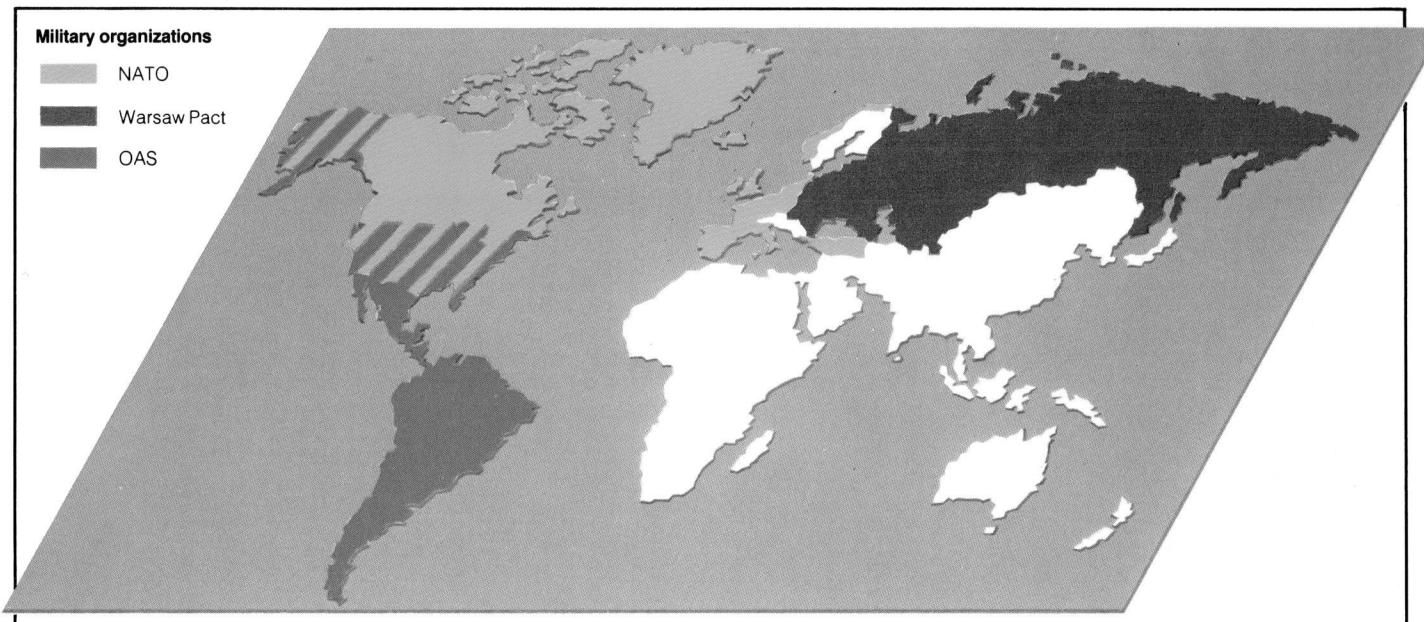

Military organizations

NATO

Warsaw Pact

OAS

Military groupings were also formed after World War II. NATO, or the North Atlantic Treaty Organization, for example, is a Western defensive alliance that was formed in 1949 to promote military aid and co-operation between Europe and North America during peacetime.

Transport and communication

TWO hundred years ago there began a revolution in the speed, availability and cost of transport. For centuries prior to the end of the eighteenth century, speeds had been limited to those of the horse on land and the sailing vessel at sea, while the carriage of heavy goods was prohibitively expensive and restricted in practice to movement by water. The period since then, however, has seen one transforming event after another — road improvement, canal building, railway construction, the steamship, pipeline, aeroplane and hovercraft. Men who sailed before the mast on the old clipper ship have lived to travel by supersonic jet. Modes of transport have superseded one another rapidly. Since World War II an extensive network of motorways has been built in Britain and much traffic that used to be carried by rail now goes by road, despite the fact that road transport uses energy less efficiently.

The transport revolution
The revolution in transport, in turn, made other changes possible. The Industrial Revolution of the nineteenth century involved, among other things, the assembly of huge quantities of raw materials, such as coal or iron ore. It involved also the transfer of other materials, such as cotton or rubber, from distant parts of the world to the new industrial areas, and the new industry necessitated the concentration of workers near to mines or factories in regions that may previously have had only a sparse population. Basic to all these changes was a transport system that could ensure rapid, predictable flows of traffic to keep industry supplied.

Transport was a key factor also in the "urban revolution" of the same period, as population drained away from the countryside and into the new industrial towns. These new townsmen no longer produced their own food: they had to be supplied from farms elsewhere, and supplied as cheaply as possible. As the nineteenth century drew to a close, the cheapest sources of food were found, on the whole, in countries thousands of miles away from the city markets — in the Americas and Australasia.

Such rapid changes in transport technology have inevitably meant that its development has seen a good deal of waste: waste of capital

invested in quickly-outmoded facilities, and waste in the construction of competing routes. Scarcely had the canals in Britain been built when they were superseded by the railways and, in regions such as Britain and North America, not only by one railway but by two or three. Every day, hundreds of empty seats cross the Atlantic in aircraft which fly not so much because there are enough passengers to fill them as for reasons of prestige or competitive pressure. New types of plane, car or train are outdated almost before they can complete the transfer from drawing board to assembly line. A rational transport policy, whereby everybody and everything travelled by the most economical transport mode available, would represent a huge saving in world resources of capital and energy. At present, however, no such policy for transport is in sight.

On land the railway dominated the nineteenth century as road transport has dominated the twentieth. Railways are still being built here and there, but almost exclusively either to tap a particular mineral deposit or for strategic purposes. Some regions have never seen the railway and probably never will. By contrast, every year sees the extension of road networks to accommodate some 430 million motor vehicles that now use them.

This last figure indicates another aspect of the transport revolution. There was a time when travel was the privilege of a few: most people never had the opportunity to travel for pleasure. It is estimated today, however, that there are 300 million tourists worldwide each year: that is, one in 14 of the world's population makes a journey purely for pleasure. Travel has truly been democratized.

Economy of scale
Technical changes in transportation continue, and economies are being made in what has been, in the past, a wasteful industry. The most dramatic of these economies is represented by the rise of the supertanker, the bulk carrier and the jumbo jet — the economies of scale in using a large vehicle. Economies have been made also in loading and unloading techniques as a result of the "container revolution", which has placed small cargoes in easily-handled modules of standard size, and produced the roll-on, roll-off vessel that cuts out trans-

▲ **"Containerization"** *has been the major development in the transport of goods in the last two decades. Containers are all of an internationally agreed size and can be quickly loaded into purpose-built vessels.*

◄ **Road transport** *has benefited in the last half-century by the investment by governments in motorway systems. It is, however, not as efficient as rail transport in terms of energy consumption, and threatens the environment.*

shipment of cargo altogether. These changes have been necessary if only because of the great increase in international waterborne commerce — from some 900 million tonnes in 1955 to 3.3 billion tonnes in 1984 , the bulk of this increase accounted for by the movement of oil.

Communications
If the past two decades have seen revolutionary changes in transport, there have been equally striking developments in communications. These began in 1843 with the transmission of messages by key and code down electric wires: they continued with the telephone, the radio (or wire-less), television and the satellite, and have reached their present degree of sophistication with the involvement of computers, data storage and instant electronic recall of information.

It seems clear that the impact of these changes has still to be fully felt. Already, however, we can see how business structures and, indeed, whole industries, can be transformed by electronics. Branch offices, for example, have immedi-

ate access to central records; executives can "sit in on" conferences at which they are not physically present; and machines are built by other machines rather than by human hand.

The contribution of satellites to the development of communications systems has been particularly dramatic. A number of tasks which previously involved the presence on the ground of a human agent — for example, to map land use or military installations — can now be done much faster and just as effectively from the sky. Satellite pictures help weather forecasters and mineral prospectors, and people across the world can watch an event on television as it happens, instead of the next day or even the following week.

All these developments — whether in transportation or communications systems — are a far cry from the relatively recent days when news was conveyed by runners, goods were moved by barge and empires were administered by issue of orders which could take years to be received and even longer to be implemented.

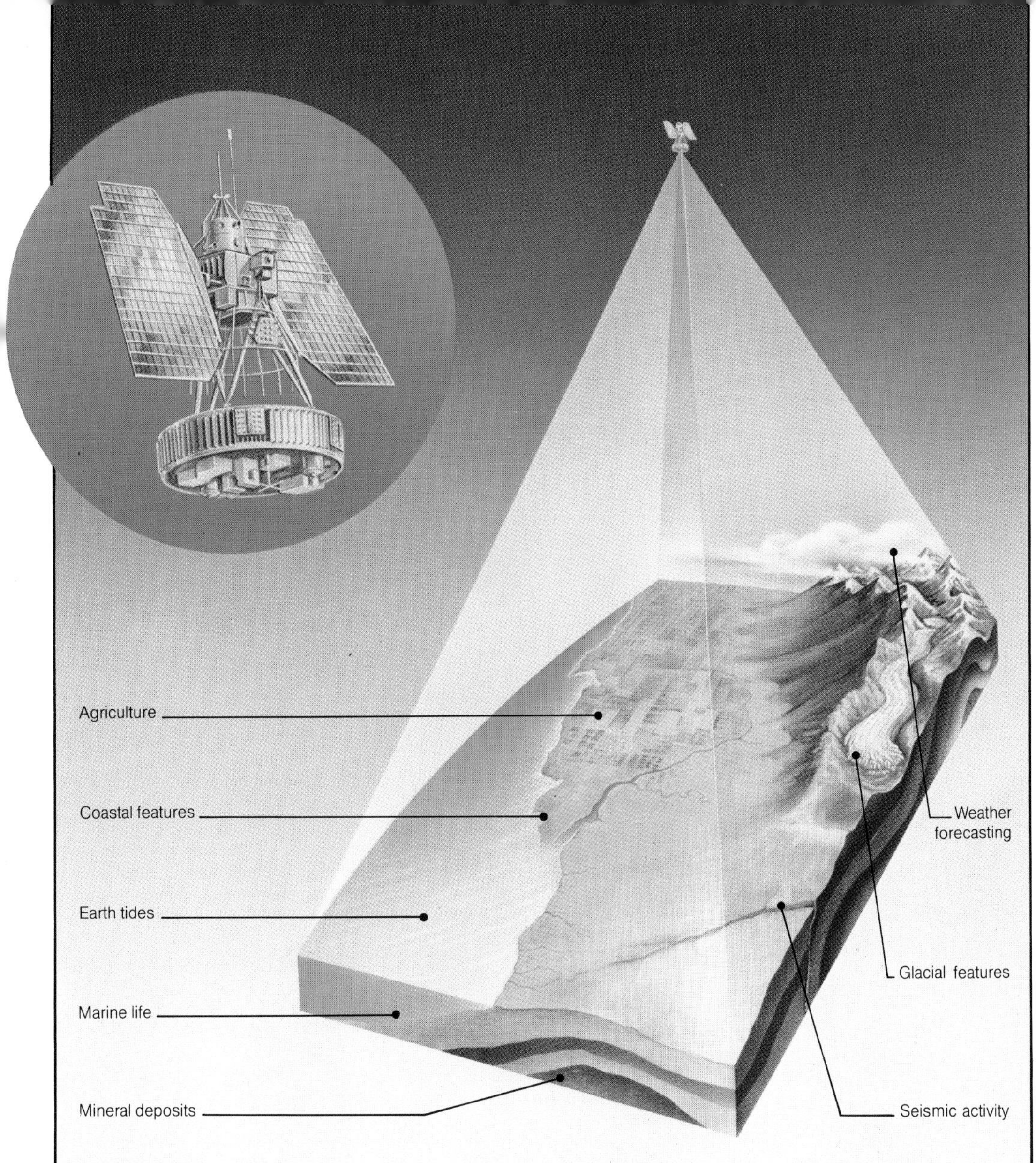

Agriculture

Coastal features

Earth tides

Marine life

Mineral deposits

Weather forecasting

Glacial features

Seismic activity

▲ **Supertankers** *can be loaded and unloaded quickly with the aid of specialized port facilities and they require few crew members.*

▼ **Transport by air,** *especially of passengers, has increased enormously in the last 30 years, particularly over long distances.*

The first satellites for meteorological purposes were launched in the early 1960s. By means of multi-band cameras and infra-red and microwave sensors that can discriminate conditions on earth far better than the human eye, satellites now provide a wealth of information from their constant surveillance of much of the globe. Satellites can also be used for defence purposes. Sophisticated infra-red sensors can detect exhaust plume emissions from missiles as they are launched and thus give an early warning of possible attack.

▲ **Traffic flow** *through the city centre can be monitored from the traffic control room by means of close circuit television cameras mounted in strategic places throughout the city. Details are then relayed to the traffic police in the streets. Highly sophisticated communications systems have revolutionized many industries.*

The shrinking world

As with other aspects of man's activities, from consumption of the earth's resources to the increase in human numbers, the development of transport systems has shown an exponential growth in the speed of the various modes of travel since the take-off point in the nineteenth century. But what of the future of transport? Since social and commercial life depends upon an efficient transport system and as concern for increasingly depleted resources and a threatened environment grows, governments are playing an ever greater role in decision-making within the transport sector. Support for public transport systems, for instance, could see the future development of extensive and rapid mass-transit systems at the expense of private transport which is being made to carry an ever heavier burden of taxation.

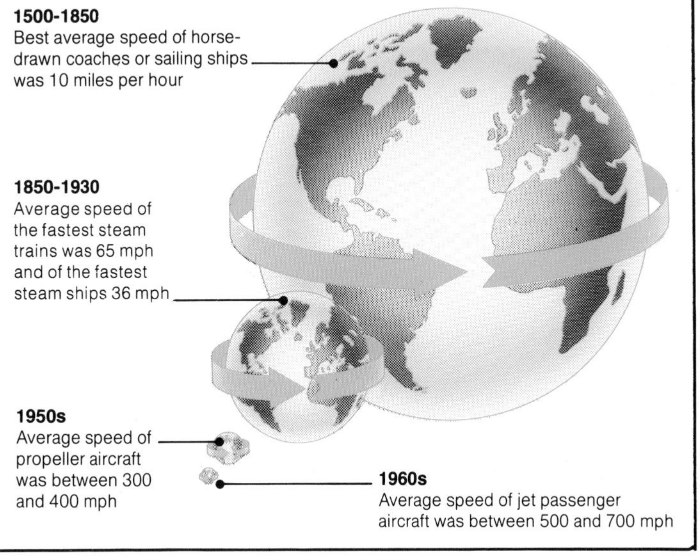

1500-1850
Best average speed of horse-drawn coaches or sailing ships was 10 miles per hour

1850-1930
Average speed of the fastest steam trains was 65 mph and of the fastest steam ships 36 mph

1950s
Average speed of propeller aircraft was between 300 and 400 mph

1960s
Average speed of jet passenger aircraft was between 500 and 700 mph

Industry and technology

WITHIN the last 30 years there have been a number of changes in the overall pattern of world industry or, at least, of industrial science and technology, which are the mainsprings of industrial advance. Before World War II most industrial research was carried out in university laboratories, supported by meagre funds. The technological fruits of that research were, in turn, developed by private companies with their own capital. In both fields — scientific research and technological development — the countries of Western Europe maintained the lead which they had established in the nineteenth century. In the 1950s and 1960s, however, three major changes took place.

Significant developments

In the first place there was an explosive growth in the amount of scientific and technological knowledge and output. Second, there was a massive assumption by government departments and agencies of responsibility for supporting industrial research and development. Third, the United States became the pre-eminent centre of world industry, both in its role as the discoverer of new technologies and in the command which it has come to exercise over worldwide industrial empires. By 1970 the United States was spending 3.5 per cent of its gross national product — about $30 billion, or more than twice the total investment of the rest of the western world — on industrial research and development. This massive capital investment by the government has given the USA its present dominance of industries such as electronics and aerospace.

There have also been changes of direction in other areas. In industries such as chemicals, transport, steel and paper production, there has been a shift away from the simple search for "bigger and better" products. Industry has begun to direct its attention to finding safer chemical products, quieter industrial plants and goods which are both destructible and made from synthetic materials. In such ways industry is beginning to respond to the need for a reduction in the consumption of the earth's natural resources and to the concern of the public that the environment should be protected.

Several trends have manifested themselves in the organization of industry. There has been a move away from adapting organization to technological requirements and towards adapting technology to human and organizational needs. There has been a shift away from plants of maximum size to medium-sized and small units which are more responsive both to market changes and to technological changes in production methods. This change has been especially noticeable in the chemicals and electronics industries and in mechanical engineering works.

In the last 20 years it has been the low-income countries (annual per capita income of less than US $250) and the middle-income countries (more than US $250) that have shown an increase in manufacturing as a percentage of gross domestic product. For all countries, however, the rate of industrial growth has slowed down during the 1970s. A growth rate of 8.9 per cent in low-income countries between 1965 and 1973 fell to 7.4 between 1973 and 1984 . In industrial states for the same periods the growth rate fell from 5.1 to 1.8 per cent.

Energy and industrial growth

Undoubtedly, the major cause of this trend has been the increasing cost of energy. Industry will not take strides forward again until alternatives to non-renewable sources of energy (chiefly oil and natural gas) are developed. The high cost of energy in the 1970s is only partly the result of the decision of the oil-exporting countries to raise their prices. It is in the very nature of a non-renewable commodity that the more it is used, the more expensive it becomes. As the most easily exploitable oil fields become exhausted, the cost of developing less accessible and smaller resource deposits automatically rises. This cost is passed on to the major consumer items: housing (fuel and electricity), clothing (synthetic materials based on petroleum) and food (fertilizers and pesticides made from petroleum and natural gas).

This steady and irreversible rise in the price of non-renewable energy sources leads necessarily to industrial stagnation. It produces inflation, a shortage of capital and an unwillingness to invest in high-risk manufacturing enterprises (because the basic cost of energy is so unstable). The future of industry depends upon the current search to find marketable ways of exploiting alternative sources of energy, and the making of plans today for using alternative energy tomorrow.

Technological breakthrough

Two developments, pioneered in the United States, represent a startling technological advance. One is the manufacture of integrated circuits — postage stamp sized chips containing electric currents sufficiently elaborate to operate complex computer systems. Production began in the early 1960s and the results have been successful enough for the product to enter the mass market in the form of digital watches and pocket calculators.

A more recent and equally important development is the photovoltaic cell. This is a thin, chemically-treated slice of silicon, mounted on a metal base. When light hits it, an electric current is generated. This development could eventually provide the answer to a substantial proportion of our electricity demands. The difficulty is to create a market large enough to reduce costs to the point where the cells could be made in large quantities.

Creating a demand

A vicious circle is in operation: because the demand for photovoltaic cells is at present too low to support an efficient scale of production, the cost of the cells remains too high for them to compete on the energy market. The demand has therefore to be created and only governments have the resources to create such a demand. It was huge orders from the American defence department, placed deliberately in order to stimulate production, that made integrated circuits competitive. If any new commodity is to have the same degree of success, a similar stimulation from governments — on a scale that private industry cannot meet — will have to be provided.

This final point helps to explain why, when one looks globally at industrial and technological development, and despite intense efforts in recent decades to transform many Third World countries from subsistence-level, agricultural economies to industrialized, manufacturing economies, the world remains divided into a relatively rich, industrial north and a relatively poor, agricultural south.

▲ **The North American farmer** has tended to become a small link in a vast agricultural production line that has earned itself the title of agribusiness. Investment in the farm is massive and trends in food production are dictated by the large food corporations.

▲ **Assembly line work,** *such as this Ford production line in Detroit, represents for many workers a sophisticated form of drudgery. Wages are high to compensate for the repetitiveness of the work.*

◀ **Textiles** *have played a pioneer role in the economic development of Third World countries. Mechanization exacerbates already high levels of under-employment.*

▶ **Since the advent** *of the transistor radio, electronic devices have become more diverse and increasingly sophisticated. The range of their application today extends from telecommunications to data processing and automatic control. The latter raises serious questions about possibly greater unemployment in the future.*

The labour shift

The growth of service industries has been the most significant development within the economic structure of developed countries since World War II. More than 60 per cent of all workers in the United States are employed in the service sector. A service industry is distinguished from other industries in that it supplies the needs of industry or the consumer in the form of such things as banking and insurance, entertainment, education, transport and communications, legal or financial advice, medical and social services, government and the distribution and sale of goods by wholesalers and retailers. The increase in services reflects greater per capita income levels. As people earn more than is required to meet their basic needs they desire and can afford more services. The growth of services does not necessarily reflect a proportional increase in demand. Service industries are labour-intensive and output per worker is not as great as in other sectors. Service industries (personal servants excepted) are of much less significance in developing countries where most growth has been in the retail trade.

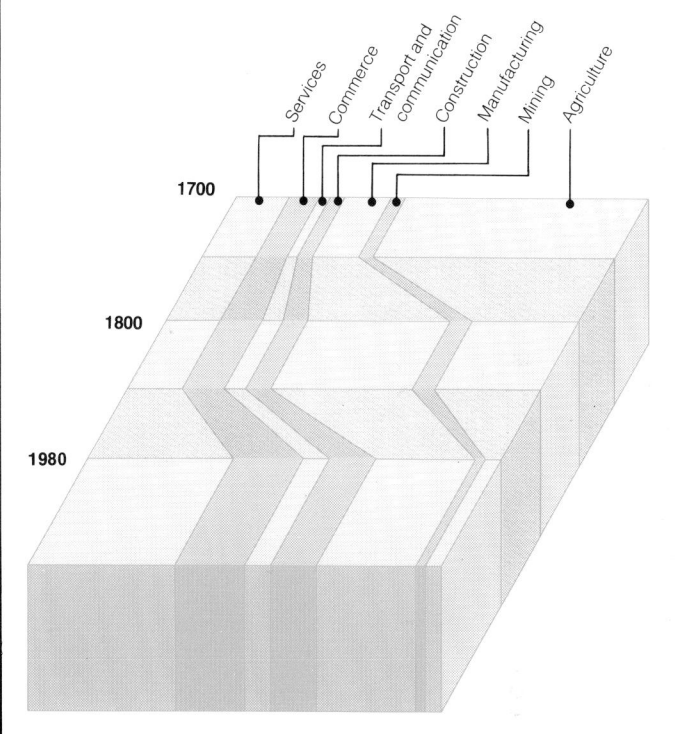

Industrial relations

Good industrial relations have become an increasingly important ingredient for the economic well-being of a nation. The purpose of trade unions is to represent the interests of workers and unions now exist in most countries of the world. The level of organization, however, varies enormously from one country to another. It depends, for instance, on social attitudes, political policies and the economic framework of the country. Disputes and strikes are an inevitable part of a democratic system of industrial relations. Britain does not fare too badly within a league of developed countries, but strikes in Britain differ from many other countries in one important respect: a large proportion of them are unofficial, that is, they are in breach of union rules.

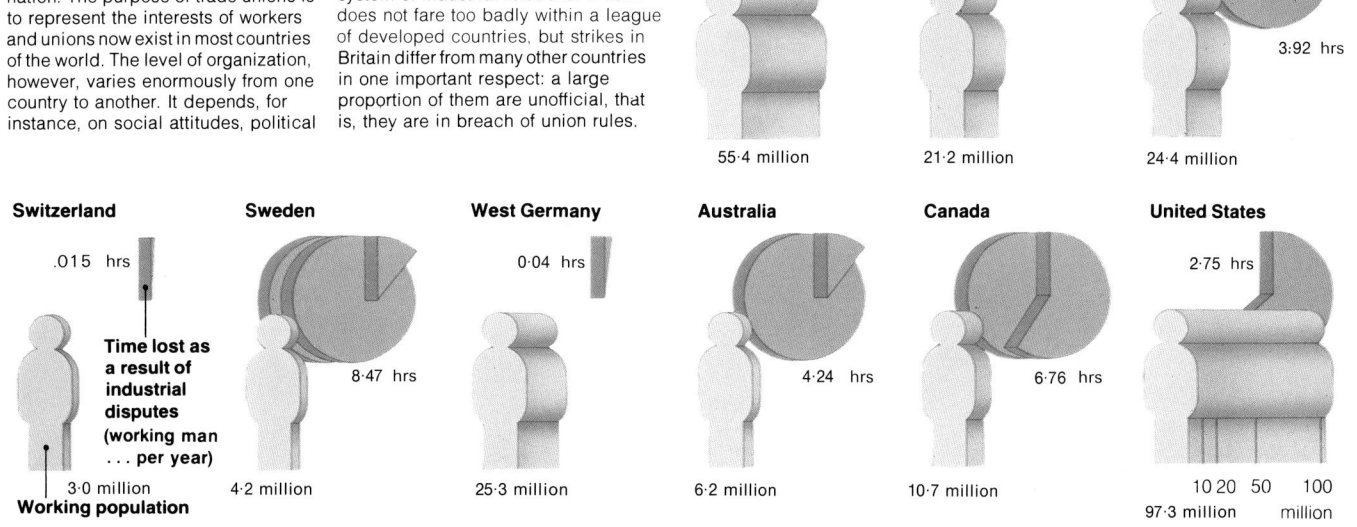

Japan
.13 hrs
55·4 million

France
0·632 hrs
21·2 million

United Kingdom
3·92 hrs
24·4 million

Switzerland
.015 hrs
3·0 million
Working population

Time lost as a result of industrial disputes (working man . . . per year)

Sweden
8·47 hrs
4·2 million

West Germany
0·04 hrs
25·3 million

Australia
4·24 hrs
6·2 million

Canada
6·76 hrs
10·7 million

United States
2·75 hrs
10 20 50 100
97·3 million   million

The quality of life

THAT people should wish for an improvement in the quality of life for themselves and their children seems to most of those people who live in the world's developed countries both reasonable and "normal". For them change is constant and advance is taken for granted. It is important to realize, however, that this state of affairs is relatively recent in the history even of the developed world, and it does not apply, even today, to millions of inhabitants of the developing countries.

The element of choice
What underlies an improvement in the quality of life is the idea of choice: the freedom of human beings, either individually or as communities, to choose among several possibilities the one that best serves their own interests, whether it be type of work, location and kind of dwelling, or use of leisure time. In a society where the dawn to dusk efforts of every single member of the community are required merely to keep starvation at bay, there are no such choices. Everybody must live wherever the work is, in whatever kind of shelter is available, and there is little opportunity for leisure activities.

Sometimes, of course, the absence of choice is imposed not by economic necessity but by political and social restraint. In the feudal society of medieval Europe, for example, most of the population were tied to the soil: they had no right to move from their birthplace, or to withhold their labour when it was required by their overlord. For many centuries, in fact, the only changes that occurred were almost always disastrous — the passage of marauding armies, or the withdrawal of common rights by the landlord. In any totalitarian society, choice is the privilege of those who rule that society.

Industrialization and choice
In the developed world, freedom of choice broadened gradually with the breakdown of feudalism and serfdom, with a growing diversity of work opportunities (especially after the onset of industrialization), with an increasing margin in the economy above the level of mere survival, and with the coming of cheap and rapid movement by public transport. Even so, change was no friend to the first generation or so of the new, freer society. Craftsmen were rendered unemployed by factory-based machines, and small farmers were dispossessed. Thousands of country people found themselves in the new slums of the industrial cities, their only "choice" being to starve on the land or work 12- or 16-hour days in the factories. It has taken time for choice to percolate down through society so that today even the most poorly paid worker has some choice about where he lives or how he spends his leisure hours.

Improvement of the quality of life is a goal also in the centrally planned economies of the Communist world no less than in Western Europe or North America, although the emphasis is on improvement for the community as a whole, rather than for its individual members. Even in these countries, however, it is impossible in practice to eliminate the idea of personal incentive and achievement: in sport, in recreation, in striving for a better job, or in the rewards that come with higher output per worker.

What of the less-developed world, however? There is no reason to suppose that, given the opportunity, millions of inhabitants in developing countries would not welcome the same range of choice that is enjoyed by others. At the moment, most of these people are tied to particular patches of earth which afford their only means of subsistence, and if and when they have the opportunity and the courage to break away, they are as likely as not to find themselves in the shanty towns that have grown up on the outskirts of many large cities in less-developed countries. There they live in appalling conditions and experience great deprivation.

A standard of living
The term normally used to identify differences in the quality of life is standard of living, although the two concepts are subtly different in character. Standard of living is generally expressed by the level of income per person. If we compare nation with nation in this respect, the differences in standards are enormous: $16,330 per person in Switzerland (1984 figures) compared with $260 in India, $360 in Sri Lanka, or $280 per person in Rwanda. Within these countries, needless to say, the range variation about the average figure is great. In many Latin American countries, for example, the idea of an "average" standard of living is meaningless.

Nevertheless, it is the policy of more or less every government, whatever its political complexion, to raise the standard of living of its people. Standards may rise, however, without a corresponding improvement in the quality of life. In general we can say that advance in either will be accompanied by certain signs of change within the society or economy that reflect the improvement of living standards.

Indications of change
As the standard of living rises, it will probably be marked by a decrease in the proportion of the population engaged in primary production — in working on the land, or in forestry, fishing or mining — which implies a broadening variety of other forms of occupation — in manufacturing, transport, education and other service industries. In other words, the society requires fewer people to supply its basic needs. In the United States today only three workers out of ten actually produce anything at all, by farming the land or manufacturing goods.

▲ **The clamour** for extensive, unpolluted open spaces in which to spend our leisure time has meant that millions of hectares in the form of national parks or game reserves have been put aside for just that purpose. Areas of outstanding natural beauty are now protected by law from human encroachment that could damage the environment.

Another indicator is an increase in the volume of circulation, whether of goods or of people, within society. This implies a greater and wider range of demand for commodities beyond those produced locally, and a greater freedom, financial and personal, to come and go at will. Finally, an improvement in the quality of life will be marked by the increased allocation of resources, especially of land, to leisure pursuits, from golf courses and waterfronts to national parks, in some cases the size of a small country. This involves setting aside some part of land resources from ordinary productive use, and expresses a growing concern for the facilities available to the population when they are not working in offices or factories.

There is an increasing awareness now, however, that the path to industrialization and a higher standard of living in the past will not lead to an improvement in the quality of life in the future. That improvement may well necessitate a fourth indication of change within society — the conservation of the earth's limited resources and the protection of the natural and our man-made environment.

Labour migration

The migration of people has been a recurrent theme throughout history, but a high degree of individual mobility is a characteristic of recent times. Migration has been an essential part of the processes of urbanization and industrialization. To a large extent this has reflected the greater job opportunities and higher income levels in urban centres. For similar reasons, rural-urban migration has been on the increase in less-developed countries. Migration represents one way by which people can improve their standard of living. On the other hand, the post-war prosperity of Europe, for example, has been increased by a vast pool of immigrant labour. The economic recession of recent years, however, has meant that many countries have closed their doors to unlimited foreign labour and only let migrant workers in according to the needs of the country. To some extent, therefore, a migrant workforce may shield the native workforce from the effects of a recessionary period as a contraction in employment will result in fewer migrant workers being admitted or allowed to stay in the host country. In times of growth, on the other hand, immigrant workers will help support economic expansion.

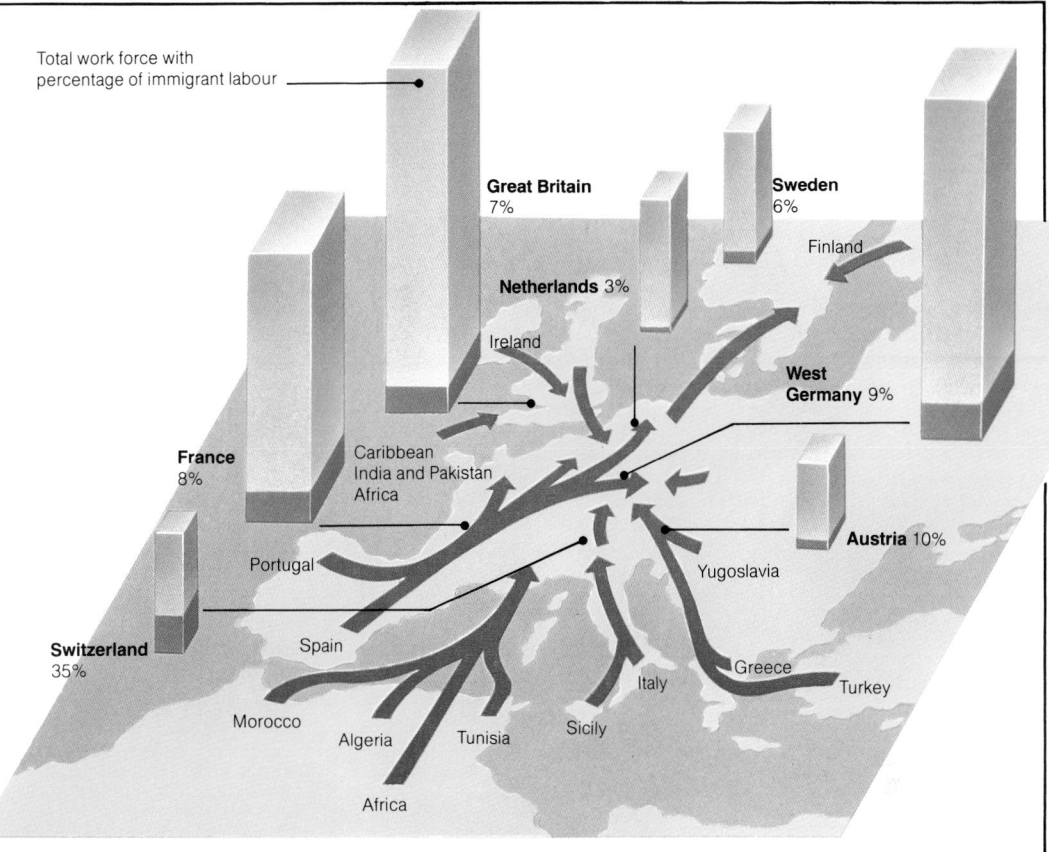

Total work force with percentage of immigrant labour

Great Britain 7%
Sweden 6%
Finland
Netherlands 3%
Ireland
West Germany 9%
Caribbean India and Pakistan Africa
France 8%
Austria 10%
Portugal
Yugoslavia
Switzerland 35%
Spain
Italy
Greece
Turkey
Morocco
Algeria
Tunisia
Sicily
Africa

▶ **The greater opportunities** *for migrant workers in post-war Europe has meant an escape from poverty for, for example, millions of Turkish factory workers in West Germany.*

▼ **In the West** *we tend to take social improvement for granted, but for the underprivileged in New York's Bowery, life in the developed world offers little opportunity.*

▼ **An ever-shorter** *working week and more leisure time leads to increasing demands for leisure facilities. Many sports, such as American baseball, are now big business ventures.*

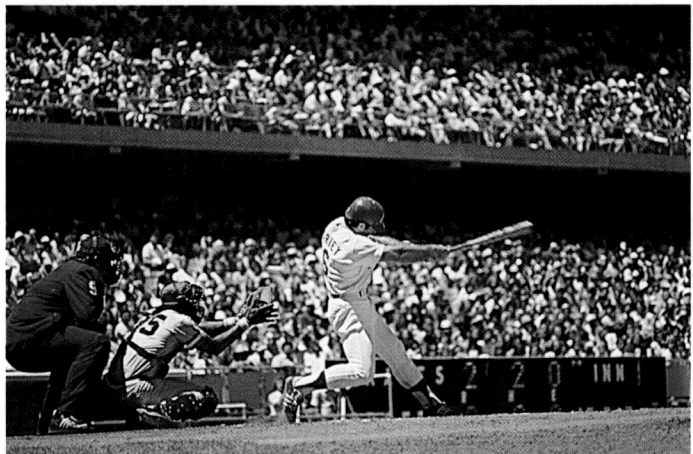

Life expectancy

Not only do we expect better opportunities in life and an ever-higher standard of living, we also expect a healthier and longer life than did our forebears. With the advances of medical science, the length of life the average new-born baby in the developed world can expect has more than doubled in the last two centuries to about 70 years today. Although death rates in many Asian and South American countries have been dramatically reduced, death rates in parts of the African continent have only just begun to decline and remain very high.

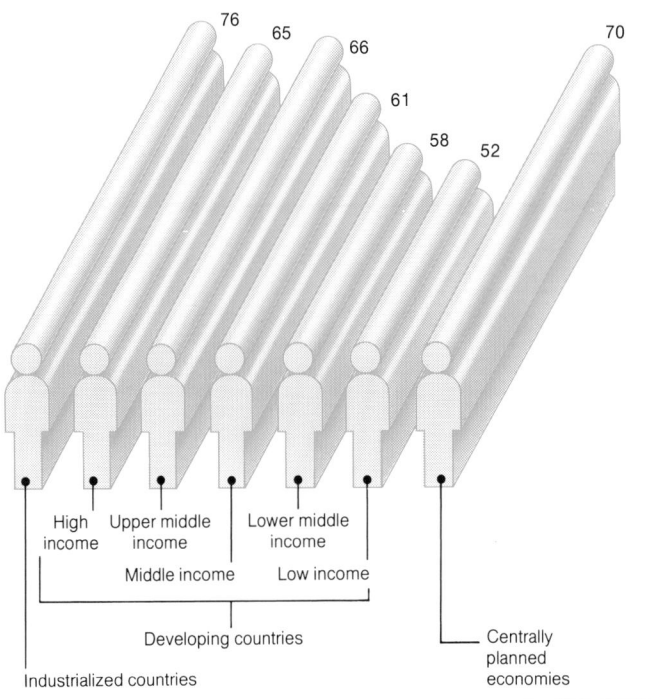

76
65
66
61
58
52
70

High income
Upper middle income
Lower middle income
Middle income
Low income
Developing countries
Industrialized countries
Centrally planned economies

One earth

WITH people everywhere, both in less-developed and developed countries, clamouring for an improved standard of living, it is necessary to appreciate what this implies for an earth whose resources are finite. One way of defining standard of living is as the total amount of resources consumed in a year by the average person in a nation or community. At present, people in countries with a high standard of living are consuming huge and varied quantities of materials derived, in one way or another, from the earth — not only more food per person than their bodies actually require,

but steel and petrol for their cars and a whole range of goods, in fact, that are part of everyday life. Such a community leaves behind it mountains of waste. By contrast, the total resource consumption in a poor community may be represented by small amounts of food and clothing.

Between these levels of consumption there is manifestly no comparison. Yet if we are to visualize that, in the course of time, all living standards will rise and converge upon the highest level we now know, then that implies a colossal drain on the earth's resources. To envisage all of mankind living as North Americans or

Western Europeans currently do, in the present state of our knowledge and technology, is an extremely daunting prospect.

Resources and technology
In past eras, inequalities in living standards were confronted very simply: groups preyed on one another, and the strong grew rich while the poor starved. Not only is this unacceptable by present-day standards, but a new factor has been introduced into the competition for resources — the technical ability to use them. A community with a high level of technology can, in practice, reach out and tap the resources of others: by contrast, a country richly endowed with natural resources may not have the technical expertise to exploit them, and so may have to bring in outsiders and share its wealth with them in return for their assistance. All this means,

however, is that, without resorting to force, the rich grow richer, often at the expense of the poor.

There are several possible remedies for this situation. One is to set up a world organization with sufficient power to introduce some form of international rationing. However, not only would it be exceedingly difficult to decide what constituted "fair shares" for nations with entirely different needs and lifestyles, but such an arrangement could, in practice, only be introduced with the consent and help of the most wealthy nations, and they would naturally be the losers by it.

A question of distribution
The second possibility is that the largest consumers of resources should limit their usage and leave more for the rest of mankind. It has even been agreed that the living standards of the rich would not

▲ **The rehabilitation** of land spoiled by man's activities has become an exact science. Here in Wales colliery spoil is spread over toxic metal waste and planted with a special strain of grass whose short root system does not reach the toxic soil beneath the top layer.

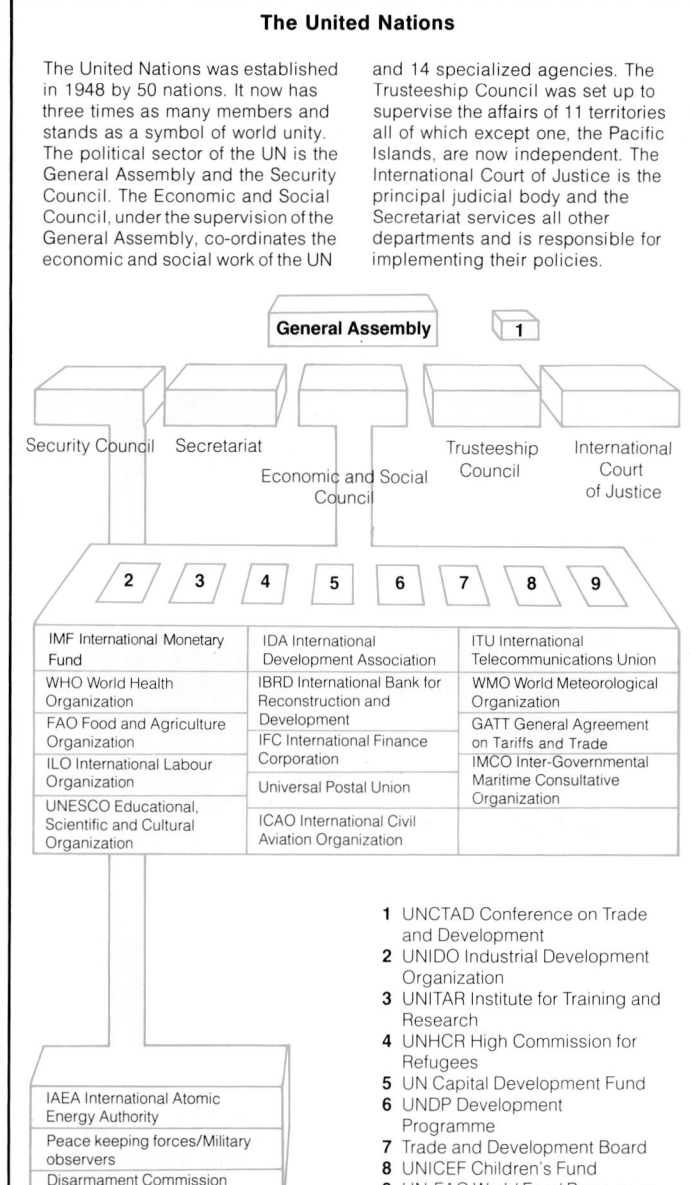

The United Nations

The United Nations was established in 1948 by 50 nations. It now has three times as many members and stands as a symbol of world unity. The political sector of the UN is the General Assembly and the Security Council. The Economic and Social Council, under the supervision of the General Assembly, co-ordinates the economic and social work of the UN

and 14 specialized agencies. The Trusteeship Council was set up to supervise the affairs of 11 territories all of which except one, the Pacific Islands, are now independent. The International Court of Justice is the principal judicial body and the Secretariat services all other departments and is responsible for implementing their policies.

General Assembly 1

Security Council Secretariat

Economic and Social Council

Trusteeship Council

International Court of Justice

2 3 4 5 6 7 8 9

IMF International Monetary Fund	IDA International Development Association	ITU International Telecommunications Union
WHO World Health Organization	IBRD International Bank for Reconstruction and Development	WMO World Meteorological Organization
FAO Food and Agriculture Organization	IFC International Finance Corporation	GATT General Agreement on Tariffs and Trade
ILO International Labour Organization	Universal Postal Union	IMCO Inter-Governmental Maritime Consultative Organization
UNESCO Educational, Scientific and Cultural Organization	ICAO International Civil Aviation Organization	

IAEA International Atomic Energy Authority

Peace keeping forces/Military observers

Disarmament Commission

1 UNCTAD Conference on Trade and Development
2 UNIDO Industrial Development Organization
3 UNITAR Institute for Training and Research
4 UNHCR High Commission for Refugees
5 UN Capital Development Fund
6 UNDP Development Programme
7 Trade and Development Board
8 UNICEF Children's Fund
9 UN-FAO World Food Programme

necessarily fall. Their present consumption patterns are so wasteful of resources that any loss in supply could be recouped by the proper use of the resources they still possessed. By eliminating waste, improving efficiency and recycling materials, the developed countries could live on a lot less.

All this is true, and there is no doubt that the average consumer in the developed world today has a far more tender conscience, and a far greater awareness of the needs of others, than was the case a few decades ago, thanks in part to the development of communications and the immediate coverage of famine, catastrophe and living conditions worldwide. Reduced consumption by the well-to-do will not, however, solve the problem of transferring the resources saved by one country in order to supply the needs of another. If the United States were to reduce its consumption of petroleum, this would not necessarily make it cheaper or easier for a poor and oil-less state such as Bangladesh to obtain petroleum. The connection between supply and demand is not that simple. While there is, therefore, an obvious argument that there should be fairness for all, the machinery for achieving this has yet to be created, at least on an international level.

The provision of aid
The only workable alternative to these two ideas, and one which has received a lot of attention in the years since World War II, is that of giving technical aid. Since it is the difference in technical standards and capacities which chiefly distinguish the rich nation from the poor one, a levelling up of those standards ought to lead directly towards an equalization of living standards. Furthermore, it should be possible to do this with a minimum of disturbance to ordinary trade relations, and without the need to move large quantities of food and materials from one place to another. By upgrading the poor nation's ability to make use of its own resources, the poor may gain much and the rich will lose little, at least in the short term. Over a longer period, however, the technically-advanced nation is creating competitors for its own producers. But it is reasonable to expect that, by the time that happens, the advanced economy will have moved on again to different levels of technology.

Experience has shown, however, that aid from the developed countries to the developing has been double-edged. Much of the aid has been in the form of loans, on which interest has to be paid, or there are strings attached, such as the demand that purchases of equipment for the developing economy shall be made only from the aid-granting country. Sometimes technical aid to agriculture benefits only the large farmers and makes life more difficult for the small operator, and industries are established which are not only controlled but also staffed largely by technicians from abroad, so that their presence makes little impact on unemployment in the area.

What this means is not that aid should be stopped, but that it should take carefully chosen forms, and that the basic objective of every aid programme should be to give the maximum assistance to those most in need. In the world today, it is not by the condition of the average man, and certainly not by the wealth of the richest, but by the circumstances of the most needy that future generations will judge us.

◄ **Massive foreign aid** *is granted to developing countries each year. Aid at times of catastrophe is widely publicized — less well known is the work of the United Nations and other international organizations in assisting economic development in the less developed world.*

▶ **Proponents of an alternative society** *advocate a return to a pre-industrial way of life in which men live more simply and without generating the problems of modern times. The Amish of Pennsylvania, however, have never succumbed to the pressures of American society and have lived in relative seclusion for the past two centuries.*

▲ **The most constructive form** *of aid to less-developed countries is education and the introduction of a technology that is best suited to their requirements.*

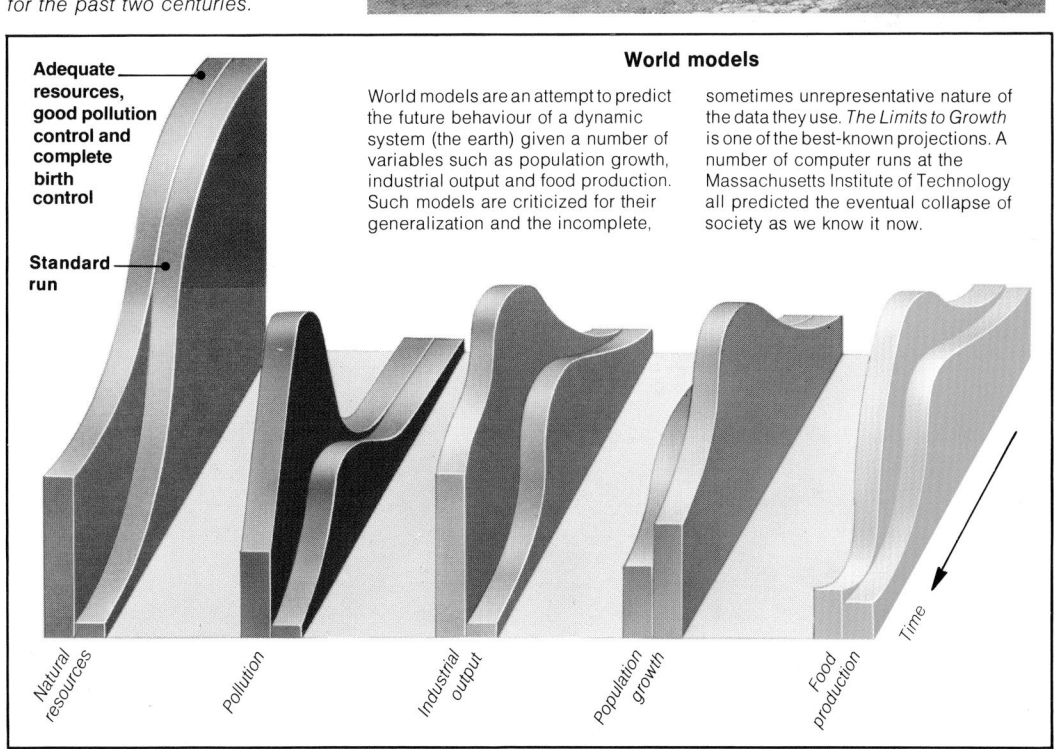

World models

World models are an attempt to predict the future behaviour of a dynamic system (the earth) given a number of variables such as population growth, industrial output and food production. Such models are criticized for their generalization and the incomplete, sometimes unrepresentative nature of the data they use. *The Limits to Growth* is one of the best-known projections. A number of computer runs at the Massachusetts Institute of Technology all predicted the eventual collapse of society as we know it now.

Adequate resources, good pollution control and complete birth control

Standard run

Natural resources

Pollution

Industrial output

Population growth

Food production

Time

Earth data

The earth's dimensions

Superficial area	510,000,000km²
Land surface	149,000,000km²
Land surface as % of total area	29.2%
Water surface	361,000,000km²
Water surface as % of total area	70.8%
Equatorial circumference	40,077km
Meridional circumference	40,009km
Equatorial diameter	12,757km
Polar diameter	12,714km
Volume	$1,083,230 \times 10^6$km³
Mass	5.9×10^{21} tonnes

The earth's surface

Highest point (Mount Everest, Tibet-Nepal border)	8,848m
Lowest point (Dead Sea, Israel-Jordan)	395m below sea level
Greatest ocean depth (Challenger Deep, Mariana Trench)	11,022m
Average height of land	840m
Average depth of sea	3,808m

The largest oceans and seas

Pacific Ocean	165,721,000km²
Atlantic Ocean	81,660,000km²
Indian Ocean	73,442,000km²
Arctic Ocean	14,351,000km²
Mediterranean Sea	2,966,000km²
Bering Sea	2,274,000km²
Caribbean Sea	1,942,000km²
Mexico, Gulf of	1,813,000km²
Okhotsk, Sea of	1,528,000km²
East China Sea	1,248,000km²

The longest rivers

	LENGTH	LOCATION
Nile	6,669km	Africa
Amazon	6,516km	South America
Mississippi-Missouri	6,050km	North America
Yangtze-Kiang	5,989km	Asia
Ob-Irtysh	5,149km	Asia
Amur	4,666km	Asia
Zaire	4,373km	Africa
Hwang Ho (Yellow River)	4,344km	Asia
Lena	4,256km	Asia
Mackénzie	4,240km	North America

The largest lakes and inland seas

	AREA	LOCATION
Caspian Sea	393,896km²	Asia
Lake Superior	82,413km²	North America
Lake Victoria	69,484km²	Africa
Aral Sea	68,681km²	Asia
Lake Huron	59,596km²	North America
Lake Michigan	58,015km²	North America
Lake Tanganyika	32,893km²	Africa
Great Bear Lake	31,792km²	North America
Lake Baykal	30,510km²	Asia
Lake Nyasa	29,604km²	Africa

The highest mountains

	HEIGHT	LOCATION
Everest	8,848m	Tibet-Nepal
K2 (Godwin Austen)	8,616m	Kashmir
Kanchenjunga	8,591m	Nepal-Sikkim
Makalu	8,481m	Tibet-Nepal
Dhaulagiri	8,177m	Nepal
Nanga Parbat	8,131m	Kashmir
Annapurna	8,078m	Nepal
Gasherbrum	8,073m	Kashmir
Gosainthan	8,019m	Tibet
Nanda Devi	7,822m	India

The largest islands

	AREA	LOCATION
Greenland	2,175,000km²	Atlantic
New Guinea	885,780km²	Pacific
Borneo	743,330km²	Pacific
Madagascar	587,045km²	Indian
Baffin	476,070km²	Arctic
Sumatra	473,600km²	Indian
Honshu	230,540km²	Pacific
Great Britain	218,050km²	Atlantic
Ellesmere	212,690km²	Arctic
Victoria	212,200km²	Arctic

The continents

	AREA
Asia	44,250,000km²
Africa	30,264,000km²
North America	24,398,000km²
South America	17,807,800km²
Antarctica	13,209,000km²
Europe	9,906,000km²
Australia and New Zealand	8,842,400km²

The greatest waterfalls

	HEIGHT	LOCATION
Angel	980m	Venezuela
Tugela	853m	South Africa
Mongefossen	774m	Norway
Yosemite	738m	California
Mardalsfossen	655m	Norway
Cuquenan	610m	Venezuela
Sutherland	579m	New Zealand
Reichenbach	548m	Switzerland
Wollomombi	518m	Australia
Ribbon	491m	California

Notable volcanoes

	HEIGHT	LOCATION
Etna	3,340m	Sicily
Fuji	3,778m	Japan
Mauna Loa	4,160m	Hawaii
Ngaurone	2,290m	New Zealand
Njamiagira	3,059m	Zaire
Nyiragongo	3,472m	Zaire
Pacaya	2,546m	Guatemala
Popocatepetl	5,456m	Mexico
Saint Helens	2,744m	USA
Stromboli	927m	Italy
Tristan da Cunha	2,026m	Atlantic Ocean
Vesuvius	1,278m	Italy

GENERAL REFERENCE

Abbreviations of measures used — ft Feet; mm {Millimetres / Millimeters} cm {Centimetres / Centimeters} m {Metres / Meters} Km. {Kilometres / Kilometers} mb Millibars

City and Town symbols in order of size

∴ Sites of Archæological or Historical Importance

—— International Boundaries

– – – International Boundaries (Undemarcated or Undefined)

········ Internal Boundaries

～～ Principal Roads

-‑-‑-‑ Tracks, Seasonal and other Roads

–]‑-‑[– Road Tunnels

〜 Principal Railways

〜 Other Railways

-‑-‑-‑ Railways under construction

–]‑-‑[– Railway Tunnels

············ Principal Canals

⊐⊏ Passes

✿ Principal Airports

– – – – 3386 Principal Shipping Routes (Distances in Nautical Miles)

〜 Perennial Streams

-‑-‑-‑ Seasonal Streams

Seasonal Lakes, Salt Flats

Swamps, Marshes

ᴗ Wells in Desert

Permanent Ice

▲ 8848 Height above sea-level ⎫
▼ 8050 Depth below sea-level ⎬ in metres
1134 Height of lake-level ⎭

CONVERSION SCALE

ft	m
30 000	8000
24 000	7000
18 000	6000
	5000
12 000	4000
9000	3000
6000	2000
3000	1000
	500
Sea-Level 0	0 Sea-Level
	500
1000	1000
	2000
	3000
2000	4000
	5000
3000	6000
4000	7000
	8000
5000	9000
	10 000
6000	11 000
	12 000
7000	
fathoms	m

THE WORLD
Physical
1:150 000 000

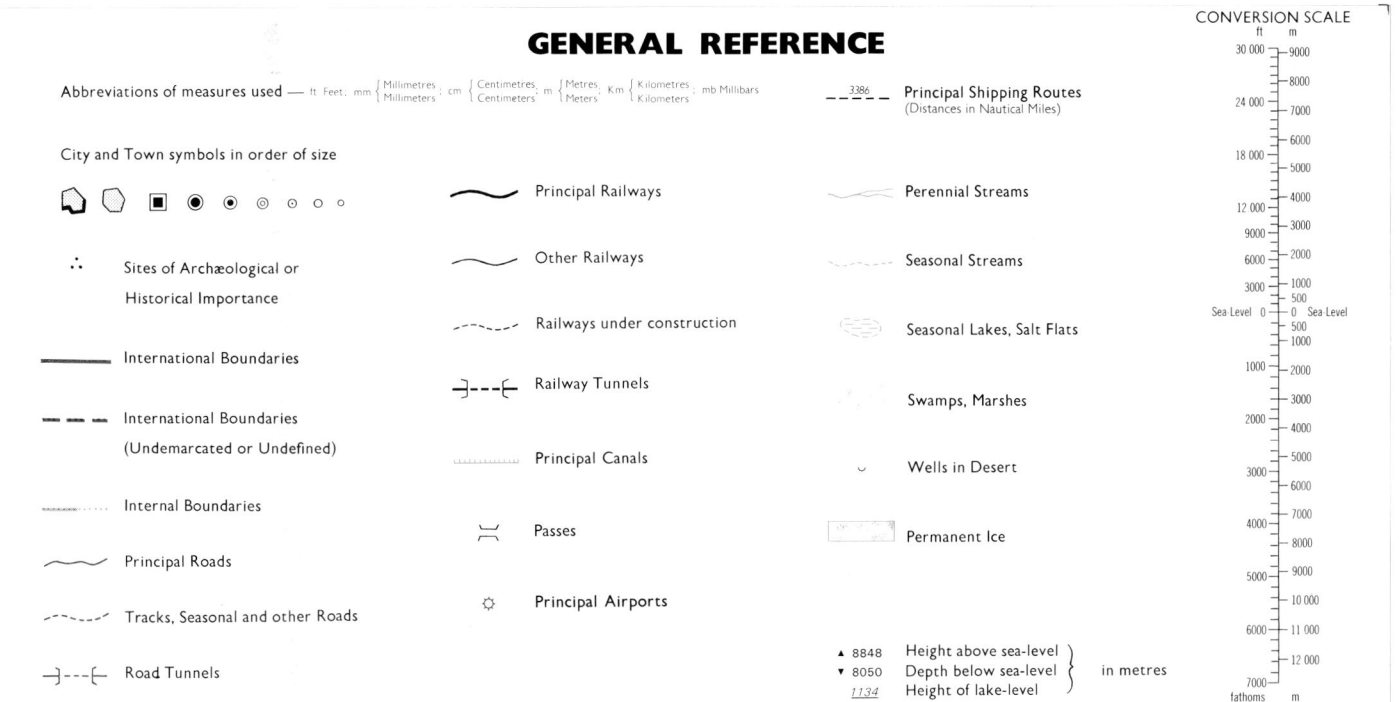

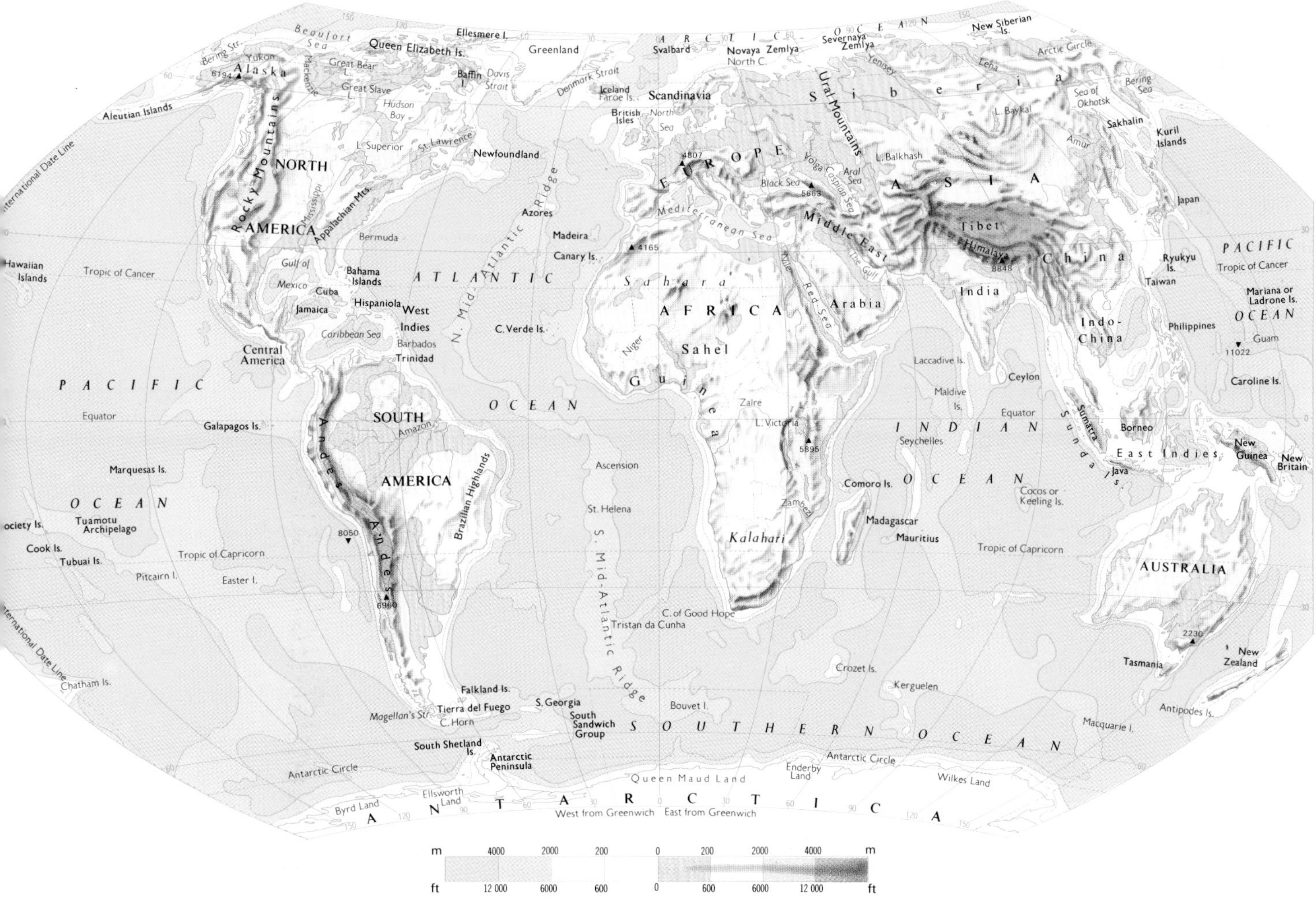

| m | 4000 | 2000 | 200 | 0 | 200 | 2000 | 4000 | m |
| ft | 12 000 | 6000 | 600 | 0 | 600 | 6000 | 12 000 | ft |

Projection: *Hammer Equal Area*

Projection: *Hammer Equal Area*

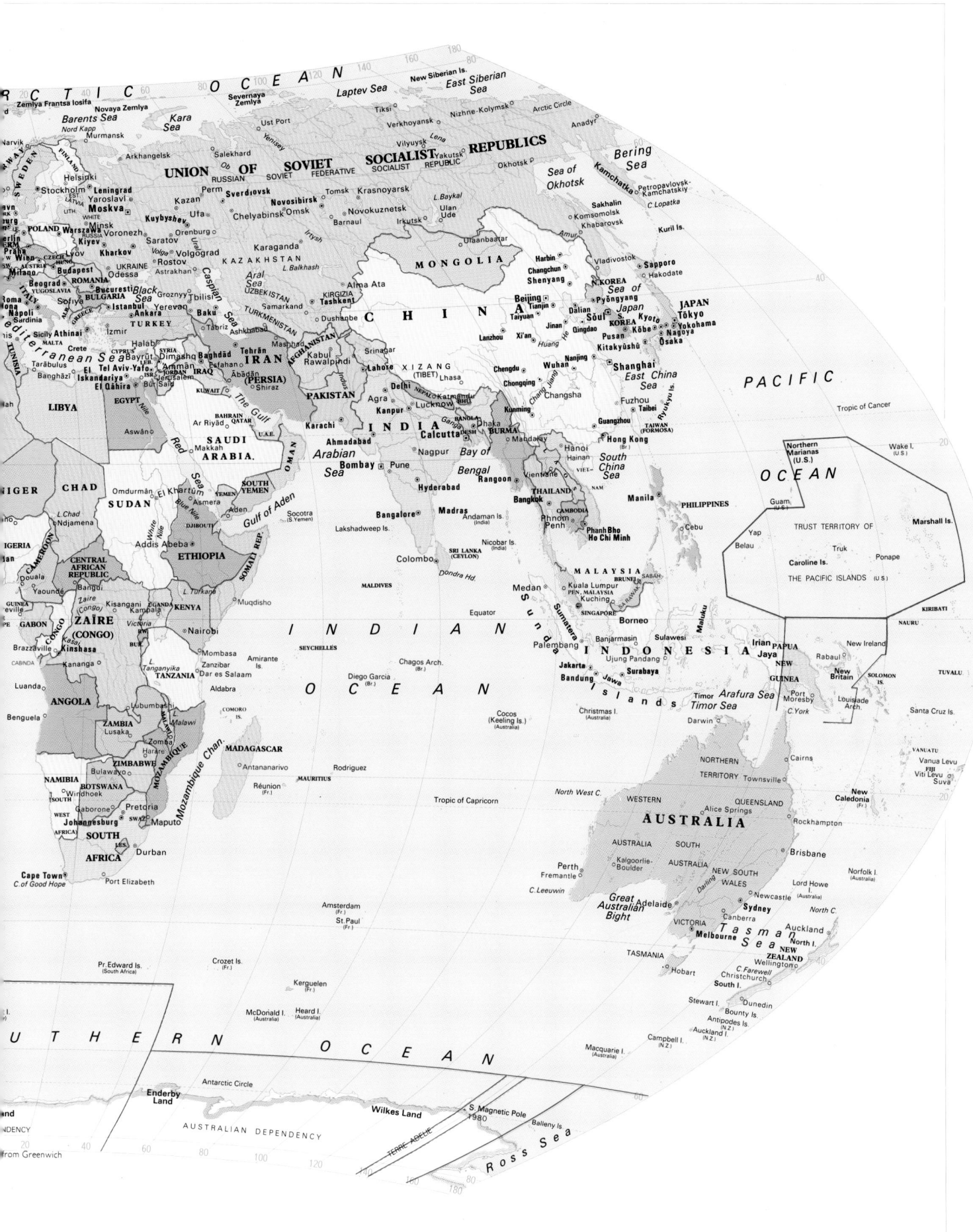

1:20 000 000

100 0 100 200 300 400 500 miles
100 0 200 400 600 800 km

Projection Bonne West from Greenwich 0 East from Greenwich
ROCKALL Sea areas named in weather forecasts

Seas, Oceans and Water Bodies

ATLANTIC OCEAN
NORWEGIAN SEA
NORTH SEA
BALTIC SEA
MEDITERRANEAN SEA
ADRIATIC SEA
BLACK SEA
CASPIAN SEA
Aegean Sea
Ionian Sea
Tyrrhenian Sea
Ligurian Sea
White Sea
Irish Sea
Bay of Biscay
G. of Lions
Sea of Azov
Gulf of Bothnia
G. of Finland
G. of Riga
Kattegat
Skagerrak
Str. of Otranto
Str. of Messina
Str. of Bonifacio
Str. of Gibraltar

Land Features

Ural Mountains
Tundra
Lapland
Scandinavia
Kjölen
Finland
Kola Peninsula
Kanin Peninsula
Volga Uplands
Obshchiy Syrt
Central Russian Uplands
European Plain
Pripyat Marshes
Ukraine
Crimea
Caucasus
Anatolia
Taurus
Carpathians
Transylvanian Alps
Plain of Hungary
Bakony For.
Wallachia
Balkans
Rhodope
Balkan Peninsula
Pindus
Morea
Dinaric Alps
Apennines
Alps
Sudetes
Erz Geb.
Harz
Bohemian For.
Black For.
Vosges
Jura
Ardennes
Eifel
Central Massif
Cévennes
Pyrenees
Iberian Peninsula
Old Castile
New Castile
Cantabrian Mts.
Sierra Morena
Sierra Nevada
Andalusia
Maritime Atlas
Plateau of the Shotts
British Isles
Great Britain
Ireland
Iceland
Faeroes
Hebrides
Shetland Is.
Orkney Is.
Corsica
Sardinia
Sicily
Calabria
Jutland
Gotland
Öland
Brittany
Dogger Bank
Fisher Bank
Portland

Sea Areas (weather forecasts)

VIKING
NORTH UTSIRE
SOUTH UTSIRE
FORTIES
CROMARTY
FORTH
TYNE
DOGGER
FISHER
GERMAN BIGHT
HUMBER
THAMES
DOVER
WIGHT
PORTLAND
PLYMOUTH
BISCAY
FINISTERRE
SOLE
LUNDY
FASTNET
IRISH SEA
SHANNON
ROCKALL
MALIN
HEBRIDES
BAILEY
FAIR ISLE
FAEROES
SOUTH EAST ICELAND

Rivers and Lakes

Ob
Ural
Pechora
Mezen
N. Dvina
Onega
L. Onega
L. Ladoga
Volga
Kama
Oka
Don
Donets
Dnepr (Dnieper)
Bug
Dnestr (Dniester)
Prut
Danube
Tisza
Drava
Sava
Mures
Morava
Maritsa
Vardar
Rhine
Rhône
Seine
Loire
Garonne
Gironde
Dordogne
Ebro
Tagus
Douro
Guadiana
Guadalquivir
Elbe
Weser
Oder (Odra)
Wisła (Vistula)
Niemen
W. Dvina
Neva
L. Chudskoye
Vänern
Vättern
Mälaren
Indals
Ume
Tornë
Tana
Terek
Kuban
Kura
Rion
Araks
Euphrates
Kizil Irmak
Sakarya
Tuz
Tsimlyansk Res.
Rybinsk Res.
Kuybyshev Res.

Spot Heights

5633
5165
2211
3770
1951 (Cyprus)
5121
3263
2914 (Gran Sasso)
1277 (Vesuvius)
2655 (Tatra)
1142 (Harz)
1617
1894
2123
2469
3734 (Norway)
2119 (Iceland)
1491 (Iceland)
1343
1085 (Snowdon)
3404
3478
3482

Arctic Circle
North Cape
Nordkinn
L. Inari

Crete
Cyprus
Malta
Balearic Is.
Ionian Is.

C. Matapan
C. St. Vincent
C. Trafalgar
C. Spartel
C. Finisterre
C. Ortegal
C. de Roca
C. de Gata
C. Blanco
C. Bon
C. Clear
Land's End

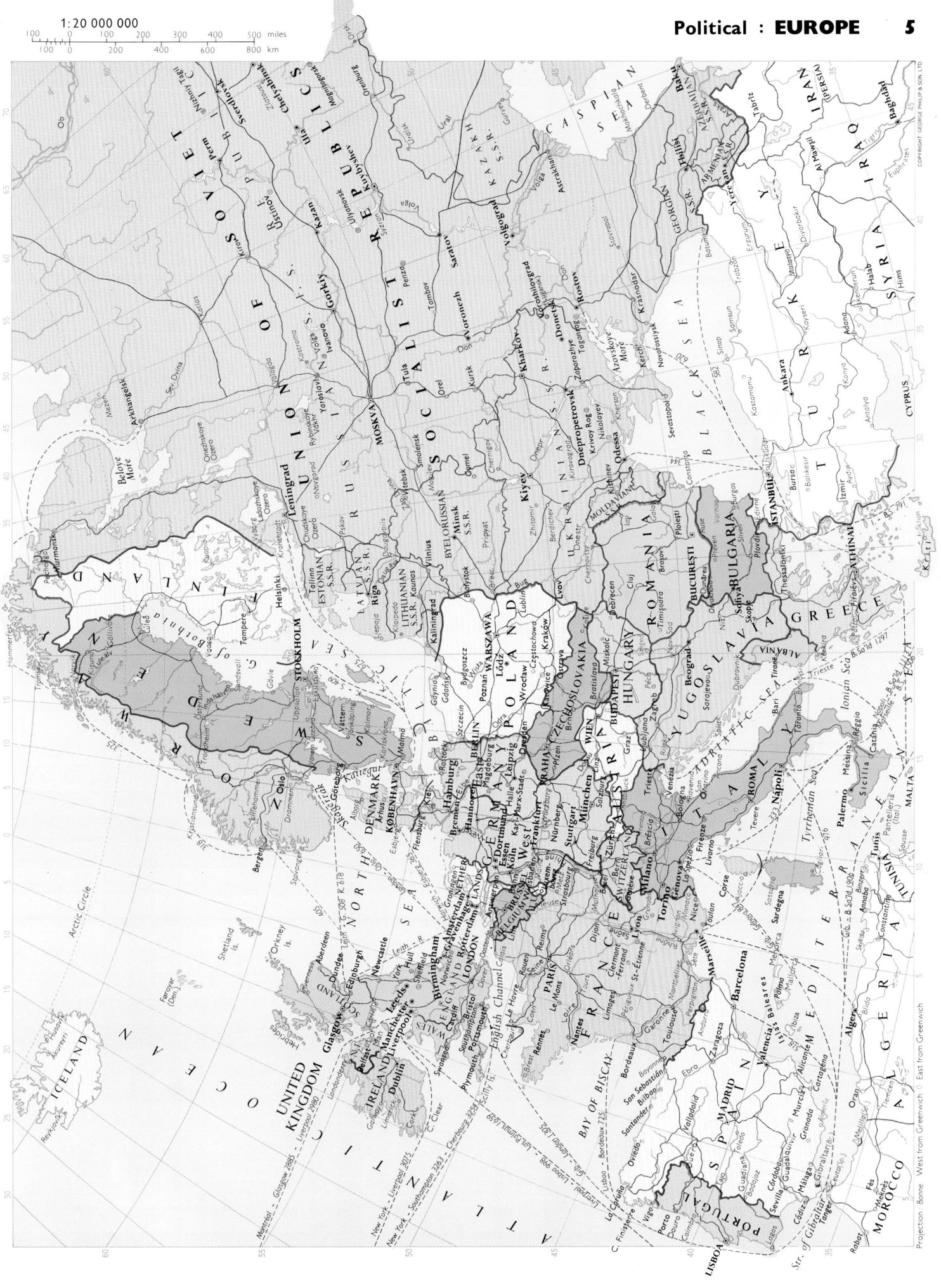

1:20 000 000

COPYRIGHT GEORGE PHILIP & SON LTD

Projection: Bonne West from Greenwich 0 East from Greenwich

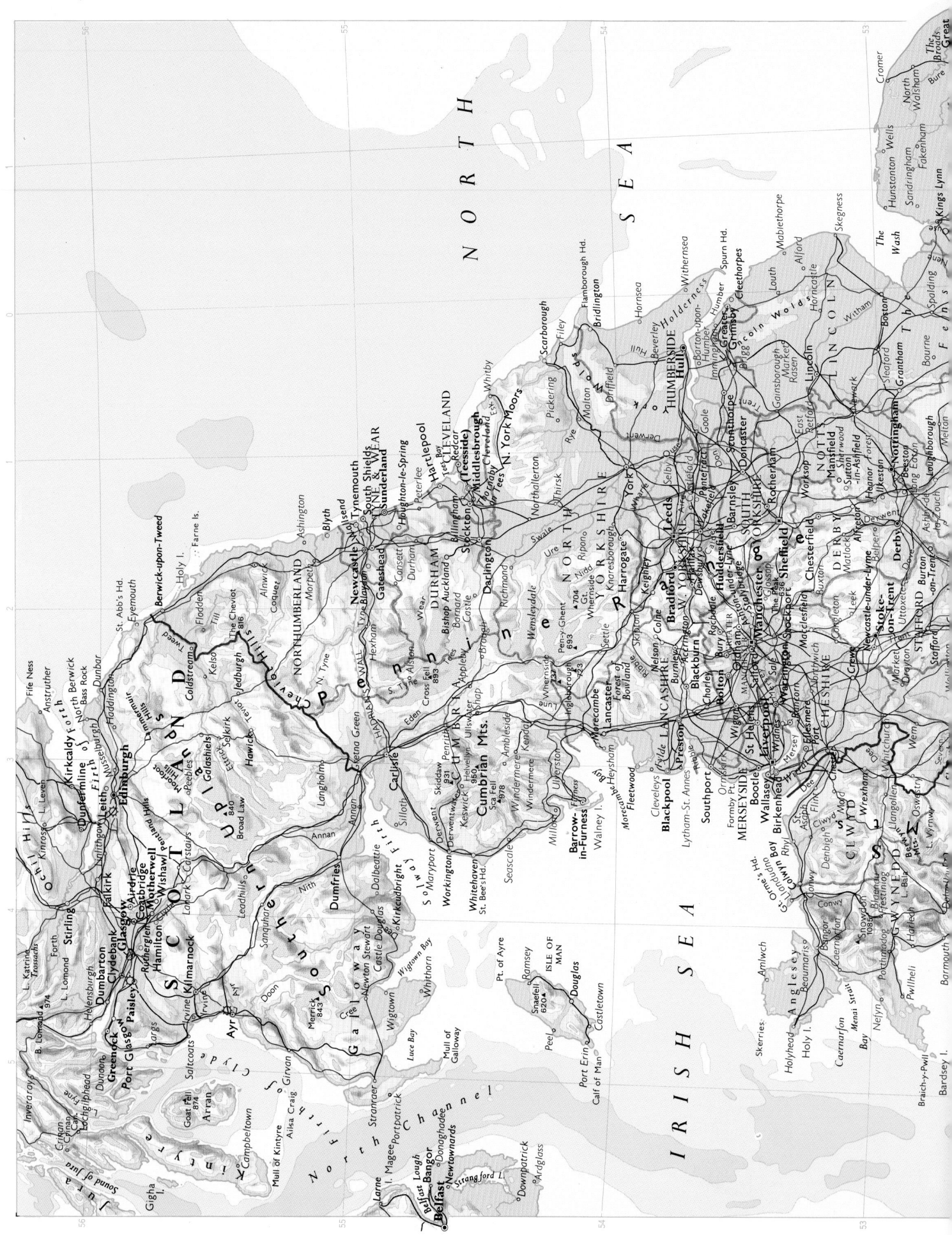

1 : 2 000 000

10 0 10 20 30 40 50 miles
10 0 10 20 30 40 50 60 70 80 km

Projection: Conical with two standard parallels.

East from Greenwich · West from Greenwich

COPYRIGHT GEORGE PHILIP & SON LTD.

ENGLISH CHANNEL

FRANCE

Rouen · Dieppe · Le Havre · Fécamp · Étretat · St-Valery-en-Caux · Yvetot · Caudebec · Louviers · Elbeuf · Bernay · Lisieux · Pont l'Évêque · Honfleur · Trouville · Seine · C. d'Antifer · C. de la Hève · Arromanches · Vierville · Bayeux · Caen · Isigny · Carentan · Périers · St-Lô · Quineville · Valognes · Barfleur · Cherbourg · C. de la Hague · Barneville · Le Tréport

Channel Islands · Alderney · Guernsey · St. Peter Port · Sark · Jersey · St. Helier

SCILLY ISLES On same Scale · Isles of Scilly · St. Mary's · St. Ives · Penzance · Land's End

Lowestoft · Sizewell · Southwold · Aldeburgh · Orford Ness · Felixstowe · The Naze · Walton-on-the-Naze · Harwich · Clacton · Mersea · Foulness · Shoeburyness · **Southend** · Maldon · Burnham · North Foreland · Margate · Ramsgate · Broadstairs · Deal · South Foreland · **Dover** · Folkestone · Hythe · New Romney · Dungeness · Rye · **Hastings** · Bexhill · **Eastbourne** · Beachy Hd. · Newhaven · **Brighton** · **Hove** · **Worthing** · Littlehampton · Bognor Regis · Selsey Bill · **Portsmouth** · Hayling I. · Southsea · Ryde · **ISLE OF WIGHT** · Cowes · Newport · Ventnor · St. Catherine's Point · The Needles · Lymington · Christchurch · **Bournemouth** · Poole · Swanage · St. Alban's Hd. · **Weymouth** · Portland Bill · Portland I. · I. of Purbeck

SUFFOLK · **Ipswich** · Beccles · Bungay · Diss · Harleston · Saxmundham · Stowmarket · Woodbridge · Sudbury · **Colchester** · Halstead · Braintree · **ESSEX** · Chelmsford · Basildon · **Cambridge** · Newmarket · St. Edmunds · Thetford · Brandon · Mildenhall · Bury · Haverhill · Saffron Walden · Bishop's Stortford · Harlow · Epping · Brentwood · **LONDON** · Enfield · Barnet · Harrow · Ealing · Croydon · Bromley · Dartford · Gravesend · Tilbury · Rochester · Chatham · Gillingham · Sittingbourne · Sheerness · **KENT** · Sheppey · Whitstable · Herne Bay · **Canterbury** · Ashford · Maidstone · Tunbridge Wells · Tonbridge · Sevenoaks · East Grinstead · **EAST SUSSEX** · Lewes · Crowborough · Battle · Uckfield · Haywards Heath · **WEST SUSSEX** · Horsham · Chichester · Havant · Petersfield · **SURREY** · Guildford · Woking · Leatherhead · Reigate · Redhill · Dorking · Haslemere · Leith Hill · **The Weald** · **North Downs** · **South Downs**

CAMBRIDGE · Peterborough · Fletton · **Huntingdon** · St. Ives · St. Neots · Ramsey · **BEDFORD** · Biggleswade · Hitchin · Letchworth · Stevenage · Baldock · **HERTFORD** · St. Albans · Hatfield · Welwyn · **Luton** · Dunstable · Watford · Hemel Hempstead · **BUCKS** · Aylesbury · High Wycombe · Marlow · Maidenhead · Slough · Windsor · Staines · Kingston · Richmond · **Reading** · Wokingham · Bracknell · Farnborough · Aldershot · Alton · Basingstoke · **HANTS** · Winchester · Eastleigh · **Southampton** · Fareham · Gosport · Andover · Whitchurch · Stockbridge · Romsey · New Forest · Lyndhurst

NORTHAMPTON · Kettering · Corby · Wellingborough · Rushden · Market Harborough · Daventry · Towcester · Brackley · Banbury · **OXFORD** · Bicester · Witney · Woodstock · Chipping Norton · Abingdon · Wantage · Didcot · Wallingford · **BERKS** · Newbury · Hungerford · Berkshire Downs · Vale of White Horse

WARWICK · **Coventry** · **Birmingham** · **West Bromwich** · **Wolverhampton** · Dudley · Tipton · Stourbridge · Halesowen · **WEST MIDLANDS** · Nuneaton · Hinckley · Rugby · Leamington · Warwick · Stratford-on-Avon · Redditch · **Worcester** · Kidderminster · Bromsgrove · **HEREFORD & WORCESTER** · Malvern · Malvern Hills · Ledbury · Tewkesbury · **Hereford** · Ross-on-Wye · Leominster · Ludlow · **SHROPSHIRE** · Clee Hills · Bridgnorth · Cleobury

GLOUCESTER · **Cheltenham** · Stroud · Cirencester · **AVON** · **Bristol** · **Bath** · Chippenham · Trowbridge · Frome · Radstock · Midsomer Norton · Keynsham · Clevedon · Weston-super-Mare · **Mendip Hills** · Wells · Glastonbury · Street · Shepton Mallet · Bruton · Cheddar · **SOMERSET** · Bridgwater · Taunton · Wellington · Yeovil · Chard · Crewkerne · Ilminster · Langport · Quantock Hills · Polden Hills · **WILTS** · **Swindon** · Marlborough · Devizes · Calne · Salisbury · Salisbury Plain · Stonehenge · Amesbury · Mere · Wilton · Warminster · Westbury · **DORSET** · Dorchester · Blandford · Shaftesbury · Sherborne · Wimborne · Bridport · Lyme Regis · Beaminster · Sturminster

WALES · **POWYS** · **DYFED** · **GWENT** · **MID GLAMORGAN** · **SOUTH GLAMORGAN** · **WEST GLAMORGAN** · **Cardiff** · **Newport** · **Swansea** · Barry · Penarth · Bridgend · Port Talbot · Neath · Llanelli · Pontypridd · Merthyr Tydfil · Aberdare · Rhondda · Ebbw Vale · Tredegar · Abergavenny · Pontypool · Cwmbran · Caerphilly · Maesteg · Porthcawl · Brecon · Brecon Beacons · Black Mts. · Builth Wells · Llandrindod Wells · Rhayader · Radnor Forest · Hay-on-Wye · Knighton · Montgomery · Newtown · Welshpool · Machynlleth · Llanidloes · Aberystwyth · Borth · Aberaeron · New Quay · Cardigan · Newcastle Emlyn · Carmarthen · Llandeilo · Llandovery · Ammanford · Kidwelly · Burry Port · Carmarthen Bay · Tenby · Pembroke · Milford Haven · Haverfordwest · Fishguard · St. David's · St. David's Hd. · St. Bride's Bay · Cardigan Bay · Tywyn · Dovey · Plynlimon · Tregaron

CORNWALL · **Plymouth** · Devonport · Saltash · Liskeard · Looe · Fowey · St. Austell · Mevagissey · Truro · Falmouth · Redruth · Camborne · **Penzance** · St. Michael's Mount · Helston · Lizard · Newquay · Padstow · Wadebridge · Bodmin · Bodmin Moor · Brown Willy · Camelford · Boscastle · Bude · Launceston

DEVON · **Exeter** · **Torquay (Torbay)** · Paignton · Teignmouth · Dawlish · Newton Abbot · Totnes · Dartmouth · Kingsbridge · Salcombe · Start Pt. · Plymouth Sound · Dartmoor · Yes Tor · Okehampton · Tavistock · Crediton · Tiverton · Cullompton · Honiton · Sidmouth · Exmouth · Budleigh Salterton · Axminster · Barnstaple · Bideford · Ilfracombe · Lynton · Lynmouth · Minehead · Exmoor · Dunkery Beacon · Holsworthy · Hartland Point · Lundy

Bristol Channel

m / ft legend:
3000 · 1200 · 600 · 300 · 150 · 0 — 1000 · 400 · 200 · 100 · 0 (m)
ft: 50 · 100 · 200 · 300 (below sea level)

1 : 2 000 000

10 0 10 20 30 40 50 miles
10 0 10 20 30 40 50 60 70 80 km

ORKNEY IS.
On same scale

Hoy · Scapa Flow · South Ronaldsay
North Ronaldsay
Westray · Eday · Sanday · Stronsay
Rousay · Shapinsay
Stromness · *Mainland* · **ORKNEY**
Hoy · Kirkwall · Scapa Flow
South Ronaldsay
Pentland Firth
Dunnet Hd. · John O'Groats

Orkney Is.
Pentland Firth
C. Wrath · Durness · Strathy Pt. · Dunnet Hd. · **Thurso** · John O'Groats
L. Laxford · Strathy · Dounreay · Noss Hd.
Butt of Lewis · Eddrachillis Bay · Tongue · Halladale · **Wick**
Flannan Is. · L. Roag · Broad Bay · Ben Hope ▲927 · Naver · Lybster
Stornoway · Lochinver · Enard Bay · L. Assynt · B. More Assynt · Reay Forest · Loch Shin · Helmsdale · Ord of Caithness
Lewis · Eye Pen. · Rubha Hunish · Brora
WESTERN · Tarbert · L. Seaforth · Ullapool · Oykell · Lairg · **Brora**
ISLES · *Harris* · L. Broom · Golspie
Sound of Harris · L. Eye · L. Dearg 1081 · Dornoch · Dornoch Firth
North Uist · Lochmaddy · L. Gairloch · Tain · Tarbat Ness
Monach Is. · Benbecula · Trotternish · L. Torridon · Fannich · Ben Wyvis 1045 · Strathpeffer · Cromarty · *Moray Firth* · Lossiemouth · Cullen · Portsoy · Kinnaird's Head
South Uist · Portree · Raasay · Rona · Conon · **Dingwall** · Fortrose · Nairn · **Elgin** · Buckie · Banff · Macduff · Fraserburgh
Lochboisdale · Scalpay · Stromeferry · Farrar · Beauly · Culloden Moor · Findhorn · Forres · Rothes · Keith · *BUCHAN* · Rattray Head
Ben More · Cuillin Hills · Dornie · **HIGHLAND** · **Inverness** · Grantown-on-Spey · Dufftown · Huntly · Turriff · Deveron · Ythan · Peterhead
Canna · Glen Affric · Fort Augustus · Aviemore · Monadhliath Mts. · Cairn Gorm 1245 · *GRAMPIAN* · Buchan Ness
Rhum · Glen Garry · Kingussie · Cairngorm Mts. · Ellon · Effin
Eigg · Mallaig · Morar · Arkaig · Newtonmore · Cairn Toul 1292 · Ben Macdhui 1311 · Tomintoul · Alford · Inverurie · **Aberdeen**
Barra Hd. · Arisaig · L. Moidart · L. Shiel · **Fort William** · Ben Nevis 1343 · *Badenoch* · L. Tilt · Lochnagar 1154 · Ballater · Aboyne · Dee · Girdle Ness
Coll · Pt. of Ardnamurchan · Ardgour · Glen Coe · Rannoch Moor · Blair Atholl · Balmoral · Banchory
GRAMPIAN HIGHLANDS · Forest of Atholl · Braemar · N.E. · Laurencekirk · Inverbervie
Tobermory · **Morvern** · Ballachulish · L. Rannoch · L. Tummel · Pass of Killiecrankie · Braes of Angus · Stonehaven
Tiree · Staffa · Mull · Ben More 966 · Lismore · Ben Cruachan 1124 · Aberfeldy · Pitlochry · Kirriemuir · Brechin · **Montrose**
Iona · **Oban** · Ben Lawers 1214 · L. Tay · Blairgowrie · Forfar
Colonsay · Inveraray · L. Awe · Killin · Crieff · Dunkeld · **TAYSIDE** · Arbroath
Breadalbane · Ben More 1174 · B. Vorlich 983 · **Dundee** · Broughty Ferry
ATLANTIC OCEAN · B. Vorlich 942 · Ben Lomond 974 · Callander · **Perth** · Scone · Cupar · St. Andrews · Fife Ness
Crinan · Lochgilphead · Trossachs · L. Katrine · L. Lomond · **CENTRAL** · Dunblane · Ochil Hills · Kinross · Leven · *FIFE* · Anstruther
Rubh' a' Mhail · Jura · Tarbert · Helensburgh · Dunoon · **Dumbarton** · **Stirling** · Bannockburn · **Alloa** · Cowdenbeath · **Glenrothes** · Buckhaven · Bass Rock
Islay · Bowmore · Sound of Jura · Rothesay · Bute · **Greenock** · **Clydebank** · Kirkintilloch · **Falkirk** · Boness · **Dunfermline** · **Kirkcaldy** · North Berwick · Dunbar
Gigha · **Port Glasgow** · **Cumbernauld** · **Grangemouth** · Linlithgow · **Leith** · Firth of Forth · Prestonpans · St. Abbs Hd.
Port Ellen · Largs · **Paisley** · Renfrew · **Glasgow** · **Airdrie** · **Edinburgh** · **Livingston** · Bathgate · Dalkeith · *LOTHIAN* · Eyemouth
Ardrossan · Saltcoats · **Johnstone** · Rutherglen · **Coatbridge** · **Motherwell** · Penicuik · Pentland Hills · Duns · **Berwick-upon-Tweed**
KINTYRE · *STRATHCLYDE* · E. Kilbride · **Wishaw** · Carstairs · Peebles · Moorfoot Hills · Coldstream · Holy I.
Goat Fell 874 · **Hamilton** · Lanark · Biggar · Broad Law 840 · Galashiels · Melrose · Kelso · Flodden · Till
Arran · Brodick · Troon · Irvine · **Kilmarnock** · Tweed · **Galashiels** · Selkirk · Jedburgh · The Cheviot 816
Campbeltown · Prestwick · Ayr · Cumnock · *SOUTHERN UPLANDS* · Hawick · *BORDERS* · Cheviot Hills
Ailsa Craig · Girvan · Leadhills · Moffat · Teviot · N. Tyne · **ENGLAND**
Mull of Kintyre · Dalmellington · Doon · Sanquhar · Nith · Langholm · Hexham
Rathlin · Fair Hd. · **DUMFRIES AND GALLOWAY** · Lockerbie · Esk · Hadrian's Wall
Ballycastle · Merrick 843 · Ken · **Dumfries** · Gretna Green · Annan · **Carlisle** · S. Tyne · Alston
Galloway · Newton Stewart · Castle Douglas · Dalbeattie · Cross Fell 893
NORTHERN · Stranraer · Wigtown · Gatehouse of Fleet · Kirkcudbright · Solway Firth · Penrith · Wear
IRELAND · Portpatrick · L. Ryan · Whithorn · Wigtown Bay · Workington · Derwent · Skiddaw 931 · Ullswater · Tees · Barnard Castle
Belfast · Bangor · Newtownards · Mull of Galloway · Luce Bay · **Cumbrian Mts.**

SHETLAND IS.
On same scale

Unst · Fetlar
Yell Sound · Yell · Whalsay
SHETLAND · Mainland · Lerwick · Bressay
Foula · Scalloway · Sumburgh Hd.

ft · m
3000 · 1000
1200 · 400
600 · 200
300 · 100
0 · 0
50 · 150
100 · 300
m · ft

Projection: Conical with two standard parallels.
West from Greenwich
COPYRIGHT. GEORGE PHILIP & SON. LTD.

NORTH SEA
North Minch · *Little Minch* · *Inner Hebrides* · *Sound of Harris*
Glen More · *Strath Spey* · *Strathmore*
Firth of Lorn · *Firth of Clyde* · *North Channel*
Belfast Lough

1:2 000 000

10 0 10 20 30 40 50 miles
10 0 10 20 30 40 50 60 70 80 km

ATLANTIC OCEAN

Kintyre
Campbeltown
Mull of Kintyre
Arran
Ailsa Craig
Rathlin I.
Fair Hd.
Giant's Causeway
Portrush
Malin Hd.
Carndonagh
Inishowen Pen.
Moville
Buncrana
Ballycastle
Ballymoney
▲554 Trostan
Coleraine
Limavady
Londonderry
Strabane
Ballymena
Larne
I. Magee
Portpatrick
Stranraer

North Channel

Sheep Haven Horn Hd.
Tory I.
Bloody Foreland
Gweedore
Errigal 752
Derryveagh Mts.
Aran I.
Letterkenny
Lough Swilly

DONEGAL
Gweebarra B.
Glenties
Bluestack
676
Finn
Lifford
Sperrin Mts.
Sawel 683
Magherafelt
Cookstown
Antrim
Carrickfergus
Belfast L.
Bangor
Donaghadee
Newtownards
Ards Pen.
Strangford L.

Loughros More B.
Rossan Pt.
Rathlin O Birne I.
Killybegs
Donegal
Ballyshannon
Bundoran
L. Erne
Irvinestown
Enniskillen
Omagh
Dungannon
Neagh
16
Belfast
Lisburn
Portadown
Lurgan (Craigavon)
Armagh
Banbridge
Downpatrick
Dundrum
Slieve Donard 852
Newcastle
Dundrum Bay

NORTHERN IRELAND

Donegal Bay
Upper Erne
Clones
Belturbet
Annalee
Cootehill
Monaghan
Castleblayney
Carling ford L.
Greenore
Dundalk
Dundalk Bay

Broad Haven
Erris Hd.
Belmullet
Mullet Peninsula
Blacksod Bay
Downpatrick Hd.
Killala B.
Killala
Sligo B.
Sligo
Colloney
L. Allen
Arrow
Leitrim
Fing
Cavan
Carrickmacross
Kingscourt
Louth
Ardee
Warrenpoint
Mourne Mts.
Sl. Gullion 577
Newry

SLIGO
LEITRIM
CAVAN
MONAGHAN

Achill Hd.
Achill
Achill I.
Clare I.
Clew Bay
Croagh Patrick 765
Westport
Castlebar
L. Conn
Nephin 806
Ballina
Ox Mts.
Moy
Boyle
Carrick-on-Shannon
L. Gowna
Granard
Longford
Oldcastle
Ceanannas Mor (Kells)
Blackwater
Drogheda
Balbriggan

MAYO
ROSCOMMON
LONGFORD
MEATH
LOUTH

Inishbofin
Killary Harbour
Mweelrea ▲819
L. Mask
Ballinrobe
Robe
Castlereagh
Roscommon
Suck
L. Ree
Athboy
Navan
An Uaimh (Navan)
Trim
Boyne
Swords
Lambay I.

Clifden
Twelve Pins
Connemara
Slyne Hd.
L. Corrib
Tuam
GALWAY
Galway
Clare
Athenry
Loughrea
Ballinasloe
Clara
Tullamore
Edenderry
Daingean
Droichead Nua
Maynooth
DUBLIN
Ireland's Eye
Howth Head
Dublin (Baile Atha Cliath)
Dublin Bay
Dun Laoghaire
Bray
Kippure 754

CONNACHT
IRELAND
WESTMEATH
Athlone
Mullingar

Galway Bay
Inishmore
Aran Is.
Slieve Aughty
Gort
Portumna
L. Derg
Birr
Sl. Bloom
Mountmellick
Portlaoise
OFFALY
Bog
KILDARE
Kildare
Naas
Celbridge
Poulaphouca Res.
Wicklow
Wicklow Hd.
Rathdrum
Mizen Hd.

LEINSTER
LAOIS
WICKLOW

Hags Hd.
Ennistymon
Liscannor Bay
Mal Bay
Miltown Malbay
Ennis
CLARE
Killaloe
Nenagh
Keeper 694
Ardnacrusha
Templemore
Thurles
Roscrea
Kilkenny
Carlow
Tullow
Muine Bheag
Mt. Leinster 796
Shillelagh
Gorey
Arklow
Avoca
Lugnaquilla 923

Kilkee
Kilrush
Loop Hd.
R. Shannon
Foynes
Rathkeale
Limerick
Golden Vale
Tipperary
Cashel
Thurles
Cahir
Slievenamon 722
Carrick-on-Suir
Clonmel
New Ross
Waterford
Wexford
Rosslare
Greenore Pt.
Tuscar Rock

LIMERICK
TIPPERARY
KILKENNY
WEXFORD

Kerry Hd.
Brandon Bay
Tralee Bay
Brandon Mt. 953
Dingle
Dingle Bay
Sl. Mish
Tralee
Maine
Laune
Killarney
Macgillycuddy's Reeks
Carrauntoohill 1040
Lakes of Killarney
Listowel
Newcastle
Rath Luirc (Charleville)
Kanturk
Newmarket
Mitchelstown
Mallow
Fermoy
Galtymore 920
Galty Mts.
Knockmealdown Mts.
Comeragh Mts.
Lismore
Dungarvan
Dungarvan Bay
Tramore
Waterford Harbour
Hook Hd.
Saltee Is.
Carnsore Pt.

KERRY
MUNSTER
WATERFORD

Gt. Blasket I.
Valentia Harbour
Valentia I.
Skellig Rocks
Cahirciveen
Kenmare
Kenmare River
Caha Mts.
Glengarriff
Bantry
Bantry Bay
Bear I.
Castletown Bearhaven
Crow Hd.
Dunmanus Hd.
Mizen Hd.
Fastnet Rock
Skull
Baltimore
Clear I.
C. Clear
Galley Hd.
Clonakilty Bay
Clonakilty
Skibbereen
Bandon
Boggeragh Mts.
Macroom
Blarney
Cork
Midleton
Youghal
Youghal Harbour
Lee
Passage West
Cobh
Crosshaven
Kinsale
Cork Harbour
Old Head of Kinsale

CORK

Irish Sea
St. George's Channel
St. David's Hd.

Projection: Conical with two standard parallels.
West from Greenwich
COPYRIGHT. GEORGE PHILIP & SON. LTD.

Towns underlined in Northern Ireland give their
names to the Districts in which they stand

The remaining Districts are:—

1	Fermanagh	5	Castlereagh
2	Moyle	6	Ards
3	Newtownabbey	7	Down
4	North Down	8	Newry & Mourne

ft m
3000 1000
1200 400
600 200
300 100
0
100 300
200 600
m ft

1:4 000 000

20 0 20 40 60 miles
20 0 20 40 60 80 km

The DISTRICTS of Northern Ireland have been numbered and can be identified by reference to this table.

1 Londonderry   14 Craigavon
2 Limavady   15 Armagh
3 Coleraine   16 Newry & Mourne
4 Ballymoney   17 Banbridge
5 Moyle   18 Down
6 Larne   19 Lisburn
7 Ballymena   20 Antrim
8 Magherafelt   21 Newtownabbey
9 Cookstown   22 Carrickfergus
10 Strabane   23 North Down
11 Omagh   24 Ards
12 Fermanagh   25 Castlereagh
13 Dungannon   26 Belfast

ORKNEY
Kirkwall
59
HIGHLAND

SHETLAND
Lerwick
60

Metropolitan Counties :-
On 1st April 1986 the administrative functions of the six metropolitan counties such as planning, education, transportation, libraries and social services were transferred to the city and town boroughs and various non-elected residuary bodies.

Stornoway
WESTERN
ISLES

HIGHLAND
Inverness
GRAMPIAN
SCOTLAND
Aberdeen

TAYSIDE
Dundee

FIFE
Glenrothes
CENTRAL
Stirling
Edinburgh
LOTHIAN
Glasgow
STRATHCLYDE

BORDERS
Newtown
St. Boswells

NORTH

DUMFRIES
AND
GALLOWAY
Dumfries
NORTHUMBERLAND
Carlisle
Newcastle
TYNE AND WEAR
Durham
SEA

CUMBRIA
DURHAM
CLEVELAND
Middlesbrough
Northallerton

ATLANTIC

OCEAN

58

56

Lifford
DONEGAL
Londonderry
NORTHERN
Tyrone
IRELAND
Fermanagh
Sligo
LEITRIM
Monaghan
Carrick-on-
Shannon
MONAGHAN
Cavan
SLIGO
MAYO
Castlebar
ROSCOMMON
Longford
LONGFORD
Roscommon
Mullingar
WESTMEATH
CAVAN
LOUTH
Dundalk
An Uaimh
(Navan)
MEATH
GALWAY
Galway
IRELAND
Tullamore
OFFALY
DUBLIN
Dublin
KILDARE
Naas
Port Laoise
LAOIS
WICKLOW
Wicklow
CLARE
Ennis
Carlow
CARLOW
Limerick
TIPPERARY
KILKENNY
WEXFORD
LIMERICK
Kilkenny
Clonmel
Wexford
KERRY
Tralee
CORK
WATERFORD
Waterford
Cork

NORTH YORKSHIRE

ISLE OF
MAN
Douglas

IRISH SEA

HUMBERSIDE
Hull
LANCASHIRE
Preston
WEST YORKSHIRE
Wakefield
Barnsley
SOUTH YORKSHIRE
GREATER MANCHESTER
MERSEYSIDE
Manchester
Liverpool
ENGLAND
Lincoln
DERBYSHIRE
NOTTINGHAMSHIRE
LINCOLNSHIRE
Chester
CHESHIRE
Matlock
Nottingham
Caernarfon
Mold
GWYNEDD
CLWYD
Stafford
STAFFORDSHIRE
Leicester
LEICESTERSHIRE
NORFOLK
Norwich
Shrewsbury
SHROPSHIRE
WEST MIDLANDS
Birmingham
WARWICKSHIRE
Warwick
NORTHAMPTONSHIRE
Northampton
CAMBRIDGESHIRE
SUFFOLK
WALES
POWYS
HEREFORD AND WORCESTER
Worcester
Bedford
BEDFORDSHIRE
Cambridge
Ipswich
Llandrindod Wells
Hertford
HERTFORDSHIRE
ESSEX
Chelmsford
DYFED
Gloucester
GLOUCESTERSHIRE
Oxford
OXFORDSHIRE
Aylesbury
BUCKINGHAMSHIRE
GREATER LONDON
Carmarthen
GWENT
Cwmbran
Reading
BERKSHIRE
Kingston
Maidstone
WEST GLAMORGAN
MID GLAMORGAN
Swansea
Cardiff
SOUTH GLAMORGAN
Bristol
AVON
Trowbridge
WILTSHIRE
SURREY
KENT
SOMERSET
HAMPSHIRE
Winchester
WEST SUSSEX
EAST SUSSEX
Lewes
Taunton
DORSET
Chichester
DEVON
Exeter
Dorchester
Newport
ISLE OF WIGHT

CORNWALL
Truro

NORTH CHANNEL

WESTMEATH

St. George's Channel

CELTIC

SEA

ENGLISH CHANNEL

FRANCE

50

52

54

○ Norwich   Administrative headquarters
MERSEYSIDE   Metropolitan counties
Antrim   Former Northern Ireland counties

Projection: Conical with two standard parallels

West from Greenwich () East from Greenwich
COPYRIGHT. GEORGE PHILIP & SON, LTD.

1:2 500 000

Projection: Conical with two standard parallels

East from Greenwich

1:5 000 000

50   50   100 miles
50   0   50   100   150 km

FRENCH DEPARTMENTS

01	Ain	A.
02	Aisne	Ai.
03	Allier	Al.
04	Alpes-de-Haute-Provence	A.H.P.
05	Alpes-Maritimes	A.M.
06	Ardèche	Ard.
07	Ardennes	Ard.
08	Ariège	Ari.
09	Aube	Aub.
10	Aude	Aud.
11	Aveyron	Av.
12	Bouches-du-Rhône	B.Rh.
13	Calvados	C.
14	Cantal	Ca.
15	Charente	Ch.
16	Charente-Maritime	Ch.M.
17	Cher	Che.
18	Corrèze	Co.
19	Corse-du-Sud	C.O.
20	Corse Haute-Corse	
21	Côte-d'Or	C.O.
22	Côtes-du-Nord	C.N.
23	Creuse	Cr.
24	Dordogne	D.
25	Doubs	Do.
26	Drôme	Dr.
27	Eure	E.
28	Eure-et-Loir	E.L.
29	Finistère	F.
30	Gard	G.
31	Haute-Garonne	H.G.
32	Gers	Ge.
33	Gironde	Gi.
34	Hérault	H.
35	Ille-et-Vilaine	I.V.
36	Indre	I.
37	Indre-et-Loire	I.L.
38	Isère	Is.
39	Jura	J.
40	Landes	L.
41	Loir-et-Cher	L.C.
42	Loire	Loi.
43	Haute-Loire	H.L.
44	Loire-Atlantique	L.A.
45	Loiret	Loi.
46	Lot	Lot
47	Lot-et-Garonne	L.G.
48	Lozère	Loz.
49	Maine-et-Loire	M.L.
50	Manche	Ma.
51	Marne	M.
52	Haute-Marne	H.M.
53	Mayenne	May.
54	Meurthe-et-Moselle	M.M.
55	Meuse	Meu.
56	Morbihan	Mo.
57	Moselle	Mos.
58	Nièvre	N.
59	Nord	No.
60	Oise	O.
61	Orne	Or.
62	Pas-de-Calais	P.C.
63	Puy-de-Dôme	P.D.
64	Pyrénées-Atlantiques	P.A.
65	Hautes-Pyrénées	H.P.
66	Pyrénées-Orientales	P.O.
67	Bas-Rhin	B.R.
68	Haut-Rhin	H.R.
69	Rhône	Rh.
70	Haute-Saône	H.S.
71	Saône-et-Loire	S.L.
72	Sarthe	Sa.
73	Savoie	S.M.
74	Haute-Savoie	H.Sa.
75	Paris	P.
76	Seine-Maritime	S.M.
77	Seine-et-Marne	S.M.
78	Yvelines	Y.
79	Deux-Sèvres	D.S.
80	Somme	So.
81	Tarn	T.
82	Tarn-et-Garonne	T.G.
83	Var	Va.
84	Vaucluse	Va.
85	Vendée	Ve.
86	Vienne	Vi.
87	Haute-Vienne	H.V.
88	Vosges	Vo.
89	Yonne	Y.
90	Belfort	B.
91	Essonne	Es.
92	Hauts-de-Seine	H.Se.
93	Seine-St-Denis	S.S.d-D
94	Val-de-Marne	V.M.
95	Val-d'Oise	V.O.

CORSICA
On same scale

Corse
Haute-Corse
Corse du Sud
Corse
Mt. Rotondo 2625
Monte Cinto 2710

MEDITERRANEAN SEA

ENGLISH CHANNEL

BAY OF BISCAY

GERMANY

BELGIUM

SWITZERLAND

ITALY

SPAIN

ANDORRA

East from Greenwich

West from Greenwich

Projection: Conical with two standard parallels

m	ft
3000	9000
2000	6000
1000	3000
400	1200
200	600
0	0

1:5 000 000

50 0 50 100 miles

50 0 50 100 150 km

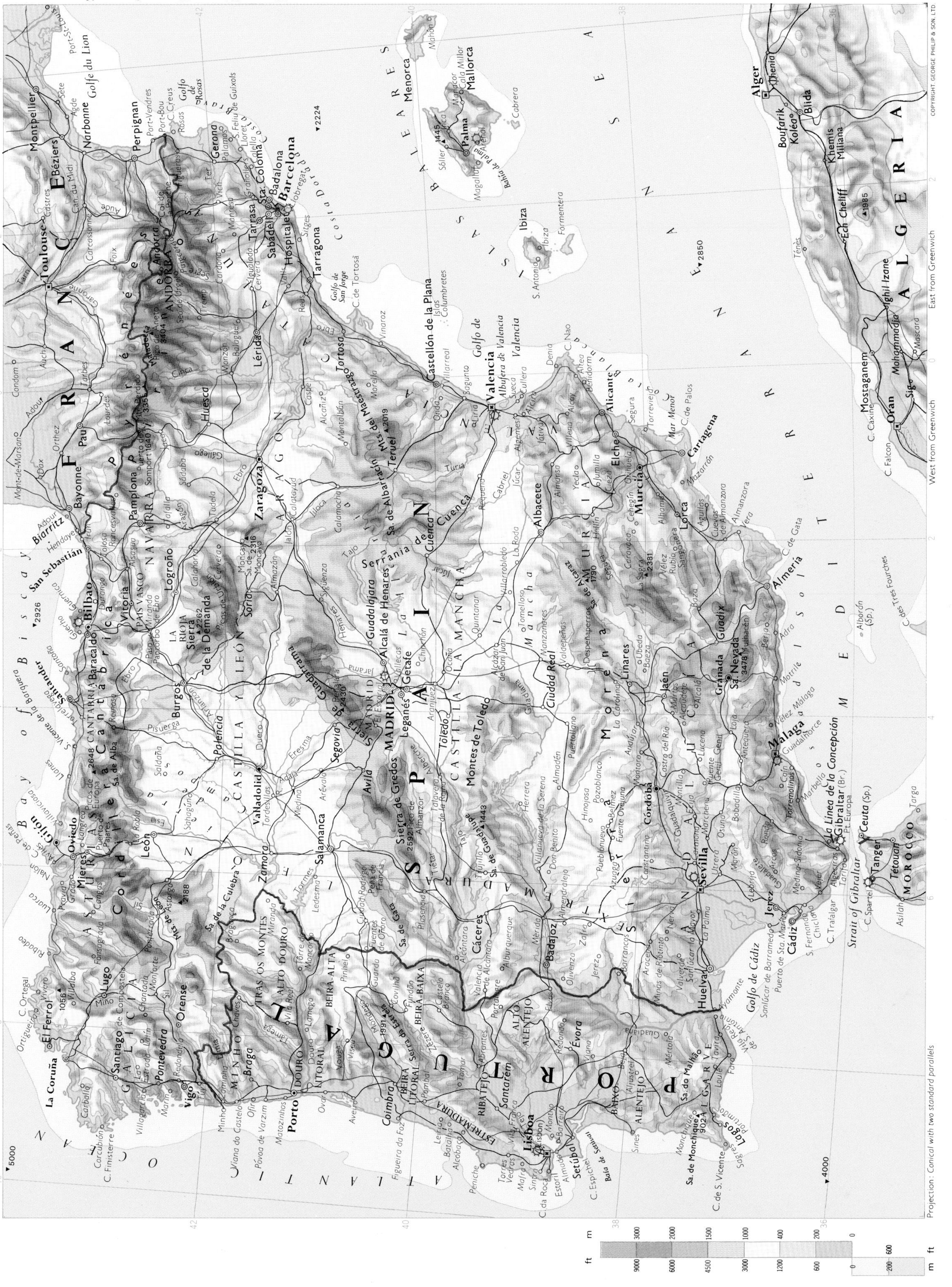

East from Greenwich

West from Greenwich

Projection: Conical with two standard parallels

FRANCE

Montpellier · Béziers · Narbonne · Toulouse · Perpignan · Bayonne · Biarritz · Pau

PYRÉNÉES · ANDORRA

Gerona · Barcelona · Badalona · Hospitalet · Sabadell · Tarrasa · Sta. Coloma · Tarragona

Huesca · Lérida · Zaragoza · ARAGON · Pamplona · NAVARRA · Logroño

San Sebastián · Bilbao · Baracaldo · PAÍS VASCO · Vitoria · CANTABRIA

Santander · Gijón · Oviedo · Mieres · ASTURIAS · CORDILLERA CANTÁBRICA

Castellón de la Plana · VALENCIA · Sagunto · **Valencia** · Alicante · Elche · Murcia · MURCIA · Lorca · Cartagena

Teruel · Cuenca · Serranía de Cuenca · Albacete

Burgos · CASTILLA Y LEÓN · Soria · Guadalajara · Alcalá de Henares · **MADRID** · Getafe · Leganés

Palencia · Valladolid · Segovia · Ávila · Sierra de Gredos · Toledo · Montes de Toledo · CASTILLA-LA MANCHA

León · Zamora · Salamanca · **SPAIN**

La Coruña · Santiago de Compostela · Lugo · Orense · Pontevedra · Vigo · GALICIA

PORTUGAL · MINHO · Braga · Porto · DOURO · BEIRA ALTA · BEIRA LITORAL · BEIRA BAIXA · Coimbra · TRÁS OS MONTES

Ciudad Real · Linares · Jaén · Córdoba · Granada · Sa. Nevada · Guadix · Almería

EXTREMADURA · Cáceres · Badajoz · ANDALUCÍA · SIERRA MORENA

Sevilla · Huelva · Jerez · Cádiz · Gibraltar (Br.) · La Línea de la Concepción · Ceuta (Sp.) · Málaga · Marbella

Lisboa · Setúbal · ESTREMADURA · Santarém · RIBATEJO · ALTO ALENTEJO · BAIXO ALENTEJO · Évora · ALGARVE

MOROCCO · Tánger · Tetouan · Ceuta · Strait of Gibraltar

ALGERIA · Alger · Blida · Koléa · Boufarik · Oran · Mostaganem · Ech Cheliff

BALEARES · Mallorca · Palma · Menorca · Ibiza · Formentera · Cabrera

Bay of Biscay · ATLANTIC OCEAN · MEDITERRANEAN SEA

Golfe du Lion · Golfo de Valencia · Golfo de Cádiz · Golfo de San Jorge

ft m 9000 3000 · 6000 2000 · 4500 1500 · 3000 1000 · 1200 400 · 600 200 · 0 · m ft

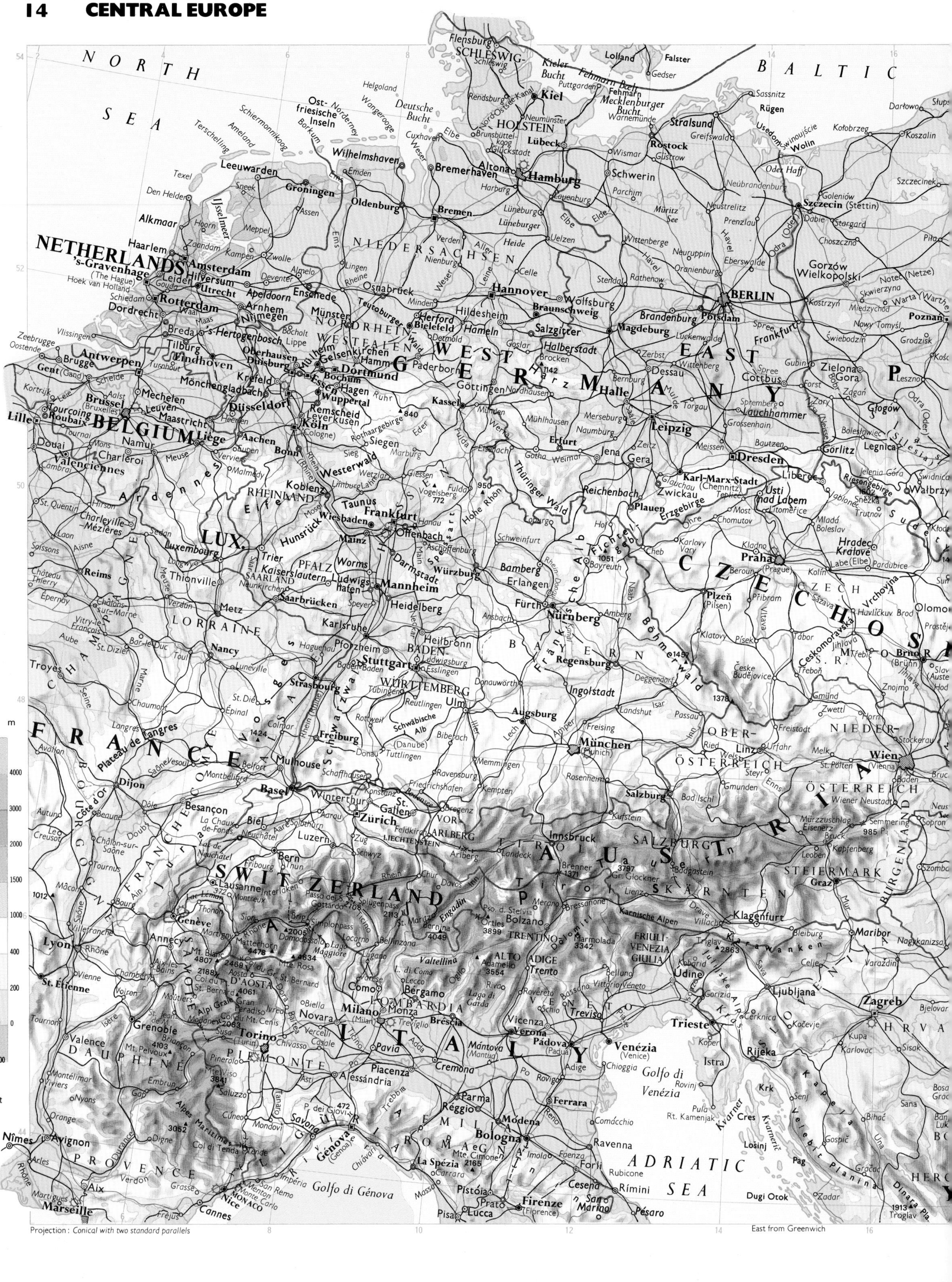

NORTH SEA

BALTIC

NETHERLANDS

BELGIUM

LUX.

FRANCE

WEST GERMANY

EAST GERMANY

CZECHOSL.

ÖSTERREICH AUSTRIA

SWITZERLAND

ITALY

ADRIATIC SEA

Projection: Conical with two standard parallels

East from Greenwich

ft m

12 000   4000

9000   3000

6000   2000

4500   1500

3000   1000

1200   400

600   200

0   0

200   600

m   ft

1:5 000 000

50   50   100 miles
50   50   100   150 km

CENTRAL
EUROPE
POLITICAL
1:25 000 000

DENMARK
København
WEST GERMANY POLAND Warszawa
EAST Berlin
Bonn U.S.S.R.
LUX. Praha
CZECHOSLOVAKIA
FRANCE Bern AUSTRIA Wien Budapest HUNGARY ROMÂNIA
SWITZ. LIECH.
MONACO ITALY SAN MARINO Beograd Bucureşti
YUGOSLAVIA
Roma BULGARIA
Sofiya

SEA
Zatoka Gdańska
Wejherowo Zelenogradsk Kaliningrad (Königsberg) Chernyakhovsk Vilnius
Sopot Gdynia Gusev LITHUANIAN S.S.R.
Gdańsk (Danzig) R.S.F.S.R. Altius Varena
Starogard Braniewo ▲309 Suwałki Lida
Elbląg Kętrzyn Gizycko Augustów Grodno
Malbork Olsztyn Sokółka ▲238 BYELORUSSIAN
Grudziądz Mława Ostróda Białystok S.S.R.
Toruń Rypin Ciechanów Ostrów Mazowiecka Brańsk Hajnówka Bereza
Włocławek Płock Warszawa (Warsaw) Mińsk Mazowiecki Brest Zhabinka
Łódź Radom Lublin Chełm Kovel Pripyat Polesye
Częstochowa Kielce Krasnik Zamość Lutsk Rovno
Opole Tarnów Przeworsk Lvov Ternopol U.S.S.R.
Kraków Rzeszów Przemyśl UKRAINIAN S.S.R.
Ostrava Tatry 2655 Ivano-Frankovsk Chernovtsy Vinnitsa
SLOVAKIA Košice Uzhgorod Mukachevo MOLDAVIAN
Miskolc Nyíregyháza Satu Mare Baia Mare Botoşani Iaşi Kishinev
BUDAPEST Debrecen Oradea Cluj-Napoca Tîrgu Mureş Bacău Odessa
HUNGARY Kecskemét Arad Alba-Iulia Sibiu Braşov Galaţi
Szeged Timişoara ROMANIA Carpaţii Meridionali Brăila
Novi Sad Reşiţa Turnu-Severin Ploieşti Constanţa
Beograd (Belgrade) Craiova BUCUREŞTI (Bucharest) BLACK
YUGOSLAVIA BULGARIA SEA
Sarajevo Ruse (Ruschuk) Tolbukhin

COPYRIGHT. GEORGE PHILIP & SON. LTD.

Bristol
LONDON
Exmoor
Southampton
Dartmoor
Brighton
Plymouth
Portsmouth
Land's End
Scilly Is.
Lizard Pt.

's-Gravenhage
Hoek van Holland   Amsterdam
Harwich   Rotterdam
Oostende   NETH.
Vlissingen
Dunkerque   Gent   Antwerpen   Mechelen
Calais   Lille   BELGIUM   Aachen
Boulogne   Brussel   Namur   Liège   Bonn
Amiens   Douai   Ardennes   LUX.
St-Quentin   Verdun

Osnabrück   W.   E. BERLIN
Hannover   Weser   Spree   Frank
Münster   Braunschweig   Potsdam   Magdeburg
GERMANY   Mulde   Dresde
Dortmund   z Halle   Leipzig   Karl-Marx-St
Essen   Kassel   Erfurt   (Chemnitz)
Düsseldorf   Köln   Fulda   Thüringer   Erzgeb.
Koblenz   Wiesbaden   Wald   Praha
Mainz   Frankfurt   Würzburg   Böhmerwald   Plzeň
Trier   Darmstadt   Nürnberg   Regensburg

English Channel
Channel Is.
I. d'Ouessant
Pte. St-Mathieu
Brest
Pte. de Penmarch

Cherbourg
Jersey
St-Malo
Dieppe   Somme
Le Havre   Rouen
Caen   Seine

Lorient
Belle-Ile
St-Nazaire

Rennes
Alençon
Sarthe   Le Mans
Vannes   Angers
Loire   Tours
Nantes   Vienne

Versailles   PARIS
Seine   Marne   Reims   Châlons
Orléans   Troyes
Cher   Loire
Bourges   Dijon

Épinal   Vosges
Metz   Nancy   Strasbourg
Toul   Rhin   Freiburg
Belfort   Basel
Besançon   Bern   SWITZERLAND

Darmstadt   Heidelberg
Mannheim   Karlsruhe
Stuttgart   Ulm   Augsburg
München   Salzburg
Bodensee   Linz
Zürich   LIECHT.   Inn
Innsbruck   Brenner   A u
Bern   Lausanne   Ortles   Klagen
Genève   Lac Léman   Passo de   Drava

45
Bay of Biscay
5365

La Rochelle
Rochefort
Charente   Angoulême
Gironde   Périgueux
Bordeaux   Dordogne   Lot
Garonne

5098

FRANCE
Limoges   Vichy   Clermont-Ferrand
Mt. Dore   St-Étienne   Lyon
1886   Auvergne
Grenoble   Torino
Cévennes   Isère
Rhône   Durance

Mt. Blanc   Genève
4807   Como   Bergamo
Novara   Milano   Brescia
Lago di Garda   Vicenza
Po   Verona   Padova   Venézia
Alessándria
Parma   Réggio   Ferrara
Génova   Módena   Bologna
La Spézia   Forlì
Firenze   Rimini

Lubljana
Udine   Gorizia   Trieste
Rijek
G. di Venézia   Pula

C. Ortegal
La Coruña   El Ferrol
C. Finisterre   Gijón   Santander   Bilbao   San Sebastián
Pontevedra   Oviedo   Picos de   Cordillera   Cantábrica
Vigo   Orense   León   Europa   Burgos   Vitoria   Pamplona
Santiago   Compos   Palencia   Logroño   Ebro
Porto   Braga   Valladolid   Pyrenees   Pico de Aneto
Douro   3404   ANDORRA

Cannes
MONACO   Menton
Nice
Golfo di   La
Génova   Spézia
Ligurian Sea   Elba
C. Corse
Mt. Cinto 2710   Bastia
Corse   ROMA
(Corsica)   SAN MARINO
Ancona
Arezzo   Siena
Perúgia
Mti. Sabini   Pesc
Gran Sasso
2914

40
PORTUGAL
Sa. da Estrela   Sa. de Gata
Coimbra
Ciudad   Salamanca
Rodrigo   SPAIN
MADRID
Sa. de Guadarrama
Tajo   Guadalajara
Cuenca
Teruel

Zaragoza   Lérida
Tortosa
Tarragona
Barcelona
Ebro

Golfe du Lion
Perpignan
C. Creus
Narbonne
Béziers   Nîmes   Avignon
Montpellier   Marseille   Nice
Sète   Toulon
Toulouse

Golfo di
Génova
Livorno   Arno
Pisa
Civitavécchia
Tevere
Roma

Lisboa
Évora
Badajoz
Guadiana
Alcántara
Cáceres
Toledo
La   Ciudad Real
Mancha
Júcar   Albacete
Castellón
Valencia

Islas Baleares
Menorca (Minorca)
Palma   Mahón
Ibiza   Mallorca (Majorca)
Cabrera
Formentera

Sássari   Olbia
Bouches de Bonifacio
Caprera
Sardegna
(Sardinia)   Mti. del Gennargentu 1834
Cágliari   3719

Volturno   Gaeta
Vesúvi   Nápoli
1277   Capri   Salerno

Sierra Morena
Córdoba   Linares
Jaén   Granada
Sevilla   Guadalquivir
Huelva   Segura   Murcia
Tinto   Lorca
Alicante

C. Nao
Ibiza

Cádiz   Jérez
C. Trafalgar   Sa. Nevada 3478
Str. of Gibraltar   Málaga   Mulhacén
Tanger   Gibraltar (Br.)   Almería
Algeciras   Ceuta (Sp.)   C. de Gata
Larache   Alborán (Sp.)
Tétouan   Melilla (Sp.)
Ouezzane   Ghazaouet

Cartagena

MEDITER

Tyrrhenian Sea
2887
2850

ft   m
12 000   4000
6000   2000
3000   1000
1200   400
600   200
0   0
200   600
1000   3000
2000   6000
3000   9000
m   ft

35

MOROCCO
Rabat   Fès
Meknès
Haut Atlas
3737

Alger   Tizi Ouzou
Oran   Chéliff   Bejaia   Skikda   Annaba
Mostaganem   Constantine
Sidi-Bel-Abbès   Sétif
Tlemcen   Plateaux
Oujda   Hauts
Moulouya
Chott ech Chergui
Djelfa

Bizerte
Tunis
Carthage
Pantelleria (It.)
G. de Hammamet
Kairouan   Sousse
Chott el   Batna
Hodna   Tébessa
Biskra
Chott Melrir

Isole Éolie o Lip
(Æolian Is.)
Palermo   Mes
Trápani   Sicilia
Isole Égadi   3340
Marsala   Catani
Agrigento   Siracus
Caltanissetta
C. Bon

MALTA
Gozo
Valletta
Lampedusa (It.)

Béchar
Figuig
Ain Sefra
A t l a s   S a h a r i e n
ALGERIA
Touggourt
Chott Djerid
Tozeur
Gabès   Djerba
Sfax   Iles Kerkenna

30
Beni Abbès
El Goléa
Ghardaïa
Ouargla
Hassi Messaoud
Ft. Lallemand
Mizdah

TUNISIA

Tarābulus
Al Khum
Jabal Nafūsah
Tarābulus

1:10 000 000

50   100   150   200 miles
50   0   100   200   300 km

POLAND
Płock
Warszawa
Poznań
Łódź
Brest
Pinsk
Polesye
Chernigov
Desna
Konotop
Sumy
Belgorod
Volgograd
Radom
Wisła (Vistula)
Lublin
Pripyat
Pripyat
Nezhin
Kazanskaya
Chorzów
Kraków
Lutsk
Rovno
Zhitomir
Kiyev
Pereyaslav-Khmelnitskiy
Poltava
Kharkov
Wrocław
Legnica
Tarnów
Przemyśl
Lvov
Vinnitsa
S. S. R.
Belaya Tserkov
Kremenchug
Slavyansk
Voroshilovgrad
Kamensk-Shakhtinskiy
Ostrava
Jablunkovský Pr.
Kielce
U.
Kamenets-Podol'skiyU
Mogilev-Podol'skiy
Cherkassy
(Dnieper)
Pavlograd
Gorlovka
Makeyevka
Shakhty
Tsimlyanskoye Vdkhr.
950
Slavkov
Tatry
Carpathians
2655
Kolomyya
Prut
Balta
Pervomaysk
Dněprodzerzhinsk
Dnepropetrovsk
Donetsk
Don
Novocherkassk
2305
Chernovtsy
MOLDAVIAN
Uman
Voznesensk
Kirovograd
Krivoy Rog
Zaporozhye
Taganrog
Rostov
Azov
CHOSLOVAKIA
Banská Stiavnica
Miskolc
Debrecen
Pietrosul
Beltsy
S. S. R.
Bug
Nikolayev
Melitopol
Zhdanov (Mariupol)
Berdyansk
Yeisk
Manych
Košice
Iaşi
Kishinev
S.
Kherson
Perekop
Tikhoretsk
Stavropol
Bratislava
Hron
Tisza
Tokaj
Sóret
Pietrosul
2102
Bendery
Tiraspol
Odessa
Karkinitskiy Zaliv
Krymskaya (Crimea)
Feodosiya
Novorossiysk
Armavir
Budapest
Oradea
Cluj-Napoca
Ismail
Belgorod Dnestrovskiy
Sea of Azov
Kerch
Krasnodar
Maykop
HUNGARY
Kecskemét
Hódmezővásárhely
Körös
Szeged
Arad
ROMANIA
Mureş
Sibiu
Braşov (Oraşul Stalin)
Galaţi
Sulina
M. Tarkhankut
Yevpatoriya
Simferopol
1545
Yalta
Novorossiysk
Tuapse
Pécs
Subotica
Timişoara
Negoiu
2535
Braşov
Brăila
Karkinitskiy Zaliv
Sevastopol
Balaklava
Bálaton
Sombor
Novi Sad
Petrovaradin
Carpaţii Meridionali
Ploieşti
Sukhumi
Zagreb
Drava
Porţile de Fier
Turnu-Severin
Piteşti
Constanţa
BLACK SEA
Poti
YUGOSLAVIA
Brod
Sava
Smederevo
Craiova
Bucureşti
Silistra
2211
İnce Burnu
Sinop
Batumi
Banja Luka
Beograd
Morava
Dunărea (Danube)
Ruse
Tolbuhin
İnebolu
Rize
BOSNA
Sarajevo
Niš
Stara Pleven
Tŭrnovo
Varna
Samsun
Trabzon
Durmitor
2522
Novi Pazar
Shipchenski
Sliven
Burgas
Kastamonu
2565
Kuzey Anadolu Dağları
Mostar
Planina
Çankırı
Giresun
Tirebolu
Erzincan
Dalmacija
CRNA GORA
Sofiya
BULGARIA
Plovdiv
Zonguldak
Ereğli
Amasya
Sıvas
Keban
Lástovo
Dubrovnik (Ragusa)
Cetinje
Musala
2925
Maritsa
Edirne
İstanbul
Karadeniz Boğazı (Bosporus)
Üsküdar
İzmit
Bolu
Tokat
Malatya
Kotor
Shkodrë
2764
Skopje
Rhodopi Planina
Tekirdağ
Marmara Denizi
İznik Gölü
Bursa
Beypazarı
Ankara
Yozgat
Kırşehir
Kayseri
Gürün
Gaziantep
ALBANIA
Tiranë
Durrës
Elbasan
Vardar
Strumica
Serrat
Kavála
Alexandroúpolis
Enez
Çanakkale
Bandırma
Bilecik
Sakarya
Eskişehir
Sivrihisar
Ercıyas Dağı
3770
Maraş
Bari
Barletta
Bitola
Athos
2033
Gökçeada (Gallipoli)
Troy
Balıkesir
Kütahya
Afyon Karahisar
Tuz Gölü
Seyhan
Adana
Gaziantep
Brindisi
Táranto
Oros Olimbos
2917
Límnos
Çanakkale Boğazı
Ayvalık
Bolvadin
TURKEY
Aksaray
Niğde
Tarsus
Mersin
İskenderun Körfezi
Halab
Golfo di Táranto
Vlorë
Lárisa
Vólos
Vóreioi Sporádhes
Lésvos
Manisa
Turgutlu
Cörüksu Çayı
Eğridir Gölü
Beyşehir Gölü
Konya
Karaman
İskenderun
Antakya
İskenderun Körfezi
SYRIA
La Sila
4929
Kérkira
Kérkira
Notia Pindhos
Évvoia
Khíos
İzmir
Alaşehir
Isparta
Burdur
Torós Dağları
Silifke
Al Lādhiqīyah
Bāniyās
Hamáh
Catanzaro
Levkás
Návpaktos
GREECE
Thívai
Andros
Sámos
Aydın
Denizli
Muğla
Antalya
Mersin
3083
Hims
Réggio
C. Spartivento di Messina
Kefallinía
Korinthiakós Kólpos
Athínai
Piraievs
Kikládhes
Náxos
Ikaría
Dhodhekánisos
Antalya Körfezi
Elmalı
3086
Nicosia
Famagusta
Tarābulus
Bayrūt (Beirut)
Dimashq (Damascus)
Ţ. Sila
Kérkira
Pátrai
Korinthos
Peloponnisos
Olympia
Spárti
Míkonos
Síros
Mílos
İos
Thira
Ródhos
Megiste (Kastellórizon)
1951
Larnaca
CYPRUS
Limassol
Morphou
2814
'Akko
Hefa (Haifa)
Jabal ad Durūz
Bosra
Ionian Sea
Zákinthos
Kalamáta
Pílos
Ákra Taínaron
5121
Kíthira
Andikíthira
Khaniá
Ídhi Oros
Iráklion
2456
Kárpathos
Ródhos
4486
LEBANON
Saydā
esh Shaykh
Tel Aviv-Yafo
Jerusalem
'Ammān
Jordan
4135
A
N
E
A
N
S
E
A
3174
CYPRUS
ISRAEL
Gaza
Dead Sea
-395
JORDAN
Cyrene
Darnah
Al Marj (Barce)
Khalij Bômba
Tubruq
Rashid
Bahra el Burullus
Dumyât
Bur Sa'id
El 'Arîsh
Petra
Ma'ān
BYA
Banghāzi
Khalīj Surt
Barqa
El 'Alamein
Matrûh
Salûm
Khalig el Salûm
El Iskandarîya
El Mahalla el Kubra
Tanta
El Qantara
Ismâ 'ilîya
Bur Sa'id
Suez Canal
El Suweis
Gebel el Tih
Al 'Aqabah
Elat
Khalīj al 'Aqabah
EGYPT
El Qâhira (Cairo)
El Faiyûm
Beni Suef
Nile
Gebel
2637
Sinai

─ ─ ─ ─ ─ Division between Greeks
and Turks in Cyprus;
Turks to the north.

COPYRIGHT. GEORGE PHILIP & SON. LTD.

MALTA
1:1 000 000

S.E. EUROPE
POLITICAL
1:25 000 000

Projection: Conical with two standard parallels

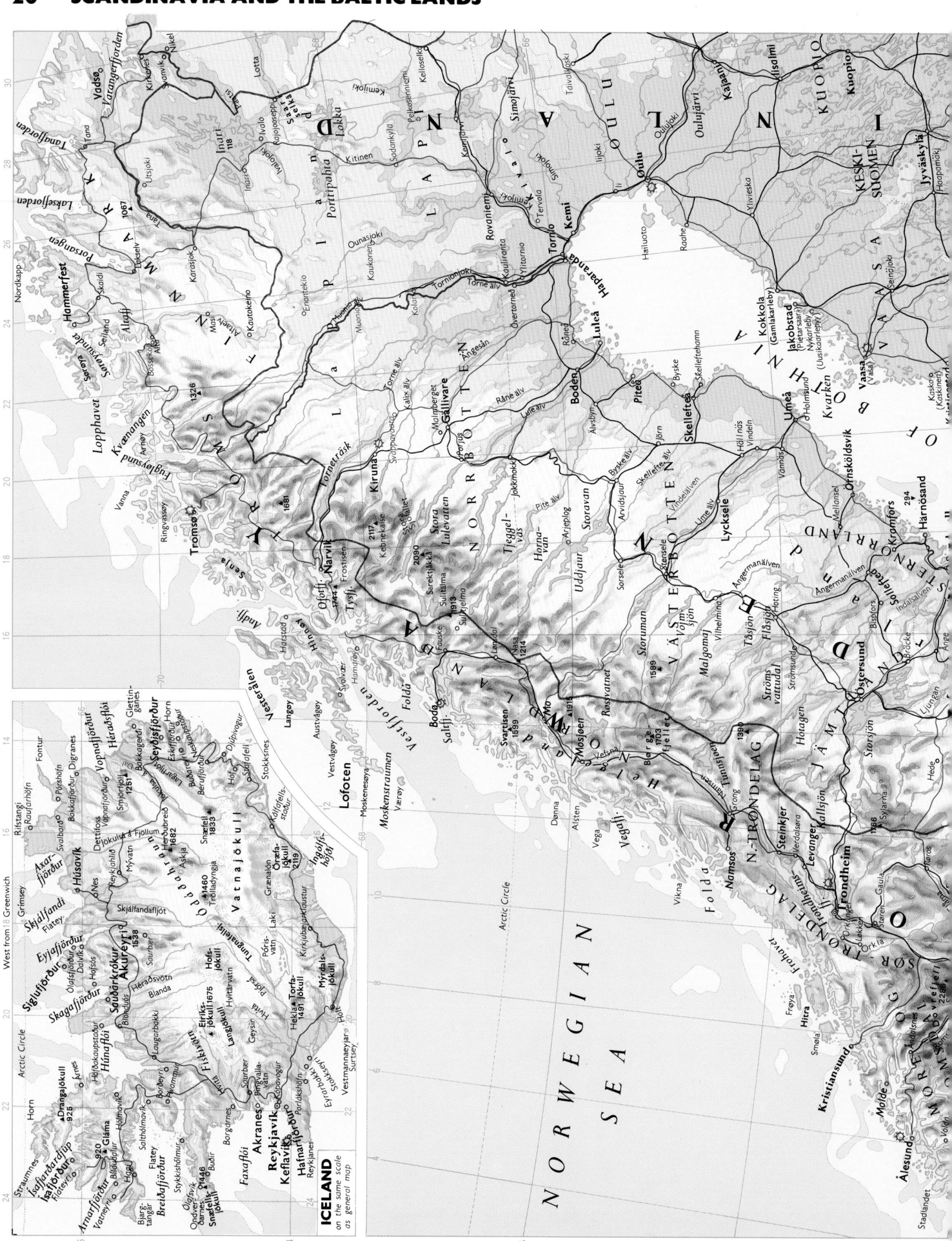

ICELAND
on the same scale
as general map

1:5 000 000

20 10 0   20   40   60   80   100 miles
40 20 0   40   80   120   160 km

Projection: Conical with two standard parallels   East from Greenwich

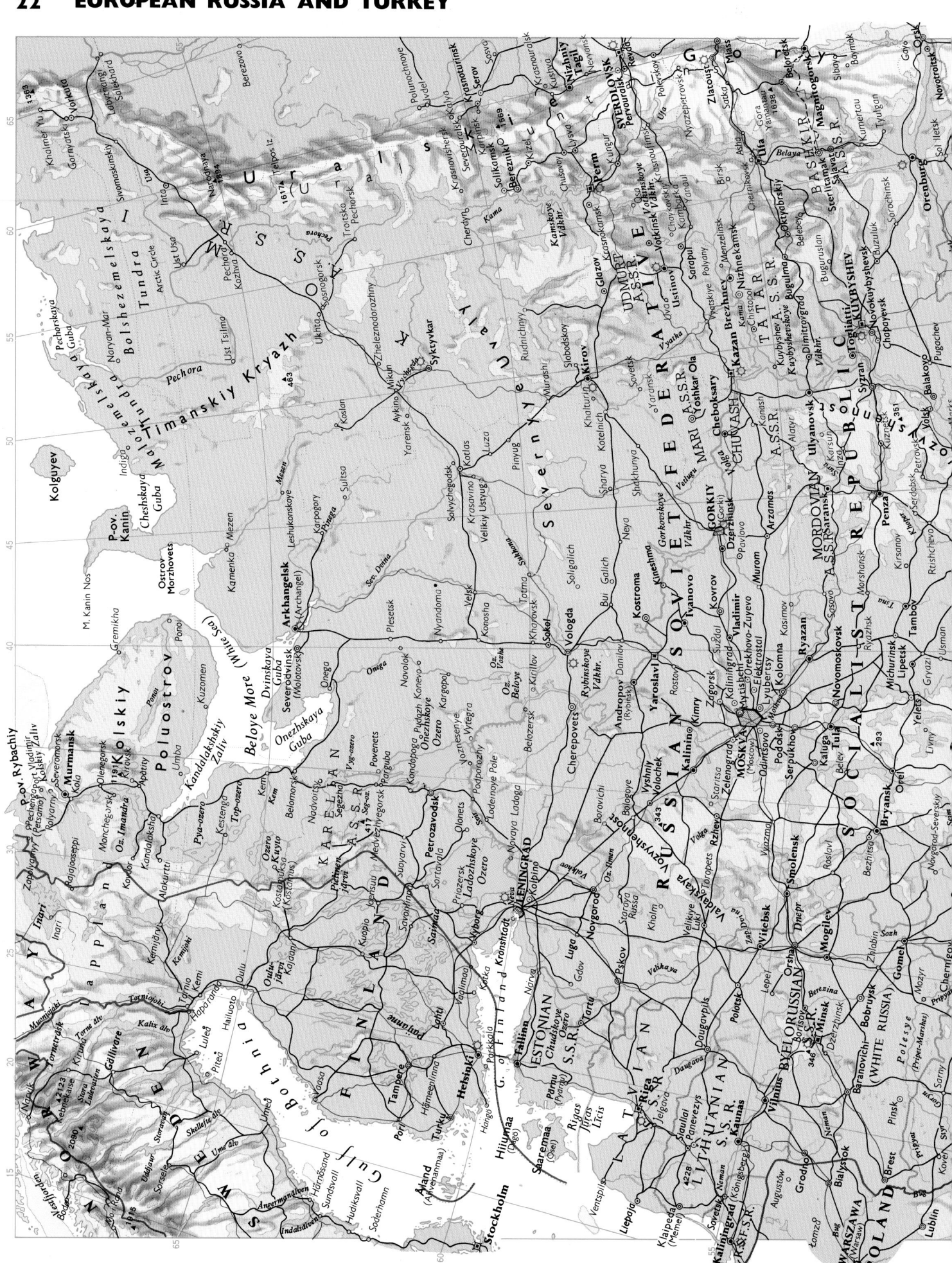

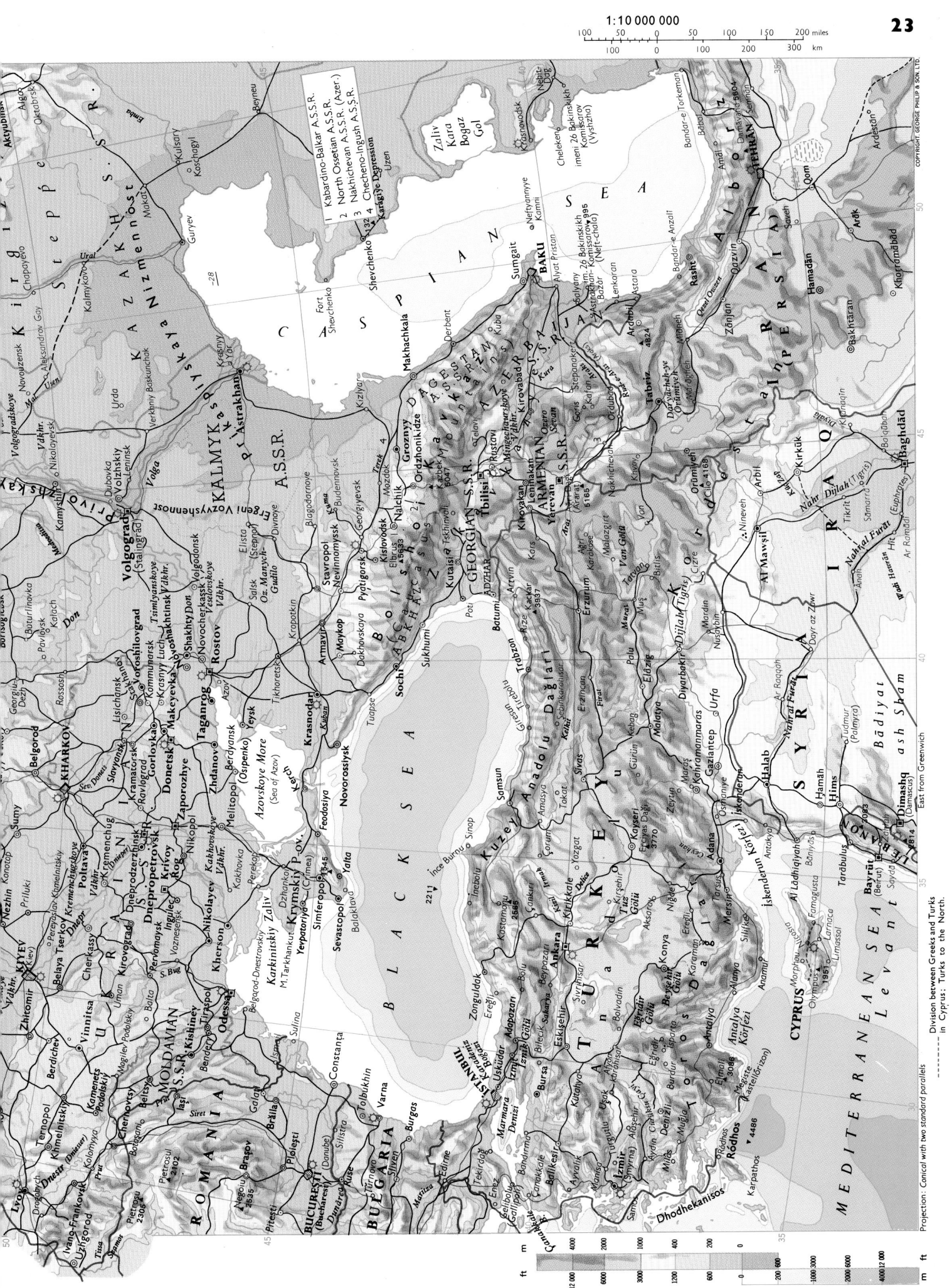

R.S.F.S.R.
1. Daghestan A.S.S.R.
2. Kabardino–Balkar A.S.S.R.
3. Mari A.S.S.R.
4. Mordovian A.S.S.R.
5. North Ossetian A.S.S.R.
6. Tatar A.S.S.R.
7. Udmurt A.S.S.R.
8. Chuvash A.S.S.R.
9. Checheno–Ingush A.S.S.R.
AZERBAIJAN
10. Nakhichevan A.S.S.R.
GEORGIA
11. Abkhaz A.S.S.R.
12. Adzhar A.S.S.R.

Projection: Conical Orthomorphic with two standard parallels

East from Greenwich

1:20 000 000

| 100 | 0 | 100 | 200 | 300 | 400 | 500 miles |

| 100 | 0 | 200 | 400 | 600 | 800 km |

OCEAN

Laptev Sea

East Siberian Sea

Mys Dezhneva (East C.)

St. Lawrence I. (U.S.A.)

Chukotskoye More

Bering Sea

Severnaya Zemlya

Ostrov Komsomolets

Ostrov Oktyabrskoy Revolyutsii

Ostrov Bolshevik

Ostrov Pioner

Ostrov Shmidt

Mys Arkticheskiy

Ostrov Novosibirskye Ostrova

Ostrov Novaya Sibir

Ostrova Delong

Ostrov Vrangelya

Severnaya Zemlya

PoluoByrranga GoryGoryo Taymyr

Ozer Taymyr

Nordvik

Tiksi

Norilsk

Gory Putorana

YAKUT A.S.S.R.

Verkhoyansk

Khrebet Cherskogo

Srednekolymsk

Sredinnyy Khrebet

Koryakskiy Khrebet

Okhotsko Kolymskoye

Poluostrov Kamchatka

Petropavlovsk-Kamchatskiy

Magadan

Arctic Circle

Vilyuysk

Yakutsk

Olekminsk

Sea of Okhotsk

Okhotsk

Sakhalin

Nikolayevsk-na-Am.

Kirensk

Bratsk

Nizhneudinsk

Krasnoyarsk

Kansk

Stanovoy Khrebet

Stanovoy Khrebet

Komsomolsk

Khabarovsk

Yuzhno-Sakhalinsk

Sovetskaya Gavan

Sapporo

Hakodate

Hokkaido

Irkutsk

Ulan Ude

BURYAT A.S.S.R.

Chita

Blagoveshchensk

Birobidzhan

Ussuriysk

Vladivostok

Nakhodka

Sea of JAPAN

Honshu

Niigata

Kanazawa

To-yama

Ulaanbaatar (Ulan Bator)

MONGOLIA

Hangayn Nuruu

Hentiyn Nuruu

Choybalsan

Qiqihar

Harbin

Jilin

Changchun

Shenyang

Fushun

Anshan

Dandong

North

P'yongyang

Nampo

Wonsan

Chongjin

Vladivostok

Edrengiyn Nuruu

GOBI

DESERT

Baotou

Hohhot

Zhangjiakou

Beijing

Zhangye

Yingkou

Dalian

Dandong

Seoul

Inch'on

South

Taejon

Taegu

Pusan

COPYRIGHT. GEORGE PHILIP & SON. LTD.

	Boundaries of U.S.S.R.
	Boundaries of S.S.R.
	Boundaries of A.S.S.R.

1:50 000 000

250   0   250   500   750   1000 miles
250   0   500   1000   1500   km

COPYRIGHT. GEORGE PHILIP & SON, LTD.

Projection: Bonne

East from Greenwich

PACIFIC OCEAN

ARCTIC OCEAN

INDIAN OCEAN

Aleutian Is.
7822
6642
4750
Bering Str.
C. Dezhneva
Kamchatka Peninsula
Klyuchevskaya Vol.
Bering Sea
Sredinny Ra.
Sea of Okhotsk
Kuril Is.
9370
Hokkaido
Honshu
Shikoku
Kyushu
Japan
Sea of Japan
Sakhalin
La Pérouse Str.
Korea Str.
Korea
Yellow Sea
East China Sea
Ryukyu Is.
Tropic of Cancer
Bonin Is.
10 654
Caroline Is.
Guam
Palau Is.
10 497
Cape Johnson Deep
Philippine Is.
Mindanao
Luzon
Formosa
Hainan
New Guinea
Australia
Halmahera
Ceram
Banda Sea
Celebes Sea
Moluccas
Arafura Sea
Timor
Flores
Bali
Java Sea
Borneo
Sulu Sea
Palawan
4101
Kinabalu
Celebes
Makasar Strait
Sumatra
Sunda Is.
Sunda Str.
Java
Str. of Malacca
Malay Peninsula
South China Sea
G. of Thailand
Nicobar Is.
Andaman Is.
Bay of Bengal
Chao Phraya
Mekong
Salween
Irrawaddy
Si-kiang
Tong king
G. of Tong king
Hong (Red) R.
Sikhote Alin Ra.
Amur
Sungari
Great Khingan Mts
Manchurian Plain
Great Plain of China
Hwang
Yangtze-Kiang
China
Koko Nor
Plateau of Mongolia
Tsangpo
Brahmaputra
Himalaya
Everest 8848
Plateau of Tibet
Kunlun Shan
Lop Nor
Tarim Basin
Takla Makan
Tarim
Turfan Basin
Tien Shan
Altai
Bogdo 4506
Sayan Mts
Selenga
Angara
L. Baikal
Yablonovy Ra.
Stanovoy Ra.
Aldan
Vilyui
Lena
Central Siberian Plateau
Lower Tunguska
Tunguska
Yenisei
Taimyr Peninsula
Chelyuskin
Severnaya Zemlya
New Siberian Is.
Wrangel I.
Kolyma
Indigirka
Gydan Ra. (Kolyma)
Verkhoyansk Range
Laptev Sea
Kara Sea
Barents Sea
Novaya Zemlya
Svalbard
Greenland
Iceland
British Isles
North Sea
Baltic Sea
Scandinavia
Finland
White Sea
Kola Pen.
North Cape
Kolguyev I.
N. Dvina
Arctic Circle
North European Plain
Central Russian Uplands
1640
Ural Mountains
1894
Narodnaya
Tobol
Irtysh
West Siberian Plain
Ob
Irtysh
Steppes
Aral Sea
Syr Darya
Amu Darya
Turanian Plain
Chu
Ili
L. Balkhash
Pamir
7495
Hindu Kush
Karakoram Ra.
8611
K2
Sutlej
Indus
Ganga
Yamuna
Narmada
Godavari
Krishna
Deccan
Eastern Ghats
Western Ghats
India
Thar
Sulaiman Ra.
Helmand
Hamun
Plateau of Iran
Zagros
Elburz Mts
5600
Great Salt Desert
Caspian Sea
Volga
Ural
Don
Dnepr
Caucasus
5633
Ararat 5165
Black Sea
Bosporus
Anatolia
Taurus Mts
Cyprus
Mediterranean Sea
Adriatic Sea
Carpathians
Danube
Oder
Elbe
Vistula
Rhine
Tigris
Euphrates
Mesopotamia
The Gulf
G. of Oman
Arabian Sea
Arabia
Ar Rub'al Khali
G. of Aden
Socotra
Râs Asir (C. Guardafui)
Somali Peninsula
Red Sea
Syrian Desert
Dead Sea
Sinai Pen.
Suez Canal
Nile
Libyan Desert
Lake Victoria
Maldive Is.
Laccadive Is.
Ceylon
C. Comorin
Polk Strait
Gulf of Manaar
Chagos Arch.
Seychelles
Amirantes
Equator
Pei Hui
Shansi
Ordos

m ft
6000 18 000
4000 12 000
2000 6000
1000 3000
400 1200
200 600
0
0
200 600
2000 6000
4000 12 000
6000 18 000
8000 24 000

1:50 000 000

250 0 250 500 750 1000 miles
250 0 500 1000 1500 km

ARCTIC OCEAN

PACIFIC OCEAN

INDIAN OCEAN

U. S. S. R.

CHINA

MONGOLIA

INNER MONGOLIA

MANCHURIA

INDIA

PAKISTAN

AFGHANISTAN

IRAN (PERSIA)

IRAQ

SAUDI ARABIA

TURKEY

SYRIA

JORDAN

EGYPT

LIBYA

SUDAN

ETHIOPIA

SOMALI REP.

KENYA

TANZANIA

ZAIRE

ZAMBIA

MALAWI

UGANDA

RWANDA

BURUNDI

OMAN

UNITED ARAB EMIRATES

QATAR

BAHRAIN

KUWAIT

YEMEN

SOUTH YEMEN

DJIBOUTI

XINJIANG UYGUR

XIZANG (TIBET)

NEPAL

BHUTAN

BANGLADESH

BURMA

THAILAND (SIAM)

LAOS

VIETNAM

CAMBODIA

MALAYSIA

INDONESIA

PHILIPPINES

BRUNEI

SRI LANKA (CEYLON)

SINGAPORE

KOREA

JAPAN

AUSTRALIA

NEW GUINEA

Borneo

Sumatera

Java

Sulawesi

Seram

Timor

Luzon

Mindanao

Taiwan (Formosa)

Hainan

HONG KONG (Br.)

Macau (Port.)

Maluku (Moluccas)

Irian Jaya

UNITED KINGDOM

ICELAND

EUROPE

AFRICA

Cities and places:
London, Paris, Roma, Berlin, Wien, Warszawa, Beograd, Thessaloniki, Athinai, Istanbul, Ankara, Izmir, Bursa, Erzurum, Odesa, Moskva, Leningrad, Murmansk, Arkhangelsk, Sverdlovsk, Chelyabinsk, Magnitogorsk, Orenburg, Omsk, Tomsk, Novosibirsk, Barnaul, Semipalatinsk, Alma Ata, Tashkent, Samarkand, Bukhara, Ashkhabad, Krasnovodsk, Baku, Tbilisi, Yerevan, Tabriz, Tehrān, Eşfahān, Shīrāz, Baghdad, Al Başrah, Dimashq, Halab, Bayrūt, Jerusalem, Al Qāhira (El Qâhira), El Iskandariya, Aşwān, El Khartûm, El Obeid, Addis Abeba, Mogadishu, Nairobi, Mombasa, Dar es Salaam, Kampala, Juba, Harer, Djibouti, Aden, Şan'ā', Makkah, Al Madīnah, Ar Riyāḍ, Bushehr, Zāhedān, Masqaṭ, Mashhad, Herāt, Kābul, Qandahār, Quetta, Karachi, Ahmadabad, Bombay, Hyderabad, Madras, Pondicherry, Colombo, Calcutta, Dacca, Allahabad, Kanpur, Lucknow, Varanasi, Delhi, Agra, Lahore, Peshawar, Simla, Kashi, Yining, Ürümqi, Lhasa, Lanzhou, Xi'an, Chengdu, Chongqing, Kunming, Changsha, Wuhan, Nanjing, Shanghai, Qingdao, Tianjin, Beijing, Shenyang, Changchun, Harbin, Dalian, Fuzhou, Guangzhou, Zhanjiang, Hanoi, Hué, Phnom Penh, Ho Chi Minh, Vientiane, Bangkok, Kuala Lumpur, Jakarta, Zomboanga, Davao, Manila, Rangoon, Mandalay, Myitkyina, Kuala Lumpur, Ulaanbaatar (Ulan Bator), Chita, Irkutsk, Krasnoyarsk, Kemerovo, Yakutsk, Khabarovsk, Vladivostok, Pusan, Seoul, Kitakyushu, Nagasaki, Fukuoka, Hakodate, Sapporo, Kyoto, Osaka, Yokohama, Tōkyō, Nagoya, Petropavlovsk, Okhotsk, Nikolayevsk, Magadan

Seas and waters:
Bering Sea, Sea of Okhotsk, Sea of Japan, Yellow Sea, East China Sea, South China Sea, Philippine Sea, Celebes Sea, Banda Sea, Java Sea, Sulu Sea, Bay of Bengal, Arabian Sea, The Gulf, G. of Oman, Red Sea, G. of Aden, Mediterranean Sea, Black Sea, Caspian Sea, Baltic Sea, North Sea, Barents Sea, Kara Sea, Laptev Sea, Aral Sea (Aral'skoye More), Ozero Balkhash, Ozero Baykal, Ozero Issyk-Kul'

Rivers:
Ob, Irtysh, Yenisey, Lena, Aldan, Amur, Angara, Nizhnyaya Tunguska, Syr Darya, Amu Darya, Volga, Don, Dnepr, Ural, Danube, Rhine, Huang He, Chang Jiang, Xi Jiang, Mekong, Salween, Irrawaddy, Ganga, Brahmaputra, Indus, Narmada, Godavari, Krishna, Tigris, Euphrates, Nile, Tarim He

Islands:
Aleutian Is., Kuril Is., Sakhalin, Hokkaido, Kyushu, Ryukyu - rettō, Bonin Is., Guam (U.S.), Caroline Is., Belau, Andaman Is. (India), Nicobar Is. (India), Maldives, Lakshadweep Is. (India), Seychelles, Socotra (South Yemen), Svalbard, Novaya Zemlya, Severnaya Zemlya, Ostrov Vrangelya, Mys Chukotskiy

Tropic of Cancer

Equator

Arctic Circle

East from Greenwich

Projection: Bonne

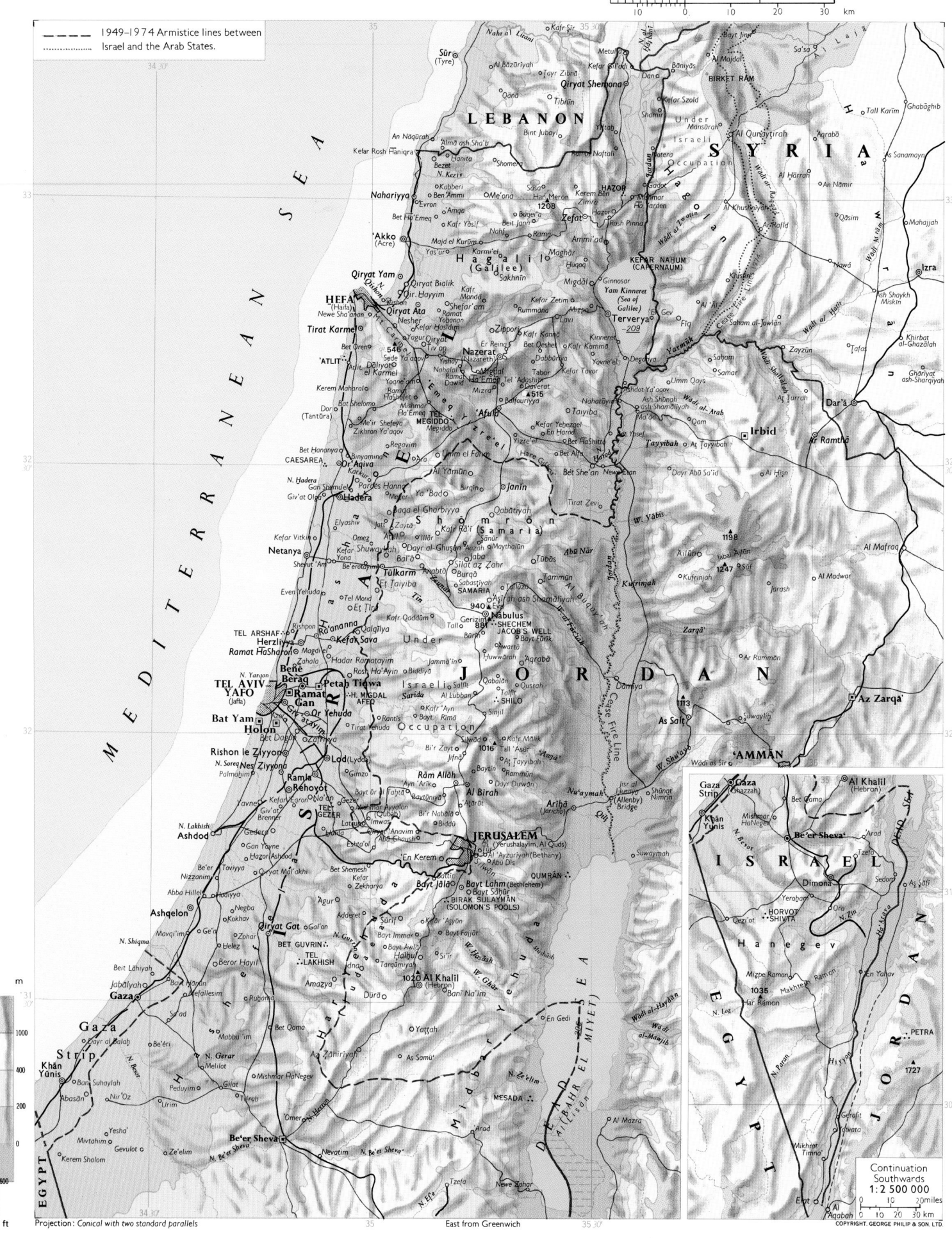

1:1 000 000

1949–1974 Armistice lines between Israel and the Arab States.

Projection: Conical with two standard parallels

East from Greenwich

Continuation Southwards 1:2 500 000

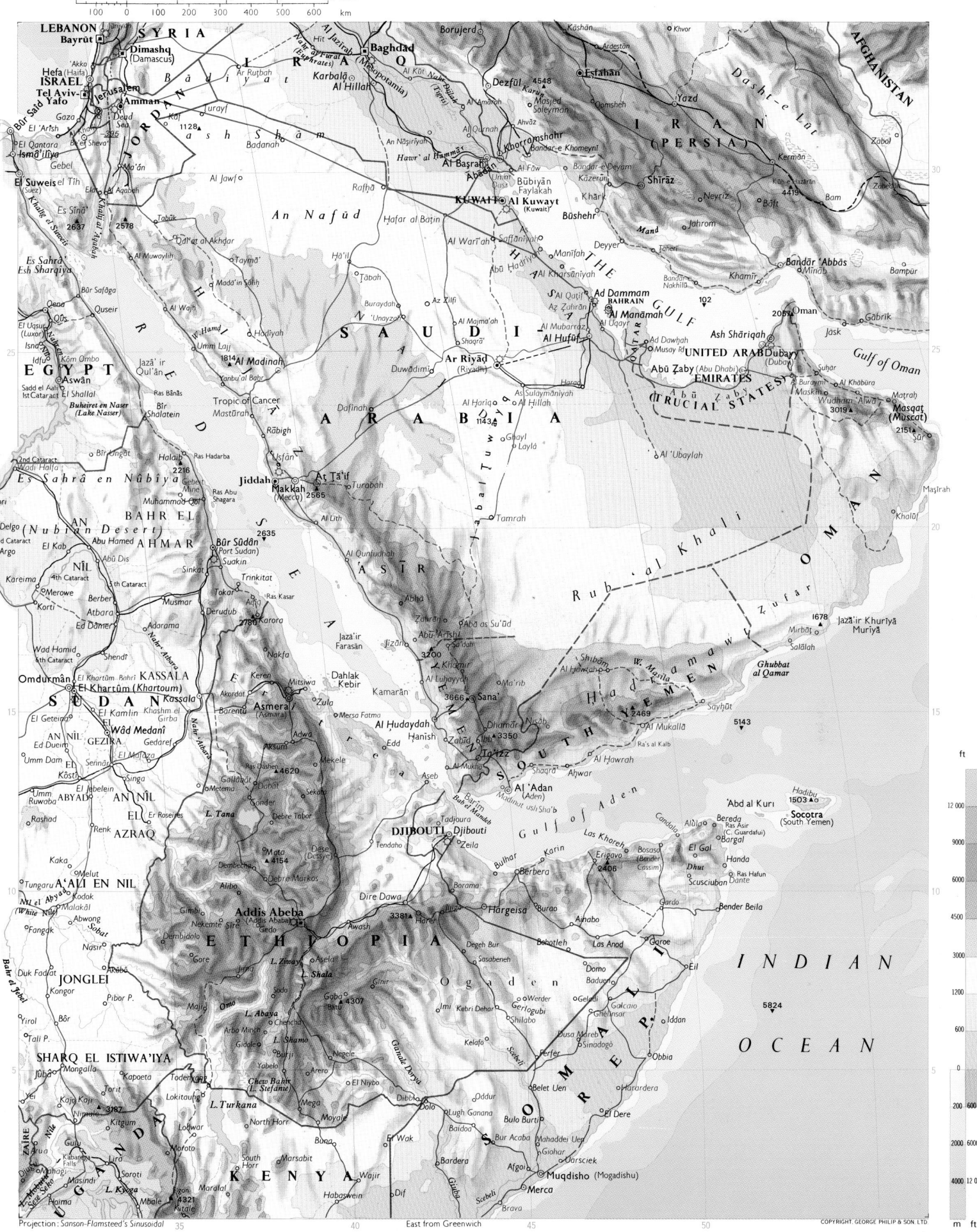

1:15 000 000

Projection: Sanson-Flamsteed's Sinusoidal

East from Greenwich

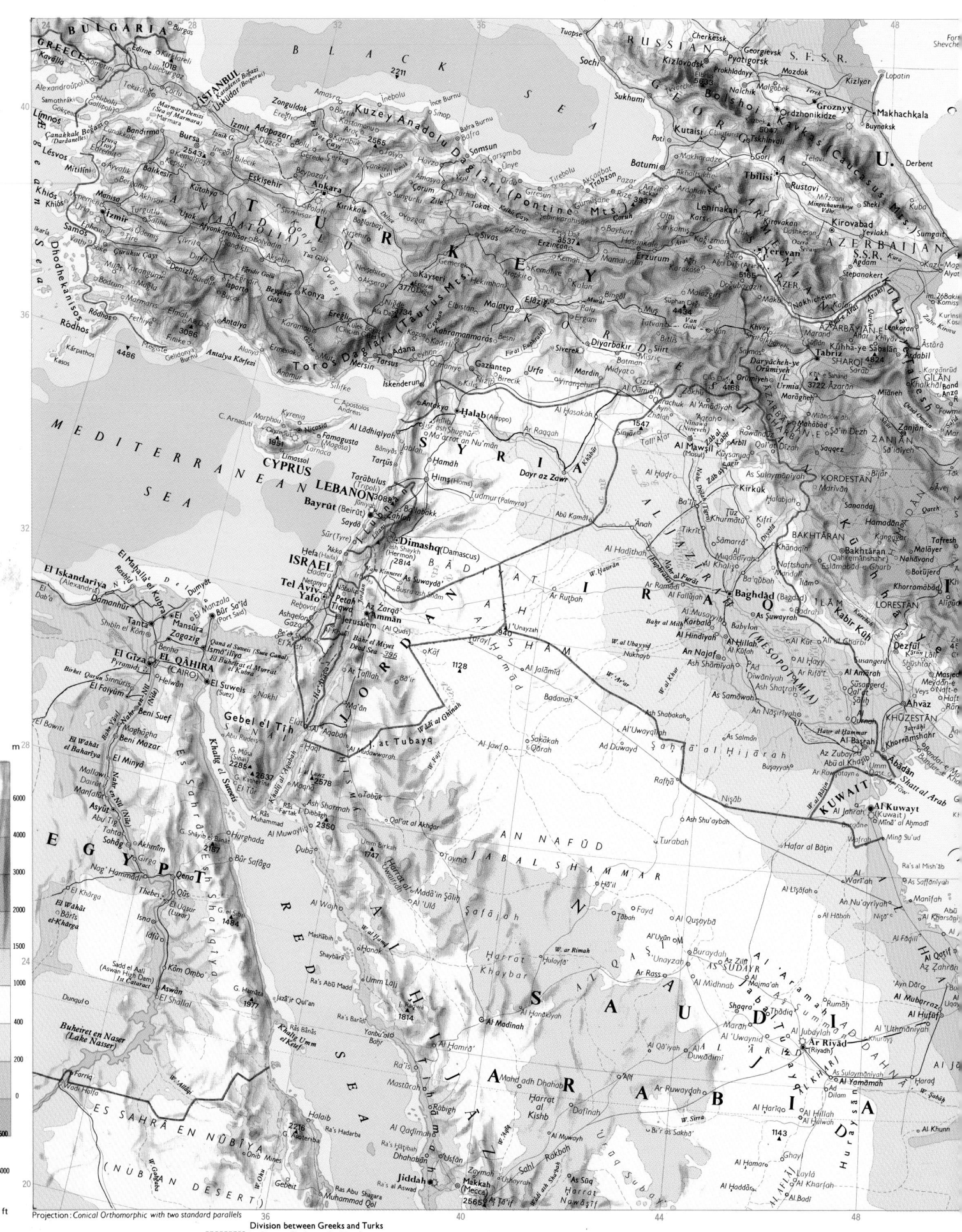

Projection: Conical Orthomorphic with two standard parallels

Division between Greeks and Turks
in Cyprus; Turks to the North.

1:10 000 000

100   100   200   300   miles
100   0   100   200   300   400   500 km

KAZAKH S.S.R.

Plato Ustyurt

Aralskoye More
Muynak

KARA-KALPAKISCHE A.S.S.R.

PESKI KYZYLKUM

UZBEK S.S.R.

KAZAKH S.S.R.

Turkestan
Chimkent
Arys
Lenger 4488
Dzhambul
Talas
Naryn

Chirchik
Tashkent
Yangi Yul
Angren
Namangan
Kokand
Andizhan
Margelan
Fergana
Osh

KIRGIZ S.S.R.

Tien Shan

Kashi (Kashgar)

CHINA

7575
7555

Nukus
Tashaus
Urgench
Turtkul
Khiva

Gizhduvan
Dzhizak
Ura-Tyube
Leninabad
Isfara
Kanibadam

Darganata
Bukhara
Kagan
Samarkand
Karshi
Shakhrisyabz

TADZHIK S.S.R.

Dushanbe
Ordzhanikidzeabad
Regar
Denau
Kurgan-Tyube
Kulyab

Pamir

Khorog

Serny Zavod
Chardzhou
Kerki
Termez
Qonduz
Talqan
Khanabad
Baghlan
Feyzabad

BADAKHSHAN

Krasnovodski Poluostrov
Krasnovodsk

Kara Bogaz Gol

TURKMEN S.S.R.

KARA KUM

Karakumskii Canal
Chamkhakly
Aqcheh
Shibarghan
Mazar-e Sharif
Kabul
Jalalabad
Peshawar
Rawalpindi
Islamabad

Nebit Dag
Kazandzhik
Kizyl Arvat

Ashkhabad

Koppeh Dagh

Mohammadabad
Tedzhen
Bairam Ali
Iolotan
Kushka

AFGHANISTAN

HINDU KUSH

Bamian
Charikar
Kabul
Ghazni
Gardez
Khowst

Qa'emshahr
Babol
Sari
Gorgan
Mashhad (Meshed)
Quchan
Kuh-e Binalud 3314
Sabzevar
Neyshabur
Kashaf
Serakhs
Tashkepri

Herat
Safed Koh

Damghan
Semnan
Shahrud
Torbat-e Heydariyeh
Torbat-e Jam
Kashmar
Khvaf
Ghuriano

DASHT-E KAVIR
(Great Salt Desert)

KHORASAN

PERSIA (IRAN)

Qom
Daryacheh-ye Namak
Kashan
Natanz
Esfahan

Anarak
Jandaq
Bejestan
Gonabad
Ferdows
Qayen
Yazdan
Shindand

Tabas
Deyhuk
Khur
Mazhan
Birjand
Sarbisheh
Farah

Dasht-e Margow

Gereshk
Qandahar
Qalat

HELMAND QANDAHAR

Rigestan

Qal'eh-ye Now

Kerman
Rafsanjan
Shahdad
Nostratabad
Zahedan (Duzdab)
Mirjaveh
Ladiz

BALUCHISTAN

Quetta
Bolan Pass

Tabas

Zabol
Zaranj
NIMRUZ

Gowd-e Zirreh

Chah Gay 2462

Dalbandin

Nushki

Shiraz
FARS
Neyriz
Sarvestan
Darab
Sabzevaran

Bam
Fahraj
Khash
Rod

Siahan Range

Central Makran Ra.

Bela
Hyderabad

Kahnuj
Hamun-e Jaz Murian
Bampur
Iranshahr
Zaboli

Nikshahr
Qasr-e Qand
Sarbaz
Pishin
Turbat

Makran Coast Range

Pasni
Gwadar

KARACHI

Mouths of the Indus

GREAT INDIAN DESERT

INDIA

Bandar Abbas
Qeshm
Minab
Jask

Gulf of Oman

Chah Bahar

ARABIAN SEA

Tropic of Cancer

Dubayy (Dubai)
Abu Zaby (Abu Dhabi)

UNITED ARAB EMIRATES

Ash Shariqah (Sharjah)
Ajman
Umm al Qaywayn
Al Fujayrah

Masqat (Muscat)

Oman (Jabal)
Suhar

OMAN

Sur
Ra's al Hadd

East from Greenwich

Continuation Southwards
on same scale

Projection: Conical with two standard parallels

ft   m
18 000   6000
12 000   4000
9000   3000
6000   2000
4500   1500
3000   1000
1200   400
600   200
0   0
200   600

m   ft

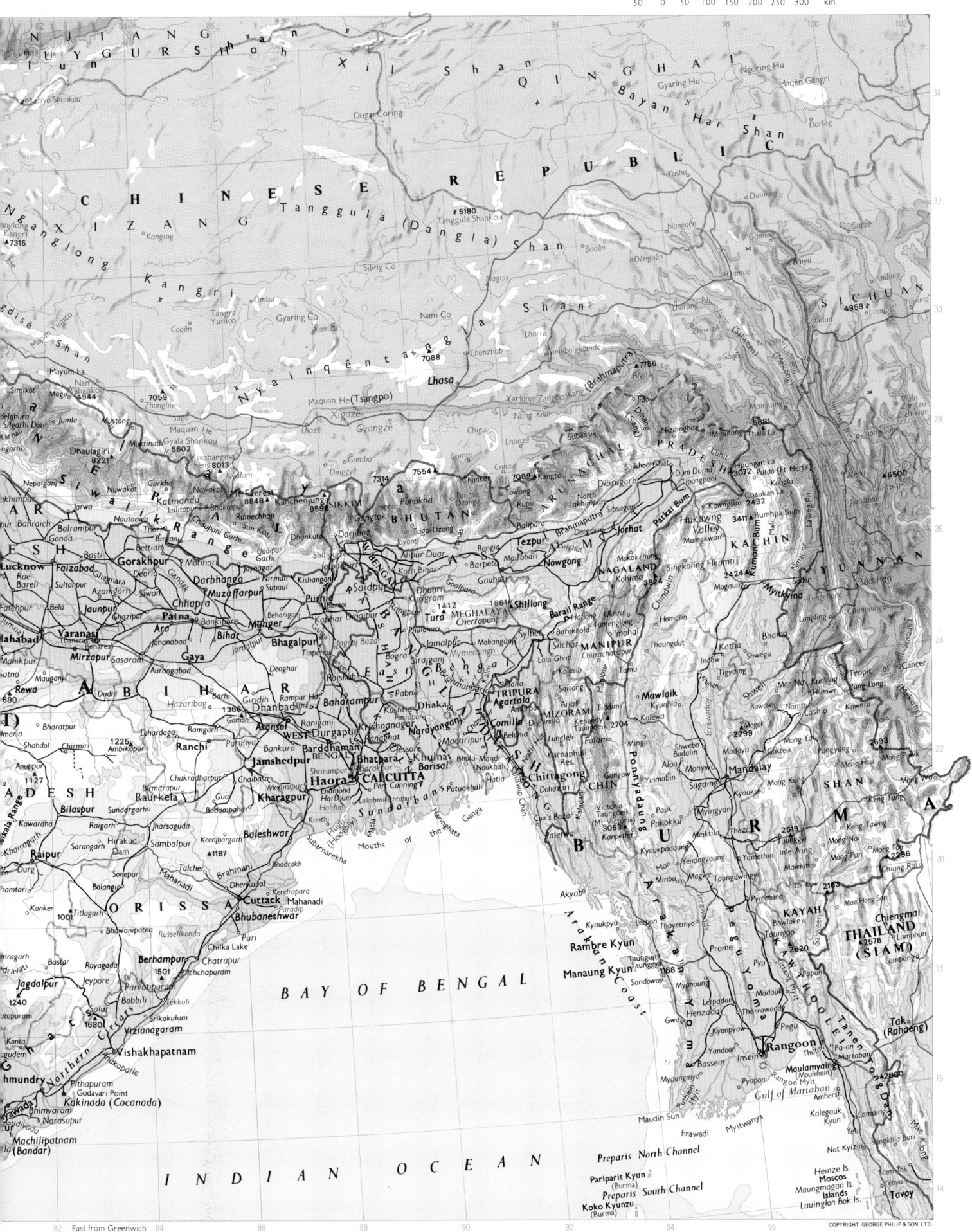

1:10 000 000

50 0 50 100 150 200 miles

50 0 50 100 150 200 250 300 km

BAY OF BENGAL

INDIAN OCEAN

CHINESE REPUBLIC

XIZANG

QINGHAI

SICHUAN

YUNNAN

BURMA

THAILAND (SIAM)

NEPAL

BHUTAN

SIKKIM

ASSAM

ARUNACHAL PRADESH

NAGALAND

MANIPUR

MIZORAM

MEGHALAYA

TRIPURA

BANGLADESH

WEST BENGAL

BIHAR

ORISSA

East from Greenwich

COPYRIGHT. GEORGE PHILIP & SON. LTD

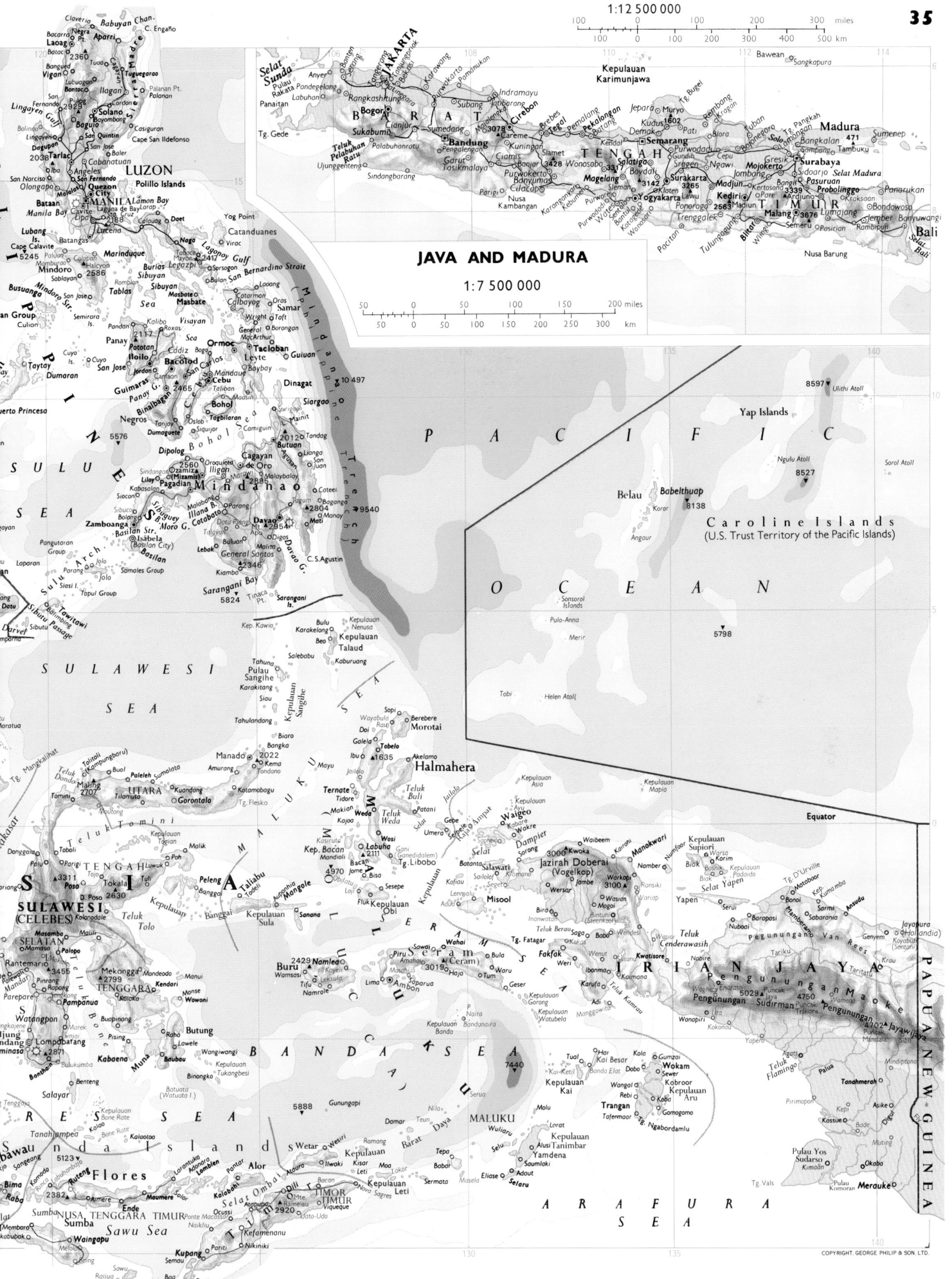

JAVA AND MADURA

1:7 500 000

1:12 500 000

COPYRIGHT. GEORGE PHILIP & SON. LTD.

SEA OF JAPAN

Suzu-misaki
Wajima Suzu
Noetsu-wan Tōkamachi
Nanao Takada Shibukawa
Himi Toyama-wan Kitaibaraki
Takaoka Nagano Yaita
Matsutō Kanazawa Toyama Matsumoto Takasaki Utsunomiya
Komotsu ISHIKAWA Ōmachi Ueda Maebashi Kiryū Tochigi Mit
Fukui Takayama 3190 Matsumoto Chichibu Kawagoe Omiya Noda
Takefu Kōfu Fuji-yoshida Urawa Kawaguchi Ichikawa
Echizen-Misaki Gero Kōfu 3776 TOKYO Chiba Funabashi
Tsuruga Kumano Ōgaki Ichinomiya Fuji Mishima Odawara Yokosuka
Sakaiminato Jizō-Zaki Maizuru Wadayama NAGOYA Fujinomiya Hiratsuka Fujisawa CHIBA
Matsue Tottori Miyazu Biwa-Ko Seto Okazaki Shizuoka Numazu YOKOHAMA Ichihara
Izumo Yonago Fukuchiyama Ayabe KYOTO Otsu Kuwana Toyota Shimizu KAWASAKI Tateyama
CHŪGOKU SHIMANE Tsuyama Himeji Amagasaki KOBE Kariya Handa Toyohashi Hamamatsu Nojima-Zaki
Hamada Gōtsu Odā Miyoshi OKAYAMA Nishinomiya OSAKA Sakai Ise TOKAIDO Ō-Shima
Masuda HIROSHIMA Kurashiki Akashi Sakai Kishiwada Toba LINE Miyake-Jima
Hagi YAMAGUCHI Fukuyama Tamashima Takatsuki NARA Owase Daiō-Misaki Irō-Zaki
Mihara Marugame Izumi-sano Wakayama Nii-Jima
Shimonoseki Iwakuni Kure Takamatsu Naruto Tanabe Shingū
Iki KITAKYŪSHŪ Onoda Ube Hōtu Imabari Awaji-Shima Kushimoto Shio-no-Misaki
FUKUOKA Iizuka Buzen Niihama TOKUSHIMA WAKAYAMA
Karatsu Yukuhashi SHIKOKU Kōchi KINKI Rebun-Tō Sōya-Misaki Sea of Okhotsk
Saga Hita Beppu EHIME Wakkanai
Imari Kurume Ōita Yawatahama Tosa-Wan Rishiri-Tō Abashiri-Wan
Sasebo Ōmuta Saiki Uwajima Muroto HOKKAIDŌ Shiretoko-Misaki
NAGASAKI Isahaya Kumamoto Bungo-Suidō Nakamura Muroto-Misaki Rumoi Asahigawa Nemuro-Kaikyō
Naga-saki Takachiho Sukumo Ashizuri-Zaki Ishikari (Otaru-Wan) HOKKAIDO Kushiro Nemuro
Amakusa Hitoyoshi Otaru SAPPORO
Minamata KYŪSHŪ Kamui-Misaki Shikotsu-Ko
Sendai MIYAZAKI Miyazaki Okushiri-Tō Uchiura-Wan Muroran Obihiro 2052
Kagoshima Kobayashi Nichinan Hakodate Esan-Misaki Erimo-Misaki
Makurazaki Kanoya Shiragami-Misaki Tsugaru-Kaikyō Shiriya-Zaki
Sata-Misaki Ōsumi-Kaikyō Aomori Hachinohe
Ōsumi-Shotō Nishin'omote Henashi-Misaki Hirosaki Towada-Ko
Yaku-shima 1935 Miyanoura-Dake Tane-ga-Shima Iwate-San 2041 Morioka Miyako
Akita TŌHOKU Kamaishi 7756
Sakata Yamagata Sendai Ishinomaki
Sado Fukushima
Niigata Kōriyama 2024 Iwaki
Noto-Hantō Toyama Nagaoka KANTŌ 8412
Kanazawa Maebashi Utsunomiya
CHŪBU TOKYO Mito Chōshi Inubō-Zaki
NAGOYA YOKOHAMA Bōsō-Hantō
Matsue Tottori Shizuoka Nojima-Zaki
CHŪGOKU KYOTO Hamamatsu Nii-Jima
Hiroshima KOBE Toyohashi Miyake-Jima
Okayama OSAKA Wakayama Hachijō-Jima
KITAKYŪSHŪ Sakai KINKI
FUKUOKA Takamatsu
Matsuyama SHIKOKU
Kumamoto Kōchi Tosa-Wan
Nagasaki SHIKOKU
KYŪSHŪ Miyazaki
Kagoshima

PACIFIC OCEAN

SEA OF JAPAN

SOUTH KOREA
Suwŏn Chungju
Taejŏn Pohang
Kunsan Chŏnju
Kwangju Chinju Taegu
Mokpo Sunchŏn Masan PUSAN
Yŏsu Korea Str.
Tsushima

1:5 000 000
East from Greenwich
Projection: Conical with two standard parallels
25 0 25 50 75 100 miles
25 0 25 50 100 150 km

1:10 000 000
East from Greenwich
100 50 0 50 100 150 200 miles
100 0 100 200 300 km
Projection: Bonne

REFERENCE TO PREFECTURES

HOKKAIDŌ DISTRICT	KINKI DISTRICT
1 Hokkaidō	24 Hyōgo
TŌHOKU DISTRICT	25 Kyōto
2 Aomori	26 Shiga
3 Akita	27 Ōsaka
4 Iwate	28 Nara
5 Yamagata	29 Mie
6 Miyagi	30 Wakayama
7 Fukushima	**CHŪGOKU DISTRICT**
CHŪBU DISTRICT	31 Tottori
8 Niigata	32 Okayama
9 Ishikawa	33 Shimane
10 Toyama	34 Hiroshima
11 Fukui	35 Yamaguchi
12 Gifu	**SHIKOKU DISTRICT**
13 Nagano	36 Kagawa
14 Yamanashi	37 Tokushima
15 Aichi	38 Ehime
16 Shizuoka	39 Kōchi
KANTŌ DISTRICT	**KYŪSHŪ DISTRICT**
17 Gumma	40 Fukuoka
18 Tochigi	41 Saga
19 Saitama	42 Nagasaki
20 Ibaraki	43 Kumamoto
21 Tōkyō	44 Ōta
22 Chiba	45 Miyazaki
23 Kanagawa	46 Kagoshima

Continuation Southwards on same scale

Ōsumi-Shotō 1935 Tane-ga-Shima
Tokara-Kaikyō Yaku-Shima
Tokara-Shima Suwanose-Jima
Nansei-Shoto
Amami-Ō-Shima
Toku-no-Shima

ft m
9000 3000
6000 2000
4500 1500
3000 1000
1200 400
600 200
0 0
200 600
2000 6000
4000 12,000
6000 18,000
8000 24,000
m ft

1:20 000 000

100   0   100   200   300   400 miles
100   0   100   200   300   400   500   600 km

U. S. S. R.

UNION OF SOVIET SOCIALIST REPUBLICS

MONGOLIA

KAZAKH S.S.R.

KIRGIZ S.S.R.

C H I N A

X I Z A N G   (T I B E T)

Q I N G H A I

NINGXIA HUIZU

XINJIANG UYGUR

Tarim Pendi

Dzungar Pendi

Kunlun Shan

Altun Shan

Qilian Shan

Tien Shan

Tannu Ola

Altai Shan

Karakoram

JAMMU & KASHMIR

NEPAL

BHUTAN

BANGLADESH

I N D I A

ASSAM

BURMA

THAILAND (SIAM)

LAOS

VIETNAM

HANOI

Haiphong

HEILONGJIANG

HARBIN

JILIN

Changchun

LIAONING

SHENYANG

NORTH KOREA

Pyongyang

SOUTH KOREA

Seoul

Pusan

JAPAN

Fukuoka

Nagasaki

YELLOW SEA

EAST CHINA SEA

SOUTH CHINA SEA

BAY OF BENGAL

TAIWAN (FORMOSA)

Taibei

PHILIPPINES

Luzon

HEBEI

BEIJING

TIANJIN

SHANDONG

QINGDAO

DALIAN

SHANXI

TAIYUAN

Datong

BAOTOU

Hohhot

SHAANXI

XI'AN

Lanzhou

GANSU

Dunhuang

Xining

HENAN

Zhengzhou

Luoyang

HUBEI

WUHAN

JIANGSU

NANJING

SHANGHAI

Hangzhou

ZHEJIANG

Ningbo

ANHUI

Hefei

JIANGXI

Nanchang

HUNAN

Changsha

SICHUAN

CHENGDU

CHONGQING

GUIZHOU

Guiyang

YUNNAN

Kunming

GUANGXI ZHUANGZU

Nanning

GUANGDONG

GUANGZHOU

Hong Kong (Br.)

Macao

Haikou

Hainan Dao

FUJIAN

Fuzhou

Xiamen

Shantou

Shanghai

Wenzhou

CALCUTTA

DELHI

Lucknow

Kanpur

Varanasi

Allahabad

Patna

Vishakhapatnam

Cuttack

Tropic of Cancer

RYUKYU Retto

Okinawa

Hainan

East from Greenwich

Projection: Bonne

COPYRIGHT GEORGE PHILIP & SON LTD.

ft   m
18 000   6000
12 000   4500
9000   3000
6000   2000
4500   1500
3000   1200
1500   600
600   400
0   200
0
200-600
2000   6000
4000   12 000
6000   18 000
m   ft

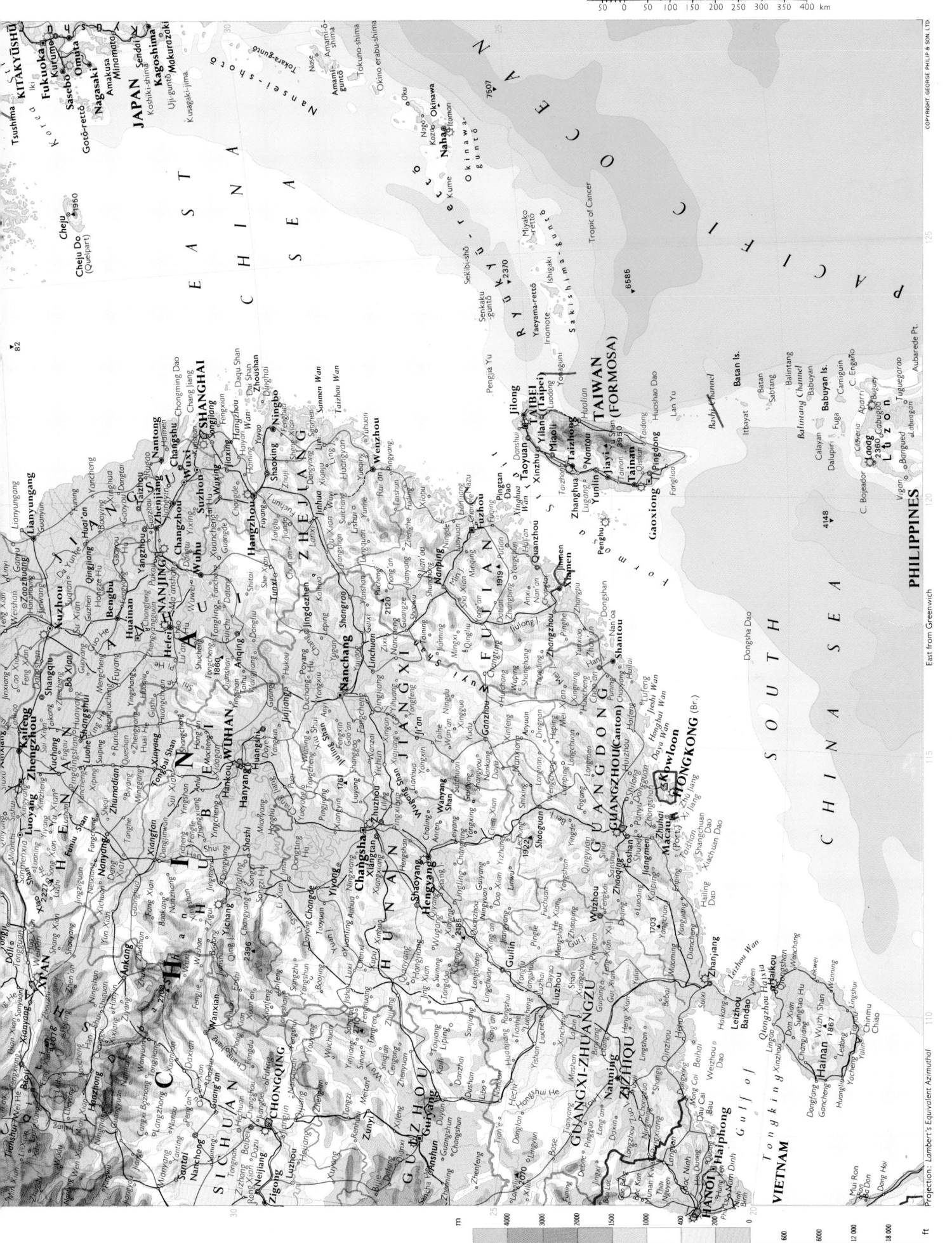

1:10 000 000

50   0   50   100   150   200   250 miles
50   0   50   100 150 200 250 300 350 400 km

P A C I F I C   O C E A N

E A S T   C H I N A   S E A

JAPAN
KITAKYŪSHŪ
Fukuoka
Kurume
Sasebo
Omuta
Nagasaki
Kagoshima
Minamoto
Amakusa
Makurozaki

Tsushima
Iki
Kōchi
Gotō-rettō

Cheju
Cheju Do
(Quelpart)

Nansei-shotō
Tokara-gunto
Amami-shima
Amami-O-shima
Tokuno-erabu-shima
Tokuno-shima

Okinawa
Naha
Okinawa-gunto

R Y U K Y U

Senkaku-gunto
Sekibi-shō
Pengjia Yu

Miyako-rettō
Yaeyama-rettō
Iriomote
Ishigaki
Sakishima-gunto

TAIWAN
(FORMOSA)
TAIBEI
(Taipei)
Jilong
Danshui
Taoyuan
Xinzhu
Miaoli
Taizhong
Zhanghua
Nantou
Yunlin
Jiayi
Tainan
Gaoxiong
Pingtung
Penghu

Tropic of Cancer

Batan Is.
Batan
Sabtang
Balintang Channel
Babuyan Is.
Calayan
Dalupiri
Fuga
Camiguin

Babuyan Channel
Aparri
Laoag
Vigan
L u z o n
PHILIPPINES

East from Greenwich

S O U T H   C H I N A   S E A

SHANGHAI
Nantong
Changshu
Songjiang
Suzhou
Wuxi
Hangzhou
J I A N G S U
Yangzhou
Zhenjiang
Changzhou
NANJING
Wuhu
Hefei
A N H U I
Huainan
Bengbu
Xuzhou
Kaifeng
Zhengzhou
Luoyang
XIAN
S H A A N X I
H E N A N
Nanyang
Zhumadian
Xinyang
WUHAN
Hankou
Hanyang
Wuchang
H U B E I
Xiangfan
Yichang
Shashi
H U N A N
Changsha
Yiyang
Changde
Shaoyang
Hengyang
Zhuzhou
Xiangtan
Z H E J I A N G
Ningbo
Shaoxing
Jiaxing
Wenzhou
J I A N G X I
Nanchang
Jiujiang
Linchuan
Ji'an
Ganzhou
F U J I A N
Nanping
Fuzhou
Quanzhou
Xiamen
Zhangzhou
Shantou
G U A N G D O N G
GUANGZHOU (Canton)
Foshan
Zhaoqing
Jiangmen
HONGKONG (Br.)
Kowloon
Macau (Port.)
Zhuhai
Zhanjiang
G U A N G X I-Z H U A N G Z U
Nanning
Liuzhou
Guilin
Wuzhou
Beihai
HAINAN
Haikou
Wuzhi Shan 1867

Z I Z H I Q U
Gulf of Tongking
Beibu Wan

VIETNAM
HANOI
Haiphong

C H I N A
S I C H U A N
CHONGQING
G U I Z H O U
Guiyang
Zunyi
Zigong
Neijiang

Dongting Hu
Poyang Hu

Projection: Lambert's Equivalent Azimuthal

COPYRIGHT. GEORGE PHILIP & SON LTD.

m   ft
12 000
9000
6000
4500
3000
1500
600
200
0

ft   m
600
6000   2000
12 000 4000
18 000 6000

Projection: Mollweide's Homolographic

ALASKA 6050 L. Athabasca Churchill *Hudson* GREENLAND C. Farewell NORTH
Bristol Bay *Gulf of Alaska* Juneau *Bay* Belcher Is. Schefferville Hamilton Inlet
Prince of Wales I. Sitka Dawson Creek Lynn Lake James *Labrador* Strait of Belle Isle
Prince Rupert Kitimat Edmonton Prince Albert Winnipeg *Bay* Anticosti Newfoundland
Queen Charlotte Is. ROCKY NORTH AMERICA St. Lawrence Québec Pr. Edward I. C. Race Southampton 3091
Vancouver Saskatoon Regina Medicine Hat Winnipeg Montréal Fredericton C. Breton I.
Vancouver I. Victoria Spokane Bismarck Duluth L. Superior Sault Ottawa Toronto Saint John Sable I. New York — Southampton
Seattle Helena Butte L. Michigan St. Paul Huron Ottawa Boston C. Sable
Tacoma Portland Boise Missouri Minneapolis Milwaukee CHICAGO L. Erie Buffalo NEW YORK
C. Blanco Cheyenne Des Moines Detroit Pittsburgh Philadelphia
Mendocino Seascarp C. Mendocino Salt Lake City Denver Kansas St. Louis Cincinnati Baltimore Washington
2419 Sacramento 4418 Santa Fé Indianapolis Appalachian Mts. Richmond ATLANTIC
6741 Oakland UNITED STATES Oklahoma Memphis Norfolk C. Hatteras
San Francisco Little Rock Atlanta New York — Recife Bermuda (U.K.)
Murray Seascarp 2091 Los Angeles El Paso Dallas Mississippi Savannah 3678
San Diego Ciudad Austin Houston New Jacksonville OCEAN
Juárez San Antonio Orleans Galveston Panamá 4550
Guadalupe 6225 SIERRA MADRE Torreón Gulf of Mexico Miami Florida BAHAMAS
Pto. Eugenia Gulf of California Monterrey Tampa Strait
Tropic of Cancer C. S. Lucas Tampico La Habana CUBA West Indies (U.S.)
Clarion Fracture Zone Revilla Gigedo Is. Aguascalientes San Luis Potosí Yucatan Channel Hispaniola 9200 St. Thomas (U.S.)
(Mexico) Guadalajara MÉXICO Veracruz Mérida HAITI DOM. REP. Virgin Is.
Honolulu Hawaii 3277 Puebla 5700 Santo PUERTO Leeward
Hawaiian Is. (U.S.) Oahu Acapulco BELIZE JAMAICA Domingo RICO Is.
GUATEMALA HONDURAS Kingston Guadeloupe (Fr.)
4711 Guatemala Tegucigalpa Caribbean Sea Martinique (Fr.)
Clipperton Fracture Zone Clipperton I. (Fr.) SALVADOR NICARAGUA Curaçao (Ne.) BARBADOS
San Salvador Managua Windward TRINIDAD & TOBAGO
3666 CENTRAL Barranquilla Is.
CURRENT AMERICA San José Caracas
Palmyra Is. (U.S.) COSTA RICA PANAMA Panamá Maracaibo
Christmas Island Ridge Cocos I. Canal Orinoco VENEZUELA
Teraina Medellín
Tabuaeran Kiritimati Bogotá COLOMBIA
Jarvis I. (U.S.) C. S. Francisco Cali
Equator 835 Quito
Galápagos ECUADOR
Malden I. (Ecuador) Guayaquil Chimborazo 6267 Manaus
KIRIBATI Starbuck I. C. Parinas Cuenca Iquitos Amazon
Vostok I. Lobos I. 706 BRAZIL
Tongareva Caroline I. Chiclayo Trujillo SOUTH
Penrhyn Is. Flint I. Marquesas Is. PERU
Manihiki Lima 6369 AMERICA
Suwarrow Is. Callao Cúzco
Leeward Is. Southeast L. Titicaca Illampu & Ancohuma
Cook Society Is. Tuamotu Archipelago Pacific Basin Arequipa La Paz 6550
Islands 1303 Windward Tahiti 8050 6866 BOLIVIA
(N.Z.) Manuae Is. Peru Arica
Austral FRENCH POLYNESIA Iquique Chile
Rarotonga Seamount Chain Antofagasta PARAGUAY
Tubuai Is. Pitcairn I. (U.K.) Tropic of Capricorn 8050 Trench Salta Asunción
(Austral Is.) Ducie I. San Félix (Chile) Tucumán Corrientes
Rapa Iti Sala-y-Gomez San Ambrosio (Chile) Paraná Pto. Alegre
(Chile) Aconcagua 6960 Córdoba
Easter Is. Arch. de Juan Fernández Valparaíso Rosario Santa Fe URUGUAY
(Chile) (Chile) Santiago Buenos Aires Paysandú
Pacific-Antarctic Ridge Alejandro Selkirk Concepción La Plata Montevideo
Robinson Crusoe ARGENTINA Río de la Plata 1355 1295
Neuquén Mar del Plata
Chile Rise SOUTH
Pacific- Chonos Arch. Buenos Aires ATLANTIC
Antarctic G. of Penas Montevideo Argentine
Basin P. Deseado Basin OCEAN
Basin WEST WIND DRIFT Wellington Sta. Cruz 6212
CAPE HORN CURRENT Punta Arenas Falkland Is. (U.K.)
Stir. of Magellan Stanley
Western Str. of Magellan Tierra del Fuego South Georgia
C. Horn

160 140 120 West from Greenwich 100 80 60 40 COPYRIGHT. GEORGE PHILIP & SON. LTD.

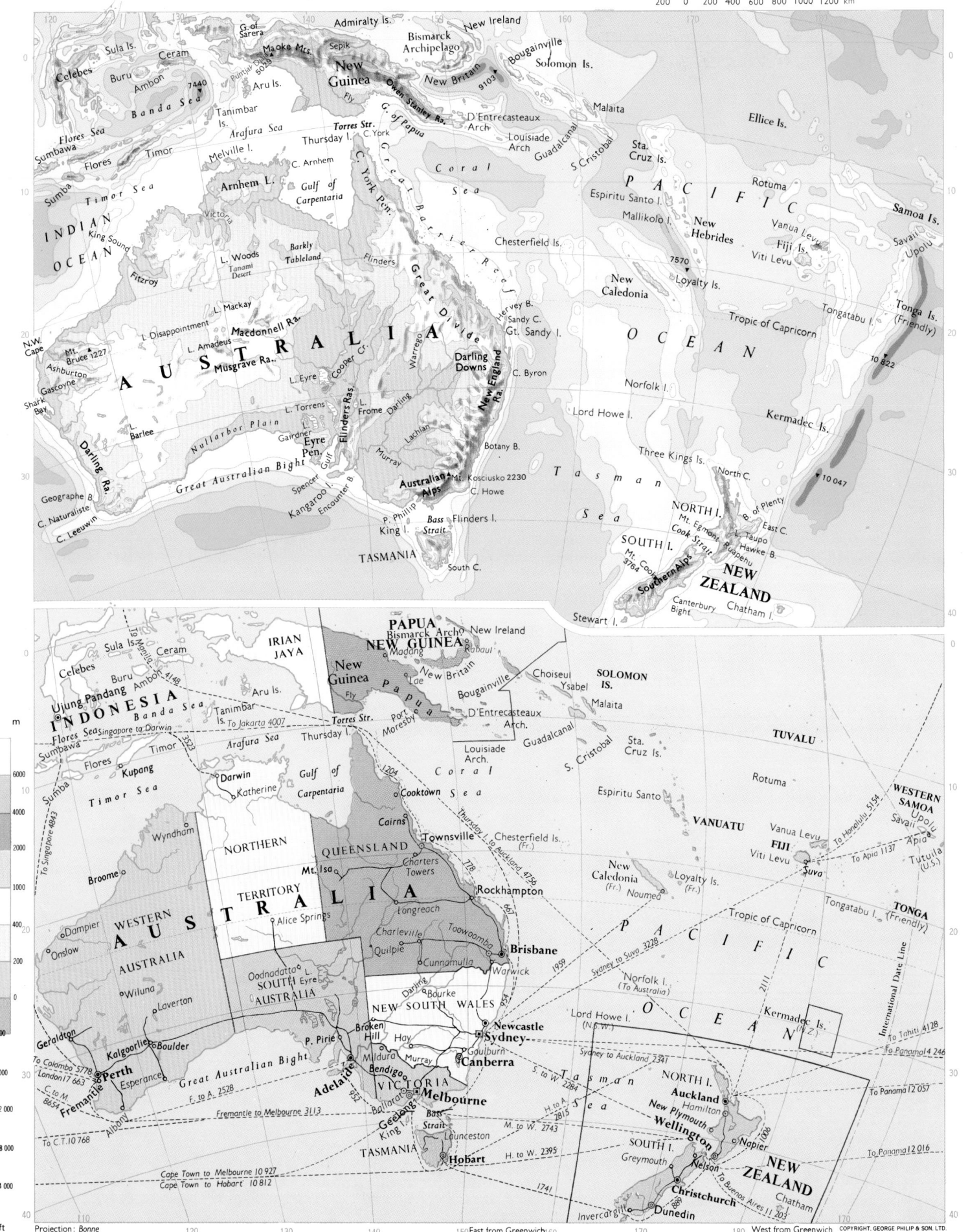

1 : 40 000 000

Projection: Bonne

East from Greenwich West from Greenwich COPYRIGHT. GEORGE PHILIP & SON. LTD.

1:6 000 000
20 0 20 40 60 80 100 miles
20 0 40 80 120 160 km

PACIFIC OCEAN

Tokelau or Union Group
WESTERN SAMOA
Rotuma (Fiji)
Vanua Levu
FIJI
Viti Levu Fiji Is.
Lau or Eastern Group
TONGA (Friendly Is.)
Niue
Savai'i
Upolu
Tutuila (U.S.)
Pukapuka (Danger)
Nassau
Suwarrow
Northern Group
Cook Is.
Palmerston Atoll
Lower Group
Rarotonga
Aitutaki
Mitiaro
Mauke
Mangaia
Îles de la Société
Rakahanga
Manihiki
Tongareva (Penrhyn) I.
Atui

Tropic of Capricorn

Macauley
Raoul (Sunday) I.
Curtis
Kermadec Is.

Three Kings Is.
Auckland
NORTH I.
Cook Strait
NEW ZEALAND
SOUTH I.
Wellington
Christchurch
Dunedin
Tasman Sea
Stewart I.
Snares
Antipodes Is.
Chatham I.
Chatham Is.
Pitt I.
Bounty Is.
Campbell I.
Auckland Is.
Macquarie I. (Austr.)

SOUTHERN OCEAN

NEW ZEALAND & DEPENDENCIES
1:60 000 000
200 0 200 400 600 800 miles
200 0 400 800 1200 km
New Zealand Territory
Self-governing Territory

NORTH ISLAND

Three Kings Is.
C. Reinga
North C.
C. Maria van Diemen
Houhora
Rangaunu Bay
Doubtless Bay
Ahipara B.
Kaitaia
Mangonui
Whangaroa Bay
Reef Pt.
Opua
B. of Islands
C. Brett
Rawene
Kaikohe
Hokianga Harb.
Hikurangi
NORTHLAND
Whangarei
Donnelly's Crossing
Whangarei Harb.
Bream Hd.
Dargaville
Waipu
Bream Bay
Waiuku
Lit. Barrier I.
C. Rodney
Gt. Barrier I.
Cuvier I.
Kaipara Harb.
Warkworth
C. Colville
Hauraki Gulf
Coromandel
Helensville
Takapuna
Devonport
Whitianga
CENTRAL AUCKLAND
Onehunga
AUCKLAND
Manukau
Papakura
Thames
Mayor I.
Pukekohe
Mercer
Waiuku
Waikato
Paeroa
Waihi
Tauranga Harb.
Huntly
Te Aroha
Morrinsville
Tauranga
Bay of Plenty
White I.
C. Runaway
East C.
Raglan
Ngaruawahia
Te Puke
Whakatane
Opotiki
Hamilton
Cambridge
SOUTH AUCKLAND
BAY OF PLENTY
Kawhia Harb.
Te Awamutu
Putaruru
Rotorua
Kawerau
Raukumara Ra.
Hikurangi
Otorohanga
Kinleith
L. Rotorua
Tarawera
Janeatua
Waipiro
Te Kuiti
FOREST
KAINGAROA
Murupara
Moutohora
Tolaga Bay
North Taranaki Bight
Mokau
Makai
Wairakei
L. Taupo
Taupo
Waikaremoana
Ormond
Gisborne
New Plymouth
Inglewood
Whangamomona
Waimarino
Rangitaiki
Poverty Bay
Mt. Egmont 2518
Stratford
Ruapehu
Waikokopu
Opunake
Eltham
Ohakune
Waiouru
Wairoa
Mahia Peninsula
Kapuni
Hawera
Raetihi
Taihape
Napier
Waverley
Mangaweka
C. Kidnappers
Hawke Bay
South Taranaki Bight
Patea
Wanganui
Marton
Hunterville
Hastings
Bulls
Holcombe
Waipawa
Palmerston N.
Feilding
Dannevirke
Waipukurau
Foxton
Woodville
Pahiatua
Shannon
Levin
Eketahuna
C. Turnagain
Otaki
Te Horo
Tararua Ra.
Masterton
Up. Hutt
Carterton
Castle Pt.
Petone
Greytown
Lr. Hutt
Martinborough
WELLINGTON
Eastbourne
Wairarapa

TASMAN SEA

C. Farewell
Golden Bay
D'Urville I.
French Pass
Collingwood
Takaka
Tasman Bay
Pelorus Sd.
Kapiti I.
Tasman Mts.
Motueka
Picton
Richmond
Havelock
Nelson
Wakefield
Cook Strait
Tadmor
Blenheim
Karamea Bight
Murchison
Seddon
MARLBOROUGH
Lyell Ra.
Inangahua Junction
Rotoiti
Ward
Seddonville
Rotoroa
Clarence
Granity
Traversc 3338
Tapuaenuku 2885
Westport
Lyell
Spenser Mts.
Reefton
Hanmer Springs
Kaikoura
Blackball
Greys
Amuri P.
Wairau
Runanga
Ahaura
Greymouth
Stillwater
Waiau
Hokitika
Kumara
Jacksons
Brunner
Hurunui
Ross
Otira Gorge
Culverden
Waiau
Abut Hd.
Arthur's Pass
Bealey
Waikari
Okarito
Waipara
SOUTH ISLAND
Coleridge
Oxford
Rangiora
Pegasus Bay
Springfield
Kaiapoi
Whitecliffs
New Brighton
Mt. Cook 3764
Riccarton
Christchurch
Haast
Methven
Staveley
Lincoln
Lyttelton
Banks Peninsula
Fairlie
Little River
Akaroa
Mt. Aspiring 3022
Tekapo
L. Ellesmere
Southbridge
Jackson B.
Okuru
Rakaia
Fairlie
Rangitata
Canterbury Plain
Haast
SOUTHERN ALPS
Ashburton
WESTLAND
Pukaki
Ohau
Temuka
Ashburton Bight
Milford Sd.
Mt. Earnslaw 2819
Wanaka
Hawea
Timaru
St. Andrews
Bligh Sd.
Sutherland Falls
Kinloch
Waimate
George Sd.
Arrowtown
Cromwell
Kurow
Waitaki
Waimate
Secretary I.
Queenstown
Clyde
Naseby
Maheno
Oamaru
Doubtful Sd.
Te Anau
Wakatipu
Alexandra
Roxburgh
Dunback
Ngapara
Breaksea Sd.
Kingston
Gore
OTAGO
Palmerston
Resolution I.
Manapouri
Lumsden
Edievale
Kelso
Waikouaiti
Dusky Sd.
Mossburn
Kaitangata
Lawrence
Fairfield
St. Kilda
Chalky Inlet
Ohai
Clyde
Milton
Port Chalmers
Tuatapere
Nightcaps
Waihola
Dunedin
Otago Harbour
Preservation Inlet
SOUTHLAND
Riverton
Winton
Clinton
Mosgiel
C. Saunders
Te Waewae B.
Orepuki
Clifden
Balclutha
Gore
Invercargill
Wyndham
Kaitangata
Hedgehope
Mataura
Nugget Pt.
Owaka
Bluff
Waikawa Harb.
Tokahoka
Halfmoon Bay
Ruapuke I.
Stewart I.
S.W. Cape
Port Pegasus

PACIFIC OCEAN

SAMOA ISLANDS
1:12 000 000
WESTERN SAMOA
Savai'i
Apia
Upolu
American Samoa
Pago Pago
Manua Is.
Tutuila
Rose I.

Futuna (Fr.)
Niuafo'ou (Tonga)
Thikombia
Thikombia
Lambasa
Vanua Levu
FIJI
Yasawa Group
Taveuni
Koro
Vanua Balavu
Lautoka
Levuka
Ovalau
Lau or Eastern Group
Viti Levu 1323
Suva
Koro Sea
Lakemba
Nadi
Moala
Vava'u
Kandavu
TONGA
Tonga (Friendly) Is.
Vatoa
Tofua I.
Tongatapu
Nuku'alofa

FIJI AND TONGA ISLANDS
1:12 000 000
50 0 50 100 150 miles
50 0 50 100 150 200 250 km

ft   m
12 000 4000
9000 3000
6000 2000
3000 1000
1200 400
600 200
0
200 600
m ft

Projection: Conical with two standard parallels

TASMANIA

Bass Strait

King Island

Flinders Island

Launceston

Devonport

New Norfolk · Glenorchy

Hobart

Furneaux Group

CORAL SEA

Great Barrier Reef

Thursday I.
Prince of Wales I.
C. York

Cape York Peninsula

Gulf of Carpentaria

Groote Eylandt

Wellesley Is.

Sir Edward Pellew Group

Mornington I.

Arnhem Land

Wessel Is.

Goulburn Is.

Cooktown
Port Douglas
Cairns
Innisfail
Mareeba
Babinda
Hinchinbrook I.
Ingham
Palm Is.
Halifax Bay
Townsville
Ayr
Bowen
Proserpine
Mackay
Cumberland Islands

Rockhampton
Yeppoon
Curtis I.
Gladstone

Hervey

Mt. Finnigan 1148
Mt. Bartle Frere 1612

Great Dividing Range

Charters Towers

Hughenden
Richmond
Winton
Cloncurry
Mt. Isa 418
Mount Isa
Selwyn Range

Normanton
Croydon
Georgetown

Burketown

Camooweal

Boulia

NORTHERN TERRITORY

Barkly Tableland

GREAT ARTESIAN BASIN

GREAT QUEENSLAND

Simpson Desert

Tennant Creek

Barrow Creek

Alice Springs
Tropic of Capricorn
Macdonnell Ranges
1128

1:8 000 000

50   0   50   100   150   200 miles
50   0   50   100   150   200   250   300 km

T A S M A N   S E A

N E W   S O U T H   W A L E S

S O U T H   A U S T R A L I A

BRISBANE

SYDNEY

CANBERRA

MELBOURNE

ADELAIDE

Newcastle

Wollongong

Broken Hill

Bass   Strait

King Island

Flinders Island

Furneaux Group

Cape Barren I.

Kangaroo I.

Lake Eyre North

Lake Eyre South

Lake Torrens

Lake Frome

Lake Gairdner

Lake Blanche

Projection: Bonne

East from Greenwich

COPYRIGHT GEORGE PHILIP & SON, LTD.

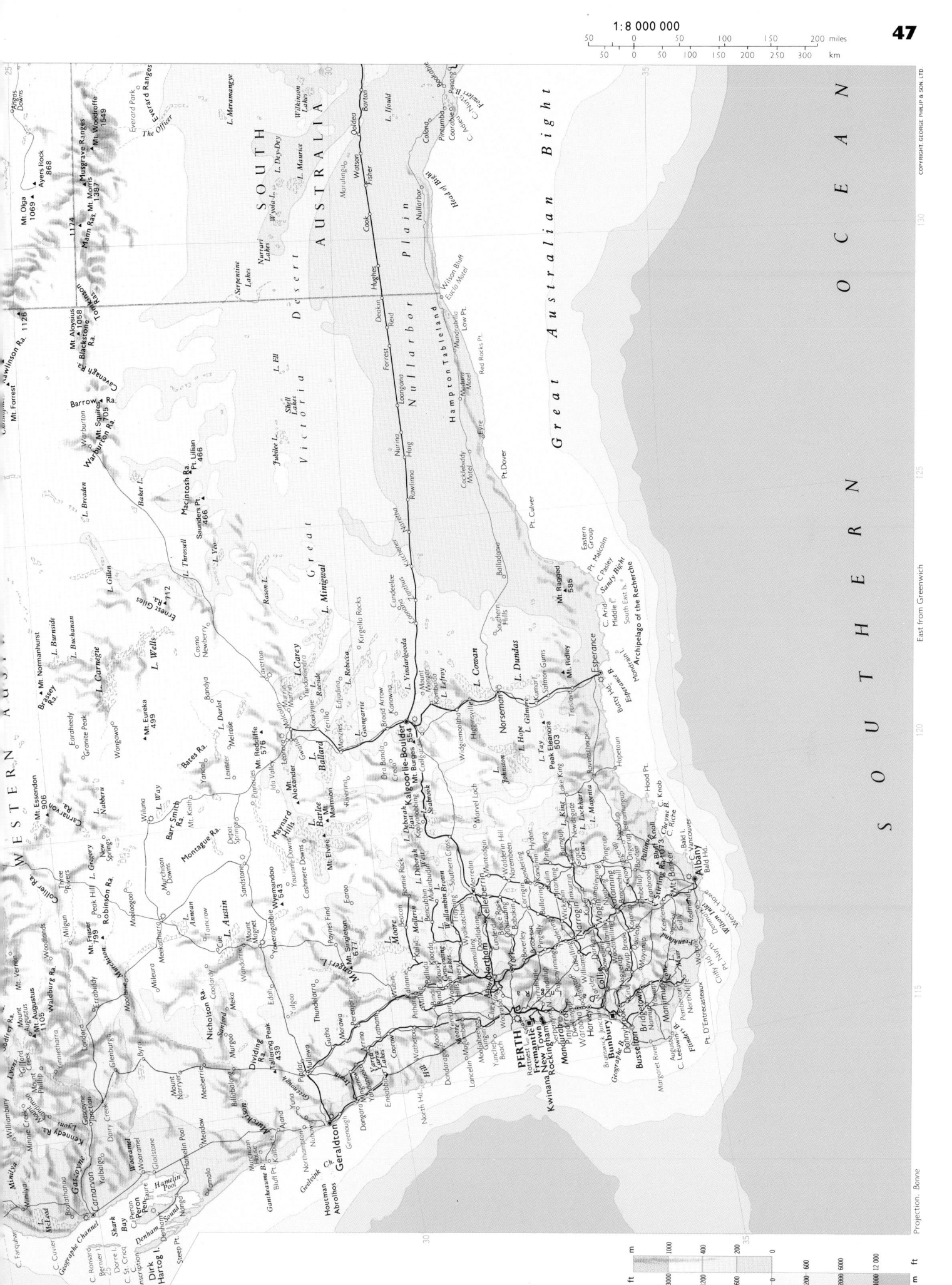

1:8 000 000

50   0   50   100   150   200 miles

50 0 50 100 150 200 250 300 km

COPYRIGHT GEORGE PHILIP & SON, LTD.

East from Greenwich

Projection. Bonne

S O U T H   A U S T R A L I A

W E S T E R N   A U S T R A L I A

S O U T H E R N   O C E A N

Great Australian Bight

Great Victoria Desert

Nullarbor Plain

Hampton Tableland

Head of Bight

PERTH
Fremantle
Kwinana
Rockingham

Geraldton

Bunbury
Busselton

Albany

Kalgoorlie-Boulder

Norseman

Esperance

Archipelago of the Recherche

Ayers Rock 868

Mt. Olga 1069

Musgrave Ranges
Mt. Woodroffe 1549

Mt. Morris 1387

Mann Ras. 1058

m   ft
1000 3000
400   1200
200   600
0   0
-200 -600
2000 6000
4000 12 000

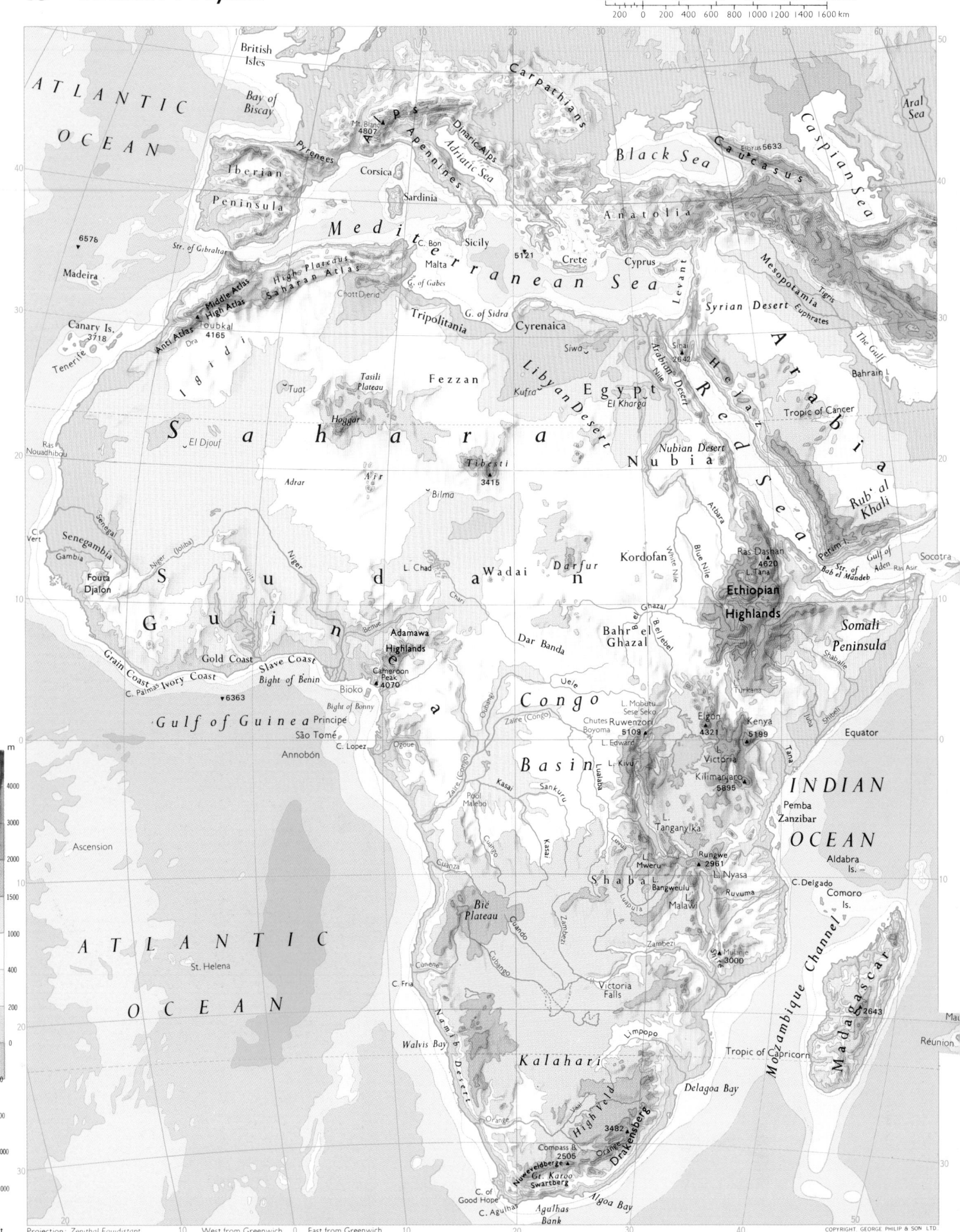

1 : 40 000 000

Scale 200 0 200 400 600 800 1000 miles
200 0 200 400 600 800 1000 1200 1400 1600 km

ATLANTIC OCEAN

British Isles

Bay of Biscay

A l p s

Carpathians

Mt. Blanc 4807

Pyrenees

Apennines

Dinaric Alps

Adriatic Sea

Black Sea

Caucasus Elbrus 5633

Caspian Sea

Aral Sea

Iberian Peninsula

Corsica

Sardinia

C. Bon

Sicily

Crete

Cyprus

Anatolia

5121

Mesopotamia

Tigris

The Gulf

6576

Madeira

Str. of Gibraltar

M e d i t e r r a n e a n   S e a

Malta

G. of Gabes

Chott Djerid

High Plateaus

Saharan Atlas

Levant

Syrian Desert

Euphrates

Bahrain I.

Tropic of Cancer

Canary Is. 3718

Tenerife

Anti Atlas

Middle Atlas

High Atlas

Toubkal 4165

Dra

I g i d i

Tripolitania

G. of Sidra

Cyrenaica

Siwa

Libyan Desert

Egypt

Kufra

El Kharga

Nile

Arabian Desert

Sinai 2642

Red Sea

Hejaz

A r a b i a

Rub' al Khali

Gulf of Aden

Str. of Bab el Mandeb

Ras Asir

Socotra

Tuat

Tasili Plateau

Fezzan

Hoggar

S a h a r a

Nubian Desert

Nubia

El Djouf

Ras Nouadhibou

Adrar

Air

Tibesti 3415

Atbara

Ras Dashan 4620

L. Tana

Perim I.

C. Vert

Senegal

Senegambia

Gambia

Niger (Joliba)

Bilma

L. Chad

Wadai

Darfur

Kordofan

White Nile

Blue Nile

Ethiopian Highlands

Somali Peninsula

Fouta Djalon

S u d a n

Volta

Niger

Benue

Char

Bahr el Ghazal

Bel Jebel

Uele

Shaballe

G u i n e a

Gold Coast

Slave Coast

Bight of Benin

Adamawa Highlands

Dar Banda

Bahr el Ghazal

L. Mobutu Sese Seko

Turkana

Grain Coast

C. Palmas

Ivory Coast

Bioko

Cameroon Peak 4070

6363

Bight of Bonny

Oubangui

Zaire (Congo)

Congo

Chutes Boyoma

Ruwenzori 5109

Elgon 4321

Kenya 5199

Equator

Gulf of Guinea

Principe

São Tomé

C. Lopez

Ogoue

Basin

L. Edward

L. Kivu

L. Victoria

Kilimanjaro 5895

INDIAN OCEAN

Annobón

Zaire (Congo)

Kasai

Sankuru

Lualaba

Pemba

Zanzibar

ATLANTIC OCEAN

Ascension

Pool Malebo

Kasai

Cuango

Cuanza

L. Tanganyika

Lerwa

Mweru

Rungwe 2961

L. Nyasa

Ruvuma

Aldabra Is.

C. Delgado

Comoro Is.

St. Helena

Bié Plateau

Cuando

Cubango

Shaba

L. Bangweulu

Lupula

L. Malawi

Mt. Mlanje 3000

Madagascar

2643

Réunion

Zambezi

Victoria Falls

Mozambique Channel

C. Fria

Cunene

Namib Desert

Orange

Walvis Bay

Kalahari

High Veld

Limpopo

Delagoa Bay

Tropic of Capricorn

3482

Compass B. 2505

Orange

Drakensberg

Nuweveldberge

Swartberg

Gr. Karoo

C. of Good Hope

C. Agulhas

Agulhas Bank

Algoa Bay

ft	m
12 000	4000
9000	3000
6000	2000
4500	1500
3000	1000
1200	400
600	200
0	0
200	600
2000	6000
4000	12 000
6000	18 000
m	ft

Projection : Zenithal Equidistant.

West from Greenwich   East from Greenwich

COPYRIGHT GEORGE PHILIP & SON LTD

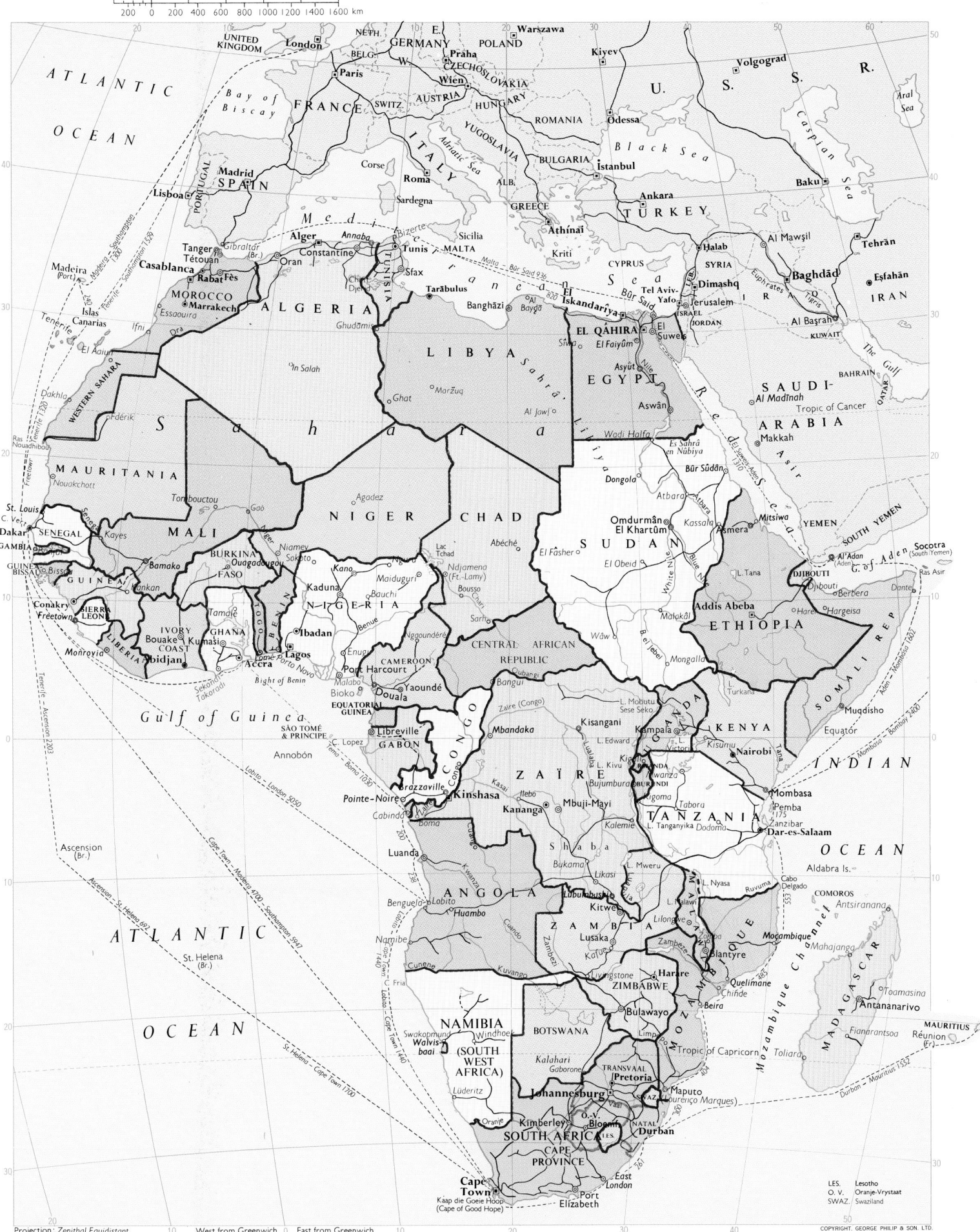

1:40 000 000

Projection: Zenithal Equidistant.

West from Greenwich 0 East from Greenwich

LES. Lesotho
O. V. Oranje-Vrystaat
SWAZ. Swaziland

COPYRIGHT. GEORGE PHILIP & SON. LTD.

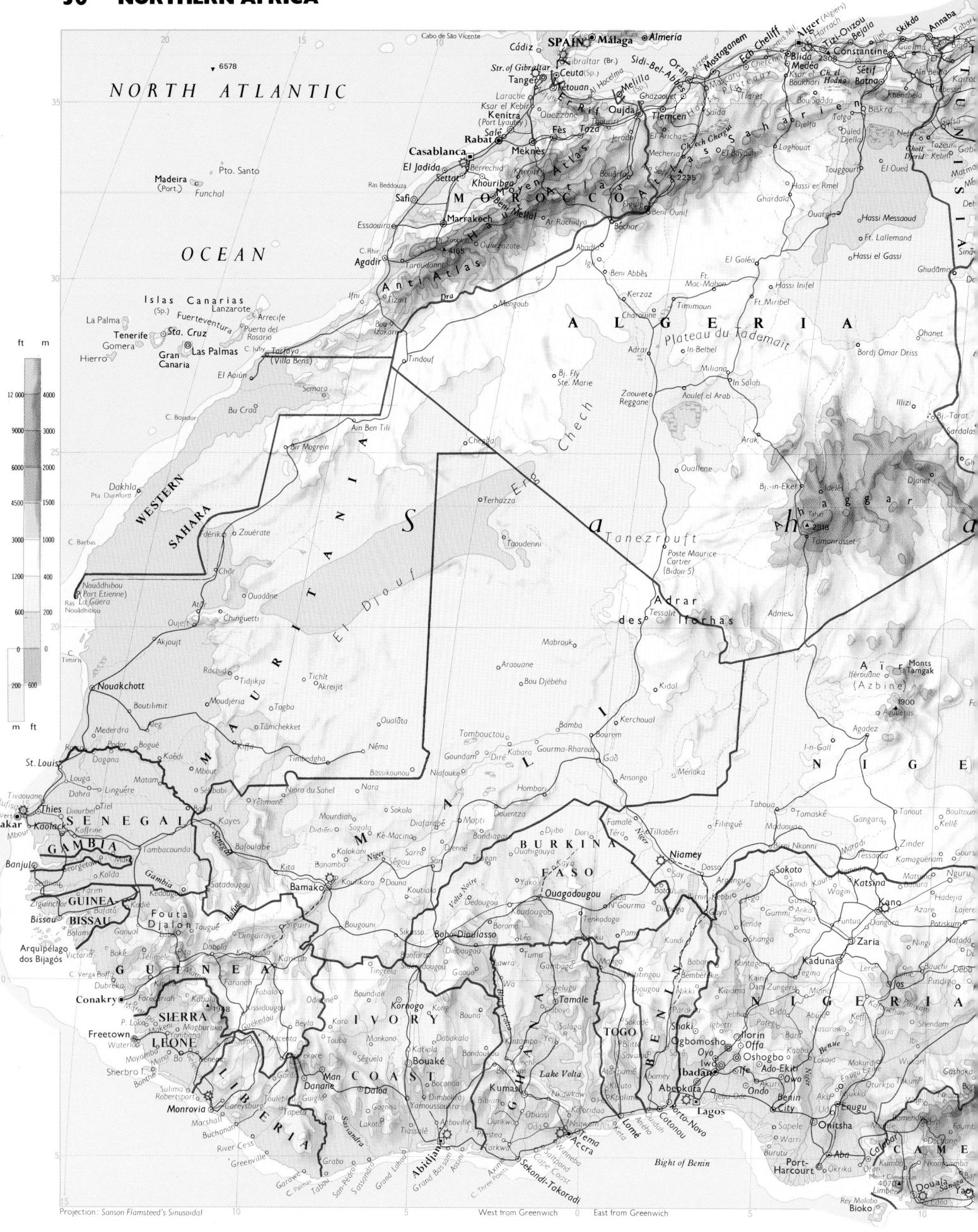

NORTH ATLANTIC

OCEAN

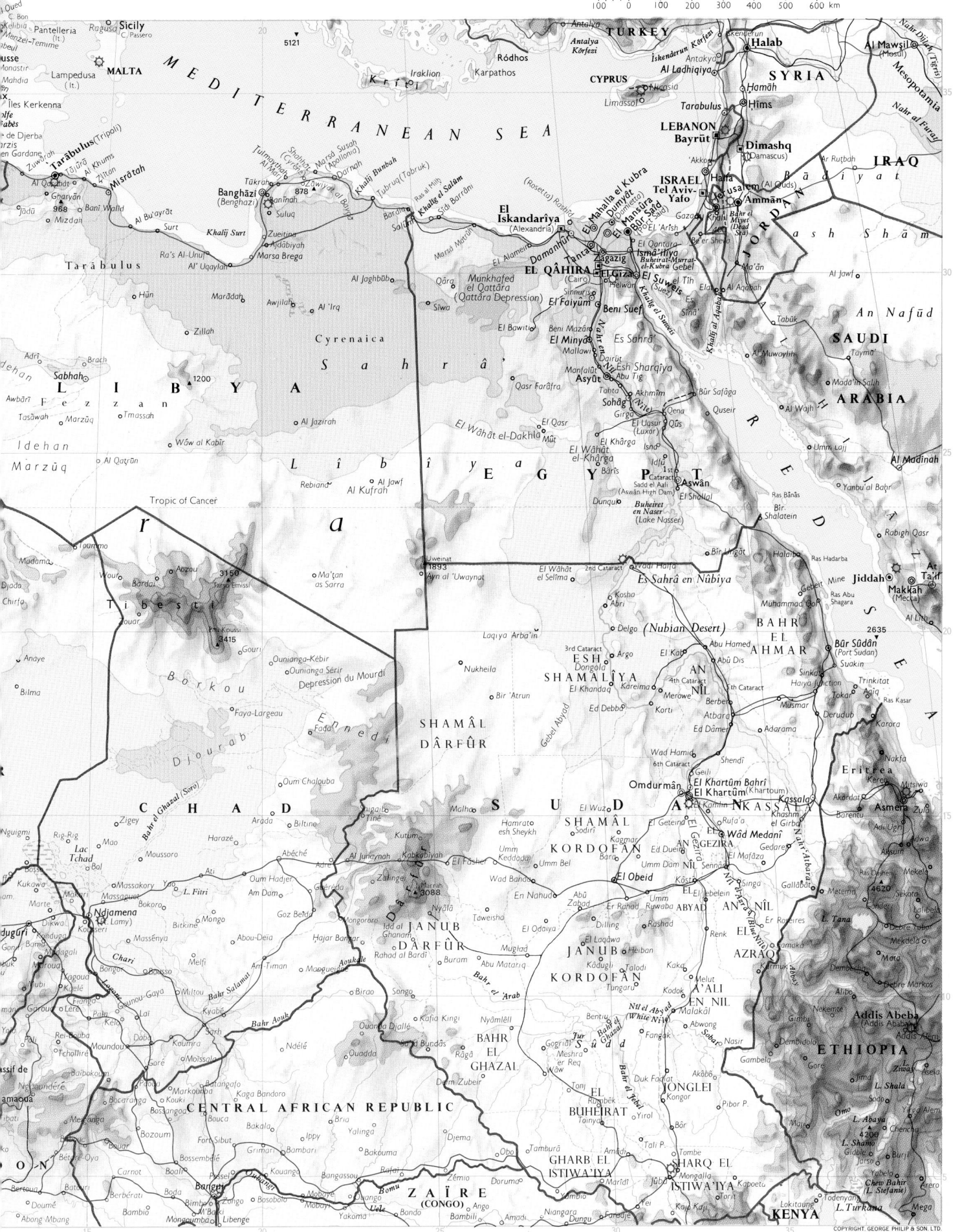

1:15 000 000

100   0   100   200   300   400 miles
100   0   100   200   300   400   500   600 km

MEDITERRANEAN SEA

TURKEY

C. Bon
Pantelleria (It.)
Menzel-Temine
Kélibia
Ragusa **Sicily**
Monastir
Mahdia
C. Passero
Lampedusa (It.)
MALTA

5121

Ródhos
Karpathos
Iraklion
Kríti

Antalya
Antalya Körfezi
İskenderun Körfezi
Antakya
Al Ladhiqiya
CYPRUS
Nicosia
Limassol

İskenderun
Halab
Al Mawşil (Mosul)
Nahr Dijlah (Tigris)

SYRIA
Hamāh
Hims
Tarabulus
Mesopotamia
Nahr al Furāt

Îles Kerkenna
Golfe
Gabès
Ile de Djerba
Zarzis
Ben Gardane
Tarābulus(Tripoli)
Tājūra
Al Khums
Zlitan
Misrātah
Gharyān
968
Banī Walīd
Mizdah
Jādu
Al Qubbah

Tükrah
Al Marj
Zāwiya al Bayḍā
(Cyrenaica)
(Apollonia)
Marsá Susah
Shaḥḥāt
Al Bayḍā
Darnah
Tulmaythah
Banghāzi
(Benghazi)
Banīnah
Suluq

878
Khalij Bunbah
Tubruq(Tobruk)
Ras al Milh

Bardīyah
Sīdī Barrāni
Salūm
Khalig el Salûm
Marsá Matrûh

LEBANON
Bayrūt
Akko
Haifa
Tel Aviv-Yafo
ISRAEL
Jerusalem (Al Quds)
Gaza
Khalil

Dimashq
(Damascus)
Ar Ruţbah
Bahr el Myet
(Dead Sea)
Ammān
JORDAN
Be'er Sheva
Al Karak
Ma'ān
Al Jawf
ash Sham

IRAQ
Bādiyat

Surt
Ajdābiyah
Marsa Brega
Al 'Uqaylah
Ra's Al-Unuf
Al Bu'ayrāt
Tarābulus

Al Jaghbūb
Qāra
Munkhafed el Qattâra
(Qattara Depression)
Sîwa

(Rosetta) Rashid
Dumyât
Damanhûr
El Iskandarîya
(Alexandria)
El Mahalla el Kubra
Tanta
Bûr Sa'îd
Zagazig
El Mansûra
Ismâ'ilîya
Buheirat-Murrat-el-Kubra
El Qântara
El 'Arîsh

El 'Alamein
Marsá Matrûh
Sinnûris
EL QÂHIRA
(Cairo)
El Gîza
Helwân
El Suweîs (Suez)
Khalig el Suweis
Et Tih
Sînâ

Jādu
Brach
Adrī
Sabhah
LIBYA
Awbārī
Tasāwah
Marzūq
Tmassah
Zillah
Marādah
Awjila
Al 'Irq

Ḥūn

El Faiyûm
Beni Suef
Beni Mazâr
El Bawîti
Mallawî
Dairût
Manfalût
Asyût

Es Sahrâ

Esh Sharqîya
Abu Tîg
Tahta
Sohâg
Akhmîm
Girga
El Uqsur (Luxor)

SAUDI
Al Jawf
Tabûk
Al Muwaylih
Taymā'
Madā'in Sāliḥ
ARABIA
Al Wajh

Bûr Safâga
Quseir

An Nafûd

Idehan
Marzūq
Fezzan
Wāw al Kabīr
Al Qaṭrūn

Libîyeg
Rebiana
Al Jawf
Al Kufrah

El Wâhât el-Dakhla
Mût
Qasr Farâfra
EGYPT
Qasr
El Khârga
El Wâhât el-Khârga
Bârîs
Isnâ
Idfû
1st Cataract
Sadd el Aali
(Aswân High Dam)
Aswân
El Shallal
Dunqul
Buheiret en Naser
(Lake Nasser)
Umm Lajj
Al Madînah

Tropic of Cancer

Tourimo
Madama
Djado
Chirfa
Wour
Bardaï
Aozou
3150
Tarso Emissi
Tibesti
Zouar
Emi Koussi
3415
Gouri
Ma'tan as Sarra
Ayn al 'Uwaynat
Uweinat
1893
El Wâhât el Selîma
2nd Cataract
Wadi Halfa
Es Sahrâ en Nûbîya
Bîr Ungât
Halaib
Ras Hadarba
Getleit Mine
Muḥammad Qol
Ras Bânâs
Bîr Shalatein

Jiddah
At Ta'if
Makkah (Mecca)
Al Līth

Anaye
Bilma
CHAD
Borkou
Ennedi
Djourab
Depression du Mourdi
Ounianga-Kébir
Ounianga Sérir
Fada
Faya-Largeau
Laqiya Arba'in
Nukheila
Bir 'Atrun
Selima
3rd Cataract
Kosha
Abri
Delgo
Argo
Dongola
El Khandaq
Kareima
Merowe
4th Cataract
5th Cataract
Abu Hamed
Abū Dis
El Kab
(Nubian Desert)
Kosho
Rabigh Qasr
2635
BAHR EL AHMAR
Bûr Sûdân (Port Sudan)
Suakin
Muḥammad Qol
Ras Abu Shagara
Sinkat
Haiya Junction
Trinkitat
Tokar
Aqîg
Ras Kasar

ESH SHAMÂLIYA
Korti
Ed Debba
Gebel Abyad
AN NÎL
Berber
Atbara
Ed Dâmer
Adarama
Derudub
Karora

Djado
Zouar
Tibesti
Zigey
Mao
Rig-Rig
Moussoro
CHAD
Biltine
Harazé
Abéché
Arada
Iriba
Tiné
Kutum
Malha
Sodirī
Hamrato esh Sheykh
Umm Keddada
SHAMÂL KORDOFAN
Bara
Umm Bel
Umm Dam
6th Cataract
Shendi
Wad Hamid
Geili
Omdurmân
El Khartûm Bahrî
El Khartûm(Khartoum)
Kamlin
Rufa'a
El Gîteina
El Dueim
AN NÎL
Wâd Medanî
GEZIRA
El Hasaheisa
El Mafâza
Gallâbat
Metema
Gedaref
Kassala
Khashm el Girba
Aroma
Asmera
Keren
Akordat
Barentu
Adi Ugri
Aksum
Mekele
4620
Ras Dashen
Debre Tabor
L. Tana
Gondar
Debre Markos

Eritrea
Nakfa
Mitsiwa
Zula

Nguigmi
Lac Tchad
N'djamena
(N. Lamy)
Massakory
Bol
Bokoro
Massaguet
Ati
Oum Hadjer
Am Dam
Mongo
Bitkine
Goz Beïda
Mongororo
Abou-Deïa
JANUB DÂRFÛR
Ghoname
Iddi
Hajar Banga
Rahad el Bardi
Buram
Muglad
Ed Damazin
El Obeid
Kosti
EL ABYAD
Er Rahad
El Odaiya
Dilling
Kadugli
Talodi
Kaka
Renk
AN NÎL EL AZRAQ
Er Roseires
Kurmuk
Famaka
Abbay
Asosa
Nekemte
Dembidolo
Gore
Gambela

Addis Abeba
(Addis Ababa)
Addis Alem

Maroua
Garoua
Rei-Bouba
Poli
Kélo
Pala
Léré
Moundou
Doba
Kyabé
Koumra
Sarh
Maïtoum
Bahr Salamat
Birao
Songo
Bahr el 'Arab
Abu Matâriq
JANUB KORDOFAN
Heiban
Talodi
Tungaru
Kodok
Melut
A'ALI EN NIL
Malakal
Abwong
Sobat
Nasir
SHARQ EL ISTIWA'IYA
Gore
L. Tana

ETHIOPIA
L. Shala

Garoua-Boulaï
Meiganga
Bertoua
Doumé
Abong-Mbang
Batouri
Bétaré-Oya
Bocaranga
Bozoum
Bossangoa
Bouca
Kaga Bandoro
Bakala
Bria
Yalinga
Ippy
CENTRAL AFRICAN REPUBLIC
Bambari
Grimari
Bakouma
Bangassou
Rafaï
Zémio
Obo
GHARB EL ISTIWA'IYA
Marîdi
SHARQ EL ISTIWA'IYA
Jûba
Kapoeta
Torit
BAHR EL GHAZAL
Raga
Deim Zubeir
Wau
Tonj
El Buheirat
Rumbek
Yirol
Bôr
Pibor P.
Akobo
Kongor
JONGLEI
Duk Faiwil
Tombe
Tali P.
Amadi
Tambura
Yambio
Maridi
Mundri

Nabounguéré
Garoua-Boulaï
Nola
Berbérati
Gamboula
Carnot
Boda
Mbaïki
Mongoumba
Zongo
Libenge
Bangui
Mobaye
Bomu
ZAÏRE (CONGO)
Yakoma
Bondo
Uele
Bambili
Ango
Bosobolo
Gemena
Dungu
Faradje
Niangara

KENYA
L. Turkana
Lokitaung
Todenyang
Mega

COPYRIGHT. GEORGE PHILIP & SON LTD.

1:7 500 000

SUDAN ETHIOPIA SOMALI REP. UGANDA KENYA ZAIRE RWANDA BURUNDI TANZANIA ZAMBIA MALAWI MOZAMBIQUE

LAKE VICTORIA 1134

LAKE TANGANYIKA

INDIAN OCEAN

Lake Turkana (Lake Rudolf) Chew Bahir (L. Stefanie)

Nairobi Mombasa and Kilindini Dar-es-Salaam Zanzibar Kampala Kigali Bujumbura (Usumbura) Dodoma Kisumu Nakuru Eldoret Arusha Moshi Tabora Mwanza Mbeya Iringa Morogoro Tanga Malindi Lamu Kilwa Kivinje Lindi Mtwara

Serengeti National Park Tsavo National Park Kilimanjaro 5895 Mt. Kenya 5199 Ruwenzori

Projection: Modified Polyconic

East from Greenwich

COPYRIGHT. GEORGE PHILIP & SON. LTD.

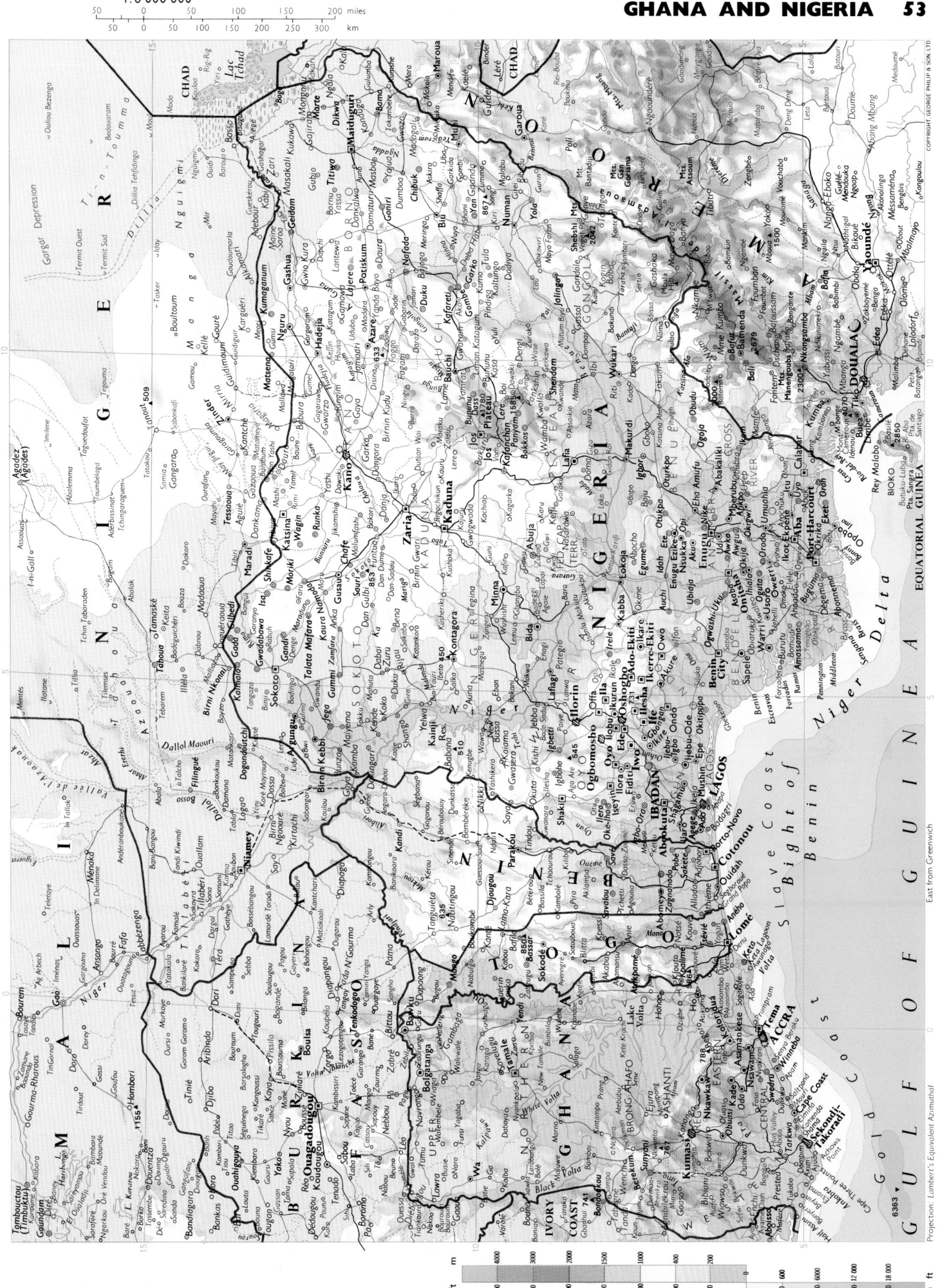

1:8 000 000

Projection: Lambert's Equivalent Azimuthal

East from Greenwich

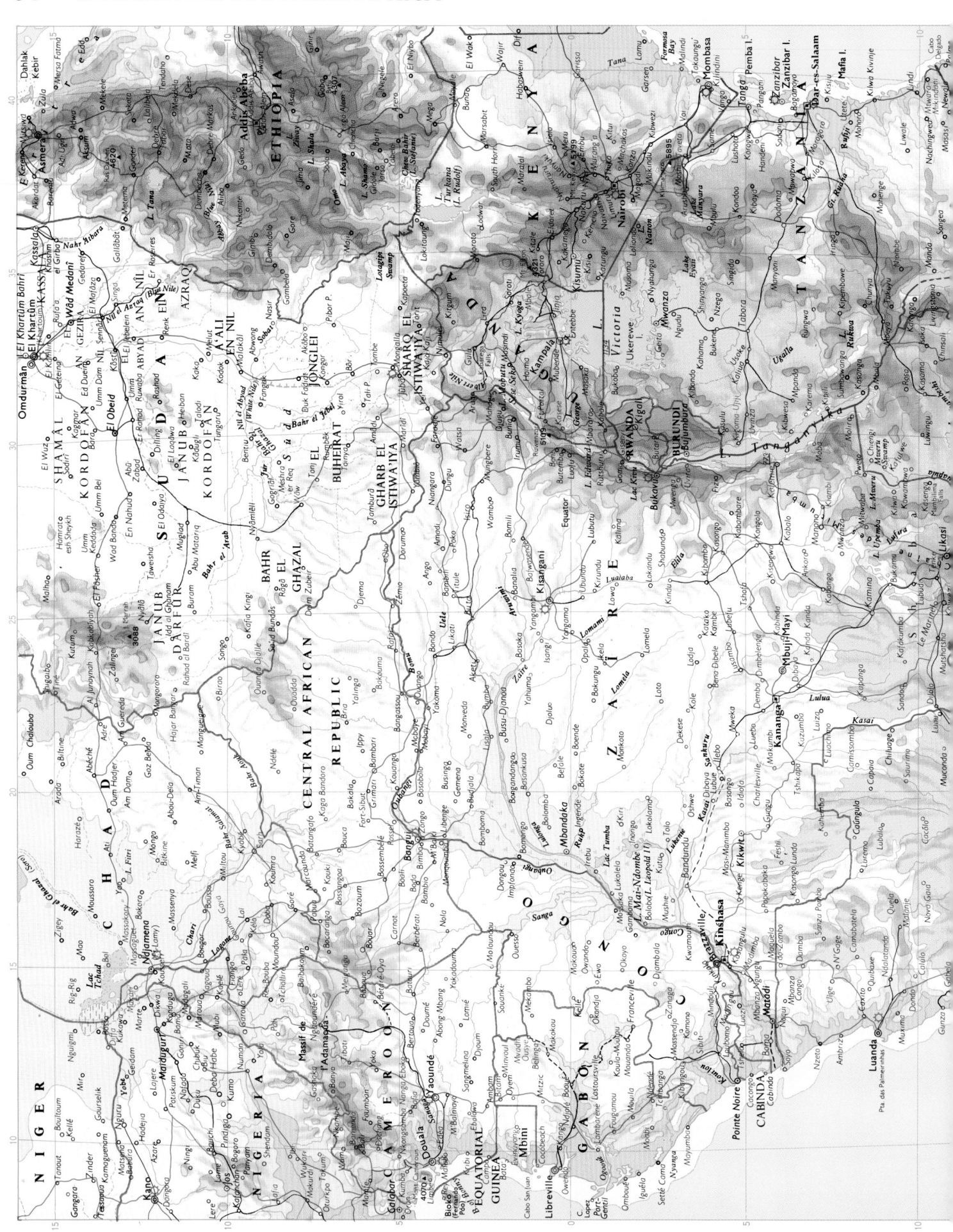

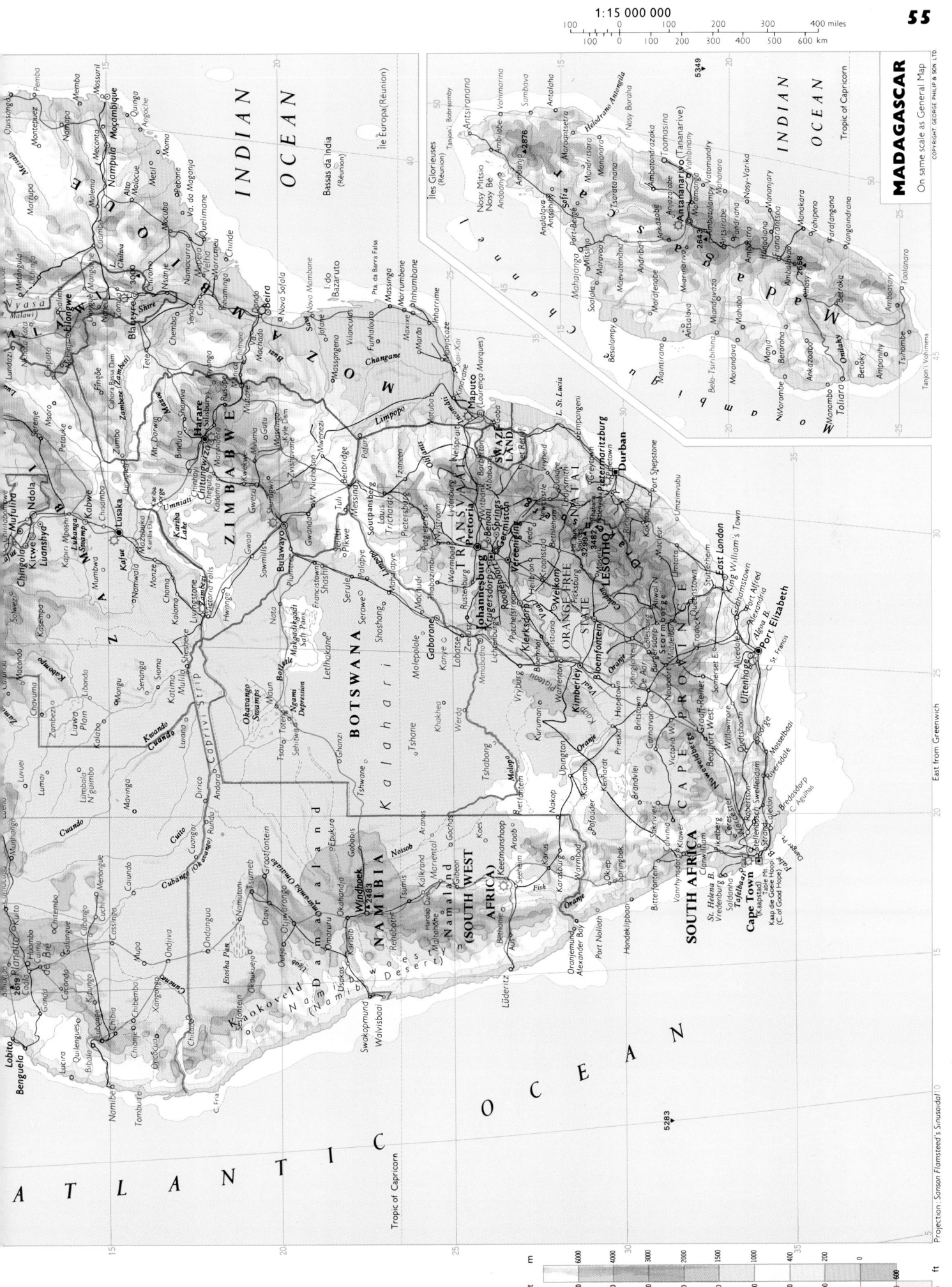

1:15 000 000

100   100   200   300   400 miles
100   0   100 200 300 400 500 600 km

MADAGASCAR
On same scale as General Map

COPYRIGHT GEORGE PHILIP & SON LTD

INDIAN

OCEAN

INDIAN

OCEAN

Tropic of Capricorn

Bassas da India
(Reunion)

Île Europa (Reunion)

Iles Glorieuses
(Reunion)

ZIMBABWE

Harare

Bulawayo

BOTSWANA

Kalahari

NAMIBIA
(SOUTH WEST
AFRICA)

Windhoek

Namib
Desert

TRANSVAAL

Pretoria

Johannesburg

ORANGE FREE
STATE

Bloemfontein

SWAZI
LAND

NATAL

Durban

Pietermaritzburg

LESOTHO

CAPE PROVINCE

East London

Port Elizabeth

SOUTH AFRICA

Cape Town

Kimberley

Maputo

Beira

INDIAN

OCEAN

ATLANTIC

OCEAN

Tropic of Capricorn

Projection: Sanson Flamsteed's Sinusoidal 10

East from Greenwich

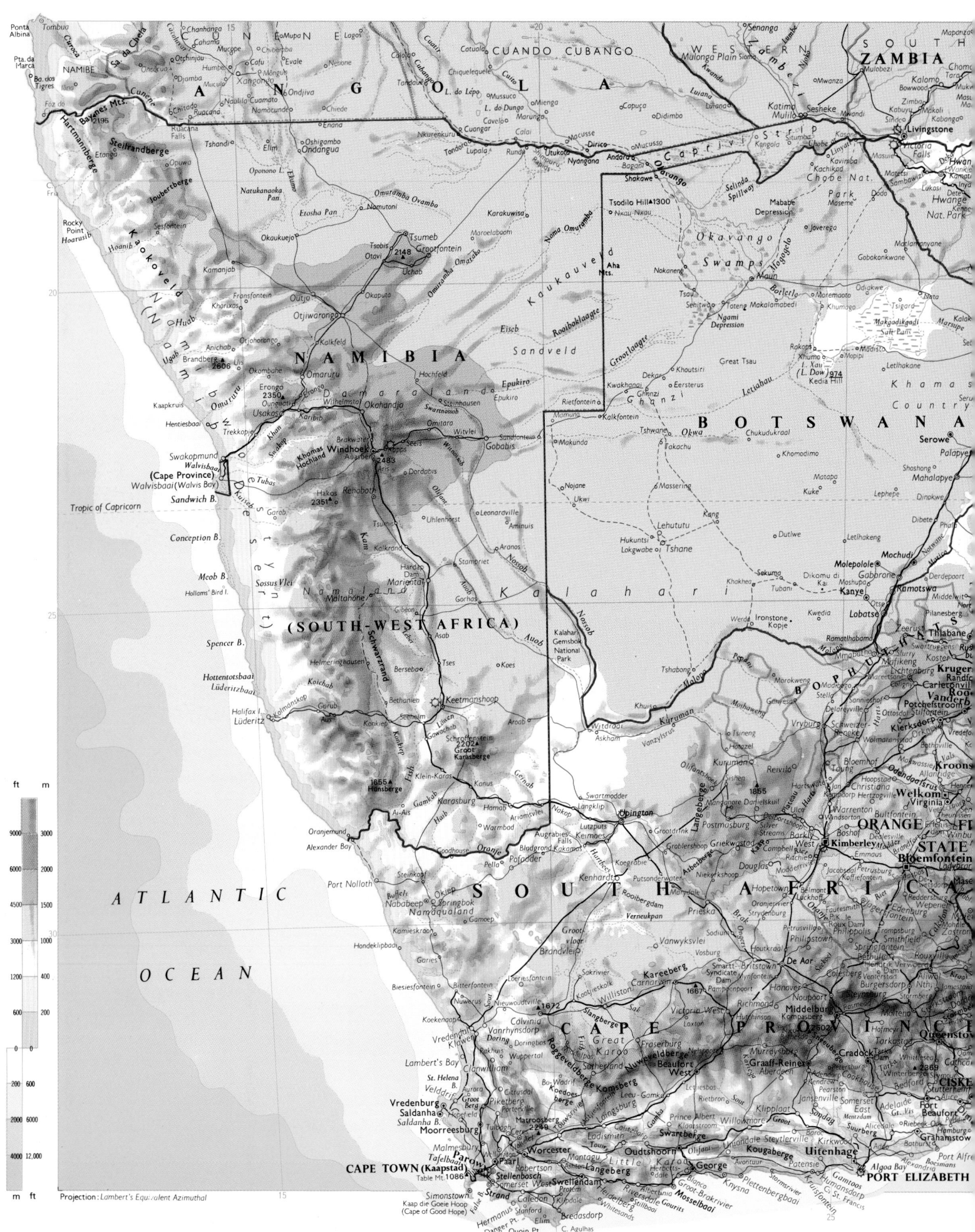

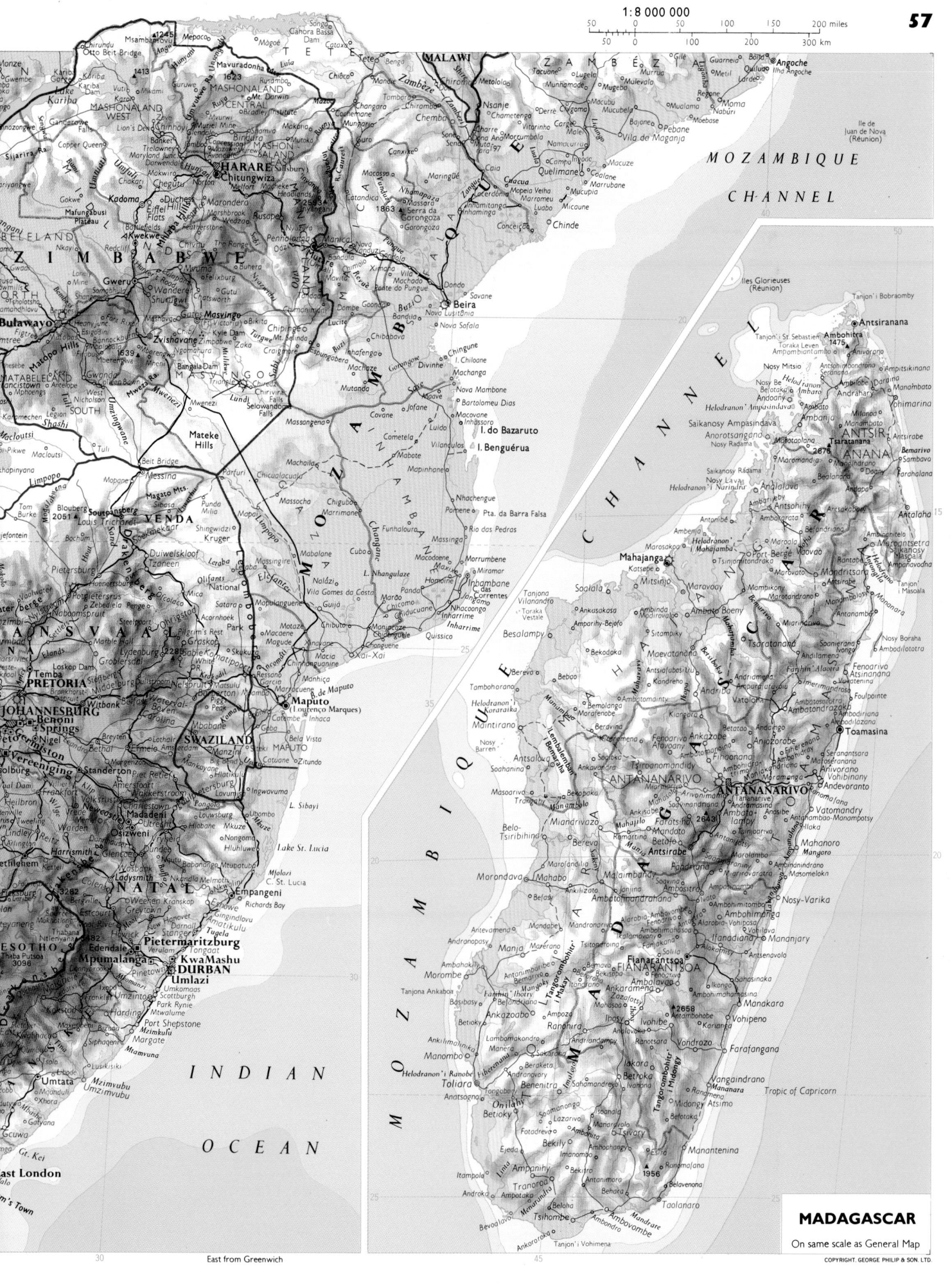

1:8 000 000

50   100   150   200 miles

50   100   200   300 km

MOZAMBIQUE

CHANNEL

Ile de
Juan de Nova
(Réunion)

Iles Glorieuses
(Réunion)

MALAWI

ZAMBÉZIA

TETE

MASHONALAND
CENTRAL

MASHONALAND
WEST

MASHON
LAND

HARARE
Chitungwiza

ZIMBABWE

Bulawayo

MATEBELELAND
SOUTH

Masvingo

MASVINGO

Mateke
Hills

VENDA

Messina

Beira
Nova Sofala

Nova Mambone

I. do Bazaruto
I. Benguérua

Mahajanga

Antsiranana

ANTSIR
ANANA

Mandritsara

Besalampy

Maintirano

MADAGASCAR

ANTANANARIVO

Antsirabe

Morondava

Toamasina

KRUGER
National
Park

PRETORIA

JOHANNESBURG
Benoni
Springs
Nigel

SWAZILAND
MAPUTO

Maputo
(Lourenço Marques)

TRANSVAAL

Lake St. Lucia

NATAL

Pietermaritzburg
KwaMashu
DURBAN
Umlazi

Fianarantsoa
FIANARANTSOA

Toliara

ESOTHO

INDIAN

OCEAN

Tropic of Capricorn

East London

MOZAMBIQUE

Taolanaro

MADAGASCAR

On same scale as General Map

East from Greenwich

COPYRIGHT. GEORGE PHILIP & SON. LTD.

1 : 35 000 000

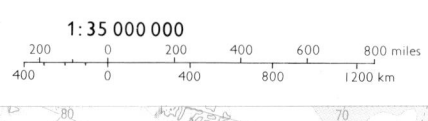

200   0   200   400   600   800 miles
400   0   400   800   1200 km

ARCTIC OCEAN

Greenland

Iceland

Asia

Bering Strait
Bering Sea
Beaufort Sea

Axel Heiberg Land
Sverdrup Is.
Parry Is.
Queen Elizabeth Islands
Ellesmere I.
Kane Basin
Thule

Melville I.
Banks I.
M'Clure Strait
Viscount Melville Sound
Prince of Wales I.
Devon I.
Bathurst
Lancaster Sound
Bylot I.
Baffin Bay
Davis Strait

Brook's Range
Alaska
Alaska Range
Mt. McKinley 6194
Yukon
Porcupine

Victoria I.
Somerset
Gulf of Boothia
Boothia Pen.
Melville Pen.
Foxe Basin
Foxe Channel
Southampton I.

Baffin Island
Cumberland Sound
Frobisher Bay
Resolution I.

Alaska Pen.
Kodiak I.
Gulf of Alaska
Mt. St. Elias 5489
Mt. Logan 6050

Mackenzie Mts.
Great Bear L.
Arctic Circle
Back
Mackenzie
Liard

Hudson Strait
Ungava Peninsula
Labrador
Hamilton Inlet

Alexander Archipelago

Great Slave L.
Peace
Athabasca L.

Chesterfield Inlet
Hudson Bay
Belcher Is.

Newfoundland
Gulf of St. Lawrence
Anticosti

Queen Charlotte Islands

Reindeer L.
Churchill
Nelson

James Bay
Eastmain

St. Pierre
C. Race
St. John's

Vancouver I.
Mt. Waddington 3994
Juan de Fuca Strait
Queen Charlotte Sound

Mt. Robson 3954
Yellowhead Pass
Kicking Horse Pass
N. Saskatchewan
S. Saskatchewan
Edmonton
Calgary
Crowsnest Pass

Regina
Winnipeg
Lake Winnipeg

Laurentian Plateau

Québec
Montréal
Ottawa
Toronto
Hamilton
Niagara Falls

Mendocino Seascarp

Seattle
Mt. Rainier 4392
Portland
Columbia
C. Blanco
C. Mendocino

Coast Range
Cascade Range
Sierra Nevada

Snake
Great Salt Lake
Wasatch Mountains

Missouri
Minneapolis
Mississippi
L. Superior
L. Huron
L. Michigan
L. Ontario
L. Erie

Chicago
Detroit

New York
Philadelphia
Washington
Chesapeake Bay
C. Cod
Nantucket I.
Long I.

Appalachian Mts.
Allegheny Mts.
Blue Ridge

ATLANTIC OCEAN

PACIFIC OCEAN

Murray Seascarp

San Francisco
Mt. Shasta 4317
Sacramento

Great Basin
Mt. Whitney 4418
S. Joaquin

Los Angeles

Grand Canyon
Colorado Plateau
Colorado
Gila

Mt. Elbert 4399
Denver
Blanca Pk. 4376
N. Platte
S. Platte

Kansas City
St. Louis
Ozark Plateau

Memphis

Cumberland Plateau
Tennessee
Atlanta
Alabama

C. Hatteras

Bermuda

Tropic of Cancer

6225

Red
Dallas
Llano Estacado
Rio Grande

Houston
New Orleans
Mississippi Delta

Florida
Bahama Islands

Clarion Fracture Zone

Revilla Gigedo Is.

Lower California
Gulf of California

Western Sierra Madre
Mexican Plateau
Eastern Sierra Madre

Gulf of Mexico

Florida Strait
Havana
Cuba
Greater Antilles
Hispaniola
Puerto Rico
Milwaukee Deep 9700

C. San Lucas

Monterrey

C. Corrientes
Guadalajara
Santiago

México
Puebla
Popocatepetl 5452
Citlaltepetl 5700
Isthmus of Tehuantepec

Gulf of Campeche
Yucatán Peninsula
C. Catoche
Yucatán Strait
Yucatán Basin
Cayman Trough 7680
Jamaica
Port-au-Prince
Venezuelan Basin

Gulf of Tehuantepec
Guatemala Trench 6662
Guatemala

Gulf of Honduras
C. Gracias a Dios
Coco
L. Nicaragua

Caribbean Sea
Colombian Basin

Sa. Nevada de Sta. Marta 5800
Andes
Sierra de Merida
G. of Venezuela
Maracaibo

Panama Canal
3837
G. of Darién
G. of Panama

Projection: Bonne   West from Greenwich   COPYRIGHT. GEORGE PHILIP & SON. LTD.

ft   m
12 000   4000
6000   2000
3000   1000
1200   400
600   200
0   0
200   600
2000   6000
4000   12 000
6000   18 000
8000   24 000
m   ft

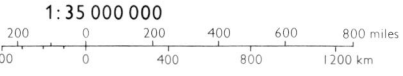

1 : 35 000 000

Projection: Bonne

ALASKA
1:30 000 000

100 0   100   200   300 miles
100 0   200   400 km

1:15 000 000

100 50 0   100   200   300   400 miles
100   0   100   200   300   400   500   600 km

GREENLAND

ATLANTIC

OCEAN

Devon Island
Lancaster Sound
Arctic Bay
Brodeur
Peninsula
Bylot I.
Pond Inlet
Pond Inlet
2136
Baffin Bay
Svartenhuk
Halvø
Angmagssalik
Milne Inlet
Scott I.
Disko
Disko B.
Christianshåb
Søndre Strømfjord
Fury & Hecla Str.
Igloolik Island
C. Hewett
Broughton Island
Padloping Island
Holsteinsborg
2850
Kong Frederik VI's Kyst
Hall Lake
Melville Peninsula
Prince Charles I.
Foxe
Basin
Godthåb
Frederikshåb
Cumberland Peninsula
2591
C. Dyer
Cape Dyer
Pangnirtung
Melville
Rae Isthmus
Repulse Bay
Wager B.
C. Dorchester
Foxe Penin.
Amadjuak L.
Cumberland Sd.
C. Mercy
Frederikshåb
Ivigtut
Southampton
Coral Harbour
Bell Pen.
Coats I.
Cape Dorset
Amadjuak
Lake Harbour
Frobisher Bay
Resolution I.
Kap Farvel
Nanortalik
Roes Welcome Sd.
Digges Is.
Nettilling L.
Mansel I.
Saglouk (Sugluk)
Invujivik
Maricourt (Wakeham)
Koartac (Notre Dame de Koartac)
Akpatok I.
Hudson Strait
C. Chidley
3809
Diggs Is.
BAFFIN
Ungava Bay
1676
Port Nouveau-Québec (George R.)
Hebron
Arnaud (Payne)
Bellin (Payne Bay)
Nutak
Payne L.
Nain
Ottawa Isl.
Portland Promontory
Inoucdjouac (Port Harrison)
Feuilles R.
Koksoak
Kuujjuaq
George R.
Whale R.
Hopedale
C. Harrison
Indian Harbour
257
Hudson
Bay
Sleeper Is.
King George Is.
L. Minto
Mélèzes
Kaniapiskau
Nain
Baker's Dozen
King George Is.
Belcher Is.
C. Henrietta Maria
Pte. Louis-XIV
À l'Eau Claire
Poste-de-la-Baleine (Great Whale River)
Grand Baleine
Petitsikapau L.
Lac Bienville
Schefferville
Rigolet
L. Melville
Cartwright
North West R.
Churchill Falls
Goose Bay
Churchill R.
Ashuanipi L.
Battle Harbour
Belle Isle
COAST OF LABRADOR
Winisk
Big Trout L.
James Bay
Akimiski I.
Charlton
Kanaaupscow
Ft. George
La Grande
Nouveau Comptoir (Paint Hills)
Eastmain
QUÉBEC
4128
Gagnon
814
Moisie
Mingan
Î. d'Anticosti
NEWFOUNDLAND
Twillingate
Lewisporte
Bonavista
Bonavista B.
Trinity B.
St. John's
Grand Falls
Harbour Grace
Carbonear
Placentia
Placentia B.
Trepassey
C. Race
Attawapiskat
Ft. Albany
Fort Rupert (Rupert House)
L. Albanel
Mistassini L.
L. Nottaway
Rupert R.
Missinaibi
Moosonee
Albany
Harricana
Nottaway
Chibougamau
Péribonca
Baie-Comeau
Betsiamites
R. St. Lawrence
Moisie
Port-Cartier
Sept-Îles
Manicouagan
St-Augustin-Saguenay
Natashquan
Romaine
Natashquan R.
Î. aux Basques
Channel-Port aux Basques
Gulf of St. Lawrence
Thunder Bay
Nakina
Kenogami
Longlac
Geraldton
Hearst
Cochrane
L. Abitibi
Taschereau
Senneterre
Matagami
Rés. de Gouin
La Tuque
Dolbeau
St-Jean
Roberval
Jonquière
Chicoutimi
Saguenay
Rivière-du-Loup
Matane
Rimouski
Pén. de Gaspé
C. de Gaspé
Gaspé
Chandler
St. Lawrence
Cabot Str.
C. North
St-Pierre et Miquelon (Fr.)
Glace Bay
Sydney
Port Hawkesbury
Heron Bay
Oba
Timmins
Noranda
Rouyn
Val d'Or
Kirkland Lake
Amos
Haileybury
Cobalt
Témiscamingue
Rés. de Cabonga
Shawinigan
Trois-Rivières
1150
Québec
Lévis
Thetford Mines
Woodstock
Edmundston
St-Léonard
Grand Falls
Fredericton
Chatham de la Madeleine
NEW BRUNSWICK
Bathurst
Newcastle
Moncton
Campbellton
Tignish
Summerside
PR. EDWARD I.
Charlottetown
Cape Breton I.
New Glasgow
Michipicoten
Franz
Sault Ste. Marie
Copper Cliff
Sudbury
North Bay
Parry Sound
Pembroke
Arnprior
Hull
Cornwall
MONTRÉAL
Lachine
St-Hyacinthe
Sorel
Sherbrooke
Bangor
Augusta
MAINE
Saint John
B. of Fundy
Windsor
Digby
Kentville
Springhill
Amherst
NOVA SCOTIA
Truro
Halifax
Dartmouth
Bridgewater
Liverpool
Shelburne
C. Sable
Yarmouth
Sable I. (Nova Scotia)
6309
Keweenaw Bay
Calumet
Marquette
Sault Ste. Marie
Lake Superior
Manistique
Escanaba
Menominee
Green Bay
Cheboygan
Petoskey
Traverse City
Cadillac
Georgian Bay
Owen Sound
Orillia
Barrie
Belleville
Kingston
Burlington
Watertown
Plattsburg
VERMONT
Montpelier
Lake Champlain
1917
Concord
NEW HAMPSHIRE
Manchester
Lowell
Lewiston
Portland
Boston
MASS.
C. Cod
Worcester
Providence
Appleton
Wausau
Manitowoc
Sheboygan
Milwaukee
Racine
Kenosha
Saginaw
Flint
Muskegon
Grand Rapids
Kalamazoo
Lake Michigan
Lake Huron
Lansing
TORONTO
Hamilton
Niagara Falls
Lake Ontario
Guelph
Kitchener
Stratford
Brantford
London
St. Catharines
Buffalo
Rochester
Syracuse
Utica
Albany
Springfield
CONN.
Waterbury
Hartford
New Haven
Bridgeport
Providence
NEW YORK
Binghamton
Elmira
Scranton
Allentown
Reading
Trenton
NEW JERSEY
Newark
NEW YORK
Jersey City
CHICAGO
Gary
INDIANA
South Bend
DETROIT
Windsor
Toledo
OHIO
Akron
Cleveland
Youngstown
Erie
Jamestown
Williamsport
PENNSYLVANIA

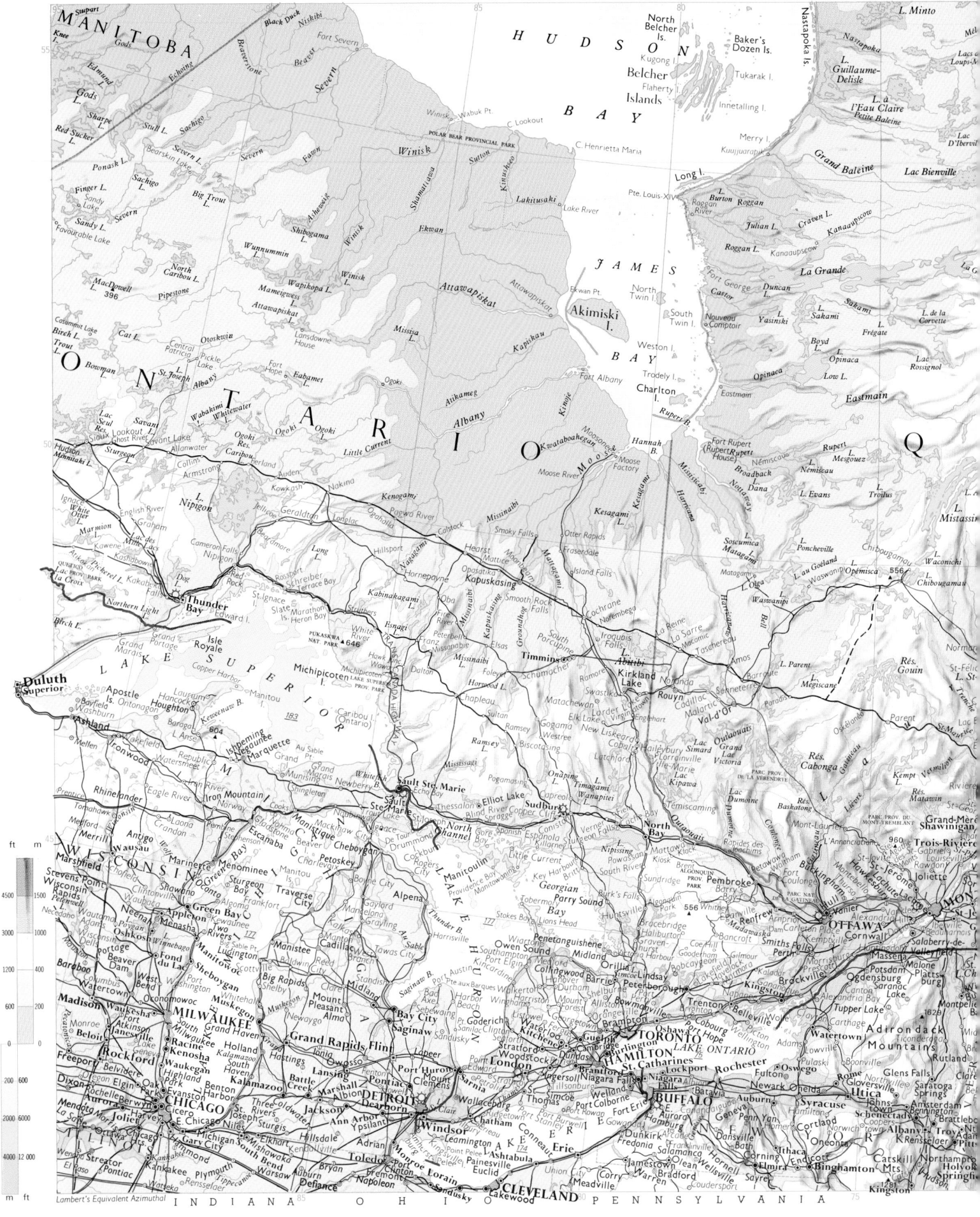

1:7 000 000

50   0   50   100   150   200 miles
50   0   50 100 150 200 250 300 km

COAST OF QUEBEC & LABRADOR

N E W F O U N D L A N D

Q U E B E C

LABRADOR

South Aulatsivik I.
High I.
Nain
Paul I.
Voisey's B.
Davis Inlet
Nunaksaluk I.
Hopedale
Big Bay
Kaipokok B.
Aillik
Makkovik
Adlavik Is.
C. Harrison
Holton
Indian Harbour
Groswater B.
Cartwright
Table B.
Island of Ponds
Separation Point
Sandwich B.
Eagle
Square Islands
Alexis
St. Lewis
Mary's Harbour
Battle Harbour
Str. of Belle Isle
Belle I.
St. Lunaire-Griquet
St. Anthony
Hare B.
Flower's Cove
Groais I.
Conche
Englee
Bell I.
Roddickton
White B.
Horse Is.
La Scie
Baie Verte
Notre Dame B.
Twillingate
Fogo I.
Carmanville
C. Freels

Erlandson L.
Whale
George
Fraser
L. de la Hutte Sauvage
Kogaluk
Mistastin
Tunungayualok I.
Champdoré
Tudor
Whitegull L.
610
Harp L.

Fort McKenzie
L. Nachicapau
Otelnuk L.
Wheeler
Chakonipau L.
Kanapiskau
Sandy
Sérigny
Wakuach
L.

Attikamagen L.
Schefferville
Kanatriktok
Nakaupi
Seal L.
Nipishish
Grand L.
L. Melville
1128
Mealy Mts.
North-West River
Goose
Happy Valley-Goose Bay
Churchill
Minipi

Petitsikapau L.
Michikamau Lake
Ossokmanuan
Winokapau L.
Churchill Falls
Little Mecatina
St. Augustin
Paradise
St. Paul
Anse-au-Loup
Forteau
Bradore Bay
Lourdes-de-Blanc-Sablon
Port Saunders
Daniel's Harbour

Néret
L. Bermen
Shabogamo L.
Opiskotish
Opiscoteo
Lac Joseph
Atikonak L.
Burnt L.
St-Paul
St-Augustin-Saguenay
Outer I.
St-Augustin

Nitchequon
L. Naococane
Kaniapiskau Lake
Labrador City
Wabush
Ashuanipi
Natashquan
Petit-Mécatina Harrington Harbour

1128
Michikamau
Pletipi
Petit Lac Manicouagan
Moisie
West Mayne
Romaine
Aguanus
Nabisipi
Olomane
Mutton Bay
L. Musquaro
Etamamu

Péribonca
Manouane
Onatchiway
Res. Manicouagan
Ste-Marguerite
1048
Manitou
Nipissis
Magpie L.
St-Jean
Lac Allard
Sheldrake
Mingan
Havre-St-Pierre
Aguanish
Natashquan
Kegaska
Gethsémoni
GROS MORNE NAT. PARK
Trout River
Bay of Islands
CORNER BROOK
814
Long Pt.
Port au Port
C. St. George
Seal Cove
Sop's Arm
White B.
Springdale
South Brook
Deer Lake
Howley
Buchans
Red Indian L.
Victoria Res.
Grey Res.
Lewisporte
Botwood
Windsor
Grand Falls
Bishop's Falls
Gander
Gander L.
Glovertown
Dark Cove
Westleyville
Bonavista
C. Bonavista
Catalina
Trinity
Trinity B.

Péribonca
L. Manouane
Ouiardes
Bétsiamites
Clarke City
Moisie
Sept-Iles
Port-Cartier
Rivière-Pentecôte
Pte. Ouest
Port-Menier
Î. d'Anticosti
Jupiter
Dét. de Jacques-Cartier
Heath Pt.
GULF OF
ST. LAWRENCE
572
NEWFOUNDLAND

Alma
Chicoutimi
Arvida
Saguenay
Port Alfred
Jonquière
Res. Pipmuacan
Godbout
Baie-Trinité
Pte. des Monts
Grande-Vallée
St-Maurice
Grande-Vallée
Sud Ouest
Petit-Cap
Rivière-au-Renard
Mont-Louis
Ste-Anne
Cap-Chat
Matane
Mont-Joli
PARC PROV. DE LA GASPÉSIE
1268
Mt. Jacques-Cartier
Gaspé
Douglastown
Percé
Grande-Rivière
Chandler

Kamouraska
Tadoussac
Bergeronnes
Grandes-Bergeronnes
Baie-Comeau
Hauterive
Betsiamites
Forestville
Mts. Chic-Chocs
Pén. de Gaspé
Bonaventure
Paspébiac
Miscou I.
Brion I.
Grande-Entrée

St. Law.
Rimouski
Bic
Trois-Pistoles
Sayabec
Amqui
Causapscal
Matapédia
Dalhousie
Chaleur Bay
Belledune
Lamèque
Shippegan
Tracadie
Îs. de la Madeleine (Quebec)
Fatima
Cap-aux-Meules
Havre-Aubert
Cap-aux-Meules
St. Paul
C. North

Rivière-du-Loup
Cabano
PARC PROV. S LAURENTIDES
Baie-St-Paul
Campbellton
Kedgwick
St. Arthur
Heath Steele
Bathurst
Neguac
Miramichi B.
North Pt.
Tignish
Alberton
PRINCE EDWARD ISLAND
Summerside
Kensington
Charlottetown
Souris
East Pt.
Pleasant Bay
CAPE BRETON NAT. PARK
532
Ingonish
Chéticamp

Montmagny
Lauzon
Lévis
QUÉBEC
1190
St-Pascal
St-Jean-Port-Joli
Edmundston
St. Leonard
819
Grand Falls
Van Buren
Caribou
NEW BRUNSWICK
Newcastle
Chatham
Collette
Richibucto
Rexton
Bay du Vin
Northumberland
Borden
Georgetown
Montague
Tormentine
Murray Hr.
Pictou
New Glasgow
Antigonish
St. Peter's
Sydney Mines
N. Sydney
Sydney
Bras d'Or
New Waterford
Glace Bay
Cape Breton Island
Louisbourg
Fourchu

Madeleine
Plessisville
Beauceville
St-Georges
Thetford Mines
Asbestos
Ft. Kent
1606
Allagash
Ashland
Presqueville
Houlton
Eagle L.
Island Falls
Chesuncook L.
Hartland
Stanley
Woodstock
Minto
Plaster Rock
Blackville
Chipman
Notre Dame
Shediac
Moncton
Petitcodiac
Elgin
Sussex
Amherst
Springhill
Parrsboro
Joggins
Oxford
Mulgrave
Chedabucto B.
Canso
L. Madame

Sherbrooke
Coaticook
East Angus
MAINE
Guilford
Greenville
Moosehead L.
Mattawamkeag
Lincoln
Millinocket
Fredericton
Gagetown
St-Georges
Jemseg
Oromocto
McAdam
St. Stephen
Calais
St. Martins
Fundy
Bay
Kentville
Windsor
Middleton
Truro
Stewiacke
Shubenacadie
Musquodoboit
Upper Musquodoboit
Sheet Hr.
Musquodoboit Hr.
ATLANTIC

Sherbrooke
Lac-Mégantic
Megantic L.
Bingham
Skowhegan
Old Town
Brewer
Bangor
Dover-Foxcroft
Bucksport
Ellsworth
Machias
Jonesport
Eastport
Grand Manan I.
Blacks Hr.
Saint John
Bridgetown
Annapolis Royal
Digby
Weymouth
St. Mary's B.
Bridgewater
Mahone Bay
Lunenburg
Dartmouth
Halifax
NOVA SCOTIA
OCEAN

Rumford
Berlin
Waterville
Augusta
Belfast
Camden
Rockland
Bar Harbor
Mt. Desert I.
Freeport
Rossignol Res.
L. Rossignol
Liverpool
Port Mouton
Sable I. (Nova Scotia)

St. Johnsbury
1917
Conway
Sebago
Auburn
Lewiston
Bath
Brunswick
Portland
Saco
Biddeford
Sanford
Wedgeport
Yarmouth
Shelburne
Clark's Harbour
C. Sable
C. Sable

Rochester
Concord
Dover
Portsmouth
Manchester
Nashua
Haverhill
Lawrence
Lowell
Lynn
Gloucester
Waltham
BOSTON
Brockton

ATLANTIC

OCEAN

Cabot Strait
Channel-Port aux Basques
Burgeo
Ramea
Francois
Harbour Breton
Hermitage
Fortune B.
Grand Bank
Fortune
Marystown
Placentia B.
Langlade
Miquelon
SAINT-PIERRE ET MIQUELON (Fr.)
St-Pierre
Argentia
Placentia
Spaniard's Bay
Harbour Grace
Carbonear
St. John's
Conception B.
Bay de Verde
Avalon Peninsula
C. Race
C. Pine
St. Mary's B.
Trepassey
Bulls

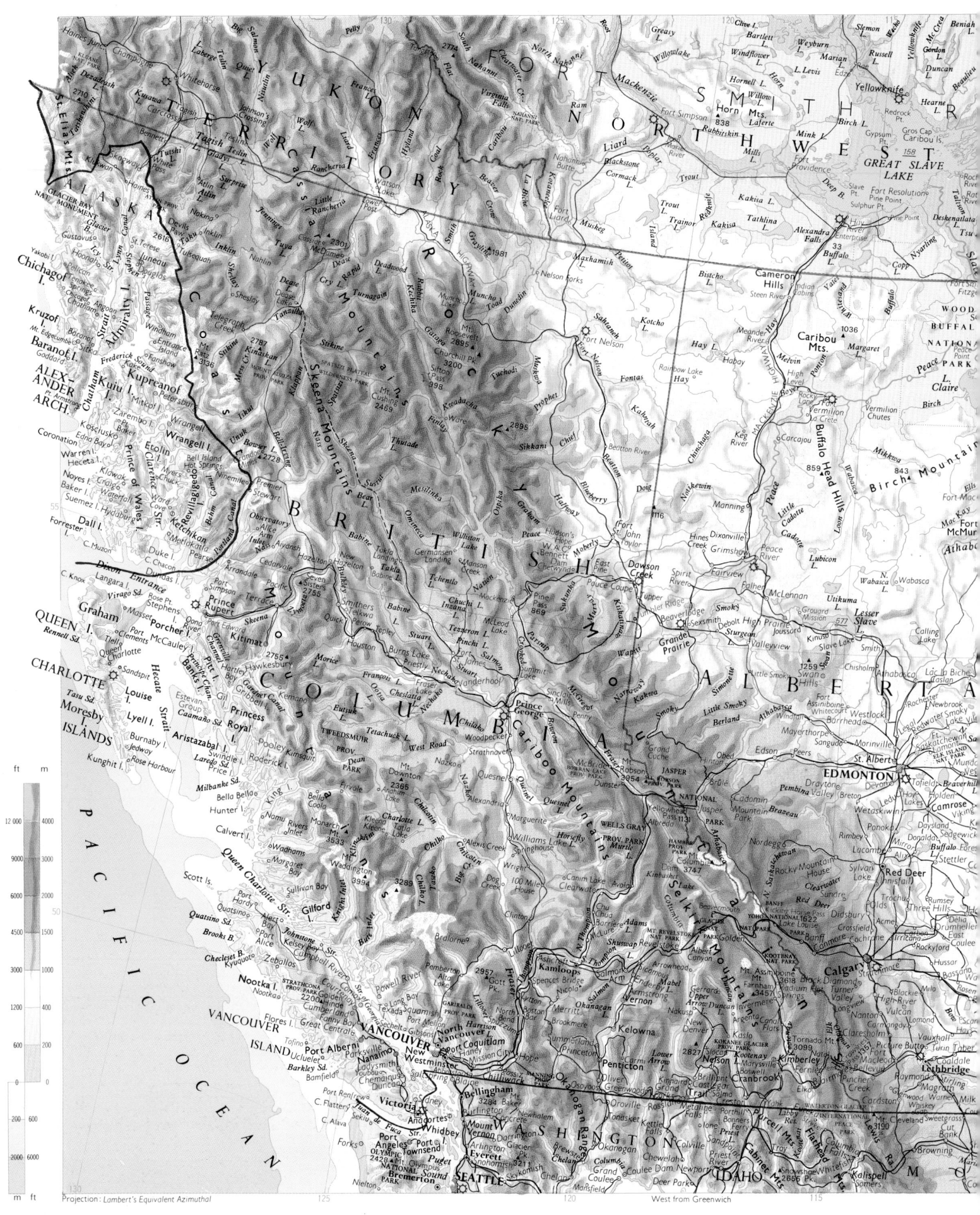

Projection: Lambert's Equivalent Azimuthal   West from Greenwich

HUDSON

BAY

KEEWATIN

REGION

MACKENZIE TERRITORIES

SASKATCHEWAN

MANITOBA

ONTARIO

Lake Athabasca

Cree L.

Reindeer L.

Southern Indian L.

LAKE WINNIPEG

Lake Winnipegoss

RIDING MOUNTAIN NATIONAL PARK

PRINCE ALBERT NAT. PARK

Cedar Lake

Churchill

Saskatoon

Prince Albert

North Battleford

Regina

Moose Jaw

Swift Current

Medicine Hat

Yorkton

Brandon

WINNIPEG

Portage la Prairie

Selkirk

Transcona

St. Boniface

Kenora

Fort Frances

Flin Flon

The Pas

Dauphin

Weyburn

Estevan

MONTANA

NORTH DAKOTA

MINNESOTA

Minot

Devils Lake

Grand Forks

Bemidji

Duluth

Williston

Fort Peck Res.

Lake of the Woods

International Falls

Lac la Croix

TRANS CANADA HIGHWAY

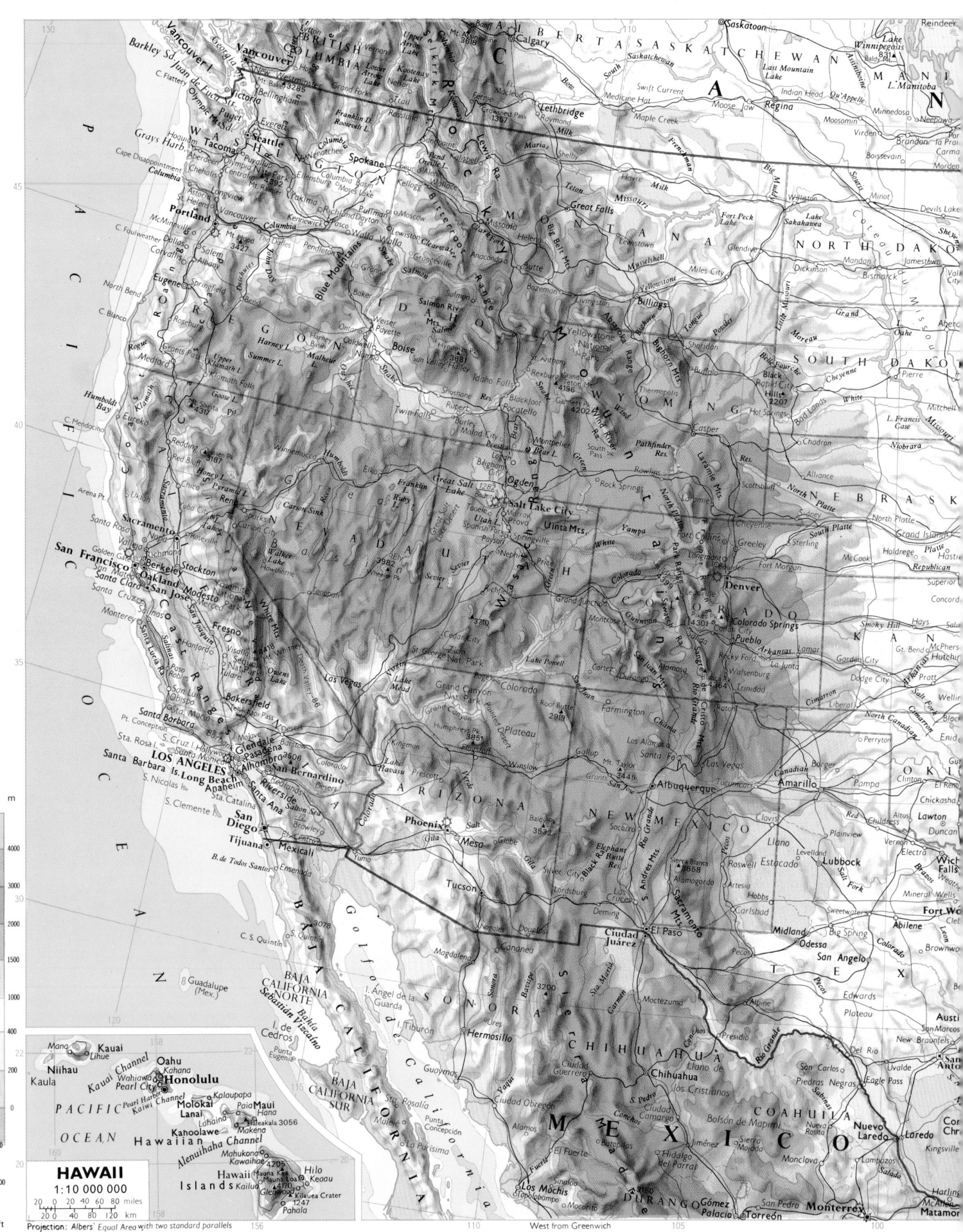

ft   m

12 000   4000

9000   3000

6000   2000

4500   1500

3000   1000

1200   400

600   200

0   0

200   600

2000   6000

m   ft

HAWAII
1:10 000 000

20 0 20 40 60 80 miles

20 0 40 80 120 km

Projection: Albers' Equal Area with two standard parallels

1:12 000 000

50   100   150   200   250   300 miles
50   0   50 100 150 200 250 300 350 400 450 km

COPYRIGHT. GEORGE PHILIP & SON. LTD.

1:6 000 000

50   0   50   100 miles

50   0   50   100   150 km

Continuation
Eastwards
On same scale

COPYRIGHT GEORGE PHILIP & SON LTD.

Projection: Alber's Equal Area with two standard parallels

West from Greenwich

ft m   6000   4500   3000   1500   1200   600   0   200-600   2000 6000   12 000   m
                                                                                              ft

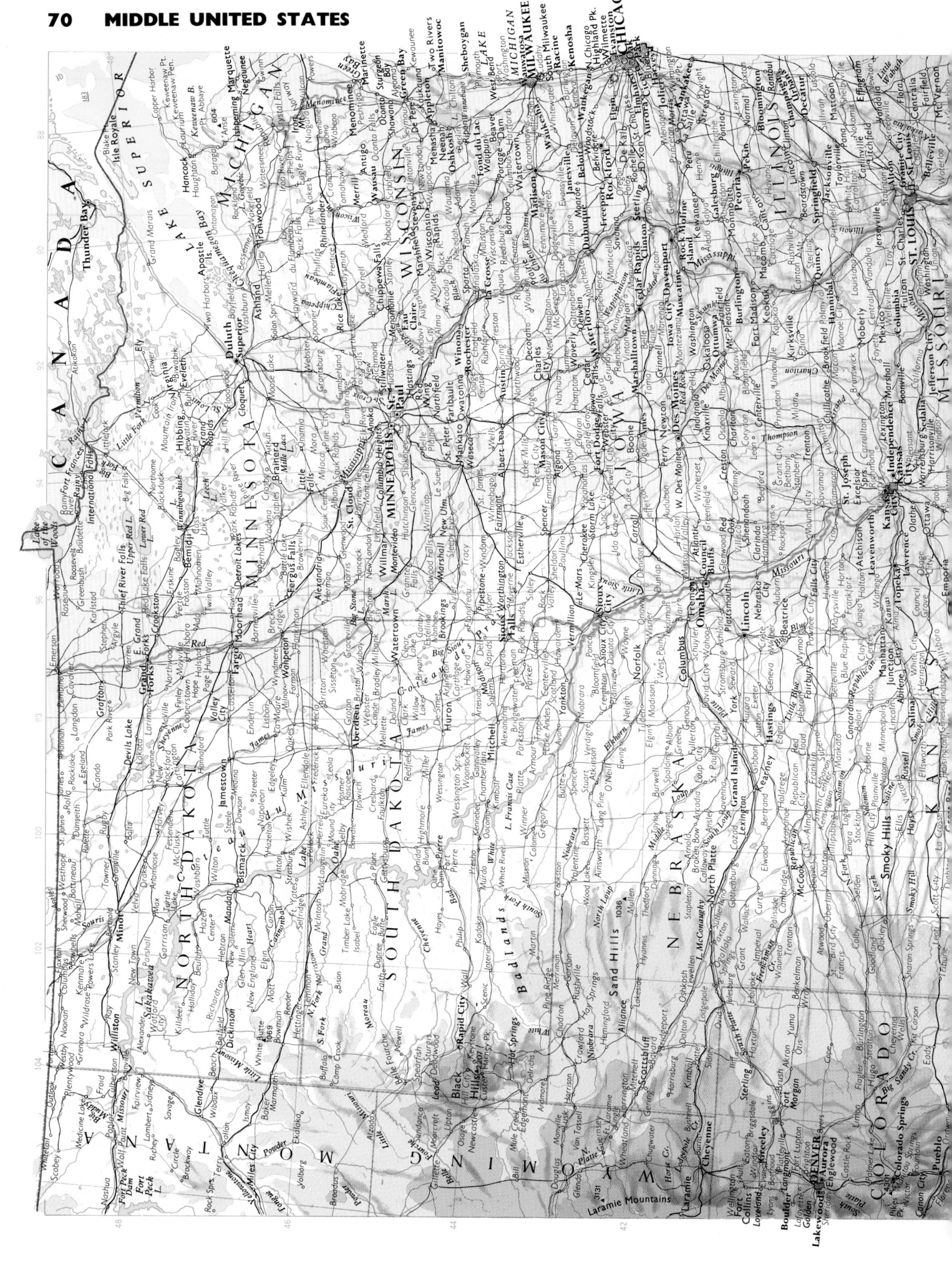

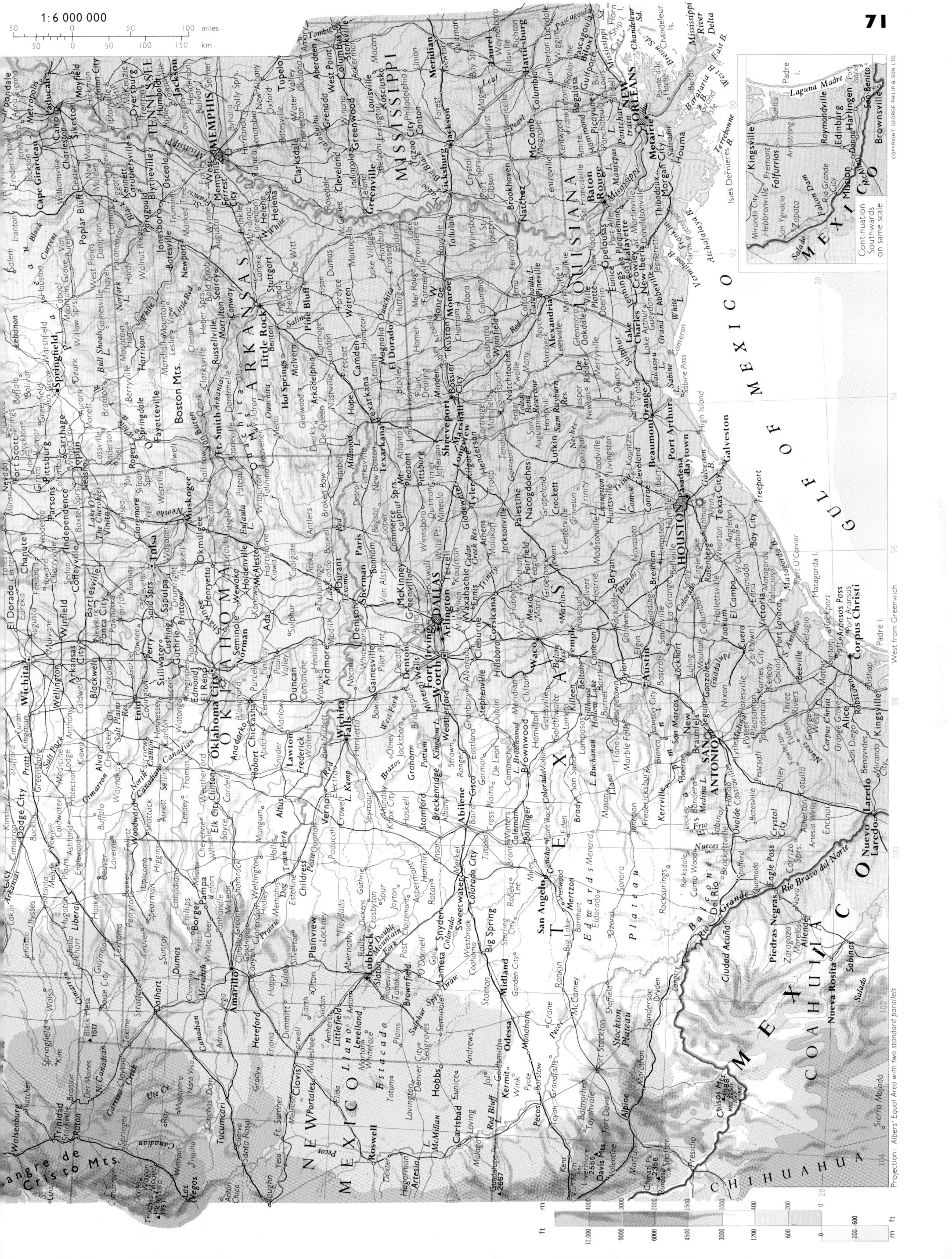

1:6 000 000

50 0 50 100 miles
50 0 50 100 150 km

TENNESSEE
MISSISSIPPI
ARKANSAS
LOUISIANA
OKLAHOMA
TEXAS
NEW MEXICO
COAHUILA
CHIHUAHUA
M E X I C O

GULF OF MEXICO

MEMPHIS
NEW ORLEANS
Baton Rouge
Little Rock
Shreveport
DALLAS
Fort Worth
HOUSTON
SAN ANTONIO
Austin
Corpus Christi
Oklahoma City
Tulsa
Wichita
Amarillo
Lubbock
San Angelo
Laredo
Nuevo Laredo

Rio Grande
Mississippi River Delta
Laguna Madre
Padre I.

West from Greenwich

Projection: Albers' Equal Area with two standard parallels

COPYRIGHT GEORGE PHILIP & SON LTD

Continuation Southwards on same scale

1:6 000 000

50 0 50 100 miles

50 0 50 100 150 km

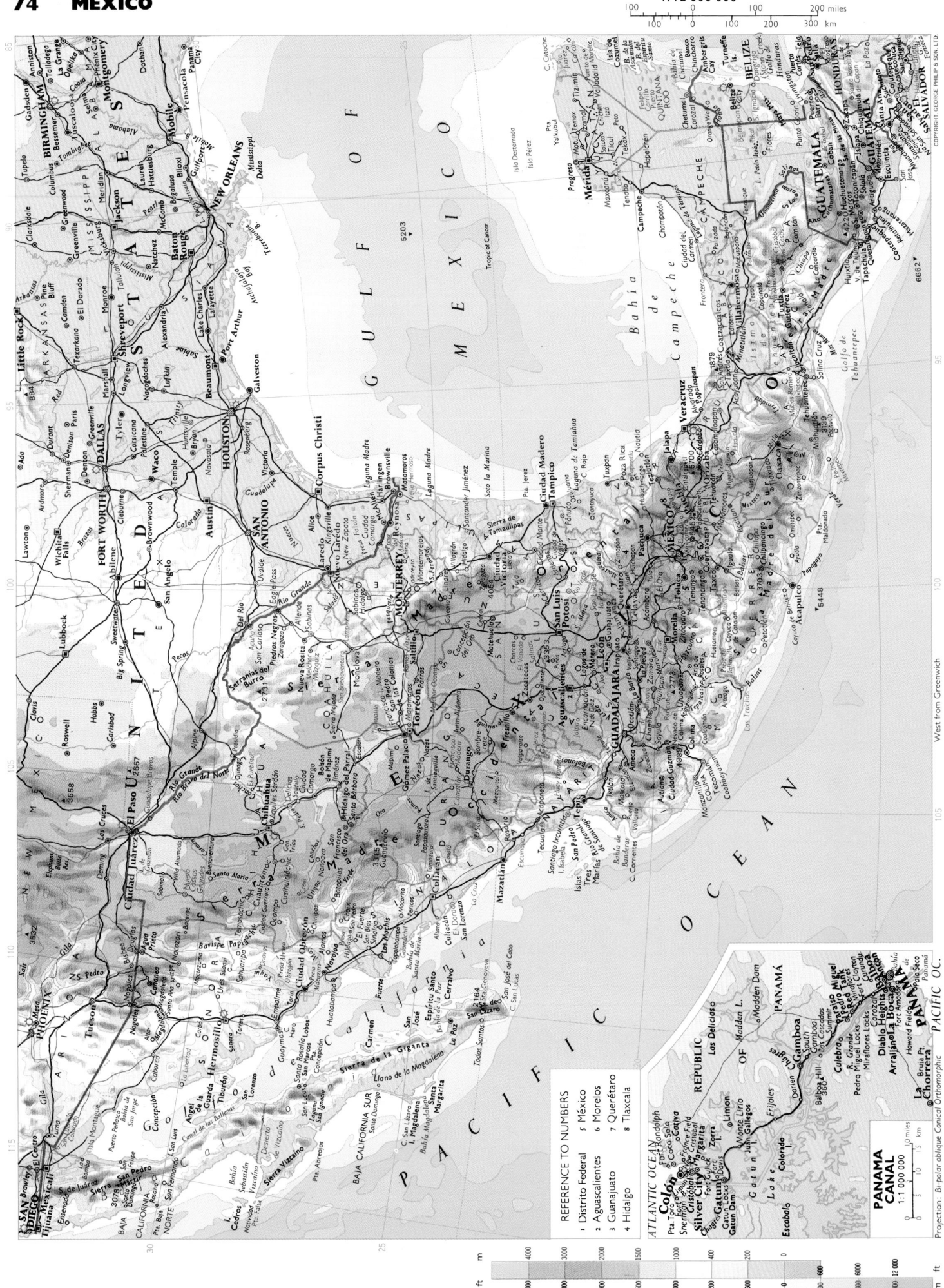

1:12 000 000

REFERENCE TO NUMBERS

1 Distrito Federal	5 México
2 Aguascalientes	6 Morelos
3 Guanajuato	7 Querétaro
4 Hidalgo	8 Tlaxcala

PANAMA CANAL
1:1 000 000

Projection: Bi-polar oblique Conical Orthomorphic

West from Greenwich

COPYRIGHT GEORGE PHILIP & SON LTD.

1:12 000 000

WINDWARD ISLANDS
1:8 000 000

TRINIDAD & TOBAGO
1:8 000 000

JAMAICA
1:8 000 000

LEEWARD ISLANDS
1:8 000 000

BERMUDA
1:1 000 000

ATLANTIC OCEAN

GULF OF MEXICO

BAHAMAS

GREAT BAHAMA BANK

FLORIDA

MIAMI

CUBA

LA HABANA

GREATER ANTILLES

JAMAICA

HAITI

DOMINICAN REP.

HISPANIOLA

PUERTO RICO (U.S.A.)

LESSER ANTILLES

CARIBBEAN SEA

VIRGIN ISLANDS

LEEWARD ISLANDS

WINDWARD ISLANDS

NETH. ANTILLES

GUADELOUPE

MARTINIQUE

ST. LUCIA

BARBADOS

GRENADA

TRINIDAD & TOBAGO

VENEZUELA

COLOMBIA

PANAMA

COSTA RICA

NICARAGUA

HONDURAS

PACIFIC OCEAN

GUIANA

PANAMA CANAL

Santiago de Cuba

Santo Domingo

Port of Spain

Caracas

MARACAIBO

BARRANQUILLA

Cartagena

Managua

Tegucigalpa

San José

COPYRIGHT GEORGE PHILIP & SON LTD.

West from Greenwich

Projection: Bi-polar oblique Conical Orthomorphic

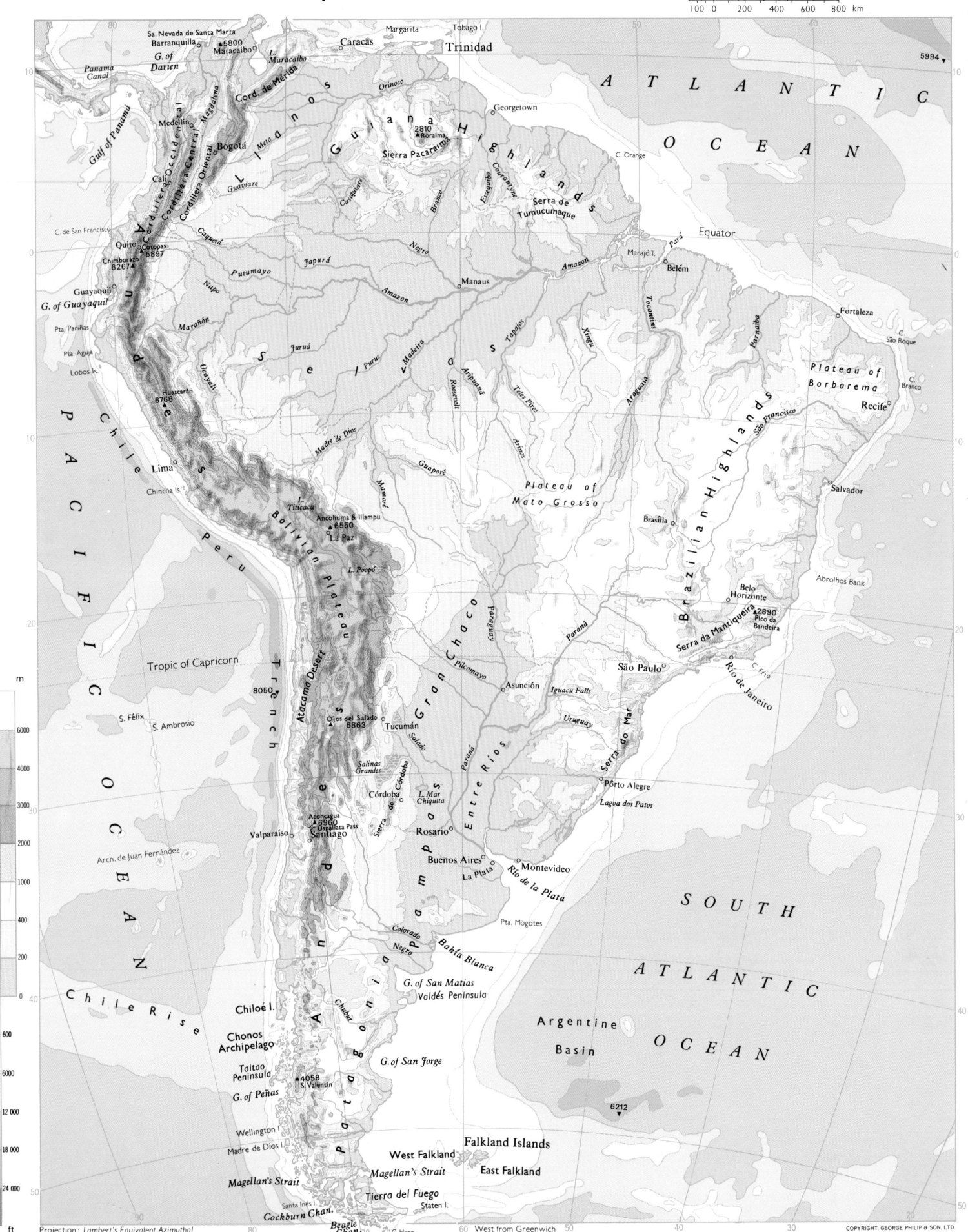

1:30 000 000

100   0   100 200 300   400   500 miles
100 0   200   400   600   800 km

Projection: Lambert's Equivalent Azimuthal

West from Greenwich

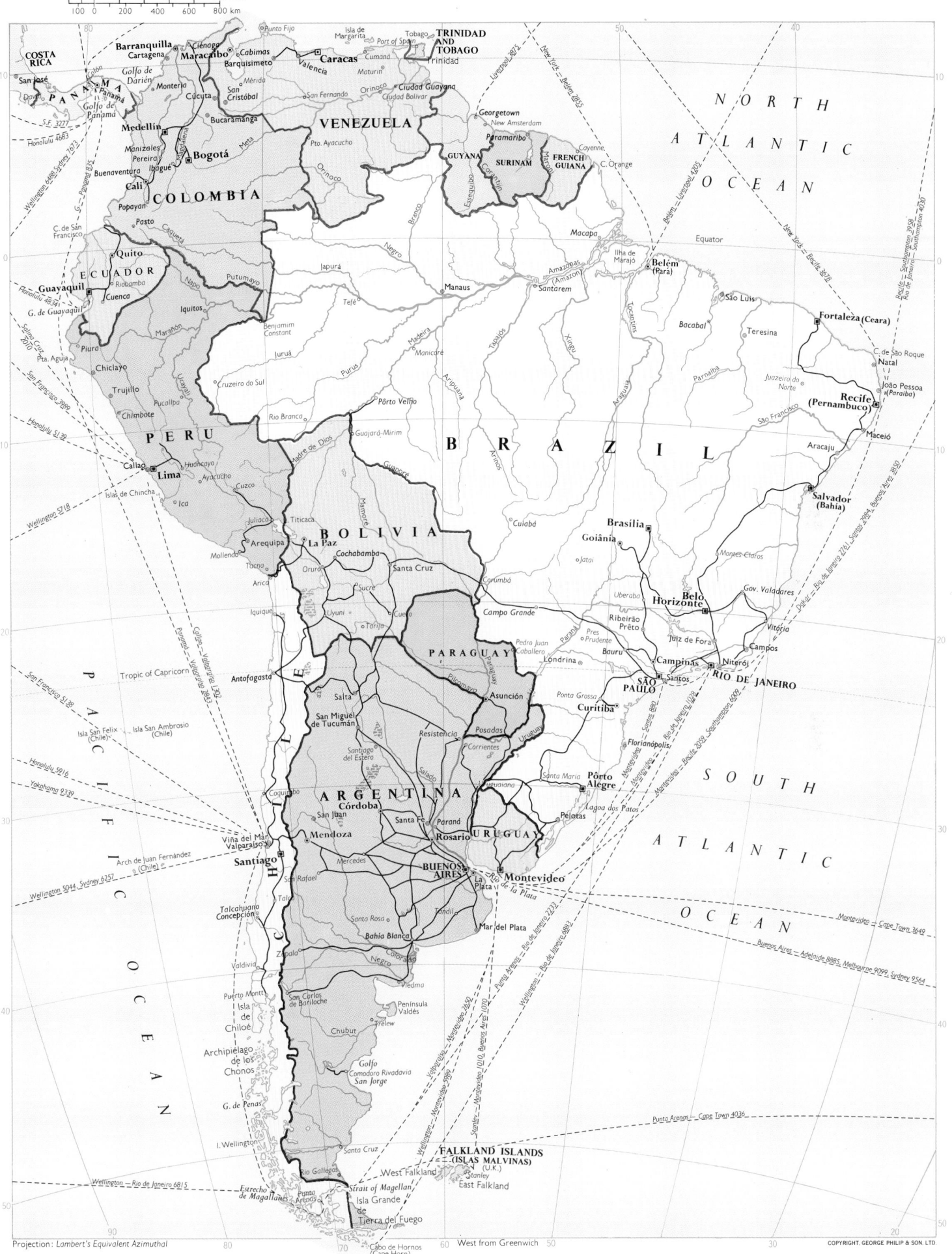

1:30 000 000

100   0   100   200   300   400   500 miles
100   0   200   400   600   800 km

Projection: Lambert's Equivalent Azimuthal

West from Greenwich

COPYRIGHT. GEORGE PHILIP & SON. LTD.

1:16 000 000

100   0   100   200   300   400   500 miles
100   0   100   200   300   400   500   600   700   800 km

ATLANTIC

A T L A N T I C   O C E A N

Paramaribo
Nieuw Amsterdam
Moengo
St. Laurent
Cayenne

FR.
GUIANA

SURINAM

C. Orange
St. Georges
Oiapoque

AMAPÁ

C. do Norte

Equator

Estuário do
Rio Amazonas
Ilha Caviana
Macapá
Ilha Mexiana

Ilha de Marajó

Belém (Pará)

Amazonas (Amazon)
Santarém

PARÁ

MARANHÃO

Bacabal

São Luís (Maranhão)

Fortaleza (Ceará)

Sobral
Cascavel

Teresina

CEARÁ
RIO GRANDE
DO NORTE
Natal

Mossoró
Macau

C. de São Roque

PIAUÍ

PARAÍBA
João Pessoa
(Paraíba)
Campina Grande

Caruaru

PERNAMBUCO
RECIFE
(Pernambuco)
Olinda

Imperatriz

Carolina

Petrolina
Juàzeiro
Paulo Afonso

ALAGOAS
Maceió

Arapiraca
SERGIPE

Aracaju
São Cristóvão
Estância

BRAZIL

GOIÁS

BAHIA

Barreiras

Feira de
Santana
Alagoinhas

Santo Amaro

Salvador (Bahia)

Jequié

Vitória da
Conquista
Ilhéus

DIST.
FED.
Brasília

Goiânia

Montes
Claros

Teófilo Otoni

Diamantina

Gov. Valadares

Linhares

MINAS GERAIS

Belo Horizonte

VITÓRIA

Campos

Juiz de Fora

Petrópolis

RIO DE JANEIRO
Niterói

SÃO
PAULO

Campinas

Marília
Piracicaba

Campo Grande

MATO GROSSO
DO SUL

MATO GROSSO

Planalto do
Mato Grosso

Fernando de Noronha
(Braz.)

Trindade
(Braz.)

COPYRIGHT: GEORGE PHILIP & SON, LTD.

1:16 000 000

100 50 0 100 200 300 miles
100 0 100 200 300 400 km

Projection: Sanson-Flamsteed's Sinusoidal

INDEX

The number in dark type which follows each name in the index refers to the page number where that feature or place will be found.

The geographical co-ordinates which follow the place name are sometimes only approximate but are close enough for the place name to be located.

An open square ☐ signifies that the name refers to an administrative division of a country while a solid square ■ follows the name of a country.

Rivers have been indexed to their mouth or to where they join another river. All rivers are followed by the symbol ➝.

The alphabetic order of names composed of two or more words is governed primarily by the first word and then by the second. This is an example of the rule:

> *East Tawas*
> *Eastbourne*
> *Easter Is.*
> *Eastern Ghats*
> *Eastleigh*

Names composed of a proper name (*Mexico*) and a description (*Gulf of*) are positioned alphabetically by the proper name. If the same word occurs in the name of a town and a geographical feature, the town name is listed first followed by the name or names of the geographical features.

Names beginning with M', Mc are all indexed as if they were spelled Mac.

Names composed of the definite article (Le, La, Les, L') and a proper name are usually alphabetized by the proper name:

> *Havre, Le*
> *Spezia, La*

If the same place name occurs twice or more in the index and the places are in different countries, they will be followed by the country and be in the latter's alphabetical order:

> *Boston, U.K.*
> *Boston, U.S.A.*

If the same place name occurs two or more times in the index and all are in the same country, each is followed by the name of the administrative subdivision in which it is located. The names are placed in the alphabetical order of the subdivisions. For example:

> *Columbus, Ga., U.S.A.*
> *Columbus, Miss., U.S.A.*
> *Columbus, Ohio, U.S.A.*

If there is a mixture of these situations, the primary order is fixed by the alphabetical sequence of the countries and the secondary order by that of the country subdivisions:

> *Rochester, U.K.*
> *Rochester, Minn., U.S.A.*
> *Rochester, N.Y., U.S.A.*

Below is a list of abbreviations used in the index.

A.S.S.R. – Autonomous Soviet Socialist Republic
Ala. – Alabama
Arch. – Archipelago
Ariz. – Arizona
Ark. – Arkansas
B. – Baie, Bahia, Bay, Boca, Bucht, Bugt
B.C. – British Columbia
Br. – British
C. – Cabo, Cap, Cape
Calif. – California
Chan. – Channel
Col. – Colombia
Colo. – Colorado
Conn. – Connecticut
Cord. – Cordillera
D.C. – District of Columbia
Del. – Delaware
Dep. – Dependency
Des. – Desert
Dist. – District
Dom. Rep. – Dominican Republic
E. – East
Fd. – Fjord

Fed. – Federal, Federation
Fla. – Florida
Fr. – France, French
G. – Golfe, Golfo, Gulf, Guba
Ga. – Georgia
Gt. – Great
Hts. – Heights
I.(s) – Ile, Ilha, Insel, Isla, Island(s)
Ill. – Illinois
Ind. – Indiana
K. – Kap, Kapp
Kans. – Kansas
Ky. – Kentucky
L. – Lac, Lacul, Lago, Lagoa, Lake, Limni, Loch, Lough
La. – Louisiana
Ld. – Land
Mad. P. – Madhya Pradesh
Man. – Manitoba
Mass. – Massachusetts
Md. – Maryland
Mich. – Michigan
Minn. – Minnesota
Miss. – Mississippi
Mo. – Missouri

Mont. – Montana
Mt.(s) – Mont, Monta, Monti, Muntii, Montaña, Mount, Mountain(s)
N. – North, Northern
N.B. – New Brunswick
N.C. – North Carolina
N. Dak. – North Dakota
N.H. – New Hampshire
N.J. – New Jersey
N. Mex. – New Mexico
N.S. – Nova Scotia
N.S.W. – New South Wales
N.Y. – New York
N.Z. – New Zealand
Nat. Park – National Park
Nebr. – Nebraska
Neth. – Netherlands
Nev. – Nevada
Nfld. – Newfoundland
Nic. – Nicaragua
Nig. – Nigeria
Okla. – Oklahoma
Ont. – Ontario
Oreg. – Oregon
P. – Pass, Paso, Pasul

Pa. – Pennsylvania
Pak. – Pakistan
Pass. – Passage
Pen. – Peninsula
Pk. – Peak
Plat. – Plateau
Prov. – Province, Provincial
Pt. – Point
Pta. – Ponta, Punta
Pte. – Pointe
Qué. – Québec
R. – Rio, River
R.S.F.S.R. – Russian Soviet Federative Socialist Republic
Ra.(s) – Range(s)
Rep. – Republic
Res. – Reserve, Reservoir
S. – South
S. Africa – South Africa
S.C. – South Carolina
S. Dak. – South Dakota
S.S.R. – Soviet Socialist Republic
Sa. – Serra, Sierra
Sask. – Saskatchewan

Scot. – Scotland
Sd. – Sound
Sp. – Spain, Spanish
St. – Saint
Str. – Strait, Stretto
Tenn. – Tennessee
Terr. – Territory
Tex. – Texas
U.K. – United Kingdom
U.S.A. – United States of America
U.S.S.R. – Union of Soviet Socialist Republics
Ut. P. – Uttar Pradesh
Va. – Virginia
Vic. – Victoria
Vt. – Vermont
Wash. – Washington
W. – West
W. Va. – West Virginia
Wis. – Wisconsin
Wyo. – Wyoming
Yug. – Yugoslavia

Aachen

A

Aachen 14 50 47N 6 4 E
Aalborg = Ålborg 21 57 2N 9 54 E
A'âli en Nîl □ 51 9 30N 31 30 E
Aalsmeer 11 52 17N 4 43 E
Aalst 11 50 56N 4 2 E
Aalten 11 51 56N 6 35 E
Aarau 14 47 23N 8 4 E
Aare ~► 14 47 33N 8 14 E
Aarhus = Århus 21 56 8N 10 11 E
Aarschot 11 50 59N 4 49 E
Aba 53 5 10N 7 19 E
Ābādān 30 30 22N 48 20 E
Ābādeh 31 31 8N 52 40 E
Abadla 50 31 2N 2 45W
Abaetetuba 79 1 40S 48 50W
Abagnar Qi 38 43 52N 116 2 E
Abakan 25 53 40N 91 10 E
Abariringa 40 2 50S 171 40W
Abarqū 31 31 10N 53 20 E
'Abasān 28 31 19N 34 21 E
Abashiri 36 44 0N 144 15 E
Abashiri-Wan 36 44 0N 144 30 E
Abay 24 49 38N 72 53 E
Abaya, L. 51 6 30N 37 50 E
Abaza 24 52 39N 90 6 E
Abbay = Nîl el Azraq ~► 51 15 38N 32 31 E
Abbaye, Pt. 68 46 58N 88 4W
Abbeville, France 12 50 6N 1 49 E
Abbeville, La., U.S.A. 71 30 0N 92 7W
Abbeville, S.C., U.S.A. 69 34 12N 82 21W
Abbieglassie 45 27 15S 147 28 E
Abbotsford, Canada 64 49 5N 122 20W
Abbotsford, U.S.A. 70 44 55N 90 20W
Abbottabad 32 34 10N 73 15 E
Abd al Kūrī 29 12 5N 52 20 E
Abéché 51 13 50N 20 35 E
Åbenrå 21 55 3N 9 25 E
Abeokuta 53 7 3N 3 19 E
Aberaeron 7 52 15N 4 16W
Aberayron = Aberaeron 7 52 15N 4 16W
Abercorn = Mbala 54 8 46S 31 24 E
Abercorn 45 25 12S 151 5 E
Aberdare 7 51 43N 3 27W
Aberdeen, Australia 45 32 9S 150 56 E
Aberdeen, Canada 65 52 20N 106 8W
Aberdeen, S. Africa 56 32 28S 24 2 E
Aberdeen, U.K. 8 57 9N 2 6W
Aberdeen, Ala., U.S.A. 69 33 49N 88 33W
Aberdeen, Idaho, U.S.A. 72 42 57N 112 50W
Aberdeen, S. Dak., U.S.A. 70 45 30N 98 30W
Aberdeen, Wash., U.S.A. 72 47 0N 123 50W
Aberdovey 7 52 33N 4 3W
Aberfeldy 8 56 37N 3 50W
Abergavenny 7 51 49N 3 1W
Abernathy 71 33 49N 101 49W
Abert, L. 72 42 40N 120 8W
Aberystwyth 7 52 25N 4 6W
Abidjan 50 5 26N 3 58W
Abilene, Kans., U.S.A. 70 39 0N 97 16W
Abilene, Tex., U.S.A. 71 32 22N 99 40W
Abingdon, U.K. 7 51 40N 1 17W
Abingdon, Ill., U.S.A. 70 40 53N 90 23W
Abingdon, Va., U.S.A. 69 36 46N 81 56W
Abington Reef 44 18 0S 149 35 E
Abitau ~► 65 59 53N 109 3W
Abitau L. 65 60 27N 107 15W
Abitibi L. 62 48 40N 79 40W
Abkhaz A.S.S.R. □ 23 43 0N 41 0 E
Abkit 25 64 10N 157 10 E
Abminga 45 26 8S 134 51 E
Abohar 32 30 10N 74 10 E
Abomey 53 7 10N 2 5 E
Abong-Mbang 54 4 0N 13 8 E
Abonnema 53 4 41N 6 49 E
Abou-Deïa 51 11 20N 19 20 E
Aboyne 8 57 4N 2 48W
Abrantes 13 39 24N 8 7W
Abreojos, Pta. 74 26 50N 113 40W
Abri 51 20 50N 30 27 E
Abrolhos, Banka 79 18 0S 38 0W
Abrud 15 46 19N 23 5 E
Abruzzi □ 18 42 15N 14 0 E
Absaroka Ra. 72 44 40N 110 0W
Abū al Khaşīb 30 30 25N 48 0 E
Abū 'Alī 30 27 20N 49 27 E
Abu 'Arīsh 29 16 53N 42 48 E
Abu Dhabi = Abū Ẓāby 31 24 28N 54 22 E
Abū Dīs, Jordan 28 31 47N 35 16 E
Abū Dīs, Sudan 51 19 12N 33 38 E
Abū Ghaush 28 31 48N 35 6 E
Abu Hamed 51 19 32N 33 13 E
Abū Kamāl 30 34 30N 41 0 E
Abū Madd, Ra's 30 24 50N 37 7 E
Abu Matariq 51 10 59N 26 9 E
Abu Rudeis 30 28 54N 33 11 E
Abu Tig 51 27 4N 31 15 E
Abû Zabad 51 12 25N 29 10 E
Abū Ẓāby 31 24 28N 54 22 E
Abuja 53 9 16N 7 2 E
Abukuma-Gawa ~► 36 38 6N 140 52 E
Abunã 78 9 40S 65 20W
Abunã ~► 78 9 41S 65 20W
Abut Hd. 43 43 7S 170 15 E
Abwong 51 9 2N 32 14 E
Acámbaro 74 20 0N 100 40W
Acaponeta 74 22 30N 105 20W
Acapulco 74 16 51N 99 56W
Acarigua 78 9 33N 69 12W
Acatlán 74 18 10N 98 3W
Acayucan 74 17 59N 94 58W
Accomac 68 37 43N 75 40W
Accra 53 5 35N 0 6W
Accrington 6 53 46N 2 22W
Aceh □ 34 4 15N 97 30 E
Achalpur 32 21 22N 77 32 E
Achill 9 53 56N 9 55W
Achill Hd. 9 53 59N 10 15W
Achill I. 9 53 58N 10 5W
Achill Sound 9 53 53N 9 55W
Achinsk 25 56 20N 90 20 E
Ackerman 71 33 20N 89 8W
Acklins I. 75 22 30N 74 0W
Acme 64 51 33N 113 30W
Aconcagua, Cerro 80 32 39S 70 0W
Aconquija, Mt. 80 27 0S 66 0W
Açores, Is. dos = Azores 2 38 44N 29 0W
Acre = 'Akko 28 32 55N 35 4 E
Acre □ 78 9 1S 71 0W
Acre ~► 78 8 45S 67 22W
Ad Dahnā 30 24 30N 48 10 E
Ad Dammām 30 26 20N 50 5 E
Ad Dawhah 31 25 15N 51 35 E
Ad Dilam 30 23 55N 47 10 E
Ad Dīwānīyah 30 32 0N 45 0 E
Ada, Minn., U.S.A. 70 47 20N 96 30W
Ada, Okla., U.S.A. 71 34 50N 96 45W
Adaja ~► 13 41 32N 4 52W
Adam 31 22 15N 57 28 E
Adamaoua, Massif de l' 51 7 20N 12 20 E
Adamawa Highlands = Adamaoua, Massif de l' 51 7 20N 12 20 E
Adamello, Mt. 18 46 10N 10 34 E
Adaminaby 45 36 0S 148 45 E
Adams, N.Y., U.S.A. 68 43 50N 76 3W
Adams, Wis., U.S.A. 70 43 59N 89 50W
Adams, Mt. 72 46 10N 121 28W
Adam's Bridge 32 9 15N 79 40 E
Adams L. 64 51 10N 119 40W
Adam's Peak 32 6 48N 80 30 E
Adana 30 37 0N 35 16 E
Adapazarı 30 40 48N 30 25 E
Adarama 51 17 10N 34 52 E
Adaut 35 8 8S 131 7 E
Adavale 45 25 52S 144 32 E
Adda ~► 18 45 8N 9 53 E
Addis Ababa = Addis Abeba 51 9 2N 38 42 E
Addis Abeba 51 9 2N 38 42 E
Addis Alem 51 9 0N 38 17 E
Addo 56 33 32S 25 45 E
Adel 69 31 10N 83 28W
Adelaide, Australia 45 34 52S 138 30 E
Adelaide, S. Africa 57 32 42S 26 20 E
Adelaide Pen. 60 68 15N 97 30W
Adelaide River 46 13 15S 131 7 E
Adele, I. 46 15 32S 123 9 E
Aden = Al 'Adan 29 12 45N 45 0 E
Aden, G. of 29 12 30N 47 30 E
Adendorp 56 32 15S 24 30 E
Adi 35 4 15S 133 30 E
Adi Ugri 51 14 58N 38 48 E
Adieu, C. 47 32 0S 132 10 E
Adieu Pt. 46 15 14S 124 35 E
Adige ~► 18 45 9N 12 20 E
Adilabad 32 19 33N 78 20 E
Adin 72 41 10N 121 0W
Adin Khel 31 32 45N 68 5 E
Adirondack Mts. 68 44 0N 74 15W
Adlavik Is. 63 55 2N 57 45W
Admer 50 20 21N 5 27 E
Admiralty G. 46 14 20S 125 55 E
Admiralty I. 60 57 40N 134 35W
Admiralty Inlet 72 48 0N 122 40W
Admiralty Is. 40 2 0S 147 0 E
Ado 53 6 36N 2 56 E
Ado Ekiti 53 7 38N 5 12 E
Adonara 35 8 15S 123 5 E
Adoni 32 15 33N 77 18W
Adour ~► 12 43 32N 1 32W
Adra 13 36 43N 3 3W
Adrano 18 37 40N 14 49 E
Adrar 50 27 51N 0 11W
Adré 51 13 40N 22 20 E
Adrī 51 27 32N 13 2 E
Adrian, Mich., U.S.A. 68 41 55N 84 0W
Adrian, Tex., U.S.A. 71 35 19N 102 37W
Adriatic Sea 16 43 0N 16 0 E
Adua 35 1 45S 129 50 E
Adwa 51 14 15N 38 52 E
Adzhar A.S.S.R. □ 23 42 0N 42 0 E
Ægean Sea 17 37 0N 25 0 E
Æolian Is. = Eólie, Is. 18 38 30N 14 50 E
Aerht'ai Shan 37 46 40N 92 45 E
Afars & Issas, Terr. of = Djibouti ■ 29 12 0N 43 0 E
Afghanistan ■ 31 33 0N 65 0 E
Afgoi 29 2 7N 44 59 E
'Afif 30 23 53N 42 56 E
Afognak I. 60 58 10N 152 50W
Africa 48 10 0N 20 0 E
Afuá 79 0 15S 50 20W
Afula 28 32 37N 35 17 E
Afyonkarahisar 30 38 45N 30 33 E
Agadès = Agadez 53 16 58N 7 59 E
Agadez 53 16 58N 7 59 E
Agadir 50 30 28N 9 55W
Agano ~► 36 37 57N 139 8 E
Agapa 25 71 27N 89 15 E
Agartala 33 23 50N 91 23 E
Agassiz 64 49 14N 121 46W
Agats 35 5 33S 138 0 E
Agattu I. 60 52 25N 172 30 E
Agboville 50 5 55N 4 15W
Agde 12 43 19N 3 28 E
Agen 12 44 12N 0 38 E
Aghil Mts. 32 36 0N 77 0 E
Aginskoye 25 51 6N 114 32 E
Agra 32 27 17N 77 58 E
Agri ~► 18 40 13N 16 44 E
Ağri Daği 30 39 50N 44 15 E
Ağri Karakose 30 39 44N 43 3 E
Agrigento 18 37 19N 13 33 E
Agrinion 19 38 37N 21 27 E
Água Clara 79 20 25S 52 45W
Agua Prieta 74 31 20N 109 32W
Aguadas 78 5 40N 75 38W
Aguadilla 75 18 27N 67 10W
Aguanish 63 50 14N 62 2W
Aguanus ~► 63 50 13N 62 5W
Aguarico ~► 78 0 59S 75 11W
Aguas Blancas 80 24 15S 69 55W
Aguascalientes 74 21 53N 102 12W
Aguascalientes □ 74 22 0N 102 20W
Aguilas 13 37 23N 1 35W
Agulhas, C. 56 34 52S 20 0 E
Agung 34 8 20S 115 28 E
'Agur 28 31 42N 34 55 E
Agusan ~► 35 9 0N 125 30 E
Aha Mts. 56 19 45S 21 0 E
Ahaggar 50 23 0N 6 30 E
Ahar 30 38 35N 47 0 E
Ahipara B. 43 35 5S 173 5 E
Ahiri 32 19 30N 80 0 E
Ahmadabad 32 23 0N 72 40 E
Ahmadnagar 32 19 7N 74 46 E
Ahmadpur 32 29 12N 71 10 E
Ahmedabad = Ahmadabad 32 23 0N 72 40 E
Ahmednagar = Ahmadnagar 32 19 7N 74 46 E
Ahuachapán 75 13 54N 89 52W
Ahvāz 30 31 20N 48 40 E
Ahvenanmaa = Åland 21 60 15N 20 0 E
Aḥwar 29 13 30N 46 40 E
Aichi □ 36 35 0N 137 15 E
Aigues-Mortes 12 43 35N 4 12 E
Aihui 38 50 10N 127 30 E
Aija 78 9 50S 77 45W
Aiken 69 33 34N 81 50W
Aillik 63 55 11N 59 18W
Ailsa Craig 8 55 15N 5 7W
'Ailūn 28 32 18N 35 47 E
Aim 25 59 0N 133 55 E
Aimere 35 8 45S 121 3 E
Aimorés 79 19 30S 41 4W
Ain □ 12 46 5N 5 20 E
Ain Banaiyan 31 23 0N 51 0 E
Aïn Beïda 50 35 50N 7 29 E
Aïn Ben Tili 50 25 59N 9 27W
Aïn-Sefra 50 32 47N 0 37W
Ainabo 29 9 0N 46 25 E
Ainsworth 70 42 33N 99 52W
Aïr 50 18 30N 8 0 E
Airdrie 8 55 53N 3 57W
Aire ~► 6 53 42N 0 55W
Airlie Beach 44 20 16S 148 43 E
Aisne □ 12 49 42N 3 40 E
Aisne ~► 12 49 26N 2 50 E
Aitkin 70 46 32N 93 43W
Aiud 15 46 19N 23 44 E
Aix-en-Provence 12 43 32N 5 27 E
Aix-la-Chapelle = Aachen 14 50 47N 6 4 E
Aiyansh 64 55 17N 129 2W
Áíyina 19 37 45N 23 26 E
Aiyion 19 38 15N 22 5 E
Aizawl 33 23 40N 92 44 E
Aizuwakamatsu 36 37 30N 139 56 E
Ajaccio 12 41 55N 8 40 E
Ajanta Ra. 32 20 28N 75 50 E
Ajdâbiyah 51 30 54N 20 4 E
'Ajmān 31 25 25N 55 30 E
Ajmer 32 26 28N 74 37 E
Ajo 73 32 18N 112 54W
Ak Dağ 30 36 30N 30 0 E
Akaroa 43 43 49S 172 59 E
Akashi 36 34 45N 135 0 E
Akelamo 35 1 35N 129 40 E
Akershus fylke □ 21 60 0N 11 10 E
Aketi 54 2 38N 23 47 E
Akhelóös ~► 19 38 36N 21 14 E
Akhisar 30 38 56N 27 48 E
Akhmîm 51 26 31N 31 47 E
Akimiski I. 62 52 50N 81 30W
Akita 36 39 45N 140 7 E
Akita □ 36 39 40N 140 30 E
Akjoujt 50 19 45N 14 15W
'Akko 28 32 55N 35 4 E
Akkol 24 45 0N 75 39 E
Aklavik 60 68 12N 135 0W
Akobo ~► 51 7 48N 33 3 E
Akola 32 20 42N 77 2 E
Akordat 51 15 30N 37 40 E
Akosombo Dam 53 6 20N 0 5 E
Akpatok I. 61 60 25N 68 8W
Akranes 20 64 19N 21 58W
Akreïjit 50 18 19N 9 11W
Akron, Colo., U.S.A. 70 40 13N 103 15W
Akron, Ohio, U.S.A. 68 41 7N 81 31W
Aksai Chih 32 35 15N 79 55 E
Aksaray 30 38 25N 34 2 E
Aksarka 24 66 31N 67 50 E
Aksay 24 51 11N 53 0 E
Akşehir 30 38 18N 31 30 E
Aksenovo Zilovskoye 25 53 20N 117 40 E
Aksu 37 41 5N 80 10 E
Aksum 51 14 5N 38 40 E
Aktogay 24 46 57N 79 40 E
Aktyubinsk 23 50 17N 57 10 E
Aku 53 6 40N 7 18 E
Akure 53 7 15N 5 5 E
Akureyri 20 65 40N 18 6W
Akyab = Sittwe 33 20 18N 92 45 E
Al 'Adan 29 12 45N 45 0 E
Al Aḥsā 30 25 50N 49 0 E
Al Amādīyah 30 37 5N 43 30 E
Al Amārah 30 31 55N 47 15 E
Al 'Aqabah 28 29 31N 35 0 E
Al 'Aramah 30 25 30N 46 0 E
Al Ashkhara 31 21 50N 59 30 E
Al 'Ayzarīyah 28 31 47N 35 15 E
Al Badī' 30 22 0N 46 35 E
Al Başrah 30 30 30N 47 50 E
Al Bāzūrīyah 28 33 15N 35 16 E
Al Bīrah 28 31 55N 35 12 E
Al Bu'ayrāt 51 31 24N 15 44 E
Al Buqay'ah 28 32 15N 35 30 E
Al Fallūjah 30 33 20N 43 55 E
Al Fāw 30 30 0N 48 30 E
Al Fujayrah 31 25 7N 56 18 E
Al Hābah 30 27 10N 47 0 E
Al Haddār 30 21 58N 45 57 E
Al Ḥadīthah 30 34 0N 41 13 E
Al Hāmad 30 31 30N 39 30 E
Al Ḥamar 30 22 23N 46 6 E
Al Ḥamrā' 30 24 2N 38 55 E
Al Ḥarīq 30 23 29N 46 27 E
Al Harīr, W. ~► 28 32 44N 35 59 E
Al Ḥasakah 30 36 35N 40 45 E
Al Ḥawrah 29 13 50N 47 35 E
Al Ḥayy 30 32 5N 46 5 E
Al Ḥijāz 29 26 0N 37 30 E
Al Ḥillah, Iraq 30 32 30N 44 25 E
Al Ḥillah, Si. Arabia 30 23 35N 46 50 E
Al Hindīyah 30 32 30N 44 10 E
Al Ḥiṣnn 28 32 29N 35 52 E
Al Hoceïma 50 35 8N 3 58W
Al Ḥudaydah 29 14 50N 43 0 E
Al Hufūf 30 25 25N 49 45 E
Al Ḥulwah 30 23 24N 46 48 E
Al Irq 51 29 5N 21 35 E
Al Ittihad = Madīnat ash Sha'b 29 12 50N 45 0 E
Al Jāfūrah 30 25 0N 50 15 E
Al Jaghbūb 51 29 42N 24 38 E
Al Jahrah 30 29 25N 47 40 E
Al Jalāmīd 30 31 20N 39 45 E
Al Jawf, Libya 51 24 10N 23 24 E
Al Jawf, Si. Arabia 30 29 55N 39 40 E
Al Jazirah, Asia 30 33 30N 44 0 E
Al Jazirah, Libya 51 26 10N 21 20 E
Al Jubayl 30 27 0N 49 50 E
Al Jubaylah 30 24 55N 46 25 E
Al Junaynah 51 13 27N 22 45 E
Al Khābūra 31 23 57N 57 5 E
Al Khalīl 28 31 32N 35 6 E
Al Khalūf 29 20 30N 58 13 E
Al Kharfah 30 22 0N 46 35 E
Al Kharj 30 24 0N 47 0 E
Al Kufrah 51 24 17N 23 15 E
Al Kūt 30 32 30N 46 0 E
Al Kuwayt 30 29 30N 48 0 E
Al Lādhiqīyah 30 35 30N 35 45 E
Al Lubban 28 32 9N 35 14 E
Al Luḥayyah 29 15 45N 42 40 E
Al Madīnah 29 24 35N 39 52 E
Al-Mafraq 28 32 17N 36 14 E
Al Majma'ah 30 25 57N 45 22 E
Al Manāmah 31 26 10N 50 30 E
Al Marj 51 32 25N 20 30 E
Al Mawşil 30 36 15N 43 5 E
Al Mazra 28 31 16N 35 31 E
Al Midhnab 30 25 50N 44 18 E
Al Miqdādīyah 30 34 0N 45 0 E
Al Mish'āb 30 28 12N 48 36 E
Al Mubarraz 30 25 30N 49 40 E
Al Muḥarraq 31 26 15N 50 40 E
Al Mukallā 29 14 33N 49 2 E
Al Mukhā 29 13 18N 43 15 E
Al Musayyib 30 32 40N 44 25 E
Al Muwayliḥ 30 27 40N 35 30 E
Al Owuho = Otukpa 53 7 9N 7 41 E
Al Qadīmah 30 22 20N 39 13 E
Al Qā'iyah 30 24 33N 43 15 E
Al Qāmishli 30 37 10N 41 10 E
Al Qaşabát 51 32 39N 14 1 E
Al Qaşīm 30 26 0N 43 0 E
Al Qaţīf 30 26 35N 50 0 E
Al Qaţrūn 51 24 56N 15 3 E
Al Quaisūmah 30 28 10N 46 20 E
Al Quds = Jerusalem 28 31 47N 35 10 E
Al Qurayyāt 31 23 17N 58 53 E
Al Qurnah 30 31 1N 47 25 E
Al 'Ulā 30 26 35N 38 0 E
Al Uqaylah ash Sharqīgah 51 30 12N 19 10 E
Al Uqayr 30 25 40N 50 15 E
Al 'Uthmānīyah 30 25 5N 49 22 E
Al 'Uwaynid 30 24 50N 46 0 E
Al' 'Uwayqīlah 30 30 30N 42 10 E
Al 'Uyūn 30 26 30N 43 50 E
Al Wakrah 31 25 10N 51 40 E
Al Wari'āh 30 27 51N 47 25 E
Al Yamāmah 30 24 5N 47 30 E
Al Yāmūn 28 32 29N 35 14 E
Alabama □ 69 33 0N 87 0W
Alabama ~► 69 31 8N 87 57W
Alagoa Grande 79 7 3S 35 35W
Alagoas □ 79 9 0S 36 0W
Alagoinhas 79 12 7S 38 20W
Alajuela 75 10 2N 84 8W
Alakamisy 57 21 19S 47 14 E
Alakurtti 22 67 0N 30 30 E
Alameda 73 35 10N 106 43W
Alamo 73 36 21N 115 10W
Alamogordo 73 32 59N 106 0W
Alamos 74 27 0N 109 0W
Alamosa 73 37 30N 106 0W
Åland 21 60 15N 20 0 E
Ålands hav 21 60 0N 19 30 E
Alandur 32 13 0N 80 15 E
Alanya 30 36 38N 32 0 E
Alaotra, Farihin' 57 17 30S 48 30 E
Alapayevsk 24 57 52N 61 42 E
Alaşehir 23 38 23N 28 30 E
Alaska □ 60 65 0N 150 0W
Alaska, G. of 60 58 0N 145 0W
Alaska Highway 64 60 0N 130 0W
Alaska Pen. 60 56 0N 160 0W
Alaska Range 60 62 50N 151 0W
Alataw Shankou 37 45 5N 81 57 E
Alatyr 22 54 45N 46 35 E
Alausi 78 2 0S 78 50W
Alava, C. 72 48 10N 124 40W
Alawoona 45 34 45S 140 30 E
Alba 18 44 41N 8 1 E
Alba Iulia 15 46 8N 23 39 E
Albacete 13 39 0N 1 50W
Albacutya, L. 45 35 45S 141 58 E
Albania ■ 19 41 0N 20 0 E
Albany, Australia 47 35 1S 117 58 E
Albany, Ga., U.S.A. 69 31 40N 84 10W
Albany, Minn., U.S.A. 70 45 37N 94 38W
Albany, N.Y., U.S.A. 68 42 35N 73 47W
Albany, Oreg., U.S.A. 72 44 41N 123 0W
Albany, Tex., U.S.A. 71 32 45N 99 20W
Albany ~► 62 52 17N 81 31W
Albardón 80 31 20S 68 30W
Albarracín, Sierra de 13 40 30N 1 30W
Albatross B. 44 12 45S 141 30 E
Albemarle 69 35 27N 80 15W
Albemarle Sd. 69 36 0N 76 30W
Alberche ~► 13 39 58N 4 46W

Angellala

Albert, L. = Mobutu Sese Seko, L. **54** 1 30N 31 0 E
Albert, L. **45** 35 30S 139 10 E
Albert Canyon **64** 51 8N 117 41W
Albert Edward Ra. **46** 18 17S 127 57 E
Albert Lea **70** 43 32N 93 20W
Albert Nile → **54** 3 36N 32 2 E
Alberta □ **64** 54 40N 115 0W
Albertinia **56** 34 11S 21 34 E
Alberton **63** 46 50N 64 0W
Albertville = Kalemie **54** 5 55S 29 9 E
Albi **12** 43 56N 2 9 E
Albia **70** 41 0N 92 50W
Albina **79** 5 37N 54 15W
Albina, Ponta **56** 15 52S 11 44 E
Albion, Idaho, U.S.A. **72** 42 21N 113 37W
Albion, Mich., U.S.A. **68** 42 15N 84 45W
Albion, Nebr., U.S.A. **70** 41 47N 98 0W
Ålborg **21** 57 2N 9 54 E
Alborz, Reshteh-ye Kūhhā-ye **31** 36 0N 52 0 E
Albreda **64** 52 35N 119 10W
Albuquerque **73** 35 5N 106 47W
Albuquerque, Cayos de **75** 12 10N 81 50W
Alburquerque **13** 39 15N 6 59W
Albury **45** 36 3S 146 56 E
Alcalá de Henares **13** 40 28N 3 22W
Alcalá la Real **13** 37 27N 3 57W
Alcamo **18** 37 59N 12 55 E
Alcaníz **13** 41 2N 0 8W
Alcântara, Brazil **79** 2 20S 44 30W
Alcántara, Spain **13** 39 41N 6 57W
Alcantara L. **65** 60 57N 108 9W
Alcaraz, Sierra de **13** 38 40N 2 20W
Alcaudete **13** 37 35N 4 5W
Alcázar de San Juan **13** 39 24N 3 12W
Alcira **13** 39 9N 0 30W
Alcoa **69** 35 50N 84 0W
Alcobaça **13** 39 32N 9 0W
Alcova **72** 42 37N 106 52W
Alcoy **13** 38 43N 0 30W
Aldabra Is. **3** 9 22S 46 28 E
Aldan **25** 58 40N 125 30 E
Aldan → **25** 63 28N 129 35 E
Aldeburgh **7** 52 9N 1 35 E
Alder **72** 45 27N 112 3W
Alderney **7** 49 42N 2 12W
Aldershot **7** 51 15N 0 43W
Aledo **70** 41 10N 90 50W
Aleg **50** 17 3N 13 55W
Alegrete **80** 29 40S 56 0W
Aleisk **24** 52 40N 83 0 E
Alejandro Selkirk, I. **41** 33 50S 80 15W
Aleksandrovsk-Sakhalinskiy **25** 50 50N 142 20 E
Aleksandrovskiy Zavod **25** 50 40N 117 50 E
Aleksandrovskoye **24** 60 35N 77 50 E
Alemania **80** 25 40S 65 30W
Alençon **12** 48 27N 0 4 E
Alenuihaha Chan. **66** 20 25N 156 0W
Aleppo = Ḥalab **30** 36 10N 37 15 E
Aléria **18** 42 5N 9 26 E
Alert Bay **64** 50 30N 126 55W
Alès **12** 44 9N 4 5 E
Alessándria **18** 44 54N 8 37 E
Ålesund **20** 62 28N 6 12 E
Aleutian Is. **60** 52 0N 175 0W
Aleutian Trench **40** 48 0N 180 0 E
Alexander **70** 47 51N 103 40W
Alexander, Mt. **47** 28 58S 120 16 E
Alexander Arch. **60** 57 0N 135 0W
Alexander B. **56** 28 36S 16 33 E
Alexander Bay **56** 28 40S 16 30 E
Alexander City **69** 32 58N 85 57W
Alexandra, Australia **45** 37 8S 145 40 E
Alexandra, N.Z. **43** 45 14S 169 25 E
Alexandra Falls **64** 60 29N 116 18W
Alexandretta = İskenderun **30** 36 32N 36 10 E
Alexandria = El Iskandarîya **51** 31 0N 30 0 E
Alexandria, Australia **44** 19 5S 136 40 E
Alexandria, B.C., Canada **64** 52 35N 122 27W
Alexandria, Ont., Canada **62** 45 19N 74 38W
Alexandria, S. Africa **56** 33 38S 26 28 E
Alexandria, Ind., U.S.A. **68** 40 18N 85 40W
Alexandria, La., U.S.A. **71** 31 20N 92 30W
Alexandria, Minn., U.S.A. **70** 45 50N 95 20W
Alexandria, S. Dak., U.S.A. **70** 43 40N 97 45W
Alexandria, Va., U.S.A. **68** 38 47N 77 1W
Alexandria Bay **68** 44 20N 75 52W
Alexandrina, L. **45** 35 25S 139 10 E
Alexandroúpolis **19** 40 50N 25 54 E
Alexis → **63** 52 33N 56 8W
Alexis Creek **64** 52 10N 123 20W
Alford **8** 57 13N 2 42W
Alfreton **6** 53 6N 1 22W
Alga **23** 49 53N 57 20 E
Algarve **13** 36 58N 8 20W
Algeciras **13** 36 9N 5 28W
Algemesí **13** 39 11N 0 27W
Alger **50** 36 42N 3 8 E
Algeria ■ **50** 28 30N 2 0 E
Alghero **18** 40 34N 8 20 E
Algiers = Alger **50** 36 42N 3 8 E
Algoa B. **56** 33 50S 25 45 E
Algoma **68** 44 35N 87 27W
Algona **70** 43 4N 94 14W
Alhama de Murcia **13** 37 51N 1 25W
Alhambra **73** 34 2N 118 10W
Alhucemas = Al Hoceïma **50** 35 8N 3 58W
'Alī al Gharbī **30** 32 30N 46 45 E
'Alī Khēl **32** 33 57N 69 43 E
Aliákmon → **19** 40 30N 22 36 E
Alibo **51** 9 52N 37 5 E
Alicante **13** 38 23N 0 30W
Alice, S. Africa **56** 32 48S 26 55 E
Alice, U.S.A. **71** 27 47N 98 1W
Alice →, Queens., Australia **44** 24 2S 144 50 E
Alice →, Queens., Australia **44** 15 35S 142 20 E
Alice Arm **64** 55 29N 129 31W
Alice Downs **46** 17 45S 127 56 E
Alice Springs **44** 23 40S 133 50 E
Alicedale **56** 33 15S 26 4 E
Aliceville **69** 33 9N 88 10W
Alick Cr. → **44** 20 55S 142 20 E
Alida **65** 49 25N 101 55W
Aligarh, Ut. P., India **32** 27 55N 78 10 E
Aligarh, India **32** 27 55N 78 10 E
Alīgūdarz **30** 33 25N 49 45 E
Alingsås **21** 57 56N 12 31 E
Alipur **32** 29 25N 70 55 E
Alipur Duar **33** 26 30N 89 35 E
Aliquippa **68** 40 38N 80 18W
Aliwal North **56** 30 45S 26 45 E
Alix **64** 52 24N 113 11W
Aljustrel **13** 37 55N 8 10W
Alkmaar **11** 52 37N 4 45 E
All American Canal **73** 32 45N 115 0W
Allahabad **33** 25 25N 81 58 E
Allakh-Yun **25** 60 50N 137 5 E
Allan **65** 51 53N 106 4W
Allanmyo **33** 19 30N 95 17 E
Allanridge **56** 27 45S 26 40 E
Allanwater **62** 50 14N 90 10W
Allegan **68** 42 32N 85 52W
Allegheny → **68** 40 27N 80 0W
Allegheny Mts. **68** 38 0N 80 0W
Allen, Bog of **9** 53 15N 7 0W
Allen, L. **9** 54 12N 8 5W
Allenby Br. = Jisr al Ḥusayn **28** 31 53N 35 33 E
Allende **74** 28 20N 100 50W
Allentown **68** 40 36N 75 30W
Alleppey **32** 9 30N 76 28 E
Alliance, Nebr., U.S.A. **70** 42 10N 102 50W
Alliance, Ohio, U.S.A. **68** 40 53N 81 7W
Allier □ **12** 46 25N 3 0 E
Allier → **12** 46 57N 3 4 E
Alliston **62** 44 9N 79 52W
Alloa **8** 56 7N 3 49W
Allora **45** 28 2S 152 0 E
Alma, Canada **63** 48 35N 71 40W
Alma, Ga., U.S.A. **69** 31 33N 82 28W
Alma, Kans., U.S.A. **70** 39 1N 96 22W
Alma, Mich., U.S.A. **68** 43 25N 84 40W
Alma, Nebr., U.S.A. **70** 40 10N 99 25W
Alma, Wis., U.S.A. **70** 44 19N 91 54W
'Almā ash Sha'b **28** 33 7N 35 9 E
Alma Ata **24** 43 15N 76 57 E
Almada **13** 38 40N 9 9W
Almaden, Australia **44** 17 22S 144 40 E
Almadén, Spain **13** 38 49N 4 52W
Almanor, L. **72** 40 15N 121 11W
Almansa **13** 38 51N 1 5W
Almanzor, Pico de **13** 40 15N 5 18W
Almanzora → **13** 37 14N 1 46W
Almazán **13** 41 30N 2 30W
Almeirim **79** 1 30S 52 34W
Almelo **11** 52 22N 6 42 E
Almendralejo **13** 38 41N 6 26W
Almería **13** 36 52N 2 27W
Almirante **75** 9 10N 82 30W
Almora **32** 29 38N 79 40 E
Alnwick **6** 55 25N 1 42W
Alon **33** 22 12N 95 5 E
Alor **35** 8 15S 124 30 E
Alor Setar **34** 6 7N 100 22 E
Aloysius Mt. **47** 26 0S 128 38 E
Alpena **68** 45 6N 83 24W
Alpes-de-Haute-Provence □ **12** 44 8N 6 10 E
Alpes-Maritimes □ **12** 43 55N 7 10 E
Alpha **44** 23 39S 146 37 E
Alphonse **3** 7 0S 52 45 E
Alpine, Ariz., U.S.A. **73** 33 57N 109 4W
Alpine, Tex., U.S.A. **71** 30 25N 103 35W
Alps **14** 47 0N 8 0 E
Alroy Downs **44** 19 20S 136 5 E
Alsace **12** 48 15N 7 25 E
Alsask **65** 51 21N 109 59W
Alsásua **13** 42 54N 2 10W
Alsten **20** 65 58N 12 40 E
Alta **20** 69 57N 23 10 E
Alta Gracia **80** 31 40S 64 30W
Alta Lake **64** 50 10N 123 0W
Altaelva → **20** 69 46N 23 45 E
Altafjorden **20** 70 5N 23 5 E
Altagracia **78** 10 45N 71 30W
Altai = Aerht'ai Shan **37** 46 40N 92 45 E
Altai Mts. **26** 46 40N 92 45 E
Altamaha → **69** 31 19N 81 17W
Altamira **79** 3 12S 52 10W
Altanbulag **37** 50 16N 106 30 E
Altar **74** 30 40N 111 50W
Altata **74** 24 30N 108 0W
Altavista **68** 37 9N 79 22W
Altay **37** 47 48N 88 10 E
Alto Adige = Trentino-Alto Adige □ **18** 46 30N 11 0 E
Alto-Alentejo **13** 39 0N 7 40W
Alto Araguaia **79** 17 15S 53 20W
Alto Cuchumatanes = Cuchumatanes, Sierra de los **75** 15 35N 91 25W
Alto Molocue **55** 15 50S 37 35 E
Alton **70** 38 55N 90 5W
Alton Downs **45** 26 7S 138 57 E
Altona **14** 53 32N 9 56 E
Altoona **68** 40 32N 78 24W
Altun Shan **37** 38 30N 88 0 E
Alturas **72** 41 36N 120 37W
Altus **71** 34 30N 99 25W
Alùla **29** 11 50N 50 45 E
Alusi **35** 7 35S 131 40 E
Alva **71** 36 50N 98 50W
Alvarado, Mexico **74** 18 40N 95 50W
Alvarado, U.S.A. **71** 32 25N 97 15W
Alvaro Obregón, Presa **74** 27 55N 109 52W
Alvear **80** 29 5S 56 30W
Alvesta **21** 56 54N 14 35 E
Alvie **45** 38 14S 143 30 E
Alvin **71** 29 23N 95 12W
Älvkarleby **21** 60 34N 17 26 E
Älvsborgs län □ **21** 58 30N 12 30 E
Älvsbyn **20** 65 40N 21 0 E
Alwar **32** 27 38N 76 34 E
Alxa Zuoqi **38** 38 50N 105 40 E
Alyaskitovyy **25** 64 45N 141 30 E
Alyata **23** 39 58N 49 25 E
Alyth **8** 56 38N 3 15W
Alzada **70** 45 3N 104 22W
Am Dam **51** 12 40N 20 35 E
Am-Timan **51** 11 0N 20 10 E
Amadeus, L. **47** 24 54S 131 0 E
Amâdi, Sudan **51** 5 29N 30 25 E
Amadi, Zaïre **54** 3 40N 26 40 E
Amadjuak **61** 64 0N 72 39W
Amadjuak L. **61** 65 0N 71 8W
Amagasaki **36** 34 42N 135 20 E
Amakusa-Shotō **36** 32 15N 130 10 E
Amalner **32** 21 5N 75 5 E
Amambay, Cordillera de **80** 23 0S 55 45W
Amangeldy **24** 50 10N 65 10 E
Amapá **79** 2 5N 50 50W
Amapá □ **79** 1 40N 52 0W
Amarante **79** 6 14S 42 50W
Amaranth **65** 50 36N 98 43W
Amargosa **79** 13 2S 39 36W
Amarillo **71** 35 14N 101 46W
Amaro, Mt. **18** 42 5N 14 6 E
Amasra **30** 41 45N 32 30 E
Amassama **53** 5 1N 6 2 E
Amasya **30** 40 40N 35 50 E
Amatikulu **57** 29 3S 31 33 E
Amatitlán **75** 14 29N 90 38W
Amazon = Amazonas → **79** 0 5S 50 0W
Amazonas □ **78** 4 0S 62 0W
Amazonas → **79** 0 5S 50 0W
Ambahakily **57** 21 36S 43 41 E
Ambala **32** 30 23N 76 56 E
Ambalavao **57** 21 50S 46 56 E
Ambalindum **44** 23 23S 135 0 E
Ambam **54** 2 20N 11 15 E
Ambanja **57** 13 40S 48 27 E
Ambarchik **25** 69 40N 162 20 E
Ambarijeby **57** 14 56S 47 41 E
Ambaro, Helodranon' **57** 13 23S 48 38 E
Ambartsevo **24** 57 30N 83 52 E
Ambato **78** 1 5S 78 42W
Ambato Boeny **57** 16 28S 46 43 E
Ambatofinandrahana **57** 20 33S 46 48 E
Ambatolampy **57** 19 20S 47 35 E
Ambatondrazaka **57** 17 55S 48 28 E
Ambatosoratra **57** 17 37S 48 31 E
Ambenja **57** 15 17S 46 58 E
Amberg **14** 49 25N 11 52 E
Ambergris Cay **74** 18 0N 88 0W
Amberley **43** 43 9S 172 44 E
Ambikapur **33** 23 15N 83 15 E
Ambilobé **57** 13 10S 49 3 E
Ambinanindrano **57** 20 5S 48 23 E
Ambleside **6** 54 26N 2 58W
Ambo **78** 10 5S 76 10W
Ambodifototra **57** 16 59S 49 52 E
Ambodilazana **57** 18 6S 49 10 E
Ambohimahasoa **57** 21 7S 47 13 E
Ambohimanga **57** 20 52S 47 36 E
Ambohitra **57** 12 30S 49 10 E
Ambon **35** 3 35S 128 20 E
Ambositra **57** 20 31S 47 25 E
Ambovombé **57** 25 11S 46 5 E
Amboy **73** 34 33N 115 51W
Amboyna I. **34** 7 50N 112 50 E
Ambriz **54** 7 48S 13 8 E
Amby **45** 26 30S 148 11 E
Amchitka I. **60** 51 30N 179 0W
Amderma **24** 69 45N 61 30 E
Ameca **74** 20 30N 104 0W
Ameca → **74** 20 40N 105 15W
Amecameca **74** 19 7N 98 46W
Ameland **11** 53 27N 5 45 E
Amen **25** 68 45N 180 0 E
American Falls **72** 42 46N 112 56W
American Falls Res. **72** 43 0N 112 50W
American Samoa ■ **43** 14 20S 170 40W
Americus **69** 32 0N 84 10W
Amersfoort, Neth. **11** 52 9N 5 23 E
Amersfoort, S. Africa **57** 26 59S 29 53 E
Amery, Australia **47** 31 9S 117 5 E
Amery, Canada **65** 56 34N 94 3W
Ames **70** 42 0N 93 40W
Amga **25** 60 50N 132 0 E
Amga → **25** 62 38N 134 32 E
Amgu **25** 45 45N 137 15 E
Amgun → **25** 52 56N 139 38 E
Amherst, Burma **33** 16 2N 97 20 E
Amherst, Canada **63** 45 48N 64 8W
Amherst, U.S.A. **71** 34 0N 102 24W
Amherstburg **62** 42 6N 83 6W
Amiata, Mte. **18** 42 54N 11 40 E
Amiens **12** 49 54N 2 16 E
Amirante Is. **3** 6 0S 53 0 E
Amisk L. **65** 54 35N 102 15W
Amite **71** 30 47N 90 31W
Amlwch **6** 53 24N 4 21W
'Ammān **28** 31 57N 35 52 E
Ammanford **7** 51 48N 4 0W
Ammi'ad **28** 32 55N 35 32 E
Amorgós **19** 36 50N 25 57 E
Amory **69** 33 59N 88 29W
Amos **62** 48 35N 78 5W
Amoy = Xiamen **38** 24 25N 118 4 E
Ampanihy **57** 24 40S 44 45 E
Ampasindava, Helodranon' **57** 13 40S 48 15 E
Ampasindava, Saikanosy **57** 13 42S 47 55 E
Ampenan **34** 8 35S 116 13 E
Ampotaka **57** 25 3S 44 41 E
Ampoza **57** 22 20S 44 44 E
Amqa **28** 32 59N 35 10 E
Amqui **63** 48 28N 67 27W
Amravati **32** 20 55N 77 45 E
Amreli **32** 21 35N 71 17 E
Amritsar **32** 31 35N 74 57 E
Amroha **32** 28 53N 78 30 E
Amsterdam, Neth. **11** 52 23N 4 54 E
Amsterdam, U.S.A. **68** 42 58N 74 10W
Amsterdam, I. **3** 38 30S 77 30 E
Amudarya → **24** 43 40N 59 0 E
Amundsen Gulf **60** 71 0N 124 0W
Amuntai **34** 2 28S 115 25 E
Amur → **25** 52 56N 141 10 E
Amurang **35** 1 5N 124 40 E
Amuri Pass **43** 42 31S 172 11 E
Amursk **25** 50 14N 136 54 E
Amurzet **25** 47 50N 131 5 E
An Nafūd **30** 28 15N 41 0 E
An Najaf **30** 32 3N 44 15 E
An Nāqūrah **28** 33 7N 35 8 E
An Nāṣirīyah **30** 31 0N 46 15 E
An Nhon **34** 13 55N 109 7 E
An Nîl □ **51** 19 30N 33 0 E
An Nîl el Abyad □ **51** 14 0N 32 15 E
An Nîl el Azraq □ **51** 12 30N 34 30 E
An Nu'ayrīyah **30** 27 30N 48 30 E
An Uaimh **9** 53 39N 6 40W
Anabar → **25** 73 8N 113 36 E
'Anabtā **28** 32 19N 35 7 E
Anaconda **72** 46 7N 113 0W
Anacortes **72** 48 30N 122 40W
Anadarko **71** 35 4N 98 15W
Anadolu **30** 38 0N 30 0 E
Anadyr **25** 64 35N 177 20 E
Anadyr → **25** 64 55N 176 5 E
Anadyrskiy Zaliv **25** 64 0N 180 0 E
'Ānah **30** 34 25N 42 0 E
Anaheim **73** 33 50N 118 0W
Anahim Lake **64** 52 28N 125 18W
Anáhuac **74** 27 14N 100 9W
Anakapalle **33** 17 42N 83 6 E
Anakie **44** 23 32S 147 45 E
Analalava **57** 14 35S 48 0 E
Anambas, Kepulauan **34** 3 20N 106 30 E
Anamoose **70** 47 55N 100 20W
Anamosa **70** 42 7N 91 30W
Anamur **30** 36 8N 32 58 E
Anan **36** 33 54N 134 40 E
Anantnag **32** 33 45N 75 10 E
Anápolis **79** 16 15S 48 50W
Anār **31** 30 55N 55 13 E
Anārak **31** 33 25N 53 40 E
Anatolia = Anadolu **30** 38 0N 30 0 E
Anatone **72** 46 9N 117 4W
Anatsogno **57** 23 33S 43 46 E
Añatuya **80** 28 20S 62 50W
Anaunethad L. **65** 60 55N 104 25W
Anaye **51** 19 15N 12 50 E
Anchorage **60** 61 10N 149 50W
Ancohuma, Nevada **78** 16 0S 68 50W
Ancón **78** 11 50S 77 10W
Ancona **18** 43 37N 13 30 E
Ancud **80** 42 0S 73 50W
Ancud, G. de **80** 42 0S 73 0W
Anda **38** 46 24N 125 19 E
Andado **44** 25 25S 135 15 E
Andalgalá **80** 27 40S 66 30W
Åndalsnes **20** 62 35N 7 43 E
Andalucía □ **13** 37 35N 5 0W
Andalusia **69** 31 19N 86 30W
Andalusia □ = Andalucía □ **13** 37 35N 5 0W
Andaman Is. **3** 12 30N 92 30 E
Andaman Sea **34** 13 0N 96 0 E
Andara **56** 18 2S 21 9 E
Andenne **11** 50 30N 5 5 E
Anderson, Calif., U.S.A. **72** 40 30N 122 19W
Anderson, Ind., U.S.A. **68** 40 5N 85 40W
Anderson, Mo., U.S.A. **71** 36 43N 94 29W
Anderson, S.C., U.S.A. **69** 34 32N 82 40W
Anderson → **60** 69 42N 129 0W
Anderson, Mt. **57** 25 5S 30 42 E
Andes **78** 5 40N 75 53W
Andes, Cord. de los **78** 20 0S 68 0W
Andfjorden **20** 69 10N 16 20 E
Andhra Pradesh □ **32** 16 0N 79 0 E
Andikíthira **19** 35 52N 23 15 E
Andizhan **24** 41 10N 72 0 E
Andkhvoy **31** 36 52N 65 8 E
Andoany **57** 13 25S 48 16 E
Andong **38** 36 40N 128 43 E
Andorra ■ **13** 42 30N 1 30 E
Andorra La Vella **13** 42 31N 1 32 E
Andover **7** 51 13N 1 29W
Andrahary, Mt. **57** 13 37S 49 17 E
Andramasina **57** 19 11S 47 35 E
Andranopasy **57** 21 17S 43 44 E
Andreanof Is. **60** 52 0N 178 0W
Andrewilla **45** 26 31S 139 17 E
Andrews, S.C., U.S.A. **69** 33 29N 79 30W
Andrews, Tex., U.S.A. **71** 32 18N 102 33W
Ándria **18** 41 13N 16 17 E
Andriba **57** 17 30S 46 58 E
Androka **57** 24 58S 44 2 E
Andropov **22** 58 5N 38 50 E
Ándros **19** 37 50N 24 57 E
Andros I. **75** 24 30N 78 0W
Andros Town **75** 24 43N 77 47W
Andújar **13** 38 3N 4 5W
Andulo **54** 11 25S 16 45 E
Anegada I. **75** 18 45N 64 20W
Anegada Passage **75** 18 15N 63 45W
Anécho **53** 6 12N 1 34 E
Aneto, Pico de **13** 42 37N 0 40 E
Angamos, Punta **80** 23 1S 70 32W
Ang'angxi **38** 47 10N 123 48 E
Angara → **25** 58 30N 97 0 E
Angarsk **25** 52 30N 104 0 E
Angas Downs **47** 25 2S 132 14 E
Angas Hills **46** 23 0S 127 50 E
Angaston **45** 34 30S 139 8 E
Ånge **20** 62 31N 15 35 E
Ángel de la Guarda, I. **74** 29 30N 113 30W
Angeles **35** 15 9N 120 33 E
Ängelholm **21** 56 15N 12 58 E
Angellala **45** 26 24S 146 54 E

Angels Camp

Angels Camp 73 38 8N 120 30W
Ångermanälven → 20 62 40N 18 0 E
Angers 12 47 30N 0 35W
Ångesån → 20 66 50N 22 15 E
Angikuni L. 65 62 0N 100 0W
Anglesey 6 53 17N 4 20W
Angleton 71 29 12N 95 23W
Ango 54 4 10N 26 5 E
Angola 68 41 40N 85 0W
Angola ■ 55 12 0S 18 0 E
Angoon 64 57 40N 134 40W
Angoulême 12 45 39N 0 10 E
Angoumois 12 45 50N 0 25 E
Angra dos Reis 80 23 0S 44 10W
Angren 24 41 1N 70 12 E
Anguilla 75 18 14N 63 5W
Angurugu 44 14 0S 136 25 E
Angus, Braes of 8 56 51N 3 10W
Anholt 21 56 42N 11 33 E
Anhua 39 28 23N 111 12 E
Anhui □ 39 32 0N 117 0 E
Anhwei □ =
Anhui □ 39 32 0N 117 0 E
Anichab 56 21 0S 14 46 E
Animas 73 31 58N 108 58W
Anivorano 57 18 44S 48 58 E
Anjidiv I. 32 14 40N 74 10 E
Anjou 12 47 20N 0 15W
Anjozorobe 57 18 22S 47 52 E
Anju 38 39 36N 125 40 E
Anka 53 12 13N 5 58 E
Ankaboa, Tanjona 57 21 58S 43 20 E
Ankang 39 32 40N 109 1 E
Ankara 30 40 0N 32 54 E
Ankaramena 57 21 57S 46 39 E
Ankazoabo 57 22 18S 44 31 E
Ankazobe 57 18 20S 47 10 E
Ankisabe 57 19 17S 46 29 E
Ankoro 54 6 45S 26 55 E
Anlu 39 31 15N 113 45 E
Ann, C. 68 42 39N 70 37W
Ann Arbor 68 42 17N 83 45W
Anna 71 37 28N 89 10W
Anna Plains 46 19 17S 121 37 E
Annaba 50 36 50N 7 46 E
Annalee → 9 54 3N 7 15W
Annam = Trung-
Phan 34 16 0N 108 0 E
Annan 8 55 0N 3 17W
Annan → 8 54 58N 3 18W
Annapolis 68 39 0N 76 30W
Annapolis Royal 63 44 44N 65 32W
Annean, L. 47 26 54S 118 14 E
Annecy 12 45 55N 6 8 E
Anning 37 24 55N 102 26 E
Anningie 46 21 50S 133 7 E
Anniston 69 33 45N 85 50W
Annobón 48 1 25S 5 36 E
Annonciation, L' 62 46 25N 74 55W
Annotto Bay 75 18 17N 77 3W
Annuello 45 34 53S 142 55 E
Anoka 70 45 10N 93 26W
Anorotsangana 57 13 56S 47 55 E
Anqing 39 30 30N 117 3 E
Anren 39 26 43N 113 18 E
Ansāb 30 29 11N 44 43 E
Ansai 38 36 50N 109 20 E
Ansbach 14 49 17N 10 34 E
Anse, L' 62 46 47N 88 28W
Anse au Loup, L' 63 51 32N 56 50W
Anshan 38 41 5N 122 58 E
Anshun 39 26 18N 105 57 E
Ansirabe 57 19 55S 47 2 E
Ansley 70 41 19N 99 24W
Anson 71 32 46N 99 54W
Anson B. 46 13 20S 130 6 E
Ansongo 53 15 25N 0 35 E
Anstruther 8 56 14N 2 40W
Ansudu 35 2 11S 139 22 E
Antabamba 78 14 40S 73 0W
Antakya 30 36 14N 36 10 E
Antalaha 57 14 57S 50 20 E
Antalya 30 36 52N 30 45 E
Antalya Körfezi 30 36 15N 31 30 E
Antananarivo 57 18 55S 47 31 E
Antananarivo □ 57 19 0S 47 0 E
Antanimbaribe 57 21 30S 44 48 E
Antequera 13 37 5N 4 33W
Antero Mt. 73 38 45N 106 15W
Anthony, Kans.,
U.S.A. 71 37 8N 98 2W
Anthony, N. Mex.,
U.S.A. 73 32 1N 106 37W
Anthony Lagoon 44 18 0S 135 30 E
Anti Atlas 50 30 0N 8 30W
Anticosti, I. d' 63 49 30N 63 0W
Antigo 70 45 8N 89 5W
Antigonish 63 45 38N 61 58W
Antigua, Guat. 75 14 34N 90 41W
Antigua, W. Indies 75 17 0N 61 50W
Antigua &
Barbuda ■ 75 17 20N 61 48W
Antilla 75 20 40N 75 50W
Antimony 73 38 7N 112 0W
Antioch 72 38 0N 121 45W
Antioquia 78 6 40N 75 55W
Antipodes Is. 40 49 45S 178 40 E
Antler 70 48 58N 101 18W
Antler → 65 49 8N 101 0W
Antlers 71 34 15N 95 35W
Antofagasta 80 23 50S 70 30W
Antofagasta de la
Sierra 80 26 5S 67 20W
Anton 71 33 49N 102 5W
Anton Chico 73 35 12N 105 5W
Antongila,
Helodrano 57 15 30S 49 50 E
Antonibé 57 15 7S 47 24 E
Antonibé, Presqu'île
d' 57 14 55S 47 20 E
Antonina 80 25 26S 48 42W
Antonito 73 37 4N 106 1W
Antrim 9 54 43N 6 13W
Antrim □ 9 54 55N 6 20W
Antrim, Mts. of 9 54 57N 6 8W
Antrim Plateau 46 18 8S 128 20 E
Antsalova 57 18 40S 44 37 E
Antsiranana 57 12 25S 49 20 E
Antsohihy 57 14 50S 47 59 E
Antsohimbondrona
Seranana 57 13 7S 48 48 E
Antwerp =
Antwerpen 11 51 13N 4 25 E
Antwerpen 11 51 13N 4 25 E
Antwerpen □ 11 51 15N 4 40 E
Anupgarh 32 29 10N 73 10 E
Anuradhapura 32 8 22N 80 28 E
Anvers = Antwerpen 11 51 13N 4 25 E
Anvik 60 62 37N 160 20W
Anxi, Fujian, China 39 25 2N 118 12 E
Anxi, Gansu, China 37 40 30N 95 43 E
Anxious B. 45 33 24S 134 45 E
Anyang 38 36 5N 114 21 E
Anyi, Jiangxi, China 39 28 49N 115 25 E
Anyi, Shanxi, China 39 35 2N 111 2 E
Anyuan 39 25 9N 115 21 E
'Anzah 28 32 22N 35 12 E
Anzhero-Sudzhensk 24 56 10N 86 0 E
Ánzio 18 41 28N 12 37 E
Aomori 36 40 45N 140 45 E
Aomori □ 36 40 45N 140 40 E
Aosta 18 45 43N 7 20 E
Aoudéras 50 17 45N 8 20 E
Aoulef el Arab 50 26 55N 1 2 E
Apache 71 34 53N 98 22W
Apalachee B. 69 30 0N 84 0W
Apalachicola 69 29 40N 85 0W
Apalachicola → 69 29 40N 85 0W
Apaporis → 78 1 23S 69 25W
Aparri 35 18 22N 121 38 E
Apàtity 22 67 34N 33 22 E
Apatzingán 74 19 0N 102 20W
Apeldoorn 11 52 13N 5 57 E
Apia 43 13 50S 171 50W
Apiacás, Serra dos 78 9 50S 57 0W
Apizaco 74 19 26N 98 9W
Aplao 78 16 0S 72 40W
Apo, Mt. 35 6 53N 125 14 E
Apollonia = Marsá
Susah 51 32 52N 21 59 E
Apolo 78 14 30S 68 30W
Apostle Is. 70 47 0N 90 30W
Apoteri 78 4 2N 58 32W
Appalachian Mts. 68 38 0N 80 0W
Appenines =
Appennini 18 41 0N 15 0 E
Appennini 18 41 0N 15 0 E
Appleby 6 54 35N 2 29W
Appleton 68 44 17N 88 25W
Approuague 79 4 20N 52 0W
Apucarana 80 23 55S 51 33W
Apulia = Púglia □ 18 41 0N 16 30 E
Apure → 78 7 37N 66 25W
Apurimac → 78 12 17S 73 56W
Aqabah = Al
'Aqabah 28 29 31N 35 0 E
'Aqabah, Khalīj al 30 28 15N 33 20 E
Āqcheh 31 37 0N 66 5 E
Aqīq 51 18 14N 38 12 E
Aqrabā 28 32 9N 35 20 E
Aqrah 30 36 46N 43 45 E
Aquidauana 79 20 30S 55 50W
Áquila, L' 18 42 21N 13 24 E
Aquiles Serdán 74 28 37N 105 54W
Ar Rachidiya 50 31 58N 4 20W
Ar Rafīd 28 32 57N 35 52 E
Ar Ramādī 30 33 25N 43 20 E
Ar Ramthā 28 32 34N 36 0 E
Ar Raqqah 30 36 0N 38 55 E
Ar Rass 30 25 50N 43 40 E
Ar Rifā'ī 30 31 50N 46 10 E
Ar Riyāḍ 29 24 41N 46 42 E
Ar Rummān 28 32 9N 35 48 E
Ar Ruṭbah 30 33 0N 40 15 E
Ar Ruwayḍah 30 23 40N 44 40 E
Ara 33 25 35N 84 32 E
'Arab, Bahr el → 51 9 0N 29 30 E
Arab, Shatt al 30 30 0N 48 31 E
Arabia 29 25 0N 45 0 E
Arabian Desert = Es
Sahrâ' Esh
Sharqîya 51 27 30N 32 30 E
Arabian Gulf = Gulf,
The 31 27 0N 50 0 E
Arabian Sea 26 16 0N 65 0 E
Arac 30 41 15N 33 21 E
Aracaju 79 10 55S 37 4W
Aracataca 78 10 38N 74 9W
Aracati 79 4 30S 37 44W
Araçatuba 79 21 10S 50 30W
Aracena 13 37 53N 6 38W
Araçuaí 79 16 52S 42 4W
'Arad, Israel 28 31 15N 35 12 E
Arad, Romania 15 46 10N 21 20 E
Arada 51 15 0N 20 20 E
Arafura Sea 35 9 0S 135 0 E
Aragón □ 13 41 25N 1 0W
Aragón → 13 42 13N 1 44W
Araguacema 79 8 50S 49 20W
Araguaia → 79 5 21S 48 41W
Araguari 79 18 38S 48 11W
Araguari → 79 1 15N 49 55W
Arak, Algeria 50 25 20N 3 45 E
Arāk, Iran 30 34 0N 49 40 E
Arakan Coast 33 19 0N 94 0 E
Arakan Yoma 33 20 0N 94 40 E
Araks = Aras, Rūd-
e → 30 39 10N 47 10 E
Aral Sea =
Aralskoye More 24 44 30N 60 0 E
Aralsk 24 46 50N 61 20 E
Aralskoye More 24 44 30N 60 0 E
Aramac 44 22 58S 145 14 E
Aran I. 9 55 0N 8 30W
Aran Is. 9 53 5N 9 42W
Aranjuez 13 40 1N 3 40W
Aranos 56 24 9S 19 7 E
Aransas Pass 71 27 55N 97 9W
Araouane 50 18 55N 3 30W
Arapahoe 70 40 22N 99 53W
Arapiraca 79 9 45S 36 39W
Arapkir 30 39 5N 38 30 E
Arapongas 80 23 29S 51 28W
Araranguá 80 29 0S 49 30W
Araraquara 79 21 50S 48 0W
Ararat 45 37 16S 143 0 E
Ararat, Mt. = Ağri
Daği 30 39 50N 44 15 E
Araripe, Chapada do 79 7 20S 40 0W
Aras, Rūd-e → 30 39 10N 47 10 E
Arauca 78 7 0N 70 40W
Arauca → 78 7 24N 66 35W
Arauco 80 37 16S 73 25W
Araxá 79 19 35S 46 55W
Araya, Pen. de 78 10 40N 64 0W
Arbatax 18 39 57N 9 42 E
Arbaza 25 52 40N 92 30 E
Arbīl 30 36 15N 44 5 E
Arborfield 65 53 6N 103 39W
Arborg 65 50 54N 97 13W
Arbroath 8 56 34N 2 35W
Arbuckle 72 39 3N 122 2W
Arcachon 12 44 40N 1 10W
Arcadia, Fla., U.S.A. 69 27 20N 81 50W
Arcadia, La., U.S.A. 71 32 34N 92 53W
Arcadia, Nebr.,
U.S.A. 70 41 29N 99 4W
Arcadia, Wis., U.S.A. 70 44 13N 91 29W
Arcata 72 40 55N 124 4W
Archangel =
Arkhangelsk 22 64 40N 41 0 E
Archer → 44 13 28S 141 41 E
Archer B. 44 13 20S 141 30 E
Arcila = Asilah 50 35 29N 6 0W
Arckaringa 45 27 56S 134 45 E
Arckaringa Cr. → 45 28 10S 135 22 E
Arco 72 43 45N 113 16W
Arcola 65 49 40N 102 30W
Arcos 13 41 12N 2 16W
Arcot 32 12 53N 79 20 E
Arcoverde 79 8 25S 37 4W
Arctic Bay 61 73 1N 85 7W
Arctic Red River 60 67 15N 134 0W
Arda → 19 41 40N 26 29 E
Ardabīl 30 38 15N 48 18 E
Ardahan 30 41 7N 42 41 E
Ardakān = Sepīdān 31 30 20N 52 5 E
Ardèche □ 12 44 42N 4 16 E
Ardee 9 53 51N 6 32W
Ardenne 11 50 0N 5 10 E
Ardennes □ 12 49 35N 4 40 E
Ardestān 31 33 20N 52 25 E
Ardgour 8 56 45N 5 25W
Ardlethan 45 34 22S 146 53 E
Ardmore, Australia 44 21 39S 139 11 E
Ardmore, Okla.,
U.S.A. 71 34 10N 97 5W
Ardmore, S. Dak.,
U.S.A. 70 43 0N 103 40W
Ardnacrusha 9 52 43N 8 38W
Ardnamurchan, Pt.
of 8 56 44N 6 14W
Ardrossan, Australia 45 34 26S 137 53 E
Ardrossan, U.K. 8 55 39N 4 50W
Ards □ 9 54 35N 5 30W
Ards Pen. 9 54 30N 5 25W
Arecibo 75 18 29N 66 42W
Areia Branca 79 5 0S 37 0W
Arendal 21 58 28N 8 46 E
Arequipa 78 16 20S 71 30W
Arero 51 4 41N 38 50 E
Arévalo 13 41 3N 4 43W
Arezzo 18 43 28N 11 50 E
Argamakmur 34 3 35S 102 0 E
Argentário, Mte. 18 42 23N 11 11 E
Argentia 63 47 18N 53 58W
Argentina ■ 80 35 0S 66 0W
Argentino, L. 80 50 10S 73 0W
Argeş → 15 44 12N 26 14 E
Arghandab → 32 31 30N 64 15 E
Argo 51 19 28N 30 30 E
Argolikós Kólpos 19 37 20N 22 52 E
Argonne 12 49 10N 5 0 E
Árgos 19 37 40N 22 43 E
Argostólion 19 38 12N 20 33 E
Arguello, Pt. 73 34 34N 120 40W
Argun → 25 53 20N 121 28 E
Argungu 53 12 40N 4 31 E
Argyle 70 48 23N 96 49W
Argyle, L. 46 16 20S 128 40 E
Århus 21 56 8N 10 11 E
Ariamsvlei 56 28 9S 19 51 E
Arica, Chile 78 18 32S 70 20W
Arica, Colombia 78 2 0S 71 50W
Arid, C. 47 34 1S 123 10 E
Aridh 30 25 0N 46 0 E
Ariège □ 12 42 56N 1 30 E
Arima 75 10 38N 61 17W
Arinos → 78 10 25S 58 20W
Ario de Rosales 74 19 12N 102 0W
Aripuanã 78 9 25S 60 30W
Aripuanã → 78 5 7S 60 25W
Ariquemes 78 9 55S 63 6W
Arisaig 8 56 55N 5 50W
Aristazabal I. 64 52 40N 129 10W
Arivaca 73 31 37N 111 25W
Arivonimamo 57 19 1S 47 11 E
Ariza 36 41 19N 2 3W
Arizona 80 35 45S 65 25W
Arizona □ 73 34 20N 111 30W
Arizpe 74 30 20N 110 11W
Arjeplog 20 66 3N 18 2 E
Arjona 78 10 14N 75 22W
Arjuno 35 7 49S 112 34 E
Arka 25 60 15N 142 0 E
Arkadelphia 71 34 5N 93 0W
Arkaig, L. 8 56 58N 5 10W
Arkalyk 24 50 13N 66 50 E
Arkansas □ 71 35 0N 92 30W
Arkansas → 71 33 48N 91 4W
Arkansas City 71 37 4N 97 3W
Arkhangelsk 22 64 40N 41 0 E
Arklow 9 52 48N 6 10W
Arkticheskiy, Mys 25 81 10N 95 0 E
Arlanzón → 13 42 3N 4 17W
Arlberg Pass 14 47 9N 10 12 E
Arlee 72 47 10N 114 4W
Arles 12 43 41N 4 40 E
Arlington, S. Africa 57 28 1S 27 53 E
Arlington, Oreg.,
U.S.A. 72 45 48N 120 6W
Arlington, S. Dak.,
U.S.A. 70 44 25N 97 4W
Arlington, Va., U.S.A. 68 38 52N 77 5W
Arlington, Wash.,
U.S.A. 72 48 11N 122 4W
Arlon 11 49 42N 5 49 E
Armagh 9 54 22N 6 40W
Armagh □ 9 54 18N 6 37W
Armagnac 12 43 50N 0 10 E
Armavir 23 45 2N 41 7 E
Armenia 78 4 35N 75 45W
Armenian S.S.R. □ 23 40 0N 44 0 E
Armidale 45 30 30S 151 40 E
Armour 70 43 20N 98 25W
Armstrong, B.C.,
Canada 64 50 25N 119 10W
Armstrong, Ont.,
Canada 62 50 18N 89 4W
Armstrong, U.S.A. 71 26 59N 97 48W
Armstrong Cr. → 46 16 35S 131 40 E
Arnaouti, C. 30 35 6N 32 17 E
Arnarfjörður 20 65 48N 23 40W
Arnaud → 61 60 0N 70 0W
Árnes 20 66 1N 21 31W
Arnett 71 36 9N 99 44W
Arnhem 11 51 58N 5 55 E
Arnhem, C. 44 12 20S 137 30 E
Arnhem B. 44 12 20S 136 10 E
Arnhem Land 44 13 10S 134 30 E
Arno → 18 43 41N 10 17 E
Arno Bay 45 33 54S 136 34 E
Arnold 70 41 29N 100 10W
Arnot 65 55 56N 96 41W
Arnøy 20 70 9N 20 40 E
Arnprior 62 45 26N 76 21W
Aroab 56 26 41S 19 39 E
Arrabury 45 26 45S 141 0 E
Arraiján 74 8 56N 79 36W
Arran 8 55 34N 5 12W
Arrandale 64 54 57N 130 0W
Arras 12 50 17N 2 46 E
Arrecife 50 28 57N 13 37W
Arrée, Mts. d' 12 48 26N 3 55W
Arriaga 74 21 55N 101 23W
Arrilalah P.O. 44 23 43S 143 54 E
Arrino 47 29 30S 115 40 E
Arrow, L. 9 54 3N 8 20W
Arrow Rock Res. 72 43 45N 115 50W
Arrowhead 64 50 40N 117 55W
Arrowtown 43 44 57S 168 50 E
Arroyo Grande 73 35 9N 120 32W
Arsenault L. 65 55 6N 108 32W
Árta 19 39 8N 21 2 E
Arteaga 74 18 50N 102 20W
Artemovsk 25 54 45N 93 35 E
Artesia =
Mosomane 56 24 2S 26 19 E
Artesia 71 32 55N 104 25W
Artesia Wells 71 28 17N 99 18W
Artesian 70 44 2N 97 54W
Arthur → 44 41 2S 144 40 E
Arthur Cr. → 44 22 30S 136 25 E
Arthur Pt. 44 22 7S 150 3 E
Arthur's Pass 43 42 54S 171 35 E
Artigas 80 30 20S 56 30W
Artillery L. 65 63 9N 107 52W
Artois 12 50 20N 2 30 E
Artvin 30 41 14N 41 44 E
Aru, Kepulauan 35 6 0S 134 30 E
Arua 54 3 1N 30 58 E
Aruanã 79 14 54S 51 10W
Aruba 75 12 30N 70 0W
Arumpo 45 33 48S 142 55 E
Arunachal
Pradesh □ 33 28 0N 95 0 E
Arusha 54 3 20S 36 40 E
Aruwimi → 54 1 13N 23 36 E
Arvada 72 44 43N 106 6W
Arvayheer 37 46 15N 102 48 E
Arvida 63 48 25N 71 14W
Arvidsjaur 20 65 35N 19 10 E
Arvika 21 59 40N 12 36 E
Arxan 38 47 11N 119 57 E
Arys 24 42 26N 68 48 E
Arzamas 22 55 27N 43 55 E
Arzew 50 35 50N 0 23W
'As Saffānīyah 30 28 5N 48 50 E
Aş Şāfī 28 31 2N 35 28 E
As Salt 28 32 2N 35 43 E
As Samāwah 30 31 15N 45 15 E
As Samū' 28 31 24N 35 4 E
As Sanamayn 28 33 3N 36 10 E
As Sulaymānīyah,
Iraq 30 35 35N 45 29 E
As Sulaymānīyah,
Si. Arabia 30 24 9N 47 18 E
As Summān 30 25 0N 47 0 E
As Sūq 30 21 58N 42 3 E
As Suwaydā' 30 32 40N 36 30 E
As Suwayh 31 22 10N 59 33 E
As Şuwayrah 30 32 55N 45 0 E
Asab 56 25 30S 18 0 E
Asahigawa 36 43 46N 142 22 E
Asamankese 53 5 50N 0 40W
Asansol 33 23 40N 87 1 E
Asbesberge 56 29 0S 23 0 E
Asbestos 63 45 47N 71 58W
Asbury Park 68 40 15N 74 1W
Ascensión, B. de la 74 19 50N 87 20W
Ascension I. 2 8 0S 14 15W
Aschaffenburg 14 49 58N 9 8 E
Áscoli Piceno 18 42 51N 13 34 E
Ascope 78 7 46S 79 8W
Aseb 29 13 0N 42 40 E
Asela 51 8 0N 39 0 E
Ash Fork 73 35 14N 112 32W
Ash Grove 71 37 21N 93 36W
Ash Shām, Bādiyat 30 32 0N 40 0 E
Ash Shāmīyah 30 31 55N 44 35 E
Ash Shāriqah 31 25 23N 55 26 E
Ash Shaṭrah 30 31 30N 46 10 E
Ash Shaykh, J. 30 33 25N 35 50 E
Ash Shu'aybah 30 27 53N 44 43 E
Ash Shu'bah 30 28 54N 44 44 E
Ash Shūnah ash
Shamālīyah 28 32 37N 35 34 E
Asha 22 55 0N 57 16 E
Ashburn 69 31 42N 83 40W
Ashburton 43 43 53S 171 48 E
Ashburton → 46 21 40S 114 56 E
Ashburton Downs 46 23 25S 117 4 E
Ashby-de-la-Zouch 6 52 45N 1 29W
Ashcroft 64 50 40N 121 20W
Ashdod 28 31 49N 34 35 E

Balashov

Ashdot Yaaqov 28 32 39N 35 35 E
Asheboro 69 35 43N 79 46W
Asherton 71 28 25N 99 43W
Asheville 69 35 39N 82 30W
Asheweig → 62 54 17N 87 12W
Ashford, Australia 45 29 15S 151 3 E
Ashford, U.K. 7 51 8N 0 53 E
Ashford, U.S.A. 72 46 45N 122 2W
Ashikaga 36 36 28N 139 29 E
Ashizuri-Zaki 36 32 44N 133 0 E
Ashkhabad 24 38 0N 57 50 E
Ashland, Kans., U.S.A. 71 37 13N 99 43W
Ashland, Ky., U.S.A. 68 38 25N 82 40W
Ashland, Maine, U.S.A. 63 46 34N 68 26W
Ashland, Mont., U.S.A. 72 45 41N 106 12W
Ashland, Nebr., U.S.A. 70 41 5N 96 27W
Ashland, Ohio, U.S.A. 68 40 52N 82 20W
Ashland, Oreg., U.S.A. 72 42 10N 122 38W
Ashland, Va., U.S.A. 68 37 46N 77 30W
Ashland, Wis., U.S.A. 70 46 40N 90 52W
Ashley 70 46 3N 99 23W
Ashmont 64 54 7N 111 35W
Ashmore Reef 46 12 14S 123 5 E
Ashq'elon 28 31 42N 34 35 E
Ashtabula 68 41 52N 80 50W
Ashton, S. Africa 56 33 50S 20 5 E
Ashton, U.S.A. 72 44 6N 111 30W
Ashton-under-Lyne 6 53 30N 2 8W
Ashuanipi, L. 63 52 45N 66 15W
Asia 26 45 0N 75 0 E
Asia, Kepulauan 35 1 0N 131 13 E
Asifabad 32 19 20N 79 24 E
Asike 35 6 39S 140 24 E
Asilah 50 35 29N 6 0W
Asinara 18 41 5N 8 15 E
Asinara, G. dell' 18 41 0N 8 30 E
Asino 24 57 0N 86 0 E
'Asīr □ 29 18 40N 42 30 E
Asir, Ras 29 11 55N 51 10 E
Askersund 21 58 53N 14 55 E
Askham 56 26 59S 20 47 E
Askja 20 65 3N 16 48W
Āsmār 31 35 10N 71 27 E
Asmara = Asmera 51 15 19N 38 55 E
Asmera 51 15 19N 38 55 E
Aso 36 33 0N 131 5 E
Asotin 72 46 20N 117 3W
Aspen 73 39 12N 106 56W
Aspermont 71 33 11N 100 15W
Aspiring, Mt. 43 44 23S 168 46 E
Asquith 65 52 8N 107 13W
Assam □ 33 26 0N 93 0 E
Asse 11 50 24N 4 10 E
Assen 11 53 0N 6 35 E
Assini 50 5 9N 3 17W
Assiniboia 65 49 40N 105 59W
Assiniboine → 65 49 53N 97 8W
Assis 80 22 40S 50 20W
Assisi 18 43 4N 12 36 E
Assynt, L. 8 58 25N 5 15W
Astara 23 38 30N 48 50 E
Asti 18 44 54N 8 11 E
Astipálaia 19 36 32N 26 22 E
Astorga 13 42 29N 6 8W
Astoria 72 46 16N 123 50W
Astrakhan 23 46 25N 48 5 E
Astrakhan-Bazàr 23 39 14N 48 30 E
Asturias 13 43 15N 6 0W
Asunción 80 25 10S 57 30W
Asunción, La 78 11 2N 63 53W
Aswân 51 24 4N 32 57 E
Aswân High Dam = Sadd el Aali 51 23 54N 32 54 E
Asyût 51 27 11N 31 4 E
At Ţafīlah 30 30 45N 35 30 E
At Tā'if 29 21 5N 40 27 E
Aţ Ţur 28 31 47N 35 14 E
Aţ Ţurrah 28 32 39N 35 59 E
Atacama, Desierto de 80 24 0S 69 20W
Atacama, Salar de 80 23 30S 68 20W
Atakpamé 53 7 31N 1 13 E
Atalaya 78 10 45S 73 50W
Atami 36 35 5N 139 4 E
Atapupu 35 9 0S 124 51 E
Atâr 50 20 30N 13 5W
Atara 25 63 10N 129 10 E
Atascadero 73 35 32N 120 44W
Atasu 24 48 30N 71 0 E
Atauro 35 8 10S 125 30 E
Atbara 51 17 42N 33 59 E
'Atbara → 51 17 40N 33 56 E
Atbasar 24 51 48N 68 20 E
Atchafalaya B. 71 29 30N 91 20W
Atchison 70 39 40N 95 10W
Ath 11 50 38N 3 47 E
Athabasca 64 54 45N 113 20W
Athabasca → 65 58 40N 110 50W
Athabasca, L. 65 59 15N 109 15W
Athboy 9 53 37N 6 55W
Athenry 9 53 18N 8 45W
Athens = Athínai 19 37 58N 23 46 E
Athens, Ala., U.S.A. 69 34 49N 86 58W
Athens, Ga., U.S.A. 69 33 56N 83 24W
Athens, Ohio, U.S.A. 68 39 25N 82 6W
Athens, Tenn., U.S.A. 69 35 45N 84 38W
Athens, Tex., U.S.A. 71 32 11N 95 48W
Atherton 44 17 17S 145 30 E
Athínai 19 37 58N 23 46 E
Athlone 9 53 26N 7 57W
Atholl, Forest of 8 56 51N 3 50W
Atholville 63 47 59N 66 43W
Áthos 19 40 9N 24 22 E
Athy 9 53 0N 7 0W
Ati 51 13 13N 18 20 E
Atico 78 16 14S 73 40W
Atikokan 62 48 45N 91 37W
Atikonak L. 63 52 40N 64 32W
Atka 25 60 50N 151 48 E
Atkinson 70 42 35N 98 59W
Atlanta, Ga., U.S.A. 69 33 50N 84 24W
Atlanta, Tex., U.S.A. 71 33 7N 94 8W
Atlantic 70 41 25N 95 0W
Atlantic City 68 39 25N 74 25W
Atlantic Ocean 2 0 0 20 0W
Atlas Mts. = Haut Atlas 50 32 30N 5 0W
Atlin 60 59 31N 133 41W
Atlin, L. 64 59 26N 133 45W
'Atlit 28 32 42N 34 56 E
Atmore 69 31 2N 87 30W
Atoka 71 34 22N 96 10W
Atoyac → 74 16 30N 97 31W
Atrak → 31 37 50N 57 0 E
Atsuta 36 43 24N 141 26 E
Attalla 69 34 2N 86 5W
Attawapiskat 62 52 56N 82 24W
Attawapiskat → 62 52 57N 82 18W
Attawapiskat, L. 62 52 18N 87 54W
Attica 68 40 20N 87 15W
Attikamagen L. 63 55 0N 66 30W
'Attīl 28 32 23N 35 4 E
Attleboro 68 41 56N 71 18W
Attock 32 33 52N 72 20 E
Attopeu 34 14 48N 106 50 E
Attur 32 11 35N 78 30 E
Atuel → 80 36 17S 66 50W
Åtvidaberg 21 58 12N 16 0 E
Atwater 73 37 21N 120 37W
Atwood 70 39 52N 101 3W
Au Sable → 68 44 25N 83 20W
Au Sable Pt. 62 46 40N 86 10W
Aube □ 12 48 15N 4 10 E
Aube → 12 48 34N 3 43 E
Auburn, Ala., U.S.A. 69 32 37N 85 30W
Auburn, Calif., U.S.A. 72 38 53N 121 4W
Auburn, Ind., U.S.A. 68 41 20N 85 0W
Auburn, N.Y., U.S.A. 68 42 57N 76 39W
Auburn, Nebr., U.S.A. 70 40 25N 95 50W
Auburn Range 45 25 15S 150 30 E
Auburndale 69 28 5N 81 45W
Aubusson 12 45 57N 2 11 E
Auch 12 43 39N 0 36 E
Auckland 43 36 52S 174 46 E
Auckland Is. 40 50 40S 166 5 E
Aude □ 12 43 8N 2 28 E
Aude → 12 43 13N 3 14 E
Auden 62 50 14N 87 53W
Audubon 70 41 43N 94 56W
Augathella 45 25 48S 146 35 E
Augrabies Falls 56 28 35S 20 20 E
Augsburg 14 48 22N 10 54 E
Augusta, Italy 18 37 14N 15 12 E
Augusta, Ark., U.S.A. 71 35 17N 91 25W
Augusta, Ga., U.S.A. 69 33 29N 81 59W
Augusta, Kans., U.S.A. 71 37 40N 97 0W
Augusta, Maine, U.S.A. 63 44 20N 69 46W
Augusta, Mont., U.S.A. 72 47 30N 112 29W
Augusta, Wis., U.S.A. 70 44 41N 91 8W
Augustów 15 53 51N 23 0 E
Augustus, Mt. 47 24 20S 116 50 E
Augustus Downs 44 18 35S 139 55 E
Augustus I. 46 15 20S 124 30 E
Ault 70 40 40N 104 42W
Aunis 12 46 5N 0 50W
Auponhia 35 1 58S 125 27 E
Aurangabad, Bihar, India 33 24 45N 84 18 E
Aurangabad, Maharashtra, India 32 19 50N 75 23 E
Aurillac 12 44 55N 2 26 E
Aurora, S. Africa 56 32 40S 18 29 E
Aurora, Colo., U.S.A. 70 39 44N 104 55W
Aurora, Ill., U.S.A. 68 41 42N 88 12W
Aurora, Mo., U.S.A. 71 36 58N 93 42W
Aurora, Nebr., U.S.A. 70 40 55N 98 0W
Aurukun Mission 44 13 20S 141 45 E
Aus 56 26 35S 16 12 E
Aust-Agder fylke □ 21 58 55N 7 40 E
Austerlitz = Slavkov 14 49 10N 16 52 E
Austin, Minn., U.S.A. 70 43 37N 92 59W
Austin, Nev., U.S.A. 72 39 30N 117 1W
Austin, Tex., U.S.A. 71 30 20N 97 45W
Austin, L. 47 27 40S 118 0 E
Austral Downs 44 20 30S 137 45 E
Austral Is. = Tubuai Is. 41 25 0S 150 0W
Austral Seamount Chain 41 24 0S 150 0W
Australia ■ 3 23 0S 135 0 E
Australian Alps 45 36 30S 148 30 E
Australian Cap. Terr. □ 45 35 30S 149 0 E
Austria ■ 14 47 0N 14 0 E
Austvågøy 20 68 20N 14 40 E
Autlán 74 19 40N 104 30W
Autun 12 46 58N 4 17 E
Auvergne, Australia 46 15 39S 130 1 E
Auvergne, France 12 45 20N 3 15 E
Auxerre 12 47 48N 3 32 E
Avallon 12 47 30N 3 53 E
Avalon Pen. 63 47 30N 53 20W
Aveiro, Brazil 79 3 10S 55 5W
Aveiro, Portugal 13 40 37N 8 38W
Āvej 30 35 40N 49 15 E
Avellaneda 80 34 50S 58 10W
Avellino 18 40 54N 14 46 E
Aversa 18 40 58N 14 11 E
Avery 72 47 22N 115 56W
Aves, I. de 75 15 45N 63 55W
Aves, Is. de 75 12 0N 67 30W
Avesta 21 60 9N 16 10 E
Aveyron □ 12 44 22N 2 45 E
Aviá Terai 80 26 45S 60 50W
Avignon 12 43 57N 4 50 E
Ávila 13 40 39N 4 43W
Avilés 13 43 35N 5 57W
Avoca, Australia 45 37 5S 143 26 E
Avoca, Ireland 9 52 52N 6 13W
Avoca → 45 35 40S 143 43 E
Avola 64 51 45N 119 19W
Avon 70 43 0N 98 3W
Avon □ 7 51 30N 2 40W
Avon →, Australia 47 31 40S 116 7 E
Avon →, Avon, U.K. 7 51 30N 2 43W
Avon →, Hants., U.K. 7 50 44N 1 45W
Avon →, Warwick, U.K. 7 52 0N 2 9W
Avonlea 65 50 0N 105 0W
Avonmouth 7 51 30N 2 42W
Avranches 12 48 40N 1 20W
'Awālī 31 26 0N 50 30 E
'Awartā 28 32 10N 35 17 E
Awash 29 9 1N 40 10 E
Awatere → 43 41 37S 174 10 E
Awbārī 51 26 46N 12 57 E
Awe, L. 8 56 15N 5 15W
Awgu 53 6 4N 7 24 E
Awjilah 51 29 8N 21 7 E
Axarfjörður 20 66 15N 16 45W
Axel Heiberg I. 58 80 0N 90 0W
Axim 50 4 51N 2 15W
Axminster 7 50 47N 3 1W
Ayabaca 78 4 40S 79 53W
Ayabe 36 35 20N 135 20 E
Ayacucho, Argentina 80 37 5S 58 20W
Ayacucho, Peru 78 13 0S 74 0W
Ayaguz 24 48 10N 80 0 E
Ayamonte 13 37 12N 7 24W
Ayan 25 56 30N 138 16 E
Ayaviri 78 14 50S 70 35W
Āybak 31 36 15N 68 5 E
Ayers Rock 47 25 23S 131 5 E
Ayíos Evstrátios 19 39 34N 24 58 E
Aykin 22 62 15N 49 56 E
Aylesbury 7 51 48N 0 49W
Aylmer L. 60 64 0N 110 8W
'Ayn 'Arīk 28 31 54N 35 8 E
Ayn Dār 30 25 55N 49 10 E
Ayn Zālah 30 36 45N 42 35 E
Ayon, Ostrov 25 69 50N 169 0 E
Ayr, Australia 44 19 35S 147 25 E
Ayr, U.K. 8 55 28N 4 37W
Ayr → 8 55 29N 4 40W
Ayre, Pt. of 6 54 27N 4 21W
Aytos 19 42 42N 27 16 E
Ayu, Kepulauan 35 0 35N 131 5 E
Ayutla 74 16 58N 99 17W
Ayvalık 30 39 20N 26 46 E
Az Zahrān 30 26 10N 50 7 E
Az Zarqā 28 32 5N 36 4 E
Az-Zilfī 30 26 12N 44 52 E
Az Zubayr 30 30 20N 47 50 E
Azamgarh 33 26 5N 83 13 E
Āzarbāyjān-e Gharbī □ 30 37 0N 44 30 E
Āzarbāyjān-e Sharqī □ 30 37 20N 47 0 E
Azare 53 11 55N 10 10 E
Azbine = Aïr 50 18 30N 8 0 E
Azerbaijan S.S.R. □ 23 40 20N 48 0 E
Azogues 78 2 35S 78 0W
Azor 28 32 2N 34 48 E
Azores 2 38 44N 29 0W
Azov 23 47 3N 39 25 E
Azov Sea = Azovskoye More 24 46 0N 36 30 E
Azovskoye More 24 46 0N 36 30 E
Azovy 24 64 55N 64 35 E
Aztec 73 36 54N 108 0W
Azúa de Compostela 75 18 25N 70 44W
Azuaga 13 38 16N 5 39W
Azuero, Pen. de 75 7 30N 80 30W
Azul 80 36 42S 59 43W

B

Ba Don 34 17 45N 106 26 E
Ba Ria 34 10 30N 107 10 E
Ba Xian 38 39 8N 116 22 E
Baa 35 10 50S 123 0 E
Baarle Nassau 11 51 27N 4 56 E
Baarn 11 52 12N 5 17 E
Bab el Mandeb 29 12 35N 43 25 E
Babahoyo 78 1 40S 79 30W
Babakin 47 32 7S 118 1 E
Babana 53 10 31N 3 46 E
Babar 35 8 0S 129 30 E
Babb 72 48 56N 113 27W
Babinda 44 17 20S 145 56 E
Babine 64 55 22N 126 37W
Babine → 64 55 45N 127 44W
Babine L. 64 54 48N 126 0W
Babo 35 2 30S 133 30 E
Bābol 31 36 40N 52 50 E
Bābol Sar 31 36 45N 52 45 E
Baboua 54 5 49N 14 58 E
Babura 53 12 51N 8 59 E
Babuyan Chan. 35 18 40N 121 30 E
Babylon 30 32 40N 44 30 E
Bacabal 79 4 15S 44 45W
Bacan 35 8 27S 126 27 E
Bacan, Kepulauan 35 0 35S 127 30 E
Bacan, Pulau 35 0 50S 127 30 E
Bacarra 35 18 15N 120 37 E
Bacău 15 46 35N 26 55 E
Bacerac 74 30 18N 108 50W
Bachelina 24 57 45N 67 20 E
Back → 60 65 10N 104 0W
Backstairs Passage 45 35 40S 138 5 E
Bacolod 35 10 40N 122 57 E
Bad → 70 44 22N 100 22W
Bad Axe 68 43 48N 82 59W
Bad Ischl 14 47 44N 13 38 E
Bad Lands 70 43 40N 102 10W
Badagara 32 11 35N 75 40 E
Badajoz 13 38 50N 6 59W
Badakhshān □ 31 36 30N 71 0 E
Badalona 13 41 26N 2 15 E
Badalzai 32 29 50N 65 35 E
Badampahar 33 22 10N 86 10 E
Badanah 30 30 58N 41 30 E
Badarinath 32 30 45N 79 30 E
Badas 34 4 33N 114 25 E
Badas, Kepulauan 34 0 45N 107 5 E
Baddo → 31 28 0N 64 20 E
Bade 35 7 10S 139 35 E
Baden 14 48 1N 16 13 E
Baden-Baden 14 48 45N 8 15 E
Baden-Württemberg □ 14 48 40N 9 0 E
Badgastein 14 47 7N 13 9 E
Badger 63 49 0N 56 4W
Bādghīsāt □ 31 35 0N 63 0 E
Badin 32 24 38N 68 54 E
Badong 39 31 1N 110 23 E
Baduen 29 7 15N 47 40 E
Badulla 32 7 1N 81 7 E
Baeza 13 37 57N 3 25W
Bafatá 50 12 8N 14 40W
Baffin B. 58 72 0N 64 0W
Baffin I. 61 68 0N 75 0W
Bafia 54 4 40N 11 10 E
Bafing → 50 13 49N 10 50W
Bafoulabé 50 13 50N 10 55W
Bāfq 31 31 40N 55 25 E
Bafra 30 41 34N 35 54 E
Bāft 31 29 15N 56 38 E
Bafut 53 6 6N 10 2 E
Bafwasende 54 1 3N 27 5 E
Bagamoyo 54 6 28S 38 55 E
Baganga 35 7 34N 126 33 E
Bagani 56 18 7S 21 41 E
Bagansiapiapi 34 2 12N 100 50 E
Bagdarin 25 54 26N 113 36 E
Bagé 80 31 20S 54 15W
Bagenalstown = Muine Bheag 9 52 42N 6 57W
Baggs 72 41 8N 107 46W
Baghdād 30 33 20N 44 30 E
Baghlān 31 36 12N 69 0 E
Baghlān □ 31 36 0N 68 30 E
Bagley 70 47 30N 95 22W
Bagotville 63 48 22N 70 54W
Baguio 35 16 26N 120 34 E
Bahama, Canal Viejo de 75 22 10N 77 30W
Bahamas ■ 75 24 0N 75 0W
Baharampur 33 24 2N 88 27 E
Bahawalpur 32 29 24N 71 40 E
Bahía = Salvador 79 13 0S 38 30W
Bahía □ 79 12 0S 42 0W
Bahía, Is. de la 75 16 45N 86 15W
Bahía Blanca 80 38 35S 62 13W
Bahía de Caráquez 78 0 40S 80 27W
Bahía Laura 80 48 10S 66 30W
Bahía Negra 78 20 5S 58 5W
Bahr Aouk → 54 8 40N 19 0 E
Bahr el Ahmar □ 51 20 0N 35 0 E
Bahr el Ghazâl □ 51 7 0N 28 0 E
Bahr Salamat → 51 9 20N 18 0 E
Bahraich 33 27 38N 81 37 E
Bahrain ■ 31 26 0N 50 35 E
Baia Mare 15 47 40N 23 35 E
Baïbokoum 51 7 46N 15 43 E
Baicheng 38 45 38N 122 42 E
Baidoa 29 3 8N 43 30 E
Baie Comeau 63 49 12N 68 10W
Baie-St-Paul 63 47 28N 70 32W
Baie Trinité 63 49 25N 67 20W
Baie Verte 63 49 55N 56 12W
Ba'ījī 30 35 0N 43 30 E
Baikal, L. = Baykal, Oz. 25 53 0N 108 0 E
Baile Atha Cliath = Dublin 9 53 20N 6 18W
Bailundo 55 12 10S 15 50 E
Bainbridge 69 30 53N 84 34W
Baing 35 10 14S 120 34 E
Bainville 70 48 8N 104 10W
Bā'ir 30 30 45N 36 55 E
Baird 71 32 25N 99 25W
Baird Mts. 60 67 10N 160 15W
Bairin Youqi 38 43 30N 118 35 E
Bairin Zuoqi 38 43 58N 119 15 E
Bairnsdale 45 37 48S 147 36 E
Baitadi 33 29 35N 80 25 E
Baixo-Alentejo 13 38 0N 8 30W
Baiyin 38 36 45N 104 14 E
Baiyu Shan 38 37 15N 107 30 E
Baja 15 46 12N 18 59 E
Baja, Pta. 74 29 50N 116 0W
Baja California 74 31 10N 115 12W
Bajimba, Mt. 45 29 17S 152 6 E
Bajo Nuevo 75 15 40N 78 50W
Bajool 44 23 40S 150 35 E
Bakala 51 6 15N 20 20 E
Bakchar 24 57 1N 82 5 E
Bakel 50 14 56N 12 20W
Baker, Calif., U.S.A. 73 35 16N 116 8W
Baker, Mont., U.S.A. 70 46 22N 104 12W
Baker, Oreg., U.S.A. 72 44 50N 117 55W
Baker, L., Australia 47 26 54S 126 5 E
Baker, L., Canada 60 64 0N 96 0W
Baker I. 40 0 10N 176 35W
Baker Lake 60 64 20N 96 3W
Baker Mt. 72 48 50N 121 49W
Bakers Creek 44 21 13S 149 7 E
Baker's Dozen Is. 62 56 45N 78 45W
Bakersfield 73 35 25N 119 0W
Bākhtarān 30 34 23N 47 0 E
Bakhtārān □ 30 34 0N 46 30 E
Bakinskikh Komissarov, im. 26 30 39 20N 49 15 E
Bakkafjörður 20 66 2N 14 48W
Bakkagerði 20 65 31N 13 49W
Bakony Forest = Bakony Hegyseg 15 47 10N 17 30 E
Bakony Hegyseg 15 47 10N 17 30 E
Bakouma 51 5 40N 22 56 E
Baku 23 40 25N 49 45 E
Bal'ā 28 32 20N 35 6 E
Bala, L. = Tegid, L. 6 52 53N 3 38W
Balabac, Str. 34 7 53N 117 5 E
Balabac I. 34 8 0N 117 0 E
Balabakk 30 34 0N 36 10 E
Balabalangan, Kepulauan 34 2 20S 117 30 E
Balaghat 32 21 49N 80 12 E
Balaghat Ra. 32 18 50N 76 30 E
Balaguer 13 41 50N 0 50 E
Balaklava, Australia 45 34 7S 138 22 E
Balaklava, U.S.S.R. 23 44 30N 33 30 E
Balakovo 22 52 4N 47 55 E
Balashov 22 51 30N 43 10 E

Balasore

Balasore = Baleshwar 33 21 35N 87 3 E
Balaton 15 46 50N 17 40 E
Balboa 75 9 0N 79 30W
Balboa Hill 74 9 6N 79 44W
Balbriggan 9 53 35N 6 10W
Balcarce 80 38 0S 58 10W
Balcarres 65 50 50N 103 35W
Balchik 19 43 28N 28 11 E
Balclutha 43 46 15S 169 45 E
Bald Hd. 47 35 6S 118 1 E
Bald I. 47 34 57S 118 27 E
Bald Knob 71 35 20N 91 35W
Baldock L. 65 56 33N 97 57W
Baldwin, Fla., U.S.A. 69 30 15N 82 10W
Baldwin, Mich., U.S.A. 68 43 54N 85 53W
Baldwinsville 68 43 10N 76 19W
Baleares, Is. 13 39 30N 3 0 E
Balearic Is. = Baleares, Is. 13 39 30N 3 0 E
Baler 35 15 46N 121 34 E
Baleshwar 33 21 35N 87 3 E
Balfe's Creek 44 20 12S 145 55 E
Balfour 57 26 38S 28 35 E
Balfouriyya 28 32 38N 35 18 E
Bali, Cameroon 53 5 54N 10 0 E
Bali, Indonesia 34 8 20S 115 0 E
Bali □ 34 8 20S 115 0 E
Bali, Selat 35 8 18S 114 25 E
Balikesir 30 39 35N 27 58 E
Balikpapan 34 1 10S 116 55 E
Balimbing 35 5 5N 119 58 E
Balipara 33 26 50N 92 45 E
Baliza 79 16 0S 52 20W
Balkan Mts. = Stara Planina 19 43 15N 23 0 E
Balkan Pen. 4 42 0N 22 0 E
Balkh 31 36 44N 66 47 E
Balkh □ 31 36 30N 67 0 E
Balkhash 24 46 50N 74 50 E
Balkhash, Ozero 24 46 0N 74 50 E
Balla 33 24 10N 91 35 E
Ballachulish 8 56 40N 5 10W
Balladonia 47 32 27S 123 51 E
Ballarat 45 37 33S 143 50 E
Ballard, L. 47 29 20S 120 10 E
Ballater 8 57 2N 3 2W
Ballenas, Canal de 74 29 10N 113 45W
Ballenas, Canal de 74 29 10N 113 45W
Ballidu 47 30 35S 116 45 E
Ballina, Australia 45 28 50S 153 31 E
Ballina, Mayo, Ireland 9 54 7N 9 10W
Ballina, Tipp., Ireland 9 52 49N 8 27W
Ballinasloe 9 53 20N 8 12W
Ballinger 71 31 45N 99 58W
Ballinrobe 9 53 36N 9 13W
Ballinskelligs B. 9 51 46N 10 11W
Ballycastle 9 55 12N 6 15W
Ballymena 9 54 53N 6 18W
Ballymena □ 9 54 53N 6 18W
Ballymoney 9 55 5N 6 30W
Ballymoney □ 9 55 5N 6 23W
Ballyshannon 9 54 30N 8 10W
Balmaceda 80 46 0S 71 50W
Balmoral, Australia 45 37 15S 141 48 E
Balmoral, U.K. 8 57 3N 3 13W
Balmorhea 71 31 2N 103 41W
Balonne → 45 28 47S 147 56 E
Balrampur 33 27 30N 82 20 E
Balranald 45 34 38S 143 33 E
Balsas → 74 17 55N 102 10W
Balta, U.S.A. 70 48 12N 100 7W
Balta, U.S.S.R. 23 48 2N 29 45 E
Baltic Sea 21 56 0N 20 0 E
Baltimore, Ireland 9 51 29N 9 22W
Baltimore, U.S.A. 68 39 18N 76 37W
Baluchistan □ 31 27 30N 65 0 E
Balygychan 25 63 56N 154 12 E
Bam 31 29 7N 58 14 E
Bama 53 11 33N 13 41 E
Bamako 50 12 34N 7 55W
Bamba 50 17 5N 1 24W
Bambari 51 5 40N 20 35 E
Bambaroo 44 18 50S 146 10 E
Bamberg, Germany 14 49 54N 10 53 E
Bamberg, U.S.A. 69 33 19N 81 1W
Bambili 54 3 40N 26 0 E
Bamenda 53 5 57N 10 11 E
Bamfield 64 48 45N 125 10W
Bāmīān □ 31 35 0N 67 0 E
Bamiancheng 38 43 15N 124 2 E
Bampūr 31 27 15N 60 21 E
Ban Don = Surat Thani 34 9 6N 99 20 E
Banaba 40 0 45S 169 50 E
Banalia 54 1 32N 25 5 E
Banam 34 11 20N 105 17 E
Banamba 50 13 29N 7 22W
Banana 44 24 28S 150 8 E
Bananal, I. do 79 11 30S 50 30W
Banaras = Varanasi 33 25 22N 83 0 E
Banbridge 9 54 21N 6 17W
Banbridge □ 9 54 21N 6 16W
Banbury 7 52 4N 1 21W
Banchory 8 57 3N 2 30W
Bancroft 62 45 3N 77 51W
Band-e Torkestān 31 35 30N 64 0 E
Banda 32 25 30N 80 26 E
Banda, Kepulauan 35 4 37S 129 50 E
Banda, La 80 27 45S 64 10W
Banda Aceh 34 5 35N 95 20 E
Banda Banda, Mt. 45 31 10S 152 28 E
Banda Elat 35 5 40S 133 5 E
Banda Sea 35 6 0S 130 0 E
Bandai-San 36 37 36N 140 4 E
Bandanaira 35 4 32S 129 54 E
Bandar = Machilipatnam 33 16 12N 81 8 E
Bandār 'Abbās 31 27 15N 56 15 E
Bandar-e Anzalī 30 37 30N 49 30 E
Bandar-e Chārak 31 26 45N 54 20 E
Bandar-e Deylam 30 30 5N 50 10 E
Bandar-e Khomeyni 30 30 30N 49 5 E
Bandar-e Lengeh 31 26 35N 54 58 E
Bandar-e Ma'shur 30 30 35N 49 10 E
Bandar-e Nakhīlū 31 26 58N 53 30 E
Bandar-e Rīg 31 29 29N 50 38 E
Bandar-e Torkeman 31 37 0N 54 10 E
Bandar Maharani = Muar 34 2 3N 102 34 E
Bandar Penggaram = Batu Pahat 34 1 50N 102 56 E
Bandar Seri Begawan 34 4 52N 115 0 E
Bandawe 55 11 58S 34 5 E
Bandeira, Pico da 79 20 26S 41 47W
Bandera, Argentina 80 28 55S 62 20W
Bandera, U.S.A. 71 29 45N 99 3W
Banderas, B. de 74 20 40N 105 30W
Bandiagara 50 14 12N 3 29W
Bandırma 30 40 20N 28 0 E
Bandon 9 51 44N 8 45W
Bandon → 9 51 40N 8 41W
Bandundu 54 3 15S 17 22 E
Bandung 35 6 54S 107 36 E
Bandya 47 27 40S 122 5 E
Banes 75 21 0N 75 42W
Banff, Canada 64 51 10N 115 34W
Banff, U.K. 8 57 40N 2 32W
Banff Nat. Park 64 51 30N 116 15W
Banfora 50 10 40N 4 40W
Bang Saphan 34 11 14N 99 28 E
Bangalore 32 12 59N 77 40 E
Bangassou 54 4 55N 23 7 E
Banggai 35 1 40S 123 30 E
Banggi, P. 34 7 17N 117 12 E
Banghāzī 51 32 11N 20 3 E
Bangil 35 7 36S 112 50 E
Bangka, Pulau, Sulawesi, Indonesia 35 1 50N 125 5 E
Bangka, Pulau, Sumatera, Indonesia 34 2 0S 105 50 E
Bangka, Selat 34 2 30S 105 30 E
Bangkalan 35 7 2S 112 46 E
Bangkinang 34 0 18N 101 5 E
Bangko 34 2 5S 102 9 E
Bangkok 34 13 45N 100 35 E
Bangladesh ■ 33 24 0N 90 0 E
Bangong Tso 32 34 0N 78 20 E
Bangor, N. Ireland, U.K. 9 54 40N 5 40W
Bangor, Wales, U.K. 6 53 13N 4 9W
Bangor, U.S.A. 63 44 48N 68 42W
Bangued 35 17 40N 120 37 E
Bangui 54 4 23N 18 35 E
Bangweulu, L. 54 11 0S 30 0 E
Bani 75 18 16N 70 22W
Banī Na'īm 28 31 31N 35 10 E
Banī Suhaylah 28 31 21N 34 19 E
Banī Walīd 51 31 36N 13 53 E
Banīnah 51 32 0N 20 12 E
Bāniyās 30 35 10N 36 0 E
Banja Luka 18 44 49N 17 11 E
Banjar 35 7 24S 108 30 E
Banjarmasin 34 3 20S 114 35 E
Banjarnegara 35 7 24S 109 42 E
Banjul 50 13 28N 16 40W
Banka Banka 44 18 50S 134 0 E
Bankipore 33 25 35N 85 10 E
Banks I., B.C., Canada 64 53 20N 130 0W
Banks I., N.W.T., Canada 60 73 15N 121 30W
Banks Pen. 43 43 45S 173 15 E
Banks Str. 44 40 40S 148 10 E
Bankura 33 23 11N 87 18 E
Bann →, Down, U.K. 9 54 30N 6 31W
Bann →, Londonderry, U.K. 9 55 10N 6 34W
Banning 73 33 58N 116 52W
Banningville = Bandundu 54 3 15S 17 22 E
Bannockburn 8 56 5N 3 55W
Bannu 32 33 0N 70 18 E
Banská Bystrica 15 48 46N 19 14 E
Banská Štiavnica 15 48 25N 18 55 E
Banswara 32 23 32N 74 24 E
Banten 35 6 5S 106 8 E
Bantry 9 51 40N 9 28W
Bantry, B. 9 51 35N 9 50W
Bantul 35 7 55S 110 19 E
Banu 32 35 35N 69 5 E
Banyak, Kepulauan 34 2 10N 97 10 E
Banyo 53 6 52N 11 45 E
Banyumas 35 7 32S 109 18 E
Banyuwangi 35 8 13S 114 21 E
Banzyville = Mobayi 54 4 15N 21 8 E
Baocheng 39 33 12N 106 56 E
Baode 38 39 1N 111 5 E
Baoding 38 38 50N 115 28 E
Baoji 39 34 20N 107 5 E
Baojing 39 28 45N 109 41 E
Baokang 39 31 54N 111 12 E
Baoshan 37 25 10N 99 5 E
Baotou 38 40 32N 110 2 E
Baoying 39 33 17N 119 20 E
Bapatla 33 15 55N 80 30 E
Bâqa el Gharbîyya 28 32 25N 35 2 E
Ba'qūbah 30 33 45N 44 50 E
Bar 19 42 8N 19 8 E
Bar Harbor 63 44 15N 68 20W
Bar-le-Duc 12 48 47N 5 10 E
Barabai 34 2 32S 115 34 E
Barabinsk 24 55 20N 78 20 E
Baraboo 70 43 28N 89 46W
Baracaldo 13 43 18N 2 59W
Baracoa 75 20 20N 74 30W
Baraga 70 46 49N 88 29W
Barahona 75 18 13N 71 7W
Barail Range 33 25 15N 93 20 E
Barakhola 33 25 0N 92 45 E
Barakpur 33 22 44N 88 30 E
Barakula 45 26 30S 150 33 E
Baralaba 44 24 13S 149 50 E
Baralzon L. 65 60 0N 98 3W
Baramula 32 34 15N 74 20 E
Baran 32 25 9N 76 40 E
Baranof I. 60 57 0N 135 10W
Baranovichi 22 53 10N 26 0 E
Barão de Melgaço 78 11 50S 60 45W
Barapasi 35 2 15S 137 5 E
Barat Daya, Kepulauan 35 7 30S 128 0 E
Barataria B. 71 29 15N 89 45W
Barbacena 79 21 15S 43 56W
Barbacoas 78 1 45N 78 0W
Barbados ■ 75 13 0N 59 30W
Barberton, S. Africa 57 25 42S 31 2 E
Barberton, U.S.A. 68 41 0N 81 40W
Barbourville 69 36 57N 83 52W
Barbuda I. 75 17 30N 61 40W
Barca, La 74 20 20N 102 40W
Barcaldine 44 23 43S 145 6 E
Barcelona, Spain 13 41 21N 2 10 E
Barcelona, Venezuela 78 10 10N 64 40W
Barcelos 78 1 0S 63 0W
Barcoo → 44 25 30S 142 50 E
Barddhaman 33 23 14N 87 39 E
Bardera 29 2 20N 42 27 E
Bardi, Ra's 30 24 17N 37 31 E
Bardia 51 31 45N 25 0 E
Bardsey I. 6 52 46N 4 47W
Bardstown 68 37 50N 85 29W
Bareilly 32 28 22N 79 27 E
Barentu 51 15 2N 37 35 E
Barga 37 30 40N 81 20 E
Bargal 29 11 25N 51 0 E
Bargara 44 24 50S 152 25 E
Barge, La 72 42 12N 110 4W
Barguzin 25 53 37N 109 37 E
Barhi 33 24 15N 85 25 E
Bari 18 41 6N 16 52 E
Bari Doab 32 30 20N 73 0 E
Barīm 29 12 39N 43 25 E
Barinas 78 8 36N 70 15W
Baring, C. 60 70 0N 117 30W
Bârîs 51 24 42N 30 31 E
Barisal 33 22 45N 90 20 E
Barisan, Bukit 34 3 30S 102 15 E
Barito → 34 4 0S 114 50 E
Barkā' 31 23 40N 58 0 E
Barkley Sound 64 48 50N 125 10W
Barkly Downs 44 20 30S 138 30 E
Barkly East 56 30 58S 27 33 E
Barkly Tableland 44 17 50S 136 40 E
Barkly West 56 28 5S 24 31 E
Barksdale 71 29 47N 100 2W
Barlee, L. 47 29 15S 119 30 E
Barletta 18 41 20N 16 17 E
Barlow L. 65 62 0N 103 0W
Barmedman 45 34 9S 147 21 E
Barmer 32 25 45N 71 20 E
Barmera 45 34 15S 140 28 E
Barmouth 6 52 44N 4 3W
Barnard Castle 6 54 33N 1 55W
Barnato 45 31 38S 145 0 E
Barnaul 24 53 20N 83 40 E
Barnesville 69 33 6N 84 9W
Barnet 7 51 37N 0 15W
Barneveld 11 52 7N 5 36 E
Barngo 44 25 3S 147 20 E
Barnhart 71 31 10N 101 8W
Barnsley 6 53 33N 1 29W
Barnstaple 7 51 5N 4 3W
Barnsville 70 46 43N 96 28W
Baro 53 8 35N 6 18 E
Baroda = Vadodara 32 22 20N 73 10 E
Baroe 56 33 13S 24 33 E
Baron Ra. 46 23 30S 127 45 E
Barpeta 33 26 20N 91 10 E
Barques, Pte. aux 68 44 5N 82 55W
Barquísimeto 78 10 4N 69 19W
Barra, Brazil 79 11 5S 43 10W
Barra, U.K. 8 57 0N 7 30W
Barra, Sd. of 8 57 4N 7 25W
Barra do Corda 79 5 30S 45 10W
Barra do Piraí 79 22 30S 43 50W
Barra Falsa, Pta. da 57 22 58S 35 37 E
Barra Hd. 8 56 47N 7 40W
Barraba 45 30 21S 150 35 E
Barrackpur = Barakpur 33 22 44N 88 30 E
Barranca, Lima, Peru 78 10 45S 77 50W
Barranca, Loreto, Peru 78 4 50S 76 50W
Barrancabermeja 78 7 0N 73 50W
Barrancas 78 8 55N 62 5W
Barrancos 13 38 10N 6 58W
Barranqueras 80 27 30S 59 0W
Barranquilla 78 11 0N 74 50W
Barras 79 4 15S 42 18W
Barraute 62 48 26N 77 38W
Barre 68 44 15N 72 30W
Barreiras 79 12 8S 45 0W
Barreirinhas 79 2 30S 42 50W
Barreiro 13 38 40N 9 6W
Barreiros 79 8 49S 35 12W
Barren, Nosy 57 18 25S 43 40 E
Barretos 79 20 30S 48 35W
Barrhead 64 54 10N 114 24W
Barrie 62 44 24N 79 40W
Barrier Ra. 45 31 0S 141 30 E
Barrière 64 51 12N 120 7W
Barrington L. 65 56 55N 100 15W
Barrington Tops 45 32 6S 151 28 E
Barringun 45 29 1S 145 41 E
Barrow 60 71 16N 156 50W
Barrow → 9 52 10N 6 57W
Barrow Creek 44 21 30S 133 55 E
Barrow I. 46 20 45S 115 20 E
Barrow-in-Furness 6 54 8N 3 15W
Barrow Pt. 44 14 20S 144 40 E
Barrow Ra. 47 26 0S 127 40 E
Barry 7 51 23N 3 19W
Barry's Bay 62 45 29N 77 41W
Barsi 32 18 10N 75 50 E
Barsoi 33 25 48N 87 57 E
Barstow, Calif., U.S.A. 73 34 58N 117 2W
Barstow, Tex., U.S.A. 71 31 28N 103 24W
Bartica 78 6 25N 58 40W
Bartin 30 41 38N 32 21 E
Bartlesville 71 36 50N 95 58W
Bartlett 71 30 46N 97 30W
Bartlett, L. 64 63 5N 118 20W
Barton 47 30 31S 132 39 E
Barton-upon-Humber 6 53 41N 0 27W
Bartow 69 27 53N 81 49W
Barú, Volcan 75 8 55N 82 35W
Bas-Rhin □ 12 48 40N 7 30 E
Bāsa'idū 31 26 35N 55 20 E
Basankusa 54 1 5N 19 50 E
Basel 14 47 35N 7 35 E
Bashkir A.S.S.R. □ 22 54 0N 57 0 E
Basilan 35 6 35N 122 0 E
Basilan Str. 35 6 50N 122 0 E
Basildon 7 51 34N 0 29 E
Basilicata □ 18 40 30N 16 0 E
Basim = Washim 32 20 3N 77 0 E
Basin 72 44 22N 108 2W
Basingstoke 7 51 15N 1 5W
Baskatong, Rés. 62 46 46N 75 50W
Basle = Basel 14 47 35N 7 35 E
Basoka 54 1 16N 23 40 E
Basongo 54 4 15S 20 20 E
Basque Provinces = Vascongadas □ 13 42 50N 2 45W
Basra = Al Başrah 30 30 30N 47 50 E
Bass Rock 8 56 5N 2 40W
Bass Str. 44 39 15S 146 30 E
Bassano 64 50 48N 112 20W
Bassano del Grappa 18 45 45N 11 45 E
Bassar 53 9 19N 0 57 E
Bassas da India 55 22 0S 39 0 E
Basse-Terre 75 16 0N 61 40W
Bassein 33 16 45N 94 30 E
Basseterre 75 17 17N 62 43W
Bassett, Nebr., U.S.A. 70 42 37N 99 30W
Bassett, Va., U.S.A. 69 36 48N 79 59W
Bassigny 12 48 0N 5 30 E
Bassikounou 50 15 55N 6 1W
Bastak 31 27 15N 54 25 E
Bastar 33 19 15N 81 40 E
Basti 33 26 52N 82 55 E
Bastia 12 42 40N 9 30 E
Bastogne 11 50 1N 5 43 E
Bastrop 71 30 5N 97 22W
Bat Yam 28 32 2N 34 44 E
Bata 54 1 57N 9 50 E
Bataan 35 14 40N 120 25 E
Batabanó 75 22 40N 82 20W
Batabanó, G. de 75 22 30N 82 30W
Batac 35 18 3N 120 34 E
Batagoy 25 67 38N 134 38 E
Batalha 13 39 40N 8 50W
Batamay 25 63 30N 129 15 E
Batang, China 37 30 1N 99 0 E
Batang, Indonesia 35 6 55S 109 45 E
Batangafo 51 7 25N 18 20 E
Batangas 35 13 35N 121 10 E
Batanta 35 0 55S 130 40 E
Batavia 68 43 0N 78 10W
Batchelor 46 13 4S 131 1 E
Bateman's B. 45 35 40S 150 12 E
Batemans Bay 45 35 44S 150 11 E
Batesburg 69 33 54N 81 32W
Batesville, Ark., U.S.A. 71 35 48N 91 40W
Batesville, Miss., U.S.A. 71 34 17N 89 58W
Batesville, Tex., U.S.A. 71 28 59N 99 38W
Bath, U.K. 7 51 22N 2 22W
Bath, Maine, U.S.A. 63 43 50N 69 49W
Bath, N.Y., U.S.A. 68 42 20N 77 17W
Bathgate 8 55 54N 3 38W
Bathurst = Banjul 50 13 28N 16 40W
Bathurst, Australia 45 33 25S 149 31 E
Bathurst, Canada 63 47 37N 65 43W
Bathurst, S. Africa 56 33 30S 26 50 E
Bathurst, C. 60 70 34N 128 0W
Bathurst B. 44 14 16S 144 25 E
Bathurst Harb. 44 43 15S 146 10 E
Bathurst I. 46 11 30S 130 10 E
Bathurst Inlet 60 66 50N 108 1W
Batinah 31 24 0N 56 0 E
Batlow 45 35 31S 148 9 E
Batman 30 37 55N 41 5 E
Batna 50 35 34N 6 15 E
Baton Rouge 71 30 30N 91 5W
Batopilas 74 27 0N 107 45W
Batouri 54 4 30N 14 25 E
Battambang 34 13 7N 103 12 E
Batticaloa 32 7 43N 81 45 E
Battīr 28 31 44N 35 8 E
Battle 7 50 55N 0 30 E
Battle → 65 52 43N 108 15W
Battle Camp 44 15 20S 144 40 E
Battle Creek 68 42 20N 85 6W
Battle Harbour 63 52 16N 55 35W
Battle Lake 70 46 20N 95 43W
Battle Mountain 72 40 45N 117 0W
Battleford 65 52 45N 108 15W
Batu 29 6 55N 39 45 E
Batu, Kepulauan 34 0 30S 98 25 E
Batu Pahat 34 1 50N 102 56 E
Batuata 35 6 12S 122 42 E
Batumi 23 41 30N 41 30 E
Baturaja 34 4 11S 104 15 E
Baturité 79 4 28S 38 45W
Bau 34 1 25N 110 9 E
Baubau 35 5 25S 122 38 E
Bauchi 53 10 22N 9 48 E
Bauchi □ 53 10 30N 10 0 E
Baudette 70 48 46N 94 35W
Bauer, C. 45 32 44S 134 4 E
Bauhinia Downs 44 24 35S 149 18 E
Bauru 79 22 10S 49 0W
Baús 79 18 22S 52 47W
Bautzen 14 51 11N 14 25 E
Bavaria = Bayern □ 14 49 7N 11 30 E
Bavispe → 74 29 30N 109 11W
Bawdwin 33 23 5N 97 20 E
Bawean 34 5 46S 112 35 E
Bawku 53 11 3N 0 19W
Bawlake 33 19 11N 97 21 E
Baxley 69 31 43N 82 23W
Baxter Springs 71 37 3N 94 45W
Bay, L. de 35 14 20N 121 11 E
Bay Bulls 63 47 19N 52 50W
Bay City, Mich., U.S.A. 68 43 35N 83 51W

Bettiah

Bay City, Oreg., U.S.A. **72** 45 45N 123 58W
Bay City, Tex., U.S.A. **71** 28 59N 95 55W
Bay de Verde **63** 48 5N 52 54W
Bay Minette **69** 30 54N 87 43W
Bay St. Louis **71** 30 18N 89 22W
Bay Springs **71** 31 58N 89 18W
Bay View **43** 39 25S 176 50 E
Bayamo **75** 20 20N 76 40W
Bayamón **75** 18 24N 66 10W
Bayan **38** 46 5N 127 24 E
Bayan Har Shan **37** 34 0N 98 0 E
Bayan Hot = Alxa Zuoqi **38** 38 50N 105 40 E
Bayan Obo **38** 41 52N 109 59 E
Bayanaul **24** 50 45N 75 45 E
Bayanhongor **37** 46 8N 102 43 E
Bayard **70** 41 48N 103 17W
Bayázeh **31** 33 30N 54 40 E
Baybay **35** 10 40N 124 55 E
Bayburt **30** 40 15N 40 20 E
Bayern □ **14** 49 7N 11 30 E
Bayeux **12** 49 17N 0 42W
Bayfield **70** 46 50N 90 48W
Baykal, Oz. **25** 53 0N 108 0 E
Baykit **25** 61 50N 95 50 E
Baykonur **24** 47 48N 65 50 E
Baymak **22** 52 36N 58 19 E
Baynes Mts. **56** 17 15S 13 0 E
Bayombong **35** 16 30N 121 10 E
Bayonne **12** 43 30N 1 28W
Bayovar **78** 5 50S 81 0W
Bayram-Ali **24** 37 37N 62 10 E
Bayreuth **14** 49 56N 11 35 E
Bayrūt **30** 33 53N 35 31 E
Bayt Awlá **28** 31 37N 35 2 E
Bayt Fajjār **28** 31 38N 35 9 E
Bayt Fūrīk **28** 32 11N 35 20 E
Bayt Ḥānūn **28** 31 32N 34 32 E
Bayt Jālā **28** 31 43N 35 11 E
Bayt Lahm **28** 31 43N 35 12 E
Bayt Rīma **28** 32 2N 35 6 E
Bayt Sāḥūr **28** 31 42N 35 13 E
Bayt Ummar **28** 31 38N 35 7 E
Bayt 'ūr al Taḥtā **28** 31 54N 35 5 E
Baytīn **28** 31 56N 35 14 E
Baytown **71** 29 42N 94 57W
Baytūniyā **28** 31 54N 35 10 E
Baza **13** 37 30N 2 47W
Bazaruto, I. do **57** 21 40S 35 28 E
Bazhong **39** 31 52N 106 46 E
Beach **70** 46 57N 103 58W
Beachport **45** 37 29S 140 0 E
Beachy Head **7** 50 44N 0 16 E
Beacon, Australia **47** 30 26S 117 52 E
Beacon, U.S.A. **68** 41 32N 73 58W
Beaconia **65** 50 25N 96 31W
Beagle, Canal **80** 55 0S 68 30W
Beagle Bay **46** 16 58S 122 40 E
Bealanana **57** 14 33N 48 44 E
Bear I. **9** 51 38N 9 50W
Bear L., B.C., Canada **64** 56 10N 126 52W
Bear L., Man., Canada **65** 55 8N 96 0W
Bear L., U.S.A. **72** 42 0N 111 20W
Bearcreek **72** 45 11N 109 6W
Beardmore **62** 49 36N 87 57W
Beardstown **70** 40 0N 90 25W
Béarn **12** 43 20N 0 30W
Bearpaw Mts. **72** 48 15N 109 30W
Bearskin Lake **62** 53 58N 91 2W
Beata, C. **75** 17 40N 71 30W
Beatrice **70** 40 20N 96 40W
Beatrice, C. **44** 14 20S 136 55 E
Beatton —► **64** 56 15N 120 45W
Beatton River **64** 57 26N 121 20W
Beatty **73** 36 58N 116 46W
Beauce, Plaine de la **12** 48 10N 1 45 E
Beauceville **63** 46 13N 70 46W
Beaudesert **45** 27 59S 153 0 E
Beaufort, Malaysia **34** 5 30N 115 40 E
Beaufort, N.C., U.S.A. **69** 34 45N 76 40W
Beaufort, S.C., U.S.A. **69** 32 25N 80 40W
Beaufort Sea **58** 72 0N 140 0W
Beaufort West **56** 32 18S 22 36 E
Beauharnois **62** 45 20N 73 52W
Beaulieu —► **64** 62 3N 113 11W
Beauly **8** 57 29N 4 27W
Beauly —► **8** 57 26N 4 28W
Beaumaris **6** 53 16N 4 7W
Beaumont **71** 30 5N 94 8W
Beaune **12** 47 2N 4 50 E
Beauséjour **65** 50 5N 96 35W
Beauvais **12** 49 25N 2 8 E
Beauval **65** 55 9N 107 37W
Beaver, Alaska, U.S.A. **60** 66 20N 147 30W
Beaver, Okla., U.S.A. **71** 36 52N 100 31W
Beaver, Utah, U.S.A. **73** 38 20N 112 45W
Beaver —►, B.C., Canada **64** 59 52N 124 20W
Beaver —►, Ont., Canada **62** 55 55N 87 48W
Beaver —►, Sask., Canada **65** 55 26N 107 45W
Beaver City **70** 40 13N 99 50W
Beaver Dam **70** 43 28N 88 50W
Beaver Falls **68** 40 44N 80 20W
Beaver Hill L. **65** 54 5N 94 50W
Beaver I. **68** 45 40N 85 31W
Beaverhill L., Alta., Canada **64** 53 27N 112 32W
Beaverhill L., N.W.T., Canada **65** 63 2N 104 22W
Beaverlodge **64** 55 11N 119 29W
Beavermouth **64** 51 32N 117 23W
Beaverstone —► **62** 54 59N 89 25W
Beawar **32** 26 3N 74 18 E
Beboa **57** 17 22S 44 33 E
Beccles **7** 52 27N 1 33 E
Bečej **19** 45 36N 20 3 E
Béchar **50** 31 38N 2 18W
Beckley **68** 37 50N 81 8W
Bedford, Canada **62** 45 7N 72 59W
Bedford, S. Africa **56** 32 40S 26 10 E
Bedford, U.K. **7** 52 8N 0 29W
Bedford, Ind., U.S.A. **68** 38 50N 86 30W
Bedford, Iowa, U.S.A. **70** 40 40N 94 41W
Bedford, Ohio, U.S.A. **68** 41 23N 81 32W
Bedford, Va., U.S.A. **68** 37 25N 79 30W
Bedford □ **7** 52 4N 0 28W
Bedford, C. **44** 15 14S 145 21 E
Bedford Downs **46** 17 19S 127 20 E
Bedourie **44** 24 30S 139 30 E
Beech Grove **68** 39 40N 86 2W
Beechworth **45** 36 22S 146 43 E
Beechy **65** 50 53N 107 24W
Beenleigh **45** 27 43S 153 10 E
Be'er Sheva' **28** 31 15N 34 48 E
Be'er Sheva' —► **28** 31 12N 34 40 E
Be'er Toviyya **28** 31 44N 34 42 E
Be'eri **28** 31 25N 34 30 E
Be'erotayim **28** 32 19N 34 59 E
Beersheba = Be'er Sheva' **28** 31 15N 34 48 E
Beeston **6** 52 55N 1 11W
Beetaloo **44** 17 15S 133 50 E
Beeville **71** 28 27N 97 44W
Befale **54** 0 25N 20 45 E
Befandriana **57** 21 55S 44 0 E
Befotaka **57** 23 49S 47 0 E
Bega **45** 36 41S 149 51 E
Behara **57** 24 55S 46 20 E
Behbehān **30** 30 30N 50 15 E
Behshahr **31** 36 45N 53 35 E
Bei Jiang —► **39** 23 2N 112 58 E
Bei'an **38** 48 10N 126 20 E
Beibei **39** 29 47N 106 22 E
Beihai **39** 21 28N 109 6 E
Beijing **38** 39 55N 116 20 E
Beijing □ **38** 39 55N 116 20 E
Beilen **11** 52 52N 6 27 E
Beilpajah **45** 32 54S 143 52 E
Beira **55** 19 50S 34 52 E
Beira-Alta **13** 40 35N 7 35W
Beira-Baixa **13** 40 2N 7 30W
Beira-Litoral **13** 40 5N 8 30W
Beirut = Bayrūt **30** 33 53N 35 31 E
Beit Lāhiyah **28** 31 32N 34 30 E
Beitaolaizhao **38** 44 58N 125 58 E
Beitbridge **55** 22 12S 30 0 E
Beizhen **38** 37 20N 118 2 E
Beja, Portugal **13** 38 2N 7 53W
Béja, Tunisia **50** 36 43N 9 12 E
Bejaia **50** 36 42N 5 2 E
Bejestān **31** 34 30N 58 5 E
Bekasi **35** 6 14S 106 59 E
Békéscsaba **15** 46 40N 21 5 E
Bekily **57** 24 13S 45 19 E
Bela, India **33** 25 50N 82 0 E
Bela, Pakistan **32** 26 12N 66 20 E
Bela Crkva **19** 44 55N 21 27 E
Bela Vista, Brazil **80** 22 12S 56 20W
Bela Vista, Mozam. **57** 26 10S 32 44 E
Belau Is. **40** 7 30N 134 30 E
Belavenona **57** 24 50S 47 4 E
Belawan **34** 3 33N 98 32 E
Belaya —► **22** 56 0N 54 32 E
Belaya Tserkov **23** 49 45N 30 10 E
Belcher Is. **62** 56 15N 78 45W
Belebey **22** 54 7N 54 7 E
Belém **79** 1 20S 48 30W
Belén, Paraguay **80** 23 30S 57 6W
Belen, U.S.A. **73** 34 40N 106 50W
Belet Uen **29** 4 30N 45 5 E
Belev **22** 53 50N 36 5 E
Belfast, S. Africa **57** 25 42S 30 2 E
Belfast, U.K. **9** 54 35N 5 56W
Belfast, U.S.A. **63** 44 30N 69 0W
Belfast □ **9** 54 35N 5 56W
Belfast, L. **9** 54 40N 5 50W
Belfield **70** 46 54N 103 11W
Belfort **12** 47 38N 6 50 E
Belfry **72** 45 10N 109 2W
Belgaum **32** 15 55N 74 35 E
Belgium ■ **11** 50 30N 5 0 E
Belgorod **23** 50 35N 36 35 E
Belgorod-Dnestrovskiy **23** 46 11N 30 23 E
Belgrade = Beograd **19** 44 50N 20 37 E
Belgrade **72** 45 50N 111 10W
Belhaven **69** 35 34N 76 35W
Beli Drim —► **19** 42 6N 20 25 E
Belinga **54** 1 10N 13 2 E
Belinyu **34** 1 35S 105 50 E
Belitung **34** 3 10S 107 50 E
Belize ■ **74** 17 0N 88 30W
Belize City **74** 17 25N 88 0W
Belkovskiy, Ostrov **25** 75 32N 135 44 E
Bell —► **62** 49 48N 77 38W
Bell Bay **44** 41 6S 146 53 E
Bell I. **63** 50 46N 55 35W
Bell-Irving —► **64** 56 12N 129 5W
Bell Peninsula **61** 63 50N 82 0W
Bell Ville **80** 32 40S 62 40W
Bella Bella **64** 52 10N 128 10W
Bella Coola **64** 52 25N 126 40W
Bella Unión **80** 30 15S 57 40W
Bella Vista **80** 28 33S 59 0W
Bellaire **68** 40 1N 80 46W
Bellary **32** 15 10N 76 56 E
Bellata **45** 29 53S 149 46 E
Belle, La **69** 26 45N 81 22W
Belle Fourche **70** 44 43N 103 52W
Belle Fourche —► **70** 44 25N 102 19W
Belle Glade **69** 26 43N 80 38W
Belle-Ile **12** 47 20N 3 10W
Belle Isle **63** 51 57N 55 25W
Belle Isle, Str. of **63** 51 30N 56 30W
Belle Plaine, Iowa, U.S.A. **70** 41 51N 92 18W
Belle Plaine, Minn., U.S.A. **70** 44 35N 93 48W
Belledune **63** 47 55N 65 50W
Bellefontaine **68** 40 20N 83 45W
Bellefonte **68** 40 56N 77 45W
Belleoram **63** 47 31N 55 25W
Belleville, Canada **62** 44 10N 77 23W
Belleville, Ill., U.S.A. **70** 38 30N 90 0W
Belleville, Kans., U.S.A. **70** 39 51N 97 38W
Bellevue, Canada **64** 49 35N 114 22W
Bellevue, U.S.A. **72** 43 25N 114 23W
Bellin **61** 60 0N 70 0W
Bellingen **45** 30 25S 152 50 E
Bellingham **72** 48 45N 122 27W
Bellinzona **14** 46 11N 9 1 E
Bello **78** 6 20N 75 33W
Bellows Falls **68** 43 10N 72 30W
Belluno **18** 46 8N 12 13 E
Bellville **71** 29 58N 96 18W
Bélmez **13** 38 17N 5 17W
Belmont, Australia **45** 33 4S 151 42 E
Belmont, S. Africa **56** 29 28S 24 22 E
Belmonte **79** 16 0S 39 0W
Belmopan **74** 17 18N 88 30W
Belmullet **9** 54 13N 9 58W
Belo Horizonte **79** 19 55S 43 56W
Belo-sur-Mer **57** 20 42S 44 0 E
Belo-Tsiribihina **57** 19 40S 44 30 E
Belogorsk **25** 51 0N 128 20 E
Beloha **57** 25 10S 45 3 E
Beloit, Kans., U.S.A. **70** 39 32N 98 9W
Beloit, Wis., U.S.A. **70** 42 35N 89 0W
Belomorsk **22** 64 35N 34 30 E
Belonia **33** 23 15N 91 30 E
Beloretsk **22** 53 58N 58 24 E
Belovo **24** 54 30N 86 0 E
Beloye, Oz. **22** 60 10N 37 35 E
Beloye More **22** 66 30N 38 0 E
Belozersk **22** 60 0N 37 30 E
Beltana **45** 30 48S 138 25 E
Belterra **79** 2 45S 55 0W
Belton, S.C., U.S.A. **69** 34 31N 82 39W
Belton, Tex., U.S.A. **71** 31 4N 97 30W
Belton Res. **71** 31 8N 97 32W
Beltsy **23** 47 48N 28 0 E
Belturbet **9** 54 6N 7 28W
Belukha **24** 49 50N 86 50 E
Beluran **34** 5 48N 117 35 E
Belvidere **70** 42 15N 88 55W
Belyando —► **44** 21 38S 146 50 E
Belyy, Ostrov **24** 73 30N 71 0 E
Belyy Yar **24** 58 26N 84 39 E
Belzoni **71** 33 12N 90 30W
Bemaraha, Lembalemban' i **57** 18 40S 44 45 E
Bemarivo **57** 21 45S 44 45 E
Bemarivo —► **57** 15 27S 47 40 E
Bemavo **57** 21 33S 45 25 E
Bembéréke **53** 10 11N 2 43 E
Bemidji **70** 47 30N 94 50W
Ben 'Ammi **28** 33 0N 35 7 E
Ben Cruachan **8** 56 26N 5 8W
Ben Dearg **8** 57 47N 4 58W
Ben Gardane **51** 33 11N 11 11 E
Ben Hope **8** 58 24N 4 36W
Ben Lawers **8** 56 33N 4 13W
Ben Lomond, N.S.W., Australia **45** 30 1S 151 43 E
Ben Lomond, Tas., Australia **44** 41 38S 147 42 E
Ben Lomond, U.K. **8** 56 12N 4 39W
Ben Macdhui **8** 57 4N 3 40W
Ben Mhor **8** 57 16N 7 21W
Ben More, Central, U.K. **8** 56 23N 4 31W
Ben More, Strathclyde, U.K. **8** 56 26N 6 2W
Ben More Assynt **8** 58 7N 4 51W
Ben Nevis **8** 56 48N 5 0W
Ben Vorlich **8** 56 22N 4 15W
Ben Wyvis **8** 57 40N 4 35W
Bena **53** 11 20N 5 50 E
Bena Dibele **54** 4 4S 22 50 E
Benagerie **45** 31 25S 140 22 E
Benalla **45** 36 30S 146 0 E
Benares = Varanasi **33** 25 22N 83 0 E
Benavides **71** 27 35N 98 28W
Benbecula **8** 57 26N 7 21W
Benbonyathe, Mt. **45** 30 25S 139 11 E
Bencubbin **47** 30 48S 117 52 E
Bend **72** 44 2N 121 15W
Bendel □ **53** 6 0N 6 0 E
Bender Beila **29** 9 30N 50 48 E
Bendering **47** 32 23S 118 18 E
Bendery **23** 46 50N 29 30 E
Bendigo **45** 36 40S 144 15 E
Benē Beraq **28** 32 6N 34 51 E
Benenitra **57** 23 27S 45 5 E
Benevento **18** 41 7N 14 45 E
Bengal, Bay of **33** 15 0N 90 0 E
Bengbu **39** 32 58N 117 20 E
Benghazi = Banghāzī **51** 32 11N 20 3 E
Bengkalis **34** 1 30N 102 10 E
Bengkulu **34** 3 50S 102 12 E
Bengkulu □ **34** 3 48S 102 16 E
Bengough **65** 49 25N 105 10W
Benguela **55** 12 37S 13 25 E
Benguérua, I. **57** 21 58S 35 28 E
Beni **54** 0 30N 29 27 E
Beni —► **78** 10 23S 65 24W
Beni Abbès **50** 30 5N 2 5W
Beni Mazâr **51** 28 32N 30 44 E
Beni Mellal **50** 32 21N 6 21W
Beni Ounif **50** 32 0N 1 10W
Beni Suef **51** 29 5N 31 6 E
Beniah L. **64** 63 23N 112 17W
Benidorm **13** 38 33N 0 9W
Benin ■ **53** 10 0N 2 0 E
Benin, Bight of **53** 5 0N 3 0 E
Benin City **53** 6 20N 5 31 E
Benjamin Constant **78** 4 40S 70 15W
Benkelman **70** 40 7N 101 32W
Benlidi **44** 24 35S 144 50 E
Bennett **64** 59 56N 134 53W
Bennett, Ostrov **25** 76 21N 148 56 E
Bennettsville **69** 34 38N 79 39W
Bennington **68** 42 52N 73 12W
Benoni **57** 26 11S 28 18 E
Benson **73** 31 59N 110 19W
Bent **31** 26 20N 59 31 E
Benteng **35** 6 10S 120 30 E
Bentinck I. **44** 17 3S 139 35 E
Benton, Ark., U.S.A. **71** 34 30N 92 35W
Benton, Ill., U.S.A. **70** 38 0N 88 55W
Benton Harbor **68** 42 10N 86 28W
Benue □ **53** 7 30N 7 30 E
Benue —► **53** 7 48N 6 46 E
Benxi **38** 41 20N 123 48 E
Beo **35** 4 25N 126 50 E
Beograd **19** 44 50N 20 37 E
Beowawe **72** 40 35N 116 30W
Beppu **36** 33 15N 131 30 E
Berau, Teluk **35** 2 30S 132 30 E
Berber **51** 18 0N 34 0 E
Berbera **29** 10 30N 45 2 E
Berbérati **54** 4 15N 15 40 E
Berbice —► **78** 6 20N 57 32W
Berdichev **23** 49 57N 28 30 E
Berdsk **24** 54 47N 83 2 E
Berdyansk **23** 46 45N 36 50 E
Berea **68** 37 35N 84 18W
Berebere **35** 2 25N 128 45 E
Bereda **29** 11 45N 51 0 E
Berekum **50** 7 29N 2 34W
Berens —► **65** 52 25N 97 2W
Berens I. **65** 52 18N 97 18W
Berens River **65** 52 25N 97 0W
Berevo, Mahajanga, Madag. **57** 17 14S 44 17 E
Berevo, Toliara, Madag. **57** 19 44S 44 58 E
Berezina —► **22** 52 33N 30 14 E
Berezniki **24** 59 24N 56 46 E
Berezovo **22** 64 0N 65 0 E
Bergama **30** 39 8N 27 15 E
Bérgamo **18** 45 42N 9 40 E
Bergen, Neth. **11** 52 40N 4 43 E
Bergen, Norway **21** 60 23N 5 20 E
Bergen-op-Zoom **11** 51 30N 4 18 E
Bergerac **12** 44 51N 0 30 E
Bergum **11** 53 13N 5 59 E
Bergville **57** 28 52S 29 18 E
Berhala, Selat **34** 1 0S 104 15 E
Berhampore = Baharampur **33** 24 2N 88 27 E
Berhampur **33** 19 15N 84 54 E
Bering Sea **60** 58 0N 167 0 E
Bering Str. **60** 66 0N 170 0W
Beringen **11** 51 3N 5 14 E
Beringovskiy **25** 63 3N 179 19 E
Berja **13** 36 50N 2 56W
Berkeley, U.K. **7** 51 41N 2 28W
Berkeley, U.S.A. **72** 37 52N 122 20W
Berkeley Springs **68** 39 38N 78 12W
Berkshire □ **7** 51 30N 1 20W
Berland —► **64** 54 0N 116 50W
Berlin, Germany **14** 52 32N 13 24 E
Berlin, Md., U.S.A. **68** 38 19N 75 12W
Berlin, N.H., U.S.A. **68** 44 29N 71 10W
Berlin, Wis., U.S.A. **68** 43 58N 88 55W
Bermejo —►, Formosa, Argentina **80** 26 51S 58 23W
Bermejo —►, San Juan, Argentina **80** 32 30S 67 30W
Bermuda ■ **2** 32 45N 65 0W
Bern **14** 46 57N 7 28 E
Bernado **73** 34 30N 106 53W
Bernalillo **73** 35 17N 106 37W
Bernardo de Irigoyen **80** 26 15S 53 40W
Bernburg **14** 51 40N 11 42 E
Berne = Bern **14** 46 57N 7 28 E
Bernier I. **47** 24 50S 113 12 E
Beror Hayil **28** 31 34N 34 38 E
Beroroha **57** 21 40S 45 10 E
Beroun **14** 49 57N 14 5 E
Berrechid **50** 33 18N 7 36W
Berri **45** 34 14S 140 35 E
Berry, Australia **45** 34 46S 150 43 E
Berry, France **12** 46 50N 2 0 E
Berry Is. **75** 25 40N 77 50W
Berryville **71** 36 23N 93 35W
Berthold **70** 48 19N 101 45W
Berthoud **70** 40 21N 105 5W
Bertoua **54** 4 30N 13 45 E
Bertrand **70** 40 35N 99 38W
Berufjörður **20** 64 48N 14 29W
Berwick **68** 41 4N 76 17W
Berwick-upon-Tweed **6** 55 47N 2 0W
Berwyn Mts. **6** 52 54N 3 26W
Besalampy **57** 16 43S 44 29 E
Besançon **12** 47 15N 6 0 E
Besar **34** 2 40S 116 0 E
Besnard L. **65** 55 25N 106 0W
Besni **30** 37 41N 37 52 E
Besor, N. —► **28** 31 28N 34 22 E
Bessemer, Ala., U.S.A. **69** 33 25N 86 57W
Bessemer, Mich., U.S.A. **70** 46 27N 90 0W
Bet Alfa **28** 32 31N 35 25 E
Bet Dagan **28** 32 1N 34 49 E
Bet Guvrin **28** 31 37N 34 54 E
Bet Ha'Emeq **28** 32 58N 35 8 E
Bet Hashitta **28** 32 31N 35 27 E
Bet Qeshet **28** 32 41N 35 21 E
Bet She'an **28** 32 30N 35 30 E
Bet Shemesh **28** 31 44N 35 0 E
Bet Yosef **28** 32 34N 35 33 E
Betafo **57** 19 50S 46 51 E
Bétaré Oya **54** 5 40N 14 5 E
Bethal **57** 26 27S 29 28 E
Bethanien **56** 26 31S 17 8 E
Bethany = Al 'Ayzarīyah **28** 31 47N 35 15 E
Bethany, S. Africa **56** 29 34S 25 59 E
Bethany, U.S.A. **70** 40 18N 94 0W
Bethel **60** 60 50N 161 50W
Bethlehem = Bayt Lahm **28** 31 43N 35 12 E
Bethlehem, S. Africa **57** 28 14S 28 18 E
Bethlehem, U.S.A. **68** 40 39N 75 24W
Bethulie **56** 30 30S 25 59 E
Béthune **12** 50 30N 2 38 E
Bethungra **45** 34 45S 147 51 E
Betioky **57** 23 48S 44 20 E
Betoota **44** 25 45S 140 42 E
Betroka **57** 23 16S 46 0 E
Betsiamites **63** 48 56N 68 40W
Betsiamites —► **63** 48 56N 68 38W
Betsiboka —► **57** 16 3S 46 36 E
Betsjoeanaland **56** 26 30S 22 30 E
Bettiah **33** 26 48N 84 33 E

Betul

Betul 32 21 58N 77 59 E
Betung 34 1 24N 111 31 E
Beulah 70 47 18N 101 47W
Beverley, Australia 47 32 9S 116 56 E
Beverley, U.K. 6 53 52N 0 26W
Beverly 72 46 55N 119 59W
Beverly Hills 73 34 4N 118 29W
Beverwijk 11 52 28N 4 38 E
Beyla 50 8 30N 8 38W
Beyneu 23 45 10N 55 3 E
Beypazarı 30 40 10N 31 56 E
Beyşehir Gölü 30 37 40N 31 45 E
Bezet 28 33 4N 35 8 E
Bezhitsa 22 53 19N 34 17 E
Béziers 12 43 20N 3 12 E
Bezwada = Vijayawada 33 16 31N 80 39 E
Bhachau 32 23 20N 70 16 E
Bhadrakh 33 21 10N 86 30 E
Bhadravati 32 13 49N 75 40 E
Bhagalpur 33 25 10N 87 0 E
Bhakra Dam 32 31 30N 76 45 E
Bhamo 33 24 15N 97 15 E
Bhandara 32 21 5N 79 42 E
Bhanrer Ra. 32 23 40N 79 45 E
Bharat = India ■ 32 20 0N 78 0 E
Bharatpur 32 27 15N 77 30 E
Bhatpara 33 22 50N 88 25 E
Bhaunagar = Bhavnagar 32 21 45N 72 10 E
Bhavnagar 32 21 45N 72 10 E
Bhawanipatna 33 19 55N 80 10 E
Bhilsa = Vidisha 32 23 28N 77 53 E
Bhilwara 32 25 25N 74 38 E
Bhima → 32 16 25N 77 17 E
Bhimavaram 33 16 30N 81 30 E
Bhind 32 26 30N 78 46 E
Bhiwandi 32 19 20N 73 0 E
Bhiwani 32 28 50N 76 9 E
Bhola 33 22 45N 90 35 E
Bhopal 32 23 20N 77 30 E
Bhubaneshwar 33 20 15N 85 50 E
Bhuj 32 23 15N 69 49 E
Bhumibol Dam 34 17 15N 98 58 E
Bhusaval 32 21 3N 75 46 E
Bhutan ■ 33 27 25N 90 30 E
Biafra, B. of = Bonny, Bight of 54 3 30N 9 20 E
Biak 35 1 10S 136 6 E
Biała Podlaska 15 52 4N 23 6 E
Białystok 15 53 10N 23 10 E
Biaro 35 2 5N 125 26 E
Biarritz 12 43 29N 1 33W
Bibai 36 43 19N 141 52 E
Bibala 55 14 44S 13 24 E
Bibby I. 65 61 55N 93 0W
Biberach 14 48 5N 9 49 E
Bibiani 50 6 30N 2 8W
Biboohra 44 16 56S 145 25 E
Bic 63 48 20N 68 41W
Biche, La → 64 59 57N 123 50W
Bickerton I. 44 13 45S 136 10 E
Bicknell, Ind., U.S.A. 68 38 50N 87 20W
Bicknell, Utah, U.S.A. 73 38 16N 111 35W
Bida 53 9 3N 5 58 E
Bidar 32 17 55N 77 35 E
Biddeford 63 43 30N 70 28W
Biddiyā 28 32 7N 35 4 E
Biddū 28 31 50N 35 8 E
Bideford 7 51 1N 4 13W
Bidon 5 = Poste Maurice Cortier 50 22 14N 1 2 E
Bié, Planalto de 55 12 0S 16 0 E
Bieber 72 41 4N 121 6W
Biel 14 47 8N 7 14 E
Bielé Karpaty 15 49 5N 18 0 E
Bielefeld 14 52 2N 8 31 E
Biella 18 45 33N 8 3 E
Bielsko-Biała 15 49 50N 19 2 E
Bien Hoa 34 10 57N 106 49 E
Bienfait 65 49 10N 102 50W
Bienne = Biel 14 47 8N 7 14 E
Bienville, L. 62 55 5N 72 40W
Biesiesfontein 56 30 57S 17 58 E
Big → 63 54 50N 58 55W
Big B. 63 55 43N 60 35W
Big Beaver 65 49 10N 105 10W
Big Belt Mts. 72 46 50N 111 30W
Big Bend 57 26 50S 31 58 E
Big Bend Nat. Park 71 29 15N 103 15W
Big Black → 71 32 0N 91 5W
Big Blue → 70 39 11N 96 40W
Big Cr. → 64 51 42N 122 41W
Big Cypress Swamp 69 26 12N 81 10W
Big Falls 70 48 11N 93 48W
Big Fork → 70 48 31N 93 43W
Big Horn Mts. = Bighorn Mts. 72 44 30N 107 30W
Big Lake 71 31 12N 101 25W
Big Muddy → 70 48 8N 104 36W
Big Pine 73 37 12N 118 17W
Big Piney 72 42 32N 110 3W
Big Quill L. 65 51 55N 104 50W
Big Rapids 68 43 42N 85 27W
Big River 65 53 50N 107 0W
Big Sable Pt. 68 44 5N 86 30W
Big Sand L. 65 57 45N 99 45W
Big Sandy 72 48 12N 110 9W
Big Sandy Cr. → 70 38 6N 102 29W
Big Sioux → 70 42 30N 96 25W
Big Spring 71 32 10N 101 25W
Big Springs 70 41 4N 102 3W
Big Stone City 70 45 20N 96 30W
Big Stone Gap 69 36 52N 82 45W
Big Stone L. 70 45 30N 96 35W
Big Timber 72 45 53N 110 0W
Big Trout L. 62 53 40N 90 0W
Bigfork 72 48 3N 114 2W
Biggar, Canada 65 52 4N 108 0W
Biggar, U.K. 8 55 38N 3 31W
Bigge I. 46 14 35S 125 10 E
Biggenden 45 25 31S 152 4 E
Bighorn 72 46 11N 107 25W
Bighorn → 72 46 9N 107 28W
Bighorn Mts. 72 44 30N 107 30W
Bigorre 12 43 10N 0 5 E
Bigstone L. 65 53 42N 95 44W
Bihać 18 44 49N 15 57 E
Bihar 33 25 5N 85 40 E
Bihar □ 33 25 0N 86 0 E
Bijagós, Arquipélago dos 50 11 15N 16 10W
Bijapur, Karnataka, India 32 16 50N 75 55 E
Bijapur, Mad. P., India 33 18 50N 80 50 E
Bījār 30 35 52N 47 35 E
Bijeljina 19 44 46N 19 17 E
Bijie 39 27 20N 105 16 E
Bijnor 32 29 27N 78 11 E
Bikaner 32 28 2N 73 18 E
Bikin 25 46 50N 134 20 E
Bikini Atoll 40 12 0N 167 30 E
Bilara 32 26 14N 73 53 E
Bilaspur 33 22 2N 82 15 E
Bilauk Taungdan 34 13 0N 99 0 E
Bilbao 13 43 16N 2 56W
Bíldudalur 20 65 41N 23 36W
Bilecik 30 40 5N 30 5 E
Bilibino 25 68 3N 166 20 E
Bilir 25 65 40N 131 20 E
Bill 70 43 18N 105 18W
Billabalong 47 27 25S 115 49 E
Billiluna 46 19 37S 127 41 E
Billingham 6 54 36N 1 18W
Billings 72 45 43N 108 29W
Billiton Is. = Belitung 34 3 10S 107 50 E
Bilma 51 18 50N 13 30 E
Biloela 44 24 24S 150 31 E
Biloxi 71 30 24N 88 53W
Bilpa Morea Claypan 44 25 0S 140 0 E
Biltine 51 14 40N 20 50 E
Bilyana 44 18 5S 145 50 E
Bima 35 8 22S 118 49 E
Bimbo 54 4 15N 18 33 E
Bimini Is. 75 25 42N 79 25W
Bin Xian 39 35 2N 108 4 E
Bina-Etawah 32 24 13N 78 14 E
Binalbagan 35 10 12N 122 50 E
Bīnālūd, Kūh-e 31 36 30N 58 30 E
Binatang 34 2 10N 111 40 E
Binbee 44 20 19S 147 56 E
Binche 11 50 26N 4 10 E
Binda 45 27 52S 147 21 E
Bindi Bindi 47 30 37S 116 22 E
Bindle 45 27 40S 148 45 E
Bindura 55 17 18S 31 18 E
Bingara, N.S.W., Australia 45 29 52S 150 36 E
Bingara, Queens., Australia 45 28 10S 144 37 E
Bingham 63 45 5N 69 50W
Bingham Canyon 72 40 31N 112 10W
Binghamton 68 42 9N 75 54W
Bingöl 30 38 53N 40 29 E
Binh Dinh = An Nhon 34 13 55N 109 7 E
Binh Son 34 15 20N 108 40 E
Binjai 34 3 20N 98 30 E
Binnaway 45 31 28S 149 24 E
Binongko 35 5 55S 123 55 E
Binscarth 65 50 37N 101 17W
Bint Jubayl 28 33 8N 35 25 E
Bintan 34 1 0N 104 0 E
Bintulu 34 3 10N 113 0 E
Bintuni 35 2 7S 133 32 E
Binyamina 28 32 32N 34 56 E
Binyang 39 23 12N 108 47 E
Binzert = Bizerte 50 37 15N 9 50 E
Bioko 53 3 30N 8 40 E
Biq'at Bet Netofa 28 32 49N 35 22 E
Bir 32 19 0N 75 54 E
Bir Autrun 51 18 15N 26 40 E
Bir Mogrein 50 25 10N 11 25W
Bi'r Nabālā 28 31 52N 35 12 E
Bîr Ungât 51 22 8N 33 48 E
Bi'r Zayt 28 31 59N 35 11 E
Bira 35 2 3S 132 2 E
Birak Sulaymān 28 31 42N 35 7 E
Birao 51 10 20N 22 47 E
Birch Hills 65 52 59N 105 25W
Birch I. 65 52 26N 99 54W
Birch L., N.W.T., Canada 64 62 4N 116 33W
Birch L., Ont., Canada 62 51 23N 92 18W
Birch L., U.S.A. 62 47 48N 91 43W
Birch Mts. 64 57 30N 113 10W
Birch River 65 52 24N 101 6W
Birchip 45 35 56S 142 55 E
Bird 65 56 30N 94 13W
Bird City 70 39 48N 101 33W
Bird I. = Aves, I. de 75 15 45N 63 55W
Bird I. 56 32 3S 18 17 E
Birdlip 7 51 50N 2 7W
Birdsville 44 25 51S 139 20 E
Birdum 46 15 39S 133 13 E
Birecik 30 37 0N 38 0 E
Bireuen 34 5 14N 96 39 E
Birkenhead 6 53 24N 3 1W
Bîrlad 15 46 15N 27 38 E
Birmingham, U.K. 7 52 30N 1 55W
Birmingham, U.S.A. 69 33 31N 86 50W
Birmitrapur 33 22 24N 84 46 E
Birni Nkonni 50 13 55N 5 15 E
Birnin Kebbi 53 12 32N 4 12 E
Birnin Kudu 53 11 30N 9 29 E
Birobidzhan 25 48 50N 132 50 E
Birqīn 28 32 27N 35 15 E
Birr 9 53 7N 7 55W
Birrie → 45 29 43S 146 37 E
Birsk 22 55 25N 55 30 E
Birtle 65 50 30N 101 5W
Birur 32 13 30N 75 55 E
Bisa 35 1 15S 127 28 E
Bisbee 73 31 30N 110 0W
Biscay, B. of 16 45 0N 2 0W
Biscayne B. 69 25 40N 80 12W
Biscostasing 62 47 18N 82 9W
Bisho 57 32 50S 27 23 E
Bishop, Calif., U.S.A. 73 37 20N 118 26W
Bishop, Tex., U.S.A. 71 27 35N 97 49W
Bishop Auckland 6 54 40N 1 40W
Bishop's Falls 63 49 2N 55 30W
Bishop's Stortford 7 51 52N 0 11 E
Biskra 50 34 50N 5 44 E
Bislig 35 8 15N 126 27 E
Bismarck 70 46 49N 100 49W
Bismarck Arch. 40 2 30S 150 0 E
Bison 70 45 34N 102 28W
Bispfors 20 63 1N 16 37 E
Bissagos = Bijagós, Arquipélago dos 50 11 15N 16 10W
Bissau 50 11 45N 15 45W
Bissett 65 51 2N 95 41W
Bistcho L. 64 59 45N 118 50W
Bistrița 15 47 9N 24 35 E
Bistrița → 15 46 30N 26 57 E
Bitam 54 2 5N 11 25 E
Bitkine 51 11 59N 18 13 E
Bitlis 30 38 20N 42 3 E
Bitola 19 41 5N 21 10 E
Bitolj = Bitola 19 41 5N 21 10 E
Bitter Creek 72 41 39N 108 36W
Bitter L. = Buheirat-Murrat-el-Kubra 51 30 15N 32 40 E
Bitterfontein 56 31 1S 18 32 E
Bitterroot → 72 46 52N 114 6W
Bitterroot Range 72 46 0N 114 20W
Biu 51 10 40N 12 3 E
Biwa-Ko 36 35 15N 136 10 E
Biwabik 70 47 33N 92 19W
Biyang 39 32 38N 113 21 E
Biysk 24 52 40N 85 0 E
Bizana 57 30 50S 29 52 E
Bizerte 50 37 15N 9 50 E
Bjargtangar 20 65 30N 24 30W
Bjelovar 18 45 56N 16 49 E
Black →, Ark., U.S.A. 71 35 38N 91 19W
Black →, Wis., U.S.A. 70 43 52N 91 22W
Black Diamond 64 50 45N 114 14W
Black Forest = Schwarzwald 14 48 0N 8 0 E
Black Hills 70 44 0N 103 50W
Black I. 65 51 12N 96 30W
Black L., Canada 65 59 12N 105 15W
Black L., U.S.A. 68 45 28N 84 15W
Black Mesa, Mt. 71 36 57N 102 55W
Black Mt. = Mynydd Du 7 51 45N 3 45W
Black Mts. 7 51 52N 3 5W
Black Range 73 33 30N 107 55W
Black River 75 18 0N 77 50W
Black River Falls 70 44 23N 90 52W
Black Sea 17 43 30N 35 0 E
Black Volta → 50 8 41N 1 33W
Black Warrior → 69 32 32N 87 51W
Blackall 44 24 25S 145 45 E
Blackball 43 42 22S 171 26 E
Blackbull 44 17 55S 141 45 E
Blackburn 6 53 44N 2 30W
Blackduck 70 47 43N 94 32W
Blackfoot 72 43 13N 112 12W
Blackfoot → 72 46 52N 113 53W
Blackfoot Res. 72 43 0N 111 35W
Blackie 64 50 36N 113 37W
Blackpool 6 53 48N 3 3W
Blacks Harbour 63 45 3N 66 49W
Blacksburg 68 37 17N 80 23W
Blacksod B. 9 54 6N 10 0W
Blackstone 68 37 6N 78 0W
Blackstone → 64 61 5N 122 55W
Blackstone Ra. 47 26 0S 128 30 E
Blackville 63 46 44N 65 50W
Blackwater 44 23 35S 148 53 E
Blackwater →, Ireland 9 51 55N 7 50W
Blackwater →, U.K. 9 54 31N 6 35W
Blackwater Cr. → 45 25 56S 144 30 E
Blackwell 71 36 55N 97 20W
Blaenau Ffestiniog 6 53 0N 3 57W
Blagodarnoye 23 45 7N 43 37 E
Blagoveshchensk 25 50 20N 127 30 E
Blaine 72 48 59N 122 43W
Blaine Lake 65 52 51N 106 52W
Blair 70 41 38N 96 10W
Blair Athol 44 22 42S 147 31 E
Blair Atholl 8 56 46N 3 50W
Blairgowrie 8 56 36N 3 20W
Blairmore 64 49 40N 114 25W
Blake Pt. 70 48 12N 88 27W
Blakely 69 31 22N 85 0W
Blanc, Mont 12 45 48N 6 50 E
Blanca, B. 80 39 10S 61 30W
Blanca Peak 73 37 35N 105 29W
Blanchard 71 35 8N 97 40W
Blanche, C. 45 33 1S 134 9 E
Blanche L., S. Austral., Australia 45 29 15S 139 40 E
Blanche L., W. Austral., Australia 46 22 25S 123 17 E
Blanco, S. Africa 56 33 55S 22 23 E
Blanco, U.S.A. 71 30 7N 98 30W
Blanco, C., C. Rica 75 9 34N 85 8W
Blanco, C., U.S.A. 72 42 50N 124 40W
Blanda → 20 65 20N 19 40W
Blandford Forum 7 50 52N 2 10W
Blanding 73 37 35N 109 30W
Blankenberge 11 51 20N 3 9 E
Blantyre 55 15 45S 35 0 E
Blarney 9 51 57N 8 35W
Blåvands Huk 21 55 33N 8 4 E
Blaydon 6 54 56N 1 47W
Blayney 45 33 32S 149 14 E
Blaze, Pt. 46 12 56S 130 11 E
Blednaya, Gora 24 76 20N 65 0 E
Bleiburg 14 46 35N 14 49 E
Blekinge län □ 21 56 20N 15 20 E
Blenheim 43 41 38S 173 57 E
Bletchley 7 51 59N 0 44W
Blida 50 36 30N 2 49 E
Bligh Sound 43 44 47S 167 32 E
Blind River 62 46 10N 82 58W
Blitar 35 8 5S 112 11 E
Blitta 53 8 23N 1 6 E
Block I. 68 41 11N 71 35W
Bloemfontein 56 29 6S 26 7 E
Bloemhof 56 27 38S 25 32 E
Blois 12 47 35N 1 20 E
Blönduós 20 65 40N 20 12W
Bloodvein → 65 51 47N 96 43W
Bloody Foreland 9 55 10N 8 18W
Bloomer 70 45 8N 91 30W
Bloomfield, Australia 44 15 56S 145 22 E
Bloomfield, Iowa, U.S.A. 70 40 44N 92 26W
Bloomfield, N. Mex., U.S.A. 73 36 46N 107 59W
Bloomfield, Nebr., U.S.A. 70 42 38N 97 40W
Bloomington, Ill., U.S.A. 70 40 27N 89 0W
Bloomington, Ind., U.S.A. 68 39 10N 86 30W
Bloomsburg 68 41 0N 76 30W
Blora 35 6 57S 111 25 E
Blouberg 57 23 8S 28 59 E
Blountstown 69 30 28N 85 5W
Blue Island 68 41 40N 87 40W
Blue Lake 72 40 53N 124 0W
Blue Mesa Res. 73 38 30N 107 15W
Blue Mts., Oreg., U.S.A. 72 45 15N 119 0W
Blue Mts., Pa., U.S.A. 68 40 30N 76 30W
Blue Mud B. 44 13 30S 136 0 E
Blue Nile = An Nîl el Azraq □ 51 12 30N 34 30 E
Blue Nile = Nîl el Azraq → 51 15 38N 32 31 E
Blue Rapids 70 39 41N 96 39W
Blue Ridge Mts. 69 36 30N 80 15W
Blue Stack Mts. 9 54 46N 8 5W
Blueberry → 64 56 45N 120 49W
Bluefield 68 37 18N 81 14W
Bluefields 75 12 20N 83 50W
Bluff, Australia 44 23 35S 149 4 E
Bluff, N.Z. 43 46 37S 168 20 E
Bluff, U.S.A. 73 37 17N 109 33W
Bluff Knoll 47 34 24S 118 15 E
Bluff Pt. 47 27 50S 114 5 E
Bluffton 68 40 43N 85 9W
Blumenau 80 27 0S 49 0W
Blunt 70 44 32N 100 0W
Bly 72 42 23N 121 0W
Blyth 6 55 8N 1 32W
Blythe 73 33 40N 114 33W
Bo 50 7 55N 11 50W
Bo Duc 34 11 58N 106 50 E
Bo Hai 38 39 0N 120 0 E
Bo Xian 39 33 50N 115 45 E
Boa Vista 78 2 48N 60 30W
Boaco 75 12 29N 85 35W
Boatman 45 27 16S 146 55 E
Bobadah 45 32 19S 146 41 E
Bobai 39 22 17N 109 59 E
Bobbili 33 18 35N 83 30 E
Bobcaygeon 62 44 33N 78 33W
Bobo-Dioulasso 50 11 8N 4 13W
Bóbr → 14 52 4N 15 4 E
Bobraomby, Tanjon' i 57 12 40S 49 10 E
Bobruysk 22 53 10N 29 15 E
Boca, La 74 8 56N 79 30W
Bôca do Acre 78 8 50S 67 27W
Boca Raton 69 26 21N 80 5W
Bocaiúva 79 17 7S 43 49W
Bocanda 50 7 5N 4 31W
Bocaranga 51 7 0N 15 35 E
Bocas del Toro 75 9 15N 82 20W
Bocholt 14 51 50N 6 35 E
Bochum 14 51 28N 7 12 E
Boda 54 4 19N 17 26 E
Bodaybo 25 57 50N 114 0 E
Boddington 47 32 50S 116 30 E
Boden 20 65 50N 21 42 E
Bodensee 14 47 35N 9 25 E
Bodhan 32 18 40N 77 44 E
Bodmin 7 50 28N 4 44W
Bodmin Moor 7 50 33N 4 36W
Bodrog → 15 48 15N 21 35 E
Bodrum 30 37 5N 27 30 E
Boegoebergdam 56 29 7S 22 9 E
Boende 54 0 24S 21 12 E
Boerne 71 29 48N 98 41W
Boffa 50 10 16N 14 3W
Bogalusa 71 30 50N 89 55W
Bogan → 45 29 59S 146 17 E
Bogan Gate 45 33 7S 147 49 E
Bogantungan 44 23 41S 147 17 E
Bogata 71 33 26N 95 10W
Boggabilla 45 28 36S 150 24 E
Boggabri 45 30 45S 150 0 E
Boggeragh Mts. 9 52 2N 8 55W
Bognor Regis 7 50 47N 0 40W
Bogo 35 11 3N 124 0 E
Bogong, Mt. 45 36 47S 147 17 E
Bogor 35 6 36S 106 48 E
Bogorodskoye 25 52 22N 140 30 E
Bogotá 78 4 34N 74 0W
Bogotol 24 56 15N 89 50 E
Bogra 33 24 51N 89 22 E
Boguchany 25 58 40N 97 30 E
Bogué 50 16 45N 14 10W
Bohemia Downs 46 18 53S 126 14 E
Bohemian Forest = Böhmerwald 14 49 30N 12 40 E
Bohena Cr. → 45 30 17S 149 42 E
Böhmerwald 14 49 30N 12 40 E
Bohol 35 9 50N 124 10 E
Bohol Sea 35 9 0N 124 0 E
Bohotleh 29 8 20N 46 25 E
Boileau, C. 46 17 40S 122 7 E
Boise 72 43 43N 116 9W
Boise City 71 36 45N 102 30W
Boissevain 65 49 15N 100 5W
Bojador C. 50 26 0N 14 30W
Bojana → 19 41 52N 19 22 E
Bojnūrd 31 37 30N 57 20 E
Bojonegoro 35 7 11S 111 54 E
Boju 53 7 22N 7 55 E
Boké 50 10 56N 14 17W
Bokhara → 45 29 55S 146 42 E
Bokkos 53 9 17N 9 1 E
Boknafjorden 21 59 14N 5 40 E
Bokoro 51 12 25N 17 14 E
Bokote 54 0 12S 21 8 E
Bokungu 54 0 35S 22 50 E

Bronte Park

Bol **51** 13 30N 15 0 E
Bolama **50** 11 30N 15 30W
Bolan Pass **31** 29 50N 67 20 E
Bolaños → **74** 21 14N 104 8W
Bolbec **12** 49 30N 0 30 E
Bole **37** 45 11N 81 37 E
Bolesławiec **14** 51 17N 15 37 E
Bolgatanga **53** 10 44N 0 53W
Boli **38** 45 46N 130 31 E
Bolinao C. **35** 16 23N 119 55 E
Bolívar, Argentina **80** 36 15S 60 53W
Bolívar, Colombia **78** 2 0N 77 0W
Bolivar, Mo., U.S.A. **71** 37 38N 93 22W
Bolivar, Tenn., U.S.A. **71** 35 14N 89 0W
Bolivia ■ **78** 17 6S 64 0W
Bolivian Plateau **76** 20 0S 67 30W
Bollnäs **21** 61 21N 16 24 E
Bollon **45** 28 2S 147 29 E
Bolobo **54** 2 6S 16 20 E
Bologna **18** 44 30N 11 20 E
Bologoye **22** 57 55N 34 0 E
Bolomba **54** 0 35N 19 0 E
Bolong **35** 7 6N 122 14 E
Bolsena, L. di **18** 42 35N 11 55 E
Bolshereche **24** 56 4N 74 45 E
Bolshevik, Ostrov **25** 78 30N 102 0 E
Bolshezemelskaya Tundra **22** 67 0N 56 0 E
Bolshoi Kavkas **23** 42 50N 44 0 E
Bolshoy Anyuy → **25** 68 30N 160 49 E
Bolshoy Atlym **24** 62 25N 66 50 E
Bolshoy Begichev, Ostrov **25** 74 20N 112 30 E
Bolshoy Lyakhovskiy, Ostrov **25** 73 35N 142 0 E
Bolsward **11** 53 3N 5 32 E
Bolton **6** 53 35N 2 26W
Bolu **30** 40 45N 31 35 E
Bolvadin **30** 38 45N 31 4 E
Bolzano **18** 46 30N 11 20 E
Bom Despacho **79** 19 43S 45 15W
Bom Jesus da Lapa **79** 13 15S 43 25W
Boma **54** 5 50S 13 4 E
Bomaderry **45** 34 52S 150 37 E
Bombala **45** 36 56S 149 15 E
Bombay **32** 18 55N 72 50 E
Bomboma **54** 2 25N 18 55 E
Bomili **54** 1 45N 27 5 E
Bomongo **54** 1 27N 18 21 E
Bomu → **54** 4 40N 22 30 E
Bon, C. **51** 37 1N 11 2 E
Bonaire **75** 12 10N 68 15W
Bonang **45** 37 11S 148 41 E
Bonanza **75** 13 54N 84 35W
Bonaparte Archipelago **46** 14 0S 124 30 E
Bonaventure **63** 48 5N 65 32W
Bonavista **63** 48 40N 53 5W
Bonavista, C. **63** 48 42N 53 5W
Bondo **54** 3 55N 23 53 E
Bondoukou **50** 8 2N 2 47W
Bondowoso **35** 7 55S 113 49 E
Bone, Teluk **35** 4 10S 120 50 E
Bone Rate **35** 7 25S 121 5 E
Bone Rate, Kepulauan **35** 6 30S 121 10 E
Bo'ness **8** 56 0N 3 38W
Bong Son = Hoai Nhon **34** 14 28N 109 1 E
Bongandanga **54** 1 24N 21 3 E
Bongor **51** 10 35N 15 20 E
Bonham **71** 33 30N 96 10W
Bonifacio **12** 41 24N 9 10 E
Bonifacio, Bouches de **18** 41 12N 9 15 E
Bonin Is. **40** 27 0N 142 0 E
Bonn **14** 50 43N 7 6 E
Bonne Terre **71** 37 57N 90 33W
Bonners Ferry **72** 48 38N 116 21W
Bonney, L. **45** 37 50S 140 20 E
Bonnie Downs **44** 22 7S 143 50 E
Bonnie Rock **47** 30 29S 118 22 E
Bonny, Bight of **54** 3 30N 9 20 E
Bonnyville **65** 54 20N 110 45W
Bonoi **35** 1 45S 137 41 E
Bontang **34** 0 10N 117 30 E
Bonthain **35** 5 34S 119 56 E
Bonthe **50** 7 30N 12 33W
Bontoc **35** 17 7N 120 58 E
Bonython Ra. **46** 23 40S 128 45 E
Boogardie **47** 28 2S 117 45 E
Bookabie **47** 31 50S 132 41 E
Booker **71** 36 29N 100 30W
Boolaboolka, L. **45** 32 38S 143 10 E
Booligal **45** 33 58S 144 53 E
Boom **11** 51 6N 4 20 E
Boonah **45** 27 58S 152 41 E
Boone, Iowa, U.S.A. **70** 42 5N 93 53W
Boone, N.C., U.S.A. **69** 36 14N 81 43W
Booneville, Ark., U.S.A. **71** 35 10N 93 54W
Booneville, Miss., U.S.A. **69** 34 39N 88 34W
Boonville, Ind., U.S.A. **68** 38 3N 87 13W
Boonville, Mo., U.S.A. **70** 38 57N 92 45W
Boonville, N.Y., U.S.A. **68** 43 31N 75 20W
Boorindal **45** 30 22S 146 11 E
Boorowa **45** 34 28S 148 44 E
Boothia, Gulf of **61** 71 0N 90 0W
Boothia Pen. **60** 71 0N 94 0W
Bootle, Cumbria, U.K. **6** 54 17N 3 24W
Bootle, Merseyside, U.K. **6** 53 28N 3 1W
Booué **54** 0 5S 11 55 E
Bophuthatswana □ **56** 25 49S 25 30 E
Boquilla, Presa de la **74** 27 40N 105 30W
Bôr, Sudan **51** 6 10N 31 40 E
Bor, Yugoslavia **19** 44 8N 22 7 E
Borah, Pk. **72** 44 19N 113 46W
Borama **29** 9 55N 43 7 E
Borås **21** 57 43N 12 56 E
Borāzjān **31** 29 22N 51 10 E
Borba **78** 4 12S 59 34W
Borda, C. **45** 35 45S 136 34 E
Bordeaux **12** 44 50N 0 36W
Borden, Australia **47** 34 3S 118 12 E
Borden, Canada **63** 46 18N 63 47W
Borders □ **8** 55 35N 2 50W
Bordertown **45** 36 19S 140 45 E
Borðeyri **20** 65 12N 21 6W
Bordj Fly Ste. Marie **50** 27 19N 2 32W
Bordj-in-Eker **50** 24 9N 5 3 E
Bordj Omar Driss **50** 28 10N 6 40 E
Bordj-Tarat **50** 25 55N 9 3 E
Borgarnes **20** 64 32N 21 55W
Børgefjellet **20** 65 20N 13 45 E
Borger, Neth. **11** 52 54N 6 44 E
Borger, U.S.A. **71** 35 40N 101 20W
Borgholm **21** 56 52N 16 39 E
Borisoglebsk **23** 51 27N 42 5 E
Borisov **22** 54 17N 28 28 E
Borja **78** 4 20S 77 40W
Borkou **51** 18 15N 18 50 E
Borkum **14** 53 36N 6 42 E
Borlänge **21** 60 29N 15 26 E
Borneo **34** 1 0N 115 0 E
Bornholm **21** 55 10N 15 0 E
Borno □ **53** 12 30N 12 30 E
Borobudur **35** 7 36S 110 13 E
Borogontsy **25** 62 42N 131 8 E
Boromo **50** 11 45N 2 58W
Borongan **35** 11 37N 125 26 E
Bororen **44** 24 13S 151 33 E
Borovichi **22** 58 25N 33 55 E
Borroloola **44** 16 4S 136 17 E
Borth **7** 52 29N 4 3W
Borujerd **30** 33 55N 48 50 E
Borzya **25** 50 24N 116 31 E
Bosa **18** 40 17N 8 32 E
Bosanska Gradiška **18** 45 10N 17 15 E
Bosaso **29** 11 12N 49 18 E
Boscastle **7** 50 42N 4 42W
Bose **39** 23 53N 106 35 E
Boshan **38** 36 28N 117 49 E
Boshoek **56** 25 30S 27 9 E
Boshof **56** 28 31S 25 13 E
Boshrūyeh **31** 33 50N 57 30 E
Bosna → **19** 45 4N 18 29 E
Bosna i Hercegovina □ **18** 44 0N 18 0 E
Bosnia = Bosna i Hercegovina □ **18** 44 0N 18 0 E
Bosnik **35** 1 5S 136 10 E
Bōsō-Hantō **36** 35 20N 140 20 E
Bosobolo **54** 4 15N 19 50 E
Bosporus = Karadeniz Boğazı **30** 41 10N 29 10 E
Bossangoa **51** 6 35N 17 30 E
Bossekop **20** 69 57N 23 15 E
Bossembélé **51** 5 25N 17 40 E
Bossier City **71** 32 28N 93 48W
Bosso **51** 13 43N 13 19 E
Bosten Hu **37** 41 55N 87 40 E
Boston, U.K. **6** 52 59N 0 2W
Boston, U.S.A. **68** 42 20N 71 0W
Boston Bar **64** 49 52N 121 30W
Boswell, Canada **64** 49 28N 116 45W
Boswell, U.S.A. **71** 34 1N 95 50W
Botany Bay **45** 34 0S 151 14 E
Bothaville **56** 27 23S 26 34 E
Bothnia, G. of **20** 63 0N 20 0 E
Bothwell **44** 42 20S 147 1 E
Botletle → **56** 20 10S 23 15 E
Botoşani **15** 47 42N 26 41 E
Botswana ■ **56** 22 0S 24 0 E
Bottineau **70** 48 49N 100 25W
Bottrop **11** 51 34N 6 59 E
Botucatu **80** 22 55S 48 30W
Botwood **63** 49 6N 55 23W
Bou Djébéha **50** 18 25N 2 45W
Bou Izakarn **50** 29 12N 9 46W
Bouaké **50** 7 40N 5 2W
Bouar **54** 6 0N 15 40 E
Bouârfa **50** 32 32N 1 58 E
Bouca **51** 6 45N 18 25 E
Boucaut B. **44** 12 0S 134 25 E
Bouches-du-Rhône □ **12** 43 37N 5 2 E
Bougainville C. **46** 13 57S 126 4 E
Bougainville Reef **44** 15 30S 147 5 E
Bougie = Bejaia **50** 36 42N 5 2 E
Bougouni **50** 11 30N 7 20W
Bouillon **11** 49 44N 5 3 E
Boulder, Colo., U.S.A. **70** 40 3N 105 10W
Boulder, Mont., U.S.A. **72** 46 14N 112 4W
Boulder City **73** 35 58N 114 50W
Boulder Dam = Hoover Dam **73** 36 0N 114 45W
Boulia **44** 22 52S 139 51 E
Boulogne-sur-Mer **12** 50 42N 1 36 E
Boultoum **53** 14 45N 10 25 E
Bouna **50** 9 10N 3 0W
Boundiali **50** 9 30N 6 20W
Bountiful **72** 40 57N 111 58W
Bounty I. **40** 48 0S 178 30 E
Bourbonnais **12** 46 28N 3 0 E
Bourem **53** 17 0N 0 24W
Bourg-en-Bresse **12** 46 13N 5 12 E
Bourges **12** 47 9N 2 25 E
Bourgogne **12** 47 0N 4 50 E
Bourke **45** 30 8S 145 55 E
Bournemouth **7** 50 43N 1 53W
Bousso **51** 10 34N 16 52 E
Boutilimit **50** 17 45N 14 40W
Bouvet I. = Bouvetøya **3** 54 26S 3 24 E
Bouvetøya **3** 54 26S 3 24 E
Bovigny **11** 50 12N 5 55 E
Bovill **72** 46 58N 116 27W
Bow Island **64** 49 50N 111 23W
Bowbells **70** 48 47N 102 19W
Bowdle **70** 45 30N 99 40W
Bowelling **47** 33 25S 116 30 E
Bowen **44** 20 0S 148 16 E
Bowen Mts. **45** 37 0S 148 0 E
Bowie, Ariz., U.S.A. **73** 32 15N 109 30W
Bowie, Tex., U.S.A. **71** 33 33N 97 50W
Bowland, Forest of **6** 54 0N 2 30W
Bowling Green, Ky., U.S.A. **68** 37 0N 86 25W
Bowling Green, Ohio, U.S.A. **68** 41 22N 83 40W
Bowling Green, C. **44** 19 19S 147 25 E
Bowman **70** 46 12N 103 21W
Bowmans **45** 34 10S 138 17 E
Bowmanville **62** 43 55N 78 41W
Bowmore **8** 55 45N 6 18W
Bowral **45** 34 26S 150 27 E
Bowraville **45** 30 37S 152 52 E
Bowron → **64** 54 3N 121 50W
Bowser L. **64** 56 30N 129 30W
Bowsman **65** 52 14N 101 12W
Boxtel **11** 51 36N 5 20 E
Boyce **71** 31 25N 92 39W
Boyer → **64** 58 27N 115 57W
Boyle **9** 53 58N 8 19W
Boyne → **9** 53 43N 6 15W
Boyne City **68** 45 13N 85 1W
Boyni Qara **31** 36 20N 67 0 E
Boynton Beach **69** 26 31N 80 3W
Boyoma, Chutes **48** 0 35N 25 23 E
Boyup Brook **47** 33 50S 116 23 E
Bozeman **72** 45 40N 111 0W
Bozen = Bolzano **18** 46 30N 11 20 E
Bozoum **51** 6 25N 16 35 E
Brabant □ **11** 50 46N 4 30 E
Brabant L. **65** 55 58N 103 43W
Brač **18** 43 20N 16 40 E
Bracadale, L. **8** 57 20N 6 30W
Bracciano, L. di **18** 42 8N 12 11 E
Bracebridge **62** 45 2N 79 19W
Brach **51** 27 31N 14 20 E
Bräcke **20** 62 45N 15 26 E
Brackettville **71** 29 21N 100 20W
Brad **15** 46 10N 22 50 E
Bradenton **69** 27 25N 82 35W
Bradford, U.K. **6** 53 47N 1 45W
Bradford, U.S.A. **68** 41 58N 78 41W
Bradley, Ark., U.S.A. **71** 33 7N 93 39W
Bradley, S. Dak., U.S.A. **70** 45 10N 97 40W
Bradore Bay **63** 51 27N 57 18W
Bradshaw **46** 15 21S 130 16 E
Brady **71** 31 8N 99 25W
Braemar **45** 33 12S 139 35 E
Braga **13** 41 35N 8 25W
Bragança, Brazil **79** 1 0S 47 2W
Bragança, Portugal **13** 41 48N 6 50W
Brahmanbaria **33** 23 58N 91 15 E
Brahmani → **33** 20 39N 86 46 E
Brahmaputra → **33** 24 2N 90 59 E
Braich-y-pwll **6** 52 47N 4 46W
Braidwood **45** 35 27S 149 49 E
Brăila **15** 45 19N 27 59 E
Brainerd **70** 46 20N 94 10W
Braintree **7** 51 53N 0 34 E
Brak → **56** 29 35S 22 55 E
Brakwater **56** 22 28S 17 3 E
Bralorne **64** 50 50N 122 50W
Brampton **62** 43 45N 79 45W
Bramwell **44** 12 8S 142 37 E
Branco → **78** 1 20S 61 50W
Brandenburg **14** 52 24N 12 33 E
Brandfort **56** 28 40S 26 30 E
Brandon **65** 49 50N 99 57W
Brandon, Mt. **9** 52 15N 10 15W
Brandon B. **9** 52 17N 10 8W
Brandvlei **56** 30 25S 20 30 E
Braniewo **15** 54 25N 19 50 E
Brańsk **15** 52 45N 22 50 E
Branson, Colo., U.S.A. **71** 37 4N 103 53W
Branson, Mo., U.S.A. **71** 36 40N 93 18W
Brantford **62** 43 10N 80 15W
Branxholme **45** 37 52S 141 49 E
Bras d'Or, L. **63** 45 50N 60 50W
Brasil, Planalto **76** 18 0S 46 30W
Brasiléia **78** 11 0S 68 45W
Brasília **79** 15 47S 47 55W
Braşov **15** 45 38N 25 35 E
Brasschaat **11** 51 19N 4 27 E
Brassey, Banjaran **34** 5 0N 117 15 E
Brassey Ra. **47** 25 8S 122 15 E
Brasstown Bald, Mt. **69** 34 54N 83 45W
Bratislava **14** 48 10N 17 7 E
Bratsk **25** 56 10N 101 30 E
Brattleboro **68** 42 53N 72 37W
Braunschweig **14** 52 17N 10 28 E
Braunton **7** 51 6N 4 9W
Brava **29** 1 20N 44 8 E
Bravo del Norte → **74** 25 57N 97 9W
Brawley **73** 32 58N 115 30W
Bray **9** 53 12N 6 6W
Bray, Mt. **44** 14 0S 134 30 E
Bray-sur-Seine **12** 48 25N 3 14 E
Brazeau → **64** 52 55N 115 14W
Brazil **68** 39 32N 87 8W
Brazil ■ **79** 12 0S 50 0W
Brazilian Highlands = Brasil, Planalto **76** 18 0S 46 30W
Brazos → **71** 28 53N 95 23W
Brazzaville **54** 4 9S 15 12 E
Brčko **19** 44 54N 18 46 E
Breadalbane, Australia **44** 23 50S 139 35 E
Breadalbane, U.K. **8** 56 30N 4 15W
Breaden, L. **47** 25 51S 125 28 E
Breaksea Sd. **43** 45 35S 166 35 E
Bream Bay **43** 35 56S 174 28 E
Bream Head **43** 35 51S 174 36 E
Brebes **35** 6 52S 109 3 E
Brechin **8** 56 44N 2 40W
Breckenridge, Colo., U.S.A. **72** 39 30N 106 2W
Breckenridge, Minn., U.S.A. **70** 46 20N 96 36W
Breckenridge, Tex., U.S.A. **71** 32 48N 98 55W
Brecon **7** 51 57N 3 23W
Brecon Beacons **7** 51 53N 3 27W
Breda **11** 51 35N 4 45 E
Bredasdorp **56** 34 33S 20 2 E
Bredbo **45** 35 58S 149 10 E
Bregenz **14** 47 30N 9 45 E
Breiðafjörður **20** 65 15N 23 15W
Brejo **79** 3 41S 42 47W
Bremen **14** 53 4N 8 47 E
Bremer I. **44** 12 5S 136 45 E
Bremerhaven **14** 53 34N 8 35 E
Bremerton **72** 47 30N 122 38W
Brenham **71** 30 5N 96 27W
Brenner Pass **14** 47 0N 11 30 E
Brent, Canada **62** 46 2N 78 29W
Brent, U.K. **7** 51 33N 0 18W
Brentwood **7** 51 37N 0 19 E
Bréscia **18** 45 33N 10 13 E
Breskens **11** 51 23N 3 33 E
Breslau = Wrocław **14** 51 5N 17 5 E
Bressanone **18** 46 43N 11 40 E
Bressay I. **8** 60 10N 1 5W
Bresse **12** 46 50N 5 10 E
Brest, France **12** 48 24N 4 31W
Brest, U.S.S.R. **22** 52 10N 23 40 E
Bretagne **12** 48 0N 3 0W
Bretçu **15** 46 7N 26 18 E
Breton **64** 53 7N 114 28W
Breton Sd. **71** 29 40N 89 12W
Brett, C. **43** 35 10S 174 20 E
Brevard **69** 35 19N 82 42W
Brewarrina **45** 30 0S 146 51 E
Brewer **63** 44 43N 68 50W
Brewster **72** 48 10N 119 51W
Brewton **69** 31 9N 87 2W
Breyten **57** 26 16S 30 0 E
Brezhnev **24** 55 42N 52 19 E
Bria **51** 6 30N 21 58 E
Briançon **12** 44 54N 6 39 E
Bribie I. **45** 27 0S 152 58 E
Bridgend **7** 51 30N 3 35W
Bridgeport, Calif., U.S.A. **73** 38 14N 119 15W
Bridgeport, Conn., U.S.A. **68** 41 12N 73 12W
Bridgeport, Nebr., U.S.A. **70** 41 42N 103 10W
Bridgeport, Tex., U.S.A. **71** 33 15N 97 45W
Bridger **72** 45 20N 108 58W
Bridgeton **68** 39 29N 75 10W
Bridgetown, Australia **47** 33 58S 116 7 E
Bridgetown, Barbados **75** 13 0N 59 30W
Bridgetown, Canada **63** 44 55N 65 18W
Bridgewater, Canada **63** 44 25N 64 31W
Bridgewater, U.S.A. **70** 43 34N 97 29W
Bridgewater, C. **45** 38 23S 141 23 E
Bridgnorth **7** 52 33N 2 25W
Bridgwater **7** 51 7N 3 0W
Bridlington **6** 54 6N 0 11W
Bridport, Australia **44** 40 59S 147 23 E
Bridport, U.K. **7** 50 43N 2 45W
Brie, Plaine de la **12** 48 35N 3 10 E
Brig **14** 46 18N 7 59 E
Brigg **6** 53 33N 0 30W
Briggsdale **70** 40 40N 104 20W
Brigham City **72** 41 30N 112 1W
Bright **45** 36 42S 146 56 E
Brighton, Australia **45** 35 5S 138 30 E
Brighton, Canada **62** 44 2N 77 44W
Brighton, U.K. **7** 50 50N 0 9W
Brighton, U.S.A. **70** 39 59N 104 50W
Brilliant **64** 49 19N 117 38W
Bríndisi **19** 40 39N 17 55 E
Brinkley **71** 34 55N 91 15W
Brinkworth **45** 33 42S 138 26 E
Brion, I. **63** 47 46N 61 26W
Brisbane **45** 27 25S 153 2 E
Brisbane → **45** 27 24S 153 9 E
Bristol, U.K. **7** 51 26N 2 35W
Bristol, Conn., U.S.A. **68** 41 44N 72 57W
Bristol, S. Dak., U.S.A. **70** 45 25N 97 43W
Bristol, Tenn., U.S.A. **69** 36 36N 82 11W
Bristol B. **60** 58 0N 160 0W
Bristol Channel **7** 51 18N 4 30W
Bristol L. **73** 34 23N 116 50W
Bristow **71** 35 55N 96 28W
British Columbia □ **64** 55 0N 125 15W
British Guiana = Guyana ■ **78** 5 0N 59 0W
British Honduras = Belize ■ **74** 17 0N 88 30W
British Isles **4** 55 0N 4 0W
Brits **57** 25 37S 27 48 E
Britstown **56** 30 37S 23 30 E
Britt **62** 45 46N 80 34W
Brittany = Bretagne **12** 48 0N 3 0W
Britton **70** 45 50N 97 47W
Brixton **44** 23 32S 144 57 E
Brlik **24** 43 40N 73 49 E
Brno **14** 49 10N 16 35 E
Broad → **69** 33 59N 82 39W
Broad Arrow **47** 30 23S 121 15 E
Broad B. **8** 58 14N 6 16W
Broad Haven **9** 54 20N 9 55W
Broad Law **8** 55 30N 3 22W
Broad Sd. **44** 22 0S 149 45 E
Broadhurst Ra. **46** 22 30S 122 30 E
Broads, The **6** 52 45N 1 30 E
Broadus **70** 45 28N 105 27W
Broadview **65** 50 22N 102 35W
Brochet **65** 57 53N 101 40W
Brochet, L. **65** 58 36N 101 35W
Brock **65** 51 26N 108 43W
Brocken **14** 51 48N 10 40 E
Brockport **68** 43 12N 77 56W
Brockville **62** 44 35N 75 41W
Brockway **70** 47 18N 105 46W
Brodeur Pen. **61** 72 30N 88 10W
Brodick **8** 55 34N 5 9W
Brogan **72** 44 14N 117 32W
Broken Bow, Nebr., U.S.A. **70** 41 25N 99 35W
Broken Bow, Okla., U.S.A. **71** 34 2N 94 43W
Broken Hill = Kabwe **55** 14 30S 28 29 E
Broken Hill **45** 31 58S 141 29 E
Bromfield **7** 52 25N 2 45W
Bromley **7** 51 20N 0 5 E
Brønderslev **21** 57 16N 9 57 E
Bronkhorstspruit **57** 25 46S 28 45 E
Bronte **71** 31 54N 100 18W
Bronte Park **44** 42 8S 146 30 E

Casper

Caldwell, Kans., U.S.A. 71 37 5N 97 37W
Caldwell, Tex., U.S.A. 71 30 30N 96 42W
Caledon 56 34 14S 19 26 E
Caledon ➝ 56 30 31S 26 5 E
Caledon B. 44 12 45S 137 0 E
Calella 13 41 37N 2 40 E
Calemba 56 16 0S 15 44 E
Calera, La 80 32 50S 71 10W
Calexico 73 32 40N 115 33W
Calf of Man 6 54 4N 4 48W
Calgary 64 51 0N 114 10W
Calhoun 69 34 30N 84 55W
Cali 78 3 25N 76 35W
Calicut 32 11 15N 75 43 E
Caliente 73 37 36N 114 34W
California 70 38 37N 92 30W
California □ 73 37 25N 120 0W
California, Baja 74 32 10N 115 12W
California, Baja, T.N. □ 74 30 0N 115 0W
California, Baja, T.S. □ 74 25 50N 111 50W
California, G. de 74 27 0N 111 0W
California, Lr. = California, Baja 74 32 10N 115 12W
Calingasta 80 31 15S 69 30W
Calipatria 73 33 8N 115 30W
Calistoga 72 38 36N 122 32W
Calitzdorp 56 33 33S 21 42 E
Callabonna, L. 45 29 40S 140 5 E
Callan 9 52 33N 7 25W
Callander 8 56 15N 4 14W
Callao 78 12 0S 77 0W
Callaway 70 41 20N 99 56W
Callide 44 24 18S 150 28 E
Calling Lake 64 55 15N 113 12W
Calliope 44 24 0S 151 16 E
Calne 6 51 26N 2 0W
Calola 56 16 25S 17 48 E
Caloundra 45 26 45S 153 10 E
Calstock 62 49 47N 84 9W
Caltagirone 18 37 13N 14 30 E
Caltanissetta 18 37 30N 14 3 E
Calulo 54 10 1S 14 56 E
Calumet 68 47 14N 88 27W
Calunda 55 12 7S 23 36 E
Calvados □ 12 49 5N 0 15W
Calvert 71 30 59N 96 40W
Calvert ➝ 44 16 17S 137 44 E
Calvert Hills 44 17 15S 137 20 E
Calvert I. 64 51 30N 128 0W
Calvert Ra. 46 24 0S 122 30 E
Calvi 12 42 34N 8 45 E
Calvinia 56 31 28S 19 45 E
Cam ➝ 7 52 21N 0 16 E
Camabatela 54 8 20S 15 26 E
Camacupa 55 11 58S 17 22 E
Camagüey 75 21 20N 78 0W
Camaná 78 16 30S 72 50W
Camaret 12 48 16N 4 37W
Camargo 78 20 38S 65 15 E
Camarón, C. 75 16 0N 85 0W
Camarones 80 44 50S 65 40W
Camas 72 45 35N 122 24W
Camas Valley 72 43 0N 123 46W
Cambay = Khambhat 32 22 23N 72 33 E
Cambodia ■ 34 12 15N 105 0 E
Camborne 7 50 13N 5 18W
Cambrai 12 50 11N 3 14 E
Cambria 73 35 39N 121 6W
Cambrian Mts. 7 52 25N 3 52W
Cambridge, Canada 62 43 23N 80 15W
Cambridge, N.Z. 43 37 54S 175 29 E
Cambridge, U.K. 7 52 13N 0 8 E
Cambridge, Idaho, U.S.A. 72 44 36N 116 40W
Cambridge, Mass., U.S.A. 68 42 20N 71 8W
Cambridge, Md., U.S.A. 68 38 33N 76 2W
Cambridge, Minn., U.S.A. 70 45 34N 93 15W
Cambridge, Nebr., U.S.A. 70 40 20N 100 12W
Cambridge, Ohio, U.S.A. 68 40 1N 81 35W
Cambridge Bay 60 69 10N 105 0W
Cambridge Gulf 46 14 55S 128 15 E
Cambridgeshire □ 7 52 12N 0 7 E
Camden, Ala., U.S.A. 69 31 59N 87 15W
Camden, Ark., U.S.A. 71 33 40N 92 50W
Camden, Maine, U.S.A. 63 44 14N 69 6W
Camden, N.J., U.S.A. 68 39 57N 75 7W
Camden, S.C., U.S.A. 69 34 17N 80 34W
Camden Sound 46 15 27S 124 25 E
Camdenton 71 38 1N 92 45W
Cameron, Ariz., U.S.A. 73 35 55N 111 31W
Cameron, La., U.S.A. 71 29 50N 93 18W
Cameron, Mo., U.S.A. 70 39 42N 94 14W
Cameron, Tex., U.S.A. 71 30 53N 97 0W
Cameron Falls 62 49 8N 88 19W
Cameron Hills 64 59 48N 118 0W
Cameroon ■ 54 6 0N 12 30 E
Cameroun, Mt. 54 4 13N 9 10 E
Cametá 79 2 12S 49 30W
Caminha 13 41 50N 8 50W
Camino 72 38 47N 120 40W
Camira Creek 45 29 15S 152 58 E
Camissombo 54 8 7S 20 38 E
Camocim 79 2 55S 40 50W
Camooweal 44 19 56S 138 7 E
Camopi ➝ 79 3 10N 52 20W
Camp Crook 70 45 36N 103 59W
Camp Wood 71 29 41N 100 0W
Campana, I. 80 48 20S 75 20W
Campania □ 18 40 50N 14 45 E
Campbell 56 28 48S 23 44 E
Campbell I. 40 52 30S 169 0 E
Campbell L. 65 63 14N 106 55W
Campbell River 64 50 5N 125 20W
Campbell Town 44 41 52S 147 30 E
Campbellsville 68 37 23N 85 21W
Campbellton 63 47 57N 66 43W
Campbelltown 45 34 4S 150 49 E
Campbeltown 8 55 25N 5 36W
Campeche 74 19 50N 90 32W
Campeche □ 74 19 50N 90 32W
Campeche, B. de 74 19 30N 93 0W
Camperdown 45 38 14S 143 9 E
Camperville 65 51 59N 100 9W
Campina Grande 79 7 20S 35 47W
Campinas 80 22 50S 47 0W
Campo 54 2 22N 9 50 E
Campo Belo 79 20 52S 45 16W
Campo Formoso 79 10 30S 40 20W
Campo Grande 79 20 25S 54 40W
Campo Maíor 79 4 50S 42 12W
Campo Mourão 79 24 3S 52 22W
Campoalegre 78 2 41N 75 20W
Campobasso 18 41 34N 14 40 E
Campos 79 21 50S 41 20W
Campos Belos 79 13 10S 47 3W
Campuya ➝ 78 1 40S 73 30W
Camrose 64 53 0N 112 50W
Camsell Portage 65 59 37N 109 15W
Can Tho 34 10 2N 105 46 E
Canada ■ 60 60 0N 100 0W
Cañada de Gómez 80 32 40S 61 30W
Canadian 71 35 56N 100 25W
Canadian ➝ 71 35 27N 95 3W
Çanakkale 30 40 8N 26 30 E
Çanakkale Boğazı 30 40 3N 26 12 E
Canal Flats 64 50 10N 115 48W
Canandaigua 68 42 55N 77 18W
Cananea 74 31 0N 110 20W
Canarias, Is. 50 28 30N 16 0W
Canarreos, Arch. de los 75 21 35N 81 40W
Canary Is. = Canarias, Is. 50 28 30N 16 0W
Canaveral, C. 69 28 28N 80 31W
Canavieiras 79 15 39S 39 0W
Canbelego 45 31 32S 146 18 E
Canberra 45 35 15S 149 8 E
Canby, Calif., U.S.A. 72 41 26N 120 58W
Canby, Minn., U.S.A. 70 44 44N 96 15W
Canby, Oreg., U.S.A. 72 45 16N 122 42W
Cancún 74 21 8N 86 44W
Candala 29 11 30N 49 58 E
Candelo 45 36 47S 149 43 E
Candia = Iráklion 19 35 20N 25 12 E
Candle L. 65 53 50N 105 18W
Cando 70 48 30N 99 14W
Canea = Khaniá 19 35 30N 24 4 E
Canelones 80 34 32S 56 17W
Cañete, Chile 80 37 50S 73 30W
Cañete, Peru 78 13 8S 76 30W
Cangas 13 42 16N 8 47W
Canguaretama 79 6 20S 35 5W
Canguçu 80 31 22S 52 43W
Cangxi 39 31 47N 105 59 E
Cangzhou 38 38 19N 116 52 E
Canim Lake 64 51 47N 120 54W
Canipaan 34 8 33N 117 15 E
Çankırı 30 40 40N 33 37 E
Canmore 64 51 7N 115 18W
Cann River 45 37 35S 149 7 E
Canna 8 57 3N 6 33W
Cannanore 32 11 53N 75 27 E
Cannes 12 43 32N 7 0 E
Cannock 6 52 42N 2 2W
Cannon Ball ➝ 70 46 20N 100 38W
Cannondale, Mt. 44 25 13S 148 57 E
Canoas 80 29 56S 51 11W
Canoe L. 65 55 10N 108 15W
Canon City 70 38 27N 105 14W
Canora 65 51 40N 102 30W
Canowindra 45 33 35S 148 38 E
Canso 63 45 20N 61 0W
Cantabria □ 13 43 10N 4 0W
Cantabrian Mts. = Cantábrica, Cordillera 13 43 0N 5 10W
Cantábrica, Cordillera 13 43 0N 5 10W
Cantal □ 12 45 5N 2 45 E
Canterbury, Australia 44 25 23S 141 53 E
Canterbury, U.K. 7 51 17N 1 5 E
Canterbury □ 43 43 45S 171 19 E
Canterbury Bight 43 44 16S 171 55 E
Canterbury Plains 43 43 55S 171 22 E
Canton = Guangzhou 39 23 5N 113 10 E
Canton, Ga., U.S.A. 69 34 13N 84 29W
Canton, Ill., U.S.A. 70 40 32N 90 0W
Canton, Miss., U.S.A. 71 32 40N 90 1W
Canton, Mo., U.S.A. 70 40 10N 91 33W
Canton, N.Y., U.S.A. 68 44 32N 75 3W
Canton, Ohio, U.S.A. 68 40 47N 81 22W
Canton, Okla., U.S.A. 71 36 5N 98 36W
Canton, S. Dak., U.S.A. 70 43 20N 96 35W
Canton L. 71 36 12N 98 40W
Canudos 78 7 13S 58 5W
Canutama 78 6 30S 64 20W
Canutillo 73 31 58N 106 36W
Canyon, Tex., U.S.A. 71 35 0N 101 57W
Canyon, Wyo., U.S.A. 72 44 43N 110 36W
Canyonlands Nat. Park 73 38 25N 109 30W
Canyonville 72 42 55N 123 14W
Cao Xian 39 34 50N 115 35 E
Cap-aux-Meules 63 47 23N 61 52W
Cap-Chat 63 49 6N 66 40W
Cap-de-la-Madeleine 62 46 22N 72 31W
Cap-Haïtien 75 19 40N 72 20W
Cap St.-Jacques = Vung Tau 34 10 21N 107 4 E
Capaia 54 8 27S 20 13 E
Capanaparo ➝ 78 7 1N 67 7W
Cape ➝ 44 20 49S 146 51 E
Cape Barren I. 44 40 25S 148 15 E
Cape Breton Highlands Nat. Park 63 46 50N 60 40W
Cape Breton I. 63 46 0N 60 30W
Cape Charles 68 37 15N 75 59W
Cape Coast 53 5 5N 1 15W
Cape Dorset 61 64 14N 76 32W
Cape Dyer 61 66 30N 61 22W
Cape Fear ➝ 69 34 30N 78 25W
Cape Girardeau 71 37 20N 89 30W
Cape Jervis 45 35 40S 138 5 E
Cape May 68 39 1N 74 53W
Cape Preston 46 20 51S 116 12 E
Cape Province □ 56 32 0S 23 0 E
Cape Tormentine 63 46 8N 63 47W
Cape Town 56 33 55S 18 22 E
Cape Verde Is. ■ 2 17 10N 25 20W
Cape York Peninsula 44 12 0S 142 30 E
Capela 79 10 30S 37 0W
Capella 44 23 2S 148 1 E
Capernaum = Kefar Nahum 28 32 54N 35 34 E
Capim ➝ 79 1 40S 47 47W
Capitan 73 33 33N 105 41W
Capraia 18 43 2N 9 50 E
Capreol 62 46 43N 80 56W
Caprera 18 41 12N 9 28 E
Capri 18 40 34N 14 15 E
Capricorn Group 44 23 30S 151 55 E
Capricorn Ra. 46 23 20S 116 50 E
Caprivi Strip 56 18 0S 23 0 E
Captain's Flat 45 35 35S 149 27 E
Caquetá ➝ 78 1 15S 69 15W
Caracal 15 44 8N 24 22 E
Caracas 78 10 30N 66 55W
Caracol 79 9 15S 43 22W
Caradoc 45 30 35S 143 5 E
Carajás, Serra dos 79 6 0S 51 30W
Carangola 79 20 44S 42 5W
Carani 47 30 57S 116 28 E
Caransebeş 15 45 28N 22 18 E
Caratasca, L. 75 15 20N 83 40W
Caratinga 79 19 50S 42 10W
Caraúbas 79 5 43S 37 33W
Caravaca 13 38 8N 1 52W
Caravelas 79 17 45S 39 15W
Caraveli 78 15 45S 73 25W
Carballo 13 43 13N 8 41W
Carberry 65 49 50N 99 25W
Carbó 74 29 42N 110 58W
Carbon 64 51 30N 113 9W
Carbonara, C. 18 39 8N 9 30 E
Carbondale, Colo., U.S.A. 72 39 30N 107 10W
Carbondale, Ill., U.S.A. 71 37 45N 89 10W
Carbondale, Pa., U.S.A. 68 41 37N 75 30W
Carbonear 63 47 42N 53 13W
Carbonia 18 39 10N 8 30 E
Carcajou 64 57 47N 117 6W
Carcasse, C. 75 18 30N 74 28W
Carcassonne 12 43 13N 2 20 E
Carcross 60 60 13N 134 45W
Cardabia 46 23 2S 113 48 E
Cardamon Hills 32 9 30N 77 15 E
Cárdenas, Cuba 75 23 0N 81 30W
Cárdenas, San Luis Potosí, Mexico 74 22 0N 99 41W
Cárdenas, Tabasco, Mexico 74 17 59N 93 21W
Cardiff 7 51 28N 3 11W
Cardigan 7 52 6N 4 41W
Cardigan B. 7 52 30N 4 30W
Cardona 13 41 56N 1 40 E
Cardross 65 49 50N 105 40W
Cardston 64 49 15N 113 20W
Cardwell 44 18 14S 146 2 E
Careen L. 65 57 0N 108 11W
Carei 15 47 40N 22 29 E
Careme 35 6 55S 108 27 E
Carey, Idaho, U.S.A. 72 43 19N 113 58W
Carey, Ohio, U.S.A. 68 40 58N 83 22W
Carey, L. 47 29 0S 122 15 E
Carey L. 65 62 12N 102 55W
Careysburg 50 6 34N 10 30W
Cargados Garajos 3 17 0S 59 0 E
Carhué 80 37 10S 62 50W
Cariacica 79 20 16S 40 25W
Caribbean Sea 75 15 0N 75 0W
Cariboo Mts. 64 53 0N 121 0W
Caribou 63 46 55N 68 0W
Caribou ➝, Man., Canada 65 59 20N 94 44W
Caribou ➝, N.W.T., Canada 64 61 27N 125 45W
Caribou I. 62 47 22N 85 49W
Caribou Is. 64 61 55N 113 15W
Caribou L., Man., Canada 65 59 21N 96 10W
Caribou L., Ont., Canada 62 50 25N 89 5W
Caribou Mts. 64 59 12N 115 40W
Carinda 45 30 28S 147 41 E
Carinhanha 79 14 15S 44 46W
Carinthia □ = Kärnten □ 14 46 52N 13 30 E
Caripito 78 10 8N 63 6W
Caritianas 78 9 20S 63 6W
Carleton Place 62 45 8N 76 9W
Carletonville 56 26 23S 27 22 E
Carlin 72 40 44N 116 5W
Carlingford, L. 9 54 0N 6 5W
Carlinville 70 39 20N 89 55W
Carlisle, U.K. 6 54 54N 2 55W
Carlisle, U.S.A. 68 40 12N 77 10W
Carlota, La 80 33 30S 63 20W
Carlow 9 52 50N 6 58W
Carlow □ 9 52 43N 6 50W
Carlsbad, Calif., U.S.A. 73 33 11N 117 25W
Carlsbad, N. Mex., U.S.A. 71 32 20N 104 14W
Carlyle, Canada 65 49 40N 102 20W
Carlyle, U.S.A. 70 38 38N 89 23W
Carmacks 60 62 5N 136 16W
Carman 65 49 30N 98 0W
Carmangay 64 50 10N 113 10W
Carmanville 63 49 23N 54 19W
Carmarthen 7 51 52N 4 20W
Carmarthen B. 7 51 40N 4 30W
Carmel-by-the-Sea 73 36 38N 121 55W
Carmel Mt. 28 32 45N 35 3 E
Carmelo 80 34 0S 58 20W
Carmen 78 9 43N 75 8W
Carmen, I. 74 26 0N 111 20W
Carmen de Patagones 80 40 50S 63 0W
Carmi 68 38 6N 88 10W
Carmila 44 21 55S 149 24 E
Carmona 13 37 28N 5 42W
Carnarvon, Queens., Australia 44 24 48S 147 45 E
Carnarvon, W. Austral., Australia 47 24 51S 113 42 E
Carnarvon, S. Africa 56 30 56S 22 8 E
Carnarvon Ra., Queens., Australia 44 25 15S 148 30 E
Carnarvon Ra., W. Austral., Australia 47 25 20S 120 45 E
Carndonagh 9 55 15N 7 16W
Carnduff 65 49 10N 101 50W
Carnegie, L. 47 26 5S 122 30 E
Carnic Alps = Karnische Alpen 14 46 36N 13 0 E
Carniche, Alpi 18 46 36N 13 0 E
Carnot 54 4 59N 15 56 E
Carnot B. 46 17 20S 122 15 E
Carnsore Pt. 9 52 10N 6 20W
Caro 68 43 29N 83 27W
Carol City 69 25 5N 80 16W
Carolina, Brazil 75 7 10S 47 30W
Carolina, S. Africa 57 26 5S 30 6 E
Carolina, La 13 38 17N 3 38W
Caroline I. 41 9 15S 150 3W
Caroline Is. 3 8 0N 150 0 E
Caron 65 50 30N 105 50W
Caroni ➝ 78 8 21N 62 43W
Caroona 45 31 24S 150 26 E
Carpathians, Mts. 15 49 30N 21 0 E
Carpaţii Meridionali 15 45 30N 25 0 E
Carpentaria, G. of 44 14 0S 139 0 E
Carpentaria Downs 44 18 44S 144 20 E
Carpinteria 73 34 25N 119 31W
Carpolac = Morea 45 36 45S 141 18 E
Carr Boyd Ra. 46 16 15S 128 35 E
Carrabelle 69 29 52N 84 40W
Carranya 46 19 14S 127 46 E
Carrara 18 44 5N 10 7 E
Carrauntoohill, Mt. 9 52 0N 9 49W
Carrick-on-Shannon 9 53 57N 8 7W
Carrick-on-Suir 9 52 22N 7 30W
Carrickfergus 9 54 43N 5 50W
Carrickfergus □ 9 54 43N 5 49W
Carrickmacross 9 54 0N 6 43W
Carrieton 45 32 25S 138 31 E
Carrington 70 47 30N 99 7W
Carrizal Bajo 80 28 5S 71 20W
Carrizo Cr. ➝ 71 36 30N 103 40W
Carrizo Springs 71 28 28N 99 50W
Carrizozo 73 33 40N 105 57W
Carroll 70 42 2N 94 55W
Carrollton, Ga., U.S.A. 69 33 36N 85 5W
Carrollton, Ill., U.S.A. 70 39 20N 90 25W
Carrollton, Ky., U.S.A. 68 38 40N 85 10W
Carrollton, Mo., U.S.A. 70 39 19N 93 24W
Carron ➝ 8 57 30N 5 30W
Carron, L. 8 57 22N 5 35W
Carrot ➝ 65 53 50N 101 17W
Carrot River 65 53 17N 103 35W
Carruthers 65 52 52N 109 16W
Çarşamba 30 41 15N 36 45 E
Carse of Gowrie 8 56 30N 3 10W
Carson 70 46 27N 101 29W
Carson City 72 39 12N 119 46W
Carson Sink 72 39 50N 118 40W
Carstairs 8 55 42N 3 41W
Cartagena, Colombia 78 10 25N 75 33W
Cartagena, Spain 13 37 38N 0 59W
Cartago, Colombia 78 4 45N 75 55W
Cartago, C. Rica 75 9 50N 85 52W
Cartersville 69 34 11N 84 48W
Carterton 43 41 2S 175 31 E
Carthage, Ark., U.S.A. 71 34 4N 92 32W
Carthage, Ill., U.S.A. 70 40 25N 91 10W
Carthage, Mo., U.S.A. 71 37 10N 94 20W
Carthage, S. Dak., U.S.A. 70 44 14N 97 38W
Carthage, Tex., U.S.A. 71 32 8N 94 20W
Cartier I. 46 12 31S 123 29 E
Cartwright 63 53 41N 56 58W
Caruaru 79 8 15S 35 55W
Carúpano 78 10 39N 63 15W
Caruthersville 71 36 10N 89 40W
Carvoeiro 78 1 30S 61 59W
Casa Grande 73 32 53N 111 51W
Casablanca 50 33 36N 7 36W
Casale Monferrato 18 45 8N 8 28 E
Casas Grandes 74 30 22N 108 0W
Cascade, Idaho, U.S.A. 72 44 30N 116 2W
Cascade, Mont., U.S.A. 72 47 16N 111 46W
Cascade Locks 72 45 44N 121 54W
Cascade Ra. 72 47 0N 121 30W
Cascavel 80 24 57S 53 28W
Caserta 18 41 5N 14 20 E
Cashel 9 52 31N 7 53W
Cashmere 72 47 31N 120 30W
Cashmere Downs 47 28 57S 119 35 E
Casiguran 35 16 22N 122 7 E
Casilda 80 33 10S 61 10W
Casino 45 28 52S 153 3 E
Casiquiare ➝ 78 2 1N 67 7W
Caslan 64 54 38N 112 31W
Casma 78 9 30S 78 20W
Caspe 13 41 14N 0 1W
Casper 72 42 52N 106 20W

Clipperton, I.

Cherryvale 71 37 20N 95 33W
Cherskiy 25 68 45N 161 18 E
Cherskogo Khrebet 25 65 0N 143 0 E
Cherwell → 7 51 46N 1 18W
Chesapeake 68 36 43N 76 15W
Chesapeake Bay 68 38 0N 76 12W
Cheshire □ 6 53 14N 2 30W
Cheshskaya Guba 22 67 20N 47 0 E
Cheslatta L. 64 53 49N 125 20W
Chester, U.K. 6 53 12N 2 53W
Chester, Calif., U.S.A. 72 40 22N 121 14W
Chester, Ill., U.S.A. 71 37 58N 89 50W
Chester, Mont., U.S.A. 72 48 31N 111 0W
Chester, Pa., U.S.A. 68 39 54N 75 20W
Chester, S.C., U.S.A. 69 34 44N 81 13W
Chesterfield 6 53 14N 1 26W
Chesterfield, Îles 40 19 52S 158 15 E
Chesterfield Inlet 60 63 30N 90 45W
Chesterton Range 45 25 30S 147 27 E
Chesuncook L. 63 46 0N 69 10W
Chéticamp 63 46 37N 60 59W
Chetumal 74 18 30N 88 20W
Chetumal, B. de 74 18 40N 88 10W
Chetwynd 64 55 45N 121 36W
Cheviot, The 6 55 29N 2 8W
Cheviot Hills 6 55 20N 2 30W
Cheviot Ra. 44 25 20S 143 45 E
Chew Bahir 51 4 40N 36 50 E
Chewelah 72 48 17N 117 43W
Cheyenne, Okla., U.S.A. 71 35 35N 99 40W
Cheyenne, Wyo., U.S.A. 70 41 9N 104 49W
Cheyenne → 70 44 40N 101 15W
Cheyenne Wells 70 38 51N 102 10W
Cheyne B. 47 34 35S 118 50 E
Chhapra 33 25 48N 84 44 E
Chhatarpur 32 24 55N 79 35 E
Chhindwara 32 22 2N 78 59 E
Chhlong 34 12 15N 105 58 E
Chi → 34 15 11N 104 43 E
Chiamis 35 7 20S 108 21 E
Chiamussu = Jiamusi 38 46 40N 130 26 E
Chiange 55 15 35S 13 40 E
Chiapa → 74 16 42N 93 0W
Chiapas □ 74 17 0N 92 45W
Chiba 36 35 30N 140 7 E
Chiba □ 36 35 30N 140 20 E
Chibabava 57 20 17S 33 35 E
Chibatu 35 7 6S 107 59 E
Chibemba, Cunene, Angola 55 15 48S 14 8 E
Chibemba, Huila, Angola 56 16 20S 15 20 E
Chibia 55 15 10S 13 42 E
Chibougamau 62 49 56N 74 24W
Chibougamau L. 62 49 50N 74 20W
Chibuk 53 10 52N 12 50 E
Chic-Chocs, Mts. 63 48 55N 66 0W
Chicacole = Srikakulam 33 18 14N 83 58 E
Chicago 68 41 53N 87 40W
Chicago Heights 68 41 29N 87 37W
Chichagof I. 64 58 0N 136 0W
Chichester 7 50 50N 0 47W
Chichibu 36 36 5N 139 10 E
Ch'ich'ihaerh = Qiqihar 38 47 26N 124 0 E
Chickasha 71 35 0N 98 0W
Chiclana de la Frontera 13 36 26N 6 9W
Chiclayo 78 6 42S 79 50W
Chico 72 39 45N 121 54W
Chico →, Chubut, Argentina 80 44 0S 67 0W
Chico →, Santa Cruz, Argentina 80 50 0S 68 30W
Chicomo 57 24 31S 34 6 E
Chicopee 68 42 6N 72 37W
Chicoutimi 63 48 28N 71 5W
Chicualacuala 57 22 6S 31 42 E
Chidambaram 32 11 20N 79 45 E
Chidenguele 57 24 55S 34 11 E
Chidley, C. 61 60 23N 64 26W
Chiede 56 17 15S 16 22 E
Chiengi 54 8 45S 29 10 E
Chiese → 18 45 8N 10 25 E
Chieti 18 42 22N 14 10 E
Chifeng 38 42 18N 118 58 E
Chignecto B. 63 45 30N 64 40W
Chiguana 78 21 0S 67 58W
Chihli, G. of = Bo Hai 38 39 0N 120 0 E
Chihuahua 74 28 40N 106 3W
Chihuahua □ 74 28 40N 106 3W
Chiili 24 44 20N 66 15 E
Chik Bollapur 32 13 25N 77 45 E
Chikmagalur 32 13 15N 75 45 E
Chilako → 64 53 53N 122 57W
Chilapa 74 17 40N 99 11W
Chilas 32 35 25N 74 5 E
Chilaw 32 7 30N 79 50 E
Chilcotin → 64 51 44N 122 23W
Childers 45 25 15S 152 17 E
Childress 71 34 30N 100 15W
Chile ■ 80 35 0S 72 0W
Chile Rise 41 38 0S 92 0W
Chilete 78 7 10S 78 50W
Chililabombwe 55 12 18S 27 43 E
Chilin = Jilin 38 43 44N 126 30 E
Chilka L. 33 19 40N 85 25 E
Chilko → 64 52 0N 123 40W
Chilko, L. 64 51 20N 124 10W
Chillagoe 44 17 7S 144 33 E
Chillán 80 36 40S 72 10W
Chillicothe, Ill., U.S.A. 70 40 55N 89 32W
Chillicothe, Mo., U.S.A. 70 39 45N 93 30W
Chillicothe, Ohio, U.S.A. 68 39 20N 82 58W
Chilliwack 64 49 10N 121 54W
Chiloane, I. 57 20 40S 34 55 E
Chiloé, I. de 80 42 30S 73 50W
Chilpancingo 74 17 30N 99 30W
Chiltern Hills 7 51 44N 0 42W
Chilton 68 44 1N 88 12W
Chiluage 54 9 30S 21 50 E
Chilumba 52 10 28S 34 12 E
Chilwa, L. 55 15 15S 35 40 E
Chimay 11 50 3N 4 20 E
Chimbay 24 42 57N 59 47 E
Chimborazo 78 1 29S 78 55W
Chimbote 78 9 0S 78 35W
Chimkent 24 42 18N 69 36 E
Chimoio 55 19 4S 33 30 E
Chin □ 33 22 0N 93 0 E
Chin Ling Shan = Qinling Shandi 39 33 50N 108 10 E
China 74 25 40N 99 20W
China ■ 37 30 0N 110 0 E
Chinan = Jinan 38 36 38N 117 1 E
Chinandega 75 12 35N 87 12W
Chinati Pk. 71 30 0N 104 25W
Chincha Alta 78 13 25S 76 7W
Chinchilla 45 26 45S 150 38 E
Chinchón 13 40 9N 3 26W
Chinchorro, Banco 74 18 35N 87 20W
Chinchou = Jinzhou 38 41 5N 121 3 E
Chincoteague 68 37 58N 75 21W
Chinde 55 18 35S 36 30 E
Chindwin → 33 21 26N 95 15 E
Chingola 55 12 31S 27 53 E
Ch'ingtao = Qingdao 38 36 5N 120 20 E
Chinguetti 50 20 25N 12 24W
Chingune 57 20 33S 35 0 E
Chinhae 38 35 9N 128 47 E
Chinhanguanine 57 25 21S 32 30 E
Chinhoyi 55 17 20S 30 8 E
Chiniot 32 31 45N 73 0 E
Chinju 38 35 12N 128 2 E
Chinle 73 36 14N 109 38W
Chinnampo 38 38 52N 125 10 E
Chino Valley 73 34 54N 112 28W
Chinon 12 47 10N 0 15 E
Chinook, Canada 65 51 28N 110 59W
Chinook, U.S.A. 72 48 35N 109 19W
Chinsali 54 10 30S 32 2 E
Chinteche 52 11 50S 34 5 E
Chióggia 18 45 13N 12 15 E
Chíos = Khíos 19 38 27N 26 9 E
Chipata 55 13 38S 32 28 E
Chipatujah 35 7 45S 108 0 E
Chipewyan L. 65 58 0N 98 27W
Chipley 69 30 45N 85 32W
Chipman 63 46 6N 65 53W
Chippenham 7 51 27N 2 7W
Chippewa → 70 44 25N 92 10W
Chippewa Falls 70 44 55N 91 22W
Chiquián 78 10 10S 77 0W
Chiquimula 75 14 51N 89 37W
Chiquinquira 78 5 37N 73 50W
Chirala 32 15 50N 80 26 E
Chirchik 24 41 29N 69 35 E
Chiricahua Pk. 73 31 53N 109 14W
Chirikof I. 60 55 50N 155 40W
Chiriquí, G. de 75 8 0N 82 10W
Chiriquí, L. de 75 9 10N 82 0W
Chirmiri 33 23 15N 82 20 E
Chiromo 55 16 30S 35 7 E
Chirripó Grande, Cerro 75 9 29N 83 29W
Chisamba 55 14 55S 28 20 E
Chisapani Garhi 33 27 30N 84 2 E
Chisholm 64 54 55N 114 10W
Chisos Mts. 71 29 20N 103 15W
Chistopol 22 55 25N 50 38 E
Chita 25 52 0N 113 35 E
Chitado 55 17 10S 14 8 E
Chitembo 55 13 30S 16 50 E
Chitral 31 35 50N 71 56 E
Chitré 75 7 59N 80 27W
Chittagong 33 22 19N 91 48 E
Chittagong □ 33 24 5N 91 0 E
Chittaurgarh 32 24 52N 74 38 E
Chittoor 32 13 15N 79 5 E
Chiusi 18 43 1N 11 58 E
Chivasso 18 45 10N 7 52 E
Chivilcoy 80 34 55S 60 0W
Chkalov = Orenburg 22 51 45N 55 6 E
Chobe National Park 56 18 0S 25 0 E
Choele Choel 80 39 11S 65 40W
Choix 74 26 40N 108 23W
Chojnice 15 53 42N 17 32 E
Chokurdakh 25 70 38N 147 55 E
Cholet 12 47 4N 0 52W
Choluteca 75 13 20N 87 14W
Choma 55 16 48S 26 59 E
Chomutov 14 50 28N 13 23 E
Chon Buri 34 13 21N 101 1 E
Chonan 38 36 48N 127 9 E
Chone 78 0 40S 80 0W
Chong'an 39 27 45N 118 0 E
Chongde 39 30 32N 120 26 E
Chongjin 38 41 47N 129 50 E
Chŏngju, N. Korea 38 39 40N 125 5 E
Chŏngju, S. Korea 38 36 39N 127 27 E
Chongli 38 40 58N 115 15 E
Chongming Dao 39 31 40N 121 30 E
Chongqing 39 29 35N 106 25 E
Chongzuo 39 22 23N 107 20 E
Chŏnju 38 35 50N 127 4 E
Chonos, Arch. de los 80 45 0S 75 0W
Chorley 6 53 39N 2 39W
Chorregon 44 22 40S 143 32 E
Chorrera, La 74 8 50N 79 50W
Chŏrwŏn 38 38 15N 127 10 E
Chorzów 15 50 18N 18 57 E
Chos-Malal 80 37 20S 70 15W
Chosan 38 40 50N 125 47 E
Chōshi 36 35 45N 140 51 E
Choszczno 14 53 7N 15 25 E
Choteau 72 47 50N 112 10W
Chotila 32 22 23N 71 15 E
Chowchilla 73 37 11N 120 12W
Choybalsan 37 48 4N 114 30 E
Christchurch, N.Z. 43 43 33S 172 47 E
Christchurch, U.K. 7 50 44N 1 33W
Christiana 56 27 52S 25 8 E
Christie B. 65 62 32N 111 10W
Christina → 65 56 40N 111 3W
Christmas Cr. → 46 18 29S 125 23 E
Christmas Creek 46 18 29S 125 23 E
Christmas I. = Kiritimati 2 1 58N 157 27W
Christmas I. 3 10 30S 105 40 E
Christopher L. 47 24 49S 127 42 E
Chu 24 43 36N 73 42 E
Chu Chua 64 51 22N 120 10W
Ch'uanchou = Quanzhou 39 24 55N 118 34 E
Chūbu □ 36 36 45N 137 30 E
Chubut → 80 43 20S 65 5W
Chuchi L. 64 55 12N 124 30W
Chudskoye, Oz. 22 58 13N 27 30 E
Chūgoku □ 36 35 0N 133 0 E
Chūgoku-Sanchi 36 35 0N 133 0 E
Chugwater 70 41 48N 104 47W
Chuka 52 0 23S 37 38 E
Chukotskiy Khrebet 25 68 0N 175 0 E
Chukotskoye More 25 68 0N 175 0W
Chula Vista 73 32 39N 117 8W
Chulman 25 56 52N 124 52 E
Chulucanas 78 5 8S 80 10W
Chulym → 24 57 43N 83 51 E
Chumbicha 80 29 0S 66 10W
Chumikan 25 54 40N 135 10 E
Chumphon 34 10 35N 99 14 E
Chuna → 25 57 47N 94 37 E
Chun'an 39 29 35N 119 3 E
Chunchŏn 38 37 58N 127 44 E
Chungking = Chongqing 39 29 35N 106 25 E
Chunya 54 8 30S 33 27 E
Chuquibamba 78 15 47S 72 44W
Chuquicamata 80 22 15S 69 0W
Chuquisaca □ 78 23 30S 63 30W
Chur 14 46 52N 9 32 E
Churachandpur 33 24 20N 93 40 E
Churchill 65 58 47N 94 11W
Churchill →, Man., Canada 65 58 47N 94 12W
Churchill →, Nfld., Canada 63 53 19N 60 10W
Churchill, C. 65 58 46N 93 12W
Churchill Falls 63 53 36N 64 19W
Churchill L. 65 55 55N 108 20W
Churchill Pk. 64 58 10N 125 10W
Churu 32 28 20N 74 50 E
Chushal 32 33 40N 78 40 E
Chusovoy 22 58 15N 57 40 E
Chuvash A.S.S.R.□ 22 55 30N 47 0 E
Ci Xian 38 36 20N 114 25 E
Cianjur 35 6 49S 107 8 E
Cibadok 35 6 53S 106 47 E
Cibatu 35 7 8S 107 59 E
Cicero 68 41 48N 87 48W
Ciechanów 15 52 52N 20 38 E
Ciego de Avila 75 21 50N 78 50W
Ciénaga 78 11 1N 74 15W
Cienfuegos 75 22 10N 80 30W
Cieszyn 15 49 45N 18 35 E
Cieza 13 38 17N 1 23W
Cijulang 35 7 42S 108 27 E
Cikajang 35 7 25S 107 48 E
Cikampek 35 6 23S 107 28 E
Cilacap 35 7 43S 109 0 E
Cilician Gates P. 30 37 20N 34 52 E
Cimahi 35 6 53S 107 33 E
Cimarron, Kans., U.S.A. 71 37 50N 100 20W
Cimarron, N. Mex., U.S.A. 71 36 30N 104 52W
Cimarron → 71 36 10N 96 17W
Cimone, Mte. 18 44 10N 10 40 E
Cîmpina 15 45 10N 25 45 E
Cîmpulung 15 45 17N 25 3 E
Cinca → 13 41 26N 0 21 E
Cincinnati 68 39 10N 84 26W
Ciney 11 50 18N 5 5 E
Cinto, Mte. 12 42 24N 8 54 E
Circle, Alaska, U.S.A. 60 65 50N 144 10W
Circle, Mont., U.S.A. 70 47 26N 105 35W
Circleville, Ohio, U.S.A. 68 39 35N 82 57W
Circleville, Utah, U.S.A. 73 38 12N 112 24W
Cirebon 35 6 45S 108 32 E
Cirencester 7 51 43N 1 59W
Cisco 71 32 25N 99 0W
Ciskei □ 57 33 0S 27 0 E
Citlaltépetl 74 19 0N 97 20W
Citrusdal 56 32 35S 19 0 E
Ciudad Altamirano 74 18 20N 100 40W
Ciudad Bolívar 78 8 5N 63 36W
Ciudad Camargo 74 27 41N 105 10W
Ciudad de Valles 74 22 0N 99 0W
Ciudad del Carmen 74 18 38N 91 50W
Ciudad Delicias = Delicias 74 28 10N 105 30W
Ciudad Guayana 78 8 0N 62 30W
Ciudad Guerrero 74 28 33N 107 28W
Ciudad Guzmán 74 19 40N 103 30W
Ciudad Juárez 74 31 40N 106 28W
Ciudad Madero 74 22 19N 97 50W
Ciudad Mante 74 22 50N 99 0W
Ciudad Obregón 74 27 28N 109 59W
Ciudad Real 13 38 59N 3 55W
Ciudad Rodrigo 13 40 35N 6 32W
Ciudad Trujillo = Santo Domingo 75 18 30N 69 59W
Ciudad Victoria 74 23 41N 99 9W
Civitanova Marche 18 43 18N 13 41 E
Civitavécchia 18 42 6N 11 46 E
Çivril 30 38 20N 29 43 E
Cizre 30 37 19N 42 10 E
Clackline 47 31 40S 116 32 E
Clacton-on-Sea 7 51 47N 1 10 E
Claire, L. 64 58 35N 112 5W
Clairemont 71 33 9N 100 44W
Clanton 69 32 48N 86 36W
Clanwilliam 56 32 11S 18 52 E
Clara 9 53 20N 7 38W
Clara → 44 19 8S 142 30 E
Clare, Australia 45 33 50S 138 37 E
Clare, U.S.A. 68 43 47N 84 45W
Clare □ 9 52 20N 9 0W
Clare → 9 53 22N 9 5W
Clare I. 9 53 48N 10 0W
Claremont 68 43 23N 72 20W
Claremont Pt. 44 14 1S 143 41 E
Claremore 71 36 40N 95 37W
Claremorris 9 53 45N 9 0W
Clarence →, Australia 45 29 25S 153 22 E
Clarence →, N.Z. 43 42 10S 173 56 E
Clarence, I. 80 54 0S 72 0W
Clarence Str., Australia 46 12 0S 131 0 E
Clarence Str., U.S.A. 64 55 40N 132 10W
Clarendon, Ark., U.S.A. 71 34 41N 91 20W
Clarendon, Tex., U.S.A. 71 34 58N 100 54W
Clarenville 63 48 10N 54 1W
Claresholm 64 50 0N 113 33W
Clarinda 70 40 45N 95 0W
Clarion 70 42 41N 93 46W
Clarion Fracture Zone 41 20 0N 120 0W
Clark 70 44 55N 97 45W
Clark Fork 72 48 9N 116 9W
Clark Fork → 72 48 9N 116 15W
Clark Hill Res. 69 33 45N 82 20W
Clarkdale 73 34 53N 112 3W
Clarke City 63 50 12N 66 38W
Clarke I. 44 40 32S 148 10 E
Clarke L. 65 54 24N 106 54W
Clarke Ra. 44 20 45S 148 20 E
Clark's Fork → 72 45 39N 108 43W
Clark's Harbour 63 43 25N 65 38W
Clarksburg 68 39 18N 80 21W
Clarksdale 71 34 12N 90 33W
Clarkston 72 46 28N 117 2W
Clarksville, Ark., U.S.A. 71 35 29N 93 27W
Clarksville, Tenn., U.S.A. 69 36 32N 87 20W
Clarksville, Tex., U.S.A. 71 33 37N 94 59W
Clatskanie 72 46 9N 123 12W
Claude 71 35 8N 101 22W
Claveria 35 18 37N 121 4 E
Clay Center 70 39 27N 97 9W
Claypool 73 33 27N 110 55W
Clayton, Idaho, U.S.A. 72 44 12N 114 31W
Clayton, N. Mex., U.S.A. 71 36 30N 103 10W
Cle Elum 72 47 15N 120 57W
Clear, C. 9 51 26N 9 30W
Clear I. 9 51 26N 9 30W
Clear L. 72 39 5N 122 47W
Clear Lake, S. Dak., U.S.A. 70 44 48N 96 41W
Clear Lake, Wash., U.S.A. 72 48 27N 122 15W
Clear Lake Res. 72 41 55N 121 10W
Clearfield, Pa., U.S.A. 68 41 0N 78 27W
Clearfield, Utah, U.S.A. 72 41 10N 112 0W
Clearmont 72 44 43N 106 29W
Clearwater, Canada 64 51 38N 120 2W
Clearwater, U.S.A. 69 27 58N 82 45W
Clearwater →, Alta., Canada 64 52 22N 114 57W
Clearwater →, Alta., Canada 65 56 44N 111 23W
Clearwater Cr. → 64 61 36N 125 30W
Clearwater Mts. 72 46 20N 115 30W
Clearwater Prov. Park 65 54 0N 101 0W
Cleburne 71 32 18N 97 25W
Cleethorpes 6 53 33N 0 2W
Cleeve Cloud 7 51 56N 2 0W
Clerke Reef 46 17 22S 119 20 E
Clermont 44 22 49S 147 39 E
Clermont-Ferrand 12 45 46N 3 4 E
Clervaux 11 50 4N 6 2 E
Cleveland, Australia 45 27 30S 153 15 E
Cleveland, Miss., U.S.A. 71 33 43N 90 43W
Cleveland, Ohio, U.S.A. 68 41 28N 81 43W
Cleveland, Okla., U.S.A. 71 36 21N 96 33W
Cleveland, Tenn., U.S.A. 69 35 9N 84 52W
Cleveland, Tex., U.S.A. 71 30 18N 95 0W
Cleveland □ 6 54 35N 1 8 E
Cleveland, C. 44 19 11S 147 1 E
Clew B. 9 53 54N 9 50W
Clewiston 69 26 44N 80 50W
Clifden, Ireland 9 53 30N 10 2W
Clifden, N.Z. 43 46 1S 167 42 E
Clifton, Australia 45 27 59S 151 53 E
Clifton, Ariz., U.S.A. 73 33 8N 109 23W
Clifton, Tex., U.S.A. 71 31 46N 97 35W
Clifton Beach 44 16 46S 145 39 E
Clifton Forge 68 37 49N 79 51W
Clifton Hills 45 27 1S 138 54 E
Climax 65 49 10N 108 20W
Clinch → 69 36 0N 84 29W
Clingmans Dome 69 35 35N 83 30W
Clint 73 31 37N 106 11W
Clinton, B.C., Canada 64 51 6N 121 35W
Clinton, Ont., Canada 62 43 37N 81 32W
Clinton, N.Z. 43 46 12S 169 23 E
Clinton, Ark., U.S.A. 71 35 37N 92 30W
Clinton, Ill., U.S.A. 70 40 8N 89 0W
Clinton, Ind., U.S.A. 68 39 40N 87 22W
Clinton, Iowa, U.S.A. 70 41 50N 90 12W
Clinton, Mass., U.S.A. 68 42 26N 71 40W
Clinton, Mo., U.S.A. 70 38 20N 93 46W
Clinton, N.C., U.S.A. 69 35 5N 78 15W
Clinton, Okla., U.S.A. 71 35 30N 99 0W
Clinton, S.C., U.S.A. 69 34 30N 81 54W
Clinton, Tenn., U.S.A. 69 36 6N 84 10W
Clinton C. 44 22 30S 150 45 E
Clinton Colden L. 60 63 58N 107 27W
Clintonville 70 44 35N 88 46W
Clipperton, I. 41 10 18N 109 13W

Dankhar Gompa

Corque 78 18 20S 67 41W
Correntes, C. das 57 24 6S 35 34 E
Corrèze □ 12 45 20N 1 45 E
Corrib, L. 9 53 5N 9 10W
Corrientes 80 27 30S 58 45W
Corrientes → 78 3 43S 74 35W
Corrientes, C., Colombia 78 5 30N 77 34W
Corrientes, C., Cuba 75 21 43N 84 30W
Corrientes, C., Mexico 74 20 25N 105 42W
Corrigan 71 31 0N 94 48W
Corrigin 47 32 20S 117 53 E
Corry 68 41 55N 79 39W
Corse 12 42 0N 9 0 E
Corse, C. 18 43 1N 9 25 E
Corse-du-Sud □ 12 41 45N 9 0 E
Corsica = Corse 12 42 0N 9 0 E
Corsicana 71 32 5N 96 30W
Cortez 73 37 24N 108 35W
Cortland 68 42 35N 76 11W
Cortona 18 43 16N 12 0 E
Çorum 30 40 30N 34 57 E
Corumbá 78 19 0S 57 30W
Corumbá de Goiás 79 16 0S 48 50W
Coruña, La 13 43 20N 8 25W
Corunna = Coruña, La 13 43 20N 8 25W
Corvallis 72 44 36N 123 15W
Corvette, L. de la 62 53 25N 74 3W
Corydon 70 40 42N 93 22W
Cosalá 74 24 28N 106 40W
Cosamaloapan 74 18 23N 95 50W
Cosenza 18 39 17N 16 14 E
Coshocton 68 40 17N 81 51W
Cosmo Newberry 47 28 0S 122 54 E
Costa Blanca 13 38 25N 0 10W
Costa Brava 13 41 30N 3 0 E
Costa del Sol 13 36 30N 4 30W
Costa Dorada 13 40 45N 1 15 E
Costa Rica ■ 75 10 0N 84 0W
Costilla 73 37 0N 105 30W
Cotabato 35 7 14N 124 15 E
Cotagaita 78 20 45S 65 40W
Côte-d'Or □ 12 47 30N 4 50 E
Coteau des Prairies 70 44 30N 97 0W
Coteau du Missouri 70 47 0N 101 0W
Cotentin 12 49 15N 1 30W
Côtes-du-Nord □ 12 48 25N 2 40W
Cotonou 53 6 20N 2 25 E
Cotopaxi, Vol. 76 0 40S 78 30W
Cotswold Hills 7 51 42N 2 10W
Cottage Grove 72 43 48N 123 2W
Cottbus 14 51 44N 14 20 E
Cottonwood 73 34 48N 112 1W
Cotulla 71 28 26N 99 14W
Coudersport 68 41 45N 78 1W
Couedic, C. du 45 36 5S 136 40 E
Coulee City 72 47 36N 119 18W
Coulonge → 62 45 52N 76 46W
Council, Alaska, U.S.A. 60 64 55N 163 45W
Council, Idaho, U.S.A. 72 44 44N 116 26W
Council Bluffs 70 41 20N 95 50W
Council Grove 70 38 41N 96 30W
Courantyne → 78 5 55N 57 5W
Courtenay 64 49 45N 125 0W
Courtrai = Kortrijk 11 50 50N 3 17 E
Coushatta 71 32 0N 93 21W
Coutts 64 49 0N 111 57W
Coventry 7 52 25N 1 31W
Coventry L. 65 61 15N 106 15W
Covilhã 13 40 17N 7 31W
Covington, Ga., U.S.A. 69 33 36N 83 50W
Covington, Ky., U.S.A. 68 39 5N 84 30W
Covington, Okla., U.S.A. 71 36 21N 97 36W
Covington, Tenn., U.S.A. 71 35 34N 89 39W
Cowal, L. 45 33 40S 147 25 E
Cowan 65 52 5N 100 45W
Cowan, L. 47 31 45S 121 45 E
Cowan L. 65 54 0N 107 15W
Cowangie 45 35 12S 141 26 E
Cowarie 45 27 45S 138 15 E
Cowcowing Lakes 47 30 55S 117 20 E
Cowdenbeath 8 56 7N 3 20W
Cowell 45 33 39S 136 56 E
Cowes 7 50 45N 1 18W
Cowra 45 33 49S 148 42 E
Coxim 79 18 30S 54 55W
Cox's Bazar 33 21 26N 91 59 E
Cox's Cove 63 49 7N 58 5W
Coyuca de Benítez 74 17 1N 100 8W
Coyuca de Catalan 74 18 18N 100 41W
Cozad 70 40 55N 99 57W
Cozumel, I. de 74 20 30N 86 40W
Craboon 45 32 3S 149 30 E
Cracow = Kraków 15 50 4N 19 57 E
Cracow 45 25 17S 150 17 E
Cradock 56 32 8S 25 36 E
Craig, Alaska, U.S.A. 64 55 30N 133 5W
Craig, Colo., U.S.A. 72 40 32N 107 33W
Craiova 15 44 21N 23 48 E
Cramsie 44 23 20S 144 15 E
Cranberry Portage 65 54 35N 101 23W
Cranbrook, Tas., Australia 44 42 0S 148 5 E
Cranbrook, W. Austral., Australia 47 34 18S 117 33 E
Cranbrook, Canada 64 49 30N 115 46W
Crandon 70 45 32N 88 52W
Crane, Oreg., U.S.A. 72 43 21N 118 39W
Crane, Tex., U.S.A. 71 31 26N 102 27W
Crater, L. 72 42 55N 122 3W
Crateús 79 5 10S 40 39W
Crato 79 7 10S 39 25W
Crawford 70 42 40N 103 25W
Crawfordsville 68 40 2N 86 51W
Crawley 7 51 7N 0 10W
Crazy Mts. 72 46 14N 110 30W
Crean L. 65 54 5N 106 9W
Crécy-en-Ponthieu 12 50 15N 1 53 E
Credo 47 30 28S 120 45 E
Cree →, Canada 65 58 57N 105 47W
Cree →, U.K. 8 54 51N 4 24W
Cree L. 65 57 30N 106 30W
Creede 73 37 56N 106 59W
Creel 74 27 45N 107 38W
Creighton 70 42 30N 97 52W
Cremona 18 45 8N 10 2 E
Cres 18 44 58N 14 25 E
Cresbard 70 45 13N 98 57W
Crescent, Okla., U.S.A. 71 35 58N 97 36W
Crescent, Oreg., U.S.A. 72 43 30N 121 37W
Crescent City 72 41 45N 124 12W
Cressy 45 38 2S 143 40 E
Crested Butte 73 38 57N 107 0W
Creston, Canada 64 49 10N 116 31W
Creston, Iowa, U.S.A. 70 41 0N 94 20W
Creston, Wash., U.S.A. 72 47 47N 118 36W
Crestview 69 30 45N 86 35W
Crete = Kríti 19 35 15N 25 0 E
Crete 70 40 38N 96 58W
Crete, La 64 58 11N 116 24W
Creus, C. 13 42 20N 3 19 E
Creuse □ 12 46 10N 2 0 E
Creuse → 12 47 0N 0 34 E
Creusot, Le 12 46 48N 4 24 E
Crewe 6 53 6N 2 28W
Crib Point 45 38 22S 145 13 E
Criciúma 80 28 40S 49 23W
Crieff 8 56 22N 3 50W
Crimea = Krymskiy Poluostrov 23 45 0N 34 0 E
Crinan 8 56 6N 5 34W
Cristóbal 74 9 19N 79 54W
Crişu Alb → 15 46 42N 21 17 E
Crişu Negru → 15 46 42N 21 16 E
Crna Gora 19 42 10N 21 30 E
Crna Gora □ 19 42 40N 19 20 E
Crna Reka → 19 41 33N 21 59 E
Croaghpatrick 9 53 46N 9 40W
Crocker, Banjaran 34 5 40N 116 30 E
Crocker I. 47 11 12S 132 32 E
Crockett 71 31 20N 95 30W
Crocodile = Krokodil → 57 25 14S 32 18 E
Crocodile Is. 44 12 3S 134 58 E
Croix, La, L. 62 48 20N 92 15W
Croker, C. 46 10 58S 132 35 E
Cromarty, Canada 65 58 3N 94 9W
Cromarty, U.K. 8 57 40N 4 2W
Cromer 6 52 56N 1 18 E
Cromwell 43 45 3S 169 14 E
Cronulla 45 34 3S 151 8 E
Crooked →, Canada 64 54 50N 122 54W
Crooked →, U.S.A. 72 44 30N 121 16W
Crooked I. 75 22 50N 74 10W
Crookston, Minn., U.S.A. 70 47 50N 96 40W
Crookston, Nebr., U.S.A. 70 42 56N 100 45W
Crooksville 68 39 45N 82 8W
Crookwell 45 34 28S 149 24 E
Crosby, Minn., U.S.A. 70 46 28N 93 57W
Crosby, N. Dak., U.S.A. 65 48 55N 103 18W
Crosbyton 71 33 37N 101 12W
Cross City 69 29 35N 83 5W
Cross Fell 6 54 44N 2 29W
Cross L. 65 54 45N 97 30W
Cross Plains 71 32 8N 99 7W
Cross River □ 53 6 0N 8 0 E
Cross Sound 60 58 20N 136 30W
Crosse, La, Kans., U.S.A. 70 38 33N 99 20W
Crosse, La, Wis., U.S.A. 70 43 48N 91 13W
Crossett 71 33 10N 91 57W
Crossfield 64 51 25N 114 0W
Crosshaven 9 51 48N 8 19W
Crotone 18 39 5N 17 6 E
Crow → 64 59 41N 124 20W
Crow Agency 72 45 40N 107 30W
Crow Hd. 9 51 34N 10 9W
Crowell 71 33 59N 99 45W
Crowley 71 30 15N 92 20W
Crown Point 68 41 24N 87 23W
Crows Nest 45 27 16S 152 4 E
Crowsnest Pass 64 49 40N 114 40W
Croydon, Australia 44 18 13S 142 14 E
Croydon, U.K. 7 51 18N 0 5W
Crozet Is. 3 46 27S 52 0 E
Cruz, C. 75 19 50N 77 50W
Cruz, La 74 23 55N 106 54W
Cruz Alta 80 28 45S 53 40W
Cruz del Eje 80 30 45S 64 50W
Cruzeiro 79 22 33S 45 0W
Cruzeiro do Sul 78 7 35S 72 35W
Cry L. 64 58 45N 129 0W
Crystal Brook 45 33 21S 138 12 E
Crystal City, Mo., U.S.A. 70 38 15N 90 23W
Crystal City, Tex., U.S.A. 71 28 40N 99 50W
Crystal Falls 68 46 9N 88 11W
Crystal River 69 28 54N 82 35W
Crystal Springs 71 31 59N 90 25W
Csongrád 15 46 43N 20 12 E
Cuamato 56 17 2S 15 7 E
Cuamba 55 14 45S 36 22 E
Cuando → 55 17 30S 23 15 E
Cuando Cubango □ 56 16 25S 20 0 E
Cuangar 56 17 36S 18 39 E
Cuanza → 48 9 2S 13 30 E
Cuarto → 80 33 25S 63 2W
Cuauhtémoc 74 28 25N 106 52W
Cuba 73 36 0N 107 0W
Cuba ■ 75 22 0N 79 0W
Cuballing 47 32 50S 117 10 E
Cubango → 56 18 50S 22 25 E
Cuchi 55 14 37S 16 58 E
Cuchumatanes, Sierra de los 75 15 35N 91 25W
Cúcuta 78 7 54N 72 31W
Cudahy 68 42 54N 87 50W
Cuddalore 32 11 46N 79 45 E
Cuddapah 32 14 30N 78 47 E
Cuddapan, L. 44 25 45S 141 26 E
Cudgewa 45 36 10S 147 42 E
Cue 47 27 25S 117 54 E
Cuenca, Ecuador 78 2 50S 79 9W
Cuenca, Spain 13 40 5N 2 10W
Cuenca, Serranía de 13 39 55N 1 50W
Cuernavaca 74 18 50N 99 20W
Cuero 71 29 5N 97 17W
Cuervo 71 35 5N 104 25W
Cuevas del Almanzora 13 37 18N 1 58W
Cuevo 78 20 15S 63 30W
Cuiabá 79 15 30S 56 0W
Cuiabá → 79 17 5S 56 36W
Cuillin Hills 8 57 14N 6 15W
Cuillin Sd. 8 57 4N 6 20W
Cuiluan 38 47 51N 128 32 E
Cuima 55 13 25S 15 45 E
Cuito → 56 18 1S 20 48 E
Cuitzeo, L. de 74 19 55N 101 5W
Cukai 34 4 13N 103 25 E
Culbertson 70 48 9N 104 30W
Culcairn 45 35 41S 147 3 E
Culebra, Sierra de la 13 41 55N 6 20W
Culgoa → 45 29 56S 146 20 E
Culiacán 74 24 50N 107 23W
Culion 35 11 54N 120 1 E
Cullarin Range 45 34 30S 149 30 E
Cullen, Australia 46 13 58S 131 54 E
Cullen, U.K. 8 57 45N 2 50W
Cullen Pt. 44 11 57S 141 54 E
Cullera 13 39 9N 0 17W
Cullman 69 34 13N 86 50W
Culloden Moor 8 57 29N 4 7W
Culpeper 68 38 29N 77 59W
Culuene → 79 12 56S 52 51W
Culver, Pt. 47 32 54S 124 43 E
Culverden 43 42 47S 172 49 E
Cumaná 78 10 30N 64 5W
Cumberland, Canada 64 49 40N 125 0W
Cumberland, Md., U.S.A. 68 39 40N 78 43W
Cumberland, Wis., U.S.A. 70 45 32N 92 3W
Cumberland → 69 36 15N 87 0W
Cumberland I. 69 30 52N 81 30W
Cumberland Is. 44 20 35S 149 10 E
Cumberland L. 65 54 3N 102 18W
Cumberland Pen. 61 67 0N 64 0W
Cumberland Plateau 69 36 0N 84 30W
Cumberland Sd. 61 65 30N 66 0W
Cumborah 45 29 40S 147 45 E
Cumbria □ 6 54 35N 2 55W
Cumbrian Mts. 6 54 30N 3 0W
Cumbum 32 15 40N 79 10 E
Cummins 45 34 16S 135 43 E
Cumnock, Australia 45 32 59S 148 46 E
Cumnock, U.K. 8 55 27N 4 18W
Cundeelee 47 30 43S 123 26 E
Cunderdin 47 31 37S 117 12 E
Cunene → 56 17 20S 11 50 E
Cúneo 18 44 23N 7 31 E
Cunnamulla 45 28 2S 145 38 E
Cupar, Canada 65 50 57N 104 10W
Cupar, U.K. 8 56 20N 3 0W
Cupica, G. de 78 6 25N 77 30W
Curaçao 75 12 10N 69 0W
Curaray → 78 2 20S 74 5W
Curiapo 78 8 33N 61 5W
Curicó 80 34 55S 71 20W
Curitiba 80 25 20S 49 10W
Currabubula 45 31 16S 150 44 E
Currais Novos 79 6 13S 36 30W
Curralinho 79 1 45S 49 46W
Currant 72 38 51N 115 32W
Curraweena 45 30 47S 145 54 E
Currawilla 44 25 10S 141 20 E
Current → 71 37 15N 91 10W
Currie, Australia 44 39 56S 143 53 E
Currie, U.S.A. 72 40 16N 114 45W
Currie, Mt. 57 30 29S 29 21 E
Currituck Sd. 69 36 20N 75 50W
Curtis 70 40 41N 100 32W
Curtis Group 44 39 30S 146 37 E
Curtis I. 44 23 35S 151 10 E
Curuápanema → 79 2 25S 55 2W
Curuçá 79 0 43S 47 50W
Çürüksu Çayi → 23 37 27N 27 11 E
Curundu 74 8 59N 79 38W
Curup 34 4 26S 102 13 E
Cururupu 79 1 50S 44 50W
Curuzú Cuatiá 80 29 50S 58 5W
Cushing 71 35 59N 96 46W
Cushing, Mt. 64 57 35N 126 57W
Cusihuiriáchic 74 28 10N 106 50W
Custer 70 43 45N 103 38W
Cut Bank 72 48 40N 112 15W
Cuthbert 69 31 47N 84 47W
Cuttaburra → 45 29 43S 144 22 E
Cuttack 33 20 25N 85 57 E
Cuvier, C. 47 23 14S 113 22 E
Cuvier I. 43 36 27S 175 50 E
Cuxhaven 14 53 51N 8 41 E
Cuyahoga Falls 68 41 8N 81 30W
Cuyo 35 10 50N 121 5 E
Cuzco, Bolivia 78 20 0S 66 50W
Cuzco, Peru 78 13 32S 72 0W
Cwmbran 7 51 39N 3 0W
Cyclades = Kikládhes 19 37 20N 24 30 E
Cygnet 44 43 8S 147 1 E
Cynthiana 68 38 23N 84 10W
Cypress Hills 65 49 40N 109 30W
Cyprus ■ 30 35 0N 33 0 E
Cyrenaica 51 27 0N 23 0 E
Cyrene = Shaḥḥāt 51 32 48N 21 54 E
Czar 65 52 27N 110 50W
Czechoslovakia ■ 14 49 0N 17 0 E
Czeremcha 15 52 31N 23 21 E
Częstochowa 15 50 49N 19 7 E

D

Da Hinggan Ling 38 48 0N 121 0 E
Da Lat 34 11 56N 108 25 E
Da Nang 34 16 4N 108 13 E
Da Qaidam 37 37 50N 95 15 E
Da Yunhe → 39 34 25N 120 5 E
Da'an 38 45 30N 124 7 E
Daba Shan 39 32 0N 109 0 E
Dabakala 50 8 15N 4 20W
Dabbūrīya 28 32 42N 35 22 E
Dąbie 14 53 27N 14 45 E
Dabo 34 0 30S 104 33 E
Dabola 50 10 50N 11 5W
Daboya 53 9 30N 1 20W
Dabrowa Tarnówska 15 50 10N 20 59 E
Dacca = Dhaka 33 23 43N 90 26 E
Dacca □ = Dhaka □ 33 24 25N 90 25 E
Dadanawa 78 2 50N 59 30W
Dade City 69 28 20N 82 12W
Dadiya 53 9 35N 11 24 E
Dadra and Nagar Haveli □ 32 20 5N 73 0 E
Dadu 32 26 45N 67 45 E
Daet 35 14 2N 122 55 E
Dafang 39 27 9N 105 39 E
Dagana 50 16 30N 15 35W
Daghestan A.S.S.R. □ 23 42 30N 47 0 E
Dagö = Hiiumaa 22 58 50N 22 45 E
Dagupan 35 16 3N 120 20 E
Dahlak Kebir 29 15 50N 40 10 E
Dahlonega 69 34 35N 83 59W
Dahod 32 22 50N 74 15 E
Dahomey = Benin ■ 53 10 0N 2 0 E
Dahra 50 15 22N 15 30W
Dai Shan 39 30 25N 122 10 E
Dai Xian 38 39 4N 112 58 E
Daingean 9 53 18N 7 15W
Daintree 44 16 20S 145 20 E
Daiō-Misaki 36 34 15N 136 45 E
Dairût 51 27 34N 30 43 E
Daisetsu-Zan 36 43 30N 142 57 E
Dajarra 44 21 42S 139 30 E
Dakar 50 14 34N 17 29W
Dakhla 50 23 50N 15 53W
Dakhla, El Wâhât el- 51 25 30N 28 50 E
Dakhovskaya 23 44 13N 40 13 E
Dakingari 53 11 37N 4 1 E
Dakota City 70 42 27N 96 28W
Đakovica 19 42 22N 20 26 E
Dalachi 38 36 48N 105 0 E
Dalai Nur 38 43 20N 116 45 E
Dalälven 21 60 12N 16 43 E
Dalandzadgad 37 43 27N 104 30 E
Dalarö 21 59 8N 18 24 E
Dālbandīn 31 29 0N 64 23 E
Dalbeattie 8 54 55N 3 50W
Dalby 45 27 10S 151 17 E
Dalgaranger, Mt. 47 27 50S 117 5 E
Dalhart 71 36 10N 102 30W
Dalhousie 63 48 5N 66 26W
Dali, Shaanxi, China 39 34 48N 109 58 E
Dali, Yunnan, China 37 25 40N 100 10 E
Dalian 38 38 50N 121 40 E
Daliang Shan 37 28 0N 102 45 E
Dāliyat el Karmel 28 32 43N 35 2 E
Dalkeith 8 55 54N 3 5W
Dall I. 64 54 59N 133 25W
Dallarnil 45 25 19S 152 2 E
Dallas, Oreg., U.S.A. 72 45 0N 123 15W
Dallas, Tex., U.S.A. 71 32 50N 96 50W
Dalmacija □ 18 43 20N 17 0 E
Dalmatia = Dalmacija □ 18 43 20N 17 0 E
Dalmellington 8 55 20N 4 25W
Dalnegorsk 25 44 32N 135 33 E
Dalneretchensk 25 45 50N 133 40 E
Daloa 50 7 0N 6 30W
Dalton, Canada 62 48 11N 84 1W
Dalton, Ga., U.S.A. 69 34 47N 84 58W
Dalton, Nebr., U.S.A. 70 41 27N 103 0W
Dalvík 20 65 58N 18 32W
Daly → 46 13 35S 130 19 E
Daly L. 65 56 32N 105 39W
Daly Waters 44 16 15S 133 24 E
Daman 32 20 25N 72 57 E
Damanhûr 51 31 0N 30 30 E
Damar 35 7 7S 128 40 E
Damaraland 56 21 0S 17 0 E
Damascus = Dimashq 30 33 30N 36 18 E
Damaturu 53 11 45N 11 55 E
Damāvand 31 35 47N 52 0 E
Damāvand, Qolleh-ye 31 35 56N 52 10 E
Damba 54 6 44S 15 20 E
Dāmghān 31 36 10N 54 17 E
Damietta = Dumyât 51 31 24N 31 48 E
Daming 38 36 15N 115 6 E
Dāmīya 28 32 6N 35 34 E
Damoh 32 23 50N 79 28 E
Dampier 46 20 41S 116 42 E
Dampier, Selat 35 0 40S 131 0 E
Dampier Arch. 46 20 38S 116 32 E
Dan Xian 39 19 31N 109 33 E
Dana 35 11 0S 122 52 E
Dana, L. 62 50 53N 77 20W
Danbury 68 41 23N 73 29W
Danby L. 73 34 17N 115 0W
Dandaragan 47 30 40S 115 40 E
Dandeldhura 33 29 20N 80 35 E
Dandeli 32 15 5N 74 30 E
Dandenong 45 38 0S 145 15 E
Dandong 38 40 10N 124 20 E
Danforth 63 45 39N 67 57W
Danger Is. = Pukapuka 41 10 53S 165 49W
Danger Pt. 56 34 40S 19 17 E
Dangora 53 11 30N 8 7 E
Dangriga 74 17 0N 88 13W
Dangshan 39 34 27N 116 22 E
Dangtu 39 31 32N 118 25 E
Dangyang 39 30 52N 111 44 E
Daniel 72 42 56N 110 2W
Daniel's Harbour 63 50 13N 57 35W
Danielskuil 56 28 11S 23 33 E
Danilov 22 58 16N 40 13 E
Dankalwa 53 11 52N 12 12 E
Dankhar Gompa 32 32 10N 78 10 E

Eagle Pt.

Disa 32 24 18N 72 10 E
Disappointment, C. 72 46 20N 124 0W
Disappointment L. 46 23 20S 122 40 E
Disaster B. 45 37 15S 150 0 E
Discovery B. 45 38 10S 140 40 E
Disko 58 69 45N 53 30W
Disteghil Sar 32 36 20N 75 12 E
Distrito Federal □ 79 15 45S 47 45W
Diu 32 20 45N 70 58 E
Divide 72 45 48N 112 47W
Dividing Ra. 47 27 45S 116 0 E
Divinópolis 79 20 10S 44 54W
Divnoye 23 45 55N 43 21 E
Dīwāl Kol 32 34 23N 67 52 E
Dixon, Ill., U.S.A. 70 41 50N 89 30W
Dixon, Mont., U.S.A. 72 47 19N 114 25W
Dixon, N. Mex., U.S.A. 73 36 15N 105 57W
Dixon Entrance 64 54 30N 132 0W
Dixonville 64 56 32N 117 40W
Diyarbakir 30 37 55N 40 18 E
Diz Chah 31 35 30N 55 30 E
Djado 51 21 4N 12 14 E
Djakarta = Jakarta 35 6 9S 106 49 E
Djamba 56 16 45S 13 58 E
Djambala 54 2 32S 14 30 E
Djanet 50 24 35N 9 32 E
Djawa = Jawa 35 7 0S 110 0 E
Djelfa 50 34 40N 3 15 E
Djema 54 6 3N 25 15 E
Djenné 50 14 0N 4 30W
Djerid, Chott 50 33 42N 8 30 E
Djibo 53 14 9N 1 35W
Djibouti 29 11 30N 43 5 E
Djibouti ■ 29 12 0N 43 0 E
Djolu 54 0 35N 22 5 E
Djougou 53 9 40N 1 45 E
Djoum 54 2 41N 12 35 E
Djourab 51 16 40N 18 50 E
Djugu 54 1 55N 30 35 E
Djúpivogur 20 64 39N 14 17W
Dmitriya Lapteva, Proliv 25 73 0N 140 0 E
Dnepr → 23 46 30N 32 18 E
Dneprodzerzhinsk 23 48 32N 34 37 E
Dnepropetrovsk 23 48 30N 35 0 E
Dnestr → 23 46 18N 30 17 E
Dnestrovski = Belgorod 23 50 35N 36 35 E
Dnieper = Dnepr → 23 46 30N 32 18 E
Dniester = Dnestr → 23 46 18N 30 17 E
Doba 51 8 40N 16 50 E
Dobbyn 44 19 44S 140 2 E
Doberai, Jazirah 35 1 25S 133 0 E
Doblas 80 37 5S 64 0W
Dobo 35 5 45S 134 15 E
Dobruja 15 44 30N 28 15 E
Dodecanese = Dhodhekánisos 19 36 35N 27 0 E
Dodge Center 70 44 1N 92 50W
Dodge City 71 37 42N 100 0W
Dodge L. 65 59 50N 105 36W
Dodgeville 70 42 55N 90 8W
Dodoma 54 6 8S 35 45 E
Dodsland 65 51 50N 108 45W
Dodson 72 48 23N 108 16W
Doetinchem 11 51 59N 6 18 E
Dog Creek 64 51 35N 122 14W
Dog L., Man., Canada 65 51 2N 98 31W
Dog L., Ont., Canada 62 48 48N 89 30W
Dogger Bank 4 54 50N 2 0 E
Dogi 32 32 20N 62 50 E
Dogondoutchi 53 13 38N 4 2 E
Dohazari 33 22 10N 92 5 E
Doi 35 2 14N 127 49 E
Doig → 64 56 25N 120 40W
Dois Irmãos, Sa. 79 9 0S 42 30W
Dokka 21 60 49N 10 7 E
Dokkum 11 53 20N 5 59 E
Doland 70 44 55N 98 5W
Dolbeau 63 48 53N 72 18W
Dole 12 47 7N 5 31 E
Dolgellau 6 52 44N 3 53W
Dolgelley = Dolgellau 6 52 44N 3 53W
Dollart 11 53 20N 7 10 E
Dolomites = Dolomiti 18 46 30N 11 40 E
Dolomiti 18 46 30N 11 40 E
Dolores, Argentina 80 36 20S 57 40W
Dolores, U.S.A. 73 37 30N 108 30W
Dolores → 73 38 49N 108 17W
Dolphin, C. 80 51 10S 59 0W
Dolphin and Union Str. 60 69 5N 114 45W
Dombarovskiy 24 50 46N 59 32 E
Dombås 21 62 4N 9 8 E
Dombes 12 46 0N 5 0 E
Domburg 11 51 30N 3 30 E
Dominica ■ 75 15 20N 61 20W
Dominican Rep. ■ 75 19 0N 70 30W
Domo 29 7 50N 47 10 E
Domodóssola 18 46 6N 8 19 E
Domville, Mt. 45 28 1S 151 15 E
Don →, England, U.K. 6 53 41N 0 51W
Don →, Scotland, U.K. 8 57 14N 2 5W
Don →, U.S.S.R. 23 47 4N 39 18 E
Don, C. 46 11 18S 131 46 E
Don Benito 13 38 53N 5 51W
Don Martín, Presa de 74 27 30N 100 50W
Donaghadee 9 54 38N 5 32W
Donald 45 36 23S 143 0 E
Donalda 64 52 35N 112 34W
Donaldsonville 71 30 2N 91 0W
Donalsonville 69 31 3N 84 52W
Donau → 14 48 10N 17 0 E
Donauwörth 14 48 42N 10 47 E
Doncaster 6 53 31N 1 9W
Dondo, Angola 54 9 45S 14 25 E
Dondo, Mozam. 55 19 33S 34 46 E
Dondo, Teluk 35 0 29N 120 30 E
Dondra Head 32 5 55N 80 40 E
Donegal 9 54 39N 8 8W
Donegal □ 9 54 53N 8 0W
Donegal B. 9 54 30N 8 35W
Donets → 23 47 33N 40 55 E
Donetsk 23 48 0N 37 45 E
Dongara 47 29 14S 114 57 E
Dongfang 39 18 50N 108 33 E
Donggala 35 0 30S 119 40 E
Donggou 38 39 52N 124 10 E
Dongguan 39 22 58N 113 44 E
Dongguang 38 37 50N 116 30 E
Dongjingcheng 38 44 0N 129 10 E
Donglan 39 24 30N 107 21 E
Dongliu 39 30 13N 116 55 E
Dongola 51 19 9N 30 22 E
Dongou 54 2 0N 18 5 E
Dongping 38 35 55N 116 20 E
Dongshan 39 23 43N 117 30 E
Dongsheng 38 39 50N 110 0 E
Dongtai 39 32 51N 120 21 E
Dongting Hu 37 29 18N 112 45 E
Dongxing 39 21 34N 108 0 E
Dongyang 39 29 13N 120 15 E
Donington, C. 45 34 45S 136 0 E
Doniphan 71 36 40N 90 50W
Dønna, Norway 20 66 6N 12 30 E
Donna, U.S.A. 71 26 12N 98 2W
Donnaconna 63 46 41N 71 41W
Donnelly's Crossing 43 35 42S 173 38 E
Donnybrook, Australia 47 33 34S 115 48 E
Donnybrook, S. Africa 57 29 59S 29 48 E
Donor's Hill 44 18 42S 140 33 E
Doon → 8 55 26N 4 41W
Dor 28 32 37N 34 55 E
Dora, L. 46 22 0S 123 0 E
Dora Báltea → 18 45 11N 8 5 E
Dorada, La 78 5 30N 74 40W
Doran L. 65 61 13N 108 6W
Dorchester 7 50 42N 2 28W
Dorchester, C. 61 65 27N 77 27W
Dordogne □ 12 45 5N 0 40 E
Dordogne → 12 45 2N 0 36W
Dordrecht, Neth. 11 51 48N 4 39 E
Dordrecht, S. Africa 56 31 20S 27 3 E
Dore, Mts. 12 45 32N 2 50 E
Doré L. 65 54 46N 107 17W
Doré Lake 65 54 38N 107 36W
Dori 53 14 3N 0 2W
Doring → 56 31 54S 18 39 E
Doringbos 56 31 59S 19 16 E
Dorion 62 45 23N 74 3W
Dornoch 8 57 52N 4 0W
Dornoch Firth 8 57 52N 4 0W
Dorohoi 15 47 56N 26 30 E
Döröö Nuur 37 48 0N 93 0 E
Dorre I. 47 25 13S 113 12 E
Dorrigo 45 30 20S 152 44 E
Dorris 72 41 59N 121 58W
Dorset □ 7 50 48N 2 25W
Dortmund 14 51 32N 7 28 E
Doruma 54 4 42N 27 33 E
Dos Bahías, C. 80 44 58S 65 32W
Dosso 53 13 0N 3 13 E
Dothan 69 31 10N 85 25W
Douai 12 50 21N 3 4 E
Douala 54 4 0N 9 45 E
Douarnenez 12 48 6N 4 21W
Double Island Pt. 45 25 56S 153 11 E
Doubs □ 12 47 10N 6 20 E
Doubs → 12 46 53N 5 1 E
Doubtful Sd. 43 45 20S 166 49 E
Doubtless B. 43 34 55S 173 26 E
Douentza 50 14 58N 2 48W
Douglas, S. Africa 56 29 4S 23 46 E
Douglas, U.K. 6 54 9N 4 29W
Douglas, Alaska, U.S.A. 64 58 23N 134 24W
Douglas, Ariz., U.S.A. 73 31 21N 109 30W
Douglas, Ga., U.S.A. 69 31 32N 82 52W
Douglas, Wyo., U.S.A. 70 42 45N 105 20W
Douglastown 63 48 46N 64 24W
Douglasville 69 33 46N 84 43W
Doumé 54 4 15N 13 25 E
Dounreay 8 58 34N 3 44W
Dourados 80 22 9S 54 50W
Douro → 13 41 8N 8 40W
Douro Litoral □ 13 41 10N 8 20W
Dove → 6 52 51N 1 36W
Dove Creek 73 37 46N 108 59W
Dover, Australia 44 43 18S 147 2 E
Dover, U.K. 7 51 7N 1 19 E
Dover, Del., U.S.A. 68 39 10N 75 31W
Dover, N.H., U.S.A. 68 43 12N 70 51W
Dover, Ohio, U.S.A. 68 40 32N 81 30W
Dover, Pt. 47 32 32S 125 32 E
Dover, Str. of 12 51 0N 1 30 E
Dover-Foxcroft 63 45 14N 69 14W
Dovey → 7 52 32N 4 0W
Dovrefjell 20 62 15N 9 33 E
Dowagiac 68 41 58N 86 8W
Dowlat Yār 31 34 30N 65 45 E
Dowlatābād 31 28 20N 56 40W
Down □ 9 54 20N 6 0W
Downey 72 42 29N 112 3W
Downham Market 7 52 36N 0 22 E
Downieville 72 39 34N 120 50W
Downpatrick 9 54 20N 5 43W
Downpatrick Hd. 9 54 20N 9 21W
Dowshī 31 35 35N 68 43 E
Draa, Oued → 50 28 40N 11 10W
Drachten 11 53 7N 6 5 E
Dragoman, Prokhod 19 43 0N 22 53 E
Draguignan 12 43 32N 6 27 E
Drain 72 43 45N 123 17W
Drake, Australia 45 28 55S 152 25 E
Drake, U.S.A. 70 47 56N 100 21W
Drakensberg 57 31 0S 28 0 E
Dráma 19 41 9N 24 10 E
Drammen 21 59 42N 10 12 E
Drangajökull 20 66 9N 22 15W
Drau = Drava → 19 45 33N 18 55 E
Drava → 19 45 33N 18 55 E
Drayton Valley 64 53 12N 114 58W
Drenthe □ 11 52 52N 6 40 E
Dresden 14 51 2N 13 45 E
Dreux 12 48 44N 1 23 E
Driffield 6 54 0N 0 25W
Driggs 72 43 50N 111 8W
Drina → 19 44 53N 19 21 E
Drøbak 21 59 39N 10 39 E
Drogheda 9 53 45N 6 20W
Drogobych 23 49 20N 23 30 E
Droichead Nua 9 53 11N 6 50W
Droitwich 7 52 16N 2 10W
Drôme □ 12 44 38N 5 15 E
Dromedary, C. 45 36 17S 150 10 E
Dronfield 44 21 12S 140 3 E
Drumheller 64 51 25N 112 40W
Drummond 72 46 40N 113 4W
Drummond I. 62 46 0N 83 40W
Drummond Pt. 45 34 9S 135 16 E
Drummond Ra. 44 23 45S 147 10 E
Drummondville 62 45 55N 72 25W
Drumright 71 35 59N 96 38W
Druzhina 25 68 14N 145 18 E
Dry Tortugas 75 24 38N 82 55W
Dryden, Canada 65 49 47N 92 50W
Dryden, U.S.A. 71 30 3N 102 3W
Drysdale → 46 13 59S 126 51 E
Drysdale I. 44 11 41S 136 0 E
Dschang 53 5 32N 10 3 E
Du Bois 68 41 8N 78 46W
Du Quoin 70 38 0N 89 10W
Duaringa 44 23 42S 149 42 E
Dubā 30 27 10N 35 40 E
Dubai = Dubayy 31 25 18N 55 20 E
Dubawnt → 65 64 33N 100 6W
Dubawnt, L. 65 63 4N 101 42W
Dubayy 31 25 18N 55 20 E
Dubbo 45 32 11S 148 35 E
Dublin, Ireland 9 53 20N 6 18W
Dublin, Ga., U.S.A. 69 32 30N 82 34W
Dublin, Tex., U.S.A. 71 32 0N 98 20W
Dublin □ 9 53 24N 6 20W
Dublin B. 9 53 18N 6 5W
Dubois 72 44 7N 112 9W
Dubovka 23 49 5N 44 50 E
Dubréka 50 9 46N 13 31W
Dubrovnik 19 42 39N 18 6 E
Dubrovskoye 25 58 55N 111 10 E
Dubuque 70 42 30N 90 41W
Duchang 39 29 18N 116 12 E
Duchesne 72 40 14N 110 22W
Duchess 44 21 20S 139 50 E
Ducie I. 41 24 40S 124 48W
Duck Cr. → 46 22 37S 116 53 E
Duck Lake 65 52 50N 106 16W
Duck Mt. Prov. Parks 65 51 45N 101 0W
Dudhi 33 24 15N 83 10 E
Dudinka 25 69 30N 86 13 E
Dudley 7 52 30N 2 5W
Duero → 13 41 8N 8 40W
Dufftown 8 57 26N 3 9W
Dugi Otok 18 44 0N 15 0 E
Duifken Pt. 44 12 33S 141 38 E
Duisburg 14 51 27N 6 42 E
Duiwelskloof 57 23 42S 30 10 E
Duke I. 64 54 50N 131 20W
Dukhān 31 25 25N 50 50 E
Duki 32 30 14N 68 25 E
Duku 53 10 43N 10 43 E
Dulce → 80 30 32S 62 33W
Dulce, G. 75 8 40N 83 20W
Dulit, Banjaran 34 3 15N 114 30 E
Dululu 44 23 48S 150 15 E
Duluth 70 46 48N 92 10W
Dum Duma 33 27 40N 95 40 E
Dum Hadjer 51 13 18N 19 41 E
Dumaguete 35 9 17N 123 15 E
Dumai 34 1 35N 101 28 E
Dumaran 35 10 33N 119 50 E
Dumas, Ark., U.S.A. 71 33 52N 91 30W
Dumas, Tex., U.S.A. 71 35 50N 101 58W
Dumbarton 8 55 58N 4 35W
Dumbleyung 47 33 17S 117 42 E
Dumfries 8 55 4N 3 37W
Dumfries & Galloway □ 8 55 0N 4 0W
Dumoine → 62 46 13N 77 51W
Dumoine L. 62 46 55N 77 55W
Dumyât 51 31 24N 31 48 E
Dun Laoghaire 9 53 17N 6 9W
Dunaföldvár 15 46 50N 18 57 E
Dunărea → 15 45 20N 29 40 E
Dunback 43 45 23S 170 36 E
Dunbar, Australia 44 16 0S 142 22 E
Dunbar, U.K. 8 56 0N 2 32W
Dunblane 8 56 10N 3 58W
Duncan, Canada 64 48 45N 123 40W
Duncan, Ariz., U.S.A. 73 32 46N 109 6W
Duncan, Okla., U.S.A. 71 34 25N 98 0W
Duncan, L. 62 53 29N 77 58W
Duncan L. 64 62 51N 113 58W
Duncan Town 75 22 15N 75 45W
Dundalk 9 54 1N 6 25W
Dundalk Bay 9 53 55N 6 15W
Dundas 62 43 17N 79 59W
Dundas, L. 47 32 35S 121 50 E
Dundas I. 64 54 30N 130 50W
Dundas Str. 46 11 15S 131 35 E
Dundee, S. Africa 57 28 11S 30 15 E
Dundee, U.K. 8 56 29N 3 0W
Dundoo 45 27 40S 144 37 E
Dundrum 9 54 17N 5 50W
Dundrum B. 9 54 12N 5 40W
Dunedin, N.Z. 43 45 50S 170 33 E
Dunedin, U.S.A. 69 28 1N 82 45W
Dunedin → 64 59 30N 124 5W
Dunfermline 8 56 5N 3 28W
Dungannon 9 54 30N 6 47W
Dungannon □ 9 54 30N 6 55W
Dungarvan 9 52 6N 7 40W
Dungarvan Bay 9 52 5N 7 35W
Dungeness 7 50 54N 0 59 E
Dungo, L. do 56 17 15S 19 0 E
Dungog 45 32 22S 151 46 E
Dungu 54 3 40N 28 32 E
Dunhua 38 43 20N 128 14 E
Dunhuang 37 40 8N 94 36 E
Dunk I. 44 17 59S 146 29 E
Dunkeld 8 56 34N 3 36W
Dunkerque 12 51 2N 2 20 E
Dunkery Beacon 7 51 15N 3 37W
Dunkirk = Dunkerque 12 51 2N 2 20 E
Dunkirk 68 42 30N 79 18W
Dunkwa 50 6 0N 1 47W
Dunlap 70 41 50N 95 36W
Dúnleary = Dun Laoghaire 9 53 17N 6 9W
Dunmanus B. 9 51 31N 9 50W
Dunmara 44 16 42S 133 25 E
Dunmore 68 41 27N 75 38W
Dunmore Hd. 9 52 10N 10 35W
Dunn 69 35 18N 78 36W
Dunnellon 69 29 4N 82 28W
Dunnet Hd. 8 58 38N 3 22W
Dunning 70 41 52N 100 4W
Dunolly 45 36 51S 143 44 E
Dunoon 8 55 57N 4 56W
Dunqul 51 23 26N 31 37 E
Duns 8 55 47N 2 20W
Dunseith 70 48 49N 100 2W
Dunsmuir 72 41 10N 122 18W
Dunstable 7 51 53N 0 31W
Dunstan Mts. 43 44 53S 169 35 E
Dunster 64 53 8N 119 50W
Dunvegan L. 65 60 8N 107 10W
Duolun 38 42 12N 116 28 E
Dupree 70 45 4N 101 35W
Dupuyer 72 48 11N 112 31W
Dūrā 28 31 31N 35 1 E
Durack → 46 15 33S 127 52 E
Durack Range 46 16 50S 127 40 E
Durance → 12 43 55N 4 45 E
Durand 68 42 54N 83 58W
Durango, Spain 13 43 13N 2 40W
Durango, U.S.A. 73 37 16N 107 50W
Durango □ 74 25 0N 105 0W
Duranillin 47 33 30S 116 45 E
Durant 71 34 0N 96 25W
Durazno 80 33 25S 56 31W
Durazzo = Durrësi 19 41 19N 19 28 E
Durban 57 29 49S 31 1 E
Durg 33 21 15N 81 22 E
Durgapur 33 23 30N 87 20 E
Durham, Canada 62 44 10N 80 49W
Durham, U.K. 6 54 47N 1 34W
Durham, U.S.A. 69 36 0N 78 55W
Durham □ 6 54 42N 1 45W
Durham Downs 45 26 6S 141 47 E
Durmitor 16 43 10N 19 0 E
Durness 8 58 34N 4 45W
Durrësi 19 41 19N 19 28 E
Durrie 44 25 40S 140 15 E
D'Urville, Tanjung 35 1 28S 137 54 E
D'Urville I. 43 40 50S 173 55 E
Dusa Mareb 29 5 30N 46 15 E
Dushak 24 37 13N 60 1 E
Dushan 39 25 48N 107 30 E
Dushanbe 24 38 33N 68 48 E
Dusky Sd. 43 45 47S 166 30 E
Dussejour, C. 46 14 45S 128 13 E
Düsseldorf 14 51 15N 6 46 E
Dutch Harbor 60 53 54N 166 35W
Dutlwe 56 23 58S 23 46 E
Dutton → 44 20 44S 143 10 E
Duwādimi 30 24 35N 44 15 E
Duyun 39 26 18N 107 29 E
Duzce 30 40 50N 31 10 E
Duzdab = Zāhedān 31 29 30N 60 50 E
Dvina, Sev. → 22 64 32N 40 30 E
Dvinsk = Daugavpils 22 55 53N 26 32 E
Dvinskaya Guba 22 65 0N 39 0 E
Dwarka 32 22 18N 69 8 E
Dwellingup 47 32 43S 116 4 E
Dwight 68 41 5N 88 25W
Dyer, C. 61 66 40N 61 0W
Dyersburg 71 36 2N 89 20W
Dyfed □ 7 52 0N 4 30W
Dynevor Downs 45 28 10S 144 20 E
Dysart 65 50 57N 104 2W
Dzamin Üüd 37 43 50N 111 58 E
Dzerzhinsk, Byelorussian S.S.R., U.S.S.R. 22 53 40N 27 1 E
Dzerzhinsk, R.S.F.S.R., U.S.S.R. 22 56 14N 43 30 E
Dzhalinda 25 53 26N 124 0 E
Dzhambul 24 42 54N 71 22 E
Dzhankoi 23 45 40N 34 20 E
Dzhardzhan 25 68 10N 124 10 E
Dzhelinde 25 70 0N 114 20 E
Dzhetygara 24 52 11N 61 12 E
Dzhezkazgan 24 47 44N 67 40 E
Dzhikimde 25 59 1N 121 47 E
Dzhizak 24 40 6N 67 50 E
Dzhugdzur, Khrebet 25 57 30N 138 0 E
Dzhungarskiye Vorota 24 45 0N 82 0 E
Dzungaria = Junggar Pendi 37 44 30N 86 0 E
Dzungarian Gate = Alataw Shankou 37 45 5N 81 57 E
Dzungarian Gates = Dzhungarskiye Vorota 24 45 0N 82 0 E
Dzuumod 37 47 45N 106 58 E

E

Eabamet, L. 62 51 30N 87 46W
Eads 70 38 30N 102 46W
Eagle, Alaska, U.S.A. 60 64 44N 141 7W
Eagle, Colo., U.S.A. 72 39 39N 106 55W
Eagle → 63 53 36N 57 26W
Eagle Butt 70 45 1N 101 12W
Eagle Grove 70 42 37N 93 53W
Eagle L., Calif., U.S.A. 72 40 35N 120 50W
Eagle L., Maine, U.S.A. 63 46 23N 69 22W
Eagle Lake 71 29 35N 96 21W
Eagle Nest 73 36 33N 105 13W
Eagle Pass 71 28 45N 100 35W
Eagle Pt. 46 16 11S 124 23 E

Eagle River

Eagle River 70 45 55N 89 17W
Ealing 7 51 30N 0 19W
Earaheedy 47 25 34S 121 29 E
Earl Grey 65 50 57N 104 43W
Earle 71 35 18N 90 26W
Earlimart 73 35 53N 119 16W
Earn → 8 56 20N 3 19W
Earn, L. 8 56 23N 4 14W
Earnslaw, Mt. 43 44 32S 168 27 E
Earoo 47 29 34S 118 22 E
Earth 71 34 18N 102 30W
Easley 69 34 52N 82 35W
East Angus 63 45 30N 71 40W
East B. 71 29 2N 89 16W
East Bengal 33 24 0N 90 0 E
East Beskids = Vychodné Beskydy 15 49 30N 22 0 E
East C. 43 37 42S 178 35 E
East Chicago 68 41 40N 87 30W
East China Sea 37 30 5N 126 0 E
East Coulee 64 51 23N 112 27W
East Falkland 80 51 30S 58 30W
East Germany ■ 14 52 0N 12 0 E
East Grand Forks 70 47 55N 97 5W
East Helena 72 46 37N 111 58W
East Indies 34 0 0 120 0 E
East Jordan 68 45 10N 85 7W
East Kilbride 8 55 46N 4 10W
East Lansing 68 42 44N 84 29W
East Liverpool 68 40 39N 80 35W
East London 57 33 0S 27 55 E
East Main = Eastmain 62 52 10N 78 30W
East Orange 68 40 46N 74 13W
East Pacific Ridge 41 15 0S 110 0W
East Pakistan = Bangladesh ■ 33 24 0N 90 0 E
East Pine 64 55 48N 120 12W
East Pt. 63 46 27N 61 58W
East Point 69 33 40N 84 28W
East Retford 6 53 19N 0 55W
East St. Louis 70 38 37N 90 4W
East Schelde → = Oosterschelde 11 51 33N 4 0 E
East Siberian Sea 25 73 0N 160 0 E
East Sussex □ 7 51 0N 0 20 E
East Tawas 68 44 17N 83 31W
East Toorale 45 30 27S 145 28 E
Eastbourne, N.Z. 43 41 19S 174 55 E
Eastbourne, U.K. 7 50 46N 0 18 E
Eastend 65 49 32N 108 50W
Easter Islands 41 27 0S 109 0W
Eastern Cr. → 44 20 40S 141 35 E
Eastern Ghats 32 14 0N 78 50 E
Eastern Group = Lau 43 17 0S 178 30W
Eastern Group 47 33 30S 124 30 E
Easterville 65 53 8N 99 49W
Eastland 71 32 26N 98 45W
Eastleigh 7 50 58N 1 21W
Eastmain 62 52 10N 78 30W
Eastmain → 62 52 27N 78 26W
Eastman 69 32 13N 83 20W
Easton, Md., U.S.A. 68 38 47N 76 7W
Easton, Pa., U.S.A. 68 40 41N 75 15W
Easton, Wash., U.S.A. 72 47 14N 121 8W
Eastport 63 44 57N 67 0W
Eaton 70 40 35N 104 42W
Eatonia 65 51 13N 109 25W
Eatonton 69 33 22N 83 24W
Eau Claire 70 44 46N 91 30W
Ebagoola 44 14 15S 143 12 E
Ebbw Vale 7 51 47N 3 12W
Ebeltoft 21 56 12N 10 41 E
Eberswalde 14 52 49N 13 50 E
Eboli 18 40 39N 15 2 E
Ebolowa 54 2 55N 11 10 E
Ebro → 13 40 43N 0 54 E
Ech Cheliff 50 36 10N 1 20 E
Echo Bay, N.W.T., Canada 60 66 5N 117 55W
Echo Bay, Ont., Canada 62 46 29N 84 4W
Echoing → 65 55 51N 92 5W
Echternach 11 49 49N 6 25 E
Echuca 45 36 10S 144 20 E
Ecija 13 37 30N 5 10W
Eclipse Is. 46 13 54S 126 19 E
Ecuador ■ 78 2 0S 78 0W
Ed Dâmer 51 17 27N 34 0 E
Ed Debba 51 18 0N 30 51 E
Ed Dueim 51 14 0N 32 10 E
Edah 47 28 16S 117 10 E
Edam, Canada 65 53 11N 108 46W
Edam, Neth. 11 52 31N 5 3 E
Eday 8 59 11N 2 47W
Edd 29 14 0N 41 38 E
Eddrachillis B. 8 58 16N 5 10W
Eddystone 7 50 11N 4 16W
Eddystone Pt. 44 40 59S 148 20 E
Ede, Neth. 11 52 4N 5 40 E
Ede, Nigeria 53 7 45N 4 29 E
Édea 54 3 51N 10 9 E
Edehon L. 65 60 25N 97 15W
Eden, Australia 45 37 3S 149 55 E
Eden, N.C., U.S.A. 69 36 29N 79 53W
Eden, Tex., U.S.A. 71 31 16N 99 50W
Eden, Wyo., U.S.A. 72 42 2N 109 27W
Eden → 6 54 57N 3 2W
Eden L. 65 56 38N 100 15W
Edenburg 56 29 43S 25 58 E
Edendale 57 29 39S 30 18 E
Edenderry 9 53 21N 7 3W
Edenton 69 36 5N 76 36W
Edenville 57 27 37S 27 34 E
Edgar 70 40 25N 98 0W
Edge Hill 7 52 7N 1 28W
Edgefield 69 33 50N 81 59W
Edgeley 70 46 27N 98 41W
Edgemont 70 43 15N 103 53W
Edhessa 19 40 48N 22 5 E
Edievale 43 45 49S 169 22 E
Edina 70 40 6N 92 10W
Edinburg 71 26 22N 98 10W
Edinburgh 8 55 57N 3 12W
Edirne 30 41 40N 26 34 E
Edithburgh 45 35 5S 137 43 E
Edjudina 47 29 48S 122 23 E
Edmond 71 35 37N 97 30W
Edmonds 72 47 47N 122 22W
Edmonton, Australia 44 17 2S 145 46 E
Edmonton, Canada 64 53 30N 113 30W
Edmund L. 65 54 45N 93 17W
Edmundston 63 47 23N 68 20W
Edna 71 29 0N 96 40W
Edna Bay 64 55 55N 133 40W
Edremit 30 39 34N 27 0 E
Edson 64 53 35N 116 28W
Edward → 45 35 0S 143 30 E
Edward, L. 54 0 25S 29 40 E
Edward I. 62 48 22N 88 37W
Edwards Plateau 71 30 30N 101 5W
Edzo 64 62 49N 116 4W
Eekloo 11 51 11N 3 33 E
Ef'e, Nahal 28 31 9N 35 13 E
Effingham 68 39 8N 88 30W
Égadi, Ísole 18 37 55N 12 16 E
Eganville 62 45 32N 77 5W
Egeland 70 48 42N 99 6W
Egenolf L. 65 59 3N 100 0W
Eger = Cheb 14 50 9N 12 28 E
Eger 15 47 53N 20 27 E
Egersund 21 58 26N 6 1 E
Egg L. 65 55 5N 105 30W
Eginbah 46 20 53S 119 47 E
Egmont, C. 43 39 16S 173 45 E
Egmont, Mt. 43 39 17S 174 5 E
Eğridir 30 37 52N 30 51 E
Eğridir Gölü 30 37 53N 30 50 E
Egume 53 7 30N 7 14 E
Egvekinot 25 66 19N 179 50W
Egypt ■ 51 28 0N 31 0 E
Eha Amufu 53 6 30N 7 46 E
Ehime □ 36 33 30N 132 40 E
Eidsvold 45 25 25S 151 12 E
Eidsvoll 21 60 19N 11 14 E
Eifel 14 50 10N 6 45 E
Eigg 8 56 54N 6 10W
Eighty Mile Beach 46 19 30S 120 40 E
Eil 29 8 0N 49 50 E
Eil, L. 8 56 50N 5 15W
Eildon, L. 45 37 10S 146 0 E
Eileen L. 65 62 16N 107 37W
Einasleigh 44 18 32S 144 5 E
Einasleigh → 44 17 30S 142 17 E
Eindhoven 11 51 26N 5 30 E
Eire ■ 9 53 0N 8 0W
Eiríksjökull 20 64 46N 20 24W
Eirunepé 78 6 35S 69 53W
Eisenach 14 50 58N 10 18 E
Eisenerz 14 47 32N 14 54 E
Ekalaka 70 45 55N 104 30W
Eket 53 4 38N 7 56 E
Eketahuna 43 40 38S 175 43 E
Ekibastuz 24 51 50N 75 10 E
Ekimchan 25 53 0N 133 0W
Ekwan → 62 53 12N 82 15W
Ekwan Pt. 62 53 16N 82 7W
El Aaiún 50 27 9N 13 12W
El Aat 28 32 50N 35 45 E
El Alamein 51 30 48N 28 58 E
El Aricha 50 34 13N 1 10W
El Arîhā 28 31 52N 35 27 E
El Arish, Australia 44 17 35S 146 1 E
El 'Arîsh, Egypt 51 31 8N 33 50 E
El Asnam = Ech Cheliff 50 36 10N 1 20 E
El Bawiti 51 28 25N 28 45 E
El Bayadh 50 33 40N 1 1 E
El Bluff 75 11 59N 83 40W
El Buheirat □ 51 7 0N 30 0 E
El Cajon 73 32 49N 117 0W
El Callao 78 7 18N 61 50W
El Campo 71 29 10N 96 20W
El Centro 73 32 50N 115 40W
El Cerro 78 17 30S 61 40W
El Cuy 80 39 55S 68 25W
El Cuyo 74 21 30N 87 40W
El Dere 29 3 50N 47 8 E
El Diviso 78 1 22N 78 14W
El Djouf 50 20 0N 9 0W
El Dorado, Ark., U.S.A. 71 33 10N 92 40W
El Dorado, Kans., U.S.A. 71 37 55N 96 56W
El Dorado, Venezuela 78 6 55N 61 37W
El Escorial 13 40 35N 4 7W
El Faiyûm 51 29 19N 30 50 E
El Fâsher 51 13 33N 25 26 E
El Ferrol 13 43 29N 8 15W
El Fuerte 74 26 30N 108 40W
El Gal 29 10 58N 50 20 E
El Geteina 51 14 50N 32 27 E
El Gezira □ 51 15 0N 33 0 E
El Gîza 51 30 0N 31 10 E
El Goléa 50 30 30N 2 50 E
El Harrach 50 36 45N 3 5 E
El Iskandarîya 51 31 0N 30 0 E
El Jadida 50 33 11N 8 17W
El Jebelein 51 12 40N 32 55 E
El Kab 51 19 27N 32 46 E
El Kala 50 36 50N 8 30 E
El Kamlin 51 15 3N 33 11 E
El Kef 50 36 12N 8 47 E
El Khandaq 51 18 30N 30 30 E
El Khârga 51 25 30N 30 33 E
El Khartûm 51 15 31N 32 35 E
El Khartûm Bahrî 51 15 40N 32 31 E
El Laqâwa 51 11 25N 29 1 E
El Mafâza 51 13 38N 34 30 E
El Mahalla el Kubra 51 31 0N 31 0 E
El Mansûra 30 31 0N 31 19 E
El Minyâ 51 28 7N 30 33 E
El Obeid 51 13 8N 30 10 E
El Odaiya 51 12 8N 28 12 E
El Oro 74 19 48N 100 8W
El Oued 50 33 20N 6 58 E
El Palmito, Presa 74 25 40N 105 30W
El Paso 73 31 50N 106 30W
El Portal 73 37 44N 119 49W
El Progreso 75 15 26N 87 51W
El Pueblito 74 29 3N 105 4W
El Qâhira 51 30 1N 31 14 E
El Qantara 51 30 51N 32 20 E
El Qasr 51 25 44N 28 42 E
El Reno 71 35 30N 98 0W
El Salvador ■ 75 13 50N 89 0W
El Sauce 75 13 0N 86 40W
El Shallal 51 24 0N 32 53 E
El Suweis 51 29 58N 32 31 E
El Tigre 78 8 44N 64 15W
El Tocuyo 78 9 47N 69 48W
El Turbio 80 51 45S 72 5W
El Uqsur 51 25 41N 32 38 E
El Venado 74 22 56N 101 10W
El Vigía 78 8 38N 71 39W
El Wak 54 2 49N 40 56 E
El Wuz 51 15 0N 30 7 E
Elandsvlei 56 32 19S 19 31 E
Elat 28 29 30N 34 56 E
Elâzığ 30 38 37N 39 14 E
Elba, Italy 18 42 48N 10 15 E
Elba, U.S.A. 69 31 27N 86 4W
Elbasani 19 41 9N 20 9 E
Elbe → 14 53 50N 9 0 E
Elbert, Mt. 73 39 5N 106 27W
Elberta 68 44 35N 86 14W
Elberton 69 34 7N 82 51W
Elbeuf 12 49 17N 1 2 E
Elbidtan 30 38 13N 37 12 E
Elbing = Elbląg 15 54 10N 19 25 E
Elbląg 15 54 10N 19 25 E
Elbow 65 51 7N 106 35W
Elbrus 23 43 21N 42 30 E
Elburg 11 52 26N 5 50 E
Elburz Mts. = Alborz, Reshteh-ye Kūhhā-ye 31 36 0N 52 0 E
Elche 13 38 15N 0 42W
Elcho I. 44 11 55S 135 45 E
Eldon 70 38 20N 92 38W
Eldora 70 42 20N 93 5W
Eldorado, Canada 65 59 35N 108 30W
Eldorado, Mexico 74 24 20N 107 22W
Eldorado, Ill., U.S.A. 68 37 50N 88 25W
Eldorado, Tex., U.S.A. 71 30 52N 100 35W
Eldorado Springs 71 37 54N 93 59W
Eldoret 54 0 30N 35 17 E
Electra 71 34 0N 99 0W
Elefantes → 57 24 10S 32 40 E
Elektrostal 22 55 41N 38 32 E
Elephant Butte Res. 73 33 45N 107 30W
Eleuthera 75 25 0N 76 20W
Elgin, Canada 63 45 48N 65 10W
Elgin, U.K. 8 57 39N 3 20W
Elgin, Ill., U.S.A. 68 42 0N 88 20W
Elgin, N. Dak., U.S.A. 70 46 24N 101 46W
Elgin, Nebr., U.S.A. 70 41 58N 98 3W
Elgin, Nev., U.S.A. 73 37 21N 114 20W
Elgin, Oreg., U.S.A. 72 45 37N 118 0W
Elgin, Tex., U.S.A. 71 30 21N 97 22W
Elgon, Mt. 54 1 10N 34 30 E
Eliase 35 8 21S 130 48 E
Elida 71 33 56N 103 41W
Elim 56 34 35S 19 45 E
Elisabethville = Lubumbashi 55 11 40S 27 28 E
Elista 23 46 16N 44 14 E
Elizabeth, Australia 45 34 42S 138 41 E
Elizabeth, U.S.A. 68 40 37N 74 12W
Elizabeth City 69 36 18N 76 16W
Elizabethton 69 36 20N 82 13W
Elizabethtown 68 37 40N 85 54W
Elk City 71 35 25N 99 25W
Elk Island Nat. Park 64 53 35N 112 59W
Elk Lake 62 47 40N 80 25W
Elk Point 65 53 54N 110 55W
Elk River, Idaho, U.S.A. 72 46 50N 116 8W
Elk River, Minn., U.S.A. 70 45 17N 93 34W
Elkedra 44 21 9S 135 33 E
Elkedra → 44 21 8S 136 22 E
Elkhart, Ind., U.S.A. 68 41 42N 85 55W
Elkhart, Kans., U.S.A. 71 37 3N 101 54W
Elkhorn 65 49 59N 101 14W
Elkhorn → 70 41 7N 98 15W
Elkhovo 19 42 10N 26 40 E
Elkin 69 36 17N 80 50W
Elkins 68 38 53N 79 53W
Elko, Canada 64 49 20N 115 10W
Elko, U.S.A. 72 40 50N 115 50W
Ell, L. 47 29 13S 127 46 E
Ellendale, Australia 46 17 56S 124 48 E
Ellendale, U.S.A. 70 46 3N 98 30W
Ellensburg 72 47 0N 120 30W
Ellenville 68 41 42N 74 23W
Ellery, Mt. 45 37 28S 148 47 E
Ellesmere I. 58 79 30N 80 0W
Ellice Is. = Tuvalu ■ 3 8 0S 178 0 E
Ellinwood 70 38 27N 98 37W
Elliot, Australia 44 17 33S 133 32 E
Elliot, S. Africa 57 31 22S 27 48 E
Elliot Lake 62 46 25N 82 35W
Elliotdale = Xhora 57 31 55S 28 38 E
Ellis 70 39 0N 99 39W
Ellisville 71 31 38N 89 12W
Ellon 8 57 21N 2 5W
Ellore = Eluru 33 16 48N 81 8 E
Ells → 64 57 18N 111 40W
Ellsworth 70 38 47N 98 15W
Ellwood City 68 40 52N 80 19W
Elma, Canada 65 49 52N 95 55W
Elma, U.S.A. 72 47 0N 123 30W
Elmalı 30 36 44N 29 56 E
Elmenteita 52 0 32S 36 14 E
Elmhurst 68 41 52N 87 58W
Elmira 68 42 8N 76 49W
Elmore 45 36 30S 144 37 E
Eloy 73 32 46N 111 33W
Elrose 65 51 12N 108 0W
Elsas 62 48 32N 82 55W
Elsinore = Helsingør 21 56 2N 12 35 E
Elsinore 73 38 40N 112 2W
Eltham 43 39 26S 174 19 E
Eluru 33 16 48N 81 8 E
Elvas 13 38 50N 7 10W
Elverum 21 60 53N 11 34 E
Elvire → 46 17 51S 128 11 E
Elwood, Ind., U.S.A. 68 40 20N 85 50W
Elwood, Nebr., U.S.A. 70 40 38N 99 51W
Ely, U.K. 7 52 24N 0 16 E
Ely, Minn., U.S.A. 70 47 54N 91 52W
Ely, Nev., U.S.A. 72 39 10N 114 50W
Elyashiv 28 32 23N 34 55 E
Elyria 68 41 22N 82 8W
Emāmrūd 31 36 30N 55 0 E
Emba 24 48 50N 58 8 E
Emba → 23 46 38N 53 14 E
Embarcación 80 23 10S 64 0W
Embarras Portage 65 58 27N 111 28W
Embetsu 36 44 44N 141 47 E
Embrun 12 44 34N 6 30 E
Embu 54 0 32S 37 38 E
Emden 14 53 22N 7 12 E
'Emeq Yizre'el 28 32 35N 35 12 E
Emerald 44 23 32S 148 10 E
Emerson 65 49 0N 97 10W
Emery 73 38 59N 111 17W
Emilia-Romagna □ 18 44 33N 10 40 E
Emmeloord 11 52 44N 5 46 E
Emmen 11 52 48N 6 57 E
Emmet 44 24 45S 144 30 E
Emmetsburg 70 43 3N 94 40W
Emmett 72 43 51N 116 33W
Empalme 74 28 1N 110 49W
Empangeni 57 28 50S 31 52 E
Empedrado 80 28 0S 58 46W
Emperor Seamount Chain 40 40 0N 170 0 E
Emporia, Kans., U.S.A. 70 38 25N 96 10W
Emporia, Va., U.S.A. 69 36 41N 77 32W
Emporium 68 41 30N 78 17W
Empress 65 50 57N 110 0W
Ems → 14 53 22N 7 15 E
Emu 38 43 40N 128 6 E
Emu Park 44 23 13S 150 50 E
En Gedi 28 31 28N 35 25 E
En Gev 28 32 47N 35 38 E
En Harod 28 32 33N 35 22 E
'En Kerem 28 31 47N 35 6 E
En Nahud 51 12 45N 28 25 E
Enana 56 17 30S 16 23 E
Enaratoli 35 3 55S 136 21 E
Enard B. 8 58 5N 5 20W
Encanto, C. 35 15 45N 121 38 E
Encarnación 80 27 15S 55 50W
Encarnación de Diaz 74 21 30N 102 13W
Encinal 71 28 3N 99 25W
Encino 73 34 38N 105 40W
Encounter B. 45 35 45S 138 45 E
Ende 35 8 45S 121 40 E
Endeavour 65 52 10N 102 39W
Endeavour Str. 44 10 45S 142 0 E
Enderbury I. 40 3 8S 171 5W
Enderby 64 50 35N 119 10W
Enderby I. 46 20 35S 116 30 E
Enderlin 70 46 37N 97 41W
Endicott, N.Y., U.S.A. 68 42 6N 76 2W
Endicott, Wash., U.S.A. 72 47 0N 117 45W
Endyalgout I. 46 11 40S 132 35 E
Enez 23 40 45N 26 5 E
Enfield 7 51 39N 0 4W
Engadin 14 46 45N 10 10 E
Engaño, C., Dom. Rep. 75 18 30N 68 20W
Engaño, C., Phil. 35 18 35N 122 23 E
Engcobo 57 31 37S 28 0 E
Engels 22 51 28N 46 6 E
Engemann L. 65 58 0N 106 55W
Enggano 34 5 20S 102 40 E
Enghien 11 50 37N 4 2 E
Engkilili 34 1 3N 111 42 E
England 71 34 30N 91 58W
England □ 5 53 0N 2 0W
Englee 63 50 45N 56 5W
Englehart 62 47 49N 79 52W
Engler L. 65 59 8N 106 52W
Englewood, Colo., U.S.A. 70 39 40N 105 0W
Englewood, Kans., U.S.A. 71 37 7N 99 59W
English → 65 50 35N 93 30W
English Bazar = Ingraj Bazar 33 24 58N 88 10 E
English Channel 7 50 0N 2 0W
English River 62 49 14N 91 0W
Enid 71 36 26N 97 52W
Enkhuizen 11 52 42N 5 17 E
Enna 18 37 34N 14 15 E
Ennadai 65 61 8N 100 53W
Ennadai L. 65 61 0N 101 0W
Ennedi 51 17 15N 22 0 E
Enngonia 45 29 21S 145 50 E
Ennis, Ireland 9 52 51N 8 59W
Ennis, Mont., U.S.A. 72 45 20N 111 42W
Ennis, Tex., U.S.A. 71 32 15N 96 40W
Enniscorthy 9 52 30N 6 35W
Enniskillen 9 54 20N 7 40W
Ennistimon 9 52 56N 9 18W
Enns → 14 48 14N 14 32 E
Enontekiö 20 68 23N 23 37 E
Enping 39 22 16N 112 21 E
Enriquillo, L. 75 18 20N 72 5W
Enschede 11 52 13N 6 53 E
Ensenada 74 31 50N 116 50W
Enshi 39 30 18N 109 29 E
Entebbe 54 0 4N 32 28 E
Enterprise, Canada 64 60 47N 115 45W
Enterprise, Oreg., U.S.A. 72 45 30N 117 18W
Enterprise, Utah, U.S.A. 73 37 37N 113 36W
Entrecasteaux, Pt. d' 43 34 50S 115 56 E
Enugu 53 6 20N 7 30 E
Enugu Ezike 53 7 0N 7 29 E
Enumclaw 72 47 12N 122 0W
Eólie, Is. 18 38 30N 14 50 E
Epe, Neth. 11 52 21N 5 59 E
Epe, Nigeria 53 6 36N 3 59 E
Épernay 12 49 3N 3 56 E
Ephesus 30 37 50N 27 33 E
Ephraim 72 39 21N 111 37W
Ephrata 72 47 20N 119 32W
Épinal 12 48 10N 6 27 E

Feuilles

Epping 7 51 42N 0 8 E
Epukiro 56 21 40S 19 9 E
Equatorial Guinea ■ 54 2 0N 8 0 E
Er Rahad 51 12 45N 30 32 E
Er Rif 50 35 1N 4 1W
Er Roseires 51 11 55N 34 30 E
Erāwadī Myit → = Irrawaddy → 33 15 50N 95 6 E
Ercha 25 69 45N 147 20 E
Erciyaş Dağı 30 38 30N 35 30 E
Erdao Jiang → 38 43 0N 127 0 E
Erechim 80 27 35S 52 15W
Ereğli, Konya, Turkey 30 37 31N 34 4 E
Ereğli, Zonguldak, Turkey 30 41 15N 31 30 E
Erenhot 38 43 48N 111 59 E
Eresma → 13 41 26N 40 45W
Erewadi Myitwanya 33 15 30N 95 0 E
Erfenisdam 56 28 30S 26 50 E
Erfurt 14 50 58N 11 2 E
Ergani 30 38 17N 39 49 E
Erğene → 19 41 1N 26 22 E
Ergeni Vozvyshennost 23 47 0N 44 0 E
Ergun Zuoqi 38 50 47N 121 31 E
Eriboll, L. 8 58 28N 4 41W
Érice 18 38 4N 12 34 E
Erie 68 42 10N 80 7W
Erie, L. 68 42 15N 81 0W
Erigavo 29 10 35N 47 20 E
Eriksdale 65 50 52N 98 7W
Erímanthos 19 37 57N 21 50 E
Erimo-misaki 36 41 50N 143 15 E
Eritrea □ 51 14 0N 38 30 E
Erlangen 14 49 35N 11 0 E
Erldunda 44 25 14S 133 12 E
Ermelo, Neth. 11 52 18N 5 35 E
Ermelo, S. Africa 57 26 31S 29 59 E
Ermenak 30 36 38N 33 0 E
Ermoúpolis = Síros 19 37 28N 24 57 E
Ernakulam = Cochin 32 9 59N 76 22 E
Erne → 9 54 30N 8 16W
Erne, Lough 9 54 26N 7 46W
Ernest Giles Ra. 47 27 0S 123 45 E
Erode 32 11 24N 77 45 E
Eromanga 45 26 40S 143 11 E
Erongo 56 21 39S 15 58 E
Errabiddy 47 25 25S 117 5 E
Erramala Hills 32 15 30N 78 15 E
Errigal, Mt. 9 55 2N 8 8W
Erris Hd. 9 54 19N 10 0W
Erskine 70 47 37N 96 0W
Erwin 69 36 10N 82 28W
Erzgebirge 14 50 25N 13 0 E
Erzin 25 50 15N 95 10 E
Erzincan 30 39 46N 39 30 E
Erzurum 30 39 57N 41 15 E
Es Sahrâ' Esh Sharqîya 51 27 30N 32 30 E
Es Sînâ' 51 29 0N 34 0 E
Esan-Misaki 36 41 40N 141 10 E
Esbjerg 21 55 29N 8 29 E
Escalante 73 37 47N 111 37W
Escalante → 73 37 17N 110 53W
Escalón 74 26 46N 104 20W
Escambia → 69 30 32N 87 15W
Escanaba 68 45 44N 87 5W
Esch-sur-Alzette 11 49 32N 6 0 E
Escobal 74 9 6N 80 1W
Escondido 73 33 9N 117 4W
Escuinapa 74 22 50N 105 50W
Escuintla 75 14 20N 90 48W
Eşfahān 31 33 0N 51 30 E
Esh Sham = Dimashq 30 33 30N 36 18 E
Esh Shamâlîya □ 51 19 0N 29 0 E
Eshowe 57 28 50S 31 30 E
Eshta'ol 28 31 47N 35 0 E
Esk →, Dumf. & Gall., U.K. 8 54 58N 3 4W
Esk →, N. Yorks., U.K. 6 54 27N 0 36W
Eskifjörður 20 65 3N 13 55W
Eskilstuna 21 59 22N 16 32 E
Eskimo Pt. 65 61 10N 94 15W
Eskişehir 30 39 50N 30 35 E
Esla → 13 41 29N 6 3W
Eslāmābād-e Gharb 30 34 10N 46 30 E
Esmeraldas 78 1 0N 79 40W
Espanola 62 46 15N 81 46W
Esperance 47 33 45S 121 55 E
Esperance B. 47 33 48S 121 55 E
Esperanza 80 31 29S 61 3W
Espichel, C. 13 38 22N 9 16W
Espinal 78 4 9N 74 53W
Espinazo, Sierra del = Espinhaço, Serra do 79 17 30S 43 30W
Espinhaço, Serra do 79 17 30S 43 30W
Espírito Santo □ 79 20 0S 40 45W
Espíritu Santo, B. del 74 19 15N 87 0W
Espíritu Santo, I. 74 24 30N 110 23W
Espungabera 57 20 29S 32 45 E
Esquel 80 42 55S 71 20W
Esquina 80 30 0S 59 30W
Essaouira 50 31 32N 9 42W
Essen, Belgium 11 51 28N 4 28 E
Essen, W. Germany 14 51 28N 6 59 E
Essequibo → 78 6 50N 58 30W
Essex □ 7 51 48N 0 30 E
Esslingen 14 48 43N 9 19 E
Essonne □ 12 48 30N 2 20 E
Estados, I. de Los 80 54 40S 64 30W
Estância, Brazil 79 11 16S 37 26W
Estancia, U.S.A. 73 34 50N 106 1W
Estcourt 57 29 0S 29 53 E
Estelí 75 13 9N 86 22W
Estelline, S. Dak., U.S.A. 70 44 39N 96 52W
Estelline, Tex., U.S.A. 71 34 35N 100 27W
Esterhazy 65 50 37N 102 5W
Estevan 65 49 10N 102 59W
Estevan Group 64 53 3N 129 38W
Estherville 70 43 25N 94 50W
Eston 65 51 8N 108 40W
Estonian S.S.R. □ 22 58 30N 25 30 E
Estoril 13 38 42N 9 23W
Estrada, La 13 42 43N 8 27W
Estrêla, Serra da 13 40 10N 7 45W
Estremadura 13 39 0N 9 0W
Estrondo, Serra do 79 7 20S 48 0W
Esztergom 15 47 47N 18 44 E
Eţ Ţira 28 32 14N 34 56 E
Etadunna 45 28 43S 138 38 E
Etamamu 63 50 18N 59 59W
Etanga 56 17 55S 13 0 E
Etawah 32 26 48N 79 6 E
Etawah → 69 34 20N 84 15W
Etawney L. 65 57 50N 96 50W
Ete 53 7 2N 7 28 E
Ethel Creek 46 23 5S 120 11 E
Ethelbert 65 51 32N 100 25W
Ethiopia ■ 29 8 0N 40 0 E
Ethiopian Highlands 48 10 0N 37 0 E
Etive, L. 8 56 30N 5 12W
Etna 18 37 45N 15 0 E
Etolin I. 64 56 5N 132 20W
Etosha Pan 56 18 40S 16 30 E
Etowah 69 35 20N 84 30W
Étroits, Les 63 47 24N 68 54W
Ettrick Water 8 55 31N 2 55W
Etzatlán 74 20 48N 104 5W
Euboea = Évvoia 19 38 30N 24 0 E
Euclid 68 41 32N 81 31W
Eucumbene, L. 45 36 2S 148 40 E
Eudora 71 33 5N 91 17W
Eufaula, Ala., U.S.A. 69 31 55N 85 11W
Eufaula, Okla., U.S.A. 71 35 20N 95 33W
Eufaula, L. 71 35 15N 95 28W
Eugene 72 44 0N 123 8W
Eugowra 45 33 22S 148 24 E
Eulo 45 28 10S 145 3 E
Eunice, La., U.S.A. 71 30 35N 92 28W
Eunice, N. Mex., U.S.A. 71 32 30N 103 10W
Eupen 11 50 37N 6 3 E
Euphrates = Furāt, Nahr al → 30 31 0N 47 25 E
Eure □ 12 49 10N 1 0 E
Eure-et-Loir □ 12 48 22N 1 30 E
Eureka, Calif., U.S.A. 72 40 50N 124 0W
Eureka, Kans., U.S.A. 71 37 50N 96 20W
Eureka, Mont., U.S.A. 72 48 53N 115 6W
Eureka, Nev., U.S.A. 72 39 32N 116 2W
Eureka, S. Dak., U.S.A. 70 45 49N 99 38W
Eureka, Utah, U.S.A. 72 40 0N 112 9W
Eureka, Mt. 47 26 35S 121 35 E
Euroa 45 36 44S 145 35 E
Europa, I. 55 22 20S 40 22 E
Europa, Picos de 13 43 10N 4 49W
Europa, Pta. de 13 36 3N 5 21W
Europa Pt. = Europa, Pta. de 13 36 3N 5 21W
Europe 4 50 0N 20 0 E
Europoort 11 51 57N 4 10 E
Eustis 69 28 54N 81 36W
Eutsuk L. 64 53 20N 126 45W
Eva Downs 44 18 1S 134 52 E
Eval 28 32 15N 35 15 E
Evale 56 16 33S 15 44 E
Evans 70 40 25N 104 43W
Evans Head 45 29 7S 153 27 E
Evans L. 62 50 50N 77 0W
Evanston, Ill., U.S.A. 68 42 0N 87 40W
Evanston, Wyo., U.S.A. 72 41 10N 111 0W
Evansville, Ind., U.S.A. 68 38 0N 87 35W
Evansville, Wis., U.S.A. 70 42 47N 89 18W
Eveleth 70 47 29N 92 46W
Even Yahuda 28 32 16N 34 53 E
Evensk 25 62 12N 159 30 E
Everard, L. 45 31 30S 135 0 E
Everard Ras. 47 27 5S 132 28 E
Everest, Mt. 33 28 5N 86 58 E
Everett 72 48 0N 122 10W
Everglades 69 26 0N 80 30W
Everglades City 69 25 52N 81 23W
Everglades Nat. Park 69 25 27N 80 53W
Evergreen 69 31 28N 86 55W
Everson 72 48 57N 122 22W
Evesham 7 52 6N 1 57W
Evinayong 54 1 26N 10 35 E
Évora 13 38 33N 7 57W
Évreux 12 49 0N 1 8 E
Évvoia 19 38 30N 24 0 E
Ewe, L. 8 57 49N 5 38W
Ewing 70 42 18N 98 22W
Ewo 54 0 48S 14 45 E
Exaltación 78 13 10S 65 20W
Excelsior Springs 70 39 20N 94 10W
Exe → 7 50 38N 3 27W
Exeter, U.K. 7 50 43N 3 31W
Exeter, Calif., U.S.A. 73 36 17N 119 9W
Exeter, Nebr., U.S.A. 70 40 43N 97 30W
Exmoor 7 51 10N 3 59W
Exmouth, Australia 46 21 54S 114 10 E
Exmouth, U.K. 7 50 37N 3 26W
Exmouth G. 46 22 15S 114 15 E
Expedition Range 44 24 30S 149 12 E
Extremadura □ 13 39 30N 6 5W
Exuma Sound 75 24 30N 76 20W
Eyasi, L. 54 3 30S 35 0 E
Eyeberry L. 65 63 8N 104 43W
Eyemouth 8 55 53N 2 5W
Eyjafjörður 20 66 15N 18 30W
Eyrarbakki 20 63 52N 21 9W
Eyre 47 32 15S 126 18 E
Eyre (North), L. 45 28 30S 137 20 E
Eyre (South), L. 45 29 18S 137 25 E
Eyre Cr. → 45 26 40S 139 0 E
Eyre Mts. 43 45 25S 168 25 E
Eyre Pen. 45 33 30S 137 17 E

F

Fabens 73 31 30N 106 8W
Fabriano 18 43 20N 12 52 E
Facatativá 78 4 49N 74 22W
Fachi 50 18 6N 11 34 E
Fada 51 17 13N 21 34 E
Fada-n-Gourma 53 12 10N 0 30 E
Faddeyevskiy, Ostrov 25 76 0N 150 0 E
Fāḍilī 30 26 55N 49 10 E
Faenza 18 44 17N 11 53 E
Fagam 53 11 1N 10 1 E
Făgăras 15 45 48N 24 58 E
Fagernes 21 60 59N 9 14 E
Fagersta 21 60 1N 15 46 E
Fagnano, L. 80 54 30S 68 0W
Fahraj 31 29 0N 59 0 E
Fahūd 31 22 18N 56 28 E
Fair Hd. 9 55 14N 6 10W
Fairbank 73 31 44N 110 12W
Fairbanks 60 64 50N 147 50W
Fairbury 70 40 5N 97 5W
Fairfax 71 36 37N 96 45W
Fairfield, Ala., U.S.A. 69 33 30N 87 0W
Fairfield, Calif., U.S.A. 72 38 14N 122 1W
Fairfield, Idaho, U.S.A. 72 43 21N 114 46W
Fairfield, Ill., U.S.A. 68 38 20N 88 20W
Fairfield, Iowa, U.S.A. 70 41 0N 91 58W
Fairfield, Mont., U.S.A. 72 47 40N 112 0W
Fairfield, Tex., U.S.A. 71 31 40N 96 0W
Fairford 65 51 37N 98 38W
Fairhope 69 30 35N 87 50W
Fairlie 43 44 5S 170 49 E
Fairmont, Minn., U.S.A. 70 43 37N 94 30W
Fairmont, W. Va., U.S.A. 68 39 29N 80 10W
Fairplay 73 39 9N 105 40W
Fairport 68 43 8N 77 29W
Fairview, Australia 44 15 31S 144 17 E
Fairview, Canada 64 56 5N 118 25W
Fairview, N. Dak., U.S.A. 70 47 49N 104 7W
Fairview, Okla., U.S.A. 71 36 19N 98 30W
Fairview, Utah, U.S.A. 72 39 50N 111 0W
Fairweather, Mt. 60 58 55N 137 45W
Faisalabad 32 31 30N 73 5 E
Faith 70 45 2N 102 4W
Faizabad 33 26 45N 82 10 E
Fajardo 75 18 20N 65 39W
Fakfak 35 3 0S 132 15 E
Faku 38 42 32N 123 21 E
Falaise 12 48 54N 0 12W
Falam 33 23 0N 93 45 E
Falcon Dam 71 26 50N 99 20W
Falfurrias 71 27 14N 98 8W
Falher 64 55 44N 117 15W
Falkenberg 21 56 54N 12 30 E
Falkirk 8 56 0N 3 47W
Falkland Is. 80 51 30S 59 0W
Falkland Sd. 80 52 0S 60 0W
Falköping 21 58 12N 13 33 E
Fall River 68 41 45N 71 5W
Fall River Mills 72 41 1N 121 30W
Fallbrook 73 33 25N 117 12W
Fallon, Mont., U.S.A. 70 46 52N 105 8W
Fallon, Nev., U.S.A. 72 39 31N 118 51W
Falls City, Nebr., U.S.A. 70 40 0N 95 40W
Falls City, Oreg., U.S.A. 72 44 54N 123 29W
Falmouth, Jamaica 75 18 30N 77 40W
Falmouth, U.K. 7 50 9N 5 5W
Falmouth, U.S.A. 68 38 40N 84 20W
False B. 56 34 15S 18 40 E
Falso, C. 75 15 12N 83 21W
Falster 21 54 45N 11 55 E
Falsterbo 21 55 23N 12 50 E
Falun 21 60 37N 15 37 E
Famagusta 30 35 8N 33 55 E
Family L. 65 51 54N 95 27W
Fan Xian 38 35 55N 115 38 E
Fandriana 57 20 14S 47 21 E
Fang Xian 39 32 3N 110 40 E
Fangchang 39 31 5N 118 4 E
Fangcheng 39 33 18N 112 59 E
Fangliao 39 22 22N 120 38 E
Fangzheng 38 49 50N 128 48 E
Fanjiatun 38 43 40N 125 0 E
Fannich, L. 8 57 40N 5 0W
Fanny Bay 64 49 37N 124 48W
Fano 18 43 50N 13 0 E
Fanshaw 64 57 11N 133 30W
Fao = Al Fāw 30 30 0N 48 30 E
Faradje 54 3 50N 29 45 E
Farafangana 57 22 49S 47 50 E
Farāh 31 32 20N 62 7 E
Farāh □ 31 32 25N 62 10 E
Farahalana 57 14 26S 50 10 E
Faranah 50 10 3N 10 45W
Farasān, Jazā'ir 29 16 45N 41 55 E
Faratsiho 57 19 24S 46 57 E
Fareham 7 50 52N 1 11W
Farewell, C. 43 40 29S 172 43 E
Farewell C. = Farvel, Kap 58 59 48N 43 55W
Fargo 70 46 52N 96 40W
Fari'a → 28 32 12N 35 27 E
Faribault 70 44 15N 93 19W
Farim 50 12 27N 15 9W
Farīmān 31 35 40N 59 49 E
Farina 45 30 3S 138 15 E
Farmerville 71 32 48N 92 23W
Farmington, N. Mex., U.S.A. 73 36 45N 108 28W
Farmington, Utah, U.S.A. 72 41 0N 111 12W
Farmville 68 37 19N 78 22W
Farnborough 7 51 17N 0 46W
Farne Is. 6 55 38N 1 37W
Faro, Brazil 79 2 10S 56 39W
Faro, Portugal 13 37 2N 7 55W
Fårö, Sweden 21 57 55N 19 5 E
Faroe Is. = Føroyar 5 62 0N 7 0W
Farquhar, C. 47 23 50S 113 36 E
Farquhar Is. 3 11 0S 52 0 E
Farrar → 8 57 30N 4 30W
Farrars Cr. → 44 25 35S 140 43 E
Farrāshband 31 28 57N 52 5 E
Farrell 68 41 13N 80 29W
Farrell Flat 45 33 48S 138 48 E
Farrukhabad-cum-Fatehgarh 32 27 30N 79 32 E
Fārs □ 31 29 30N 55 0 E
Fársala 19 39 17N 22 23 E
Farsund 21 58 5N 6 55 E
Fartak, Râs 30 28 5N 34 34 E
Farvel, Kap 58 59 48N 43 55W
Farwell 71 34 25N 103 0W
Faryab 32 28 7N 57 14 E
Fāryāb □ 31 36 0N 65 0 E
Fasā 31 29 0N 53 39 E
Fastnet Rock 9 51 22N 9 37W
Fatagar, Tanjung 35 2 46S 131 57 E
Fatehgarh 32 27 25N 79 35 E
Fatehpur, Raj., India 32 28 0N 74 40 E
Fatehpur, Ut. P., India 33 25 56N 81 13 E
Fatima 63 47 24N 61 53W
Faulkton 70 45 4N 99 8W
Faure I. 47 25 52S 113 50 E
Fauresmith 56 29 44S 25 17 E
Fauske 20 67 17N 15 25 E
Favara 18 37 19N 13 39 E
Favignana 18 37 56N 12 18 E
Favourable Lake 62 52 50N 93 39W
Fawn → 62 55 20N 87 35W
Faxaflói 20 64 29N 23 0W
Faya-Largeau 51 17 58N 19 6 E
Fayd 30 27 1N 42 52 E
Fayette, Ala., U.S.A. 69 33 40N 87 50W
Fayette, Mo., U.S.A. 70 39 10N 92 40W
Fayetteville, Ark., U.S.A. 71 36 0N 94 5W
Fayetteville, N.C., U.S.A. 69 35 0N 78 58W
Fayetteville, Tenn., U.S.A. 69 35 8N 86 30W
Fazilka 32 30 27N 74 2 E
Fdérik 50 22 40N 12 45W
Feale → 9 52 26N 9 40W
Fear, C. 69 33 51N 78 0W
Feather → 72 38 47N 121 36W
Featherston 43 41 6S 175 20 E
Fécamp 12 49 45N 0 22 E
Fehmarn 14 54 26N 11 10 E
Fehmarn Bælt 14 54 35N 11 20 E
Fei Xian 39 35 18N 117 59 E
Feilding 43 40 13S 175 35 E
Feira de Santana 79 12 15S 38 57W
Feldkirch 14 47 15N 9 37 E
Felipe Carrillo Puerto 74 19 38N 88 3W
Felixstowe 7 51 58N 1 22 E
Femunden 20 62 10N 11 53 E
Fen He → 38 35 36N 110 42 E
Feng Xian, Jiangsu, China 39 34 43N 116 35 E
Feng Xian, Shaanxi, China 39 33 54N 106 40 E
Fengcheng, Jiangxi, China 39 28 12N 115 48 E
Fengcheng, Liaoning, China 38 40 28N 124 5 E
Fengdu 39 29 55N 107 41 E
Fengfeng 38 36 28N 114 8 E
Fenghua 39 29 40N 121 25 E
Fenghuang 39 27 57N 109 29 E
Fengjie 39 31 5N 109 36 E
Fengkai 39 23 24N 111 30 E
Fengle 39 31 29N 112 29 E
Fengning 38 41 10N 116 33 E
Fengtai 38 39 50N 116 18 E
Fengxian 39 30 55N 121 26 E
Fengxiang 39 34 29N 107 25 E
Fengxin 39 28 41N 115 18 E
Fengyang 39 32 51N 117 29 E
Fengzhen 38 40 25N 113 2 E
Fenit 9 52 17N 9 51W
Fennimore 70 42 58N 90 41W
Fenoarivo Afovoany 57 18 26S 46 34 E
Fenoarivo Atsinanana 57 17 22S 49 25 E
Fens, The 6 52 45N 0 2 E
Fenton 68 42 47N 83 44W
Fenyang 38 37 18N 111 48 E
Feodosiya 23 45 2N 35 28 E
Ferdows 31 33 58N 58 2 E
Ferfer 29 5 4N 45 9 E
Fergana 24 40 23N 71 19 E
Fergus 62 43 43N 80 24W
Fergus Falls 70 46 18N 96 7W
Ferland 62 50 19N 88 27W
Fermanagh □ 9 54 21N 7 40W
Fermoy 9 52 4N 8 18W
Fernandina Beach 69 30 40N 81 30W
Fernando de Noronha 79 4 0S 33 10W
Fernando Póo = Bioko 53 3 30N 8 40 E
Ferndale, Calif., U.S.A. 72 40 37N 124 12W
Ferndale, Wash., U.S.A. 72 48 51N 122 41W
Fernie 64 49 30N 115 5W
Fernlees 44 23 51S 148 7 E
Fernley 72 39 36N 119 14W
Ferozepore = Firozpur 32 30 55N 74 40 E
Ferrara 18 44 50N 11 36 E
Ferreñafe 78 6 42S 79 50W
Ferriday 71 31 35N 91 33W
Ferron 73 39 3N 111 3W
Ferryland 63 47 2N 52 53W
Fertile 70 47 31N 96 18W
Fès 50 34 0N 5 0W
Feshi 54 6 8S 18 10 E
Fessenden 70 47 42N 99 38W
Fethiye 30 36 36N 29 10 E
Fetlar 8 60 36N 0 52W
Feuilles → 61 58 47N 70 4W

Gereshk

Gereshk 31 31 47N 64 35 E
Gering 70 41 51N 103 30W
Gerizim 28 32 13N 35 15 E
Gerlach 72 40 43N 119 27W
Gerlogubi 29 6 53N 45 3 E
Germansen Landing 64 55 43N 124 40W
Germany, East ■ 14 52 0N 12 0 E
Germany, West ■ 14 52 0N 9 0 E
Germiston 57 26 15S 28 10 E
Gerona 13 41 58N 2 46 E
Gerrard 64 50 30N 117 17W
Gers □ 12 43 35N 0 30 E
Geser 35 3 50S 130 54 E
Gethsémani 63 50 13N 60 40W
Gettysburg, Pa., U.S.A. 68 39 47N 77 18W
Gettysburg, S. Dak., U.S.A. 70 45 3N 99 56W
Gévaudan 12 44 40N 3 40 E
Geyser 72 47 17N 110 30W
Geysir 20 64 19N 20 18W
Ghaghara → 33 25 45N 84 40 E
Ghana ■ 53 8 0N 1 0W
Ghanzi 56 21 50S 21 34 E
Ghanzi □ 56 21 50S 21 45 E
Gharb el Istiwa'iya □ 51 5 0N 30 0 E
Ghardaïa 50 32 20N 3 37 E
Gharyān 51 32 10N 13 0 E
Ghat 50 24 59N 10 11 E
Ghawdex = Gozo 16 36 0N 14 13 E
Ghayl 30 21 40N 46 20 E
Ghazal, Bahr el →, Chad 51 13 0N 15 47 E
Ghazâl, Bahr el →, Sudan 51 9 31N 30 25 E
Ghazaouet 50 35 8N 1 50W
Ghaziabad 32 28 42N 77 26 E
Ghazipur 33 25 38N 83 35 E
Ghaznī 31 33 30N 68 28 E
Ghaznī □ 31 32 10N 68 20 E
Ghèlinsor 29 6 28N 46 39 E
Ghent = Gent 11 51 2N 3 42 E
Ghizao 32 33 20N 65 44 E
Ghowr □ 31 34 0N 64 20 E
Ghugus 32 19 58N 79 12 E
Ghūriān 31 34 17N 61 25 E
Gia Lai = Pleiku 34 13 57N 108 0 E
Gian 35 5 45N 125 20 E
Giant's Causeway 9 55 15N 6 30W
Giarabub = Al Jaghbūb 51 29 42N 24 38 E
Giarre 18 37 44N 15 10 E
Gibara 75 21 9N 76 11W
Gibb River 46 16 26S 126 26 E
Gibbon 70 40 49N 98 45W
Gibraltar 13 36 7N 5 22W
Gibraltar, Str. of 13 35 55N 5 40W
Gibson Desert 46 24 0S 126 0 E
Gibsons 64 49 24N 123 32W
Giddings 71 30 11N 96 58W
Gidole 51 5 40N 37 25 E
Giessen 14 50 34N 8 40 E
Gifford Creek 47 24 3S 116 16 E
Gifu 36 35 30N 136 45 E
Gifu □ 36 35 40N 137 0 E
Giganta, Sa. de la 74 25 30N 111 30W
Gigha 8 55 42N 5 45W
Gijón 13 43 32N 5 42W
Gil I. 64 53 12N 129 15W
Gila → 73 32 43N 114 33W
Gila Bend 73 33 0N 112 46W
Gila Bend Mts. 73 33 15N 113 0W
Gīlān □ 30 37 0N 50 0 E
Gilbert → 44 16 35S 141 15 E
Gilbert Is. = Kiribati ■ 3 1 0N 176 0 E
Gilbert Plains 65 51 9N 100 28W
Gilbert River 44 18 9S 142 52 E
Gilberton 44 19 16S 143 35 E
Gilford I. 64 50 40N 126 30W
Gilgandra 45 31 43S 148 39 E
Gilgil 52 0 30S 36 20 E
Gilgit 32 35 50N 74 15 E
Gillam 65 56 20N 94 40W
Gillen, L. 47 26 11S 124 38 E
Gilles, L. 45 32 50S 136 45 E
Gillette 70 44 20N 105 30W
Gilliat 44 20 40S 141 28 E
Gillingham 7 51 23N 0 34 E
Gilmer 71 32 44N 94 55W
Gilmore 45 35 20S 148 12 E
Gilmore, L. 47 32 29S 121 37 E
Gilmour 62 44 48N 77 37W
Gilroy 73 37 1N 121 37W
Gimbi 51 9 3N 35 42 E
Gimli 65 50 40N 97 0W
Gimzo 28 31 56N 34 56 E
Gin Gin 45 25 0S 151 58 E
Gindie 44 23 44S 148 8 E
Gingin 47 31 22S 115 54 E
Ginir 29 7 6N 40 40 E
Giohar 29 2 48N 45 30 E
Gióna, Óros 19 38 38N 22 14 E
Girard 71 37 30N 94 50W
Girardot 78 4 18N 74 48W
Girdle Ness 8 57 9N 2 2W
Giresun 30 40 55N 38 30 E
Girga 51 26 17N 31 55 E
Giridih 33 24 10N 86 21 E
Girilambone 45 31 16S 146 57 E
Gironde □ 12 44 45N 0 30W
Gironde → 12 45 32N 1 7W
Giru 44 19 30S 147 5 E
Girvan 8 55 15N 4 50W
Gisborne 43 38 39S 178 5 E
Gisenyi 54 1 41S 29 15 E
Gitega 54 3 26S 29 56 E
Giuba → 29 1 30N 42 35 E
Giurgiu 15 43 52N 25 57 E
Giv'at Brenner 28 31 52N 34 47 E
Giv'atayim 28 32 4N 34 49 E
Giza = El Gîza 51 30 0N 31 10 E
Gizhiga 25 62 3N 160 30 E
Gizhiginskaya, Guba 25 61 0N 158 0 E
Giżycko 15 54 2N 21 48 E
Gjirokastra 19 40 7N 20 10 E
Gjoa Haven 60 68 20N 96 8W
Gjøvik 21 60 47N 10 43 E
Glace Bay 63 46 11N 59 58W
Glacier B. 64 58 30N 136 10W
Glacier Nat. Park 64 51 15N 117 30W
Glacier Park 72 48 30N 113 18W
Glacier Peak Mt. 72 48 7N 121 7W
Gladewater 71 32 30N 94 58W
Gladstone, Queens., Australia 44 23 52S 151 16 E
Gladstone, S. Austral., Australia 45 33 15S 138 22 E
Gladstone, W. Austral., Australia 47 25 57S 114 17 E
Gladstone, Canada 65 50 13N 98 57W
Gladstone, U.S.A. 68 45 52N 87 1W
Gladwin 68 43 59N 84 29W
Gladys L. 64 59 50N 133 0W
Gláma 20 65 48N 23 0W
Glåma → 21 59 12N 10 57 E
Glasco 70 39 25N 97 50W
Glasgow, U.K. 8 55 52N 4 14W
Glasgow, Ky., U.S.A. 68 37 2N 85 55W
Glasgow, Mont., U.S.A. 72 48 12N 106 35W
Glastonbury 7 51 9N 2 42W
Glauchau 14 50 50N 12 33 E
Glazov 22 58 9N 52 40 E
Gleiwitz = Gliwice 15 50 22N 18 41 E
Glen Affric 8 57 15N 5 0W
Glen Canyon Dam 73 37 0N 111 25W
Glen Canyon Nat. Recreation Area 73 37 30N 111 0W
Glen Coe 6 56 40N 5 0W
Glen Garry 8 57 3N 5 7W
Glen Innes 45 29 44S 151 44 E
Glen Mor 8 57 12N 4 37 E
Glen Moriston 8 57 10N 4 58W
Glen Orchy 8 56 27N 4 52W
Glen Spean 8 56 53N 4 40W
Glen Ullin 70 46 48N 101 46W
Glen Valley 45 36 54S 147 28 E
Glenburgh 47 25 26S 116 6 E
Glencoe, S. Africa 57 28 11S 30 11 E
Glencoe, U.S.A. 70 44 45N 94 10W
Glendale, Ariz., U.S.A. 73 33 40N 112 8W
Glendale, Calif., U.S.A. 73 34 7N 118 18W
Glendale, Oreg., U.S.A. 72 42 44N 123 29W
Glendive 70 47 7N 104 40W
Glendo 70 42 30N 105 0W
Glenelg 45 34 58S 138 31 E
Glenelg → 45 38 4S 140 59 E
Glenflorrie 46 22 55S 115 59 E
Glengarriff 9 51 45N 9 33W
Glengyle 44 24 48S 139 37 E
Glenmora 71 31 1N 92 34W
Glenmorgan 45 27 14S 149 42 E
Glenns Ferry 72 43 0N 115 15W
Glenorchy 44 42 49S 147 18 E
Glenore 44 17 50S 141 12 E
Glenormiston 44 22 55S 138 50 E
Glenreagh 45 30 2S 153 1 E
Glenrock 72 42 53N 105 55W
Glenrothes 8 56 12N 3 11W
Glens Falls 68 43 20N 73 40W
Glenties 9 54 48N 8 18W
Glenville 68 38 56N 80 50W
Glenwood, Alta., Canada 64 49 21N 113 31W
Glenwood, Nfld., Canada 63 49 0N 54 58W
Glenwood, Ark., U.S.A. 71 34 20N 93 30W
Glenwood, Hawaii, U.S.A. 66 19 29N 155 10W
Glenwood, Iowa, U.S.A. 70 41 7N 95 41W
Glenwood, Minn., U.S.A. 70 45 38N 95 21W
Glenwood Sprs. 72 39 39N 107 21W
Gliwice 15 50 22N 18 41 E
Globe 73 33 25N 110 53W
Głogów 14 51 37N 16 5 E
Glorieuses, Is. 57 11 30S 47 20 E
Glossop 6 53 27N 1 56W
Gloucester, Australia 45 32 0S 151 59 E
Gloucester, U.K. 7 51 52N 2 15W
Gloucester I. 44 20 0S 148 30 E
Gloucestershire □ 7 51 44N 2 10W
Gloversville 68 43 5N 74 18W
Glovertown 63 48 40N 54 3W
Glückstadt 14 53 46N 9 28 E
Gmünd 14 48 45N 15 0 E
Gmunden 14 47 55N 13 48 E
Gniezno 15 52 30N 17 35 E
Gnowangerup 47 33 58S 117 59 E
Go Cong 34 10 22N 106 40 E
Goa 32 15 33N 73 59 E
Goa □ 32 15 33N 73 59 E
Goalen Hd. 45 36 33S 150 4 E
Goalpara 33 26 10N 90 40 E
Goat Fell 8 55 37N 5 11W
Goba, Ethiopia 29 7 1N 39 59 E
Goba, Mozam. 57 26 15S 32 13 E
Gobabis 56 22 30S 19 0 E
Gobi 38 44 0N 111 0 E
Gochas 56 24 59S 18 55 E
Godavari → 33 16 25N 82 18 E
Godavari Point 33 17 0N 82 20 E
Godbout 63 49 20N 67 38W
Goderich 62 43 45N 81 43W
Godhra 32 22 49N 73 40 E
Gods → 65 56 22N 92 51W
Gods L. 65 54 40N 94 15W
Godthåb 2 64 10N 51 35W
Godwin Austen = K2, Mt. 32 35 58N 76 32 E
Goeie Hoop, Kaap die = Good Hope, C. of 56 34 24S 18 30 E
Goéland, L. au 62 49 50N 76 48W
Goeree 11 51 50N 4 0 E
Goes 11 51 30N 3 55 E
Gogama 62 47 35N 81 43W
Gogango 44 23 40S 150 2 E
Gogebic, L. 70 46 20N 89 34W
Gogra = Ghaghara → 33 25 45N 84 40 E
Goiânia 79 16 43S 49 20W
Goiás 79 15 55S 50 10W
Goiás □ 79 12 10S 48 0W
Goio-Ere 80 24 12S 53 1W
Gojra 32 31 10N 72 40 E
Gokteik 33 22 26N 97 0 E
Golan Heights = Hagolan 28 33 0N 35 45 E
Golconda 72 40 58N 117 32W
Gold Beach 72 42 25N 124 25W
Gold Coast 45 28 0S 153 25 E
Gold Hill 72 42 28N 123 2W
Golden, Canada 64 51 20N 116 59W
Golden, U.S.A. 70 39 42N 105 15W
Golden Bay 43 40 40S 172 50 E
Golden Gate 72 37 54N 122 30W
Golden Hinde 64 49 40N 125 44W
Golden Prairie 65 50 13N 109 37W
Golden Vale 9 52 33N 8 17W
Goldendale 72 45 53N 120 48W
Goldfield 73 37 45N 117 13W
Goldfields 65 59 28N 108 29W
Goldsand L. 65 57 2N 101 8W
Goldsboro 69 35 24N 77 59W
Goldsmith 71 32 0N 102 40W
Goldsworthy 46 20 21S 119 30 E
Goldthwaite 71 31 25N 98 32W
Goleniów 14 53 35N 14 50 E
Golfito 75 8 41N 83 5W
Goliad 71 28 40N 97 22W
Golspie 8 57 58N 3 58W
Goma 54 2 11S 29 18 E
Gombe 53 10 19N 11 2 E
Gomel 22 52 28N 31 0 E
Gomera 50 28 7N 17 14W
Gómez Palacio 74 25 40N 104 0W
Gomogomo 35 6 39S 134 43 E
Gomoh 33 23 52N 86 10 E
Gompa = Ganta 50 7 15N 8 59W
Gonābād 31 34 15N 58 45 E
Gonaïves 75 19 20N 72 42W
Gonâve, G. de la 75 19 29N 72 42W
Gonbab-e Kāvūs 31 37 20N 55 25 E
Gonda 33 27 9N 81 58 E
Gonder 51 12 39N 37 30 E
Gondia 32 21 23N 80 10 E
Gonghe 37 36 18N 100 32 E
Gongola □ 53 8 0N 12 0 E
Gongola → 53 9 30N 12 4 E
Gongolgon 45 30 21S 146 54 E
Goniri 51 11 30N 12 15 E
Gonzales, Calif., U.S.A. 73 36 35N 121 30W
Gonzales, Tex., U.S.A. 71 29 30N 97 30W
Good Hope, C. of 56 34 24S 18 30 E
Gooderham 62 44 54N 78 21W
Goodeve 65 51 4N 103 10W
Gooding 72 43 0N 114 44W
Goodland 70 39 22N 101 44W
Goodnight 71 35 4N 101 13W
Goodooga 45 29 3S 147 28 E
Goodsoil 65 54 24N 109 13W
Goodsprings 73 35 51N 115 30W
Goole 6 53 42N 0 52W
Goolgowi 45 33 58S 145 41 E
Goomalling 47 31 15S 116 49 E
Goombalie 45 29 59S 145 26 E
Goondiwindi 45 28 30S 150 21 E
Goongarrie 47 30 3S 121 9 E
Goonyella 44 21 47S 147 58 E
Goor 11 52 13N 6 33 E
Gooray 45 28 25S 150 2 E
Goose → 63 53 20N 60 35W
Goose L. 72 42 0N 120 30W
Gop 32 22 5N 69 50 E
Gorakhpur 33 26 47N 83 23 E
Gorda, Punta 75 14 20N 83 10W
Gordan B. 46 11 35S 130 10 E
Gordon, Australia 45 32 7S 138 20 E
Gordon, U.S.A. 70 42 49N 102 12W
Gordon → 44 42 27S 145 30 E
Gordon Downs 46 18 48S 128 33 E
Gordon L., Alta., Canada 65 56 30N 110 25W
Gordon L., N.W.T., Canada 64 63 5N 113 11W
Gordon River 47 34 10S 117 15 E
Gordonia 56 28 13S 21 10 E
Gordonvale 44 17 5S 145 50 E
Gore, Australia 45 28 17S 151 30 E
Goré, Chad 51 7 59N 16 31 E
Gore, Ethiopia 51 8 12N 35 32 E
Gore, N.Z. 43 46 5S 168 58 E
Gore Bay 62 45 57N 82 28W
Gorey 9 52 41N 6 18W
Gorgān 31 36 55N 54 30 E
Gorgona, I. 78 3 0N 78 10W
Gorinchem 11 51 50N 4 59 E
Gorízia 18 45 56N 13 37 E
Gorki = Gorkiy 22 56 20N 44 0 E
Gorkiy 22 56 20N 44 0 E
Gorkovskoye Vdkhr. 22 57 2N 43 4 E
Görlitz 14 51 10N 14 59 E
Gorlovka 23 48 19N 38 5 E
Gorman 71 32 15N 98 43W
Gorna Oryakhovitsa 19 43 7N 25 40 E
Gorno-Altaysk 24 51 50N 86 5 E
Gorno Slinkino 24 60 5N 70 0 E
Gornyatski 22 67 32N 64 3 E
Gorongose → 57 20 30S 34 40 E
Gorontalo 35 0 35N 123 5 E
Gort 9 53 4N 8 50W
Gorzów Wielkopolski 14 52 43N 15 15 E
Gosford 45 33 23S 151 18 E
Goshen, S. Africa 56 25 50S 25 0 E
Goshen, U.S.A. 68 41 36N 85 46W
Goslar 14 51 55N 10 23 E
Gospič 18 44 35N 15 23 E
Gosport 7 50 48N 1 8W
Gosse → 44 19 32S 134 37 E
Göta kanal 21 58 50N 13 58 E
Göteborg 21 57 43N 11 59 E
Göteborgs och Bohus län □ 21 58 30N 11 30 E
Gotha 14 50 56N 10 42 E
Gothenburg 70 40 58N 100 8W
Gotland 21 57 30N 18 33 E
Gotō-Rettō 36 32 55N 129 5 E
Gotska Sandön 21 58 24N 19 15 E
Göttingen 14 51 31N 9 55 E
Gottwaldov 15 49 14N 17 40 E
Goubangzi 38 41 20N 121 52 E
Gouda 11 52 1N 4 42 E
Gough I. 2 40 10S 9 45W
Gouin, Rés. 62 48 35N 74 40W
Goulburn 45 34 44S 149 44 E
Goulburn Is. 44 11 40S 133 20 E
Gounou-Gaya 51 9 38N 15 31 E
Gouri 51 19 36N 19 36 E
Gourits → 56 34 21S 21 52 E
Gourma Rharous 53 16 55N 1 50W
Gourock Ra. 45 36 0S 149 25 E
Govan 65 51 20N 105 0W
Governador Valadares 79 18 15S 41 57W
Gowan Ra. 44 25 0S 145 0 E
Gowanda 68 42 29N 78 58W
Gowd-e Zirreh 31 29 45N 62 0 E
Gower, The 7 51 35N 4 10W
Gowna, L. 9 53 52N 7 35W
Gowrie, Carse of 8 56 30N 3 10W
Goya 80 29 10S 59 10W
Goyder Lagoon 45 27 3S 138 58 E
Goyllarisquisga 78 10 31S 76 24W
Goz Beïda 51 12 10N 21 20 E
Gozo 16 36 0N 14 13 E
Graaff-Reinet 56 32 13S 24 32 E
Gračac 18 44 18N 15 57 E
Grace 72 42 38N 111 46W
Grace, L. (North) 47 33 10S 118 20 E
Grace, L. (South) 47 33 15S 118 25 E
Graceville 70 45 36N 96 23W
Gracias a Dios, C. 75 15 0N 83 10W
Grado 13 43 23N 6 4W
Gradule 45 28 32S 149 15 E
Grady 71 34 52N 103 15W
Graénalon, L. 20 64 10N 17 20W
Grafton, Australia 45 29 38S 152 58 E
Grafton, U.S.A. 70 48 30N 97 25W
Graham, Canada 62 49 20N 90 30W
Graham, N.C., U.S.A. 69 36 5N 79 22W
Graham, Tex., U.S.A. 71 33 7N 98 38W
Graham → 64 56 31N 122 17W
Graham Bell, Os. 24 80 5N 70 0 E
Graham I. 64 53 40N 132 30W
Graham Mt. 73 32 46N 109 58W
Grahamdale 65 51 23N 98 30W
Grahamstown 56 33 19S 26 31 E
Grajaú 79 5 50S 46 4W
Grajaú → 79 3 41S 44 48W
Grampian □ 8 57 0N 3 0W
Grampian Mts. 8 56 50N 4 0W
Grampians, The 45 37 0S 142 20 E
Gran Canaria 50 27 55N 15 35W
Gran Chaco 80 25 0S 61 0W
Gran Paradiso 18 45 33N 7 17 E
Gran Sasso d'Italia 18 42 25N 13 30 E
Granada, Nic. 75 11 58N 86 0W
Granada, Spain 13 37 10N 3 35W
Granada, U.S.A. 71 38 5N 102 20W
Granard 9 53 47N 7 30W
Granbury 71 32 28N 97 48W
Granby 62 45 25N 72 45W
Grand →, Mo., U.S.A. 70 39 23N 93 6W
Grand →, S. Dak., U.S.A. 70 45 40N 100 32W
Grand Bahama 75 26 40N 78 30W
Grand Bank 63 47 6N 55 48W
Grand Bassam 50 5 10N 3 49W
Grand-Bourg 75 15 53N 61 19W
Grand Canyon 73 36 3N 112 9W
Grand Canyon National Park 73 36 15N 112 20W
Grand Cayman 75 19 20N 81 20W
Grand Coulee 72 47 48N 119 1W
Grand Coulee Dam 72 48 0N 118 50W
Grand Falls 63 48 56N 55 40W
Grand Forks, Canada 64 49 0N 118 30W
Grand Forks, U.S.A. 70 48 0N 97 3W
Grand Haven 68 43 3N 86 13W
Grand I. 68 46 30N 86 40W
Grand Island 70 40 59N 98 25W
Grand Isle 71 29 15N 89 58W
Grand Junction 73 39 0N 108 30W
Grand Lac Victoria 62 47 35N 77 35W
Grand Lahou 50 5 10N 5 0W
Grand L., N.B., Canada 63 45 57N 66 7W
Grand L., Nfld., Canada 63 49 0N 57 30W
Grand L., Nfld., Canada 63 53 40N 60 30W
Grand L., U.S.A. 71 29 55N 92 45W
Grand Lake 72 40 20N 105 54W
Grand Manan I. 63 44 45N 66 52W
Grand Marais, Canada 70 47 45N 90 25W
Grand Marais, U.S.A. 68 46 39N 85 59W
Grand-Mère 62 46 36N 72 40W
Grand Portage 62 47 58N 89 41W
Grand Rapids, Canada 65 53 12N 99 19W
Grand Rapids, Mich., U.S.A. 68 42 57N 86 40W
Grand Rapids, Minn., U.S.A. 70 47 15N 93 29W
Grand St-Bernard, Col du 14 45 50N 7 10 E
Grand Teton 72 43 54N 111 50W
Grand Valley 72 39 30N 108 2W
Grand View 65 51 10N 100 42W
Grande →, Argentina 80 24 20S 65 2W
Grande →, Bolivia 78 15 51S 64 39W
Grande →, Bahia, Brazil 79 11 30S 44 30W
Grande →, Minas Gerais, Brazil 79 20 6S 51 4W
Grande →, U.S.A. 71 25 57N 97 9W

H

Hospet

Heber Springs 71 35 29N 91 59W
Hebert 65 50 30N 107 10W
Hebgen, L. 72 44 50N 111 15W
Hebi 38 35 57N 114 7 E
Hebrides 8 57 30N 7 0W
Hebrides, Inner Is. 8 57 20N 6 40W
Hebrides, Outer Is. 8 57 30N 7 40W
Hebron = Al Khalīl 28 31 32N 35 6 E
Hebron, Canada 61 58 5N 62 30W
Hebron, N. Dak., U.S.A. 70 46 56N 102 2W
Hebron, Nebr., U.S.A. 70 40 15N 97 33W
Hecate Str. 64 53 10N 130 30W
Hechi 39 24 40N 108 2 E
Hechuan 39 30 2N 106 12 E
Hecla 70 45 56N 98 8W
Hecla I. 65 51 10N 96 43W
Hede 20 62 23N 13 30 E
Hedemora 21 60 18N 15 58 E
Hedley 71 34 53N 100 39W
Heemstede 11 52 22N 4 37 E
Heerde 11 52 24N 6 2 E
Heerenveen 11 52 57N 5 55 E
Heerlen 11 50 55N 6 0 E
Ḥefa 28 32 46N 35 0 E
Hefei 39 31 52N 117 18 E
Hegang 38 47 20N 130 19 E
Heidelberg, Germany 14 49 23N 8 41 E
Heidelberg, C. Prov., S. Africa 56 34 6S 20 59 E
Heidelberg, Trans., S. Africa 57 26 30S 28 23 E
Heilbron 57 27 16S 27 59 E
Heilbronn 14 49 8N 9 13 E
Heilongjiang □ 38 48 0N 126 0 E
Heilunkiang = Heilongjiang □ 38 48 0N 126 0 E
Heinola 21 61 13N 26 2 E
Heinze Is. 33 14 25N 97 45 E
Hejaz = Al Ḥijāz 29 26 0N 37 30 E
Hejian 38 38 25N 116 5 E
Hejiang 39 28 43N 105 46 E
Hekimhan 30 38 50N 38 0 E
Hekla 20 63 56N 19 35W
Hekou 37 22 30N 103 59 E
Helan Shan 38 39 0N 105 55 E
Helena, Ark., U.S.A. 71 34 30N 90 35W
Helena, Mont., U.S.A. 72 46 40N 112 0W
Helensburgh 8 56 0N 4 44W
Helensville 43 36 41S 174 29 E
Ḥelez 28 31 36N 34 39 E
Helgoland 14 54 10N 7 51 E
Heligoland = Helgoland 14 54 10N 7 51 E
Hellendoorn 11 52 24N 6 27 E
Hellevoetsluis 11 51 50N 4 8 E
Hellín 13 38 31N 1 40W
Helmand □ 31 31 20N 64 0 E
Helmand → 31 31 12N 61 34 E
Helmand, Hamun 31 31 15N 61 15 E
Helmond 11 51 29N 5 41 E
Helmsdale 8 58 7N 3 40W
Helper 72 39 44N 110 56W
Helsingborg 21 56 3N 12 42 E
Helsingfors 21 60 15N 25 3 E
Helsingør 21 56 2N 12 35 E
Helsinki 21 60 15N 25 3 E
Helston 7 50 7N 5 17W
Helvellyn 6 54 31N 3 1W
Helwân 51 29 50N 31 20 E
Hemet 73 33 45N 116 59W
Hemingford 70 42 21N 103 4W
Hemphill 71 31 21N 93 49W
Hempstead 71 30 5N 96 5W
Hemse 21 57 15N 18 22 E
Henan □ 39 34 0N 114 0 E
Henares → 13 40 24N 3 30W
Henderson, Ky., U.S.A. 68 37 50N 87 38W
Henderson, N.C., U.S.A. 69 36 20N 78 25W
Henderson, Nev., U.S.A. 73 36 2N 115 0W
Henderson, Pa., U.S.A. 69 35 25N 88 40W
Henderson, Tex., U.S.A. 71 32 5N 94 49W
Hendersonville 69 35 21N 82 28W
Hendon 45 28 5S 151 50 E
Heng Xian 39 22 40N 109 17 E
Hengdaohezi 38 44 52N 129 0 E
Hengelo 11 52 3N 6 19 E
Hengshan, Hunan, China 39 27 16N 112 45 E
Hengshan, Shaanxi, China 38 37 58N 109 5 E
Hengshui 38 37 41N 115 40 E
Hengyang 39 26 52N 112 33 E
Henlopen, C. 68 38 48N 75 5W
Hennenman 56 27 59S 27 1 E
Hennessey 71 36 8N 97 53W
Henrietta 71 33 50N 98 15W
Henrietta, Ostrov 25 77 6N 156 30 E
Henrietta Maria C. 62 55 9N 82 20W
Henry 70 41 5N 89 20W
Henryetta 71 35 30N 96 0W
Hentiyn Nuruu 37 48 30N 108 30 E
Henty 45 35 30S 147 0 E
Henzada 33 17 38N 95 26 E
Heping 39 24 29N 115 0 E
Heppner 72 45 21N 119 34W
Hepu 39 21 40N 109 12 E
Héraðsflói 20 65 42N 14 12W
Héraðsvötn → 20 65 45N 19 25W
Herald Cays 44 16 58S 149 9 E
Herāt 31 34 20N 62 7 E
Herāt □ 31 35 0N 62 0 E
Hérault □ 12 43 34N 3 15 E
Herbert → 44 18 31S 146 17 E
Herbert Downs 44 23 7S 139 9 E
Herberton 44 17 20S 145 25 E
Hercegnovi 19 42 30N 18 33 E
Hercegovina = Bosna i Hercegovina □ 18 44 0N 18 0 E
Herðubreið 20 65 11N 16 21W
Hereford, U.K. 7 52 4N 2 42W
Hereford, U.S.A. 71 34 50N 102 28W
Hereford and Worcester □ 7 52 10N 2 30W
Herentals 11 51 12N 4 51 E
Herford 14 52 7N 8 40 E
Herington 70 38 43N 97 0W
Herjehogna 21 61 43N 12 7 E
Herkimer 68 43 0N 74 59W
Herman 70 45 51N 96 8W
Hermann 70 38 40N 91 25W
Hermannsburg Mission 46 23 57S 132 45 E
Hermanus 56 34 27S 19 12 E
Hermidale 45 31 30S 146 42 E
Hermiston 72 45 50N 119 16W
Hermitage 43 43 44S 170 5 E
Hermite, I. 80 55 50S 68 0W
Hermon, Mt. = Ash Shaykh, J. 30 33 25N 35 50 E
Hermosillo 74 29 10N 111 0W
Hernád → 15 47 56N 21 8 E
Hernandarias 80 25 20S 54 40W
Hernando 71 34 50N 89 59W
Herne 11 51 33N 7 12 E
Herne Bay 7 51 22N 1 8 E
Herning 21 56 8N 8 58 E
Heroica = Caborca 74 30 40N 112 10W
Heroica Nogales = Nogales 74 31 20N 110 56W
Heron Bay 62 48 40N 86 25W
Herreid 70 45 53N 100 5W
Herrera 13 37 26N 4 55W
Herrick 44 41 5S 147 55 E
Herrin 71 37 50N 89 0W
Herstal 11 50 40N 5 38 E
Hertford 7 51 47N 0 4W
Hertford □ 7 51 51N 0 5W
's-Hertogenbosch 11 51 42N 5 17 E
Hertzogville 56 28 9S 25 30 E
Hervey Bay 44 25 3S 153 5 E
Herzliyya 28 32 10N 34 50 E
Hesse = Hessen □ 14 50 40N 9 20 E
Hessen □ 14 50 40N 9 20 E
Hettinger 70 46 0N 102 38W
Hevron → 28 31 12N 34 42 E
Hewett, C. 61 70 16N 67 45W
Hexham 6 54 58N 2 7W
Hexigten Qi 38 43 18N 117 30 E
Hexrivier 56 33 30S 19 35 E
Heysham 6 54 5N 2 53W
Heywood 45 38 8S 141 37 E
Hi-no-Misaki 36 35 26N 132 38 E
Hialeah 69 25 49N 80 17W
Hiawatha, Kans., U.S.A. 70 39 55N 95 33W
Hiawatha, Utah, U.S.A. 72 39 29N 111 1W
Hibbing 70 47 30N 93 0W
Hibbs B. 44 42 35S 145 15 E
Hibernia Reef 46 12 0S 123 23 E
Hickory 69 35 46N 81 17W
Hicks Pt. 45 37 49S 149 17 E
Hida-Sammyaku 36 36 30N 137 40 E
Hidalgo 74 24 15N 99 26W
Hidalgo, Presa M. 74 26 30N 108 35W
Hidalgo del Parral 74 26 58N 105 40W
Hierro 50 27 44N 18 0 E
Higashiōsaka 36 34 40N 135 37 E
Higgins 71 36 9N 100 1W
Higginsville 47 31 42S 121 38 E
High Atlas = Haut Atlas 50 32 30N 5 0W
High I. 63 56 40N 61 10W
High Island 71 29 32N 94 22W
High Level 64 58 31N 117 8W
High Point 69 35 57N 79 58W
High Prairie 64 55 30N 116 30W
High River 64 50 30N 113 50W
High Springs 69 29 50N 82 40W
High Wycombe 7 51 37N 0 45W
Highbury 44 16 25S 143 9 E
Highland □ 8 57 30N 5 0W
Highland Park 68 42 10N 87 50W
Highmore 70 44 35N 99 26W
Highrock L. 65 57 5N 105 32W
Hiiumaa 22 58 50N 22 45 E
Ḥijārah, Şaḩrā' al 30 30 25N 44 30 E
Ḥijāz □ 29 24 0N 40 0 E
Hijo = Tagum 35 7 33N 125 53 E
Hiko 73 37 30N 115 13W
Hikone 36 35 15N 136 10 E
Hildesheim 14 52 9N 9 55 E
Hill → 47 30 23S 115 3 E
Hill City, Idaho, U.S.A. 72 43 20N 115 2W
Hill City, Kans., U.S.A. 70 39 25N 99 51W
Hill City, Minn., U.S.A. 70 46 57N 93 35W
Hill City, S. Dak., U.S.A. 70 43 58N 103 35W
Hill Island L. 65 60 30N 109 50W
Hillegom 11 52 18N 4 35 E
Hillingdon 7 51 33N 0 29W
Hillman 68 45 5N 83 52W
Hillmond 65 53 26N 109 41W
Hillsboro, Kans., U.S.A. 70 38 22N 97 10W
Hillsboro, N. Dak., U.S.A. 70 47 23N 97 9W
Hillsboro, N.H., U.S.A. 68 43 8N 71 56W
Hillsboro, N. Mex., U.S.A. 73 33 0N 107 35W
Hillsboro, Oreg., U.S.A. 72 45 31N 123 0W
Hillsboro, Tex., U.S.A. 71 32 0N 97 10W
Hillsdale 68 41 55N 84 40W
Hillside 46 21 45S 119 23 E
Hillsport 62 49 27N 85 34W
Hillston 45 33 30S 145 31 E
Hilo 66 19 44N 155 5W
Hilversum 11 52 14N 5 10 E
Himachal Pradesh □ 32 31 30N 77 0 E
Himalaya, Mts. 33 29 0N 84 0 E
Himatnagar 32 23 37N 72 57 E
Himeji 36 34 50N 134 40 E
Himi 36 36 50N 137 0 E
Ḥimş 30 34 40N 36 45 E
Hinchinbrook I. 44 18 20S 146 15 E
Hinckley, U.K. 7 52 33N 1 21W
Hinckley, U.S.A. 72 39 18N 112 41W
Hindmarsh L. 45 36 5S 141 55 E
Hindu Kush 31 36 0N 71 0 E
Hindubagh 32 30 56N 67 57 E
Hindupur 32 13 49N 77 32 E
Hines Creek 64 56 20N 118 40W
Hinganghat 32 20 30N 78 52 E
Hingham 72 48 34N 110 29W
Hingoli 32 19 41N 77 15 E
Hinna = Imi 29 6 28N 42 10 E
Hinsdale 72 48 26N 107 2W
Hinton, Canada 64 53 26N 117 34W
Hinton, U.S.A. 68 37 40N 80 51W
Hippolytushoef 11 52 54N 4 58 E
Hirakud Dam 33 21 32N 83 45 E
Hiratsuka 36 35 19N 139 21 E
Hirosaki 36 40 34N 140 28 E
Hiroshima 36 34 24N 132 30 E
Hiroshima □ 36 34 50N 133 0 E
Hisar 32 29 12N 75 45 E
Hispaniola 75 19 0N 71 0W
Hita 36 33 20N 130 58 E
Hitachi 36 36 36N 140 39 E
Hitchin 7 51 57N 0 16W
Hitoyoshi 36 32 13N 130 45 E
Hitra 20 63 30N 8 45 E
Ḥiyyon, N. → 28 30 25N 35 10 E
Hjalmar L. 65 61 33N 109 25W
Hjälmaren 21 59 18N 15 40 E
Hjørring 21 57 29N 9 59 E
Hluhluwe 57 28 1S 32 15 E
Ho 53 6 37N 0 27 E
Ho Chi Minh City = Phanh Bho Ho Chi Minh 34 10 58N 106 40 E
Hoai Nhon 34 14 28N 109 1 E
Hoare B. 61 65 17N 62 30W
Hobart, Australia 44 42 50S 147 21 E
Hobart, U.S.A. 71 35 0N 99 5W
Hobbs 71 32 40N 103 3W
Hoboken 11 51 11N 4 21 E
Hobro 21 56 39N 9 46 E
Hoburgen 21 56 55N 18 7 E
Hodgson 65 51 13N 97 36W
Hódmezövásárhely 15 46 28N 20 22 E
Hodna, Chott el 50 35 30N 5 0 E
Hodonín 14 48 50N 17 10 E
Hoek van Holland 11 52 0N 4 7 E
Hoëveld 57 26 30S 30 0 E
Hof, Germany 14 50 18N 11 55 E
Hof, Iceland 20 64 33N 14 40W
Höfðakaupstaður 20 65 50N 20 19W
Hofmeyr 56 31 39S 25 50 E
Hofsjökull 20 64 49N 18 48W
Hofsós 20 65 53N 19 26W
Hōfu 36 34 3N 131 34 E
Hogan Group 44 39 13S 147 1 E
Hogansville 69 33 14N 84 50W
Hogeland 72 48 51N 108 40W
Hoh Xil Shan 37 35 0N 89 0 E
Hohe Rhön 14 50 24N 9 58 E
Hohe Venn 11 50 30N 6 5 E
Hohenwald 69 35 35N 87 30W
Hohhot 38 40 52N 111 40 E
Hoi An 34 15 30N 108 19 E
Hoisington 70 38 33N 98 50W
Hokianga Harbour 43 35 31S 173 22 E
Hokitika 43 42 42S 171 0 E
Hokkaidō □ 36 43 30N 143 0 E
Holbrook, Australia 45 35 42S 147 18 E
Holbrook, U.S.A. 73 35 54N 110 10W
Holden, Canada 64 53 13N 112 11W
Holden, U.S.A. 72 39 0N 112 26W
Holdenville 71 35 5N 96 25W
Holderness 6 53 45N 0 5W
Holdfast 65 50 58N 105 25W
Holdrege 70 40 26N 99 22W
Holguín 75 20 50N 76 20W
Hollams Bird I. 56 24 40S 14 30 E
Holland 68 42 47N 86 7W
Hollandia = Jayapura 35 2 28S 140 38 E
Holleton 47 31 55S 119 0 E
Hollidaysburg 68 40 26N 78 25W
Hollis 71 34 45N 99 55W
Hollister, Calif., U.S.A. 73 36 51N 121 24W
Hollister, Idaho, U.S.A. 72 42 21N 114 40W
Holly 70 38 7N 102 7W
Holly Hill 69 29 15N 81 3W
Holly Springs 71 34 45N 89 25W
Hollywood, Calif., U.S.A. 66 34 7N 118 25W
Hollywood, Fla., U.S.A. 69 26 0N 80 9W
Holman Island 60 70 42N 117 41W
Hólmavík 20 65 42N 21 40W
Holmes Reefs 44 16 27S 148 0 E
Holmsund 20 63 41N 20 20 E
Holon 28 32 2N 34 47 E
Holroyd → 44 14 10S 141 36 E
Holstebro 21 56 22N 8 37 E
Holsworthy 7 50 48N 4 21W
Holt 20 63 33N 19 48W
Holton, Canada 63 54 31N 57 12W
Holton, U.S.A. 70 39 28N 95 44W
Holtville 73 32 50N 115 27W
Holwerd 11 53 22N 5 54 E
Holy Cross 60 62 10N 159 52W
Holy I., England, U.K. 6 55 42N 1 48W
Holy I., Wales, U.K. 6 53 17N 4 37W
Holyhead 6 53 18N 4 38W
Holyoke, Colo., U.S.A. 70 40 39N 102 18W
Holyoke, Mass., U.S.A. 68 42 14N 72 37W
Holyrood 63 47 27N 53 8W
Homalin 33 24 55N 95 0 E
Hombori 53 15 20N 1 38W
Home B. 61 68 40N 67 10W
Home Hill 44 19 43S 147 25 E
Homedale 72 43 42N 116 59W
Homer, Alaska, U.S.A. 60 59 40N 151 35W
Homer, La., U.S.A. 71 32 50N 93 4W
Homestead, Australia 44 20 20S 145 40 E
Homestead, Fla., U.S.A. 69 25 29N 80 27W
Homestead, Oreg., U.S.A. 72 45 5N 116 57W
Hominy 71 36 26N 96 24W
Homoine 57 23 55S 35 8 E
Homs = Ḥimş 30 34 40N 36 45 E
Hon Chong 34 10 25N 104 30 E
Honan = Henan □ 39 34 0N 114 0 E
Honbetsu 36 43 7N 143 37 E
Honda 78 5 12N 74 45W
Hondeklipbaai 56 30 19S 17 17 E
Hondo 71 29 22N 99 6W
Hondo → 74 18 25N 88 21W
Honduras ■ 75 14 40N 86 30W
Honduras, G. de 75 16 50N 87 0W
Hønefoss 21 60 10N 10 18 E
Honey L. 72 40 13N 120 14W
Honfleur 12 49 25N 0 13 E
Hong → 26 20 17N 106 34 E
Hong Kong ■ 39 22 11N 114 14 E
Hong'an 39 31 20N 114 40 E
Honghai Wan 39 22 40N 115 0 E
Honghu 39 29 50N 113 30 E
Hongjiang 39 27 7N 109 59 E
Hongshui He → 39 23 48N 109 30 E
Hongtong 38 36 16N 111 40 E
Honguedo, Détroit d' 63 49 15N 64 0W
Hongze Hu 39 33 15N 118 35 E
Honiara 40 9 27S 159 57 E
Honiton 7 50 48N 3 11W
Honjō 36 39 23N 140 3 E
Honolulu 66 21 19N 157 52W
Honshū 36 36 0N 138 0 E
Hood, Pt. 47 34 23S 119 34 E
Hood Mt. 72 45 24N 121 41W
Hood River 72 45 45N 121 31W
Hoodsport 72 47 24N 123 7W
Hoogeveen 11 52 44N 6 30 E
Hoogezand 11 53 11N 6 45 E
Hooghly → = Hughli → 33 21 56N 88 4 E
Hook Hd. 9 52 8N 6 57W
Hook I. 44 20 4S 149 0 E
Hook of Holland = Hoek van Holland 11 52 0N 4 7 E
Hooker 71 36 55N 101 10W
Hooker Creek 46 18 23S 130 38 E
Hoopeston 68 40 30N 87 40W
Hoopstad 56 27 50S 25 55 E
Hoorn 11 52 38N 5 4 E
Hoover Dam 73 36 0N 114 45W
Hope, Canada 64 49 25N 121 25 E
Hope, Ark., U.S.A. 71 33 40N 93 36W
Hope, N. Dak., U.S.A. 70 47 21N 97 42W
Hope, L. 45 28 24S 139 18 E
Hope Pt. 60 68 20N 166 50W
Hope Town 75 26 35N 76 57W
Hopedale 63 55 28N 60 13W
Hopefield 56 33 3S 18 22 E
Hopei = Hebei □ 38 39 0N 116 0 E
Hopelchén 74 19 46N 89 50W
Hopetoun, Vic., Australia 45 35 42S 142 22 E
Hopetoun, W. Austral., Australia 47 33 57S 120 7 E
Hopetown 56 29 34S 24 3 E
Hopkins 70 40 31N 94 45W
Hopkins, L. 46 24 15S 128 35 E
Hopkinsville 69 36 52N 87 26W
Hopland 72 39 0N 123 7W
Hoquiam 72 46 50N 123 55W
Hordaland fylke □ 21 60 25N 6 15 E
Horden Hills 46 20 15S 130 0 E
Hormoz 31 27 35N 55 0 E
Hormoz, Jaz. ye 31 27 8N 56 28 E
Hormozgān □ 31 27 30N 56 0 E
Hormuz Str. 31 26 30N 56 30 E
Horn, Austria 14 48 39N 15 40 E
Horn, Ísafjarðarsýsla, Iceland 20 66 28N 22 28W
Horn, Suður-Múlasýsla, Iceland 20 65 10N 13 31W
Horn → 64 61 30N 118 1W
Horn, Cape = Hornos, C. de 80 55 50S 67 30W
Horn Head 9 55 13N 8 0W
Horn I., Australia 44 10 37S 142 17 E
Horn I., U.S.A. 69 30 17N 88 40W
Horn Mts. 64 62 15N 119 15W
Hornavan 20 66 15N 17 30 E
Hornbeck 71 31 22N 93 20W
Hornbrook 72 41 58N 122 37W
Horncastle 6 53 13N 0 8W
Hornell 68 42 23N 77 41W
Hornell L. 64 62 20N 119 25W
Hornepayne 62 49 14N 84 48W
Hornos, C. de 80 55 50S 67 30W
Hornsby 45 33 42S 151 2 E
Hornsea 6 53 55N 0 10W
Horqin Youyi Qianqi 38 46 5N 122 3 E
Horqueta 80 23 15S 56 55W
Horse Cr. → 70 41 57N 103 58W
Horse Is. 63 50 15N 55 50W
Horsefly L. 64 52 25N 121 0W
Horsens 21 55 52N 9 51 E
Horsham, Australia 45 36 44S 142 13 E
Horsham, U.K. 7 51 4N 0 20W
Horten 21 59 25N 10 32 E
Horton 70 39 42N 95 30W
Horton → 60 69 56N 126 52W
Horwood, L. 62 48 5N 82 20W
Hose, Gunung-Gunung 34 2 5N 114 6 E
Hoshangabad 32 22 45N 77 45 E
Hoshiarpur 32 31 30N 75 58 E
Hosmer 70 45 36N 99 29W
Hospet 32 15 15N 76 20 E

Jenkins

İnegöl 30 40 5N 29 31 E
Infante, Kaap 56 34 27S 20 51 E
Infiernillo, Presa del 74 18 9N 102 0W
Ingende 54 0 12S 18 57 E
Ingham 44 18 43S 146 10 E
Ingleborough 6 54 11N 2 23W
Inglewood, Queens., Australia 45 28 25S 151 2 E
Inglewood, Vic., Australia 45 36 29S 143 53 E
Inglewood, N.Z. 43 39 9S 174 14 E
Inglewood, U.S.A. 73 33 58N 118 21W
Ingólfshöfði 20 63 48N 16 39W
Ingolstadt 14 48 45N 11 26 E
Ingomar 72 46 35N 107 21W
Ingonish 63 46 42N 60 18W
Ingraj Bazar 33 24 58N 88 10 E
Ingulec 23 47 42N 33 14 E
Ingwavuma 57 27 9S 31 59 E
Inhaca, I. 57 26 1S 32 57 E
Inhafenga 57 20 36S 33 53 E
Inhambane 57 23 54S 35 30 E
Inhambane □ 57 22 30S 34 20 E
Inhaminga 55 18 26S 35 0 E
Inharrime 57 24 30S 35 0 E
Inharrime → 57 24 30S 35 0 E
Ining = Yining 37 43 58N 81 10 E
Inírida → 78 3 55N 67 52W
Inishbofin 9 53 35N 10 12W
Inishmore 9 53 8N 9 45W
Inishowen 9 55 14N 7 15W
Injune 45 25 53S 148 32 E
Inklin 64 58 56N 133 5W
Inklin → 64 58 50N 133 10W
Inkom 72 42 51N 112 15W
Inle L. 33 20 30N 96 58 E
Inn → 14 48 35N 13 28 E
Innamincka 45 27 44S 140 46 E
Inner Hebrides 8 57 0N 6 30W
Inner Mongolia = Nei Monggol Zizhiqu □ 38 42 0N 112 0 E
Inner Sound 8 57 30N 5 55W
Innetalling I. 62 56 0N 79 0W
Innisfail, Australia 44 17 33S 146 5 E
Innisfail, Canada 64 52 0N 113 57W
Innsbruck 14 47 16N 11 23 E
Inny → 9 53 30N 7 50W
Inongo 54 1 55S 18 30 E
Inoucdjouac 61 58 25N 78 15W
Inowrocław 15 52 50N 18 12 E
Inquisivi 78 16 50S 67 10W
Inscription, C. 47 25 29S 112 59 E
Insein 33 16 50N 96 5 E
Inta 22 66 5N 60 8 E
Interior 70 43 46N 101 59W
International Falls 70 48 36N 93 25W
Intiyaco 80 28 43S 60 5W
Inútil, B. 80 53 30S 70 15W
Inuvik 60 68 16N 133 40W
Inveraray 8 56 13N 5 5W
Inverbervie 8 56 50N 2 17W
Invercargill 43 46 24S 168 24 E
Inverell 45 29 45S 151 8 E
Invergordon 8 57 41N 4 10W
Invermere 64 50 30N 116 2W
Inverness, Canada 63 46 15N 61 19W
Inverness, U.K. 8 57 29N 4 12W
Inverness, U.S.A. 69 28 50N 82 20W
Inverurie 8 57 15N 2 21W
Inverway 46 17 50S 129 38 E
Investigator Group 45 34 45S 134 20 E
Investigator Str. 45 35 30S 137 0 E
Inya 24 50 28N 86 37 E
Inyo Mts. 73 37 0N 118 0W
Inyokern 73 35 38N 117 48W
Inza 22 53 55N 46 25 E
Iola 71 38 0N 95 20W
Iona 8 56 20N 6 25W
Ione, Calif., U.S.A. 72 38 20N 120 56W
Ione, Wash., U.S.A. 72 48 44N 117 29W
Ionia 68 42 59N 85 7W
Ionian Is. = Iónioi Nísoi 19 38 40N 20 0 E
Ionian Sea 17 37 30N 17 30 E
Iónioi Nísoi 19 38 40N 20 0 E
Íos 19 36 41N 25 20 E
Iowa □ 70 42 18N 93 30W
Iowa City 70 41 40N 91 35W
Iowa Falls 70 42 30N 93 15W
Ipameri 79 17 44S 48 9W
Ipatinga 79 19 32S 42 30W
Ipiales 78 0 50N 77 37W
Ipin = Yibin 37 28 45N 104 32 E
Ípiros □ 19 39 30N 20 30 E
Ipixuna 78 7 0S 71 40W
Ipoh 34 4 35N 101 5 E
Ippy 51 6 5N 21 7 E
Ipswich, Australia 45 27 35S 152 40 E
Ipswich, U.K. 7 52 4N 1 9 E
Ipswich, U.S.A. 70 45 28N 99 1W
Ipu 79 4 23S 40 44W
Iquique 78 20 19S 70 5W
Iquitos 78 3 45S 73 10W
Iracoubo 79 5 30N 53 10W
Iráklion 19 35 20N 25 12 E
Iran ■ 31 33 0N 53 0 E
Iran, Gunung-Gunung 34 2 20N 114 50 E
Īrānshahr 31 27 15N 60 40 E
Irapuato 74 20 40N 101 30W
Iraq ■ 30 33 0N 44 0 E
Irbid 28 32 35N 35 48 E
Irebu 54 0 40S 17 46 E
Ireland ■ 9 53 0N 8 0W
Ireland's Eye 9 53 25N 6 4W
Irele 53 7 40N 5 40 E
Iret 25 60 3N 154 20 E
Iri 38 35 59N 127 0 E
Irian Jaya □ 35 4 0S 137 0 E
Iringa 54 7 48S 35 43 E
Iriri → 79 3 52S 52 37W
Irish Republic ■ 9 53 0N 8 0W
Irish Sea 6 54 0N 5 0W
Irkineyeva 25 58 30N 96 49 E
Irkutsk 25 52 18N 104 20 E
Irma 65 52 55N 111 14W
Iron Baron 45 32 58S 137 11 E
Iron Gate = Portile de Fier 15 44 42N 22 30 E
Iron Knob 45 32 46S 137 8 E
Iron Mountain 68 45 49N 88 4W
Iron River 70 46 6N 88 40W
Ironbridge 7 52 38N 2 29W
Ironstone Kopje 56 25 17S 24 5 E
Ironton, Mo., U.S.A. 71 37 40N 90 40W
Ironton, Ohio, U.S.A. 68 38 35N 82 40W
Ironwood 70 46 30N 90 10W
Iroquois Falls 62 48 46N 80 41W
Irrara Cr. → 45 29 35S 145 31 E
Irrawaddy □ 33 17 0N 95 0 E
Irrawaddy → 33 15 50N 95 6 E
Irtysh → 24 61 4N 68 52 E
Irumu 54 1 32N 29 53 E
Irún 13 43 20N 1 52W
Irvine, Canada 65 49 57N 110 16W
Irvine, U.K. 8 55 37N 4 40W
Irvine, U.S.A. 68 37 42N 83 58W
Irvinestown 9 54 28N 7 38W
Irwin → 47 29 15S 114 54 E
Irwin, Pt. 47 35 5S 116 55 E
Irymple 45 34 14S 142 8 E
Isa 53 13 14N 6 24 E
Isaac → 44 22 55S 149 20 E
Isabel 70 45 27N 101 22W
Isabela, I. 74 21 51N 105 55W
Isabella 35 6 40N 122 10 E
Isabella, Cord. 75 13 30N 85 25W
Isabella Ra. 46 21 0S 121 4 E
Ísafjarðardjúp 20 66 10N 23 0W
Ísafjörður 20 66 5N 23 9W
Isangi 54 0 52N 24 10 E
Isar → 14 48 49N 12 58 E
Íschia 18 40 45N 13 51 E
Isdell → 46 16 27S 124 51 E
Ise 36 34 25N 136 45 E
Ise-Wan 36 34 43N 136 43 E
Isère □ 12 45 15N 5 40 E
Isère → 12 44 59N 4 51 E
Iseyin 53 8 0N 3 36 E
Ishikari-Wan 36 43 25N 141 1 E
Ishikawa □ 36 36 30N 136 30 E
Ishim 24 56 10N 69 30 E
Ishim → 24 57 45N 71 10 E
Ishinomaki 36 38 32N 141 20 E
Ishkuman 32 36 30N 73 50 E
Ishpeming 68 46 30N 87 40W
Isil Kul 24 54 55N 71 16 E
Isiolo 54 0 24N 37 33 E
Isipingo Beach 57 30 0S 30 57 E
Isiro 54 2 53N 27 40 E
Isisford 44 24 15S 144 21 E
İskenderun 30 36 32N 36 10 E
İskenderun Körfezi 23 36 40N 35 50 E
Iskut → 64 56 45N 131 49W
Isla → 8 56 32N 3 20W
Islamabad 32 33 40N 73 10 E
Island → 64 60 25N 121 12W
Island Falls, Canada 62 49 35N 81 20W
Island Falls, U.S.A. 63 46 0N 68 16W
Island L. 65 53 47N 94 25W
Island Lagoon 45 31 30S 136 40 E
Island Pt. 47 30 20S 115 1 E
Island Pond 68 44 50N 71 50W
Islands, B. of 63 49 11N 58 15W
Islay 8 55 46N 6 10W
Isle aux Morts 63 47 35N 59 0W
Isle of Wight □ 7 50 40N 1 20W
Isle Royale 70 48 0N 88 50W
Isleta 73 34 58N 106 46W
Ismail 23 45 22N 28 46 E
Ismâ'ilîya 30 30 37N 32 18 E
Ismay 70 46 33N 104 44W
Isna 51 25 17N 32 30 E
Isoka 52 10 4S 32 42 E
Isparta 30 37 47N 30 30 E
Íspica 18 36 47N 14 53 E
Israel ■ 28 32 0N 34 50 E
Isseka 47 28 30S 114 35 E
Issyk-Kul, Ozero 24 42 25N 77 15 E
İstanbul 30 41 0N 29 0 E
Istokpoga, L. 69 27 22N 81 14W
Istra 18 45 10N 14 0 E
Istria = Istra 18 45 10N 14 0 E
Itabaiana 79 7 18S 35 19W
Itaberaba 79 12 32S 40 18W
Itabira 79 19 37S 43 13W
Itabuna 79 14 48S 39 16W
Itaipu Dam 80 25 30S 54 30W
Itaituba 79 4 10S 55 50W
Itajaí 80 27 50S 48 39W
Italy ■ 18 42 0N 13 0 E
Itampolo 57 24 41S 43 57 E
Itapecuru-Mirim 79 3 24S 44 20W
Itaperuna 79 21 10S 41 54W
Itapicuru →, Bahia, Brazil 79 11 47S 37 32W
Itapicuru →, Maranhão, Brazil 79 2 52S 44 12W
Itapipoca 79 3 30S 39 35W
Itaquatiara 78 2 58S 58 30W
Itaquí 80 29 8S 56 30W
Itatuba 78 5 46S 63 20W
Itchen → 7 50 57N 1 20W
Ithaca = Itháki 19 38 25N 20 40 E
Ithaca 68 42 25N 76 30W
Itháki 19 38 25N 20 40 E
Ito 36 34 58N 139 5 E
Itonamas → 78 12 28S 64 24W
Itu 53 5 10N 7 58 E
Ituaçu 79 13 50S 41 18W
Ituiutaba 79 19 0S 49 25W
Itumbiara 79 18 20S 49 10W
Ituna 65 51 10N 103 24W
Iturbe 80 23 0S 65 25W
Iturup, Ostrov 25 45 0N 148 0 E
Ivalo 20 68 38N 27 35 E
Ivalojoki → 20 68 40N 27 40 E
Ivanhoe, N.S.W., Australia 45 32 56S 144 20 E
Ivanhoe, N. Terr., Australia 46 15 41S 128 41 E
Ivanhoe L. 65 60 25N 106 30W
Ivano-Frankovsk 23 48 40N 24 40 E
Ivanovo 22 57 5N 41 0 E
Ivato 57 20 37S 47 10 E
Ivdel 22 60 42N 60 24 E
Iviza = Ibiza 13 38 54N 1 26 E
Ivohibe 57 22 31S 46 57 E
Ivory Coast ■ 50 7 30N 5 0W
Ivrea 18 45 30N 7 52 E
Ivugivik 61 62 24N 77 55W
Iwahig 34 8 36N 117 32 E
Iwaki 36 37 3N 140 55 E
Iwakuni 36 34 15N 132 8 E
Iwamizawa 36 43 12N 141 46 E
Iwanai 36 42 58N 140 30 E
Iwanuma 36 38 7N 140 51 E
Iwata 36 34 42N 137 51 E
Iwate □ 36 39 30N 141 30 E
Iwate-San 36 39 51N 141 0 E
Iwo 53 7 39N 4 9 E
Ixiamas 78 13 50S 68 5W
Ixopo 57 30 11S 30 5 E
Ixtepec 74 16 32N 95 10W
Ixtlán del Río 74 21 5N 104 21W
Izabel, L. de 75 15 30N 89 10W
Izamal 74 20 56N 89 1W
Izegem 11 50 55N 3 12 E
Izhevsk = Ustinov 22 56 51N 53 14 E
İzmir 23 38 25N 27 8 E
İzmit 30 40 45N 29 50 E
Izra 28 32 51N 36 15 E
Izumi-sano 36 34 23N 135 18 E
Izumo 36 35 20N 132 46 E

J

Jaba' 28 32 20N 35 13 E
Jabalpur 32 23 9N 79 58 E
Jabālyah 28 31 32N 34 27 E
Jablah 30 35 20N 36 0 E
Jablonec 14 50 43N 15 10 E
Jaboatão 79 8 7S 35 1W
Jaburu 78 5 30S 64 0W
Jaca 13 42 35N 0 33W
Jacareí 80 23 20S 46 0W
Jacarèzinho 80 23 5S 50 0W
Jackman 63 45 35N 70 17W
Jacksboro 71 33 14N 98 15W
Jackson, Australia 45 26 39S 149 39 E
Jackson, Ala., U.S.A. 69 31 32N 87 53W
Jackson, Calif., U.S.A. 72 38 19N 120 47W
Jackson, Ky., U.S.A. 68 37 35N 83 22W
Jackson, Mich., U.S.A. 68 42 18N 84 25W
Jackson, Minn., U.S.A. 70 43 35N 95 0W
Jackson, Miss., U.S.A. 71 32 20N 90 10W
Jackson, Mo., U.S.A. 71 37 25N 89 42W
Jackson, Ohio, U.S.A. 68 39 0N 82 40W
Jackson, Tenn., U.S.A. 69 35 40N 88 50W
Jackson, Wyo., U.S.A. 72 43 30N 110 49W
Jackson, L. 72 43 55N 110 40W
Jackson Bay 43 43 58S 168 42 E
Jacksons 43 42 46S 171 32 E
Jacksonville, Ala., U.S.A. 69 33 49N 85 45W
Jacksonville, Fla., U.S.A. 69 30 15N 81 38W
Jacksonville, Ill., U.S.A. 70 39 42N 90 15W
Jacksonville, N.C., U.S.A. 69 34 50N 77 29W
Jacksonville, Oreg., U.S.A. 72 42 19N 122 56W
Jacksonville, Tex., U.S.A. 71 31 58N 95 19W
Jacksonville Beach 69 30 19N 81 26W
Jacmel 75 18 14N 72 32W
Jacob Lake 73 36 45N 112 12W
Jacobabad 32 28 20N 68 29 E
Jacobina 79 11 11S 40 30W
Jacob's Well 28 32 13N 35 13 E
Jacques-Cartier, Mt. 63 48 57N 66 0W
Jacundá → 79 1 57S 50 26W
Jadotville = Likasi 54 10 55S 26 48 E
Jādū 51 32 0N 12 0 E
Jaén, Peru 78 5 25S 78 40W
Jaén, Spain 13 37 44N 3 43W
Jaffa = Tel Aviv-Yafo 28 32 4N 34 48 E
Jaffa, C. 45 36 58S 139 40 E
Jaffna 32 9 45N 80 2 E
Jagadhri 32 30 10N 77 20 E
Jagdalpur 33 19 3N 82 0 E
Jagersfontein 56 29 44S 25 27 E
Jagraon 32 30 50N 75 25 E
Jagtial 32 18 50N 79 0 E
Jaguariaíva 80 24 10S 49 50W
Jaguaribe → 79 4 25S 37 45W
Jagüey Grande 75 22 35N 81 7W
Jahrom 31 28 30N 53 31 E
Jailolo 35 1 5N 127 30 E
Jailolo, Selat 35 0 5N 129 5 E
Jaipur 32 27 0N 75 50 E
Jakarta 35 6 9S 106 49 E
Jakobstad 20 63 40N 22 43 E
Jal 71 32 8N 103 8W
Jalai Nur 38 49 27N 117 42 E
Jalalabad 31 34 30N 70 29 E
Jalapa 75 14 39N 89 59W
Jalapa Enríquez 74 19 32N 96 55W
Jalas, Jabal al 30 27 30N 36 30 E
Jalgaon, Maharashtra, India 32 21 2N 76 31 E
Jalgaon, Maharashtra, India 32 21 0N 75 42 E
Jalingo 53 8 55N 11 25 E
Jalisco □ 74 20 0N 104 0W
Jalna 32 19 48N 75 38 E
Jalón → 13 41 47N 1 4W
Jalpa 74 21 38N 102 58W
Jalpaiguri 33 26 32N 88 46 E
Jalq 31 27 35N 62 46 E
Jaluit I. 40 6 0N 169 30 E
Jamaari 53 11 44N 9 53 E
Jamaica ■ 75 18 10N 77 30W
Jamalpur, Bangla. 33 24 52N 89 56 E
Jamalpur, India 33 25 18N 86 28 E
Jamanxim → 79 4 43S 56 18W
Jambe 35 1 15S 132 10 E
Jambi 34 1 38S 103 30 E
Jambi □ 34 1 30S 102 30 E
James → 70 42 52N 97 18W
James B. 62 51 30N 80 0W
James Ranges 46 24 10S 132 30 E
Jamestown, Australia 45 33 10S 138 32 E
Jamestown, S. Africa 56 31 6S 26 45 E
Jamestown, Ky., U.S.A. 68 37 0N 85 5W
Jamestown, N. Dak., U.S.A. 70 46 54N 98 42W
Jamestown, N.Y., U.S.A. 68 42 5N 79 18W
Jamestown, Tenn., U.S.A. 69 36 25N 85 0W
Jamkhandi 32 16 30N 75 15 E
Jammā'īn 28 32 8N 35 12 E
Jammu 32 32 43N 74 54 E
Jammu & Kashmir □ 32 34 25N 77 0 E
Jamnagar 32 22 30N 70 6 E
Jamrud 32 33 59N 71 24 E
Jamshedpur 33 22 44N 86 12 E
Jämtlands län □ 20 62 40N 13 50 E
Jan Kempdorp 56 27 55S 24 51 E
Jan L. 65 54 56N 102 55W
Jand 32 33 30N 72 6 E
Jandaq 31 34 3N 54 22 E
Jandowae 45 26 45S 151 7 E
Janesville 70 42 39N 89 1W
Janīn 28 32 28N 35 18 E
Januária 79 15 25S 44 25W
Janub Dârfûr □ 51 11 0N 25 0 E
Janub Kordofân □ 51 12 0N 30 0 E
Jaora 32 23 40N 75 10 E
Japan ■ 36 36 0N 136 0 E
Japan, Sea of 36 40 0N 135 0 E
Japan Trench 40 32 0N 142 0 E
Japen = Yapen 35 1 50S 136 0 E
Japurá → 78 3 8S 64 46W
Jaque 78 7 27N 78 8W
Jara, La 73 37 16N 106 0W
Jarama → 13 40 2N 3 39W
Jarash 28 32 17N 35 54 E
Jardines de la Reina, Is. 75 20 50N 78 50W
Jargalant = Hovd 37 48 2N 91 37 E
Jargalant 37 48 2N 91 37 E
Jarosław 15 50 2N 22 42 E
Jarrahdale 47 32 24S 116 5 E
Jarso 51 5 15N 37 30 E
Jarvis I. 41 0 15S 159 55W
Jarwa 33 27 38N 82 30 E
Jäsk 31 25 38N 57 45 E
Jasło 15 49 45N 21 30 E
Jasper, Canada 64 52 55N 118 5W
Jasper, Ala., U.S.A. 69 33 48N 87 16W
Jasper, Fla., U.S.A. 69 30 31N 82 58W
Jasper, Minn., U.S.A. 70 43 52N 96 22W
Jasper, Tex., U.S.A. 71 30 59N 93 58W
Jasper Nat. Park 64 52 50N 118 8W
Jassy = Iaşi 17 47 10N 27 40 E
Jászberény 15 47 30N 19 55 E
Jataí 79 17 58S 51 48W
Jatibarang 35 6 28S 108 18 E
Jatinegara 35 6 13S 106 52 E
Játiva 13 39 0N 0 32W
Jatt 28 32 24N 35 2 E
Jaú 79 22 10S 48 30W
Jauja 78 11 45S 75 15W
Jaunpur 33 25 46N 82 44 E
Java = Jawa 35 7 0S 110 0 E
Java Sea 34 4 35S 107 15 E
Java Trench 40 10 0S 110 0W
Javhlant = Ulyasutay 37 47 56N 97 28 E
Jawa 35 7 0S 110 0 E
Jay 71 36 25N 94 46W
Jaya, Puncak 35 3 57S 137 17 E
Jayanti 33 26 45N 89 40 E
Jayapura 35 2 28S 140 38 E
Jayawijaya, Pegunungan 35 5 0S 139 0 E
Jaynagar 33 26 43N 86 9 E
Jayton 71 33 17N 100 35W
Jean 73 35 47N 115 20W
Jean Marie River 60 61 32N 120 38W
Jean Rabel 75 19 50N 73 5W
Jeanerette 71 29 52N 91 38W
Jeanette, Ostrov 25 76 43N 158 0 E
Jebba 53 9 9N 4 48 E
Jebel, Bahr el → 51 9 30N 30 25 E
Jedburgh 8 55 28N 2 33W
Jedda = Jiddah 29 21 29N 39 10 E
Jędrzejów 15 50 35N 20 15 E
Jedway 64 52 17N 131 14W
Jefferson, Iowa, U.S.A. 70 42 3N 94 25W
Jefferson, Tex., U.S.A. 71 32 45N 94 23W
Jefferson, Wis., U.S.A. 70 43 0N 88 49W
Jefferson, Mt., Nev., U.S.A. 72 38 51N 117 0W
Jefferson, Mt., Oreg., U.S.A. 72 44 45N 121 50W
Jefferson City, Mo., U.S.A. 70 38 34N 92 10W
Jefferson City, Tenn., U.S.A. 69 36 8N 83 30W
Jeffersonville 68 38 20N 85 42W
Jega 53 12 15N 4 23 E
Jelenia Góra 14 50 50N 15 45 E
Jelgava 22 56 41N 23 49 E
Jellicoe 62 49 40N 87 30W
Jemaja 34 3 5N 105 45 E
Jember 35 8 11S 113 41 E
Jembongan 34 6 45N 117 20 E
Jemeppe 11 50 37N 5 30 E
Jena, Germany 14 50 56N 11 33 E
Jena, U.S.A. 71 31 41N 92 7W
Jenkins 68 37 13N 82 41W

Khalmer Yu

Kampot 34 10 36N 104 10 E
Kampuchea = Cambodia ■ 34 12 15N 105 0 E
Kampung → 35 5 44S 138 24 E
Kampungbaru = Tolitoli 35 1 5N 120 50 E
Kamrau, Teluk 35 3 30S 133 36 E
Kamsack 65 51 34N 101 54W
Kamskoye Vdkhr. 22 58 0N 56 0 E
Kamuchawie L. 65 56 18N 101 59W
Kamui-Misaki 36 43 20N 140 21 E
Kamyshin 23 50 10N 45 24 E
Kanaaupscow 62 54 2N 76 30W
Kanab 73 37 3N 112 29W
Kanab Creek 73 37 0N 112 40W
Kanagawa □ 36 35 20N 139 20 E
Kanairiktok → 63 55 2N 60 18W
Kananga 54 5 55S 22 18 E
Kanarraville 73 37 34N 113 12W
Kanash 22 55 30N 47 32 E
Kanawha → 68 38 50N 82 8W
Kanazawa 36 36 30N 136 38 E
Kanchanaburi 34 14 2N 99 31 E
Kanchenjunga 33 27 50N 88 10 E
Kanchipuram 32 12 52N 79 45 E
Kanda Kanda 54 6 52S 23 48 E
Kandahar = Qandahār 31 31 32N 65 30 E
Kandalaksha 22 67 9N 32 30 E
Kandalakshkiy Zaliv 22 66 0N 35 0 E
Kandalu 32 29 55N 63 20 E
Kandangan 34 2 50S 115 20 E
Kandi 53 11 7N 2 55 E
Kandla 32 23 0N 70 10 E
Kandos 45 32 45S 149 58 E
Kandy 32 7 18N 80 43 E
Kane 68 41 39N 78 53W
Kane Basin 58 79 1N 73 0W
Kangaroo I. 45 35 45S 137 0 E
Kangaroo Mts. 44 23 25S 142 0 E
Kangavar 30 34 40N 48 0 E
Kangean, Kepulauan 34 6 55S 115 23 E
Kanggye 38 41 0N 126 35 E
Kangnŭng 38 37 45N 128 54 E
Kango 54 0 11N 10 5 E
Kangto 33 27 50N 92 35 E
Kaniapiskau → 63 56 40N 69 30W
Kaniapiskau L. 63 54 10N 69 55W
Kanin, P-ov. 22 68 0N 45 0 E
Kanin Nos, Mys 22 68 45N 43 20 E
Kaniva 45 36 22S 141 18 E
Kankakee 68 41 6N 87 50W
Kankakee → 68 41 23N 88 16W
Kankan 50 10 23N 9 15W
Kanker 33 20 10N 81 40 E
Kankunskiy 25 57 37N 126 8 E
Kannapolis 69 35 32N 80 37W
Kannauj 32 27 3N 79 56 E
Kannod 32 22 45N 76 40 E
Kano 53 12 2N 8 30 E
Kano □ 53 11 45N 9 0 E
Kanowit 34 2 14N 112 20 E
Kanowna 47 30 32S 121 31 E
Kanoya 36 31 25N 130 50 E
Kanpetlet 33 21 10N 93 59 E
Kanpur 32 26 28N 80 20 E
Kansas □ 70 38 40N 98 0W
Kansas → 70 39 7N 94 36W
Kansas City, Kans., U.S.A. 70 39 0N 94 40W
Kansas City, Mo., U.S.A. 70 39 3N 94 30W
Kansk 25 56 20N 95 37 E
Kansu = Gansu □ 38 36 0N 104 0 E
Kantang 34 7 25N 99 31 E
Kantché 53 13 31N 8 30 E
Kanturk 9 52 10N 8 55W
Kanuma 36 36 34N 139 42 E
Kanus 56 27 50S 18 39 E
Kanye 56 25 0S 25 28 E
Kaohsiung = Gaoxiong 39 22 38N 120 18 E
Kaokoveld 56 19 15S 14 30 E
Kaolack 50 14 5N 16 8W
Kapanga 54 8 30S 22 40 E
Kapchagai 24 43 51N 77 14 E
Kapela 18 44 40N 15 40 E
Kapfenberg 14 47 26N 15 18 E
Kapiri Mposhi 55 13 59S 28 43 E
Kāpīsā □ 31 35 0N 69 20 E
Kapiskau → 62 52 47N 81 55W
Kapit 34 2 0N 112 55 E
Kapiti I. 43 40 50S 174 56 E
Kapoeta 51 4 50N 33 35 E
Kaposvár 15 46 25N 17 47 E
Kapps 56 22 32S 17 18 E
Kapuas → 34 0 25S 109 20 E
Kapuas Hulu, Pegunungan 34 1 30N 113 30 E
Kapunda 45 34 20S 138 56 E
Kapuskasing 62 49 25N 82 30W
Kapuskasing → 62 49 49N 82 0W
Kaputar, Mt. 45 30 15S 150 10 E
Kara 24 69 10N 65 0 E
Kara Bogaz Gol, Zaliv 23 41 0N 53 30 E
Kara Kalpak A.S.S.R. □ 24 43 0N 60 0 E
Kara Kum = Karakum, Peski 24 39 30N 60 0 E
Kara Sea 24 75 0N 70 0 E
Karabük 30 41 12N 32 37 E
Karabutak 24 49 59N 60 14 E
Karachi 32 24 53N 67 0 E
Karad 32 17 15N 74 10 E
Karadeniz Boğazı 30 41 10N 29 10 E
Karaganda 24 49 50N 73 10 E
Karagayly 24 49 26N 76 0 E
Karaginskiy, Ostrov 25 58 45N 164 0 E
Karagiye Depression 23 43 27N 51 45 E
Karaikal 32 10 59N 79 50 E
Karaikkudi 32 10 0N 78 45 E
Karaj 31 35 48N 51 0 E
Karakas 24 48 20N 83 30 E
Karakitang 35 3 14N 125 28 E
Karakoram Pass 32 35 33N 77 50 E
Karakoram Ra. 32 35 30N 77 0 E
Karakum, Peski 24 39 30N 60 0 E
Karalon 25 57 5N 115 50 E
Karaman 30 37 14N 33 13 E
Karamay 37 45 30N 84 58 E
Karambu 34 3 53S 116 6 E
Karamea Bight 43 41 22S 171 40 E
Karanganyar 35 7 38S 109 37 E
Karasburg 56 28 0S 18 44 E
Karasino 24 66 50N 86 50 E
Karasjok 20 69 27N 25 30 E
Karasuk 24 53 44N 78 2 E
Karatau 24 43 10N 70 28 E
Karatau, Khrebet 24 43 30N 69 30 E
Karawanken 18 46 30N 14 40 E
Karazhal 24 48 2N 70 49 E
Karbalā 30 32 36N 44 3 E
Karcag 15 47 19N 20 57 E
Karda 25 55 0N 103 16 E
Kardhítsa 19 39 23N 21 54 E
Kareeberge 56 30 59S 21 50 E
Karelian A.S.S.R. □ 22 65 30N 32 30 E
Kargānrūd 30 37 55N 49 0 E
Kargasok 24 59 3N 80 53 E
Kargat 24 55 10N 80 15 E
Kargil 32 34 32N 76 12 E
Kargopol 22 61 30N 38 58 E
Kariba Dam 55 16 30S 28 35 E
Kariba Gorge 55 16 30S 28 50 E
Kariba L. 55 16 40S 28 25 E
Karibib 56 22 0S 15 56 E
Karimata, Kepulauan 34 1 25S 109 0 E
Karimata, Selat 34 2 0S 108 40 E
Karimnagar 32 18 26N 79 10 E
Karimunjawa, Kepulauan 34 5 50S 110 30 E
Karin 29 10 50N 45 52 E
Kariya 36 34 58N 137 1 E
Karkaralinsk 24 49 26N 75 30 E
Karkinitskiy Zaliv 23 45 56N 33 0 E
Karkur 28 32 29N 34 57 E
Karl-Marx-Stadt 14 50 50N 12 55 E
Karlovac 18 45 31N 15 36 E
Karlovy Vary 14 50 13N 12 51 E
Karlsborg 21 58 33N 14 33 E
Karlshamn 21 56 10N 14 51 E
Karlskoga 21 59 22N 14 33 E
Karlskrona 21 56 10N 15 35 E
Karlsruhe 14 49 3N 8 23 E
Karlstad, Sweden 21 59 23N 13 30 E
Karlstad, U.S.A. 70 48 38N 96 30W
Karnal 32 29 42N 77 2 E
Karnali → 33 29 0N 83 20 E
Karnaphuli Res. 33 22 40N 92 20 E
Karnataka □ 32 13 15N 77 0 E
Karnes City 71 28 53N 97 53W
Karnische Alpen 14 46 36N 13 0 E
Kärnten □ 14 46 52N 13 30 E
Karonga 54 9 57S 33 55 E
Karoonda 45 35 1S 139 59 E
Karora 51 17 44N 38 15 E
Kárpathos 19 35 37N 27 10 E
Karpinsk 22 59 45N 60 1 E
Karpogory 22 63 59N 44 27 E
Kars 30 40 40N 43 5 E
Karsakpay 24 47 55N 66 40 E
Karshi 24 38 53N 65 48 E
Karsun 22 54 14N 46 57 E
Kartaly 24 53 3N 60 40 E
Karufa 35 3 50S 133 20 E
Karumba 44 17 31S 140 50 E
Karungu 54 0 50S 34 10 E
Karwar 32 14 55N 74 13 E
Kasai → 54 3 30S 16 10 E
Kasama 54 10 16S 31 9 E
Kasane 56 17 34S 24 50 E
Kasanga 54 8 30S 31 10 E
Kasangulu 54 4 33S 15 15 E
Kasaragod 32 12 30N 74 58 E
Kasba L. 65 60 20N 102 10W
Kasempa 55 13 30S 25 44 E
Kasenga 54 10 20S 28 45 E
Kashabowie 62 48 40N 90 26W
Kāshān 31 34 5N 51 30 E
Kashi 37 39 30N 76 2 E
Kashiwazaki 36 37 22N 138 33 E
Kashk-e Kohneh 31 34 55N 62 30 E
Kāshmar 31 35 16N 58 26 E
Kashmir 32 34 0N 76 0 E
Kashun Noerh = Gaxun Nur 37 42 22N 100 30 E
Kasimov 22 54 55N 41 20 E
Kasiruta 35 0 25S 127 12 E
Kaskaskia → 70 37 58N 89 57W
Kaskattama → 65 57 3N 90 4W
Kaskinen 20 62 22N 21 15 E
Kaskö 20 62 22N 21 15 E
Kaslo 64 49 55N 116 55W
Kasmere L. 65 59 34N 101 10W
Kasongo 54 4 30S 26 33 E
Kasongo Lunda 54 6 35S 16 49 E
Kásos 19 35 20N 26 55 E
Kassala 51 15 30N 36 0 E
Kassalâ □ 51 15 20N 36 26 E
Kassel 14 51 19N 9 32 E
Kassue 35 6 58S 139 21 E
Kastamonu 30 41 25N 33 43 E
Kastellorizon = Megiste 17 36 8N 29 34 E
Kastoría 19 40 30N 21 19 E
Kasulu 54 4 37S 30 5 E
Kasur 32 31 5N 74 25 E
Kata 25 58 46N 102 40 E
Katako Kombe 54 3 25S 24 20 E
Katamatite 45 36 6S 145 41 E
Katangi 32 21 56N 79 50 E
Katangli 25 51 42N 143 14 E
Katha 33 24 10N 96 30 E
Katherine 46 14 27S 132 20 E
Kathiawar 32 22 20N 71 0 E
Katihar 33 25 34N 87 36 E
Katima Mulilo 56 17 28S 24 13 E
Katingan = Mendawai → 34 3 30S 113 0 E
Katiola 50 8 10N 5 10W
Katkopberg 56 30 0S 20 0 E
Katmandu 33 27 45N 85 20 E
Katoomba 45 33 41S 150 19 E
Katowice 15 50 17N 19 5 E
Katrine, L. 8 56 15N 4 30W
Katrineholm 21 59 9N 16 12 E
Katsepe 57 15 45S 46 15 E
Katsina 53 13 0N 7 32 E
Katsuura 36 35 10N 140 20 E
Kattegatt 21 57 0N 11 20 E
Katwe 52 0 8S 29 52 E
Katwijk-aan-Zee 11 52 12N 4 24 E
Kauai 66 22 0N 159 30W
Kauai Chan. 66 21 45N 158 50W
Kaufman 71 32 35N 96 20W
Kaukauna 68 44 20N 88 13W
Kaukauveld 56 20 0S 20 15 E
Kaukonen 20 67 31N 24 53 E
Kauliranta 20 66 27N 23 41 E
Kaunas 22 54 54N 23 54 E
Kaura Namoda 53 12 37N 6 33 E
Kautokeino 20 69 0N 23 4 E
Kavacha 25 60 16N 169 51 E
Kavali 32 14 55N 80 1 E
Kavála 19 40 57N 24 28 E
Kavkaz, Bolshoi 23 42 50N 44 0 E
Kaw 79 4 30N 52 15W
Kawagoe 36 35 55N 139 29 E
Kawaguchi 36 35 52N 139 45 E
Kawaihae 66 20 3N 155 50W
Kawambwa 54 9 48S 29 3 E
Kawardha 33 22 0N 81 17 E
Kawasaki 36 35 35N 139 42 E
Kawene 62 48 45N 91 15W
Kawerau 43 38 7S 176 42 E
Kawhia Harbour 43 38 5S 174 51 E
Kawio, Kepulauan 35 4 30N 125 30 E
Kawnro 33 22 48N 99 8 E
Kawthoolei □ = Kawthule □ 33 18 0N 97 30 E
Kawthule □ 33 18 0N 97 30 E
Kaya 53 13 4N 1 10W
Kayah □ 33 19 15N 97 15 E
Kayan → 34 2 55N 117 35 E
Kaycee 72 43 45N 106 46W
Kayeli 35 3 20S 127 10 E
Kayenta 73 36 46N 110 15W
Kayes 50 14 25N 11 30W
Kayoa 35 0 1N 127 28 E
Kayrunnera 45 30 40S 142 30 E
Kayseri 30 38 45N 35 30 E
Kaysville 72 41 2N 111 58W
Kayuagung 34 3 24S 104 50 E
Kazachinskoye 25 56 16N 107 36 E
Kazachye 25 70 52N 135 58 E
Kazakh S.S.R. □ 23 50 0N 70 0 E
Kazan 22 55 48N 49 3 E
Kazanlúk 19 42 38N 25 20 E
Kāzerūn 31 29 38N 51 40 E
Kazumba 54 6 25S 22 5 E
Kazym → 24 63 54N 65 50 E
Ké-Macina 50 13 58N 5 22W
Kéa 19 37 35N 24 22 E
Keams Canyon 73 35 53N 110 9W
Kearney 70 40 45N 99 3W
Keban 23 38 50N 38 50 E
Kebnekaise 20 67 53N 18 33 E
Kebri Dehar 29 6 45N 44 17 E
Kebumen 35 7 42S 109 40 E
Kechika → 64 59 41N 127 12W
Kecskemét 15 46 57N 19 42 E
Kedgwick 63 47 40N 67 20W
Kedia Hill 56 21 28S 24 37 E
Kediri 35 7 51S 112 1 E
Kédougou 50 12 35N 12 10W
Keeley L. 65 54 54N 108 8W
Keeling Is. = Cocos Is. 3 12 10S 96 55 E
Keene 68 42 57N 72 17W
Keeper Hill 9 52 46N 8 17W
Keer-Weer, C. 44 14 0S 141 32 E
Keetmanshoop 56 26 35S 18 8 E
Keewatin 70 47 23N 93 0W
Keewatin □ 65 63 20N 95 0W
Keewatin → 65 56 29N 100 46W
Kefallinía 19 38 20N 20 30 E
Kefamenanu 35 9 28S 124 29 E
Kefar 'Eqron 28 31 52N 34 49 E
Kefar Ḥasidim 28 32 47N 35 5 E
Kefar Naḥum 28 32 54N 35 34 E
Kefar Sava 28 32 11N 34 54 E
Kefar Szold 28 33 11N 35 39 E
Kefar Vitkin 28 32 22N 34 53 E
Kefar Yehezqel 28 32 34N 35 22 E
Kefar Yona 28 32 20N 34 54 E
Kefar Zekharya 28 31 43N 34 57 E
Kefar Zetim 28 32 48N 35 27 E
Keffi 53 8 55N 7 43 E
Keflavík 20 64 2N 22 35W
Keg River 64 57 54N 117 55W
Kegaska 63 50 9N 61 18W
Keighley 6 53 52N 1 54W
Keimoes 56 28 41S 20 59 E
Keith, Australia 45 36 6S 140 20 E
Keith, U.K. 8 57 33N 2 58W
Keith Arm 60 64 20N 122 15W
Kekri 32 26 0N 75 10 E
Kël 25 69 30N 124 10 E
Kelan 38 38 43N 111 31 E
Kelang 34 3 2N 101 26 E
Kelibia 51 36 50N 11 3 E
Kellé 54 0 8S 14 38 E
Keller 72 48 2N 118 44W
Kellerberrin 47 31 36S 117 38 E
Kellogg 72 47 30N 116 5W
Kelloselkä 20 66 56N 28 53 E
Kells = Ceanannus Mor 9 53 42N 6 53W
Kélo 51 9 10N 15 45 E
Kelowna 64 49 50N 119 25W
Kelsey Bay 64 50 25N 126 0W
Kelso, N.Z. 43 45 54S 169 15 E
Kelso, U.K. 8 55 36N 2 27W
Kelso, U.S.A. 72 46 10N 122 57W
Keluang 34 2 3N 103 18 E
Kelvington 65 52 10N 103 30W
Kem 22 65 0N 34 38 E
Kem → 22 64 57N 34 41 E
Kema 35 1 22N 125 8 E
Kemah 30 39 32N 39 5 E
Kemano 64 53 35N 128 0W
Kemerovo 24 55 20N 86 5 E
Kemi 20 65 44N 24 34 E
Kemi älv = Kemijoki → 20 65 47N 24 32 E
Kemijärvi 20 66 43N 27 22 E
Kemijoki → 20 65 47N 24 32 E
Kemmerer 72 41 52N 110 30W
Kemmuna = Comino 18 36 0N 14 20 E
Kemp L. 71 33 45N 99 15W
Kempsey 45 31 1S 152 50 E
Kempt, L. 62 47 25N 74 22W
Kempten 14 47 42N 10 18 E
Kemptville 62 45 0N 75 38W
Kendal, Indonesia 34 6 56S 110 14 E
Kendal, U.K. 6 54 19N 2 44W
Kendall 45 31 35S 152 44 E
Kendall → 44 14 4S 141 35 E
Kendallville 68 41 25N 85 15W
Kendari 35 3 50S 122 30 E
Kendawangan 34 2 32S 110 17 E
Kende 53 11 30N 4 12 E
Kendenup 47 34 30S 117 38 E
Kendrapara 33 20 35N 86 30 E
Kendrew 56 32 32S 24 30 E
Kendrick 72 46 43N 116 41W
Kenedy 71 28 49N 97 51W
Kenema 50 7 50N 11 14W
Keng Tawng 33 20 45N 98 18 E
Keng Tung 33 21 0N 99 30 E
Kenge 54 4 50S 17 4 E
Kenhardt 56 29 19S 21 12 E
Kenitra 50 34 15N 6 40W
Kenmare, Ireland 9 51 52N 9 35W
Kenmare, U.S.A. 70 48 40N 102 4W
Kenmare → 9 51 40N 10 0W
Kennebec 70 43 56N 99 54W
Kennedy Ra. 47 24 45S 115 10 E
Kennedy Taungdeik 33 23 15N 93 45 E
Kennet → 7 51 24N 0 58W
Kenneth Ra. 47 23 50S 117 8 E
Kennett 71 36 7N 90 0W
Kennewick 72 46 11N 119 2W
Kénogami 63 48 25N 71 15W
Kenogami → 62 51 6N 84 28W
Kenora 65 49 47N 94 29W
Kenosha 68 42 33N 87 48W
Kensington, Canada 63 46 28N 63 34W
Kensington, U.S.A. 70 39 48N 99 2W
Kensington Downs 44 22 31S 144 19 E
Kent, Ohio, U.S.A. 68 41 8N 81 20W
Kent, Oreg., U.S.A. 72 45 11N 120 45W
Kent, Tex., U.S.A. 71 31 5N 104 12W
Kent □ 7 51 12N 0 40 E
Kent Group 44 39 30S 147 20 E
Kent Pen. 60 68 30N 107 0W
Kentau 24 43 32N 68 36 E
Kentland 68 40 45N 87 25W
Kenton 68 40 40N 83 35W
Kentucky □ 68 37 20N 85 0W
Kentucky → 68 38 41N 85 11W
Kentucky L. 69 36 25N 88 0W
Kentville 63 45 6N 64 29W
Kentwood 71 31 0N 90 30W
Kenya ■ 54 1 0N 38 0 E
Kenya, Mt. 54 0 10S 37 18 E
Keokuk 70 40 25N 91 24W
Kepi 35 6 32S 139 19 E
Kepsut 30 39 40N 28 9 E
Kerala □ 32 11 0N 76 15 E
Kerang 45 35 40S 143 55 E
Keraudren, C. 46 19 58S 119 45 E
Kerch 23 45 20N 36 20 E
Kerchoual 50 17 12N 0 20 E
Kerem Maharal 28 32 39N 34 59 E
Keren 51 15 45N 38 28 E
Kerguelen 3 49 15S 69 10 E
Kericho 54 0 22S 35 15 E
Kerinci 34 1 40S 101 15 E
Kerki 24 37 50N 65 12 E
Kérkira 19 39 38N 19 50 E
Kerkrade 11 50 53N 6 4 E
Kermadec Is. 40 30 0S 178 15W
Kermadec Trench 40 30 30S 176 0W
Kermān 31 30 15N 57 1 E
Kermān □ 31 30 0N 57 0 E
Kermānshāh = Bākhtarān 30 34 23N 47 0 E
Kermit 71 31 56N 103 3W
Kern → 73 35 16N 119 18W
Kerrobert 65 51 56N 109 8W
Kerrville 71 30 1N 99 8W
Kerry □ 9 52 7N 9 35W
Kerry Hd. 9 52 26N 9 56W
Kertosono 35 7 38S 112 9 E
Kerulen → 37 48 48N 117 0 E
Kerzaz 50 29 29N 1 37W
Kesagami → 62 51 40N 79 45W
Kesagami L. 62 50 23N 80 15W
Keski-Suomen lääni □ 20 62 0N 25 30 E
Kestell 57 28 17S 28 42 E
Kestenga 22 66 0N 31 50 E
Keswick 6 54 35N 3 9W
Ket → 24 58 55N 81 32 E
Keta 53 5 49N 1 0 E
Ketapang 34 1 55S 110 0 E
Ketchikan 60 55 25N 131 40W
Ketchum 72 43 41N 114 27W
Kettering 7 52 24N 0 44W
Kettle → 65 56 40N 89 34W
Kettle Falls 72 48 41N 118 2W
Kevin 72 48 45N 111 58W
Kewanee 70 41 18N 89 55W
Kewaunee 68 44 27N 87 30W
Keweenaw B. 68 46 56N 88 23W
Keweenaw Pen. 68 47 30N 88 0W
Keweenaw Pt. 68 47 26N 87 40W
Key Harbour 62 45 50N 80 45W
Key West 75 24 33N 82 0W
Keyser 68 39 26N 79 0W
Keystone 70 43 54N 103 27W
Kezhma 25 58 59N 101 9 E
Khabarovo 24 69 30N 60 30 E
Khabarovsk 25 48 30N 135 5 E
Khābūr → 30 35 0N 40 30 E
Khairpur 32 27 32N 68 49 E
Khakhea 56 24 48S 23 22 E
Khalkhāl 30 37 37N 48 32 E
Khalkís 19 38 27N 23 42 E
Khalmer-Sede = Tazovskiy 24 67 30N 78 44 E
Khalmer Yu 22 67 58N 65 1 E

Lafia

Kong 50 8 54N 4 36W
Kong, Koh 34 11 20N 103 0 E
Kongju 38 36 30N 127 0 E
Konglu 33 27 13N 97 57 E
Kongolo 54 5 22S 27 0 E
Kongor 51 7 1N 31 27 E
Kongsberg 21 59 39N 9 39 E
Kongsvinger 21 60 12N 12 2 E
Königsberg = Kaliningrad 22 54 42N 20 32 E
Konin 15 52 12N 18 15 E
Konjic 19 43 42N 17 58 E
Konkiep 56 26 49S 17 15 E
Konosha 22 61 0N 40 5 E
Konotop 23 51 12N 33 7 E
Konqi He → 37 40 45N 90 10 E
Końskie 15 51 15N 20 23 E
Konstanz 14 47 39N 9 10 E
Kontagora 53 10 23N 5 27 E
Kontum 34 14 24N 108 0 E
Konya 30 37 52N 32 35 E
Konya Ovasi 30 38 30N 33 0 E
Konza 54 1 45S 37 7 E
Kookynie 47 29 17S 121 22 E
Kooline 46 22 57S 116 20 E
Kooloonong 45 34 48S 143 10 E
Koolyanobbing 47 30 48S 119 36 E
Koondrook 45 35 33S 144 8 E
Koorawatha 45 34 2S 148 33 E
Koorda 47 30 48S 117 35 E
Kooskia 72 46 9N 115 59W
Kootenai → 72 49 15N 117 39W
Kootenay L. 64 49 45N 116 50W
Kootenay Nat. Park 64 51 0N 116 0W
Kootjieskolk 56 31 15S 20 21 E
Kopaonik Planina 19 43 10N 21 50 E
Kópavogur 20 64 6N 21 55W
Koper 18 45 31N 13 44 E
Kopervik 21 59 17N 5 17 E
Kopeysk 24 55 7N 61 37 E
Kopi 45 33 24S 135 40 E
Köping 21 59 31N 16 3 E
Kopparberg 21 59 52N 15 0 E
Kopparbergs län □ 21 61 20N 14 15 E
Koppeh Dāgh 31 38 0N 58 0 E
Koppies 57 27 20S 27 30 E
Korab 19 41 44N 20 40 E
Korça 19 40 37N 20 50 E
Korce = Korça 19 40 37N 20 50 E
Korčula 18 42 57N 17 8 E
Kordestan 30 35 30N 42 0 E
Kordestān □ 30 36 0N 47 0 E
Korea, North ■ 38 40 0N 127 0 E
Korea, South ■ 38 36 0N 128 0 E
Korea Bay 38 39 0N 124 0 E
Korea Strait 39 34 0N 129 30 E
Koreh Wells 52 0 3N 38 45 E
Korhogo 50 9 29N 5 28W
Korim 35 0 58S 136 10 E
Korinthiakós Kólpos 19 38 16N 22 30 E
Kórinthos 19 37 56N 22 55 E
Kōriyama 36 37 24N 140 23 E
Koro, Fiji 43 17 19S 179 23 E
Koro, Ivory C. 50 8 32N 7 30W
Koro, Mali 50 14 1N 2 58W
Koro Sea 43 17 30S 179 45W
Korogwe 54 5 5S 38 25 E
Koroit 45 38 18S 142 24 E
Körös → 15 46 43N 20 12 E
Korraraika, Helodranon' i 57 17 45S 43 57 E
Korsakov 25 46 36N 142 42 E
Korshunovo 25 58 37N 110 10 E
Korsör 21 55 20N 11 9 E
Korti 51 18 6N 31 33 E
Kortrijk 11 50 50N 3 17 E
Koryakskiy Khrebet 25 61 0N 171 0 E
Kos 19 36 50N 27 15 E
Koschagyl 23 46 40N 54 0 E
Kościan 14 52 5N 16 40 E
Kosciusko 71 33 3N 89 34W
Kosciusko, Mt. 45 36 27S 148 16 E
Kosciusko I. 64 56 0N 133 40W
Kosha 51 20 50N 30 30 E
K'oshih = Kashi 37 39 30N 76 2 E
Kosi-meer 57 27 0S 32 50 E
Košice 15 48 42N 21 15 E
Koslan 22 63 28N 48 52 E
Kosŏng 38 38 40N 128 22 E
Kosovska-Mitrovica 19 42 54N 20 52 E
Kostamuksa 22 62 34N 32 44 E
Koster 56 25 52S 26 54 E
Kôstî 51 13 8N 32 43 E
Kostroma 22 57 50N 40 58 E
Koszalin 14 54 11N 16 8 E
Kota 32 25 14N 75 49 E
Kota Baharu 34 6 7N 102 14 E
Kota Belud 34 6 21N 116 26 E
Kota Kinabalu 34 6 0N 116 4 E
Kota Tinggi 34 1 44N 103 53 E
Kotaagung 34 5 38S 104 29 E
Kotabaru 34 3 20S 116 20 E
Kotabumi 34 4 49S 104 54 E
Kotagede 35 7 54S 110 26 E
Kotamobagu 35 0 57N 124 31 E
Kotaneelee → 64 60 11N 123 42W
Kotawaringin 34 2 28S 111 27 E
Kotcho L. 64 59 7N 121 12W
Kotelnich 22 58 20N 48 10 E
Kotelnyy, Ostrov 25 75 10N 139 0 E
Kotka 21 60 28N 26 58 E
Kotlas 22 61 15N 47 0 E
Kotli 32 33 30N 73 55 E
Kotor 19 42 25N 18 47 E
Kotri 32 25 22N 68 22 E
Kottayam 32 9 35N 76 33 E
Kotturu 32 14 45N 76 10 E
Kotuy → 25 71 54N 102 6 E
Kotzebue 60 66 50N 162 40W
Kouango 54 5 0N 20 10 E
Koudougou 50 12 10N 2 20W
Kougaberge 56 33 48S 23 50 E
Kouilou → 54 4 10S 12 5 E
Kouki 54 7 22N 17 3 E
Koula Moutou 54 1 15S 12 25 E
Koulen 34 13 50N 104 40 E
Koulikoro 50 12 40N 7 50W
Koumala 44 21 38S 149 15 E
Koumra 51 8 50N 17 35 E
Kounradskiy 24 46 59N 75 0 E
Kountze 71 30 20N 94 22W
Kouroussa 50 10 45N 9 45W
Kousseri 51 12 0N 14 55 E
Koutiala 50 12 25N 5 23W
Kovdor 22 67 34N 30 24 E
Kovel 22 51 10N 24 20 E
Kovrov 22 56 25N 41 25 E
Kowkash 62 50 20N 87 12W
Kowloon 39 22 20N 114 15 E
Koyabuti 35 2 36S 140 37 E
Koyuk 60 64 55N 161 20W
Koyukuk → 60 64 56N 157 30W
Kozan 30 37 35N 35 50 E
Kozáni 19 40 19N 21 47 E
Kozhikode = Calicut 32 11 15N 75 43 E
Kozhva 22 65 10N 57 0 E
Kpalimé 53 6 57N 0 44 E
Kra, Isthmus of = Kra, Kho Khot 34 10 15N 99 30 E
Kra, Kho Khot 34 10 15N 99 30 E
Kragan 35 6 43S 111 38 E
Kragerø 21 58 52N 9 25 E
Kragujevac 19 44 2N 20 56 E
Krakatau = Rakata, Pulau 34 6 10S 105 20 E
Kraków 15 50 4N 19 57 E
Kraksaan 35 7 43S 113 23 E
Kraljevo 19 43 44N 20 41 E
Kramatorsk 23 48 50N 37 30 E
Kramfors 20 62 55N 17 48 E
Krankskop 57 28 0S 30 47 E
Krasavino 22 60 58N 46 29 E
Kraskino 25 42 44N 130 48 E
Kraśnik 15 50 55N 22 5 E
Krasnodar 23 45 5N 39 0 E
Krasnokamsk 22 58 4N 55 48 E
Krasnoselkupsk 24 65 20N 82 10 E
Krasnoturinsk 22 59 46N 60 12 E
Krasnoufimsk 22 56 57N 57 46 E
Krasnouralsk 22 58 21N 60 3 E
Krasnovishersk 22 60 23N 57 3 E
Krasnovodsk 23 40 0N 52 52 E
Krasnoyarsk 25 56 8N 93 0 E
Krasnyy Luch 23 48 13N 39 0 E
Krasnyy Yar 23 46 43N 48 23 E
Kratie 34 12 32N 106 10 E
Krau 35 3 19S 140 5 E
Krawang 35 6 19S 107 18 E
Krefeld 14 51 20N 6 32 E
Kremenchug 23 49 5N 33 25 E
Kremenchugskoye Vdkhr. 23 49 20N 32 30 E
Kremmling 72 40 10N 106 30W
Kremnica 15 48 45N 18 50 E
Kribi 54 2 57N 9 56 E
Krishna → 33 15 57N 80 59 E
Krishnanagar 33 23 24N 88 33 E
Kristiansand 21 58 9N 8 1 E
Kristianstad 21 56 2N 14 9 E
Kristianstads län □ 21 56 15N 14 0 E
Kristiansund 20 63 7N 7 45 E
Kristiinankaupunki 20 62 16N 21 21 E
Kristinehamn 21 59 18N 14 13 E
Kristinestad 20 62 16N 21 21 E
Kríti 19 35 15N 25 0 E
Krivoy Rog 23 47 51N 33 20 E
Krk 18 45 8N 14 40 E
Krokodil → 57 25 14S 32 18 E
Kronobergs län □ 21 56 45N 14 30 E
Kronshtadt 22 60 5N 29 45 E
Kroonstad 56 27 43S 27 19 E
Kropotkin, R.S.F.S.R., U.S.S.R. 23 45 28N 40 28 E
Kropotkin, R.S.F.S.R., U.S.S.R. 25 59 0N 115 30 E
Krosno 15 49 42N 21 46 E
Krotoszyn 15 51 42N 17 23 E
Kruger Nat. Park 57 23 30S 31 40 E
Krugersdorp 57 26 5S 27 46 E
Kruisfontein 56 33 59S 24 43 E
Krung Thep = Bangkok 34 13 45N 100 35 E
Kruševac 19 43 35N 21 28 E
Kruzof I. 64 57 10N 135 40W
Krymskiy Poluostrov 23 45 0N 34 0 E
Ksar el Boukhari 50 35 51N 2 52 E
Ksar el Kebir 50 35 0N 6 0W
Ksar es Souk = Ar Rachidiya 50 31 58N 4 20W
Kuala 34 2 55N 105 47 E
Kuala Kubu Baharu 34 3 34N 101 39 E
Kuala Lipis 34 4 10N 102 3 E
Kuala Lumpur 34 3 9N 101 41 E
Kuala Trengganu 34 5 20N 103 8 E
Kualajelai 34 2 58S 110 46 E
Kualakapuas 34 2 55S 114 20 E
Kualakurun 34 1 10S 113 50 E
Kualapembuang 34 3 14S 112 38 E
Kualasimpang 34 4 17N 98 3 E
Kuandang 35 0 56N 123 1 E
Kuandian 38 40 45N 124 45 E
Kuangchou = Guangzhou 39 23 5N 113 10 E
Kuantan 34 3 49N 103 20 E
Kuba 23 41 21N 48 32 E
Kubak 31 27 10N 63 10 E
Kuban → 23 45 20N 37 30 E
Kucing 34 1 33N 110 25 E
Kuda 32 23 10N 71 15 E
Kudat 34 6 55N 116 55 E
Kudus 35 6 48S 110 51 E
Kudymkar 24 59 1N 54 39 E
Kueiyang = Guiyang 39 26 32N 106 40 E
Kufrinjah 28 32 20N 35 41 E
Kufstein 14 47 35N 12 11 E
Kugong I. 62 56 18N 79 50W
Kūh-e 'Alījūq 31 31 30N 51 41 E
Kūh-e Dīnār 31 30 40N 51 0 E
Kūh-e-Hazārām 31 29 35N 57 20 E
Kūh-e-Jebāl Bārez 31 29 0N 58 0 E
Kūh-e Sorkh 31 35 30N 58 45 E
Kūh-e Taftān 31 28 40N 61 0 E
Kūhak 31 27 12N 63 10 E
Kūhhā-ye-Bashākerd 31 26 45N 59 0 E
Kūhhā-ye Sabalān 30 38 15N 47 45 E
Kūhpāyeh 31 32 44N 52 20 E
Kuile He → 38 49 32N 124 42 E
Kuito 55 12 22S 16 55 E
Kuji 36 40 11N 141 46 E
Kukawa 51 12 58N 13 27 E
Kukerin 47 33 13S 118 0 E
Kulasekarappattinam 32 8 20N 78 0 E
Kuldja = Yining 37 43 58N 81 10 E
Kulin 47 32 40S 118 2 E
Kulja 47 30 28S 117 18 E
Kulm 70 46 22N 98 58W
Kulsary 23 46 59N 54 1 E
Kulumbura 46 13 55S 126 35 E
Kulunda 24 52 35N 78 57 E
Kulwin 45 35 0S 142 42 E
Kulyab 24 37 55N 69 50 E
Kum Tekei 24 43 10N 79 30 E
Kuma → 23 44 55N 47 0 E
Kumaganum 53 13 8N 10 38 E
Kumagaya 36 36 9N 139 22 E
Kumai 34 2 44S 111 43 E
Kumamba, Kepulauan 35 1 36S 138 45 E
Kumamoto 36 32 45N 130 45 E
Kumamoto □ 36 32 55N 130 55 E
Kumanovo 19 42 9N 21 42 E
Kumara 43 42 37S 171 12 E
Kumarl 47 32 47S 121 33 E
Kumasi 50 6 41N 1 38W
Kumba 54 4 36N 9 24 E
Kumbarilla 45 27 15S 150 55 E
Kumertau 22 52 46N 55 47 E
Kumla 21 59 8N 15 10 E
Kumo 53 10 1N 11 12 E
Kumon Bum 33 26 30N 97 15 E
Kunama 45 35 35S 148 4 E
Kunashir, Ostrov 25 44 0N 146 0 E
Kundip 47 33 42S 120 10 E
Kungala 45 29 58S 153 7 E
Kunghit I. 64 52 6N 131 3W
Kungrad 24 43 6N 58 54 E
Kungsbacka 21 57 30N 12 5 E
Kungur 22 57 25N 56 57 E
Kungurri 44 21 3S 148 46 E
Kuningan 35 6 59S 108 29 E
Kunlong 33 23 20N 98 50 E
Kunlun Shan 33 36 0N 86 30 E
Kunming 37 25 1N 102 41 E
Kunsan 38 35 59N 126 45 E
Kunshan 39 31 22N 120 58 E
Kununurra 46 15 40S 128 50 E
Kunwarara 44 22 55S 150 9 E
Kunya-Urgench 24 42 19N 59 10 E
Kuopio 20 62 53N 27 35 E
Kuopion lääni □ 20 63 25N 27 10 E
Kupa → 18 45 28N 16 24 E
Kupang 35 10 19S 123 39 E
Kuqa 37 41 35N 82 30 E
Kura → 23 39 50N 49 20 E
Kuranda 44 16 48S 145 35 E
Kurashiki 36 34 40N 133 50 E
Kurayoshi 36 35 26N 133 50 E
Kure 36 34 14N 132 32 E
Kurgaldzhino 24 50 35N 70 20 E
Kurgan 24 55 26N 65 18 E
Kuria Maria Is. = Khūrīyā Mūrīyā, Jazā 'ir 29 17 30N 55 58 E
Kuridala 44 21 16S 140 29 E
Kurigram 33 25 49N 89 39 E
Kuril Is. = Kurilskiye Ostrova 25 45 0N 150 0 E
Kuril Trench 40 44 0N 153 0 E
Kurilsk 25 45 14N 147 53 E
Kurilskiye Ostrova 25 45 0N 150 0 E
Kurmuk 51 10 33N 34 21 E
Kurnool 32 15 45N 78 0 E
Kurow 43 44 44S 170 29 E
Kurrajong 45 33 33S 150 42 E
Kurri Kurri 45 32 50S 151 28 E
Kursk 22 51 42N 36 11 E
Kuršumlija 19 43 9N 21 19 E
Kuruktag 37 41 0N 89 0 E
Kuruman 56 27 28S 23 28 E
Kuruman → 56 26 56S 20 39 E
Kurume 36 33 15N 130 30 E
Kurunegala 32 7 30N 80 23 E
Kurya 25 61 15N 108 10 E
Kusawa L. 64 60 20N 136 13W
Kushiro 36 43 0N 144 25 E
Kushiro → 36 42 59N 144 23 E
Kushka 24 35 20N 62 18 E
Kushtia 33 23 55N 89 5 E
Kushva 22 58 18N 59 45 E
Kuskokwim → 60 60 17N 162 27W
Kuskokwim Bay 60 59 50N 162 56W
Kussharo-Ko 36 43 38N 144 21 E
Kustanay 24 53 10N 63 35 E
Kütahya 30 39 30N 30 2 E
Kutaisi 23 42 19N 42 40 E
Kutaraja = Banda Aceh 34 5 35N 95 20 E
Kutch, Gulf of = Kachchh, Gulf of 32 22 50N 69 15 E
Kutch, Rann of = Kachchh, Rann of 32 24 0N 70 0 E
Kutno 15 52 15N 19 23 E
Kuttabul 44 21 5S 148 48 E
Kutu 54 2 40S 18 11 E
Kutum 51 14 10N 24 40 E
Kuujjuaq 61 58 6N 68 15W
Kuwait = Al Kuwayt 30 29 30N 48 0 E
Kuwait ■ 30 29 30N 47 30 E
Kuwana 36 35 0N 136 43 E
Kuybyshev, R.S.F.S.R., U.S.S.R. 22 53 8N 50 6 E
Kuybyshev, R.S.F.S.R., U.S.S.R. 24 55 27N 78 19 E
Kuybyshevskoye Vdkhr. 22 55 2N 49 30 E
Kūysanjaq 30 36 5N 44 38 E
Kuyto, Oz. 22 64 40N 31 0 E
Kuyumba 25 60 58N 96 59 E
Kuzey Anadolu Dağlari 30 41 30N 35 0 E
Kuznetsk 22 53 12N 46 40 E
Kuzomen 22 66 22N 36 50 E
Kvænangen 20 70 5N 21 15 E
Kvarner 18 44 50N 14 10 E
Kvarnerič 18 44 43N 14 37 E
Kwabhaca 57 30 51S 29 0 E
Kwadacha → 64 57 28N 125 38W
Kwakhanai 56 21 39S 21 16 E
Kwakoegron 79 5 12N 55 25W
KwaMashu 57 29 45S 30 58 E
Kwamouth 54 3 9S 16 12 E
Kwando → 56 18 27S 23 32 E
Kwangju 38 35 9N 126 54 E
Kwangsi-Chuang = Guangxi Zhuangzu Zizhiqu □ 39 24 0N 109 0 E
Kwangtung = Guangdong □ 39 23 0N 113 0 E
Kwara □ 53 8 0N 5 0 E
Kwataboahegan → 62 51 9N 80 50W
Kwatisore 35 3 18S 134 50 E
Kweichow = Guizhou □ 39 27 0N 107 0 E
Kwekwe 55 18 58S 29 48 E
Kwiguk 60 63 45N 164 35W
Kwinana New Town 47 32 15S 115 47 E
Kwoka 35 0 31S 132 27 E
Kyabé 51 9 30N 19 0 E
Kyabra Cr. → 45 25 36S 142 55 E
Kyabram 45 36 19S 145 4 E
Kyakhta 25 50 30N 106 25 E
Kyangin 33 18 20N 95 20 E
Kyaukpadaung 33 20 52N 95 8 E
Kyaukpyu 33 19 28N 93 30 E
Kyaukse 33 21 36N 96 10 E
Kyle Dam 55 20 15S 31 0 E
Kyle of Lochalsh 8 57 17N 5 43W
Kyneton 45 37 10S 144 29 E
Kynuna 44 21 37S 141 55 E
Kyō-ga-Saki 36 35 45N 135 15 E
Kyoga, L. 54 1 35N 33 0 E
Kyogle 45 28 40S 153 0 E
Kyongju 38 35 51N 129 14 E
Kyongpyaw 33 17 12N 95 10 E
Kyōto 36 35 0N 135 45 E
Kyōto □ 36 35 15N 135 45 E
Kyren 25 51 45N 101 45 E
Kyrenia 30 35 20N 33 20 E
Kystatyam 25 67 20N 123 10 E
Kytal Ktakh 25 65 30N 123 40 E
Kyulyunken 25 64 10N 137 5 E
Kyunhla 33 23 25N 95 15 E
Kyuquot 64 50 3N 127 25W
Kyūshū 36 33 0N 131 0 E
Kyūshū-Sanchi 36 32 35N 131 17 E
Kyustendil 19 42 16N 22 41 E
Kyusyur 25 70 39N 127 15 E
Kywong 45 34 58S 146 44 E
Kyzyl 25 51 50N 94 30 E
Kyzyl-Kiya 24 40 16N 72 8 E
Kyzylkum, Peski 24 42 30N 65 0 E
Kzyl-Orda 24 44 48N 65 28 E

L

Labak 35 6 32N 124 5 E
Labe = Elbe → 14 53 50N 9 0 E
Labé 50 11 24N 12 16W
Laberge, L. 64 61 11N 135 12W
Labis 34 2 22N 103 2 E
Laboulaye 80 34 10S 63 30W
Labrador, Coast of □ 63 53 20N 61 0W
Labrador City 63 52 57N 66 55W
Lábrea 78 7 15S 64 51W
Labuan, Pulau 34 5 21N 115 13 E
Labuha 35 0 30S 127 30 E
Labuhan 35 6 22S 105 50 E
Labuhanbajo 35 8 28S 120 1 E
Labuk, Telok 34 6 10N 117 50 E
Labytnangi 22 66 39N 66 21 E
Lac Allard 63 50 33N 63 24W
Lac Bouchette 63 48 16N 72 11W
Lac du Flambeau 70 46 1N 89 51W
Lac Édouard 62 47 40N 72 16W
Lac La Biche 64 54 45N 111 58W
Lac la Martre 60 63 8N 117 16W
Lac-Mégantic 63 45 35N 70 53W
Lac Seul, Res. 62 50 25N 92 30W
Lacantúm → 74 16 36N 90 40W
Laccadive Is. = Lakshadweep Is. 3 10 0N 72 30 E
Lacepede B. 45 36 40S 139 40 E
Lacepede Is. 46 16 55S 122 0 E
Lachine 62 45 30N 73 40W
Lachlan → 45 34 22S 143 55 E
Lachute 62 45 39N 74 21W
Lackawanna 68 42 49N 78 50W
Lacombe 64 52 30N 113 44W
Laconia 68 43 32N 71 30W
Lacrosse 72 46 51N 117 58W
Ladakh Ra. 32 34 0N 78 0 E
Ladismith 56 33 28S 21 15 E
Lādīz 31 28 55N 61 15 E
Ladoga, L. = Ladozhskoye Ozero 22 61 15N 30 30 E
Ladozhskoye Ozero 22 61 15N 30 30 E
Lady Grey 56 30 43S 27 13 E
Ladybrand 56 29 9S 27 29 E
Ladysmith, Canada 64 49 0N 123 49W
Ladysmith, S. Africa 57 28 32S 29 46 E
Ladysmith, U.S.A. 70 45 27N 91 4W
Lae 40 6 40S 147 2 E
Læsø 21 57 15N 10 53 E
Lafayette, Colo., U.S.A. 70 40 0N 105 2W
Lafayette, Ga., U.S.A. 69 34 44N 85 15W
Lafayette, Ind., U.S.A. 68 40 22N 86 52W
Lafayette, La., U.S.A. 71 30 18N 92 0W
Lafayette, Tenn., U.S.A. 69 36 35N 86 0W
Laferte → 64 61 53N 117 44W
Lafia 53 8 30N 8 34 E

Longxi

Lévis 63 46 48N 71 9W
Levis, L. 64 62 37N 117 58W
Levkás 19 38 40N 20 43 E
Levkôsia = Nicosia 30 35 10N 33 25 E
Lewellen 70 41 22N 102 5W
Lewes, U.K. 7 50 53N 0 2 E
Lewes, U.S.A. 68 38 45N 75 8W
Lewis 8 58 10N 6 40W
Lewis, Butt of 8 58 30N 6 12W
Lewis Ra., Australia 46 20 3S 128 50 E
Lewis Ra., U.S.A. 72 48 0N 113 15W
Lewisburg 69 35 29N 86 46W
Lewisporte 63 49 15N 55 3W
Lewiston 72 46 25N 117 0W
Lewistown, Mont., U.S.A. 72 47 0N 109 25W
Lewistown, Pa., U.S.A. 68 40 37N 77 33W
Lexington, Ill., U.S.A. 70 40 37N 88 47W
Lexington, Ky., U.S.A. 68 38 6N 84 30W
Lexington, Miss., U.S.A. 71 33 8N 90 2W
Lexington, Mo., U.S.A. 70 39 7N 93 55W
Lexington, N.C., U.S.A. 69 35 50N 80 13W
Lexington, Nebr., U.S.A. 70 40 48N 99 45W
Lexington, Oreg., U.S.A. 72 45 29N 119 46W
Lexington, Tenn., U.S.A. 69 35 38N 88 25W
Lexington Park 68 38 16N 76 27W
Leyte 35 11 0N 125 0 E
Lhasa 37 29 25N 90 58 E
Lhazê 37 29 5N 87 38 E
Lhokkruet 34 4 55N 95 24 E
Lhokseumawe 34 5 10N 97 10 E
Lhuntsi Dzong 33 27 39N 91 10 E
Li Shui → 39 29 24N 112 1 E
Li Xian, Gansu, China 39 34 10N 105 5 E
Li Xian, Hunan, China 39 29 36N 111 42 E
Lianga 35 8 38N 126 6 E
Liangdang 39 33 56N 106 18 E
Lianhua 39 27 3N 113 54 E
Lianjiang 39 26 12N 119 27 E
Lianping 39 24 26N 114 30 E
Lianshanguan 38 40 53N 123 43 E
Lianyungang 39 34 40N 119 11 E
Liao He → 38 41 0N 121 50 E
Liaocheng 38 36 28N 115 58 E
Liaodong Bandao 38 40 0N 122 30 E
Liaodong Wan 38 40 20N 121 10 E
Liaoning □ 38 42 0N 122 0 E
Liaoyang 38 41 15N 122 58 E
Liaoyuan 38 42 58N 125 2 E
Liaozhong 38 41 23N 122 50 E
Liard → 64 61 51N 121 18W
Libau = Liepaja 22 56 30N 21 0 E
Libby 72 48 20N 115 33W
Libenge 54 3 40N 18 55 E
Liberal, Kans., U.S.A. 71 37 4N 101 0W
Liberal, Mo., U.S.A. 71 37 35N 94 30W
Liberec 14 50 47N 15 7 E
Liberia 75 10 40N 85 30W
Liberia ■ 50 6 30N 9 30W
Libertad, La 74 29 55N 112 41W
Liberty, Mo., U.S.A. 70 39 15N 94 24W
Liberty, Tex., U.S.A. 71 30 5N 94 50W
Libo 39 25 22N 107 53 E
Libobo, Tanjung 35 0 54S 128 28 E
Libode 57 31 33S 29 2 E
Libonda 55 14 28S 23 12 E
Libourne 12 44 55N 0 14W
Libramont 11 49 55N 5 23 E
Libreville 54 0 25N 9 26 E
Libya ■ 51 27 0N 17 0 E
Libyan Desert 48 25 0N 25 0 E
Licantén 80 35 55S 72 0W
Licata 18 37 6N 13 55 E
Lichfield 6 52 40N 1 50W
Lichtenburg 56 26 8S 26 8 E
Lichuan 39 30 18N 108 57 E
Lida 73 37 30N 117 30W
Lidköping 21 58 31N 13 14 E
Liechtenstein ■ 14 47 8N 9 35 E
Liège 11 50 38N 5 35 E
Liège □ 11 50 32N 5 35 E
Liegnitz = Legnica 14 51 12N 16 10 E
Lienyünchiangshih = Lianyungang 39 34 40N 119 11 E
Lienz 14 46 50N 12 46 E
Liepaja 22 56 30N 21 0 E
Lier 11 51 7N 4 34 E
Lièvre → 62 45 31N 75 26W
Liffey → 9 53 21N 6 20W
Lifford 9 54 50N 7 30W
Lightning Ridge 45 29 22S 148 0 E
Liguria □ 18 44 30N 9 0 E
Ligurian Sea 18 43 20N 9 0 E
Lihou Reefs and Cays 44 17 25S 151 40 E
Lihue 66 21 59N 159 24W
Lijiang 37 26 55N 100 20 E
Likasi 54 10 55S 26 48 E
Likati 54 3 20N 24 0 E
Liling 39 27 42N 113 29 E
Lille 12 50 38N 3 3 E
Lille Bælt 21 55 20N 9 45 E
Lillehammer 21 61 8N 10 30 E
Lillesand 21 58 15N 8 23 E
Lilleshall 7 52 45N 2 22W
Lillestrøm 21 59 58N 11 5 E
Lillian Point, Mt. 47 27 40S 126 6 E
Lillooet → 64 49 15N 121 57W
Lilongwe 55 14 0S 33 48 E
Liloy 35 8 4N 122 39 E
Lima, Indonesia 35 3 37S 128 4 E
Lima, Peru 78 12 0S 77 0W
Lima, Mont., U.S.A. 72 44 41N 112 38W
Lima, Ohio, U.S.A. 68 40 42N 84 5W
Limassol 30 34 42N 33 1 E
Limavady 9 55 3N 6 58W
Limavady □ 9 55 0N 6 55W
Limay → 80 39 0S 68 0W
Limay Mahuida 80 37 10S 66 45W
Limbang 34 4 42N 115 6 E
Limbe 54 4 1N 9 10 E
Limbri 45 31 3S 151 5 E
Limbunya 46 17 14S 129 50 E
Limburg □, Belgium 11 51 2N 5 25 E
Limburg □, Neth. 11 51 20N 5 55 E
Limeira 80 22 35S 47 28W
Limerick 9 52 40N 8 38W
Limerick □ 9 52 30N 8 50W
Limestone → 65 56 31N 94 7W
Limfjorden 21 56 55N 9 0 E
Limia → 13 41 41N 8 50W
Limmen Bight 44 14 40S 135 35 E
Limmen Bight → 44 15 7S 135 44 E
Límnos 19 39 50N 25 5 E
Limoeiro do Norte 79 5 5S 38 0W
Limoges 12 45 50N 1 15 E
Limón, C. Rica 75 10 0N 83 2W
Limon, Panama 74 9 17N 79 45W
Limon, U.S.A. 70 39 18N 103 38W
Limon B. 74 9 22N 79 56W
Limousin 12 45 30N 1 30 E
Limpopo → 57 25 5S 33 30 E
Limuru 54 1 2S 36 35 E
Linares, Chile 80 35 50S 71 40W
Linares, Mexico 74 24 50N 99 40W
Linares, Spain 13 38 10N 3 40W
Lincheng 38 37 25N 114 30 E
Linchuan 39 27 57N 116 15 E
Lincoln, Argentina 80 34 55S 61 30W
Lincoln, N.Z. 43 43 38S 172 30 E
Lincoln, U.K. 6 53 14N 0 32W
Lincoln, Ill., U.S.A. 70 40 10N 89 20W
Lincoln, Kans., U.S.A. 70 39 6N 98 9W
Lincoln, Maine, U.S.A. 63 45 27N 68 29W
Lincoln, N. Mex., U.S.A. 73 33 30N 105 26W
Lincoln, Nebr., U.S.A. 70 40 50N 96 42W
Lincoln □ 6 53 14N 0 32W
Lincoln Wolds 6 53 20N 0 5W
Lincolnton 69 35 30N 81 15W
Lind 72 47 0N 118 33W
Linden, Guyana 78 6 0N 58 10W
Linden, U.S.A. 71 33 0N 94 20W
Lindi 54 9 58S 39 38 E
Lindian 38 47 11N 124 52 E
Lindsay, Canada 62 44 22N 78 43W
Lindsay, Calif., U.S.A. 73 36 14N 119 6W
Lindsay, Okla., U.S.A. 71 34 51N 97 37W
Lindsborg 70 38 35N 97 40W
Línea de la Concepción, La 13 36 15N 5 23W
Linfen 38 36 3N 111 30 E
Ling Xian 38 37 22N 116 30 E
Lingao 39 19 56N 109 42 E
Lingayen 35 16 1N 120 14 E
Lingayen G. 35 16 10N 120 15 E
Lingchuan 39 25 26N 110 21 E
Lingen 14 52 32N 7 21 E
Lingga 34 0 12S 104 37 E
Lingga, Kepulauan 34 0 10S 104 30 E
Lingle 70 42 10N 104 18W
Lingling 39 26 17N 111 37 E
Lingshan 39 22 25N 109 18 E
Lingshi 38 36 48N 111 48 E
Lingshui 39 18 27N 110 0 E
Lingtai 39 35 0N 107 40 E
Linguéré 50 15 25N 15 5W
Lingyuan 38 41 10N 119 15 E
Lingyun 39 25 2N 106 35 E
Linhai 39 28 50N 121 8 E
Linhares 79 19 25S 40 4W
Linhe 38 40 48N 107 20 E
Linjiang 38 41 50N 127 0 E
Linköping 21 58 28N 15 36 E
Linkou 38 45 15N 130 18 E
Linlithgow 8 55 58N 3 38W
Linnhe, L. 8 56 36N 5 25W
Linqing 38 36 50N 115 42 E
Lins 80 21 40S 49 44W
Lintao 38 35 18N 103 52 E
Lintlaw 65 52 4N 103 14W
Linton, Canada 63 47 15N 72 16W
Linton, Ind., U.S.A. 68 39 0N 87 10W
Linton, N. Dak., U.S.A. 70 46 21N 100 12W
Linville 45 26 50S 152 11 E
Linwu 39 25 19N 112 31 E
Linxi 38 43 36N 118 2 E
Linxia 37 35 36N 103 10 E
Linyanti → 56 17 50S 25 5 E
Linyi 39 35 5N 118 21 E
Linz 14 48 18N 14 18 E
Lion, G. du 12 43 0N 4 0 E
Lion's Head 62 44 58N 81 15W
Lipa 35 13 57N 121 10 E
Lípari, Is. 18 38 30N 14 50 E
Lipetsk 22 52 37N 39 35 E
Liping 39 26 15N 109 7 E
Lippe → 14 51 39N 6 38 E
Lipscomb 71 36 16N 100 16W
Liptrap C. 45 38 50S 145 55 E
Lira 54 2 17N 32 57 E
Liria 13 39 37N 0 35W
Lisala 54 2 12N 21 38 E
Lisboa 13 38 42N 9 10W
Lisbon = Lisboa 13 38 42N 9 10W
Lisbon 70 46 30N 97 46W
Lisburn 9 54 30N 6 9W
Lisburne, C. 60 68 50N 166 0W
Liscannor, B. 9 52 57N 9 24W
Lishi 38 37 31N 111 8 E
Lishui 39 28 28N 119 54 E
Lisianski I. 40 26 2N 174 0W
Lisichansk 23 48 55N 38 30 E
Lisieux 12 49 10N 0 12 E
Lismore, Australia 45 28 44S 153 21 E
Lismore, Ireland 9 52 8N 7 58W
Lisse 11 52 16N 4 33 E
Lista, Norway 21 58 7N 6 39 E
Lista, Sweden 21 59 19N 16 16 E
Liston 45 28 39S 152 6 E
Listowel, Canada 62 43 44N 80 58W
Listowel, Ireland 9 52 27N 9 30W
Litang, China 39 23 12N 109 8 E
Litang, Malaysia 35 5 27N 118 31 E
Litani →, Lebanon 28 33 20N 35 14 E
Litani →, Surinam 30 3 40N 54 0W
Litchfield, Ill., U.S.A. 70 39 10N 89 40W
Litchfield, Minn., U.S.A. 70 45 5N 94 31W
Lithgow 45 33 25S 150 8 E
Líthinon, Ákra 19 34 55N 24 44 E
Lithuanian S.S.R. □ 22 55 30N 24 0 E
Litoměřice 14 50 33N 14 10 E
Little Abaco I. 75 26 50N 77 30W
Little Barrier I. 43 36 12S 175 8 E
Little Belt Mts. 72 46 50N 111 0W
Little Blue → 70 39 41N 96 40W
Little Bushman Land 56 29 10S 18 10 E
Little Cadotte → 64 56 41N 117 6W
Little Churchill → 65 57 30N 95 22W
Little Colorado → 73 36 11N 111 48W
Little Current 62 45 55N 82 0W
Little Current → 62 50 57N 84 36W
Little Falls, Minn., U.S.A. 70 45 58N 94 19W
Little Falls, N.Y., U.S.A. 68 43 3N 74 50W
Little Fork → 70 48 31N 93 35W
Little Grand Rapids 65 52 0N 95 29W
Little Humboldt → 72 41 0N 117 43W
Little Inagua I. 75 21 40N 73 50W
Little Karoo 56 33 45S 21 0 E
Little Lake 73 35 58N 117 58W
Little Minch 8 57 35N 6 45W
Little Missouri → 70 47 30N 102 25W
Little Namaqualand 56 29 0S 17 9 E
Little Ouse → 7 52 25N 0 50 E
Little Red → 71 35 11N 91 27W
Little River 43 43 45S 172 49 E
Little Rock 71 34 41N 92 10W
Little Sable Pt. 68 43 40N 86 32W
Little Sioux → 70 41 49N 96 4W
Little Smoky → 64 54 44N 117 11W
Little Snake → 72 40 27N 108 26W
Little Wabash → 68 37 54N 88 5W
Littlefield 71 33 57N 102 17W
Littlefork 70 48 24N 93 35W
Littlehampton 7 50 48N 0 32W
Littleton 68 44 19N 71 47W
Liuba 39 33 38N 106 55 E
Liucheng 39 24 38N 109 14 E
Liukang Tenggaja 35 6 45S 118 50 E
Liuwa Plain 55 14 20S 22 30 E
Liuyang 39 28 10N 113 37 E
Liuzhou 39 24 22N 109 22 E
Live Oak 69 30 17N 83 0W
Liveringa 46 18 3S 124 10 E
Livermore, Mt. 71 30 45N 104 8W
Liverpool, Australia 45 33 54S 150 58 E
Liverpool, Canada 63 44 5N 64 41W
Liverpool, U.K. 6 53 25N 3 0W
Liverpool Plains 45 31 15S 150 15 E
Liverpool Ra. 45 31 50S 150 30 E
Livingston, Guat. 75 15 50N 88 50W
Livingston, Mont., U.S.A. 72 45 40N 110 40W
Livingston, Tex., U.S.A. 71 30 44N 94 54W
Livingstone 55 17 46S 25 52 E
Livingstone Mts. 52 9 40S 34 20 E
Livingstonia 54 10 38S 34 5 E
Livny 22 52 30N 37 30 E
Livonia 68 42 25N 83 23W
Livorno 18 43 32N 10 18 E
Livramento 80 30 55S 55 30W
Liwale 54 9 48S 37 58 E
Lizard I. 44 14 42S 145 30 E
Lizard Pt. 7 49 57N 5 11W
Ljubljana 18 46 4N 14 33 E
Ljungan → 20 62 18N 17 23 E
Ljungby 21 56 49N 13 55 E
Ljusdal 21 61 46N 16 3 E
Ljusnan → 21 61 12N 17 8 E
Ljusne 21 61 13N 17 7 E
Llancanelo, Salina 80 35 40S 69 8W
Llandeilo 7 51 53N 4 0W
Llandovery 7 51 59N 3 49W
Llandrindod Wells 7 52 15N 3 23W
Llandudno 6 53 19N 3 51W
Llanelli 7 51 41N 4 11W
Llanes 13 43 25N 4 50W
Llangollen 6 52 58N 3 10W
Llanidloes 7 52 28N 3 31W
Llano 71 30 45N 98 41W
Llano → 71 30 50N 98 25W
Llano Estacado 71 34 0N 103 0W
Llanos 78 5 0N 71 35W
Llera 74 23 19N 99 1W
Llobregat → 13 41 19N 2 9 E
Lloret de Mar 13 41 41N 2 53 E
Lloyd B. 44 12 45S 143 27 E
Lloyd L. 65 57 22N 108 57W
Lloydminster 65 53 17N 110 0W
Llullaillaco, Volcán 80 24 43S 68 30W
Loa 73 38 18N 111 40W
Loa → 80 21 26S 70 41W
Lobatse 56 25 12S 25 40 E
Lobería 80 38 10S 58 40W
Lobito 55 12 18S 13 35 E
Lobos, I. 74 27 15N 110 30W
Lobos, Is. 76 6 57S 80 45W
Locarno 14 46 10N 8 47 E
Lochaber 8 56 55N 5 0W
Lochcarron 8 57 25N 5 30W
Loche, La 65 56 29N 109 26W
Lochem 11 52 9N 6 26 E
Loches 12 47 7N 1 0 E
Lochgelly 8 56 7N 3 18W
Lochgilphead 8 56 2N 5 37W
Lochinver 8 58 9N 5 15W
Lochnagar, Australia 44 23 33S 145 38 E
Lochnagar, U.K. 8 56 57N 3 14W
Lochy → 8 56 52N 5 3W
Lock 45 33 34S 135 46 E
Lock Haven 68 41 7N 77 31W
Lockeport 63 43 47N 65 4W
Lockerbie 8 55 7N 3 21W
Lockhart 71 29 55N 97 40W
Lockhart, L. 47 33 15S 119 3 E
Lockney 71 34 7N 101 27W
Lockport 68 43 12N 78 42W
Lod 28 31 57N 34 54 E
Lodeinoye Pole 22 60 44N 33 33 E
Lodge Grass 72 45 21N 107 20W
Lodgepole 70 41 12N 102 40W
Lodgepole Cr. → 70 41 20N 104 30W
Lodhran 32 29 32N 71 30 E
Lodi 72 38 12N 121 16W
Lodja 54 3 30S 23 23 E
Lodwar 54 3 10N 35 40 E
Łódź 15 51 45N 19 27 E
Loeriesfontein 56 31 0S 19 26 E
Lofoten 20 68 30N 15 0 E
Logan, Kans., U.S.A. 70 39 40N 99 35W
Logan, Ohio, U.S.A. 68 39 25N 82 22W
Logan, Utah, U.S.A. 72 41 45N 111 50W
Logan, W. Va., U.S.A. 68 37 51N 81 59W
Logan, Mt. 60 60 31N 140 22W
Logan Pass 64 48 41N 113 44W
Logansport, Ind., U.S.A. 68 40 45N 86 21W
Logansport, La., U.S.A. 71 31 58N 93 58W
Logroño 13 42 28N 2 27W
Lohardaga 33 23 27N 84 45 E
Loi-kaw 33 19 40N 97 17 E
Loimaa 21 60 50N 23 5 E
Loir → 12 47 33N 0 32W
Loir-et-Cher □ 12 47 40N 1 20 E
Loire □ 12 45 40N 4 5 E
Loire → 12 47 16N 2 10W
Loire-Atlantique □ 12 47 25N 1 40W
Loiret □ 12 47 55N 2 30 E
Loja, Ecuador 78 3 59S 79 16W
Loja, Spain 13 37 10N 4 10W
Loji 35 1 38S 127 28 E
Lokandu 54 2 30S 25 45 E
Lokeren 11 51 6N 3 59 E
Lokichokio 52 4 19N 34 13 E
Lokitaung 54 4 12N 35 48 E
Lokka 20 67 55N 27 35 E
Løkken Verk 20 63 7N 9 43 E
Lokoja 53 7 47N 6 45 E
Lokolama 54 2 35S 19 50 E
Lokwei 39 19 5N 110 31 E
Loliondo 54 2 2S 35 39 E
Lolland 21 54 45N 11 30 E
Lolo 72 46 50N 114 8W
Lom 19 43 48N 23 12 E
Loma 72 47 59N 110 29W
Lomami → 54 0 46N 24 16 E
Lombadina 46 16 31S 122 54 E
Lombardia □ 18 45 35N 9 45 E
Lombardy = Lombardia □ 18 45 35N 9 45 E
Lomblen 35 8 30S 123 32 E
Lombok 34 8 45S 116 30 E
Lomé 53 6 9N 1 20 E
Lomela 54 2 19S 23 15 E
Lomela → 54 0 15S 20 40 E
Lometa 71 31 15N 98 25W
Lomié 54 3 13N 13 38 E
Lomond 64 50 24N 112 36W
Lomond, L. 8 56 8N 4 38W
Lompobatang 35 5 24S 119 56 E
Lompoc 73 34 41N 120 32W
Łomza 15 53 10N 22 2 E
Loncoche 80 39 20S 72 50W
Londa 32 15 30N 74 30 E
Londiani 52 0 10S 35 33 E
London, Canada 62 42 59N 81 15W
London, U.K. 7 51 30N 0 5W
London, Ky., U.S.A. 68 37 11N 84 5W
London, Ohio, U.S.A. 68 39 54N 83 28W
London, Greater □ 7 51 30N 0 5W
Londonderry 9 55 0N 7 20W
Londonderry □ 9 55 0N 7 20W
Londonderry, C. 46 13 45S 126 55 E
Londonderry, I. 80 55 0S 71 0W
Londrina 80 23 18S 51 10W
Lone Pine 73 36 35N 118 2W
Long Beach, Calif., U.S.A. 73 33 46N 118 12W
Long Beach, Wash., U.S.A. 72 46 20N 124 1W
Long Branch 68 40 19N 74 0W
Long Creek 72 44 43N 119 6W
Long Eaton 6 52 54N 1 16W
Long I., Australia 44 22 8S 149 53 E
Long I., Bahamas 75 23 20N 75 10W
Long I., U.S.A. 68 40 50N 73 20W
Long L. 62 49 30N 86 50W
Long Pine 70 42 33N 99 41W
Long Pt. 63 48 47N 58 46W
Long Range Mts. 63 49 30N 57 30W
Long Xian 39 34 55N 106 55 E
Long Xuyen 34 10 19N 105 28 E
Long'an 39 23 10N 107 40 E
Longchuan 39 24 5N 115 17 E
Longde 38 35 30N 106 20 E
Longford, Australia 44 41 32S 147 3 E
Longford, Ireland 9 53 43N 7 50W
Longford □ 9 53 42N 7 45W
Longhua 38 41 18N 117 45 E
Longiram 34 0 5S 115 45 E
Longjiang 38 47 20N 123 12 E
Longkou 38 37 40N 120 18 E
Longlac 62 49 45N 86 25W
Longlin 39 24 47N 105 20 E
Longmen 39 23 40N 114 18 E
Longmont 70 40 10N 105 4W
Longnan 39 24 55N 114 47 E
Longnawan 34 1 51N 114 55 E
Longone → 51 10 0N 15 40 E
Longquan 39 28 7N 119 10 E
Longreach 44 23 28S 144 14 E
Longshan 39 29 29N 109 25 E
Longsheng 39 25 48N 110 0 E
Longton 44 20 58S 145 55 E
Longtown 7 51 58N 2 59W
Longview, Canada 64 50 32N 114 10W
Longview, Tex., U.S.A. 71 32 30N 94 45W
Longview, Wash., U.S.A. 72 46 9N 122 58W
Longxi 38 34 53N 104 40 E

Maracay

Madre, Sierra, Phil. 35 17 0N 122 0 E
Madre de Dios → 78 10 59S 66 8W
Madre de Dios, I. 80 50 20S 75 10W
Madre del Sur, Sierra 74 17 30N 100 0W
Madre Occidental, Sierra 74 27 0N 107 0W
Madre Oriental, Sierra 74 25 0N 100 0W
Madrid 13 40 25N 3 45W
Madura, Selat 35 7 30S 113 20 E
Madura Motel 47 31 55S 127 0 E
Madurai 32 9 55N 78 10 E
Madurantakam 32 12 30N 79 50 E
Mae Sot 34 16 43N 98 34 E
Maebashi 36 36 24N 139 4 E
Maesteg 7 51 36N 3 40W
Maestra, Sierra 75 20 15N 77 0W
Maestrazgo, Mts. del 13 40 30N 0 25W
Maevatanana 57 16 56S 46 49 E
Mafeking 65 52 40N 101 10W
Mafeteng 56 29 51S 27 15 E
Maffra 45 37 53S 146 58 E
Mafia I. 54 7 45S 39 50 E
Mafikeng 56 25 50S 25 38 E
Mafra, Brazil 80 26 10S 50 0W
Mafra, Portugal 13 38 55N 9 20W
Magadan 25 59 38N 150 50 E
Magadi 54 1 54S 36 19 E
Magaliesburg 57 26 0S 27 32 E
Magallanes, Estrecho de 80 52 30S 75 0W
Magangué 78 9 14N 74 45W
Magburaka 50 8 47N 12 0W
Magdalena, Argentina 80 35 5S 57 30W
Magdalena, Bolivia 78 13 13S 63 57W
Magdalena, Malaysia 34 4 25N 117 55 E
Magdalena, Mexico 74 30 50N 112 0W
Magdalena, U.S.A. 73 34 10N 107 20W
Magdalena →, Colombia 78 11 6N 74 51W
Magdalena →, Mexico 74 30 40N 112 25W
Magdalena, B. 74 24 30N 112 10W
Magdalena, Llano de la 74 25 0N 111 30W
Magdeburg 14 52 8N 11 36 E
Magdelaine Cays 44 16 33S 150 18 E
Magdi'el 28 32 10N 34 54 E
Magee 71 31 53N 89 45W
Magee, I. 9 54 48N 5 44W
Magelang 35 7 29S 110 13 E
Magellan's Str. = Magallanes, Estrecho de 80 52 30S 75 0W
Magenta, L. 47 33 30S 119 2 E
Maggiore, L. 18 46 0N 8 35 E
Maghâr 28 32 54N 35 24 E
Magherafelt 9 54 44N 6 37W
Magnitogorsk 22 53 27N 59 4 E
Magnolia, Ark., U.S.A. 71 33 18N 93 12W
Magnolia, Miss., U.S.A. 71 31 8N 90 28W
Magog 63 45 18N 72 9W
Magosa = Famagusta 30 35 8N 33 55 E
Magpie L. 63 51 0N 64 41W
Magrath 64 49 25N 112 50W
Maguarinho, C. 79 0 15S 48 30W
Maguse L. 65 61 40N 95 10W
Maguse Pt. 65 61 20N 93 50W
Magwe 33 20 10N 95 0 E
Mahābād 30 36 50N 45 45 E
Mahabo 57 20 23S 44 40 E
Mahagi 54 2 20N 31 0 E
Mahajamba → 57 15 33S 47 8 E
Mahajamba, Helodranon' i 57 15 24S 47 5 E
Mahajanga 57 15 40S 46 25 E
Mahajanga □ 57 17 0S 47 0 E
Mahajilo → 57 19 42S 45 22 E
Mahakam → 34 0 35S 117 17 E
Mahalapye 56 23 1S 26 51 E
Maḥallāt 31 33 55N 50 30 E
Mahanadi → 33 20 20N 86 25 E
Mahanoro 57 19 54S 48 48 E
Maharashtra □ 32 20 30N 75 30 E
Mahari Mts. 52 6 20S 30 0 E
Mahasolo 57 19 7S 46 22 E
Mahbubnagar 32 16 45N 77 59 E
Mahdia 51 35 28N 11 0 E
Mahé 3 5 0S 55 30 E
Mahenge 54 8 45S 36 41 E
Maheno 43 45 10S 170 50 E
Mahesana 32 23 39N 72 26 E
Mahia Pen. 43 39 9S 177 55 E
Mahnomen 70 47 22N 95 57W
Mahón 13 39 53N 4 16 E
Mahone Bay 63 44 30N 64 20W
Mai-Ndombe, L. 54 2 0S 18 20 E
Maicurú → 79 2 14S 54 17W
Maidenhead 7 51 31N 0 42W
Maidstone, Canada 65 53 5N 109 20W
Maidstone, U.K. 7 51 16N 0 31 E
Maiduguri 53 12 0N 13 20 E
Maijdi 33 22 48N 91 10 E
Maikala Ra. 33 22 0N 81 0 E
Main →, Germany 14 50 0N 8 18 E
Main →, U.K. 9 54 49N 6 20W
Main Centre 65 50 35N 107 21W
Maine 12 48 0N 0 0 E
Maine □ 63 45 20N 69 0W
Maine → 9 52 10N 9 40W
Maine-et-Loire □ 12 47 31N 0 30W
Maingkwan 33 26 15N 96 37 E
Mainit, L. 35 9 31N 125 30 E
Mainland, Orkney, U.K. 8 59 0N 3 10W
Mainland, Shetland, U.K. 8 60 15N 1 22W
Maintirano 57 18 3S 44 1 E
Mainz 14 50 0N 8 17 E
Maipú 80 36 52S 57 50W
Maiquetía 78 10 36N 66 57W
Mairabari 33 26 30N 92 22 E
Maisi, Pta. de 75 20 10N 74 10W
Maitland, N.S.W., Australia 45 32 33S 151 36 E
Maitland, S. Austral., Australia 45 34 23S 137 40 E
Maiz, Is. del 75 12 15N 83 4W
Maizuru 36 35 25N 135 22 E
Majalengka 35 6 50S 108 13 E
Majd el Kurūm 28 32 56N 35 15 E
Majene 35 3 38S 118 57 E
Maji 51 6 12N 35 30 E
Major 65 51 52N 109 37W
Majorca, I. = Mallorca 13 39 30N 3 0 E
Maka 50 13 40N 14 10W
Makale 35 3 6S 119 51 E
Makari 54 12 35N 14 28 E
Makarikari = Makgadikgadi Salt Pans 56 20 40S 25 45 E
Makarovo 25 57 40N 107 45 E
Makasar = Ujung Pandang 35 5 10S 119 20 E
Makasar, Selat 35 1 0S 118 20 E
Makat 23 47 39N 53 19 E
Makedhonía □ 19 40 39N 22 0 E
Makedonija □ 19 41 53N 21 40 E
Makena 66 20 39N 156 27W
Makeni 50 8 55N 12 5W
Makeyevka 23 48 0N 38 0 E
Makgadikgadi Salt Pans 56 20 40S 25 45 E
Makhachkala 23 43 0N 47 30 E
Makian 35 0 20N 127 20 E
Makindu 54 2 18S 37 50 E
Makinsk 24 52 37N 70 26 E
Makkah 29 21 30N 39 54 E
Makkovik 63 55 10N 59 10W
Maklakovo 25 58 16N 92 29 E
Makó 15 46 14N 20 33 E
Makokou 54 0 40N 12 50 E
Makoua 54 0 5S 15 50 E
Makrai 32 22 2N 77 0 E
Makran 31 26 13N 61 30 E
Makran Coast Range 31 25 40N 64 0 E
Maksimkin Yar 24 58 42N 86 50 E
Mākū 30 39 15N 44 31 E
Makumbi 54 5 50S 20 43 E
Makunda 56 22 30S 20 7 E
Makurazaki 36 31 15N 130 20 E
Makurdi 53 7 43N 8 35 E
Makwassie 56 27 17S 26 0 E
Mal B. 9 52 50N 9 30W
Mala, Pta. 75 7 28N 80 2W
Malabang 35 7 36N 124 3 E
Malabar Coast 32 11 0N 75 0 E
Malacca, Str. of 34 3 0N 101 0 E
Malad City 72 42 10N 112 20 E
Málaga, Spain 13 36 43N 4 23W
Malaga, U.S.A. 71 32 12N 104 2W
Málaga □ 13 36 38N 4 58W
Malaimbandy 57 20 20S 45 36 E
Malakâl 51 9 33N 31 40 E
Malakand 32 34 40N 71 55 E
Malakoff 71 32 10N 95 55W
Malamyzh 25 50 0N 136 50 E
Malang 35 7 59S 112 45 E
Malange 54 9 36S 16 17 E
Mälaren 21 59 30N 17 10 E
Malargüe 80 35 32S 69 30W
Malartic 62 48 9N 78 9W
Malatya 30 38 25N 38 20 E
Malawi ■ 55 11 55S 34 0 E
Malawi, L. 55 12 30S 34 30 E
Malay Pen. 34 7 25N 100 0 E
Malaybalay 35 8 5N 125 7 E
Malāyer 30 34 19N 48 51 E
Malaysia ■ 34 5 0N 110 0 E
Malazgirt 30 39 10N 42 33 E
Malbaie, La 63 47 40N 70 10W
Malbon 44 21 5S 140 17 E
Malbooma 45 30 41S 134 11 E
Malbork 15 54 3N 19 1 E
Malcolm 47 28 51S 121 25 E
Malcolm, Pt. 47 33 48S 123 45 E
Maldegem 11 51 14N 3 26 E
Malden 71 36 35N 90 0W
Malden I. 41 4 3S 155 1W
Maldives ■ 3 5 0N 73 0 E
Maldonado 80 35 0S 55 0W
Maldonado, Punta 74 16 19N 98 35W
Malé Karpaty 14 48 30N 17 20 E
Maléa, Ákra 19 36 28N 23 7 E
Malegaon 32 20 30N 74 38 E
Malema 55 14 57S 37 20 E
Malgomaj 20 64 40N 16 30 E
Malha 51 15 8N 25 10 E
Malhão, Sa. do 13 37 25N 8 0W
Malheur → 72 44 3N 116 59W
Malheur L. 72 43 19N 118 42W
Mali ■ 50 17 0N 3 0W
Mali → 33 25 40N 97 40 E
Malih → 28 32 20N 35 34 E
Malik 35 0 39S 123 16 E
Malili 35 2 42S 121 6 E
Malindi 54 3 12S 40 5 E
Malines = Mechelen 11 51 2N 4 29 E
Maling 35 1 0N 121 0 E
Malita 35 6 19N 125 39 E
Mallacoota Inlet 45 37 34S 149 40 E
Mallaig 8 57 0N 5 50W
Mallawi 51 27 44N 30 44 E
Mallorca 13 39 30N 3 0 E
Mallow 9 52 8N 8 40W
Malmberget 20 67 11N 20 40 E
Malmédy 11 50 25N 6 2 E
Malmesbury 56 33 28S 18 41 E
Malmö 21 55 36N 12 59 E
Malmöhus län □ 21 55 45N 13 30 E
Malolos 35 14 50N 120 49 E
Malone 68 44 50N 74 19W
Malozemelskaya Tundra 22 67 0N 50 0 E
Malpelo 78 4 3N 81 35W
Malta, Idaho, U.S.A. 72 42 15N 113 30W
Malta, Mont., U.S.A. 72 48 20N 107 55W
Malta ■ 18 35 50N 14 30 E
Maltahöhe 56 24 55S 17 0 E
Malton 6 54 9N 0 48W
Maluku 35 1 0S 127 0 E
Maluku □ 35 3 0S 128 0 E
Malvan 32 16 2N 73 30 E
Malvern, U.K. 7 52 7N 2 19W
Malvern, U.S.A. 71 34 22N 92 50W
Malvern Hills 7 52 0N 2 19W
Malvinas, Is. = Falkland Is. 80 51 30S 59 0W
Malyy Lyakhovskiy, Ostrov 25 74 7N 140 36 E
Mama 25 58 18N 112 54 E
Mamahatun 30 39 50N 40 23 E
Mamaia 15 44 18N 28 37 E
Mamanguape 79 6 50S 35 4W
Mamasa 35 2 55S 119 20 E
Mambasa 52 1 22N 29 3 E
Mamberamo → 35 2 0S 137 50 E
Mambilima Falls 54 10 31S 28 45 E
Mamburao 35 13 13N 120 39 E
Mameigwess L. 62 52 35N 87 50W
Mamfe 53 5 50N 9 15 E
Mammoth 73 32 46N 110 43W
Mamoré → 78 10 23S 65 53W
Mamou 50 10 15N 12 0W
Mamuju 35 2 41S 118 50 E
Man 50 7 30N 7 40W
Man, I. of 6 54 15N 4 30W
Man Na 33 23 27N 97 19 E
Mana 79 5 45N 53 55W
Manaar, Gulf of = Mannar, G. of 32 8 30N 79 0 E
Manacapuru 78 3 16S 60 37W
Manacor 13 39 34N 3 13 E
Manado 35 1 29N 124 51 E
Managua 75 12 6N 86 20W
Managua, L. 75 12 20N 86 30W
Manakara 57 22 8S 48 1 E
Manambao → 57 17 35S 44 0 E
Manambato 57 13 43S 49 7 E
Manambolo → 57 19 18S 44 22 E
Manambolosy 57 16 2S 49 40 E
Mananara 57 16 10S 49 46 E
Mananara → 57 23 21S 47 42 E
Mananjary 57 21 13S 48 20 E
Manantenina 57 24 17S 47 19 E
Manaos = Manaus 78 3 0S 60 0W
Manapouri 43 45 34S 167 39 E
Manapouri, L. 43 45 32S 167 32 E
Manas 37 44 17N 85 56 E
Manas → 33 26 12N 90 40 E
Manasir 31 24 30N 51 10 E
Manassa 73 37 12N 105 58W
Manaung 33 18 45N 93 40 E
Manaus 78 3 0S 60 0W
Manawan L. 65 55 24N 103 14W
Manay 35 7 17N 126 33 E
Mancelona 68 44 54N 85 5W
Mancha, La 13 39 10N 2 54W
Manche □ 12 49 10N 1 20W
Manchegorsk 22 67 40N 32 40 E
Manchester, U.K. 6 53 30N 2 15W
Manchester, Conn., U.S.A. 68 41 47N 72 30W
Manchester, Ga., U.S.A. 69 32 53N 84 32W
Manchester, Iowa, U.S.A. 70 42 28N 91 27W
Manchester, Ky., U.S.A. 68 37 9N 83 45W
Manchester, N.H., U.S.A. 68 42 58N 71 29W
Manchester L. 65 61 28N 107 29W
Mand → 31 28 20N 52 30 E
Manda 54 10 30S 34 40 E
Mandabé 57 21 0S 44 55 E
Mandal 21 58 2N 7 25 E
Mandalay 33 22 0N 96 4 E
Mandale = Mandalay 33 22 0N 96 4 E
Mandalī 30 33 43N 45 28 E
Mandan 70 46 50N 101 0W
Mandar, Teluk 35 3 35S 119 15 E
Mandasor = Mandsaur 32 24 3N 75 8 E
Mandaue 35 10 20N 123 56 E
Mandi 32 31 39N 76 58 E
Mandimba 55 14 20S 35 40 E
Mandioli 35 0 40S 127 20 E
Mandla 33 22 39N 80 30 E
Mandoto 57 19 34S 46 17 E
Mandrare → 57 25 10S 46 30 E
Mandritsara 57 15 50S 48 49 E
Mandsaur 32 24 3N 75 8 E
Mandurah 47 32 36S 115 48 E
Mandvi 32 22 51N 69 22 E
Mandya 32 12 30N 77 0 E
Maneroo 44 23 22S 143 53 E
Maneroo Cr. → 44 23 21S 143 53 E
Manfalût 51 27 20N 30 52 E
Manfred 45 33 19S 143 45 E
Mangaia 43 21 55S 157 55W
Mangalia 15 43 50N 28 35 E
Mangalore 32 12 55N 74 47 E
Manggar 34 2 50S 108 10 E
Manggawitu 35 4 8S 133 32 E
Mangkalihat, Tanjung 35 1 2N 118 59 E
Mangla Dam 32 33 9N 73 44 E
Mangnai 37 37 52N 91 43 E
Mango 53 10 20N 0 30 E
Mangoche 55 14 25S 35 16 E
Mangoky → 57 21 29S 43 41 E
Mangole 35 1 50S 125 55 E
Mangonui 43 35 1S 173 32 E
Mangueigne 51 10 30N 21 15 E
Mangueira, L. da 80 33 0S 52 50W
Mangum 71 34 50N 99 30W
Manhattan 70 39 10N 96 40W
Manhiça 57 25 23S 32 49 E
Manhuaçu 79 20 15S 42 2W
Mania → 57 19 42S 45 22 E
Manica 57 18 58S 32 59 E
Manica e Sofala □ 57 19 10S 33 45 E
Manicoré 78 5 48S 61 16W
Manicouagan → 63 49 30N 68 30W
Manīfah 30 27 44N 49 0 E
Manifold 44 22 41S 150 40 E
Manifold, C. 44 22 41S 150 50 E
Manigotagan 65 51 6N 96 18W
Manihiki 41 10 24S 161 1W
Manila, Phil. 35 14 40N 121 3 E
Manila, U.S.A. 72 41 0N 109 44W
Manila Bay 35 14 0N 120 0 E
Manilla 45 30 45S 150 43 E
Manipur □ 33 25 0N 94 0 E
Manipur → 33 23 45N 94 20 E
Manisa 30 38 38N 27 30 E
Manistee 68 44 15N 86 20W
Manistee → 68 44 15N 86 21W
Manistique 68 45 59N 86 18W
Manito L. 65 52 43N 109 43W
Manitoba □ 65 55 30N 97 0W
Manitoba, L. 65 51 0N 98 45W
Manitou 65 49 15N 98 32W
Manitou I. 62 47 22N 87 30W
Manitou Is. 68 45 8N 86 0W
Manitou L. 63 50 55N 65 17W
Manitou Springs 70 38 52N 104 55W
Manitoulin I. 62 45 40N 82 30W
Manitowaning 62 45 46N 81 49W
Manitowoc 68 44 8N 87 40W
Manizales 78 5 5N 75 32W
Manja 57 21 26S 44 20 E
Manjacaze 57 24 45S 34 0 E
Manjakandriana 57 18 55S 47 47 E
Manjhand 32 25 50N 68 10 E
Manjil 30 36 46N 49 30 E
Manjimup 47 34 15S 116 6 E
Manjra → 32 18 49N 77 52 E
Mankato, Kans., U.S.A. 70 39 49N 98 11W
Mankato, Minn., U.S.A. 70 44 8N 93 59W
Mankayane 57 26 40S 31 4 E
Mankono 50 8 1N 6 10W
Mankota 65 49 25N 107 5W
Manly 45 33 48S 151 17 E
Manmad 32 20 18N 74 28 E
Mann Ranges, Mts. 47 26 6S 130 5 E
Manna 34 4 25S 102 55 E
Mannahill 45 32 25S 140 0 E
Mannar 32 9 1N 79 54 E
Mannar, G. of 32 8 30N 79 0 E
Mannar I. 32 9 5N 79 45 E
Mannheim 14 49 28N 8 29 E
Manning, Canada 64 56 53N 117 39W
Manning, U.S.A. 69 33 40N 80 9W
Manning Prov. Park 64 49 5N 120 45W
Mannington 68 39 35N 80 25W
Mannum 45 34 50S 139 20 E
Mano 50 8 3N 12 2W
Manokwari 35 0 54S 134 0 E
Manombo 57 22 57S 43 28 E
Manono 54 7 15S 27 25 E
Manouane, L. 63 50 45N 70 45W
Manresa 13 41 48N 1 50 E
Mans, Le 12 48 0N 0 10 E
Mansa 54 11 13S 28 55 E
Mansel I. 61 62 0N 80 0W
Mansfield, Australia 45 37 4S 146 6 E
Mansfield, U.K. 6 53 8N 1 12W
Mansfield, La., U.S.A. 71 32 2N 93 40W
Mansfield, Ohio, U.S.A. 68 40 45N 82 30W
Mansfield, Wash., U.S.A. 72 47 51N 119 44W
Manson Creek 64 55 37N 124 32W
Manta 78 1 0S 80 40W
Mantalingajan, Mt. 34 8 55N 117 45 E
Manteca 73 37 50N 121 12W
Manteo 69 35 55N 75 41W
Mantes-la-Jolie 12 49 0N 1 41 E
Manthani 32 18 40N 79 35 E
Manti 72 39 23N 111 32W
Mantiqueira, Serra da 79 22 0S 44 0W
Manton 68 44 23N 85 25W
Mántova 18 45 20N 10 42 E
Mänttä 20 62 0N 24 40 E
Mantua = Mántova 18 45 20N 10 42 E
Manu 78 12 10S 70 51W
Manua Is. 43 14 13S 169 35W
Manuae 41 19 30S 159 0W
Manuel Alves → 79 11 19S 48 28W
Manui 35 3 35S 123 5 E
Manville 70 42 48N 104 36W
Many 71 31 36N 93 28W
Manyara, L. 54 3 40S 35 50 E
Manych-Gudilo, Oz. 23 46 24N 42 38 E
Manyoni 54 5 45S 34 55 E
Manzai 32 32 12N 70 15 E
Manzanares 13 39 0N 3 22W
Manzanillo, Cuba 75 20 20N 77 31W
Manzanillo, Mexico 74 19 0N 104 20W
Manzanillo, Pta. 75 9 30N 79 40W
Manzano Mts. 73 34 30N 106 45W
Manzhouli 38 49 35N 117 25 E
Manzini 57 26 30S 31 25 E
Mao 51 14 4N 15 19 E
Maoke, Pegunungan 35 3 40S 137 30 E
Maoming 39 21 50N 110 54 E
Mapam Yumco 33 30 45N 81 28 E
Mapia, Kepulauan 35 0 50N 134 20 E
Mapimí 74 25 50N 103 50W
Mapimí, Bolsón de 74 27 30N 104 15W
Mapinhane 57 22 20S 35 0 E
Maple Creek 65 49 55N 109 29W
Mapleton 72 44 4N 123 58W
Mapuera → 78 1 5S 57 2W
Maputo 57 25 58S 32 32 E
Maputo, B. de 57 25 50S 32 45 E
Maqnā 30 28 25N 34 50 E
Maquela do Zombo 54 6 0S 15 15 E
Maquinchao 80 41 15S 68 50W
Maquoketa 70 42 4N 90 40W
Mar, Serra do 80 25 30S 49 0W
Mar Chiquita, L. 80 30 40S 62 50W
Mar del Plata 80 38 0S 57 30W
Mara 52 1 30S 34 32 E
Maraā 78 1 52S 65 25W
Marabá 79 5 20S 49 5W
Maracá, I. de 79 2 10N 50 30W
Maracaibo 78 10 40N 71 37W
Maracaibo, L. de 78 9 40N 71 30W
Maracay 78 10 15N 67 28W

Marādah

Marādah 51 29 15N 19 15 E
Maradi 53 13 29N 7 20 E
Marāgheh 30 37 30N 46 12 E
Marāh 30 25 0N 45 35 E
Marajó, I. de 79 1 0S 49 30W
Maralal 54 1 0N 36 38 E
Maralinga 47 30 13S 131 32 E
Marama 45 35 10S 140 10 E
Marampa 50 8 45N 12 28W
Marana 73 32 30N 111 9W
Maranboy 46 14 40S 132 39 E
Marand 30 38 30N 45 45 E
Maranguape 79 3 55S 38 50W
Maranhão = São Luís 79 2 39S 44 15W
Maranhão □ 79 5 0S 46 0W
Maranoa → 45 27 50S 148 37 E
Marañón → 78 4 30S 73 35W
Marão 57 24 18S 34 2 E
Marathon, Australia 44 20 51S 143 32 E
Marathon, Canada 62 48 44N 86 23W
Marathón, Greece 19 38 11N 23 58 E
Marathon, U.S.A. 71 30 15N 103 15W
Maratua 35 2 10N 118 35 E
Marbella 13 36 30N 4 57W
Marble Bar 46 21 9S 119 44 E
Marble Falls 71 30 30N 98 15W
Marburg 14 50 49N 8 36 E
March 7 52 33N 0 5 E
Marche 12 46 5N 1 20 E
Marche □ 18 43 22N 13 10 E
Marche-en-Famenne 11 50 14N 5 19 E
Marches = Marche □ 18 43 22N 13 10 E
Marcus 40 24 0N 153 45 E
Marcus Necker Ridge 40 20 0N 175 0 E
Mardan 32 34 20N 72 0 E
Mardie 46 21 12S 115 59 E
Mardin 30 37 20N 40 43 E
Maree L. 8 57 40N 5 30W
Mareeba 44 16 59S 145 28 E
Marek = Stanke Dimitrov 19 42 17N 23 9 E
Marek 35 4 41S 120 24 E
Maremma 18 42 45N 11 15 E
Marengo 70 41 42N 92 5W
Marerano 57 21 23S 44 52 E
Marfa 71 30 15N 104 0W
Margaret Bay 64 51 20N 127 35W
Margaret L. 64 58 56N 115 25W
Margarita 74 9 20N 79 55W
Margarita, I. de 78 11 0N 64 0W
Margate, S. Africa 57 30 50S 30 20 E
Margate, U.K. 7 51 23N 1 24 E
Margelan 24 40 27N 71 42 E
Marguerite 64 52 30N 122 25W
Mari A.S.S.R. □ 22 56 30N 48 0 E
Maria I., N. Terr., Australia 44 14 52S 135 45 E
Maria I., Tas., Australia 44 42 35S 148 0 E
Maria van Diemen, C. 43 34 29S 172 40 E
Marian L. 64 63 0N 116 15W
Mariana Trench 40 13 0N 145 0 E
Marianao 75 23 8N 82 24W
Marianna, Ark., U.S.A. 71 34 48N 90 48W
Marianna, Fla., U.S.A. 69 30 45N 85 15W
Marias → 72 47 56N 110 30W
Mariato, Punta 75 7 12N 80 52W
Ma'rib 29 15 25N 45 21 E
Maribor 18 46 36N 15 40 E
Marico → 56 23 35S 26 57 E
Maricopa, Ariz., U.S.A. 73 33 5N 112 2W
Maricopa, Calif., U.S.A. 73 35 7N 119 27W
Marīdī 51 4 55N 29 25 E
Marie-Galante 75 15 56N 61 16W
Mariecourt 61 61 30N 72 0W
Mariehamn 21 60 5N 19 55 E
Marienberg 11 52 30N 6 35 E
Marienbourg 11 50 6N 4 31 E
Mariental 56 24 36S 18 0 E
Mariestad 21 58 43N 13 50 E
Marietta, Ga., U.S.A. 69 34 0N 84 30W
Marietta, Ohio, U.S.A. 68 39 27N 81 27W
Mariinsk 24 56 10N 87 20 E
Marília 79 22 13S 50 0W
Marillana 46 22 37S 119 16 E
Marín 13 42 23N 8 42W
Marina Plains 44 14 37S 143 57 E
Marinduque 35 13 25N 122 0 E
Marine City 68 42 45N 82 29W
Marinel, Le 54 10 25S 25 17 E
Marinette 68 45 4N 87 40W
Maringá 80 23 26S 52 2W
Marion, Ala., U.S.A. 69 32 33N 87 20W
Marion, Ill., U.S.A. 71 37 45N 88 55W
Marion, Ind., U.S.A. 68 40 35N 85 40W
Marion, Iowa, U.S.A. 70 42 2N 91 36W
Marion, Kans., U.S.A. 70 38 25N 97 2W
Marion, Mich., U.S.A. 68 44 7N 85 8W
Marion, N.C., U.S.A. 69 35 42N 82 0W
Marion, Ohio, U.S.A. 68 40 38N 83 8W
Marion, S.C., U.S.A. 69 34 11N 79 22W
Marion, Va., U.S.A. 69 36 51N 81 29W
Marion, L. 69 33 30N 80 15W
Marion I. 3 47 0S 38 0 E
Mariposa 73 37 31N 119 59W
Mariscal Estigarribia 78 22 3S 60 40W
Maritsa → 19 41 40N 26 34 E
Marīvān 30 35 30N 46 25 E
Markazī □ 31 35 0N 49 30 E
Marked Tree 71 35 35N 90 24W
Marken 11 52 26N 5 12 E
Market Drayton 6 52 55N 2 30W
Market Harborough 7 52 29N 0 55W
Markham L. 65 62 30N 102 35W
Markovo 25 64 40N 169 40 E
Marks 22 51 45N 46 50 E
Marksville 71 31 10N 92 2W
Marla 45 27 19S 133 33 E
Marlborough 44 22 46S 149 52 E
Marlborough □ 43 41 45S 173 33 E
Marlborough Downs 7 51 25N 1 55W
Marlin 71 31 25N 96 50W
Marlow 71 34 40N 97 58W
Marmagao 32 15 25N 73 56 E
Marmara 30 40 35N 27 38 E
Marmara, Sea of = Marmara Denizi 30 40 45N 28 15 E
Marmara Denizi 30 40 45N 28 15 E
Marmaris 30 36 50N 28 14 E
Marmarth 70 46 21N 103 52W
Marmion L. 62 48 55N 91 20W
Marmion Mt. 47 29 16S 119 50 E
Marmolada, Mte. 18 46 25N 11 55 E
Marmora 62 44 28N 77 41W
Marne □ 12 48 50N 4 10 E
Marne → 12 48 48N 2 24 E
Maroala 57 15 23S 47 59 E
Maroantsetra 57 15 26S 49 44 E
Maromandia 57 14 13S 48 5 E
Marondera 55 18 5S 31 42 E
Maroni → 79 5 30N 54 0W
Maroochydore 45 26 29S 153 5 E
Maroona 45 37 27S 142 54 E
Marosakoa 57 15 26S 46 38 E
Maroua 53 10 40N 14 20 E
Marovoay 57 16 6S 46 39 E
Marquard 56 28 40S 27 28 E
Marquesas Is. 41 9 30S 140 0W
Marquette 68 46 30N 87 21W
Marracuene 57 25 45S 32 35 E
Marrakech 50 31 9N 8 0W
Marrawah 44 40 55S 144 42 E
Marree 45 29 39S 138 1 E
Marrilla 46 22 31S 114 25 E
Marrimane 57 22 58S 33 34 E
Marromeu 57 18 15S 36 25 E
Marrowie Creek 45 33 23S 145 40 E
Marrupa 55 13 8S 37 30 E
Mars, Le 70 43 0N 96 0W
Marsá Matrûh 51 31 19N 27 9 E
Marsá Susah 51 32 52N 21 59 E
Marsabit 54 2 18N 38 0 E
Marsala 18 37 48N 12 25 E
Marsaxlokk 18 35 47N 14 32 E
Marsden 45 33 47S 147 32 E
Marseille 12 43 18N 5 23 E
Marseilles = Marseille 12 43 18N 5 23 E
Marsh I. 71 29 35N 91 50W
Marsh L. 70 45 5N 96 0W
Marshall, Liberia 50 6 8N 10 22W
Marshall, Ark., U.S.A. 71 35 58N 92 40W
Marshall, Mich., U.S.A. 68 42 17N 84 59W
Marshall, Minn., U.S.A. 70 44 25N 95 45W
Marshall, Mo., U.S.A. 70 39 8N 93 15W
Marshall, Tex., U.S.A. 71 32 29N 94 20W
Marshall → 44 22 59S 136 59 E
Marshall Is. 40 9 0N 171 0 E
Marshalltown 70 42 5N 92 56W
Marshfield, Mo., U.S.A. 71 37 20N 92 58W
Marshfield, Wis., U.S.A. 70 44 42N 90 10W
Marstrand 21 57 53N 11 35 E
Mart 71 31 34N 96 51W
Martaban 33 16 30N 97 35 E
Martaban, G. of 33 16 5N 96 30 E
Martapura, Kalimantan, Indonesia 34 3 22S 114 47 E
Martapura, Sumatera, Indonesia 34 4 19S 104 22 E
Marte 53 12 23N 13 46 E
Martelange 11 49 49N 5 43 E
Martha's Vineyard 68 41 25N 70 35W
Martin, S. Dak., U.S.A. 70 43 11N 101 45W
Martin, Tenn., U.S.A. 71 36 23N 88 51W
Martin, L. 69 32 45N 85 50W
Martinborough 43 41 14S 175 29 E
Martinique 75 14 40N 61 0W
Martinique Passage 75 15 15N 61 0W
Martinsburg 68 39 30N 77 57W
Martinsville, Ind., U.S.A. 68 39 29N 86 23W
Martinsville, Va., U.S.A. 69 36 41N 79 52W
Marton 43 40 4S 175 23 E
Martos 13 37 44N 3 58W
Marudi 34 4 11N 114 19 E
Ma'ruf 31 31 30N 67 6 E
Marugame 36 34 15N 133 40 E
Marulan 45 34 43S 150 3 E
Marunga 56 17 28S 20 2 E
Marwar 32 25 43N 73 45 E
Mary 24 37 40N 61 50 E
Mary Frances L. 65 63 19N 106 13W
Mary Kathleen 44 20 44S 139 48 E
Maryborough = Port Laoise 9 53 2N 7 20W
Maryborough, Queens., Australia 45 25 31S 152 37 E
Maryborough, Vic., Australia 45 37 0S 143 44 E
Maryfield 65 49 50N 101 35W
Maryland □ 68 39 10N 76 40W
Maryport 6 54 43N 3 30W
Mary's Harbour 63 52 18N 55 51W
Marystown 63 47 10N 55 10W
Marysvale 73 38 25N 112 17W
Marysville, Canada 64 49 35N 116 0W
Marysville, Calif., U.S.A. 72 39 14N 121 40W
Marysville, Kans., U.S.A. 70 39 50N 96 49W
Marysville, Ohio, U.S.A. 68 40 15N 83 20W
Maryvale 45 28 4S 152 12 E
Maryville 69 35 50N 84 0W
Marzūq 51 25 53N 13 57 E
Masada = Mesada 28 31 20N 35 19 E
Masai Steppe 52 4 30S 36 30 E
Masaka 54 0 21S 31 45 E
Masalembo, Kepulauan 34 5 35S 114 30 E
Masalima, Kepulauan 34 5 4S 117 5 E
Masamba 35 2 30S 120 15 E
Masan 38 35 11N 128 32 E
Masandam, Ras 31 26 30N 56 30 E
Masasi 54 10 45S 38 52 E
Masaya 75 12 0N 86 7W
Masbate 35 12 21N 123 36 E
Mascara 50 35 26N 0 6 E
Mascarene Is. 3 22 0S 55 0 E
Mascota 74 20 30N 104 50W
Masela 35 8 9S 129 51 E
Maseru 56 29 18S 27 30 E
Mashābih 30 25 35N 36 30 E
Mashan 39 23 40N 108 11 E
Mashhad 31 36 20N 59 35 E
Mashike 36 43 31N 141 30 E
Mashkel, Hamun-i- 31 28 30N 63 0 E
Mashki Chāh 31 29 5N 62 30 E
Mashonaland Central □ 57 17 30S 31 0 E
Mashonaland East □ 57 18 0S 32 0 E
Mashonaland West □ 57 17 30S 29 30 E
Masi 20 69 26N 23 40 E
Masi Manimba 54 4 40S 17 54 E
Masindi 54 1 40N 31 43 E
Masisea 78 8 35S 74 22W
Masisi 52 1 23S 28 49 E
Masjed Soleyman 30 31 55N 49 18 E
Mask, L. 9 53 36N 9 24W
Masoala, Tanjon' i 57 15 59S 50 13 E
Masoarivo 57 19 3S 44 19 E
Masohi 35 3 20S 128 55 E
Masomeloka 57 20 17S 48 37 E
Mason 71 30 45N 99 15W
Mason City 70 43 9N 93 12W
Masqat 31 23 37N 58 36 E
Massa 18 44 2N 10 7 E
Massachusetts □ 68 42 25N 72 0W
Massada 28 33 41N 35 36 E
Massaguet 51 12 28N 15 26 E
Massakory 51 13 0N 15 49 E
Massangena 57 21 34S 33 0 E
Massawa = Mitsiwa 51 15 35N 39 25 E
Massena 68 44 52N 74 55W
Massénya 51 11 21N 16 9 E
Masset 64 54 2N 132 10W
Massif Central 12 45 30N 3 0 E
Massillon 68 40 47N 81 30W
Massinga 57 23 15S 35 22 E
Masterton 43 40 56S 175 39 E
Mastuj 32 36 20N 72 36 E
Mastung 31 29 50N 66 56 E
Masuda 36 34 40N 131 51 E
Masvingo 55 20 8S 30 49 E
Mataboor 35 1 41S 138 3 E
Matachewan 62 47 56N 80 39W
Matad 37 47 11N 115 27 E
Matadi 54 5 52S 13 31 E
Matagalpa 75 13 0N 85 58W
Matagami 62 49 45N 77 34W
Matagami, L. 62 49 50N 77 40W
Matagorda 71 28 43N 96 0W
Matagorda B. 71 28 30N 96 15W
Matagorda I. 71 28 10N 96 40W
Matak, P. 34 3 18N 106 16 E
Matakana 45 32 59S 145 54 E
Matam 50 15 34N 13 17W
Matamoros, Coahuila, Mexico 74 25 33N 103 15W
Matamoros, Puebla, Mexico 74 18 2N 98 17W
Matamoros, Tamaulipas, Mexico 74 25 50N 97 30W
Ma'ṭan as Sarra 51 21 45N 22 0 E
Matane 63 48 50N 67 33W
Matanuska 60 61 39N 149 19W
Matanzas 75 23 0N 81 40W
Matapan, C. = Taínaron, Ákra 19 36 22N 22 27 E
Matapédia 63 48 0N 66 59W
Matara 32 5 58N 80 30 E
Mataram 34 8 41S 116 10 E
Matarani 78 77 0S 72 10W
Mataranka 46 14 55S 133 4 E
Matatiele 57 30 20S 28 49 E
Mataura 43 46 11S 168 51 E
Matehuala 74 23 40N 100 40W
Matera 18 40 40N 16 37 E
Matheson Island 65 51 45N 96 56W
Mathis 71 28 4N 97 48W
Mathura 32 27 30N 77 40 E
Mati 35 6 55N 126 15 E
Matías Romero 74 16 53N 95 2W
Matima 56 20 15S 24 26 E
Matlock 6 53 8N 1 32W
Matmata 50 33 37N 9 59 E
Mato Grosso □ 79 14 0S 55 0W
Mato Grosso, Planalto do 79 15 0S 55 0W
Matochkin Shar 24 73 10N 56 40 E
Matosinhos 13 41 11N 8 42W
Matrah 31 23 37N 58 30 E
Matsena 53 13 5N 10 5 E
Matsue 36 35 25N 133 10 E
Matsumae 36 41 26N 140 7 E
Matsumoto 36 36 15N 138 0 E
Matsusaka 36 34 34N 136 32 E
Matsutō 36 36 31N 136 34 E
Matsuyama 36 33 45N 132 45 E
Mattagami → 62 50 43N 81 29W
Mattancheri 32 9 50N 76 15 E
Mattawa 62 46 20N 78 45W
Mattawamkeag 63 45 30N 68 21W
Matterhorn 14 45 58N 7 39 E
Matthew Town 75 20 57N 73 40W
Matthew's Ridge 78 7 37N 60 10W
Mattice 62 49 40N 83 20W
Matuba 57 24 28S 32 49 E
Matucana 78 11 55S 76 25W
Matun 32 33 22N 69 58 E
Maturín 78 9 45N 63 11W
Mau Ranipur 32 25 16N 79 8 E
Maud, Pt. 46 23 6S 113 45 E
Maude 45 34 29S 144 18 E
Maudin Sun 33 16 0N 94 30 E
Maués 78 3 20S 57 45W
Mauganj 33 24 50N 81 55 E
Maui 66 20 45N 156 20 E
Mauke 43 20 9S 157 20W
Maulamyaing 33 16 30N 97 40 E
Maumee 68 41 35N 83 40W
Maumee → 68 41 42N 83 28W
Maumere 35 8 38S 122 13 E
Maun 56 20 0S 23 26 E
Mauna Kea 66 19 50N 155 28W
Mauna Loa 66 21 8N 157 10W
Maungmagan Kyunzu 33 14 0N 97 48 E
Maupin 72 45 12N 121 9W
Maurepas L. 71 30 18N 90 35W
Maures 12 43 15N 6 15 E
Maurice L. 47 29 30S 131 0 E
Mauritania ■ 50 20 50N 10 0W
Mauritius ■ 3 20 0S 57 0 E
Mauston 70 43 48N 90 5W
Mavinga 55 15 50S 20 21 E
Mavqi'im 28 31 38N 34 32 E
Mawk Mai 33 20 14N 97 37 E
Mawlaik 33 23 40N 94 26 E
Max 70 47 50N 101 20W
Maxcanú 74 20 40N 92 0W
Maxesibeni 57 30 49S 29 23 E
Maxhamish L. 64 59 50N 123 17W
Maxixe 57 23 54S 35 17 E
Maxwelton 44 20 43S 142 41 E
May Downs 44 22 38S 148 55 E
May Pen 75 17 58N 77 15W
Maya → 25 54 31N 134 41 E
Maya Mts. 74 16 30N 89 0W
Mayaguana 75 22 30N 72 44W
Mayagüez 75 18 12N 67 9W
Mayarí 75 20 40N 75 41W
Maybell 72 40 30N 108 4W
Maydena 44 42 45S 146 30 E
Mayenne 12 48 20N 0 38W
Mayenne □ 12 48 10N 0 40W
Mayer 73 34 28N 112 17W
Mayerthorpe 64 53 57N 115 8W
Mayfield 69 36 45N 88 40W
Mayhill 73 32 58N 105 30W
Maykop 23 44 35N 40 25 E
Maynard Hills 47 28 28S 119 49 E
Mayne → 44 23 40S 141 55 E
Maynooth 9 53 22N 6 38W
Mayo 60 63 38N 135 57W
Mayo □ 9 53 47N 9 7W
Mayo L. 60 63 45N 135 0W
Mayon Volcano 35 13 15N 123 41 E
Mayor I. 43 37 16S 176 17 E
Mayson L. 65 57 55N 107 10W
Maysville 68 38 39N 83 46W
Maythalūn 28 32 21N 35 16 E
Mayu 35 1 30N 126 30 E
Mayville 70 47 30N 97 23W
Mayya 25 61 44N 130 18 E
Mazabuka 55 15 52S 27 44 E
Mazagán = El Jadida 50 33 11N 8 17W
Mazagão 79 0 7S 51 16W
Mazán 78 3 30S 73 0W
Māzandarān □ 31 36 30N 52 0 E
Mazar-e Sharīf 31 36 41N 67 0 E
Mazarredo 80 47 10S 66 50W
Mazarrón 13 37 38N 1 19W
Mazaruni → 78 6 25N 58 35W
Mazatenango 75 14 35N 91 30W
Mazatlán 74 23 10N 106 30W
Māzhān 31 32 30N 59 0 E
Mazīnān 31 36 19N 56 56 E
Mazoe → 55 16 20S 33 30 E
Mazu Dao 39 26 10N 119 55 E
Mazurian Lakes = Mazurski, Pojezierze 15 53 50N 21 0 E
Mazurski, Pojezierze 15 53 50N 21 0 E
Mbabane 57 26 18S 31 6 E
Mbaïki 54 3 53N 18 1 E
Mbala 54 8 46S 31 24 E
Mbale 54 1 8N 34 12 E
Mbalmayo 54 3 33N 11 33 E
Mbamba Bay 54 11 13S 34 49 E
Mbandaka 54 0 1N 18 18 E
Mbanza Congo 54 6 18S 14 16 E
Mbanza Ngungu 54 5 12S 14 53 E
Mbarara 54 0 35S 30 40 E
Mbashe → 57 32 15S 28 54 E
Mbeya 54 8 54S 33 29 E
Mbini □ 54 1 30N 10 0 E
Mbour 50 14 22N 16 54W
Mbout 50 16 1N 12 38W
Mbuji-Mayi 54 6 9S 23 40 E
Mbulu 54 3 45S 35 30 E
Mchinji 55 13 47S 32 58 E
Mdina 18 35 51N 14 25 E
Mead, L. 73 36 1N 114 44W
Meade 71 37 18N 100 25W
Meadow 47 26 35S 114 40 E
Meadow Lake 65 54 10N 108 26W
Meadow Lake Prov. Park 65 54 27N 109 0W
Meadow Valley Wash → 73 36 39N 114 35W
Meadville 68 41 39N 80 9W
Meaford 62 44 36N 80 35W
Mealy Mts. 63 53 10N 58 0W
Meander River 64 59 2N 117 42W
Meares, C. 72 45 37N 124 0W
Mearim → 79 3 4S 44 35W
Meath □ 9 53 32N 6 40W
Meath Park 65 53 27N 105 22W
Meaux 12 48 58N 2 50 E
Mecca = Makkah 29 21 30N 39 54 E
Mecca 73 33 37N 116 3W
Mechelen 11 51 2N 4 29 E
Mecheria 50 33 35N 0 18W
Mecklenburger Bucht 14 54 20N 11 40 E
Meconta 55 14 59S 39 50 E
Meda 46 17 22S 123 59 E

Nairobi

Nairobi .... 54 1 17S 36 48 E
Naivasha .... 54 0 40S 36 30 E
Najafābād .... 31 32 40N 51 15 E
Najd .... 30 26 30N 42 0 E
Najibabad .... 32 29 40N 78 20 E
Najin .... 38 42 12N 130 15 E
Nakadōri-Shima ... 36 32 57N 129 4 E
Nakamura .... 36 33 0N 133 0 E
Nakfa .... 51 16 40N 38 32 E
Nakhichevan
A.S.S.R. □ ..... 23 39 14N 45 30 E
Nakhodka .... 25 42 53N 132 54 E
Nakhon Phanom .. 34 17 23N 104 43 E
Nakhon Ratchasima 34 14 59N 102 12 E
Nakhon Sawan ... 34 15 35N 100 10 E
Nakhon Si
Thammarat ..... 34 8 29N 100 0 E
Nakina, B.C.,
Canada 64 59 12N 132 52W
Nakina, Ont.,
Canada 62 50 10N 86 40W
Nakskov .... 21 54 50N 11 8 E
Naktong → ..... 38 35 7N 128 57 E
Nakuru .... 54 0 15S 36 4 E
Nakusp 64 50 20N 117 45W
Nal → .... 32 25 20N 65 30 E
Nalchik .... 23 43 30N 43 33 E
Nalgonda .... 32 17 6N 79 15 E
Nallamalai Hills ... 32 15 30N 78 50 E
Nalón → 13 43 32N 6 4W
Nālūt .... 51 31 54N 11 0 E
Nam Co .... 37 30 30N 90 45 E
Nam-Phan .... 34 10 30N 106 0 E
Namacunde ...... 56 17 18S 15 50 E
Namacurra ...... 57 17 30S 36 50 E
Namak, Daryācheh-
ye .... 31 34 30N 52 0 E
Namak, Kavir-e ... 31 34 30N 57 30 E
Namaland .... 56 24 30S 17 0 E
Namangan .... 24 41 0N 71 40 E
Namapa .... 55 13 43S 39 50 E
Namaqualand .... 56 30 0S 17 25 E
Namasagali ...... 52 1 2N 33 0 E
Namber .... 35 1 2S 134 49 E
Nambour .... 45 26 32S 152 58 E
Nambucca Heads . 45 30 37S 153 0 E
Nameh .... 34 2 34N 116 21 E
Namew L. 65 54 14N 101 56W
Namib Desert =
Namibwoestyn .. 56 22 30S 15 0 E
Namibe .... 55 15 7S 12 11 E
Namibe □ .... 56 16 35S 12 30 E
Namibia ■ .... 56 22 0S 18 9 E
Namibwoestyn .... 56 22 30S 15 0 E
Namlea .... 35 3 18S 127 5 E
Namoi → .... 45 30 12S 149 30 E
Nampa 72 43 34N 116 34W
Nampula .... 55 15 6S 39 15 E
Namrole .... 35 3 46S 126 46 E
Namse Shankou .. 33 30 0N 82 25 E
Namsen → ..... 20 64 27N 11 42 E
Namsos .... 20 64 29N 11 30 E
Namtay .... 25 62 43N 129 37 E
Namtu .... 33 23 5N 97 28 E
Namu 64 51 52N 127 50W
Namur .... 11 50 27N 4 52 E
Namur □ .... 11 50 17N 5 0 E
Namutoni .... 56 18 49S 16 55 E
Namwala .... 55 15 44S 26 30 E
Nanaimo 64 49 10N 124 0W
Nanam .... 38 41 44N 129 40 E
Nanan .... 39 24 59N 118 21 E
Nanango .... 45 26 40S 152 0 E
Nan'ao, China .... 39 23 28N 117 5 E
Nanao, Japan .... 36 37 0N 137 0 E
Nanbu .... 39 31 18N 106 3 E
Nanchang .... 39 28 42N 115 55 E
Nancheng .... 39 27 33N 116 35 E
Nanching = Nanjing 39 32 2N 118 47 E
Nanchong .... 39 30 43N 106 2 E
Nanchuan .... 39 29 9N 107 6 E
Nancy .... 12 48 42N 6 12 E
Nanda Devi ...... 32 30 23N 79 59 E
Nandan .... 39 24 58N 107 29 E
Nanded .... 32 19 10N 77 20 E
Nandewar Ra. .... 45 30 15S 150 35 E
Nandi .... 43 17 42S 177 20 E
Nandurbar .... 32 21 20N 74 15 E
Nandyal .... 32 15 30N 78 30 E
Nanga .... 47 26 7S 113 45 E
Nanga-Eboko .... 54 4 41N 12 22 E
Nanga Parbat .... 32 35 10N 74 35 E
Nangapinoh ..... 34 0 20S 111 44 E
Nangarhár □ .... 31 34 20N 70 0 E
Nangatayap ..... 34 1 32S 110 34 E
Nanjiang .... 39 32 28N 106 51 E
Nanjing .... 39 32 2N 118 47 E
Nankang .... 39 25 40N 114 45 E
Nanking = Nanjing 39 32 2N 118 47 E
Nanning .... 39 22 48N 108 20 E
Nannup .... 47 33 59S 115 48 E
Nanpi .... 38 38 2N 116 45 E
Nanping .... 39 26 38N 118 10 E
Nansei-Shotō .... 37 26 0N 128 0 E
Nantes 12 47 12N 1 33W
Nanticoke 68 41 12N 76 1W
Nanton 64 50 21N 113 46W
Nantong .... 39 32 1N 120 52 E
Nantucket I. 58 41 16N 70 3W
Nanuque 79 17 50S 40 21W
Nanutarra .... 46 22 32S 115 30 E
Nanxiong .... 39 25 6N 114 15 E
Nanyang .... 39 33 11N 112 30 E
Nanyuan .... 38 39 44N 116 22 E
Nanyuki .... 54 0 2N 37 4 E
Nanzhang .... 39 31 45N 111 50 E
Náo, C. de la .... 13 38 44N 0 14 E
Naococane L. 63 52 50N 70 45W
Naoetsu .... 36 37 12N 138 10 E
Naoli He → .... 38 47 18N 134 9 E
Napa 72 38 18N 122 17W
Napanee 62 44 15N 77 0W
Napier .... 43 39 30S 176 56 E
Napier Broome B. . 46 14 2S 126 37 E
Napier Downs .... 46 17 11S 124 36 E
Napier Pen. ..... 44 12 4S 135 43 E
Naples = Nápoli .. 18 40 50N 14 17 E
Naples 69 26 10N 81 45W
Napo → 78 3 20S 72 40W
Napoleon, N. Dak.,
U.S.A. 70 46 32N 99 49W
Napoleon, Ohio,
U.S.A. 68 41 24N 84 7W
Nápoli .... 18 40 50N 14 17 E
Nappa Merrie .... 45 27 36S 141 7 E
Nara, Japan ..... 36 34 40N 135 49 E
Nara, Mali 50 15 10N 7 20W
Nara □ .... 36 34 30N 136 0 E
Nara Visa 71 35 39N 103 10W
Naracoorte .... 45 36 58S 140 45 E
Naradhan .... 45 33 34S 146 17 E
Narasapur .... 33 16 26N 81 40 E
Narathiwat .... 34 6 30N 101 48 E
Narayanganj ..... 33 23 40N 90 33 E
Narayanpet ..... 32 16 45N 77 30 E
Narbonne .... 12 43 11N 3 0 E
Nardò .... 19 40 10N 18 0 E
Narembeen ..... 47 32 7S 118 24 E
Nares Stræde 58 80 0N 70 0W
Naretha .... 47 31 0S 124 45 E
Narin .... 32 36 5N 69 0 E
Narindra,
Helodranon' i ... 57 14 55S 47 30 E
Narmada → .... 32 21 38N 72 36 E
Narodnaya .... 22 65 5N 60 0 E
Narok .... 52 1 55S 35 52 E
Narooma .... 45 36 14S 150 4 E
Narrabri .... 45 30 19S 149 46 E
Narran → .... 45 28 37S 148 12 E
Narrandera .... 45 34 42S 146 31 E
Narraway → 64 55 44N 119 55W
Narrogin .... 47 32 58S 117 14 E
Narromine .... 45 32 12S 148 12 E
Narsimhapur .... 32 22 54N 79 14 E
Narva .... 22 59 23N 28 12 E
Narvik .... 20 68 28N 17 26 E
Naryan-Mar .... 22 68 0N 53 0 E
Naryilco .... 45 28 37S 141 53 E
Narym .... 24 59 0N 81 30 E
Narymskoye .... 24 49 10N 84 15 E
Naryn .... 24 41 26N 75 58 E
Nasa .... 20 66 29N 15 23 E
Nasarawa .... 53 8 32N 7 41 E
Naseby .... 43 45 1S 170 10 E
Naser, Buheirat en 51 23 0N 32 30 E
Nashua, Iowa,
U.S.A. 70 42 55N 92 34W
Nashua, Mont.,
U.S.A. 72 48 10N 106 25W
Nashua, N.H., U.S.A. 68 42 50N 71 25W
Nashville, Ark.,
U.S.A. 71 33 56N 93 50W
Nashville, Ga.,
U.S.A. 69 31 3N 83 15W
Nashville, Tenn.,
U.S.A. 69 36 12N 86 46W
Nasik .... 32 19 58N 73 50 E
Nasirabad .... 32 26 15N 74 45 E
Naskaupi → 63 53 47N 60 51W
Nass → 64 55 0N 129 40W
Nassau 75 25 0N 77 20W
Nassau, B. 80 55 20S 68 0W
Nasser, L. = Naser,
Buheirat en ..... 51 23 0N 32 30 E
Nässjö .... 21 57 39N 14 42 E
Nat Kyizin .... 33 14 57N 97 59 E
Nata .... 56 20 12S 26 12 E
Natagaima 78 3 37N 75 6W
Natal, Brazil 79 5 47S 35 13W
Natal, Canada 64 49 43N 114 51W
Natal, Indonesia ... 34 0 35N 99 7 E
Natal □ .... 57 28 30S 30 30 E
Naṭanz .... 31 33 30N 51 55 E
Natashquan 63 50 14N 61 46W
Natashquan → .. 63 50 7N 61 50W
Natchez 71 31 35N 91 25W
Natchitoches 71 31 47N 93 4W
Nathalia .... 45 36 1S 145 13 E
Nathdwara .... 32 24 55N 73 50 E
Natimuk .... 45 36 42S 142 0 E
Nation → 64 55 30N 123 32W
National City 73 32 39N 117 7W
Natitingou .... 53 10 20N 1 26 E
Natividad, I. 74 27 50N 115 10W
Natoma 70 39 14N 99 0W
Natron, L. .... 54 2 20S 36 0 E
Natuna Besar,
Kepulauan ..... 34 4 0N 108 15 E
Natuna Selatan,
Kepulauan ..... 34 2 45N 109 0 E
Naturaliste C. .... 44 40 50S 148 15 E
Naubinway 62 46 7N 85 27W
Naumburg .... 14 51 10N 11 48 E
Nauru ■ .... 3 1 0S 166 0 E
Naushahra =
Nowshera ...... 32 34 0N 72 0 E
Nauta 78 4 31S 73 35W
Nautanwa .... 33 27 20N 83 25 E
Nautla 74 20 20N 96 50W
Navajo Res. 73 36 55N 107 30W
Navalcarnero 13 40 17N 4 5W
Navan = An Uaimh 9 53 39N 6 40W
Navarino, I. 80 55 0S 67 40W
Navarra □ 13 42 40N 1 40W
Navasota 71 30 20N 96 5W
Navassa 75 18 30N 75 0W
Naver → 8 58 34N 4 15W
Navoi .... 24 40 9N 65 22 E
Navojoa 74 27 0N 109 30W
Navolok .... 22 62 33N 39 57 E
Návpaktos .... 19 38 23N 21 50 E
Návplion .... 19 37 33N 22 50 E
Navsari .... 32 20 57N 72 59 E
Nawabshah .... 32 26 15N 68 25 E
Nawakot .... 33 27 55N 85 10 E
Nawalgarh .... 32 27 50N 75 15 E
Nawāsīf, Harrat ... 30 21 20N 42 10 E
Náxos .... 19 37 8N 25 25 E
Nāy Band .... 31 27 20N 52 40 E
Nayakhan .... 25 61 56N 159 0 E
Nayarit □ 74 22 0N 105 0W
Nazareth = Nazerat 28 32 42N 35 17 E
Nazas 74 25 10N 104 6W
Nazas → 74 25 35N 103 25W
Naze, The .... 7 51 53N 1 19 E
Naẓerat .... 28 32 42N 35 17 E
Nazir Hat .... 33 22 35N 91 49 E
Nazko 64 53 1N 123 37W
Nazko → 64 53 7N 123 34W
Ncheu .... 55 14 50S 34 47 E
Ndala .... 54 4 45S 33 15 E
Ndalatando .... 54 9 12S 14 48 E
Ndélé .... 51 8 25N 20 36 E
Ndendé .... 54 2 22S 11 23 E
Ndjamena .... 51 12 10N 14 59 E
Ndjolé .... 54 0 10S 10 45 E
Ndola .... 55 13 0S 28 34 E
Neagh, Lough 9 54 35N 6 25W
Neah Bay 72 48 25N 124 40W
Neale L. .... 46 24 15S 130 0 E
Near Is. .... 60 53 0N 172 0 E
Neath 7 51 39N 3 49W
Nebine Cr. → .... 45 29 27S 146 56 E
Nebit Dag .... 23 39 30N 54 22 E
Nebo .... 44 59 12N 32 25 E
Nebraska □ 70 41 30N 100 0W
Nebraska City 70 40 40N 95 52W
Nébrodi, Monti .... 18 37 55N 14 50 E
Necedah 70 44 2N 90 7W
Nechako → 64 53 30N 122 44W
Neches → 71 29 55N 93 52W
Neckar → .... 14 49 31N 8 26 E
Necochea 80 38 30S 58 50W
Needles 73 34 50N 114 35W
Needles, The 7 50 39N 1 35W
Neemuch = Nimach 32 24 30N 74 56 E
Neenah 68 44 10N 88 30W
Neepawa 65 50 15N 99 30W
Neft-chala = imeni
26 Bakinskikh
Komissarov .... 23 39 19N 49 12 E
Nefta .... 50 33 53N 7 50 E
Neftyannyye Kamni 23 40 20N 50 55 E
Negapatam =
Nagappattinam . 32 10 46N 79 51 E
Negaunee 68 46 30N 87 36W
Negba .... 28 31 40N 34 41 E
Negele .... 29 5 20N 39 36 E
Negev Desert =
Hanegev .... 28 30 50N 35 0 E
Negoiul, Vf. .... 15 45 38N 24 35 E
Negombo .... 32 7 12N 79 50 E
Negotin .... 19 44 16N 22 37 E
Negra Pt. .... 35 18 40N 120 50 E
Negro →,
Argentina 80 41 2S 62 47W
Negro →, Brazil . 78 3 0S 60 0W
Negro →, Uruguay 80 33 24S 58 22W
Negros .... 35 9 30N 122 40 E
Nehbandān ..... 31 31 35N 60 5 E
Nei Monggol
Zizhiqu □ ...... 38 42 0N 112 0 E
Neidpath 65 50 12N 107 20W
Neihart 72 47 0N 110 44W
Neijiang .... 39 29 35N 104 55 E
Neilton 72 47 24N 123 52W
Neisse → .... 14 52 4N 14 46 E
Neiva 78 2 56N 75 18W
Neixiang .... 39 33 10N 111 52 E
Nejanilini L. 65 59 33N 97 48W
Nekemte .... 51 9 4N 36 30 E
Neksø .... 21 55 4N 15 8 E
Nelia .... 44 20 39S 142 12 E
Neligh 70 42 11N 98 2W
Nelkan .... 25 57 40N 136 4 E
Nellore .... 32 14 27N 79 59 E
Nelma .... 25 47 39N 139 0 E
Nelson, Canada ... 64 49 30N 117 20W
Nelson, N.Z. ...... 43 41 18S 173 16 E
Nelson, U.K. 6 53 50N 2 14W
Nelson, U.S.A. 73 35 35N 113 16W
Nelson □ .... 43 42 11S 172 15 E
Nelson → 65 54 33N 98 2W
Nelson, C. .... 45 38 26S 141 32 E
Nelson, Estrecho .. 80 51 30S 75 0W
Nelson Forks 64 59 30N 124 0W
Nelson House 65 55 47N 98 51W
Nelson L. 65 55 48N 100 7W
Nelspoort .... 56 32 7S 23 0 E
Nelspruit .... 57 25 29S 30 59 E
Néma 50 16 40N 7 15W
Neman → .... 22 55 25N 21 10 E
Nemeiben L. 65 55 20N 105 20W
Nemunas =
Neman → ..... 22 55 25N 21 10 E
Nemuro .... 36 43 20N 145 35 E
Nemuro-Kaikyō ... 36 43 30N 145 30 E
Nemuy .... 25 55 40N 136 9 E
Nen Jiang → .... 38 45 28N 124 30 E
Nenagh 9 52 52N 8 11W
Nenana 60 64 30N 149 20W
Nene → .... 6 52 38N 0 13 E
Nenjiang .... 38 49 10N 125 10 E
Nenusa, Kepulauan 35 4 45N 127 1 E
Neodesha 71 37 30N 95 37W
Neosho 71 36 56N 94 28W
Neosho → 71 35 59N 95 10W
Nepal ■ .... 33 28 0N 84 30 E
Nepalganj .... 33 28 5N 81 40 E
Nephi 72 39 43N 111 52W
Nephin 9 54 1N 9 21W
Nerchinsk .... 25 52 0N 116 39 E
Nerchinskiy Zavod . 25 51 20N 119 40 E
Néret L. 63 54 45N 70 44W
Neretva → .... 19 43 1N 17 27 E
Nerva 13 37 42N 6 30W
Nes 20 65 53N 17 24W
Nes Ziyyona 28 31 56N 34 48W
Neskaupstaður ... 20 65 9N 13 42W
Ness, Loch 8 57 15N 4 30W
Nesttun .... 21 60 19N 5 21 E
Netanya .... 28 32 20N 34 51 E
Nète → .... 11 51 7N 4 14 E
Nether Stowey 7 51 0N 3 10W
Netherbury 7 50 46N 2 45W
Netherdale .... 44 21 10S 148 33 E
Netherlands ■ .... 11 52 0N 5 30 E
Netherlands
Antilles ■ 78 12 15N 69 0W
Netherlands Guiana
= Surinam ■ ... 79 4 0N 56 0W
Nettilling L. 61 66 30N 71 0W
Netzahualcoyotl,
Presa 74 17 10N 93 30W
Neubrandenburg .. 14 53 33N 13 17 E
Neuchâtel .... 14 47 0N 6 55 E
Neuchâtel, Lac de . 14 46 53N 6 50 E
Neufchâteau ...... 11 49 50N 5 25 E
Neumünster .... 14 54 4N 9 58 E
Neunkirchen .... 14 49 23N 7 12 E
Neuquén 80 38 55S 68 0W
Neuruppin .... 14 52 56N 12 48 E
Neuse → 69 35 5N 76 30W
Neusiedler See .... 14 47 50N 16 47 E
Neuss .... 11 51 12N 6 39 E
Neustrelitz .... 14 53 22N 13 4 E
Neva → .... 22 59 50N 30 30 E
Nevada 71 37 51N 94 22W
Nevada □ 72 39 20N 117 0W
Nevada, Sierra,
Spain 13 37 3N 3 15W
Nevada, Sierra,
U.S.A. 72 39 0N 120 30W
Nevada City 72 39 20N 121 0W
Nevada de Sta.
Marta, Sa. 78 10 55N 73 50W
Nevanka .... 25 56 31N 98 55 E
Nevers .... 12 47 0N 3 9 E
Nevertire .... 45 31 50S 147 44 E
Neville 65 49 58N 107 39W
Nevinnomyssk .... 23 44 40N 42 0 E
Nevis 75 17 0N 62 30W
Nevşehir .... 30 38 33N 34 40 E
Nevyansk .... 22 57 30N 60 13 E
New Albany, Ind.,
U.S.A. 68 38 20N 85 50W
New Albany, Miss.,
U.S.A. 71 34 30N 89 0W
New Amsterdam .. 78 6 15N 57 36W
New Angledool ... 45 29 5S 147 55 E
New Bedford 68 41 40N 70 52W
New Bern 69 35 8N 77 3W
New Boston 71 33 27N 94 21W
New Braunfels 71 29 43N 98 9W
New Brighton ..... 43 43 29S 172 43 E
New Britain,
Papua N. G. .... 40 5 50S 150 20 E
New Britain, U.S.A. 68 41 41N 72 47W
New Brunswick ... 68 40 30N 74 28W
New Brunswick □ . 63 46 50N 66 30W
New Bussa .... 53 9 53N 4 31 E
New Caledonia ... 40 21 0S 165 0 E
New Castile =
Castilla La Nueva 13 39 45N 3 20W
New Castle, Ind.,
U.S.A. 68 39 55N 85 23W
New Castle, Pa.,
U.S.A. 68 41 0N 80 20W
New Cristóbal 74 9 22N 79 40W
New Delhi .... 32 28 37N 77 13 E
New Denver 64 50 0N 117 25W
New England 70 46 36N 102 47W
New England Ra. .. 45 30 20S 151 45 E
New Forest 7 50 53N 1 40W
New Glasgow 63 45 35N 62 36W
New Guinea .... 40 4 0S 136 0 E
New Hampshire □ . 68 43 40N 71 40W
New Hampton 70 43 2N 92 20W
New Hanover ..... 57 29 22S 30 31 E
New Haven 68 41 20N 72 54W
New Hazelton 64 55 20N 127 30W
New Hebrides =
Vanuatu ■ ..... 3 15 0S 168 0 E
New Iberia 71 30 2N 91 54W
New Ireland .... 40 3 20S 151 50 E
New Jersey □ 68 40 30N 74 10W
New Kensington .. 68 40 36N 79 43W
New Lexington 68 39 40N 82 15W
New Liskeard 62 47 31N 79 41W
New London, Conn.,
U.S.A. 68 41 23N 72 8W
New London, Minn.,
U.S.A. 70 45 17N 94 55W
New London, Wis.,
U.S.A. 70 44 23N 88 43W
New Madrid 71 36 40N 89 30W
New Meadows 72 45 0N 116 32W
New Mexico □ 66 34 30N 106 0W
New Norcia .... 47 30 57S 116 13 E
New Norfolk ..... 44 42 46S 147 2 E
New Orleans 71 30 0N 90 5W
New Philadelphia .. 68 40 29N 81 25W
New Plymouth, N.Z. 43 39 4S 174 5 E
New Plymouth,
U.S.A. 72 43 58N 116 49W
New Providence .. 75 25 25N 78 35W
New Radnor 7 52 15N 3 10W
New Richmond ... 70 45 6N 92 34W
New Roads 71 30 43N 91 30W
New Rockford 70 47 44N 99 7W
New Ross 9 52 24N 6 58W
New Salem 70 46 51N 101 25W
New Siberian Is. =
Novosibirskiye
Ostrava .... 25 75 0N 142 0 E
New Smyrna Beach 69 29 0N 80 50W
New South Wales □ 45 33 0S 146 0 E
New Springs ..... 47 25 49S 120 1 E
New Town 70 48 0N 102 30W
New Ulm 70 44 15N 94 30W
New Waterford ... 63 46 13N 60 4W
New Westminster . 64 49 13N 122 55W
New York □ 68 42 40N 76 0W
New York City 68 40 45N 74 0W
New Zealand ■ ... 43 40 0S 176 0 E
Newala .... 54 10 58S 39 18 E
Newark, Del., U.S.A. 68 39 42N 75 45W
Newark, N.J., U.S.A. 68 40 41N 74 12W
Newark, N.Y., U.S.A. 68 43 2N 77 10W
Newark, Ohio, U.S.A. 68 40 5N 82 24W
Newark-on-Trent .. 6 53 6N 0 48W
Newaygo 68 43 25N 85 48W
Newberg 72 45 22N 123 0W
Newberry, Mich.,
U.S.A. 68 46 20N 85 32W
Newberry, S.C.,
U.S.A. 69 34 17N 81 37W
Newbrook 64 54 24N 112 57W
Newburgh 68 41 30N 74 1W
Newbury 7 51 24N 1 19W
Newburyport 68 42 48N 70 50W
Newcastle, Australia 45 33 0S 151 46 E
Newcastle, Canada 63 47 1N 65 38W
Newcastle, S. Africa 57 27 45S 29 58 E
Newcastle, U.K. ... 9 54 13N 5 54W

Novaya Ladoga

Newcastle, U.S.A. 70 43 50N 104 12W
Newcastle Emlyn 7 52 2N 4 29W
Newcastle Ra. 46 15 45S 130 15 E
Newcastle-under-Lyme 6 53 2N 2 15W
Newcastle-upon-Tyne 6 54 59N 1 37W
Newcastle Waters 44 17 30S 133 28 E
Newdegate 47 33 6S 119 0 E
Newe Etan 28 32 30N 35 32 E
Newe Sha'anan 28 32 47N 34 59 E
Newe Zohar 28 31 9N 35 21 E
Newell 70 44 48N 103 25W
Newenham, C. 60 58 40N 162 15W
Newfoundland □ 61 53 0N 58 0W
Newhalem 64 48 41N 121 16W
Newham 7 51 31N 0 2 E
Newhaven 7 50 47N 0 4 E
Newkirk 71 36 52N 97 3W
Newman 46 23 18S 119 45 E
Newmarket, Ireland 9 52 13N 9 0W
Newmarket, U.K. 7 52 15N 0 23 E
Newnan 69 33 22N 84 48W
Newport, Gwent, U.K. 7 51 35N 3 0W
Newport, I. of W., U.K. 7 50 42N 1 18W
Newport, Salop, U.K. 7 52 47N 2 22W
Newport, Ark., U.S.A. 71 35 38N 91 15W
Newport, Ky., U.S.A. 68 39 5N 84 23W
Newport, N.H., U.S.A. 68 43 23N 72 8W
Newport, Oreg., U.S.A. 72 44 41N 124 2W
Newport, R.I., U.S.A. 68 41 13N 71 19W
Newport, Tenn., U.S.A. 69 35 59N 83 12W
Newport, Vt., U.S.A. 68 44 57N 72 17W
Newport, Wash., U.S.A. 72 48 11N 117 2W
Newport Beach 73 33 40N 117 58W
Newport News 68 37 2N 76 30W
Newquay 7 50 24N 5 6W
Newry 9 54 10N 6 20W
Newry & Mourne □ 9 54 10N 6 15W
Newton, Iowa, U.S.A. 70 41 40N 93 3W
Newton, Mass., U.S.A. 68 42 21N 71 10W
Newton, Miss., U.S.A. 71 32 19N 89 10W
Newton, N.C., U.S.A. 69 35 42N 81 10W
Newton, N.J., U.S.A. 68 41 3N 74 46W
Newton, Tex., U.S.A. 71 30 54N 93 42W
Newton Abbot 7 50 32N 3 37W
Newton Boyd 45 29 45S 152 16 E
Newton Stewart 8 54 57N 4 30W
Newtonmore 8 57 4N 4 7W
Newtown 7 52 31N 3 19W
Newtownabbey 9 54 40N 5 55W
Newtownabbey □ 9 54 45N 6 0W
Newtownards 9 54 37N 5 40W
Neya 22 58 21N 43 49 E
Neyrīz 31 29 15N 54 19 E
Neyshābūr 31 36 10N 58 50 E
Nezhin 23 51 5N 31 55 E
Nezperce 72 46 13N 116 15W
Ngabang 34 0 23N 109 55 E
Ngabordamlu, Tanjung 35 6 56S 134 11 E
Ngami Depression 56 20 30S 22 46 E
Nganglong Kangri 33 33 0N 81 0 E
Nganjuk 35 7 32S 111 55 E
Ngaoundéré 54 7 15N 13 35 E
Ngapara 43 44 57S 170 46 E
Ngawi 35 7 24S 111 26 E
Ngoring Hu 37 34 55N 97 5 E
Ngorongoro 52 3 11S 35 32 E
Ngozi 52 2 54S 29 50 E
Ngudu 54 2 58S 33 25 E
Nguigmi 53 14 20N 13 20 E
Ngukurr 44 14 44S 134 44 E
Nguru 53 12 56N 10 29 E
Nha Trang 34 12 16N 109 10 E
Nhacoongo 57 24 18S 35 14 E
Nhangutazi, L. 57 24 0S 34 30 E
Nhill 45 36 18S 141 40 E
Nhulunbuy 44 12 10S 137 20 E
Niafounké 50 16 0N 4 5W
Niagara 68 45 45N 88 0W
Niagara Falls, Canada 62 43 7N 79 5W
Niagara Falls, U.S.A. 68 43 5N 79 0W
Niah 34 3 58N 113 46 E
Niamey 53 13 27N 2 6 E
Niangara 54 3 42N 27 50 E
Nianzishan 38 47 31N 122 53 E
Nias 34 1 0N 97 30 E
Nicaragua ■ 75 11 40N 85 30W
Nicaragua, L. de 75 12 0N 85 30W
Nicastro 18 39 0N 16 18 E
Nice 12 43 42N 7 14 E
Niceville 69 30 30N 86 30W
Nichinan 36 31 38N 131 23 E
Nicholás, Canal 75 23 30N 80 5W
Nicholasville 68 37 54N 84 31W
Nicholson 46 18 2S 128 54 E
Nicholson → 44 17 31S 139 36 E
Nicholson Ra. 47 27 15S 116 45 E
Nicobar Is. 3 9 0N 93 0 E
Nicola 64 50 12N 120 40W
Nicolet 62 46 17N 72 35W
Nicolls Town 75 25 8N 78 0W
Nicosia 30 35 10N 33 25 E
Nicoya, G. de 75 10 0N 85 0W
Nicoya, Pen. de 75 9 45N 85 40W
Nidd → 6 54 1N 1 32W
Niekerkshoop 56 29 19S 22 51 E
Nienburg 14 52 38N 9 15 E
Nieu Bethesda 56 31 51S 24 34 E
Nieuw Amsterdam 79 5 53N 55 5W
Nieuw Nickerie 79 6 0N 56 59W
Nieuwoudtville 56 31 23S 19 7 E
Nieuwpoort 11 51 8N 2 45 E
Nièvre □ 12 47 10N 3 40 E
Niğde 30 38 0N 34 40 E
Nigel 57 26 27S 28 25 E
Niger □ 53 10 0N 5 0 E
Niger ■ 50 17 30N 10 0 E
Niger → 53 5 33N 6 33 E
Nigeria ■ 53 8 30N 8 0 E
Nightcaps 43 45 57S 168 2 E
Nii-Jima 36 34 20N 139 15 E
Niigata 36 37 58N 139 0 E
Niigata □ 36 37 15N 138 45 E
Niihama 36 33 55N 133 16 E
Niihau 66 21 55N 160 10W
Nijkerk 11 52 13N 5 30 E
Nijmegen 11 51 50N 5 52 E
Nijverdal 11 52 22N 6 28 E
Nike 53 6 26N 7 29 E
Nikel 20 69 24N 30 12 E
Nikiniki 35 9 49S 124 30 E
Nikki 53 9 58N 3 12 E
Nikkō 36 36 45N 139 35 E
Nikolayev 23 46 58N 32 0 E
Nikolayevsk 23 50 0N 45 35 E
Nikolayevsk-na-Amur 25 53 8N 140 44 E
Nikolskoye 25 55 12N 166 0 E
Nikopol 23 47 35N 34 25 E
Nīkshahr 31 26 15N 60 10 E
Nîl, Nahr en → 51 30 10N 31 6 E
Nîl el Abyad → 51 15 38N 32 31 E
Nîl el Azraq → 51 15 38N 32 31 E
Niland 73 33 16N 115 30W
Nile = Nîl, Nahr en → 51 30 10N 31 6 E
Niles 68 41 8N 80 40W
Nimach 32 24 30N 74 56 E
Nîmes 12 43 50N 4 23 E
Nimmitabel 45 36 29S 149 15 E
Nimneryskiy 25 57 50N 125 10 E
Nīmrūz □ 31 30 0N 62 0 E
Nimule 54 3 32N 32 3 E
Nīnawá 30 36 25N 43 10 E
Nindigully 45 28 21S 148 50 E
Ninemile 64 56 0N 130 7W
Nineveh = Nīnawá 30 36 25N 43 10 E
Ningaloo 46 22 41S 113 41 E
Ning'an 38 44 22N 129 20 E
Ningbo 39 29 51N 121 28 E
Ningde 39 26 38N 119 23 E
Ningdu 39 26 25N 115 59 E
Ningjin 38 37 35N 114 57 E
Ningming 39 22 8N 107 4 E
Ningpo = Ningbo 39 29 51N 121 28 E
Ningqiang 39 32 47N 106 15 E
Ningshan 39 33 21N 108 21 E
Ningsia Hui A.R. = Ningxia Huizu Zizhiqu □ 38 38 0N 106 0 E
Ningwu 38 39 0N 112 18 E
Ningxia Huizu Zizhiqu □ 38 38 0N 106 0 E
Ningxiang 39 28 15N 112 30 E
Ningyuan 39 25 37N 111 57 E
Ninove 11 50 51N 4 2 E
Niobrara 70 42 48N 97 59W
Niobrara → 70 42 45N 98 0W
Nioro du Sahel 50 15 15N 9 30W
Niort 12 46 19N 0 29W
Nipawin 65 53 20N 104 0W
Nipawin Prov. Park 65 54 0N 104 37W
Nipigon 62 49 0N 88 17W
Nipigon, L. 62 49 50N 88 30W
Nipin → 65 55 46N 108 35W
Nipishish L. 63 54 12N 60 45W
Nipissing L. 62 46 20N 80 0W
Nipomo 73 35 4N 120 29W
Niquelândia 79 14 33S 48 23W
Nirmal 32 19 3N 78 20 E
Nirmali 33 26 20N 86 35 E
Niš 19 43 19N 21 58 E
Nişāb 29 14 25N 46 29 E
Nishinomiya 36 34 45N 135 20 E
Niskibi → 62 56 29N 88 9W
Nisutlin → 64 60 14N 132 34W
Niţā' 30 27 15N 48 35 E
Nitchequon 63 53 10N 70 58W
Niterói 79 22 52S 43 0W
Nith → 8 55 20N 3 5W
Nitra 15 48 19N 18 4 E
Nitra → 15 47 46N 18 10 E
Niuafo'ou 43 15 30S 175 58W
Niue I. 2 19 2S 169 54W
Niut 34 0 55N 110 6 E
Nivelles 11 50 35N 4 20 E
Nivernais 12 47 0N 3 20 E
Nixon 71 29 17N 97 45W
Nizamabad 32 18 45N 78 7 E
Nizamghat 33 28 20N 95 45 E
Nizhne Kolymsk 25 68 34N 160 55 E
Nizhneangarsk 25 55 47N 109 30 E
Nizhnekamsk 22 55 38N 51 49 E
Nizhneudinsk 25 54 54N 99 3 E
Nizhnevartovsk 24 60 56N 76 38 E
Nizhneyansk 25 71 26N 136 4 E
Nizhniy Novgorod = Gorkiy 22 56 20N 44 0 E
Nizhniy Tagil 22 57 55N 59 57 E
Nizhnyaya Tunguska → 25 64 20N 93 0 E
Nizip 30 37 5N 37 50 E
Nizké Tatry 15 48 55N 20 0 E
Njombe 54 9 20S 34 50 E
Nkambe 53 6 35N 10 40 E
Nkawkaw 53 6 36N 0 49W
Nkhata Bay 54 11 33S 34 16 E
Nkhota Kota 55 12 56S 34 15 E
Nkongsamba 54 4 55N 9 55 E
Nkurenkuru 56 17 42S 18 32 E
Nmai → 33 25 30N 97 25 E
Noakhali = Maijdi 33 22 48N 91 10 E
Noatak 60 67 32N 162 59W
Nobeoka 36 32 36N 131 41 E
Noblesville 68 40 1N 85 59W
Nocera Inferiore 18 40 45N 14 37 E
Nockatunga 45 27 42S 142 42 E
Nocona 71 33 48N 97 45W
Noel 71 36 36N 94 29W
Nogales, Mexico 74 31 20N 110 56W
Nogales, U.S.A. 73 31 33N 110 56W
Nōgata 36 33 48N 130 44 E
Noggerup 47 33 32S 116 5 E
Noginsk 25 64 30N 90 50 E
Nogoa → 44 23 40S 147 55 E
Noirmoutier, I. de 12 46 58N 2 10W
Nojane 56 23 15S 20 14 E
Nok Kundi 31 28 50N 62 45 E
Nokaneng 56 19 40S 22 17 E
Nokhtuysk 25 60 0N 117 45 E
Nokomis 65 51 35N 105 0W
Nokomis L. 65 57 0N 103 0W
Nola 54 3 35N 16 4 E
Noma Omuramba → 56 18 52S 20 53 E
Noman L. 65 62 15N 108 55W
Nome 60 64 30N 165 24W
Nonacho L. 65 61 42N 109 40W
Nonda 44 20 40S 142 28 E
Nong Khai 34 17 50N 102 46 E
Nong'an 38 44 25N 125 5 E
Nongoma 57 27 58S 31 35 E
Nonoava 74 27 28N 106 44W
Noonamah 46 12 40S 131 4 E
Noonan 70 48 51N 102 59W
Noondoo 45 28 35S 148 30 E
Noonkanbah 46 18 30S 124 50 E
Noord Brabant □ 11 51 40N 5 0 E
Noord Holland □ 11 52 30N 4 45 E
Noordbeveland 11 51 35N 3 50 E
Noordoostpolder 11 52 45N 5 45 E
Noordwijk aan Zee 11 52 14N 4 26 E
Nootka 64 49 38N 126 38W
Nootka I. 64 49 32N 126 42W
Nóqui 54 5 55S 13 30 E
Noranda 62 48 20N 79 0W
Nord □ 12 50 15N 3 30 E
Nord-Ostsee Kanal 14 54 15N 9 40 E
Nord-Trøndelag fylke □ 20 64 20N 12 0 E
Nordegg 64 52 29N 116 5W
Nordhausen 14 51 29N 10 47 E
Nordkapp 20 71 10N 25 44 E
Nordkinn 4 71 8N 27 40 E
Nordland fylke □ 20 65 40N 13 0 E
Nordrhein-Westfalen □ 14 51 45N 7 30 E
Nordvik 25 74 2N 111 32 E
Nore → 9 52 40N 7 20W
Norembega 62 48 59N 80 43W
Norfolk, Nebr., U.S.A. 70 42 3N 97 25W
Norfolk, Va., U.S.A. 68 36 40N 76 15W
Norfolk □ 6 52 39N 1 0 E
Norfolk Broads 6 52 30N 1 15 E
Norfolk I. 3 28 58S 168 3 E
Norfork Res. 71 36 13N 92 15W
Norilsk 25 69 20N 88 6 E
Norley 45 27 45S 143 48 E
Norma, Mt. 44 20 55S 140 42 E
Normal 70 40 30N 89 0W
Norman 71 35 12N 97 30W
Norman → 44 17 28S 140 49 E
Norman Wells 60 65 17N 126 51W
Normanby → 44 14 23S 144 10 E
Normandie 12 48 45N 0 10 E
Normandin 62 48 49N 72 31W
Normandy = Normandie 12 48 45N 0 10 E
Normanhurst, Mt. 47 25 4S 122 30 E
Normanton 44 17 40S 141 10 E
Norquay 65 51 53N 102 5W
Norquinco 80 41 51S 70 55W
Norrbotten □ 20 66 30N 22 30 E
Norrby 20 64 55N 18 15 E
Nørresundby 21 57 5N 9 52 E
Norris 72 45 40N 111 40W
Norristown 68 40 9N 75 21W
Norrköping 21 58 37N 16 11 E
Norrland □ 20 66 50N 18 0 E
Norrtälje 21 59 46N 18 42 E
Norseman 47 32 8S 121 43 E
Norsk 25 52 30N 130 0 E
North Adams 68 42 42N 73 6W
North America 58 40 0N 100 0W
North Battleford 65 52 50N 108 17W
North Bay 62 46 20N 79 30W
North Belcher Is. 62 56 50N 79 50W
North Bend, Canada 64 49 50N 121 27W
North Bend, U.S.A. 72 43 28N 124 14W
North Berwick 8 56 4N 2 44W
North Canadian → 71 35 17N 95 31W
North C., Canada 63 47 2N 60 20W
North C., N.Z. 43 34 23S 173 4 E
North Caribou L. 62 52 50N 90 40W
North Carolina □ 69 35 30N 80 0W
North Channel, Br. Is. 8 55 0N 5 30W
North Channel, Canada 62 46 0N 83 0W
North Chicago 68 42 19N 87 50W
North Dakota □ 70 47 30N 100 0W
North Dandalup 47 32 30S 115 57 E
North Down □ 9 54 40N 5 45W
North Downs 7 51 17N 0 30 E
North East Frontier Agency = Arunachal Pradesh □ 33 28 0N 95 0 E
North East Providence Chan. 75 26 0N 76 0W
North Esk → 8 56 44N 2 25W
North European Plain 4 55 0N 20 0 E
North Foreland 7 51 22N 1 28 E
North Henik L. 65 61 45N 97 40W
North I. 43 38 0S 175 0 E
North Knife → 65 58 53N 94 45W
North Korea ■ 38 40 0N 127 0 E
North Lakhimpur 33 27 14N 94 7 E
North Las Vegas 73 36 15N 115 6W
North Loup → 70 41 17N 98 23W
North Minch 8 58 5N 5 55W
North Nahanni → 64 62 15N 123 20W
North Ossetian A.S.S.R. □ 23 43 30N 44 30 E
North Palisade 73 37 6N 118 32W
North Platte 70 41 10N 100 50W
North Platte → 70 41 15N 100 45W
North Pt. 63 47 5N 64 0W
North Portal 65 49 0N 102 33W
North Powder 72 45 2N 117 59W
North Ronaldsay 8 59 20N 2 30W
North Saskatchewan → 65 53 15N 105 5W
North Sea 4 56 0N 4 0 E
North Sporades = Voríai Sporádhes 19 39 15N 23 30 E
North Sydney 63 46 12N 60 15W
North Thompson → 64 50 40N 120 20W
North Tonawanda 68 43 5N 78 50W
North Truchas Pk. 73 36 0N 105 30W
North Twin I. 62 53 20N 80 0W
North Tyne → 6 54 59N 2 7W
North Uist 8 57 40N 7 15W
North Vancouver 64 49 25N 123 3W
North Vernon 68 39 0N 85 35W
North Wabasca L. 64 56 0N 113 55W
North Walsham 6 52 49N 1 22 E
North West C. 46 21 45S 114 9 E
North West Christmas I. Ridge 41 6 30N 165 0W
North West Frontier □ 32 34 0N 71 0 E
North West Highlands 8 57 35N 5 2W
North West Providence Channel 75 26 0N 78 0W
North West River 63 53 30N 60 10W
North West Territories □ 60 67 0N 110 0W
North York Moors 6 54 25N 0 50W
North Yorkshire □ 6 54 15N 1 25W
Northallerton 6 54 20N 1 26W
Northam 56 24 56S 27 18 E
Northampton, Australia 47 28 27S 114 33 E
Northampton, U.K. 7 52 14N 0 54W
Northampton, U.S.A. 68 42 22N 72 31W
Northampton □ 7 52 16N 0 55W
Northampton Downs 44 24 35S 145 48 E
Northcliffe 47 34 39S 116 7 E
Northern Circars 33 17 30N 82 30 E
Northern Group 43 10 0S 160 0W
Northern Indian L. 65 57 20N 97 20W
Northern Ireland □ 9 54 45N 7 0W
Northern Light, L. 62 48 15N 90 39W
Northern Marianas 40 17 0N 145 0 E
Northern Territory □ 46 16 0S 133 0 E
Northfield 70 44 30N 93 10W
Northland □ 43 35 30S 173 30 E
Northome 70 47 53N 94 15W
Northport, Ala., U.S.A. 69 33 15N 87 35W
Northport, Mich., U.S.A. 68 45 8N 85 39W
Northport, Wash., U.S.A. 72 48 55N 117 48W
Northumberland □ 7 55 12N 2 0W
Northumberland, C. 45 38 5S 140 40 E
Northumberland Is. 44 21 30S 149 50 E
Northumberland Str. 63 46 20N 64 0W
Northwich 6 53 16N 2 30W
Northwood, Iowa, U.S.A. 70 43 27N 93 0W
Northwood, N. Dak., U.S.A. 70 47 44N 97 30W
Norton 70 39 50N 99 53W
Norton Sd. 60 64 0N 164 0W
Norwalk, Conn., U.S.A. 68 41 9N 73 25W
Norwalk, Ohio, U.S.A. 68 41 13N 82 38W
Norway 68 45 46N 87 57W
Norway ■ 21 63 0N 11 0 E
Norway House 65 53 59N 97 50W
Norwegian Sea 21 66 0N 1 0 E
Norwich, U.K. 6 52 38N 1 17 E
Norwich, U.S.A. 68 42 32N 75 30W
Noshiro 36 40 12N 140 0 E
Nosok 24 70 10N 82 20 E
Noşratābād 31 29 55N 60 0 E
Noss Hd. 8 58 29N 3 4W
Nossob → 56 26 55S 20 45 E
Nosy Bé 55 13 25S 48 15 E
Nosy Boraha 57 16 50S 49 55 E
Nosy Mitsio 55 12 54S 48 36 E
Nosy Varika 57 20 35S 48 32 E
Notigi Dam 65 56 40N 99 10W
Notikewin → 64 57 2N 117 38W
Noto 18 36 52N 15 4 E
Noto-Hanto 36 37 0N 137 0 E
Notre-Dame 63 46 18N 64 46W
Notre Dame B. 63 49 45N 55 30W
Notre Dame de Koartac = Koartac 61 60 55N 69 40W
Notre Dame d'Ivugivic = Ivugivik 61 62 24N 77 55W
Nottaway → 62 51 22N 78 55W
Nottingham 6 52 57N 1 10W
Nottingham □ 6 53 10N 1 0W
Nottoway → 68 36 33N 76 55W
Notwane → 56 23 35S 26 58 E
Nouâdhibou 50 20 54N 17 0W
Nouâdhibou, Ras 50 20 50N 17 0W
Nouakchott 50 18 9N 15 58W
Nouméa 40 22 17S 166 30 E
Noupoort 56 31 10S 24 57 E
Nouveau Comptoir 62 53 0N 78 49W
Nouvelle Calédonie = New Caledonia 40 21 0S 165 0 E
Nova Casa Nova 79 9 25S 41 5W
Nova Cruz 79 6 28S 35 25W
Nova Friburgo 79 22 16S 42 30W
Nova Gaia 54 10 10S 17 35 E
Nova Iguaçu 79 22 45S 43 28W
Nova Iorque 79 7 0S 44 5W
Nova Lima 79 19 59S 43 51W
Nova Lisboa = Huambo 55 12 42S 15 54 E
Nova Mambone 57 21 0S 35 3 E
Nova Scotia □ 63 45 10N 63 0W
Nova Sofala 57 20 7S 34 42 E
Nova Venécia 79 18 45S 40 24W
Noval Iorque 79 6 48S 44 0W
Novara 18 45 27N 8 36 E
Novaya Ladoga 22 60 7N 32 16 E

Novaya Lyalya

Novaya Lyalya **24** 59 10N 60 35 E
Novaya Sibir, Ostrov **25** 75 10N 150 0 E
Novaya Zemlya **24** 75 0N 56 0 E
Nové Zámky **15** 48 2N 18 8 E
Novgorod **22** 58 30N 31 25 E
Novgorod-Severskiy **22** 52 2N 33 10 E
Novi Sad **19** 45 18N 19 52 E
Novo Remanso **79** 9 41S 42 4W
Novoaltaysk **24** 53 30N 84 0 E
Novocherkassk **23** 47 27N 40 5 E
Novokazalinsk **24** 45 48N 62 6 E
Novokuybyshevsk **22** 53 7N 49 58 E
Novokuznetsk **24** 53 45N 87 10 E
Novomoskovsk **22** 54 5N 38 15 E
Novorossiysk **23** 44 43N 37 46 E
Novorybnoye **25** 72 50N 105 50 E
Novoshakhtinsk **23** 47 46N 39 58 E
Novosibirsk **24** 55 0N 83 5 E
Novosibirskiye Ostrava **25** 75 0N 142 0 E
Novotroitsk **22** 51 10N 58 15 E
Novouzensk **23** 50 32N 48 17 E
Novska **18** 45 19N 17 0 E
Novvy Port **24** 67 40N 72 30 E
Now Shahr **31** 36 40N 51 30 E
Nowgong **33** 26 20N 92 50 E
Nowra **45** 34 53S 150 35 E
Nowshera **32** 34 0N 72 0 E
Nowy Sącz **15** 49 40N 20 41 E
Nowy Tomyśl **14** 52 19N 16 10 E
Noxon **72** 48 0N 115 43W
Noyes I. **64** 55 30N 133 40W
Nsanje **55** 16 55S 35 12 E
Nsawam **53** 5 50N 0 24W
Nsukka **53** 6 51N 7 29 E
Nûbîya, Es Sahrâ En **51** 21 30N 33 30 E
Nuboai **35** 2 10S 136 30 E
Nueces → **71** 27 50N 97 30W
Nueima → **28** 31 54N 35 25 E
Nueltin L. **65** 60 30N 99 30W
Nueva Gerona **75** 21 53N 82 49W
Nueva Imperial **80** 38 45S 72 58W
Nueva Rosita **74** 28 0N 101 11W
Nueva San Salvador **75** 13 40N 89 18W
Nuéve de Julio **80** 35 30S 61 0W
Nuevitas **75** 21 30N 77 20W
Nuevo, G. **80** 43 0S 64 30W
Nuevo Laredo **74** 27 30N 99 30W
Nuevo León □ **74** 25 0N 100 0W
Nugget Pt. **43** 46 27S 169 50 E
Nuhaka **43** 39 3S 177 45 E
Nukey Bluff, Mt. **45** 32 26S 135 29 E
Nukheila **51** 19 1N 26 21 E
Nuku'alofa **43** 21 10S 174 0W
Nukus **24** 42 20N 59 7 E
Nulato **60** 64 40N 158 10W
Nullagine → **46** 21 20S 120 20 E
Nullarbor **47** 31 28S 130 55 E
Nullarbor Plain **47** 31 10S 129 0 E
Numalla, L. **45** 28 43S 144 20 E
Numan **53** 9 29N 12 3 E
Numata **36** 36 45N 139 4 E
Numazu **36** 35 7N 138 51 E
Numbulwar **44** 14 15S 135 45 E
Numfoor **35** 1 0S 134 50 E
Numurkah **45** 36 5S 145 26 E
Nunaksaluk I. **63** 55 49N 60 20W
Nuneaton **7** 52 32N 1 29W
Nunivak **60** 60 0N 166 0W
Nunkun **32** 33 57N 76 2 E
Nunspeet **11** 52 21N 5 45 E
Nuomin He → **38** 46 45N 126 55 E
Nuremburg = Nürnberg **14** 49 26N 11 5 E
Nurina **47** 30 56S 126 33 E
Nuriootpa **45** 34 27S 139 0 E
Nürnberg **14** 49 26N 11 5 E
Nurran, L. = Terewah, L. **45** 29 52S 147 35 E
Nurrari Lakes **47** 29 1S 130 5 E
Nusa Barung **35** 8 10S 113 30 E
Nusa Kambangan **35** 7 40S 108 10 E
Nusa Tenggara Barat □ **34** 8 50S 117 30 E
Nusa Tenggara Timur □ **35** 9 30S 122 0 E
Nusaybin **23** 37 3N 41 10 E
Nushki **32** 29 35N 66 0 E
Nutak **61** 57 28N 61 59W
Nutwood Downs **44** 15 49S 134 10 E
Nuwakot **33** 28 10N 83 55 E
Nuweveldberge **56** 32 10S 21 45 E
Nuyts, C. **47** 32 2S 132 21 E
Nuyts Arch. **45** 32 35S 133 20 E
Nxau-Nxau **56** 18 57S 21 4 E
Nyah West **45** 35 16S 143 21 E
Nyahanga **54** 2 20S 33 37 E
Nyahururu **54** 0 2N 36 27 E
Nyainqentanglha Shan **37** 30 0N 90 0 E
Nyakanazi **52** 3 2S 31 10 E
Nyakanyasi **52** 1 10S 31 13 E
Nyâlâ **51** 12 2N 24 58 E
Nyandoma **22** 61 40N 40 12 E
Nyangana **56** 18 0S 20 40 E
Nyanza **52** 4 21S 29 36 E
Nyarling → **64** 60 41N 113 23W
Nyasa, L. = Malawi, L. **55** 12 30S 34 30 E
Nyazepetrovsk **22** 56 3N 59 36 E
Nybro **21** 56 44N 15 55 E
Nyda **24** 66 40N 72 58 E
Nyeri **54** 0 23S 36 56 E
Nyíregyháza **15** 47 58N 21 47 E
Nykarleby **20** 63 22N 22 31 E
Nykøbing **21** 54 56N 11 52 E
Nyköping **21** 58 45N 17 0 E
Nylstroom **57** 24 42S 28 22 E
Nymagee **45** 32 7S 146 20 E
Nynäshamn **21** 58 54N 17 57 E
Nyngan **45** 31 30S 147 8 E
Nysa **15** 50 30N 17 22 E
Nysa → **14** 52 4N 14 46 E
Nyssa **72** 43 56N 117 2W
Nyurba **25** 63 17N 118 28 E
Nzega **54** 4 10S 33 12 E
N'Zérékoré **50** 7 49N 8 48W
Nzeto **54** 7 10S 12 52 E
Nzubuka **52** 4 45S 32 50 E

O

Ō-Shima **36** 34 44N 139 24 E
Oacoma **70** 43 50N 99 26W
Oahe Dam **70** 44 28N 100 25W
Oahe L. **70** 45 30N 100 25W
Oahu **66** 21 30N 158 0W
Oak Creek **72** 40 15N 106 59W
Oak Harb. **72** 48 20N 122 38W
Oak Hill **68** 38 0N 81 7W
Oak Park **68** 41 55N 87 45W
Oak Ridge **69** 36 1N 84 12W
Oakbank **45** 33 4S 140 33 E
Oakdale, Calif., U.S.A. **73** 37 45N 120 55W
Oakdale, La., U.S.A. **71** 30 50N 92 38W
Oakengates **6** 52 42N 2 29W
Oakes **70** 46 14N 98 4W
Oakesdale **72** 47 11N 117 15W
Oakey **45** 27 25S 151 43 E
Oakham **6** 52 40N 0 43W
Oakland, Calif., U.S.A. **73** 37 50N 122 18W
Oakland, Oreg., U.S.A. **72** 43 23N 123 18W
Oakland City **68** 38 20N 87 20W
Oakley, Idaho, U.S.A. **72** 42 14N 113 55W
Oakley, Kans., U.S.A. **70** 39 8N 100 51W
Oakover → **46** 21 0S 120 40 E
Oakridge **72** 43 47N 122 31W
Oamaru **43** 45 5S 170 59 E
Oatman **73** 35 1N 114 19W
Oaxaca **74** 17 2N 96 40W
Oaxaca □ **74** 17 0N 97 0W
Ob → **24** 66 45N 69 30 E
Oba **62** 49 4N 84 7W
Oban **8** 56 25N 5 30W
Obbia **29** 5 25N 48 30 E
Obed **64** 53 30N 117 10W
Oberhausen **14** 51 28N 6 50 E
Oberlin, Kans., U.S.A. **70** 39 52N 100 31W
Oberlin, La., U.S.A. **71** 30 42N 92 42W
Oberon **45** 33 45S 149 52 E
Obi, Kepulauan **35** 1 23S 127 45 E
Óbidos **79** 1 50S 55 30W
Obihiro **36** 42 56N 143 12 E
Obilatu **35** 1 25S 127 20 E
Obluchye **25** 49 1N 131 4 E
Obo **54** 5 20N 26 32 E
Observatory Inlet **64** 55 10N 129 54W
Obshchi Syrt **4** 52 0N 53 0 E
Obskaya Guba **24** 69 0N 73 0 E
Obuasi **53** 6 17N 1 40W
Ocala **69** 29 11N 82 5W
Ocampo **74** 28 9N 108 24W
Ocaña **13** 39 55N 3 30W
Ocanomowoc **70** 43 7N 88 30W
Ocate **71** 36 12N 104 59W
Occidental, Cordillera **78** 5 0N 76 0W
Ocean, I. = Banaba **40** 0 45S 169 50 E
Ocean City **68** 39 18N 74 34W
Ocean Park **72** 46 30N 124 2W
Oceanside **73** 33 13N 117 26W
Ochil Hills **8** 56 14N 3 40W
Ochre River **65** 51 4N 99 47W
Ocilla **69** 31 35N 83 12W
Ocmulgee → **69** 31 58N 82 32W
Oconee → **69** 31 58N 82 32W
Oconto **68** 44 52N 87 53W
Oconto Falls **68** 44 52N 88 10W
Ocotal **75** 13 41N 86 31W
Ocotlán **74** 20 21N 102 42W
Octave **73** 34 10N 112 43W
Ocumare del Tuy **78** 10 7N 66 46W
Oda **53** 5 50N 0 51W
Ódáðahraun **20** 65 5N 17 0W
Odate **36** 40 16N 140 34 E
Odawara **36** 35 20N 139 6 E
Odda **21** 60 3N 6 35 E
Oddur **29** 4 11N 43 52 E
Odei → **65** 56 6N 96 54W
Ödemiş **30** 38 15N 28 0 E
Odendaalsrus **56** 27 48S 26 45 E
Odense **21** 55 22N 10 23 E
Oder → **14** 53 33N 14 38 E
Odessa, Tex., U.S.A. **71** 31 51N 102 23W
Odessa, Wash., U.S.A. **72** 47 19N 118 35W
Odessa, U.S.S.R. **23** 46 30N 30 45 E
Odiakwe **56** 20 12S 25 17 E
Odienné **50** 9 30N 7 34W
Odintsovo **22** 55 39N 37 15 E
O'Donnell **71** 33 0N 101 48W
Odorheiu Secuiesc **15** 46 21N 25 21 E
Odra → **14** 53 33N 14 38 E
Odžak **19** 45 3N 18 18 E
Odzi **57** 19 0S 32 20 E
Oeiras **79** 7 0S 42 8W
Oelrichs **70** 43 11N 103 14W
Oelwein **70** 42 41N 91 55W
Oenpelli **46** 12 20S 133 4 E
Ofanto → **18** 41 22N 16 13 E
Offa **53** 8 13N 4 42 E
Offaly □ **9** 53 15N 7 30W
Offenbach **14** 50 6N 8 46 E
Ofotfjorden **20** 68 27N 16 40 E
Oga-Hantō **36** 39 58N 139 47 E
Ogahalla **62** 50 6N 85 51W
Ōgaki **36** 35 21N 136 37 E
Ogallala **70** 41 12N 101 40W
Ogbomosho **53** 8 1N 4 11 E
Ogden, Iowa, U.S.A. **70** 42 3N 94 0W
Ogden, Utah, U.S.A. **72** 41 13N 112 1W
Ogdensburg **68** 44 40N 75 27W
Ogeechee → **69** 31 51N 81 6W
Oglio → **18** 45 2N 10 39 E
Ogmore **44** 22 37S 149 35 E
Ogoja **53** 6 38N 8 39 E
Ogoki → **62** 51 38N 85 57W
Ogoki L. **62** 50 50N 87 10W
Ogoki Res. **62** 50 45N 88 15W
Ogooué → **54** 1 0S 9 0 E
Ogowe = Ogooué → **54** 1 0S 9 0 E
Oguta **53** 5 44N 6 44 E
Ogwashi-Uku **53** 6 15N 6 30 E
Ohai **43** 44 55S 168 0 E
Ohakune **43** 39 24S 175 24 E
Ohanet **50** 28 44N 8 46 E
Ohau, L. **43** 44 15S 169 53 E
Ohey **11** 50 26N 5 8 E
Ohio □ **68** 40 20N 84 10W
Ohio → **68** 38 0N 86 0W
Ohre → **14** 50 30N 14 10 E
Ohridsko, Jezero **19** 41 8N 20 52 E
Ohrigstad **57** 24 39S 30 36 E
Oil City **68** 41 26N 79 40W
Oise □ **12** 49 28N 2 30 E
Ōita **36** 33 14N 131 36 E
Ōita □ **36** 33 15N 131 30 E
Oiticica **79** 5 3S 41 5W
Ojai **73** 34 28N 119 16W
Ojinaga **74** 29 34N 104 25W
Ojos del Salado, Cerro **80** 27 0S 68 40W
Okaba **35** 8 6S 139 42 E
Okahandja **56** 22 0S 16 59 E
Okahukura **40** 38 48S 175 14 E
Okanagan L. **64** 50 0N 119 30W
Okandja **54** 0 35S 13 45 E
Okanogan **72** 48 6N 119 43W
Okanogan → **72** 48 6N 119 43W
Okaputa **56** 20 5S 17 0 E
Okara **32** 30 50N 73 31 E
Okarito **43** 43 15S 170 9 E
Okaukuejo **56** 19 10S 16 0 E
Okavango Swamps **56** 18 45S 22 45 E
Okaya **36** 36 0N 138 10 E
Okayama **36** 34 40N 133 54 E
Okayama □ **36** 35 0N 133 50 E
Okazaki **36** 34 57N 137 10 E
Oke-Iho **53** 8 1N 3 18 E
Okeechobee **69** 27 16N 80 46W
Okeechobee, L. **69** 27 0N 80 50W
Okefenokee Swamp **69** 30 50N 82 15W
Okehampton **7** 50 44N 4 1W
Okene **53** 7 32N 6 11 E
Okha **25** 53 40N 143 0 E
Okhotsk **25** 59 20N 143 10 E
Okhotsk, Sea of **25** 55 0N 145 0 E
Okhotskiy Perevoz **25** 61 52N 135 35 E
Okhotsko Kolymskoye **25** 63 0N 157 0 E
Oki-Shotō **36** 36 5N 133 15 E
Okiep **56** 29 39S 17 53 E
Okigwi **53** 5 52N 7 20 E
Okija **53** 5 54N 6 55 E
Okitipupa **53** 6 31N 4 50 E
Oklahoma □ **71** 35 20N 97 30W
Oklahoma City **71** 35 25N 97 30W
Okmulgee **71** 35 38N 96 0W
Okolona **71** 34 0N 88 45W
Okrika **53** 4 40N 7 10 E
Oktabrsk **23** 49 28N 57 25 E
Oktyabrskiy **22** 54 28N 53 28 E
Oktyabrskoy Revolyutsii, Os. **25** 79 30N 97 0 E
Oktyabrskoye **24** 62 28N 66 3 E
Okuru **43** 43 55S 168 55 E
Okushiri-Tō **36** 42 15N 139 30 E
Okuta **53** 9 14N 3 12 E
Okwa → **56** 22 30S 23 0 E
Ola **71** 35 2N 93 10W
Ólafsfjörður **20** 66 4N 18 39W
Ólafsvík **20** 64 53N 23 43W
Olancha **73** 36 15N 118 1W
Olanchito **75** 15 30N 86 30W
Öland **21** 56 45N 16 38 E
Olary **45** 32 18S 140 19 E
Olathe **70** 38 50N 94 50W
Olavarría **80** 36 55S 60 20W
Ólbia **18** 40 55N 9 30 E
Old Bahama Chan. = Bahama, Canal Viejo de **75** 22 10N 77 30W
Old Castile = Castilla La Vieja **13** 41 55N 4 0W
Old Castle **9** 53 46N 7 10W
Old Cork **44** 22 57S 141 52 E
Old Crow **60** 67 30N 140 5 E
Old Fort → **65** 58 36N 110 24W
Old Town **63** 45 0N 68 41W
Old Wives L. **65** 50 5N 106 0W
Oldbury **7** 51 38N 2 30W
Oldenburg **14** 53 10N 8 10 E
Oldenzaal **11** 52 19N 6 53 E
Oldham **6** 53 33N 2 8W
Oldman → **64** 49 57N 111 42W
Olds **64** 51 50N 114 10W
Olean **68** 42 8N 78 25W
Olekma → **25** 60 22N 120 42 E
Olekminsk **25** 60 25N 120 30 E
Olenegorsk **22** 68 9N 33 18 E
Olenek **25** 68 28N 112 18 E
Olenek → **25** 73 0N 120 10 E
Oléron, I. d' **12** 45 55N 1 15W
Oleśnica **15** 51 13N 17 22 E
Olga **25** 43 50N 135 14 E
Olga, L. **62** 49 47N 77 15W
Olga, Mt. **47** 25 20S 130 50 E
Olifants → **57** 23 57S 31 58 E
Olifantshoek **56** 27 57S 22 42 E
Ólimbos, Óros **19** 40 6N 22 23 E
Olinda **79** 8 1S 34 51W
Oliveira **79** 20 39S 44 50W
Olivenza **13** 38 41N 7 9W
Oliver **64** 49 13N 119 37W
Oliver L. **65** 56 56N 103 22W
Ollagüe **78** 21 15S 68 10W
Olney, Ill., U.S.A. **68** 38 40N 88 0W
Olney, Tex., U.S.A. **71** 33 25N 98 45W
Olomane → **63** 50 14N 60 37W
Olomouc **14** 49 38N 17 12 E
Olonets **22** 61 10N 33 0 E
Olongapo **35** 14 50N 120 18 E
Olovo **19** 44 0N 19 0 E
Olovyannaya **25** 50 58N 115 35 E
Oloy → **25** 66 29N 159 29 E
Olsztyn **15** 53 48N 20 29 E
Olt → **15** 43 43N 24 51 E
Olteniţa **15** 44 7N 26 42 E
Olton **71** 34 16N 102 7W
Oltu **30** 40 35N 41 58 E
Olympia, Greece **19** 37 39N 21 39 E
Olympia, U.S.A. **72** 47 0N 122 58W
Olympic Mts. **72** 47 50N 123 45W
Olympic Nat. Park **72** 47 48N 123 30W
Olympus, Mt. = Ólimbos, Óros **19** 40 6N 22 23 E
Olympus, Mt. **72** 47 52N 123 40W
Om → **24** 54 59N 73 22 E
Ōmachi **36** 36 30N 137 50 E
Omagh **9** 54 36N 7 20W
Omagh □ **9** 54 35N 7 15W
Omaha **70** 41 15N 96 0W
Omak **72** 48 24N 119 31W
Oman ■ **29** 23 0N 58 0 E
Oman, G. of **31** 24 30N 58 30 E
Omaruru **56** 21 26S 16 0 E
Omaruru → **56** 22 7S 14 15 E
Omate **78** 16 45S 71 0W
Ombai, Selat **35** 8 30S 124 50 E
Omboué **54** 1 35S 9 15 E
Ombrone → **18** 42 39N 11 0 E
Omdurmân **51** 15 40N 32 28 E
Ometepe, I. de **75** 11 32N 85 35W
Ometepec **74** 16 39N 98 23W
Omez **28** 32 22N 35 0 E
Omineca → **64** 56 3N 124 16W
Omitara **56** 22 16S 18 2 E
Ōmiya **36** 35 54N 139 38 E
Ommen **11** 52 31N 6 26 E
Omo → **51** 6 25N 36 10 E
Omolon → **25** 68 42N 158 36 E
Omono-Gawa → **36** 39 46N 140 3 E
Omsk **24** 55 0N 73 12 E
Omsukchan **25** 62 32N 155 48 E
Omul, Vf. **15** 45 27N 25 29 E
Ōmura **36** 32 56N 130 0 E
Omuramba Omatako → **55** 17 45S 20 25 E
Ōmuta **36** 33 0N 130 26 E
Onaga **70** 39 32N 96 12W
Onalaska **70** 43 53N 91 14W
Onamia **70** 46 4N 93 38W
Onancock **68** 37 42N 75 49W
Onang **35** 3 2S 118 49 E
Onaping L. **62** 47 3N 81 30W
Onarhā **31** 35 30N 71 0 E
Onavas **74** 28 28N 109 30W
Onawa **70** 42 2N 96 2W
Onaway **68** 45 21N 84 11W
Oncócua **56** 16 30S 13 25 E
Onda **13** 39 55N 0 17W
Ondangua **56** 17 57S 16 4 E
Ondjiva **56** 16 48S 15 50 E
Ondo **53** 7 4N 4 47 E
Ondo □ **53** 7 0N 5 0 E
Öndörhaan **37** 47 19N 110 39 E
Öndverðarnes **20** 64 52N 24 0W
Onega **22** 64 0N 38 10 E
Onega → **22** 63 58N 37 55 E
Onega, G. of = Onezhskaya Guba **22** 64 30N 37 0 E
Onega, L. = Onezhskoye Ozero **22** 62 0N 35 30 E
Onehunga **43** 36 55S 174 48 E
Oneida **68** 43 5N 75 40W
Oneida L. **68** 43 12N 76 0W
O'Neill **70** 42 30N 98 38W
Onekotan, Ostrov **25** 49 25N 154 45 E
Oneonta, Ala., U.S.A. **69** 33 58N 86 29W
Oneonta, N.Y., U.S.A. **68** 42 26N 75 5W
Onezhskaya Guba **22** 64 30N 37 0 E
Onezhskoye Ozero **22** 62 0N 35 30 E
Ongarue **43** 38 42S 175 19 E
Ongerup **47** 33 58S 118 28 E
Ongniud Qi **38** 43 0N 118 38 E
Ongole **32** 15 33N 80 2 E
Onguren **25** 53 38N 107 36 E
Onida **70** 44 42N 100 5W
Onilahy → **57** 23 34S 43 45 E
Onitsha **53** 6 6N 6 42 E
Onoda **36** 34 2N 131 25 E
Onslow **46** 21 40S 115 12 E
Onslow B. **69** 34 20N 77 20W
Onstwedde **11** 53 2N 7 4 E
Ontake-San **36** 35 53N 137 29 E
Ontario, Calif., U.S.A. **73** 34 2N 117 40W
Ontario, Oreg., U.S.A. **72** 44 1N 117 1W
Ontario □ **62** 52 0N 88 10W
Ontario, L. **62** 43 40N 78 0W
Ontonagon **70** 46 52N 89 19W
Oodnadatta **45** 27 33S 135 30 E
Ooldea **47** 30 27S 131 50 E
Oombulgurri **46** 15 15S 127 45 E
Oona River **64** 53 57N 130 16W
Oorindi **44** 20 40S 141 1 E
Oost-Vlaanderen □ **11** 51 5N 3 50 E
Oostende **11** 51 15N 2 54 E
Oosterhout **11** 51 39N 4 47 E
Oosterschelde **11** 51 33N 4 0 E
Ootacamund **32** 11 30N 76 44 E
Ootsa L. **64** 53 50N 126 2W
Opala, U.S.S.R. **25** 51 58N 156 30 E
Opala, Zaïre **54** 0 40S 24 20 E
Opanake **32** 6 35N 80 40 E
Opasatika **62** 49 30N 82 50W
Opasquia **65** 53 16N 93 34W
Opava **15** 49 57N 17 58 E
Opelousas **71** 30 35N 92 7W
Opémisca, L. **62** 49 56N 74 52W
Opheim **72** 48 52N 106 30W
Ophir **60** 63 10N 156 40W
Ophthalmia Ra. **46** 23 15S 119 30 E
Opi **53** 6 36N 7 28 E
Opinaca → **62** 52 15N 78 2W
Opinaca L. **62** 52 39N 76 20W
Opiskotish, L. **63** 53 10N 67 50W
Opobo **53** 4 35N 7 34 E
Opole **15** 50 42N 17 58 E
Oporto = Porto **13** 41 8N 8 40W

Panama Canal

Opotiki 43 38 1S 177 19 E
Opp 69 31 19N 86 13W
Oppland fylke □ 21 61 15N 9 40 E
Opua 43 35 19S 174 9 E
Opunake 43 39 26S 173 52 E
Or Yehuda 28 32 2N 34 50 E
Ora 28 30 55N 35 1 E
Ora Banda 47 30 20S 121 0 E
Oracle 73 32 36N 110 46W
Oradea 17 47 2N 21 58 E
Öræfajökull 20 64 2N 16 39W
Orai 32 25 58N 79 30 E
Oran, Algeria 50 35 45N 0 39W
Oran, Argentina 80 23 10S 64 20W
Orange, Australia 45 33 15S 149 7 E
Orange, France 12 44 8N 4 47 E
Orange, Tex., U.S.A. 71 30 10N 93 50W
Orange, Va., U.S.A. 68 38 17N 78 5W
Orange → = Oranje → 56 28 41S 16 28 E
Orange, C. 79 4 20N 51 30W
Orange Free State □ 56 28 30S 27 0 E
Orange Grove 71 27 57N 97 57W
Orange Walk 74 18 6N 88 33W
Orangeburg 69 33 35N 80 53W
Orangeville 62 43 55N 80 5W
Oranienburg 14 52 45N 13 15 E
Oranje → 56 28 41S 16 28 E
Oranje Vrystaat □ = Orange Free State □ 56 28 30S 27 0 E
Oranjemund 56 28 38S 16 29 E
Oranjerivier 56 29 40S 24 12 E
Or'Aquiva 28 32 30N 34 54 E
Oras 35 12 9N 125 28 E
Oraşul Stalin = Braşov 15 45 38N 25 35 E
Orbetello 18 42 26N 11 11 E
Orbost 45 37 40S 148 29 E
Orchila, I. 78 11 48N 66 10W
Ord → 46 15 33S 138 15 E
Ord, Mt. 46 17 20S 125 34 E
Orderville 73 37 18N 112 43W
Ordos = Mu Us Shamo 38 39 0N 109 0 E
Ordu 30 40 55N 37 53 E
Ordway 70 38 15N 103 42W
Ordzhonikidze 23 43 0N 44 35 E
Ore Mts. = Erzgebirge 14 50 25N 13 0 E
Örebro 21 59 20N 15 18 E
Örebro län □ 21 59 27N 15 0 E
Oregon 70 42 1N 89 20W
Oregon □ 72 44 0N 121 0W
Oregon City 72 45 21N 122 35W
Orekhovo-Zuyevo 22 55 50N 38 55 E
Orel 22 52 57N 36 3 E
Orem 72 40 20N 111 45W
Orenburg 22 51 45N 55 6 E
Orense 13 42 19N 7 55W
Orepuki 43 46 19S 167 46 E
Orford Ness 7 52 6N 1 31 E
Orgūn 31 32 55N 69 12 E
Orhon Gol → 37 49 30N 106 0 E
Orient 45 28 7S 142 50 E
Oriental, Cordillera 78 6 0N 73 0W
Orihuela 13 38 7N 0 55W
Orinoco → 78 9 15N 61 30W
Orissa □ 33 20 0N 84 0 E
Oristano 18 39 54N 8 35 E
Oristano, G. di 18 39 50N 8 22 E
Orizaba 74 18 50N 97 10W
Orkanger 20 63 18N 9 52 E
Orkla → 20 63 18N 9 51 E
Orkney 56 26 58S 26 40 E
Orkney □ 8 59 0N 3 0W
Orkney Is. 8 59 0N 3 0W
Orland 72 39 46N 122 12W
Orlando 69 28 30N 81 25W
Orléanais 12 48 0N 2 0 E
Orléans 12 47 54N 1 52 E
Orléans, I. d' 63 46 54N 70 58W
Orlik 25 52 30N 99 55 E
Ormara 31 25 16N 64 33 E
Ormoc 35 11 0N 124 37 E
Ormond 43 38 33S 177 56 E
Ormond Beach 69 29 13N 81 5W
Orne □ 12 48 40N 0 5 E
Örnsköldsvik 20 63 17N 18 40 E
Oro → 74 25 35N 105 2W
Orocué 78 4 48N 71 20W
Orodo 53 5 34N 7 4 E
Orogrande 73 32 20N 106 4W
Oromocto 63 45 54N 66 29W
Oron 53 4 48N 8 14 E
Oroqen Zizhiqi 38 50 34N 123 43 E
Oroquieta 35 8 32N 123 44 E
Orós 79 6 15S 38 55W
Orotukan 25 62 16N 151 42 E
Oroville, Calif., U.S.A. 72 39 31N 121 30W
Oroville, Wash., U.S.A. 72 48 58N 119 30W
Orroroo 45 32 43S 138 38 E
Orsha 22 54 30N 30 25 E
Orsk 22 51 12N 58 34 E
Orşova 15 44 41N 22 25 E
Ortegal, C. 13 43 43N 7 52W
Orthez 12 43 29N 0 48W
Ortigueira 13 43 40N 7 50W
Ortles 18 46 31N 10 33 E
Ortón → 78 10 50S 67 0W
Ortona 18 42 21N 14 24 E
Orūmīyeh 30 37 40N 45 0 E
Orūmīyeh, Daryācheh-ye 30 37 50N 45 30 E
Oruro 78 18 0S 67 9W
Oruzgān □ 31 33 30N 66 0 E
Orvieto 18 42 43N 12 8 E
Orwell → 7 52 2N 1 12 E
Oryakhovo 19 43 40N 23 57 E
Osa 22 57 17N 55 26 E
Osa, Pen. de 75 8 0N 84 0W
Osage, Iowa, U.S.A. 70 43 15N 92 50W
Osage, Wyo., U.S.A. 70 43 59N 104 25W
Osage → 70 38 35N 91 57W
Osage City 70 38 43N 95 51W
Ōsaka 36 34 40N 135 30 E
Ōsaka □ 36 34 30N 135 30 E
Osawatomie 70 38 30N 94 55W
Osborne 70 39 30N 98 45W
Osceola, Ark., U.S.A. 71 35 40N 90 0W
Osceola, Iowa, U.S.A. 70 41 0N 93 20W
Oscoda 68 44 26N 83 20W
Ösel = Saaremaa 22 58 30N 22 30 E
Osh 24 40 37N 72 49 E
Oshawa 62 43 50N 78 50W
Oshkosh, Nebr., U.S.A. 70 41 27N 102 20W
Oshkosh, Wis., U.S.A. 70 44 3N 88 35W
Oshogbo 53 7 48N 4 37 E
Oshwe 54 3 25S 19 28 E
Osijek 19 45 34N 18 41 E
Osipenko = Berdyansk 23 46 45N 36 50 E
Osizweni 57 27 49S 30 7 E
Oskaloosa 70 41 18N 92 40W
Oskarshamn 21 57 15N 16 27 E
Oskélanéo 62 48 5N 75 15W
Oslo 21 59 55N 10 45 E
Oslob 35 9 31N 123 26 E
Oslofjorden 21 59 20N 10 35 E
Osmanabad 32 18 5N 76 10 E
Osmaniye 30 37 5N 36 10 E
Osnabrück 14 52 16N 8 2 E
Osorio 80 29 53S 50 17W
Osorno 80 40 25S 73 0W
Osoyoos 64 49 0N 119 30W
Ospika → 64 56 20N 124 0W
Osprey Reef 44 13 52S 146 36 E
Oss 11 51 46N 5 32 E
Ossa, Mt. 44 41 52S 146 3 E
Óssa, Oros 19 39 47N 22 42 E
Ossabaw I. 69 31 45N 81 8W
Ossining 68 41 9N 73 50W
Ossokmanuan L. 63 53 25N 65 0W
Ossora 25 59 20N 163 13 E
Ostend = Oostende 11 51 15N 2 54 E
Österdalälven → 21 61 30N 13 45 E
Östergötlands län □ 21 58 35N 15 45 E
Östersund 20 63 10N 14 38 E
Østfold fylke □ 21 59 25N 11 25 E
Ostfriesische Inseln 14 53 45N 7 15 E
Ostrava 15 49 51N 18 18 E
Ostróda 15 53 42N 19 58 E
Ostrołęka 15 53 4N 21 32 E
Ostrów Mazowiecka 15 52 50N 21 51 E
Ostrów Wielkopolski 15 51 36N 17 44 E
Ostrowiec-Świętokrzyski 15 50 55N 21 22 E
Ōsumi-Kaikyō 36 30 55N 131 0 E
Osuna 13 37 14N 5 8W
Oswego 68 43 29N 76 30W
Oswestry 6 52 52N 3 3W
Otago □ 43 44 44S 169 10 E
Otago Harb. 43 45 47S 170 42 E
Ōtake 36 34 12N 132 13 E
Otaki 43 40 45S 175 10 E
Otaru 36 43 10N 141 0 E
Otaru-Wan = Ishikari-Wan 36 43 25N 141 1 E
Otavalo 78 0 13N 78 20W
Otavi 56 19 40S 17 24 E
Otchinjau 56 16 30S 13 56 E
Othello 72 46 53N 119 8W
Otira Gorge 43 42 53S 171 33 E
Otis 70 40 12N 102 58W
Otjiwarongo 56 20 30S 16 33 E
Otoineppu 36 44 44N 142 16 E
Otorohanga 43 38 12S 175 14 E
Otoskwin → 62 52 13N 88 6W
Otosquen 65 53 17N 102 1W
Otranto 19 40 9N 18 28 E
Otranto, C. d' 19 40 7N 18 30 E
Otranto, Str. of 19 40 15N 18 40 E
Otse 56 25 2S 25 45 E
Ōtsu 36 35 0N 135 50 E
Ottawa, Canada 62 45 27N 75 42W
Ottawa, Ill., U.S.A. 70 41 20N 88 55W
Ottawa, Kans., U.S.A. 70 38 40N 95 6W
Ottawa → = Outaouais → 62 45 27N 74 8W
Ottawa Is. 61 59 35N 80 10W
Otter L. 65 55 35N 104 39W
Otter Rapids, Ont., Canada 62 50 11N 81 39W
Otter Rapids, Sask., Canada 65 55 38N 104 44W
Ottosdal 56 26 46S 25 59 E
Ottoshoop 56 25 45S 25 58 E
Ottumwa 70 41 0N 92 25W
Otukpa 53 7 9N 7 41 E
Oturkpo 53 7 16N 8 8 E
Otway, B. 80 53 30S 74 0W
Otway, C. 45 38 52S 143 30 E
Otwock 15 52 5N 21 20 E
Ou-Sammyaku 36 39 20N 140 35 E
Ouachita → 71 31 38N 91 49W
Ouachita, L. 71 34 40N 93 25W
Ouachita Mts. 71 34 50N 94 30W
Ouadâne 50 20 50N 11 40W
Ouadda 51 8 15N 22 20 E
Ouagadougou 53 12 25N 1 30W
Ouahran = Oran 50 35 45N 0 39W
Ouallene 50 24 41N 1 11 E
Ouanda Djallé 51 8 55N 22 53 E
Ouango 54 4 19N 22 30 E
Ouargla 50 31 59N 5 16 E
Ouarzazate 50 30 55N 6 50W
Oubangi → 54 0 30S 17 50 E
Ouddorp 11 51 50N 3 57 E
Oude Rijn → 11 52 12N 4 24 E
Oudenaarde 11 50 50N 3 37 E
Oudtshoorn 56 33 35S 22 14 E
Ouessant, I. d' 12 48 28N 5 6W
Ouesso 54 1 37N 16 5 E
Ouest, Pte. 63 49 52N 64 40W
Ouezzane 50 34 51N 5 35W
Ouidah 53 6 25N 2 0 E
Oujda 50 34 41N 1 55W
Oujeft 50 20 2N 13 0W
Ouled Djellal 50 34 28N 5 2 E
Oulu 20 65 1N 25 29 E
Oulu □ 20 65 10N 27 20 E
Oulujärvi 20 64 25N 27 15 E
Oulujoki → 20 65 1N 25 30 E
Oum Chalouba 51 15 48N 20 46 E
Ounguati 56 22 0S 15 46 E
Ounianga-Kébir 51 19 4N 20 29 E
Ounianga Sérir 51 18 54N 20 51 E
Our → 11 49 55N 6 5 E
Ouray 73 38 3N 107 40W
Ouricuri 79 7 53S 40 5W
Ouro Prêto 79 20 20S 43 30W
Ourthe → 11 50 29N 5 35 E
Ouse 44 42 38S 146 42 E
Ouse →, E. Sussex, U.K. 7 50 43N 0 3 E
Ouse →, N. Yorks., U.K. 6 54 3N 0 7 E
Outaouais → 62 45 27N 74 8W
Outardes → 63 49 24N 69 30W
Outer Hebrides 8 57 30N 7 40W
Outer I. 63 51 10N 58 35W
Outjo 56 20 5S 16 7 E
Outlook, Canada 65 51 30N 107 0W
Outlook, U.S.A. 70 48 53N 104 46W
Ouyen 45 35 1S 142 22 E
Ovalau 43 17 40S 178 48 E
Ovalle 80 30 33S 71 18W
Ovar 13 40 51N 8 40W
Overflakkee 11 51 44N 4 10 E
Overijssel □ 11 52 25N 6 35 E
Overpelt 11 51 12N 5 20 E
Overton 73 36 32N 114 31W
Övertorneå 20 66 23N 23 38 E
Ovid 70 41 0N 102 17W
Oviedo 13 43 25N 5 50W
Owaka 43 46 27S 169 40 E
Owase 36 34 7N 136 12 E
Owatonna 70 44 3N 93 10W
Owbeh 31 34 28N 63 10 E
Owego 68 42 6N 76 17W
Owen Falls 52 0 30N 33 5 E
Owen Sound 62 44 35N 80 55W
Owendo 54 0 17N 9 30 E
Owens L. 73 36 20N 118 0W
Owensboro 68 37 40N 87 5W
Owensville 70 38 20N 91 30W
Owerri 53 5 29N 7 0 E
Owl → 65 57 51N 92 44W
Owo 53 7 10N 5 39 E
Owosso 68 43 0N 84 10W
Owyhee 72 42 0N 116 3W
Owyhee → 72 43 46N 117 2W
Owyhee, L. 72 43 40N 117 16W
Ox Mts. 9 54 6N 9 0W
Oxelösund 21 58 43N 17 15 E
Oxford, N.Z. 43 43 18S 172 11 E
Oxford, U.K. 7 51 45N 1 15W
Oxford, Miss., U.S.A. 71 34 22N 89 30W
Oxford, N.C., U.S.A. 69 36 19N 78 36W
Oxford, Ohio, U.S.A. 68 39 30N 84 40W
Oxford □ 7 51 45N 1 15W
Oxford L. 65 54 51N 95 37W
Oxley 45 34 11S 144 6 E
Oxnard 73 34 10N 119 14W
Oya 34 2 55N 111 55 E
Oyama 36 36 18N 139 48 E
Oyem 54 1 34N 11 31 E
Oyen 65 51 22N 110 28W
Oykel → 8 57 55N 4 26W
Oymyakon 25 63 25N 142 44 E
Oyo 53 7 46N 3 56 E
Oyo □ 53 8 0N 3 30 E
Ozamis 35 8 15N 123 50 E
Ozark, Ala., U.S.A. 69 31 29N 85 39W
Ozark, Ark., U.S.A. 71 35 30N 93 50W
Ozark, Mo., U.S.A. 71 37 0N 93 15W
Ozark Plateau 71 37 20N 91 40W
Ozarks, L. of the 70 38 10N 92 40W
Ozona 71 30 43N 101 11W
Ozuluama 74 21 40N 97 50W

P

P.K. le Roux Dam 56 30 4S 24 40 E
Pa-an 33 16 51N 97 40 E
Paarl 56 33 45S 18 56 E
Paatsi → 20 68 55N 29 0 E
Paauilo 66 20 3N 155 22W
Pab Hills 32 26 30N 66 45 E
Pabna 33 24 1N 89 18 E
Pacaja → 79 1 56S 50 50W
Pacaraima, Sierra 78 4 0N 62 30W
Pacasmayo 78 7 20S 79 35W
Pachpadra 32 25 58N 72 10 E
Pachuca 74 20 10N 98 40W
Pacific 64 54 48N 128 28W
Pacific-Antarctic Basin 41 46 0S 95 0W
Pacific-Antarctic Ridge 41 43 0S 115 0W
Pacific Grove 73 36 38N 121 58W
Pacific Ocean 2 10 0N 140 0W
Pacitan 35 8 12S 111 7 E
Padaido, Kepulauan 35 1 5S 138 0 E
Padang 34 1 0S 100 20 E
Padangpanjang 34 0 40S 100 20 E
Padangsidempuan 34 1 30N 99 15 E
Paddockwood 65 53 30N 105 30W
Paderborn 14 51 42N 8 44 E
Padloping Island 61 67 0N 62 50W
Pádova 18 45 24N 11 52 E
Padre I. 71 27 0N 97 20W
Padstow 6 50 33N 4 57W
Padua = Pádova 18 45 24N 11 52 E
Paducah, Ky., U.S.A. 68 37 0N 88 40W
Paducah, Tex., U.S.A. 71 34 3N 100 16W
Paeroa 43 37 23S 175 41 E
Pag 18 44 30N 14 50 E
Pagadian 35 7 55N 123 30 E
Pagai Selatan 34 3 0S 100 15 E
Pagai Utara 34 2 35S 100 0 E
Pagalu = Annobón 48 1 25S 5 36 E
Pagastikós Kólpos 19 39 15N 23 0 E
Pagatan 34 3 33S 115 59 E
Page, Ariz., U.S.A. 73 36 57N 111 27W
Page, N. Dak., U.S.A. 70 47 11N 97 37W
Pago Pago 43 14 16S 170 43W
Pagosa Springs 73 37 16N 107 4W
Pagwa River 62 50 2N 85 14W
Pahala 66 19 12N 155 25W
Pahiatua 43 40 27S 175 50 E
Pahokee 69 26 50N 80 40W
Pahrump 73 36 15N 116 0W
Paia 66 20 54N 156 22W
Paignton 7 50 26N 3 33W
Päijänne, L. 21 61 30N 25 30 E
Painan 34 1 21S 100 34 E
Painesville 68 41 42N 81 18W
Paint Hills = Nouveau Comptoir 62 53 0N 78 49W
Paint L. 65 55 28N 97 57W
Paint Rock 71 31 30N 99 56W
Painted Desert 73 36 0N 111 30W
Paintsville 68 37 50N 82 50W
Pais Vasco □ 13 43 0N 2 30W
Paisley, U.K. 8 55 51N 4 27W
Paisley, U.S.A. 72 42 43N 120 40W
Paita 78 5 11S 81 9W
Pakaraima Mts. 78 6 0N 60 0W
Pakistan ■ 31 30 0N 70 0 E
Pakistan, East = Bangladesh ■ 33 24 0N 90 0 E
Pakokku 33 21 20N 95 0 E
Pakse 34 15 5N 105 52 E
Paktīā □ 31 33 0N 69 15 E
Pala 51 9 25N 15 5 E
Palacios 71 28 44N 96 12W
Palagruža 18 42 24N 16 15 E
Palam 32 19 0N 77 0 E
Palamós 13 41 50N 3 10 E
Palampur 32 32 10N 76 30 E
Palana, Australia 44 39 45S 147 55 E
Palana, U.S.S.R. 25 59 10N 159 59 E
Palanan 35 17 8N 122 29 E
Palanan Pt. 35 17 17N 122 30 E
Palangkaraya 34 2 16S 113 56 E
Palani Hills 32 10 14N 77 33 E
Palanpur 32 24 10N 72 25 E
Palapye 56 22 30S 27 7 E
Palatka, U.S.A. 69 29 40N 81 40W
Palatka, U.S.S.R. 25 60 6N 150 54 E
Palawan 34 9 30N 118 30 E
Palayankottai 32 8 45N 77 45 E
Paleleh 35 1 10N 121 50 E
Palembang 34 3 0S 104 50 E
Palencia 13 42 1N 4 34W
Palermo, Italy 18 38 8N 13 20 E
Palermo, U.S.A. 72 39 30N 121 37W
Palestine, Asia 28 32 0N 35 0 E
Palestine, U.S.A. 71 31 42N 95 35W
Paletwa 33 21 10N 92 50 E
Palghat 32 10 46N 76 42 E
Palgrave, Mt. 46 23 22S 115 58 E
Pali 32 25 50N 73 20 E
Palisade 70 40 21N 101 10W
Palitana 32 21 32N 71 49 E
Palizada 74 18 18N 92 8W
Palk Bay 32 9 30N 79 15 E
Palk Strait 32 10 0N 79 45 E
Palla Road = Dinokwe 56 23 29S 26 37 E
Pallinup 47 34 0S 117 55 E
Palm Beach 69 26 46N 80 0W
Palm Is. 44 18 40S 146 35 E
Palm Springs 73 33 51N 116 35W
Palma 54 10 46S 40 29 E
Palma → 79 12 33S 47 52W
Palma, B. de 13 39 30N 2 39 E
Palma, La, Canary Is. 50 28 40N 17 50W
Palma, La, Panama 75 8 15N 78 0W
Palma, La, Spain 13 37 21N 6 38W
Palma de Mallorca 13 39 35N 2 39 E
Palma Soriano 75 20 15N 76 0W
Palmahim 28 31 56N 34 44 E
Palmares 79 8 41S 35 28W
Palmas, C. 50 4 27N 7 46W
Pálmas, G. di 18 39 0N 8 30 E
Palmdale 73 34 36N 118 7W
Palmeira dos Índios 79 9 25S 36 37W
Palmeirinhas, Pta. das 54 9 2S 12 57 E
Palmer 60 61 35N 149 10W
Palmer → 44 15 34S 142 26 E
Palmer Lake 70 39 10N 104 52W
Palmerston North 43 40 21S 175 39 E
Palmetto 69 27 33N 82 33W
Palmi 18 38 21N 15 51 E
Palmira 78 3 32N 76 16W
Palmyra = Tudmur 30 34 36N 38 15 E
Palmyra 70 39 45N 91 30W
Palmyra Is. 41 5 52N 162 5W
Palo Alto 73 37 25N 122 8W
Palopo 35 3 0S 120 16 E
Palos, C. de 13 37 38N 0 40W
Palouse 72 46 59N 117 5W
Palparara 44 24 47S 141 28 E
Palu, Indonesia 35 1 0S 119 52 E
Palu, Turkey 30 38 45N 40 0 E
Paluan 35 13 26N 120 29 E
Pama 53 11 19N 0 44 E
Pamanukan 35 6 16S 107 49 E
Pamekasan 35 7 10S 113 28 E
Pamirs 24 37 40N 73 0 E
Pamlico → 69 35 25N 76 30W
Pamlico Sd. 69 35 20N 76 0W
Pampa 71 35 35N 100 58W
Pampa de las Salinas 80 32 1S 66 58W
Pampanua 35 4 16S 120 8 E
Pampas, Argentina 80 35 0S 63 0W
Pampas, Peru 78 12 20S 74 50W
Pamplona, Colombia 78 7 23N 72 39W
Pamplona, Spain 13 42 48N 1 38W
Pampoenpoort 56 31 3S 22 40 E
Pana 70 39 25N 89 5W
Panaca 73 37 51N 114 23W
Panaitan 35 6 36S 105 12 E
Panaji 32 15 25N 73 50 E
Panamá 75 9 0N 79 25W
Panama ■ 75 8 48N 79 55W
Panamá, G. de 75 8 4N 79 20W
Panama Canal 75 9 10N 79 37W

Port Alice

Peru, Ill., U.S.A. 70 41 18N 89 12W
Peru, Ind., U.S.A. 68 40 42N 86 0W
Peru ■ 78 8 0S 75 0W
Peru-Chile Trench 41 20 0S 72 0W
Perúgia 18 43 6N 12 24 E
Pervomaysk 23 48 10N 30 46 E
Pervouralsk 22 56 55N 60 0 E
Pésaro 18 43 55N 12 53 E
Pescara 18 42 28N 14 13 E
Peshawar 32 34 2N 71 37 E
Peshtigo 68 45 4N 87 46W
Pesqueira 79 8 20S 36 42W
Petah Tiqwa 28 32 6N 34 53 E
Petaluma 72 38 13N 122 39W
Petange 11 49 33N 5 55 E
Petatlán 74 17 31N 101 16W
Petauke 55 14 14S 31 20 E
Petawawa 62 45 54N 77 17W
Petén Itzá, L. 75 16 58N 89 50W
Peter Pond L. 65 55 55N 108 44W
Peterbell 62 48 36N 83 21W
Peterborough, Australia 45 32 58S 138 51 E
Peterborough, U.K. 7 52 35N 0 14W
Peterhead 8 57 30N 1 49W
Petersburg, Alaska, U.S.A. 60 56 50N 133 0W
Petersburg, Ind., U.S.A. 68 38 30N 87 15W
Petersburg, Va., U.S.A. 68 37 17N 77 26W
Petersburg, W. Va., U.S.A. 68 38 59N 79 10W
Petford 44 17 20S 144 58 E
Petit Bois I. 69 30 16N 88 25W
Petit-Cap 63 49 3N 64 30W
Petit Goâve 75 18 27N 72 51W
Petit Lac Manicouagan 63 51 25N 67 40W
Petitcodiac 63 45 57N 65 11W
Petite Baleine → 62 56 0N 76 45W
Petite Saguenay 63 48 15N 70 4W
Petitsikapau, L. 63 54 37N 66 25W
Petlad 32 22 30N 72 45 E
Peto 74 20 10N 88 53W
Petone 43 41 13S 174 53 E
Petoskey 68 45 22N 84 57W
Petra 28 30 20N 35 22 E
Petrich 19 41 24N 23 13 E
Petrolândia 79 9 5S 38 20W
Petrolia 62 42 54N 82 9W
Petrolina 79 9 24S 40 30W
Petropavlovsk 24 54 53N 69 13 E
Petropavlovsk-Kamchatskiy 25 53 3N 158 43 E
Petrópolis 79 22 33S 43 9W
Petroşeni 15 45 28N 23 20 E
Petroskey 68 45 22N 84 57W
Petrovaradin 19 45 16N 19 55 E
Petrovsk 22 52 22N 45 19 E
Petrovsk-Zabaykalskiy 25 51 20N 108 55 E
Petrozavodsk 22 61 41N 34 20 E
Petrus Steyn 57 27 38S 28 8 E
Petrusburg 56 29 4S 25 26 E
Peureulak 34 4 48N 97 45 E
Pevek 25 69 41N 171 19 E
Pforzheim 14 48 53N 8 43 E
Phagwara 32 31 10N 75 40 E
Phala 56 23 45S 26 50 E
Phalodi 32 27 12N 72 24 E
Phan Rang 34 11 34N 109 0 E
Phangan, Ko 34 9 45N 100 0 E
Phangnga 34 8 28N 98 30 E
Phanh Bho Ho Chi Minh 34 10 58N 106 40 E
Phatthalung 34 7 39N 100 6 E
Phelps 70 46 2N 89 2W
Phelps L. 65 59 15N 103 15W
Phenix City 69 32 30N 85 0W
Phetchabun 34 16 25N 101 8 E
Philadelphia, Miss., U.S.A. 71 32 47N 89 5W
Philadelphia, Pa., U.S.A. 68 40 0N 75 10W
Philip 70 44 4N 101 42W
Philippeville 11 50 12N 4 33 E
Philippi L. 44 24 20S 138 55 E
Philippines ■ 35 12 0N 123 0 E
Philippolis 56 30 15S 25 16 E
Philippopolis = Plovdiv 19 42 8N 24 44 E
Philipsburg 72 46 20N 113 21W
Philipstown 56 30 28S 24 30 E
Phillip, I. 45 38 30S 145 12 E
Phillips, Tex., U.S.A. 71 35 48N 101 17W
Phillips, Wis., U.S.A. 70 45 41N 90 22W
Phillipsburg 70 39 48N 99 20W
Phillott 45 27 53S 145 50 E
Philomath 72 44 28N 123 21W
Phitsanulok 34 16 50N 100 12 E
Phnom Dangrek 34 14 20N 104 0 E
Phnom Penh 34 11 33N 104 55 E
Phoenix 73 33 30N 112 10W
Phoenix Is. 40 3 30S 172 0W
Phra Nakhon Si Ayutthaya 34 14 25N 100 30 E
Phuket 34 7 52N 98 22 E
Piacenza 18 45 2N 9 42 E
Pialba 45 25 20S 152 45 E
Pian Cr. → 45 30 2S 148 12 E
Piapot 65 49 59N 109 8W
Piatra Neamţ 15 46 56N 26 21 E
Piauí □ 79 7 0S 43 0W
Piave → 18 45 32N 12 44 E
Piazza Ármerina 18 37 21N 14 20 E
Pibor Post 51 6 47N 33 3 E
Pica 78 20 35S 69 25W
Picardie 12 49 50N 3 0 E
Picardy = Picardie 12 49 50N 3 0 E
Picayune 71 30 31N 89 40W
Pichilemu 80 34 22S 72 0W
Pickerel L. 62 48 40N 91 25W
Pickle Lake 62 51 30N 90 12W
Pico Truncado 80 46 40S 68 0W
Picton, Australia 45 34 12S 150 34 E
Picton, Canada 62 44 1N 77 9W
Picton, N.Z. 43 41 18S 174 3 E
Pictou 63 45 41N 62 42W
Picture Butte 64 49 55N 112 45W
Picún Leufú 80 39 30S 69 5W
Pidurutalagala 32 7 10N 80 50 E
Piedad, La 74 20 20N 102 1W
Piedmont = Piemonte □ 18 45 0N 7 30 E
Piedmont 69 33 55N 85 39W
Piedmont Plateau 69 34 0N 81 30W
Piedras, R. de las → 78 12 30S 69 15W
Piedras Negras 74 28 35N 100 35W
Piemonte □ 18 45 0N 7 30 E
Pierce 72 46 29N 115 53W
Pierre 70 44 23N 100 20W
Piet Retief 57 27 1S 30 50 E
Pietarsaari = Jakobstad 20 63 40N 22 43 E
Pietermaritzburg 57 29 35S 30 25 E
Pietersburg 57 23 54S 29 25 E
Pietrosul 15 47 35N 24 43 E
Pigeon 68 43 50N 83 17W
Piggott 71 36 20N 90 10W
Pigüe 80 37 36S 62 25W
Pikes Peak 70 38 50N 105 10W
Piketberg 56 32 55S 18 40 E
Pikeville 68 37 30N 82 30W
Pikwitonei 65 55 35N 97 9W
Pilar, Brazil 79 9 36S 35 56W
Pilar, Paraguay 80 26 50S 58 20W
Pilas Group 35 6 45N 121 35 E
Pilbara 46 21 15S 118 16 E
Pilcomayo → 80 25 21S 57 42W
Pilibhit 32 28 40N 79 50 E
Pilica → 15 51 52N 21 17 E
Pílos 19 36 55N 21 42 E
Pilot Mound 65 49 15N 98 54W
Pilot Point 71 33 26N 97 0W
Pilot Rock 72 45 30N 118 50W
Pilsen = Plzeň 14 49 45N 13 22 E
Pima 73 32 54N 109 50W
Pimba 45 31 18S 136 46 E
Pimenta Bueno 78 11 35S 61 10W
Pimentel 78 6 45S 79 55W
Pinang 34 5 25N 100 15 E
Pinar del Río 75 22 26N 83 40W
Pincher Creek 64 49 30N 113 57W
Pinchi L. 64 54 38N 124 30W
Pinckneyville 70 38 5N 89 20W
Pińczów 15 50 32N 20 32 E
Pindar 47 28 30S 115 47 E
Pindiga 53 9 58N 10 53 E
Pindos Óros 19 40 0N 21 0 E
Pindus Mts. = Pindos Óros 19 40 0N 21 0 E
Pine 73 34 27N 111 30W
Pine → 65 58 50N 105 38W
Pine, C. 63 46 37N 53 32W
Pine, La 72 43 40N 121 30W
Pine Bluff 71 34 10N 92 0W
Pine City 70 45 46N 93 0W
Pine Falls 65 50 34N 96 11W
Pine Pass 64 55 25N 122 42W
Pine Point 64 60 50N 114 28W
Pine Ridge 70 43 0N 102 35W
Pine River, Canada 65 51 45N 100 30W
Pine River, U.S.A. 70 46 43N 94 24W
Pinega → 22 64 8N 46 54 E
Pinehill 44 23 38S 146 57 E
Pinerolo 18 44 47N 7 21 E
Pinetop 73 34 10N 109 57W
Pinetown 57 29 48S 30 54 E
Pinetree 72 43 42N 105 52W
Pineville, Ky., U.S.A. 69 36 42N 83 42W
Pineville, La., U.S.A. 71 31 22N 92 30W
Ping → 34 15 42N 100 9 E
Pingaring 47 32 40S 118 32 E
Pingding 38 37 47N 113 38 E
Pingdingshan 39 33 43N 113 27 E
Pingdong 39 22 39N 120 30 E
Pingdu 38 36 42N 119 59 E
Pingelly 47 32 32S 117 5 E
Pingguo 39 23 19N 107 36 E
Pinghe 39 24 17N 117 21 E
Pingjiang 39 28 45N 113 36 E
Pingle 39 24 40N 110 40 E
Pingliang 38 35 35N 106 31 E
Pingluo 38 38 52N 106 30 E
Pingnan 39 23 33N 110 22 E
Pingrup 47 33 32S 118 29 E
Pingtan Dao 39 25 29N 119 47 E
Pingwu 39 32 25N 104 30 E
Pingxiang, Guangxi Zhuangzu, China 39 22 6N 106 46 E
Pingxiang, Jiangxi, China 39 27 43N 113 48 E
Pingyao 38 37 12N 112 10 E
Pinhel 13 40 50N 7 1W
Pini 34 0 10N 98 40 E
Piniós → 19 39 55N 22 10 E
Pinjarra 47 32 37S 115 52 E
Pink → 65 56 50N 103 50W
Pinnacles 47 28 12S 120 26 E
Pinnaroo 45 35 17S 140 53 E
Pinos 74 22 20N 101 40W
Pinos Pt. 73 36 38N 121 57W
Pinrang 35 3 46S 119 41 E
Pinsk 22 52 10N 26 1 E
Pintados 78 20 35S 69 40W
Pintumba 47 31 30S 132 12 E
Pinyang 39 27 42N 120 31 E
Pinyug 22 60 5N 48 0 E
Pioche 73 38 0N 114 35W
Piombino 18 42 54N 10 30 E
Pioner, Os. 25 79 50N 92 0 E
Piorini, L. 78 3 15S 62 35W
Piotrków Trybunalski 15 51 23N 19 43 E
Pīp 31 26 45N 60 10 E
Pipestone 70 44 0N 96 20W
Pipestone → 62 52 53N 89 23W
Pipestone Cr. → 65 49 38N 100 15W
Pipmuacan, Rés. 63 49 45N 70 30W
Pippingarra 46 20 27S 118 42 E
Piqua 68 40 10N 84 10W
Piquiri → 80 24 3S 54 14W
Piracicaba 80 22 45S 47 40W
Piracuruca 79 3 50S 41 50W
Piræus = Piraiévs 19 37 57N 23 42 E
Piraiévs 19 37 57N 23 42 E
Pirané 80 25 42S 59 6W
Pirapora 79 17 20S 44 56W
Pírgos 19 37 40N 21 27 E
Pirin Planina 19 41 40N 23 30 E
Pirineos 13 42 40N 1 0 E
Piripiri 79 4 15S 41 46W
Pirot 19 43 9N 22 39 E
Piru 35 3 4S 128 12 E
Pisa 18 43 43N 10 23 E
Pisagua 78 19 40S 70 15W
Pisco 78 13 50S 76 12W
Písek 14 49 19N 14 10 E
Pishan 37 37 30N 78 33 E
Pising 35 5 8S 121 53 E
Pistóia 18 43 57N 10 53 E
Pistol B. 65 62 25N 92 37W
Pisuerga → 13 41 33N 4 52W
Pitarpunga, L. 45 34 24S 143 30 E
Pitcairn I. 2 25 5S 130 5W
Pite älv → 20 65 20N 21 25 E
Piteå 20 65 20N 21 25 E
Piteşti 15 44 52N 24 54 E
Pithapuram 33 17 10N 82 15 E
Pithara 47 30 20S 116 35 E
Pitlochry 8 56 43N 3 43W
Pitt I. 64 53 30N 129 50W
Pittsburg, Kans., U.S.A. 71 37 21N 94 43W
Pittsburg, Tex., U.S.A. 71 32 59N 94 58W
Pittsburgh 68 40 25N 79 55W
Pittsfield, Ill., U.S.A. 70 39 35N 90 46W
Pittsfield, Mass., U.S.A. 68 42 28N 73 17W
Pittston 68 41 19N 75 50W
Pittsworth 45 27 41S 151 37 E
Pituri → 44 22 35S 138 30 E
Piura 78 5 15S 80 38W
Pizzo 18 38 44N 16 10 E
Placentia 63 47 20N 54 0W
Placentia B. 63 47 0N 54 40W
Placerville 72 38 47N 120 51W
Placetas 75 22 15N 79 44W
Plain Dealing 71 32 56N 93 41W
Plainfield 68 40 37N 74 28W
Plains, Kans., U.S.A. 71 37 20N 100 35W
Plains, Mont., U.S.A. 72 47 27N 114 57W
Plains, Tex., U.S.A. 71 33 11N 102 50W
Plainview, Nebr., U.S.A. 70 42 25N 97 48W
Plainview, Tex., U.S.A. 71 34 10N 101 40W
Plainville 70 39 18N 99 19W
Plainwell 68 42 28N 85 40W
Plakhino 24 67 45N 86 5 E
Plankinton 70 43 45N 98 27W
Plano 71 33 0N 96 45W
Plant, La 70 45 11N 100 40W
Plant City 69 28 0N 82 8W
Plaquemine 71 30 20N 91 15W
Plasencia 13 40 3N 6 8W
Plaster Rock 63 46 53N 67 22W
Plata, La 80 35 0S 57 55W
Plata, Río de la 80 34 45S 57 30W
Platani → 18 37 23N 13 16 E
Plateau □ 53 8 0N 8 30 E
Plateau du Coteau du Missouri 70 47 9N 101 5W
Platí, Ákra 19 40 27N 24 0 E
Plato 78 9 47N 74 47W
Platte 70 43 28N 98 50W
Platte → 70 39 16N 94 50W
Platteville 70 40 18N 104 47W
Plattsburg 68 44 41N 73 30W
Plattsmouth 70 41 0N 95 50W
Plauen 14 50 29N 12 9 E
Playgreen L. 65 54 0N 98 15W
Pleasant Bay 63 46 51N 60 48W
Pleasant Hill 70 38 48N 94 14W
Pleasanton 71 29 0N 98 30W
Pleasantville 68 39 25N 74 30W
Pleiku 34 13 57N 108 0 E
Plenty → 44 23 25S 136 31 E
Plenty, Bay of 43 37 45S 177 0 E
Plentywood 70 48 45N 104 35W
Plesetsk 22 62 40N 40 10 E
Plessisville 63 46 14N 71 47W
Pletipi L. 63 51 44N 70 6W
Pleven 19 43 26N 24 37 E
Plevlja 19 43 21N 19 21 E
Płock 15 52 32N 19 40 E
Ploieşti 15 44 57N 26 5 E
Plonge, Lac la 65 55 8N 107 20W
Plovdiv 19 42 8N 24 44 E
Plummer 72 47 21N 116 59W
Plumtree 55 20 27S 27 55 E
Plymouth, U.K. 7 50 23N 4 9W
Plymouth, Ind., U.S.A. 68 41 20N 86 19W
Plymouth, N.C., U.S.A. 69 35 54N 76 46W
Plymouth, Wis., U.S.A. 68 43 42N 87 58W
Plymouth Sd. 7 50 20N 4 10W
Plynlimon = Pumlumon Fawr 7 52 29N 3 47W
Plzeň 14 49 45N 13 22 E
Po → 18 44 57N 12 4 E
Po Hai = Bo Hai 38 39 0N 120 0 E
Pobé 53 7 0N 2 56 E
Pobeda 25 65 12N 146 12 E
Pobedino 25 49 51N 142 49 E
Pobedy Pik 24 40 45N 79 58 E
Pocahontas, Ark., U.S.A. 71 36 18N 91 0W
Pocahontas, Iowa, U.S.A. 70 42 41N 94 42W
Pocatello 72 42 50N 112 25W
Pochutla 74 15 50N 96 31W
Pocomoke City 68 38 4N 75 32W
Poços de Caldas 79 21 50S 46 33W
Podgorica = Titograd 19 42 30N 19 19 E
Podkamennaya Tunguska → 25 61 50N 90 13 E
Podolsk 22 55 25N 37 30 E
Podor 50 16 40N 15 2W
Podporozhy 22 60 55N 34 2 E
Pofadder 56 29 10S 19 22 E
Pogamasing 62 46 55N 81 50W
Poh 35 0 46S 122 51 E
Pohang 38 36 1N 129 23 E
Point Edward 62 43 0N 82 30W
Point Pedro 32 9 50N 80 15 E
Point Pleasant 68 38 50N 82 7W
Pointe-à-la Hache 71 29 35N 89 55W
Pointe-à-Pitre 75 16 10N 61 30W
Pointe Noire 54 4 48S 11 53 E
Poisonbush Ra. 46 22 30S 121 30 E
Poitiers 12 46 35N 0 20 E
Pojoaque Valley 73 35 55N 106 0W
Pokaran 32 27 0N 71 50 E
Pokataroo 45 29 30S 148 36 E
Pokrovsk 25 61 29N 126 12 E
Polacca 73 35 52N 110 25W
Polan 31 25 30N 61 10 E
Poland ■ 15 52 0N 20 0 E
Polcura 80 37 17S 71 43W
Polden Hills 7 51 7N 2 50W
Polesye 22 52 0N 28 10 E
Polevskoy 22 56 26N 60 11 E
Polewali 35 3 21S 119 23 E
Poli 54 8 34N 13 15 E
Polillo Is. 35 14 56N 122 0 E
Políyiros 19 40 23N 23 25 E
Pollachi 32 10 35N 77 0 E
Pollock 70 45 58N 100 18W
Polnovat 24 63 50N 65 54 E
Polo 70 41 59N 89 38W
Polotsk 22 55 30N 28 50 E
Polson 72 47 45N 114 12W
Poltava 23 49 35N 34 35 E
Polunochnoye 22 60 52N 60 25 E
Polyarny 22 69 8N 33 20 E
Polynesia 41 10 0S 162 0W
Pombal, Brazil 79 6 45S 37 50W
Pombal, Portugal 13 39 55N 8 40W
Pomeroy, Ohio, U.S.A. 68 39 0N 82 0W
Pomeroy, Wash., U.S.A. 72 46 30N 117 33W
Pomona 73 34 2N 117 49W
Pompano Beach 69 26 12N 80 6W
Pompeys Pillar 72 46 0N 108 0W
Ponape 40 6 55N 158 10 E
Ponask, L. 62 54 0N 92 41W
Ponass L. 65 52 16N 103 58W
Ponca 70 42 38N 96 41W
Ponca City 71 36 40N 97 5W
Ponce 75 18 1N 66 37W
Ponchatoula 71 30 27N 90 25W
Poncheville, L. 62 50 10N 76 55W
Pond Inlet 61 72 40N 77 0W
Pondicherry 32 11 59N 79 50 E
Ponds, I. of 63 53 27N 55 52W
Ponferrada 13 42 32N 6 35W
Ponnani 32 10 45N 75 59 E
Ponnyadaung 33 22 0N 94 10 E
Ponoi 22 67 0N 41 0 E
Ponoi → 22 66 59N 41 17 E
Ponoka 64 52 42N 113 40W
Ponorogo 35 7 52S 111 27 E
Ponta Grossa 80 25 7S 50 10W
Ponta Pora 80 22 20S 55 35W
Pontarlier 12 46 54N 6 20 E
Pontchartrain, L. 71 30 12N 90 0W
Ponte Macassar 35 9 30S 123 58 E
Ponte Nova 79 20 25S 42 54W
Pontedera 18 43 40N 10 37 E
Pontefract 6 53 42N 1 19W
Ponteix 65 49 46N 107 29W
Pontevedra 13 42 26N 8 40W
Pontiac, Ill., U.S.A. 70 40 50N 88 40W
Pontiac, Mich., U.S.A. 68 42 40N 83 20W
Pontianak 34 0 3S 109 15 E
Pontine Is. = Ponziane, Isole 18 40 55N 13 0 E
Pontine Mts. = Kuzey Anadolu Dağlari 30 41 30N 35 0 E
Ponton → 64 58 27N 116 11W
Pontypool 7 51 42N 3 1W
Pontypridd 7 51 36N 3 21W
Ponziane, Isole 18 40 55N 13 0 E
Poochera 45 32 43S 134 51 E
Poole 7 50 42N 1 58W
Pooley I. 64 52 45N 128 15W
Poona = Pune 32 18 29N 73 57 E
Pooncarie 45 33 22S 142 31 E
Poopelloe, L. 45 31 40S 144 0 E
Poopó, L. de 78 18 30S 67 35W
Popanyinning 47 32 40S 117 2 E
Popayán 78 2 27N 76 36W
Poperinge 11 50 51N 2 42 E
Popigay 25 72 1N 110 39 E
Popilta, L. 45 33 10S 141 42 E
Popio, L. 45 33 10S 141 52 E
Poplar 70 48 3N 105 9W
Poplar →, Man., Canada 65 53 0N 97 19W
Poplar →, N.W.T., Canada 64 61 22N 121 52W
Poplar Bluff 71 36 45N 90 22W
Poplarville 71 30 55N 89 30W
Popocatepetl 74 19 10N 98 40W
Popokabaka 54 5 41S 16 40 E
Porbandar 32 21 44N 69 43 E
Porcher I. 64 53 50N 130 30W
Porcupine →, Canada 65 59 11N 104 46W
Porcupine →, U.S.A. 60 66 35N 145 15W
Pori 21 61 29N 21 48 E
Porjus 20 66 57N 19 50 E
Porkkala 21 59 59N 24 26 E
Porlamar 78 10 57N 63 51W
Poronaysk 25 49 13N 143 0 E
Poroshiri-Dake 36 42 41N 142 52 E
Porretta, Passo di 18 44 2N 10 56 E
Porsangen 20 70 40N 25 40 E
Port Adelaide 45 34 46S 138 30 E
Port Alberni 64 49 14N 124 50W
Port Alfred, Canada 63 48 18N 70 53W
Port Alfred, S. Africa 56 33 36S 26 55 E
Port Alice 64 50 20N 127 25W

Purnia 33 25 45N 87 31 E
Purukcahu 34 0 35S 114 35 E
Puruliya 33 23 17N 86 24 E
Purus → 78 3 42S 61 28W
Purwakarta 35 6 35S 107 29 E
Purwodadi, Jawa, Indonesia 35 7 7S 110 55 E
Purwodadi, Jawa, Indonesia 35 7 51S 110 0 E
Purwokerto 35 7 25S 109 14 E
Purworejo 35 7 43S 110 2 E
Pusan 38 35 5N 129 0 E
Push, La 72 47 55N 124 38W
Pushchino 25 54 10N 158 0 E
Pushkino 23 51 16N 47 0 E
Putahow L. 65 59 54N 100 40W
Putao 33 27 28N 97 30 E
Putaruru 43 38 2S 175 50 E
Puthein Myit → 33 15 56N 94 18 E
Putian 39 25 23N 119 0 E
Putignano 18 40 50N 17 5 E
Puting, Tanjung 34 3 31S 111 46 E
Putorana, Gory 25 69 0N 95 0 E
Puttalam 32 8 1N 79 55 E
Putten 11 52 16N 5 36 E
Puttgarden 14 54 28N 11 15 E
Putumayo → 78 3 7S 67 58W
Putussibau 34 0 50N 112 56 E
Puy, Le 12 45 3N 3 52 E
Puy-de-Dôme 12 45 46N 2 57 E
Puy-de-Dôme □ 12 45 40N 3 5 E
Puyallup 72 47 10N 122 22W
Puyang 38 35 40N 115 1 E
Pweto 54 8 25S 28 51 E
Pwllheli 6 52 54N 4 26W
Pya-ozero 22 66 5N 30 58 E
Pyapon 33 16 20N 95 40 E
Pyasina → 25 73 30N 87 0 E
Pyatigorsk 23 44 2N 43 6 E
Pyè 33 18 49N 95 13 E
Pyinmana 33 19 45N 96 12 E
Pyŏngyang 38 39 0N 125 30 E
Pyote 71 31 34N 103 5W
Pyramid L. 72 40 0N 119 30W
Pyrénées 12 42 45N 0 18 E
Pyrénées-Atlantiques □ 12 43 10N 0 50W
Pyrénées-Orientales □ 12 42 35N 2 26 E
Pyu 33 18 30N 96 28 E

Q

Qabalān 28 32 8N 35 17 E
Qabātiyah 28 32 25N 35 16 E
Qachasnek 57 30 6S 28 42 E
Qādib 29 12 37N 53 57 E
Qā'emshahr 31 36 30N 52 55 E
Qahremānshahr = Bākhtarān 30 34 23N 47 0 E
Qaidam Pendi 37 37 0N 95 0 E
Qalāt 31 32 15N 66 58 E
Qal'at al Akhḍar 30 28 0N 37 10 E
Qal'eh Shaharak 32 34 10N 64 20 E
Qal'eh-ye Now 31 35 0N 63 5 E
Qalqīlya 28 32 12N 34 58 E
Qam 28 32 36N 35 43 E
Qamar, Ghubbat al 29 16 20N 52 30 E
Qamruddin Karez 32 31 45N 68 20 E
Qāna 28 33 12N 35 17 E
Qandahār 31 31 32N 65 30 E
Qandahār □ 32 31 0N 65 0 E
Qâra 51 29 38N 26 30 E
Qarachuk 30 37 0N 42 2 E
Qārah 30 29 55N 40 3 E
Qarqan 37 38 5N 85 20 E
Qarqan He → 37 39 30N 88 30 E
Qāsim 28 32 59N 36 2 E
Qaṣr-e Qand 31 26 15N 60 45 E
Qasr Farâfra 51 27 0N 28 1 E
Qatar ■ 31 25 30N 51 15 E
Qattâra, Munkhafed el 51 29 30N 27 30 E
Qattâra Depression = Qattâra, Munkhafed el 51 29 30N 27 30 E
Qāyen 31 33 40N 59 10 E
Qazvin 30 36 15N 50 0 E
Qena 51 26 10N 32 43 E
Qeshm 31 26 55N 56 10 E
Qezi'ot 28 30 52N 34 26 E
Qian Xian 39 34 31N 108 15 E
Qianshan 39 30 37N 116 35 E
Qianxi 39 27 3N 106 3 E
Qianyang 39 27 18N 110 10 E
Qijiang 39 28 57N 106 35 E
Qila Safed 31 29 0N 61 30 E
Qila Saifullāh 32 30 45N 68 17 E
Qilian Shan 37 38 30N 96 0 E
Qin Ling = Qinling Shandi 39 33 50N 108 10 E
Qin'an 39 34 48N 105 40 E
Qingdao 38 36 5N 120 20 E
Qinghai □ 37 36 0N 98 0 E
Qinghai Hu 37 36 40N 100 10 E
Qingjiang, Jiangsu, China 39 33 30N 119 2 E
Qingjiang, Jiangxi, China 39 28 4N 115 29 E
Qingliu 39 26 11N 116 48 E
Qingshuihe 38 39 55N 111 35 E
Qingyang 38 36 2N 107 55 E
Qingyuan 39 23 40N 112 59 E
Qinhuangdao 38 39 56N 119 30 E
Qinling Shandi 39 33 50N 108 10 E
Qinyang 39 35 7N 112 57 E
Qinyuan 38 36 29N 112 20 E
Qinzhou 39 21 58N 108 38 E
Qiongshan 39 19 51N 110 26 E
Qiongzhou Haixia 39 20 10N 110 15 E
Qiqihar 38 47 26N 124 0 E
Qiryat 'Anavim 28 31 49N 35 7 E
Qiryat Ata 28 32 47N 35 6 E
Qiryat Bialik 28 32 50N 35 5 E
Qiryat Gat 28 31 32N 34 46 E
Qiryat Ḥayyim 28 32 49N 35 4 E
Qiryat Mal'akhi 28 31 44N 34 44 E
Qiryat Shemona 28 33 13N 35 35 E
Qiryat Yam 28 32 51N 35 4 E
Qishan 39 22 52N 120 25 E
Qishon → 28 32 49N 35 2 E
Qitai 37 44 2N 89 35 E
Qiyahe 38 53 0N 120 35 E
Qiyang 39 26 35N 111 50 E
Qom 31 34 40N 51 0 E
Qomsheh 31 32 0N 51 55 E
Qondūz 31 36 50N 68 50 E
Qondūz □ 31 36 50N 68 50 E
Qu Jiang → 39 30 1N 106 24 E
Qu Xian, Sichuan, China 39 30 48N 106 58 E
Qu Xian, Zhejiang, China 39 28 57N 118 54 E
Quairading 47 32 0S 117 21 E
Qualeup 47 33 48S 116 48 E
Quambatook 45 35 49S 143 34 E
Quambone 45 30 57S 147 53 E
Quan Long 34 9 7N 105 8 E
Quanan 71 34 20N 99 45W
Quandialla 45 34 1S 147 47 E
Quang Ngai 34 15 13N 108 58 E
Quantock Hills 7 51 8N 3 10W
Quanzhou, Fujian, China 39 24 55N 118 34 E
Quanzhou, Guangxi Zhuangzu, China 39 25 57N 111 5 E
Quaraí 80 30 15S 56 20W
Quartzsite 73 33 44N 114 16W
Quatsino 64 50 30N 127 40W
Quatsino Sd. 64 50 25N 127 58W
Qubab = Mishmar Ayyalon 28 31 52N 34 57 E
Qūchān 31 37 10N 58 27 E
Queanbeyan 45 35 17S 149 14 E
Québec 63 46 52N 71 13W
Québec □ 63 50 0N 70 0W
Queen Charlotte 64 53 15N 132 2W
Queen Charlotte Is. 64 53 20N 132 10W
Queen Charlotte Sd. 43 41 10S 174 15 E
Queen Charlotte Str. 64 51 0N 128 0W
Queen Elizabeth Is. 2 76 0N 95 0W
Queen Maud G. 60 68 15N 102 30W
Queens Chan. 46 15 0S 129 30 E
Queenscliff 45 38 16S 144 39 E
Queensland □ 44 22 0S 142 0 E
Queenstown, Australia 44 42 4S 145 35 E
Queenstown, N.Z. 43 45 1S 168 40 E
Queenstown, S. Africa 56 31 52S 26 52 E
Queimadas 79 11 0S 39 38W
Quela 54 9 10S 16 56 E
Quelimane 55 17 53S 36 58 E
Quelpart = Cheju Do 39 33 29N 126 34 E
Quemado, N. Mex., U.S.A. 73 34 17N 108 28W
Quemado, Tex., U.S.A. 71 28 58N 100 35W
Quequén 80 38 30S 58 30W
Querétaro 74 20 40N 100 23W
Querétaro □ 74 20 30N 100 0W
Queshan 39 32 55N 114 2 E
Quesnel 64 53 0N 122 30W
Quesnel → 64 52 58N 122 29W
Quesnel L. 64 52 30N 121 20W
Questa 73 36 45N 105 35W
Quetico Prov. Park 62 48 30N 91 45W
Quetta 31 30 15N 66 55 E
Quezaltenango 75 14 50N 91 30W
Quezon City 35 14 38N 121 0 E
Qui Nhon 34 13 40N 109 13 E
Quiaca, La 80 22 5S 65 35W
Quibaxe 54 8 24S 14 27 E
Quibdo 78 5 42N 76 40W
Quiberon 12 47 29N 3 9W
Quick 64 54 36N 126 54W
Quiet L. 64 61 5N 133 5W
Quilán, C. 80 43 15S 74 30W
Quilengues 55 14 12S 14 12 E
Quillabamba 78 12 50S 72 50W
Quillagua 78 21 40S 69 40W
Quillota 80 32 54S 71 16W
Quilon 32 8 50N 76 38 E
Quilpie 45 26 35S 144 11 E
Quimilí 80 27 40S 62 30W
Quimper 12 48 0N 4 9W
Quimperlé 12 47 53N 3 33W
Quincy, Calif., U.S.A. 72 39 56N 120 56W
Quincy, Fla., U.S.A. 69 30 34N 84 34W
Quincy, Ill., U.S.A. 70 39 55N 91 20W
Quincy, Mass., U.S.A. 68 42 14N 71 0W
Quincy, Wash., U.S.A. 72 47 22N 119 56W
Quines 80 32 13S 65 48W
Quinga 55 15 49S 40 15 E
Quintana Roo □ 74 19 0N 88 0W
Quintanar de la Orden 13 39 36N 3 5W
Quintanar de la Sierra 13 41 57N 2 55W
Quintero 80 32 45S 71 30W
Quinyambie 45 30 15S 141 0 E
Quipungo 55 14 37S 14 40 E
Quirindi 45 31 28S 150 40 E
Quissanga 55 12 24S 40 28 E
Quitilipi 80 26 50S 60 13W
Quitman, Ga., U.S.A. 69 30 49N 83 35W
Quitman, Miss., U.S.A. 69 32 2N 88 42W
Quitman, Tex., U.S.A. 71 32 48N 95 25W
Quito 78 0 15S 78 35W
Quixadá 79 4 55S 39 0W
Qumbu 57 31 10S 28 48 E
Qumrān 28 31 43N 35 27 E
Quneitra 28 33 7N 35 48 E
Quoin I. 46 14 54S 129 32 E
Quoin Pt. 56 34 46S 19 37 E
Quondong 45 33 6S 140 18 E
Quorn 45 32 25S 138 0 E
Qûs 51 25 55N 32 50 E
Quseir 51 26 7N 34 16 E
Qusrah 28 32 5N 35 20 E
Quthing 57 30 25S 27 36 E

R

Raahe 20 64 40N 24 28 E
Ra'ananna 28 32 12N 34 52 E
Raasay 8 57 25N 6 4W
Raasay, Sd. of 8 57 30N 6 8W
Raba 35 8 36S 118 55 E
Rabat, Malta 18 35 53N 14 25 E
Rabat, Morocco 50 34 2N 6 48W
Rabaul 40 4 24S 152 18 E
Rabbit → 64 59 41N 127 12W
Rabbit Lake 65 53 8N 107 46W
Rabbitskin → 64 61 47N 120 42W
Rābigh 30 22 50N 39 5 E
Race, C. 63 46 40N 53 5W
Rach Gia 34 10 5N 105 5 E
Racine 68 42 41N 87 51W
Radama, Nosy 57 14 0S 47 47 E
Radama, Saikanosy 57 14 16S 47 53 E
Rădăuţi 15 47 50N 25 59 E
Radford 68 37 8N 80 32W
Radhwa, Jabal 30 24 34N 38 18 E
Radisson 65 52 30N 107 20W
Radium Hot Springs 64 50 35N 116 2W
Radnor Forest 7 52 17N 3 10W
Radom 15 51 23N 21 12 E
Radomir 19 42 37N 23 4 E
Radomsko 15 51 5N 19 28 E
Radstock 7 51 17N 2 25W
Radstock, C. 45 33 12S 134 20 E
Radville 65 49 30N 104 15W
Rae 64 62 50N 116 3W
Rae Bareli 33 26 18N 81 20 E
Rae Isthmus 61 66 40N 87 30W
Raeren 11 50 41N 6 7 E
Raeside, L. 47 29 20S 122 0 E
Raetihi 43 39 25S 175 17 E
Rafaela 80 31 10S 61 30W
Rafai 54 4 59N 23 58 E
Rafḥā 30 29 35N 43 35 E
Rafsanjān 31 30 30N 56 5 E
Raft Pt. 46 16 4S 124 26 E
Ragama 32 7 0N 79 50 E
Ragged Mt. 47 33 27S 123 25 E
Raglan, Australia 44 23 42S 150 49 E
Raglan, N.Z. 43 37 55S 174 55 E
Ragusa 18 36 56N 14 42 E
Raha 35 4 55S 123 0 E
Rahad al Bardī 51 11 20N 23 40 E
Rahaeng = Tak 34 16 52N 99 8 E
Rahimyar Khan 32 28 30N 70 25 E
Raichur 32 16 10N 77 20 E
Raigarh 33 21 56N 83 25 E
Raijua 35 10 37S 121 36 E
Railton 44 41 25S 146 28 E
Rainbow Lake 64 58 30N 119 23W
Rainier 72 46 4N 122 58W
Rainier, Mt. 72 46 50N 121 50W
Rainy L. 65 48 42N 93 10W
Rainy River 65 48 43N 94 29W
Raipur 33 21 17N 81 45 E
Ra'is 30 23 33N 38 43 E
Raj Nandgaon 33 21 0N 81 0 E
Raja, Ujung 34 3 40N 96 25 E
Raja Ampat, Kepulauan 35 0 30S 130 0 E
Rajahmundry 33 17 1N 81 48 E
Rajang → 34 2 30N 112 0 E
Rajapalaiyam 32 9 25N 77 35 E
Rajasthan □ 32 26 45N 73 30 E
Rajasthan Canal 32 28 0N 72 0 E
Rajgarh 32 24 2N 76 45 E
Rajkot 32 22 15N 70 56 E
Rajojooseppi 20 68 25N 28 30 E
Rajpipla 32 21 50N 73 30 E
Rajshahi 33 24 22N 88 39 E
Rajshahi □ 33 25 0N 89 0 E
Rakaia 43 43 45S 172 1 E
Rakaia → 43 43 36S 172 15 E
Rakan, Ra's 31 26 10N 51 20 E
Rakaposhi 32 36 10N 74 25 E
Rakata, Pulau 34 6 10S 105 20 E
Rakops 56 21 1S 24 28 E
Raleigh 69 35 47N 78 39W
Raleigh B. 69 34 50N 76 15W
Ralls 71 33 40N 101 20W
Ram → 64 62 1N 123 41W
Rām Allāh 28 31 55N 35 10 E
Ram Hd. 45 37 47S 149 30 E
Rama 28 32 56N 35 21 E
Ramanathapuram 32 9 25N 78 55 E
Ramanetaka, B. de 57 14 13S 47 52 E
Ramat Gan 28 32 4N 34 48 E
Ramat HaSharon 28 32 7N 34 50 E
Ramatlhabama 56 25 37S 25 33 E
Rambipuji 35 8 12S 113 37 E
Ramea 63 47 31N 57 23W
Ramechhap 33 27 25N 86 10 E
Ramelau 35 8 55S 126 22 E
Ramgarh, Bihar, India 33 23 40N 85 35 E
Ramgarh, Raj., India 32 27 30N 70 36 E
Rāmhormoz 30 31 15N 49 35 E
Ramla 28 31 55N 34 52 E
Rammūn 28 31 55N 35 17 E
Ramnad = Ramanathapuram 32 9 25N 78 55 E
Ramon, Har 28 30 30N 34 38 E
Ramona 73 33 1N 116 56W
Ramore 62 48 30N 80 25W
Ramotswa 56 24 50S 25 52 E
Rampart 60 65 0N 150 15W
Rampur 32 28 50N 79 5 E
Rampur Hat 33 24 10N 87 50 E
Ramree Kyun 33 19 0N 94 0 E
Ramsey, Canada 62 47 25N 82 20W
Ramsey, U.K. 6 54 20N 4 21W
Ramsgate 7 51 20N 1 25 E
Ramtek 32 21 20N 79 15 E
Ranaghat 33 23 15N 88 35 E
Ranau 34 6 2N 116 40 E
Rancagua 80 34 10S 70 50W
Rancheria → 64 60 13N 129 7W
Ranchester 72 44 57N 107 12W
Ranchi 33 23 19N 85 27 E
Randers 21 56 29N 10 1 E
Randfontein 57 26 8S 27 45 E
Randolph 72 41 43N 111 10W
Råne älv → 20 65 50N 22 20 E
Rangaunu B. 43 34 51S 173 15 E
Rangeley 68 44 58N 70 33W
Rangely 72 40 3N 108 53W
Ranger 71 32 30N 98 42W
Rangia 33 26 28N 91 38 E
Rangiora 43 43 19S 172 36 E
Rangitaiki → 43 37 54S 176 49 E
Rangitata → 43 43 45S 171 15 E
Rangkasbitung 35 6 21S 106 15 E
Rangon → 33 16 28N 96 40 E
Rangoon 33 16 45N 96 20 E
Rangpur 33 25 42N 89 22 E
Rangwe 52 0 38S 34 35 E
Ranibennur 32 14 35N 75 30 E
Raniganj 33 23 40N 87 5 E
Raniwara 32 24 50N 72 10 E
Ranken → 44 20 31S 137 36 E
Rankin 71 31 16N 101 56W
Rankin Inlet 60 62 30N 93 0W
Rankins Springs 45 33 49S 146 14 E
Rannoch, L. 8 56 41N 4 20W
Rannoch Moor 8 56 38N 4 48W
Ranobe, Helodranon' i 57 23 3S 43 33 E
Ranohira 57 22 29S 45 24 E
Ranomafana, Toamasina, Madag. 57 18 57S 48 50 E
Ranomafana, Toliara, Madag. 57 24 34S 47 0 E
Ranong 34 9 56N 98 40 E
Ransiki 35 1 30S 134 10 E
Rantau 34 2 56S 115 9 E
Rantauprapat 34 2 15N 99 50 E
Rantekombola 35 3 15S 119 57 E
Rantīs 28 32 4N 35 3 E
Rantoul 68 40 18N 88 10W
Raohe 38 46 47N 134 0 E
Rapa Iti 41 27 35S 144 20W
Rāpch 31 25 40N 59 15 E
Rapid → 64 59 15N 129 5W
Rapid City 70 44 0N 103 0W
Rapid River 68 45 55N 87 0W
Rapides des Joachims 62 46 13N 77 43W
Rarotonga 41 21 30S 160 0W
Ra's al Khaymah 31 25 50N 56 5 E
Ra's al-Unuf 51 30 25N 18 15 E
Ras Bânâs 51 23 57N 35 59 E
Ras Dashen 54 13 8N 38 26 E
Râs Timirist 50 19 21N 16 30W
Rasa, Punta 80 40 50S 62 15W
Rashad 51 11 55N 31 0 E
Rashîd 51 31 21N 30 22 E
Rasht 30 37 20N 49 40 E
Rason, L. 47 28 45S 124 25 E
Rat Is. 60 51 50N 178 15 E
Rat River 64 61 7N 112 36W
Ratangarh 32 28 5N 74 35 E
Rath Luirc 9 52 21N 8 40W
Rathdrum 9 52 57N 6 13W
Rathenow 14 52 38N 12 23 E
Rathkeale 9 52 32N 8 57W
Rathlin I. 9 55 18N 6 14W
Rathlin O'Birne I. 9 54 40N 8 50W
Ratlam 32 23 20N 75 0 E
Ratnagiri 32 16 57N 73 18 E
Raton 71 37 0N 104 30W
Rattray Hd. 8 57 38N 1 50W
Ratz, Mt. 64 57 23N 132 12W
Raufarhöfn 20 66 27N 15 57W
Raukumara Ra. 43 38 5S 177 55 E
Rauma 21 61 10N 21 30 E
Raurkela 33 22 14N 84 50 E
Rāvar 31 31 20N 56 51 E
Ravenna, Italy 18 44 28N 12 15 E
Ravenna, U.S.A. 70 41 3N 98 58W
Ravensburg 14 47 48N 9 38 E
Ravenshoe 44 17 37S 145 29 E
Ravensthorpe 47 33 35S 120 2 E
Ravenswood, Australia 44 20 6S 146 54 E
Ravenswood, U.S.A. 68 38 58N 81 47W
Ravi → 32 30 35N 71 49 E
Rawalpindi 32 33 38N 73 8 E
Rawāndūz 30 36 40N 44 30 E
Rawdon 62 46 3N 73 40W
Rawene 43 35 25S 173 32 E
Rawlinna 47 30 58S 125 28 E
Rawlins 72 41 50N 107 20W
Rawlinson Range 47 24 40S 128 30 E
Rawson 80 43 15S 65 0W
Ray 70 48 21N 103 6W
Ray, C. 63 47 33N 59 15W
Rayadurg 32 14 40N 76 50 E
Rayagada 33 19 15N 83 20 E
Raychikhinsk 25 49 46N 129 25 E
Raymond, Canada 64 49 30N 112 35W
Raymond, U.S.A. 72 46 45N 123 48W
Raymondville 71 26 30N 97 50W
Raymore 65 51 25N 104 31W
Rayne 71 30 16N 92 16W
Rayville 71 32 30N 91 45W
Raz, Pte. du 12 48 2N 4 47W
Razgrad 19 43 33N 26 34 E
Ré, I. de 12 46 12N 1 30W
Reading, U.K. 7 51 27N 0 57W
Reading, U.S.A. 68 40 20N 75 53W
Realicó 80 35 0S 64 15W
Rebecca L. 47 30 0S 122 15 E
Rebi 35 6 23S 134 7 E
Rebiana 51 24 12N 22 10 E
Rebun-Tō 36 45 23N 141 2 E
Recherche, Arch. of the 47 34 15S 122 50 E
Recife 79 8 0S 35 0W
Recklinghausen 11 51 36N 7 10 E
Reconquista 80 29 10S 59 45W
Recreo 80 29 25S 65 10W
Red → = Hong → 26 20 17N 106 34 E

Red →, Canada **65** 50 24N 96 48W
Red →, Minn., U.S.A. **70** 48 10N 97 0W
Red →, Tex., U.S.A. **71** 31 0N 91 40W
Red Bay **63** 51 44N 56 25W
Red Bluff **72** 40 11N 122 11W
Red Bluff L. **71** 31 59N 103 58W
Red Cliffs **45** 34 19S 142 11 E
Red Cloud **70** 40 8N 98 33W
Red Deer **64** 52 20N 113 50W
Red Deer →, Alta., Canada **65** 50 58N 110 0W
Red Deer →, Man., Canada **65** 52 53N 101 1W
Red Deer L. **65** 52 55N 101 20W
Red Indian L. **63** 48 35N 57 0W
Red Lake **65** 51 3N 93 49W
Red Lake Falls **70** 47 54N 96 15W
Red Lodge **72** 45 10N 109 10W
Red Oak **70** 41 0N 95 10W
Red Rock **62** 48 55N 88 15W
Red Rock, L. **70** 41 30N 93 15W
Red Rock's Pt. **47** 32 13S 127 32 E
Red Sea **29** 25 0N 36 0 E
Red Sucker L. **65** 54 9N 93 40W
Red Tower Pass = Turnu Rosu Pasul **15** 45 33N 24 17 E
Red Wing **70** 44 32N 92 35W
Redbridge **7** 51 35N 0 7 E
Redcar **6** 54 37N 1 4W
Redcliff **65** 50 10N 110 50W
Redcliffe **45** 27 12S 153 0 E
Redcliffe, Mt. **47** 28 30S 121 30 E
Reddersburg **56** 29 41S 26 10 E
Redding **72** 40 30N 122 25W
Redditch **7** 52 18N 1 57W
Redfield **70** 45 0N 98 30W
Redknife → **64** 61 14N 119 22W
Redlands **73** 34 0N 117 11W
Redmond, Australia **47** 34 55S 117 40 E
Redmond, U.S.A. **72** 44 19N 121 11W
Redonda **75** 16 58N 62 19W
Redondela **13** 42 15N 8 38W
Redondo **13** 38 39N 7 37W
Redrock Pt. **64** 62 11N 115 2W
Redruth **7** 50 14N 5 14W
Redvers **65** 49 35N 101 40W
Redwater **64** 53 55N 113 6W
Redwood City **73** 37 30N 122 15W
Redwood Falls **70** 44 30N 95 2W
Ree, L. **9** 53 35N 8 0W
Reed, L. **65** 54 38N 100 30W
Reed City **68** 43 52N 85 30W
Reeder **70** 46 7N 102 52W
Reedley **73** 36 36N 119 27W
Reedsburg **70** 43 34N 90 5W
Reedsport **72** 43 45N 124 4W
Reefton **43** 42 6S 171 51 E
Refugio **71** 28 18N 97 17W
Regavim **28** 32 32N 35 2 E
Regensburg **14** 49 1N 12 7 E
Réggio di Calábria **18** 38 7N 15 38 E
Réggio nell' Emilia **18** 44 42N 10 38 E
Regina **65** 50 27N 104 35W
Rehoboth **56** 23 15S 17 4 E
Rehovot **28** 31 54N 34 48 E
Rei-Bouba **51** 8 40N 14 15 E
Reichenbach **14** 50 36N 12 19 E
Reid **47** 30 49S 128 26 E
Reid River **44** 19 40S 146 48 E
Reidsville **69** 36 21N 79 40W
Reigate **7** 51 14N 0 11W
Reims **12** 49 15N 4 1 E
Reina **28** 32 43N 35 18 E
Reina Adelaida, Arch. **80** 52 20S 74 0W
Reinbeck **70** 42 18N 92 40W
Reindeer → **65** 55 36N 103 11W
Reindeer I. **65** 52 30N 98 0W
Reindeer L. **65** 57 15N 102 15W
Reine, La **62** 48 50N 79 30W
Reinga, C. **43** 34 25S 172 43 E
Reitz **57** 27 48S 28 29 E
Reivilo **56** 27 36S 24 8 E
Rekinniki **25** 60 51N 163 40 E
Reliance **65** 63 0N 109 20W
Remarkable, Mt. **45** 32 48S 138 10 E
Rembang **35** 6 42S 111 21 E
Remeshk **31** 26 55N 58 50 E
Remich **11** 49 32N 6 22 E
Remscheid **14** 51 11N 7 12 E
Rendsburg **14** 54 18N 9 41 E
Rene **25** 66 2N 179 25W
Renfrew, Canada **62** 45 30N 76 40W
Renfrew, U.K. **8** 55 52N 4 24W
Rengat **34** 0 30S 102 45 E
Renhuai **39** 27 48N 106 24 E
Renk **51** 11 50N 32 50 E
Renkum **11** 51 58N 5 43 E
Renmark **45** 34 11S 140 43 E
Rennell Sd. **64** 53 23N 132 35W
Renner Springs T.O. **44** 18 20S 133 47 E
Rennes **12** 48 7N 1 41W
Reno **72** 39 30N 119 50W
Reno → **18** 44 37N 12 17 E
Renovo **68** 41 20N 77 47W
Rensselaer **68** 40 57N 87 10W
Renton **72** 47 30N 122 9W
Republic, Mich., U.S.A. **68** 46 25N 87 59W
Republic, Wash., U.S.A. **72** 48 38N 118 42W
Republican → **70** 39 3N 96 48W
Republican City **70** 40 9N 99 20W
Repulse Bay **61** 66 30N 86 30W
Requena, Peru **78** 5 5S 73 52W
Requena, Spain **13** 39 30N 1 4W
Reserve, Canada **65** 52 28N 102 39W
Reserve, U.S.A. **73** 33 50N 108 54W
Resht = Rasht **30** 37 20N 49 40 E
Resistencia **80** 27 30S 59 0W
Reşiţa **15** 45 18N 21 53 E
Resolution I., Canada **61** 61 30N 65 0W
Resolution I., N.Z. **43** 45 40S 166 40 E
Ressano Garcia **57** 25 25S 32 0 E
Reston **65** 49 33N 101 6W
Retalhuleu **75** 14 33N 91 46W
Réthímnon **19** 35 18N 24 30 E
Réunion **3** 21 0S 56 0 E
Reutlingen **14** 48 28N 9 13 E
Reval = Tallinn **22** 59 22N 24 48 E
Revda **22** 56 48N 59 57 E
Revelstoke **64** 51 0N 118 10W
Revilla Gigedo, Is. **41** 18 40N 112 0W
Revillagigedo I. **64** 55 50N 131 20W
Rewa **33** 24 33N 81 25 E
Rewari **32** 28 15N 76 40 E
Rexburg **72** 43 55N 111 50W
Rey Malabo **54** 3 45N 8 50 E
Reykjahlið **20** 65 40N 16 55W
Reykjanes **20** 63 48N 22 40W
Reykjavík **20** 64 10N 21 57 E
Reynolds **65** 49 40N 95 55W
Reynolds Ra. **46** 22 30S 133 0 E
Reynosa **74** 26 5N 98 18W
Rhayader **7** 52 19N 3 30W
Rheden **11** 52 0N 6 3 E
Rhein **65** 51 25N 102 15W
Rhein → **11** 51 52N 6 2 E
Rheine **14** 52 17N 7 25 E
Rheinland-Pfalz □ **14** 50 0N 7 0 E
Rhin = Rhein → **11** 51 52N 6 2 E
Rhine = Rhein → **11** 51 52N 6 2 E
Rhineland-Palatinate □ = Rheinland-Pfalz □ **14** 50 0N 7 0 E
Rhinelander **70** 45 38N 89 29W
Rhode Island □ **68** 41 38N 71 37W
Rhodes = Ródhos **19** 36 15N 28 10 E
Rhodesia = Zimbabwe ■ **55** 19 0S 30 0 E
Rhodope Mts. = Rhodopi Planina **19** 41 40N 24 20 E
Rhodopi Planina **19** 41 40N 24 20 E
Rhondda **7** 51 39N 3 30W
Rhône □ **12** 45 54N 4 35 E
Rhône → **14** 43 28N 4 42 E
Rhum **8** 57 0N 6 20W
Rhyl **6** 53 19N 3 29W
Rhymney **7** 51 32N 3 7W
Riachão **79** 7 20S 46 37W
Riasi **32** 33 10N 74 50 E
Riau □ **34** 0 0 102 35 E
Riau, Kepulauan **34** 0 30N 104 20 E
Ribadeo **13** 43 35N 7 5W
Ribatejo □ **13** 39 15N 8 30W
Ribble → **6** 54 13N 2 20W
Ribe **21** 55 19N 8 44 E
Ribeirão Prêto **79** 21 10S 47 50W
Riberalta **78** 11 0S 66 0W
Riccarton **43** 43 32S 172 37 E
Rice Lake **70** 45 30N 91 42W
Rich Hill **71** 38 5N 94 22W
Richards Bay **57** 28 48S 32 6 E
Richards L. **65** 59 10N 107 10W
Richardson → **65** 58 25N 111 14W
Richardton **70** 46 56N 102 22W
Riche, C. **47** 34 36S 118 47 E
Richey **70** 47 42N 105 5W
Richfield, Idaho, U.S.A. **72** 43 2N 114 5W
Richfield, Utah, U.S.A. **73** 38 50N 112 0W
Richibucto **63** 46 42N 64 54W
Richland, Ga., U.S.A. **69** 32 7N 84 40W
Richland, Oreg., U.S.A. **72** 44 49N 117 9W
Richland, Wash., U.S.A. **72** 46 15N 119 15W
Richland Center **70** 43 21N 90 22W
Richlands **68** 37 7N 81 49W
Richmond, N.S.W., Australia **45** 33 35S 150 42 E
Richmond, Queens., Australia **44** 20 43S 143 8 E
Richmond, N.Z. **43** 41 20S 173 12 E
Richmond, S. Africa **57** 29 51S 30 18 E
Richmond, N. Yorks., U.K. **6** 54 24N 1 43W
Richmond, Surrey, U.K. **7** 51 28N 0 18W
Richmond, Calif., U.S.A. **72** 37 58N 122 21W
Richmond, Ind., U.S.A. **68** 39 50N 84 50W
Richmond, Ky., U.S.A. **68** 37 40N 84 20W
Richmond, Mo., U.S.A. **70** 39 15N 93 58W
Richmond, Tex., U.S.A. **71** 29 32N 95 42W
Richmond, Utah, U.S.A. **72** 41 55N 111 48W
Richmond, Va., U.S.A. **68** 37 33N 77 27W
Richmond Ra., Australia **45** 29 0S 152 45 E
Richmond Ra., N.Z. **43** 41 32S 173 22 E
Richton **69** 31 23N 88 58W
Richwood **68** 38 17N 80 32W
Ridgedale **65** 53 0N 104 10W
Ridgeland **69** 32 30N 80 58W
Ridgelands **44** 23 16S 150 17 E
Ridgetown **62** 42 26N 81 52W
Ridgway **68** 41 25N 78 43W
Riding Mt. Nat. Park **65** 50 50N 100 0W
Ridley Mt. **47** 33 12S 122 7 E
Ried **14** 48 14N 13 30 E
Riet → **56** 29 0S 23 54 E
Rieti **18** 42 23N 12 50 E
Rifle **72** 39 40N 107 50W
Rifstangi **20** 66 32N 16 12W
Rig Rig **51** 14 13N 14 25 E
Riga **22** 56 53N 24 8 E
Riga, G. of = Rīgas Jūras Līcis **22** 57 40N 23 45 E
Rīgas Jūras Līcis **22** 57 40N 23 45 E
Rigby **72** 43 41N 111 58W
Rigestān □ **31** 30 15N 65 0 E
Riggins **72** 45 29N 116 26W
Rigolet **63** 54 10N 58 23W
Riihimäki **21** 60 45N 24 48 E
Rijeka **18** 45 20N 14 21 E
Rijn → **11** 52 12N 4 21 E
Rijssen **11** 52 19N 6 30 E
Rijswijk **11** 52 4N 4 22 E
Riley **72** 43 35N 119 33W
Rima → **53** 13 4N 5 10 E
Rimah, Wadi ar → **30** 26 5N 41 30 E
Rimbey **64** 52 35N 114 15W
Rímini **18** 44 3N 12 33 E
Rîmnicu Sărat **15** 45 26N 27 3 E
Rîmnicu Vîlcea **15** 45 9N 24 21 E
Rimouski **63** 48 27N 68 30W
Rinca **35** 8 45S 119 35 E
Rinconada **80** 22 26S 66 10W
Rineanna **9** 52 42N 85 7W
Ringkøbing **21** 56 5N 8 15 E
Ringling **72** 46 16N 110 56W
Ringvassøy **20** 69 56N 19 15 E
Rinía **19** 37 23N 25 13 E
Rinjani **34** 8 24S 116 28 E
Rio Branco, Brazil **78** 9 58S 67 49W
Río Branco, Uruguay **80** 32 40S 53 40W
Rio Claro **75** 10 20N 61 25W
Río Colorado **80** 39 0S 64 0W
Río Cuarto **80** 33 10S 64 25W
Rio das Pedras **57** 23 8S 35 28 E
Rio de Janeiro **79** 23 0S 43 12W
Rio de Janeiro □ **79** 22 50S 43 0W
Rio do Sul **80** 27 13S 49 37W
Río Gallegos **80** 51 35S 69 15W
Río Grande, Argentina **80** 53 50S 67 45W
Rio Grande, Brazil **80** 32 0S 52 20W
Rio Grande → **71** 25 57N 97 9W
Rio Grande City **71** 26 23N 98 49W
Río Grande del Norte → **66** 26 0N 97 0W
Rio Grande do Norte □ **79** 5 40S 36 0W
Rio Grande do Sul □ **80** 30 0S 53 0W
Rio Largo **79** 9 28S 35 50W
Río Mulatos **78** 19 40S 66 50W
Río Muni = Mbini □ **54** 1 30N 10 0 E
Rio Negro **80** 26 0S 50 0W
Rio Verde, Brazil **79** 17 50S 51 0W
Río Verde, Mexico **74** 21 56N 99 59W
Rio Vista **72** 38 11N 121 44W
Ríobamba **78** 1 50S 78 45W
Ríohacha **78** 11 33N 72 55W
Rioja, La **80** 29 20S 67 0W
Rioja, La □ **13** 42 20N 2 20W
Riosucio, Caldas, Colombia **78** 5 30N 75 40W
Ríosucio, Choco, Colombia **78** 7 27N 77 7W
Riou L. **65** 59 7N 106 25W
Ripley **71** 35 43N 89 34W
Ripon, U.K. **6** 54 8N 1 31W
Ripon, U.S.A. **68** 43 51N 88 50W
Rishiri-Tō **36** 45 11N 141 15 E
Rishon le Ẓiyyon **28** 31 58N 34 48 E
Rishpon **28** 32 12N 34 49 E
Rison **71** 33 57N 92 11W
Risør **21** 58 43N 9 13 E
Ritzville **72** 47 10N 118 21W
Rivadavia **80** 29 57S 70 35W
Rivas **75** 11 30N 85 50W
Rivera **80** 31 0S 55 50W
Riverdsale **56** 34 7S 21 15 E
Riverhead **68** 40 53N 72 40W
Riverhurst **65** 50 55N 106 50W
Riverina **47** 29 45S 120 40 E
Rivers **65** 50 2N 100 14W
Rivers □ **53** 5 0N 6 30 E
Rivers, L. of the **65** 49 49N 105 44W
Rivers Inlet **64** 51 42N 127 15W
Riverside, Calif., U.S.A. **73** 34 0N 117 22W
Riverside, Wyo., U.S.A. **72** 41 12N 106 57W
Riversleigh **44** 19 5S 138 40 E
Riverton, Australia **45** 34 10S 138 46 E
Riverton, Canada **65** 51 1N 97 0W
Riverton, N.Z. **43** 46 21S 168 0 E
Riverton, U.S.A. **72** 43 1N 108 27W
Riviera **14** 44 0N 8 30 E
Rivière-à-Pierre **63** 46 59N 72 11W
Rivière-au-Renard **63** 48 59N 64 23W
Rivière-du-Loup **63** 47 50N 69 30W
Rivière-Pentecôte **63** 49 57N 67 1W
Rivoli B. **45** 37 32S 140 3 E
Riyadh = Ar Riyāḍ **29** 24 41N 46 42 E
Rize **30** 41 0N 40 30 E
Rizhao **39** 35 25N 119 30 E
Rizzuto, C. **18** 38 54N 17 5 E
Rjukan **21** 59 54N 8 33 E
Roag, L. **8** 58 10N 6 55W
Roanne **12** 46 3N 4 4 E
Roanoke, Ala., U.S.A. **69** 33 9N 85 23W
Roanoke, Va., U.S.A. **68** 37 19N 79 55W
Roanoke → **69** 35 56N 76 43W
Roanoke I. **69** 35 55N 75 40W
Roanoke Rapids **69** 36 28N 77 42W
Roatán **75** 16 18N 86 35W
Robbins I. **44** 40 42S 145 0 E
Robe →, Australia **46** 21 42S 116 15 E
Robe →, Ireland **9** 53 38N 9 10W
Robert Lee **71** 31 55N 100 26W
Roberts **72** 43 44N 112 8W
Robertson **56** 33 46S 19 50 E
Robertson Ra. **46** 23 15S 121 0 E
Robertsport **50** 6 45N 11 26W
Robertstown **45** 33 58S 139 5 E
Roberval **63** 48 32N 72 15W
Robinson → **44** 16 3S 137 16 E
Robinson Crusoe I. **41** 33 38S 78 52W
Robinson Ranges **47** 25 40S 119 0 E
Robinson River **44** 16 45S 136 58 E
Robinvale **45** 34 40S 142 45 E
Robla, La **13** 42 50N 5 41W
Roblin **65** 51 14N 101 21W
Roboré **78** 18 10S 59 45W
Robson, Mt. **64** 53 10N 119 10W
Robstown **71** 27 47N 97 40W
Roca, C. da **13** 38 40N 9 31W
Rocas, I. **79** 4 0S 34 1W
Rocha **80** 34 30S 54 25W
Rochdale **6** 53 36N 2 10W
Rochefort, Belgium **11** 50 9N 5 12 E
Rochefort, France **12** 45 56N 0 57W
Rochelle **70** 41 55N 89 5W
Rochelle, La **12** 46 10N 1 9W
Rocher River **64** 61 23N 112 44W
Rochester, Canada **64** 54 22N 113 27W
Rochester, U.K. **7** 51 22N 0 30 E
Rochester, Ind., U.S.A. **68** 41 5N 86 15W
Rochester, Minn., U.S.A. **70** 44 1N 92 28W
Rochester, N.H., U.S.A. **68** 43 19N 70 57W
Rochester, N.Y., U.S.A. **68** 43 10N 77 40W
Rock → **64** 60 7N 127 7W
Rock Hill **69** 34 55N 81 2W
Rock Island **70** 41 30N 90 35W
Rock Port **70** 40 26N 95 30W
Rock Rapids **70** 43 25N 96 10W
Rock River **72** 41 49N 106 0W
Rock Sound **75** 24 54N 76 12W
Rock Sprs., Mont., U.S.A. **72** 46 55N 106 11W
Rock Sprs., Wyo., U.S.A. **72** 41 40N 109 10W
Rock Valley **70** 43 10N 96 17W
Rockall **4** 57 37N 13 42W
Rockdale **71** 30 40N 97 0W
Rockford **70** 42 20N 89 0W
Rockglen **65** 49 11N 105 57W
Rockhampton **44** 23 22S 150 32 E
Rockhampton Downs **44** 18 57S 135 10 E
Rockingham **47** 32 15S 115 38 E
Rockingham B. **44** 18 5S 146 10 E
Rockingham Forest **7** 52 28N 0 42W
Rocklake **70** 48 50N 99 13W
Rockland, Idaho, U.S.A. **72** 42 37N 112 57W
Rockland, Maine, U.S.A. **63** 44 6N 69 6W
Rockland, Mich., U.S.A. **70** 46 40N 89 10W
Rockmart **69** 34 1N 85 2W
Rockport **71** 28 2N 97 3W
Rocksprings **71** 30 2N 100 11W
Rockville **68** 39 7N 77 10W
Rockwall **71** 32 55N 96 30W
Rockwell City **70** 42 20N 94 35W
Rockwood **69** 35 52N 84 40W
Rocky Ford **70** 38 7N 103 45W
Rocky Gully **47** 34 30S 116 57 E
Rocky Lane **64** 58 31N 116 22W
Rocky Mount **69** 35 55N 77 48W
Rocky Mountain House **64** 52 22N 114 55W
Rocky Mts. **60** 55 0N 121 0W
Rockyford **64** 51 14N 113 10W
Rod **31** 28 10N 63 5 E
Roda, La **13** 39 13N 2 15W
Rødbyhavn **21** 54 39N 11 22 E
Roddickton **63** 50 51N 56 8W
Roderick I. **64** 52 38N 128 22W
Rodez **12** 44 21N 2 33 E
Ródhos **19** 36 15N 28 10 E
Rodney, C. **43** 36 17S 174 50 E
Rodriguez **3** 19 45S 63 20 E
Roe → **9** 55 10N 6 59W
Roebourne **46** 20 44S 117 9 E
Roebuck B. **46** 18 5S 122 20 E
Roebuck Plains **46** 17 56S 122 28 E
Roermond **11** 51 12N 6 0 E
Roes Welcome Sd. **61** 65 0N 87 0W
Roeselare **11** 50 57N 3 7 E
Rogagua, L. **78** 13 43S 66 50W
Rogaland fylke □ **21** 59 12N 6 20 E
Rogers **71** 36 20N 94 5W
Rogers City **68** 45 25N 83 49W
Rogerson **72** 42 10N 114 40W
Rogersville **69** 36 27N 83 1W
Roggan River **62** 54 25N 79 32W
Roggeveldberge **56** 32 10S 20 10 E
Rogoaguado, L. **78** 13 0S 65 30W
Rogue → **72** 42 30N 124 0W
Rohri **32** 27 45N 68 51 E
Rohtak **32** 28 55N 76 43 E
Roi Et **34** 16 4N 103 40 E
Rojas **80** 34 10S 60 45W
Rojo, C. **74** 21 33N 97 20W
Rokan → **34** 2 0N 100 50 E
Rokeby **44** 13 39S 142 40 E
Rolândia **80** 23 18S 51 23W
Rolette **70** 48 42N 99 50W
Rolla, Kans., U.S.A. **71** 37 10N 101 40W
Rolla, Mo., U.S.A. **71** 37 56N 91 42W
Rolla, N. Dak., U.S.A. **70** 48 50N 99 36W
Rolleston **44** 24 28S 148 35 E
Rollingstone **44** 19 2S 146 24 E
Roma, Australia **45** 26 32S 148 49 E
Roma, Italy **18** 41 54N 12 30 E
Roma, Sweden **21** 57 32N 18 26 E
Roman, Romania **15** 46 57N 26 55 E
Roman, U.S.S.R. **25** 66 4N 112 14 E
Romana, La **75** 18 27N 68 57W
Romang **35** 7 30S 127 20 E
Romania ■ **15** 46 0N 25 0 E
Romano, Cayo **75** 22 0N 77 30W
Romblon **35** 12 33N 122 17 E
Rome = Roma **18** 41 54N 12 30 E
Rome, Ga., U.S.A. **69** 34 20N 85 0W
Rome, N.Y., U.S.A. **68** 43 14N 75 29W
Romney **68** 39 21N 78 45W
Romney Marsh **7** 51 0N 1 0 E
Romorantin-Lanthenay **12** 47 21N 1 45 E
Romsdalen **20** 62 25N 8 0 E
Rona **8** 57 33N 6 0W
Ronan **72** 47 30N 114 6W
Roncador, Cayos **75** 13 32N 80 4W
Roncador, Serra do **79** 12 30S 52 30W
Ronceverte **68** 37 45N 80 28W
Ronda **13** 36 46N 5 12W
Rondane **21** 61 57N 9 50 E
Rondônia □ **78** 11 0S 63 0W
Rondonópolis **79** 16 28S 54 38W
Rong Xian **39** 29 23N 104 22 E
Rong'an **39** 25 14N 109 22 E
Ronge, L. la **65** 55 6N 105 17W

St. Lawrence, Gulf of

St. Lawrence, Gulf of **63** 48 25N 62 0W
St. Lawrence I. **60** 63 0N 170 0W
St. Leonard **63** 47 12N 67 58W
St. Lewis → **63** 52 26N 56 11W
St.-Lô **12** 49 7N 1 5W
St-Louis **50** 16 8N 16 27W
St. Louis, Mich., U.S.A. **68** 43 27N 84 38W
St. Louis, Mo., U.S.A. **70** 38 40N 90 12W
St. Louis → **70** 47 15N 92 45W
St. Lucia ■ **75** 14 0N 60 50W
St. Lucia, L. **57** 28 5S 32 30 E
St. Lucia Channel **75** 14 15N 61 0W
St. Lunaire-Griquet **63** 51 31N 55 28W
St. Maarten **75** 18 0N 63 5W
St.-Malo **12** 48 39N 2 1W
St-Marc **75** 19 10N 72 41W
St. Maries **72** 47 17N 116 34W
St-Martin, I. **75** 18 0N 63 0W
St. Martin L. **65** 51 40N 98 30W
St. Martins **63** 45 22N 65 34W
St. Martinsville **71** 30 10N 91 50W
St. Mary Pk. **45** 31 32S 138 34 E
St. Marys, Australia **44** 41 35S 148 11 E
St. Mary's, U.K. **7** 49 55N 6 17W
St. Marys, U.S.A. **68** 41 27N 78 33W
St. Mary's, C. **63** 46 50N 54 12W
St. Mary's B. **63** 46 50N 53 50W
St. Marys Bay **63** 44 25N 66 10W
St.-Mathieu, Pte. de **12** 48 20N 4 45W
St. Matthews, I. = Zadetkyi Kyun **34** 10 0N 98 25 E
St-Maurice → **62** 46 21N 72 31W
St. Michael's Mt. **7** 50 7N 5 30W
St.-Nazaire **12** 47 17N 2 12W
St. Neots **7** 52 14N 0 16W
St.-Omer **12** 50 45N 2 15 E
St-Pacome **63** 47 24N 69 58W
St-Pamphile **63** 46 58N 69 48W
St. Pascal **63** 47 32N 69 48W
St. Paul, Canada **64** 54 0N 111 17W
St. Paul, Ind. Oc. **3** 38 55S 77 34 E
St. Paul, Minn., U.S.A. **70** 44 54N 93 5W
St. Paul, Nebr., U.S.A. **70** 41 15N 98 30W
St. Paul, I. **63** 47 12N 60 9W
St. Peter **70** 44 21N 93 57W
St. Peter Port **7** 49 27N 2 31W
St. Peters, N.S., Canada **63** 45 40N 60 53W
St. Peters, P.E.I., Canada **63** 46 25N 62 35W
St. Petersburg **69** 27 45N 82 40W
St. Pierre, Ind. Oc. **3** 9 20S 46 0 E
St.-Pierre, St- P. & M. **63** 46 46N 56 12W
St-Pierre, L. **62** 46 12N 72 52W
St.-Pierre et Miquelon □ **63** 46 55N 56 10W
St.-Quentin **12** 49 50N 3 16 E
St. Regis **72** 47 20N 115 3W
St. Sebastien, Tanjon' i **57** 12 26S 48 44 E
St-Siméon **63** 47 51N 69 54W
St. Stephen **63** 45 16N 67 17W
St. Thomas, Canada **62** 42 45N 81 10W
St. Thomas, W. Indies **75** 18 21N 64 55W
St-Tite **62** 46 45N 72 34W
St.-Tropez **12** 43 17N 6 38 E
St. Troud = Sint Truiden **11** 50 48N 5 10 E
St.-Valéry-sur-Somme **12** 50 11N 1 38 E
St. Vincent **75** 13 10N 61 10W
St. Vincent, G. **45** 35 0S 138 0 E
St. Vincent and the Grenadines ■ **75** 13 0N 61 10W
St. Vincent Passage **75** 13 30N 61 0W
St-Vith **11** 50 17N 6 9 E
Ste-Agathe-des-Monts **62** 46 3N 74 17W
Ste Anne de Beaupré **63** 47 2N 70 58W
Ste-Anne-des-Monts **63** 49 8N 66 30W
Ste. Genevieve **70** 37 59N 90 2W
Ste-Marguerite → **63** 50 9N 66 36W
Ste.-Marie **75** 14 48N 61 1W
Ste-Marie de la Madeleine **63** 46 26N 71 0W
Ste.-Rose **75** 16 20N 61 45W
Ste. Rose du lac **65** 51 4N 99 30W
Saintes **12** 45 45N 0 37W
Saintes, I. des **75** 15 50N 61 35W
Saintonge **12** 45 40N 0 50W
Sairang **33** 23 50N 92 45 E
Sairecábur, Cerro **80** 22 43S 67 54W
Saitama □ **36** 36 25N 139 30 E
Sajama **78** 18 7S 69 0W
Sak → **56** 30 52S 20 25 E
Sakai **36** 34 30N 135 30 E
Sakākah **30** 30 0N 40 8 E
Sakakawea, L. **70** 47 30N 102 0W
Sakami, L. **62** 53 15N 77 0W
Sakarya → **23** 41 7N 30 39 E
Sakata **36** 38 55N 139 50 E
Sakeny → **57** 20 0S 45 25 E
Sakété **53** 6 40N 2 45 E
Sakhalin **25** 51 0N 143 0 E
Sakhalinskiy Zaliv **25** 54 0N 141 0 E
Sakhnīn **28** 32 52N 35 12 E
Sakon Nakhon **34** 17 10N 104 9 E
Sakrivier **56** 30 54S 20 28 E
Sala **21** 59 58N 16 35 E
Sala-y-Gómez **41** 26 28S 105 28W
Salaberry-de-Valleyfield **62** 45 15N 74 8W
Saladillo **80** 35 40S 59 55W
Salado →, Buenos Aires, Argentina **80** 35 44S 57 22W
Salado →, La Pampa, Argentina **80** 37 30S 67 0W
Salado →, Santa Fe, Argentina **80** 31 40S 60 41W
Salado →, Mexico **74** 26 52N 99 19W
Salaga **53** 8 31N 0 31W
Salālah **29** 16 56N 53 59 E
Salamanca, Chile **80** 31 46S 70 59W
Salamanca, Spain **13** 40 58N 5 39W
Salamanca, U.S.A. **68** 42 10N 78 42W
Salamis **19** 37 56N 23 30 E
Salar de Atacama **80** 23 30S 68 25W
Salar de Uyuni **78** 20 30S 67 45W
Salatiga **35** 7 19S 110 30 E
Salavat **22** 53 21N 55 55 E
Salaverry **78** 8 15S 79 0W
Salawati **35** 1 7S 130 52 E
Salayar **35** 6 7S 120 30 E
Salcombe **7** 50 14N 3 47W
Saldaña **13** 42 32N 4 48W
Saldanha **56** 33 0S 17 58 E
Saldanha B. **56** 33 6S 18 0 E
Sale, Australia **45** 38 6S 147 6 E
Salé, Morocco **50** 34 3N 6 48W
Sale, U.K. **6** 53 26N 2 19W
Salekhard **22** 66 30N 66 35 E
Salem, India **32** 11 40N 78 11 E
Salem, Ind., U.S.A. **68** 38 38N 86 6W
Salem, Mass., U.S.A. **68** 42 29N 70 53W
Salem, Mo., U.S.A. **71** 37 40N 91 30W
Salem, N.J., U.S.A. **68** 39 34N 75 29W
Salem, Ohio, U.S.A. **68** 40 52N 80 50W
Salem, Oreg., U.S.A. **72** 45 0N 123 0W
Salem, S. Dak., U.S.A. **70** 43 44N 97 23W
Salem, Va., U.S.A. **68** 37 19N 80 8W
Salen **21** 64 41N 11 27 E
Salerno **18** 40 40N 14 44 E
Salfīt **28** 32 5N 35 11 E
Salford **6** 53 30N 2 17W
Salima **55** 13 47S 34 28 E
Salina, Italy **18** 38 35N 14 50 E
Salina, U.S.A. **70** 38 50N 97 40W
Salina Cruz **74** 16 10N 95 10W
Salinas, Brazil **79** 16 10S 42 10W
Salinas, Ecuador **78** 2 10S 80 58W
Salinas, U.S.A. **73** 36 40N 121 41W
Salinas →, Mexico **74** 16 28N 90 31W
Salinas →, U.S.A. **73** 36 45N 121 48W
Salinas, B. de **75** 11 4N 85 45W
Salinas Ambargasta **80** 29 0S 65 0W
Salinas de Hidalgo **74** 22 30N 101 40W
Salinas Grandes **80** 30 0S 65 0W
Saline →, Ark., U.S.A. **71** 33 10N 92 8W
Saline →, Kans., U.S.A. **70** 38 51N 97 30W
Salinópolis **79** 0 40S 47 20W
Salisbury = Harare **55** 17 43S 31 2 E
Salisbury, Australia **45** 34 46S 138 40 E
Salisbury, U.K. **7** 51 4N 1 48W
Salisbury, Md., U.S.A. **68** 38 20N 75 38W
Salisbury, N.C., U.S.A. **69** 35 20N 80 29W
Salisbury Plain **7** 51 13N 1 50W
Salle, La **70** 41 20N 89 6W
Sallisaw **71** 35 26N 94 45W
Salmās **30** 38 11N 44 47 E
Salmo **64** 49 10N 117 20W
Salmon **72** 45 12N 113 56W
Salmon →, Canada **64** 54 3N 122 40W
Salmon →, U.S.A. **72** 45 51N 116 46W
Salmon Arm **64** 50 40N 119 15W
Salmon Falls **72** 42 48N 114 59W
Salmon Gums **47** 32 59S 121 38 E
Salmon Res. **63** 48 5N 56 0W
Salmon River Mts. **72** 45 0N 114 30W
Salo **21** 60 22N 23 10 E
Salome **73** 33 51N 113 37W
Salonica = Thessaloníki **19** 40 38N 22 58 E
Salonta **15** 46 49N 21 42 E
Salop = Shropshire □ **7** 52 36N 2 45W
Salsk **23** 46 28N 41 30 E
Salso → **18** 37 6N 13 55 E
Salt →, Canada **64** 60 0N 112 25W
Salt →, U.S.A. **73** 33 23N 112 18W
Salt Creek **45** 36 8S 139 38 E
Salt Fork → **71** 36 37N 97 7W
Salt Lake City **72** 40 45N 111 58W
Salta **80** 24 57S 65 25W
Saltcoats **8** 55 38N 4 47W
Saltee Is. **9** 52 7N 6 37W
Saltfjorden **20** 67 15N 14 10 E
Salthólmavík **20** 65 24N 21 57W
Saltillo **74** 25 30N 100 57W
Salto **80** 31 27S 57 50W
Salton Sea **73** 33 20N 115 50W
Saltpond **53** 5 15N 1 3W
Saltville **68** 36 53N 81 46W
Saluda → **69** 34 0N 81 4W
Salûm **51** 31 31N 25 7 E
Salûm, Khâlig el **51** 31 30N 25 9 E
Salur **33** 18 27N 83 18 E
Saluzzo **18** 44 39N 7 29 E
Salvador, Brazil **79** 13 0S 38 30W
Salvador, Canada **65** 52 10N 109 32W
Salvador, L. **71** 29 46N 90 16W
Salwa **31** 24 45N 50 55 E
Salween → **33** 16 31N 97 37 E
Salyany **23** 39 10N 48 50 E
Salyersville **68** 37 45N 83 4W
Salzburg **14** 47 48N 13 2 E
Salzburg □ **14** 47 15N 13 0 E
Salzgitter **14** 52 13N 10 22 E
Sam Rayburn Res. **71** 31 15N 94 20W
Sama **24** 60 12N 60 22 E
Sama de Langreo **13** 43 18N 5 40W
Samagaltai **25** 50 36N 95 3 E
Samales Group **35** 6 0N 122 0 E
Samangán □ **31** 36 15N 68 3 E
Samani **36** 42 7N 142 56 E
Samar **35** 12 0N 125 0 E
Samaria = Shōmrōn **28** 32 15N 35 13 E
Samarinda **34** 0 30S 117 9 E
Samarkand **24** 39 40N 66 55 E
Sāmarrā **30** 34 12N 43 52 E
Sambalpur **33** 21 28N 84 4 E
Sambar, Tanjung **34** 2 59S 110 19 E
Sambas **34** 1 20N 109 20 E
Sambava **57** 14 16S 50 10 E
Sambhal **32** 28 35N 78 37 E
Sambhar **32** 26 52N 75 6 E
Sambre → **11** 50 27N 4 52 E
Samchŏk **38** 37 30N 129 10 E
Same **54** 4 2S 37 38 E
Sámos **19** 37 45N 26 50 E
Samothráki **19** 40 28N 25 28 E
Sampacho **80** 33 20S 64 50W
Sampang **35** 7 11S 113 13 E
Sampit **34** 2 34S 113 0 E
Sampit, Teluk **34** 3 5S 113 3 E
Samra **30** 25 35N 41 0 E
Samsun **30** 41 15N 36 22 E
Samui, Ko **34** 9 30N 100 0 E
Samut Prakan **34** 13 32N 100 40 E
Samut Songkhram → **34** 13 24N 100 1 E
San **50** 13 15N 4 57W
San → **15** 50 45N 21 51 E
San Ambrosio **76** 26 28S 79 53W
San Andreas **72** 38 0N 120 39W
San Andrés, I. de **75** 12 42N 81 46W
San Andres Mts. **73** 33 0N 106 45W
San Andrés Tuxtla **74** 18 30N 95 20W
San Angelo **71** 31 30N 100 30W
San Antonio, Chile **80** 33 40S 71 40W
San Antonio, N. Mex., U.S.A. **73** 33 58N 106 57W
San Antonio, Tex., U.S.A. **71** 29 30N 98 30W
San Antonio → **71** 28 30N 96 50W
San Antonio, C., Argentina **80** 36 15S 56 40W
San Antonio, C., Cuba **75** 21 50N 84 57W
San Antonio de los Baños **75** 22 54N 82 31W
San Antonio Oeste **80** 40 40S 65 0W
San Augustin, C. **35** 6 20N 126 13 E
San Augustine **71** 31 30N 94 7W
San Benito **71** 26 5N 97 39W
San Bernardino **73** 34 7N 117 18W
San Bernardino Str. **35** 13 0N 125 0 E
San Bernardo **80** 33 40S 70 50W
San Bernardo, I. de **78** 9 45N 75 50W
San Blas **74** 26 4N 108 46W
San Blas, Arch. de **75** 9 50N 78 31W
San Blas, C. **69** 29 40N 85 12W
San Borja **78** 14 50S 66 52W
San Buenaventura **74** 27 5N 101 32W
San Carlos, Argentina **80** 33 50S 69 0W
San Carlos, Chile **80** 36 10S 72 0W
San Carlos, Mexico **74** 29 0N 100 54W
San Carlos, Nic. **75** 11 12N 84 50W
San Carlos, Phil. **35** 10 29N 123 25 E
San Carlos, U.S.A. **73** 33 24N 110 27W
San Carlos, Amazonas, Venezuela **78** 1 55N 67 4W
San Carlos, Cojedes, Venezuela **78** 9 40N 68 36W
San Carlos de Bariloche **80** 41 10S 71 25W
San Carlos del Zulia **78** 9 1N 71 55W
San Carlos L. **73** 33 15N 110 25W
San Clemente **73** 33 29N 117 36W
San Clemente I. **73** 32 53N 118 30W
San Cristóbal, Argentina **80** 30 20S 61 10W
San Cristóbal, Dom. Rep. **75** 18 25N 70 6W
San Cristóbal, Venezuela **78** 7 46N 72 14W
San Cristóbal de las Casas **74** 16 50N 92 33W
San Diego, Calif., U.S.A. **73** 32 43N 117 10W
San Diego, Tex., U.S.A. **71** 27 47N 98 15W
San Diego, C. **80** 54 40S 65 10W
San Felipe, Chile **80** 32 43S 70 42W
San Felipe, Mexico **74** 31 0N 114 52W
San Felipe, Venezuela **78** 10 20N 68 44W
San Felíu de Guíxols **13** 41 45N 3 1 E
San Félix **41** 26 23S 80 0W
San Fernando, Chile **80** 34 30S 71 0W
San Fernando, Mexico **74** 30 0N 115 10W
San Fernando, La Union, Phil. **35** 16 40N 120 23 E
San Fernando, Pampanga, Phil. **35** 15 5N 120 37 E
San Fernando, Spain **13** 36 28N 6 17W
San Fernando, Trin. & Tob. **75** 10 20N 61 30W
San Fernando, U.S.A. **73** 34 15N 118 29W
San Fernando → **74** 24 55N 98 10W
San Fernando de Apure **78** 7 54N 67 15W
San Fernando de Atabapo **78** 4 3N 67 42W
San Francisco, Argentina **80** 31 30S 62 5W
San Francisco, U.S.A. **73** 37 47N 122 30W
San Francisco → **73** 32 59N 109 22W
San Francisco de Macorís **75** 19 19N 70 15W
San Francisco del Monte de Oro **80** 32 36S 66 8W
San Francisco del Oro **74** 26 52N 105 50W
San Gil **78** 6 33N 73 8W
San Gottardo, Paso del **14** 46 33N 8 33 E
San Ignacio, Belize **74** 17 10N 89 0W
San Ignacio, Bolivia **78** 16 20S 60 55W
San Ignacio, Paraguay **80** 26 52S 57 3W
San Ignacio, L. **74** 26 50N 113 11W
San Ildefonso, C. **35** 16 0N 122 1 E
San Javier, Argentina **80** 30 40S 59 55W
San Javier, Bolivia **78** 16 18S 62 30W
San Joaquin → **73** 38 4N 121 51W
San Jorge, B. de **74** 31 20N 113 20W
San Jorge, G. **80** 46 0S 66 0W
San Jorge, G. de **13** 40 50N 0 55W
San José, Bolivia **78** 17 53S 60 50W
San José, C. Rica **75** 10 0N 84 2W
San José, Guat. **75** 14 0N 90 50W
San José, Mexico **74** 25 0N 110 50W
San Jose, Luzon, Phil. **35** 15 45N 120 55 E
San Jose, Mindoro, Phil. **35** 12 27N 121 4 E
San Jose, U.S.A. **73** 37 20N 121 53W
San Jose → **73** 34 58N 106 7W
San José de Jáchal **80** 30 15S 68 46W
San José de Mayo **80** 34 27S 56 40W
San José de Ocune **78** 4 15N 70 20W
San José del Cabo **74** 23 0N 109 40W
San José del Guaviare **78** 2 35N 72 38W
San Juan, Argentina **80** 31 30S 68 30W
San Juan, Mexico **74** 21 20N 102 50W
San Juan, Phil. **35** 8 25N 126 20 E
San Juan, Puerto Rico **75** 18 28N 66 8W
San Juan →, Nic. **75** 10 56N 83 42W
San Juan →, U.S.A. **73** 37 20N 110 20W
San Juan, C. **54** 1 5N 9 20 E
San Juan Bautista **73** 36 51N 121 32W
San Juan Capistrano **73** 33 29N 117 40W
San Juan de los Morros **78** 9 55N 67 21W
San Juan del Norte, B. de **75** 11 0N 83 40W
San Juan del Río **74** 20 25N 100 0W
San Juan del Sur **75** 11 20N 85 51W
San Juan Mts. **73** 38 30N 108 30W
San Julián **80** 49 15S 67 45W
San Justo **80** 30 47S 60 30W
San Lázaro, C. **74** 24 50N 112 18W
San Lázaro, Sa. **74** 23 25N 110 0W
San Leandro **73** 37 40N 122 6W
San Lorenzo **78** 1 15N 78 50W
San Lorenzo → **74** 24 15N 107 24W
San Lorenzo, I., Mexico **74** 28 35N 112 50W
San Lorenzo, I., Peru **78** 12 7S 77 15W
San Lorenzo, Mt. **80** 47 40S 72 20W
San Lucas, Bolivia **78** 20 5S 65 7W
San Lucas, Mexico **74** 27 10N 112 14W
San Lucas, C. **74** 22 50N 110 0W
San Luis, Argentina **80** 33 20S 66 20W
San Luis, U.S.A. **73** 37 3N 105 26W
San Luis, I. **74** 29 58N 114 26W
San Luis de la Paz **74** 21 19N 100 32W
San Luis Obispo **73** 35 21N 120 38W
San Luis Potosí **74** 22 9N 100 59W
San Luis Potosí □ **74** 22 10N 101 0W
San Luis Río Colorado **74** 32 29N 114 58W
San Marcos, Guat. **75** 14 59N 91 52W
San Marcos, Mexico **74** 27 13N 112 6W
San Marcos, U.S.A. **71** 29 53N 98 0W
San Marino ■ **18** 43 56N 12 25 E
San Martín, L. **80** 48 50S 72 50W
San Mateo **73** 37 32N 122 19W
San Matías **78** 16 25S 58 20W
San Matías, G. **80** 41 30S 64 0W
San Miguel, El Salv. **75** 13 30N 88 12W
San Miguel, U.S.A. **73** 35 45N 120 42W
San Miguel → **78** 13 52S 63 56W
San Miguel de Tucumán **80** 26 50S 65 20W
San Narciso **35** 15 2N 120 3 E
San Nicolás de los Arroyas **80** 33 25S 60 10W
San Nicolas I. **73** 33 16N 119 30W
San-Pédro **50** 4 50N 6 33W
San Pedro →, Chihuahua, Mexico **74** 28 20N 106 10W
San Pedro →, Nayarit, Mexico **74** 21 45N 105 30W
San Pedro →, U.S.A. **73** 33 0N 110 50W
San Pedro de las Colonias **74** 25 50N 102 59W
San Pedro de Lloc **78** 7 15S 79 28W
San Pedro de Macorís **75** 18 30N 69 18W
San Pedro del Paraná **80** 26 43S 56 13W
San Pedro Mártir, Sierra **74** 31 0N 115 30W
San Pedro Mixtepec **74** 16 2N 97 7W
San Pedro Ocampo = Melchor Ocampo **74** 24 52N 101 40W
San Pedro Sula **75** 15 30N 88 0W
San Rafael, Argentina **80** 34 40S 68 21W
San Rafael, Calif., U.S.A. **72** 37 59N 122 32W
San Rafael, N. Mex., U.S.A. **73** 35 6N 107 58W
San Ramón de la Nueva Orán **80** 23 10S 64 20W
San Remo **18** 43 48N 7 47 E
San Roque **80** 28 25S 58 45W
San Rosendo **80** 37 16S 72 43W
San Saba **71** 31 12N 98 45W
San Salvador, Bahamas **75** 24 0N 74 40W
San Salvador, El Salv. **75** 13 40N 89 10W
San Salvador de Jujuy **80** 24 10S 64 48W
San Salvador I. **75** 24 0N 74 32W
San Sebastián, Argentina **80** 53 10S 68 30W
San Sebastián, Spain **13** 43 17N 1 58W
San Simon **73** 32 14N 109 16W
San Valentin, Mte. **80** 46 30S 73 30W
San Vicente de la Barquera **13** 43 23N 4 29W

Tonantins

Tepalcatepec → 74 18 35N 101 59W
Tepic 74 21 30N 104 54W
Teplice 14 50 40N 13 48 E
Tepoca, C. 74 30 20N 112 25W
Tequila 74 20 54N 103 47W
Ter → 13 42 0N 3 12 E
Ter Apel 11 52 53N 7 5 E
Téra 53 14 0N 0 45 E
Teraina, I. 41 4 43N 160 25W
Téramo 18 42 40N 13 40 E
Terang 45 38 15S 142 55 E
Terek → 23 44 0N 47 30 E
Teresina 79 5 9S 42 45W
Terewah, L. 45 29 52S 147 35 E
Terhazza 50 23 38N 5 22W
Teridgerie Cr. → 45 30 25S 148 50 E
Termez 24 37 15N 67 15 E
Términos, L. de 74 18 35N 91 30W
Térmoli 18 42 0N 15 0 E
Ternate 35 0 45N 127 25 E
Terneuzen 11 51 20N 3 50 E
Terney 25 45 3N 136 37 E
Terni 18 42 34N 12 38 E
Ternopol 22 49 30N 25 40 E
Terowie 45 32 27S 147 52 E
Terrace 64 54 30N 128 35W
Terrace Bay 62 48 47N 87 5W
Terracina 18 41 17N 13 12 E
Terralba 18 39 42N 8 38 E
Terranova = Ólbia 18 40 55N 9 30 E
Terre Haute 68 39 28N 87 24W
Terrebonne B. 71 29 15N 90 28W
Terrell 71 32 44N 96 19W
Terrenceville 63 47 40N 54 44W
Terrick Terrick 44 24 44S 145 5 E
Territoire de Belfort □ 12 47 40N 6 55 E
Terry 70 46 47N 105 20W
Terschelling 11 53 25N 5 20 E
Teruel 13 40 22N 1 8W
Tervola 20 66 6N 24 49 E
Teryaweyna L. 45 32 18S 143 22 E
Tešanj 19 44 38N 17 59 E
Teshio 36 44 53N 141 44 E
Teshio-Gawa → 36 44 53N 141 45 E
Tesiyn Gol → 37 50 40N 93 20 E
Teslin 60 60 10N 132 43W
Teslin → 64 61 34N 134 35W
Teslin L. 64 60 15N 132 57W
Tessalit 50 20 12N 1 0 E
Tessaoua 53 13 47N 7 56 E
Test → 7 51 7N 1 30W
Tetachuck L. 64 53 18N 125 55W
Tetas, Pta. 80 23 31S 70 38W
Tete 55 16 13S 33 33 E
Teteven 19 42 58N 24 17 E
Tethul → 64 60 35N 112 12W
Teton → 72 47 58N 111 0W
Tétouan 50 35 35N 5 21W
Tetovo 19 42 1N 21 2 E
Tetuán = Tétouan 50 35 35N 5 21W
Teuco → 80 25 35S 60 11W
Teulon 65 50 23N 97 16W
Teun 35 6 59S 129 8 E
Teutoburger Wald 14 52 5N 8 20 E
Tevere → 18 41 44N 12 14 E
Teverya 28 32 47N 35 32 E
Teviot → 8 55 21N 2 51W
Tewantin 45 26 27S 153 3 E
Tewkesbury 7 51 59N 2 8W
Texada I. 64 49 40N 124 25W
Texarkana, Ark., U.S.A. 71 33 25N 94 0W
Texarkana, Tex., U.S.A. 71 33 25N 94 3W
Texas 45 28 49S 151 9 E
Texas □ 71 31 40N 98 30W
Texas City 71 29 20N 94 55W
Texel 11 53 5N 4 50 E
Texhoma 71 36 32N 101 47W
Texline 71 36 26N 103 0W
Texoma L. 71 34 0N 96 38W
Teyvareh 31 33 30N 64 24 E
Teziutlán 74 19 50N 97 22W
Tezpur 33 26 40N 92 45 E
Tezzeron L. 64 54 43N 124 30W
Tha-anne → 65 60 31N 94 37W
Thaba Nchu 56 29 17S 26 52 E
Thaba Putsoa 57 29 45S 28 0 E
Thabana Ntlenyana 57 29 30S 29 16 E
Thabazimbi 57 24 40S 27 21 E
Thailand ■ 34 16 0N 102 0 E
Thailand, G. of 34 11 30N 101 0 E
Thakhek 34 17 25N 104 45 E
Thal 32 33 28N 70 33 E
Thala La 33 28 25N 97 23 E
Thallon 45 28 39S 148 49 E
Thame → 7 51 35N 1 8W
Thames 43 37 7S 175 34 E
Thames →, Canada 62 42 20N 82 25W
Thames →, U.K. 7 51 30N 0 35 E
Thane 32 19 12N 72 59 E
Thanet, I. of 7 51 21N 1 20 E
Thangoo 46 18 10S 122 22 E
Thangool 44 24 38S 150 42 E
Thanh Pho Ho Chi Minh = Phanh Bho Ho Chi Minh 34 10 58N 106 40 E
Thanjavur 32 10 48N 79 12 E
Thanlwin Myit → 33 20 0N 98 0 E
Thar Desert 32 28 0N 72 0 E
Tharad 32 24 30N 71 44 E
Thargomindah 45 27 58S 143 46 E
Tharrawaddy 33 17 38N 95 48 E
Thásos 19 40 40N 24 40 E
Thatcher, Ariz., U.S.A. 73 32 54N 109 46W
Thatcher, Colo., U.S.A. 71 37 38N 104 6W
Thaton 33 16 55N 97 22 E
Thaungdut 33 24 30N 94 40 E
Thayer 71 36 34N 91 34W
Thayetmyo 33 19 20N 95 10 E
Thazi 33 21 0N 96 5 E
The Alberga → 45 27 6S 135 33 E
The Bight 75 24 19N 75 24W
The Dalles 72 45 40N 121 11W
The English Company's Is. 44 11 50S 136 32 E
The Frome → 45 29 8S 137 54 E
The Grenadines, Is. 75 12 40N 61 20W
The Hague = 's-Gravenhage 11 52 7N 4 17 E
The Hamilton → 45 26 40S 135 19 E
The Lynd 44 19 12S 144 20 E
The Macumba → 45 27 52S 137 12 E
The Neales → 45 28 8S 136 47 E
The Officer → 47 27 46S 132 30 E
The Pas 65 53 45N 101 15W
The Rock 45 35 15S 147 2 E
The Salt Lake 45 30 6S 142 8 E
The Stevenson → 45 27 6S 135 33 E
The Warburton → 45 28 4S 137 28 E
Thebes = Thívai 19 38 19N 23 19 E
Thedford 70 41 59N 100 31W
Theebine 45 25 57S 152 34 E
Thekulthili L. 65 61 3N 110 0W
Thelon → 65 62 35N 104 3W
Theodore 44 24 55S 150 3 E
Thermaïkos Kólpos 19 40 15N 22 45 E
Thermopolis 72 43 35N 108 10W
Thermopylae P. 19 38 48N 22 35 E
Thessalía □ 19 39 30N 22 0 E
Thessalon 62 46 20N 83 30W
Thessaloníki 19 40 38N 22 58 E
Thessaloniki, Gulf of = Thermaïkos Kólpos 19 40 15N 22 45 E
Thessaly = Thessalía □ 19 39 30N 22 0 E
Thetford 7 52 25N 0 44 E
Thetford Mines 63 46 8N 71 18W
Theunissen 56 28 26S 26 43 E
Thevenard 45 32 9S 133 38 E
Thibodaux 71 29 48N 90 49W
Thicket Portage 65 55 19N 97 42W
Thief River Falls 70 48 15N 96 48W
Thiérache 12 49 51N 3 45 E
Thies 50 14 50N 16 51W
Thika 54 1 1S 37 5 E
Thikombia 43 15 44S 179 55W
Thimphu 33 27 31N 89 45 E
þingvallavatn 20 64 11N 21 9W
Thionville 12 49 20N 6 10 E
Thíra 19 36 23N 25 27 E
Thirsk 6 54 15N 1 20W
Thisted 21 56 58N 8 40 E
Thistle I. 45 35 0S 136 8 E
Thívai 19 38 19N 23 19 E
þjórsá → 20 63 47N 20 48W
Thlewiaza →, Man., Canada 65 59 43N 100 5W
Thlewiaza →, N.W.T., Canada 65 60 29N 94 40W
Thoa → 65 60 31N 109 47W
Thomas, Okla., U.S.A. 71 35 48N 98 48W
Thomas, W. Va., U.S.A. 68 39 10N 79 30W
Thomas, L. 45 26 4S 137 58 E
Thomaston 69 32 54N 84 20W
Thomasville, Ala., U.S.A. 69 31 55N 87 42W
Thomasville, Ga., U.S.A. 69 30 50N 84 0W
Thomasville, N.C., U.S.A. 69 35 55N 80 4W
Thompson, Canada 65 55 45N 97 52W
Thompson, U.S.A. 73 39 0N 109 50W
Thompson →, Canada 64 50 15N 121 24W
Thompson →, U.S.A. 70 39 46N 93 37W
Thompson Falls 72 47 37N 115 20W
Thompson Landing 65 62 56N 110 40W
Thompson Pk. 72 41 0N 123 3W
Thomson → 44 25 11S 142 53 E
Thomson's Falls = Nyahururu 54 0 2N 36 27 E
þórisvatn 20 64 20N 18 55W
þorlákshöfn 20 63 51N 21 22W
Thornaby on Tees 6 54 36N 1 19W
þórshöfn 20 66 12N 15 20W
Thouin, C. 46 20 20S 118 10 E
Thrace = Thráki □ 19 41 9N 25 30 E
Thráki □ 19 41 9N 25 30 E
Three Forks 72 45 55N 111 32W
Three Hills 64 51 43N 113 15W
Three Hummock I. 44 40 25S 144 55 E
Three Lakes 70 45 48N 89 10W
Three Points, C. 50 4 42N 2 6W
Three Rivers, Australia 47 25 10S 119 5 E
Three Rivers, U.S.A. 71 28 30N 98 10W
Three Sisters, Mt. 72 44 10N 121 46W
Throssell, L. 47 27 33S 124 10 E
Throssell Ra. 46 22 3S 121 43 E
Thubun Lakes 65 61 30N 112 0W
Thuin 11 50 20N 4 17 E
Thun 14 46 45N 7 38 E
Thundelarra 47 28 53S 117 7 E
Thunder B. 68 45 0N 83 20W
Thunder Bay 62 48 20N 89 15W
Thung Song 34 8 10N 99 40 E
Thunkar 33 27 55N 91 0 E
Thüringer Wald 14 50 35N 11 0 E
Thurles 9 52 40N 7 53W
Thurloo Downs 45 29 15S 143 30 E
Thursday I. 44 10 30S 142 3 E
Thurso, Canada 62 45 36N 75 15W
Thurso, U.K. 8 58 34N 3 31W
Thutade L. 64 57 0N 126 55W
Thylungra 45 26 4S 143 28 E
Thysville = Mbanza Ngungu 54 5 12S 14 53 E
Tia 45 31 10S 150 34 E
Tian Shan 37 43 0N 84 0 E
Tiandu 39 18 18N 109 36 E
Tian'e 39 25 1N 107 9 E
Tianhe 39 24 48N 108 40 E
Tianjin 38 39 8N 117 10 E
Tianshui 39 34 32N 105 40 E
Tianyang 39 23 42N 106 53 E
Tianzhen 38 40 24N 114 5 E
Tiaret 50 35 20N 1 21 E
Tiassalé 50 5 58N 4 57W
Tibati 51 6 22N 12 30 E
Tiber = Tevere → 18 41 44N 12 14 E
Tiber Res. 72 48 20N 111 15W
Tiberias = Teverya 28 32 47N 35 32 E
Tiberias, L. = Yam Kinneret 28 32 45N 35 35 E
Tibesti 51 21 0N 17 30 E
Tibet = Xizang □ 37 32 0N 88 0 E
Tibnīn 28 33 12N 35 24 E
Tibooburra 45 29 26S 142 1 E
Tiburón 74 29 0N 112 30W
Tichît 50 18 21N 9 29W
Ticino → 14 45 9N 9 14 E
Ticonderoga 68 43 50N 73 28W
Ticul 74 20 20N 89 31W
Tiddim 33 23 28N 93 45 E
Tidjikja 50 18 29N 11 35W
Tidore 35 0 40N 127 25 E
Tiel, Neth. 11 51 53N 5 26 E
Tiel, Senegal 50 14 55N 15 5W
Tieling 38 42 20N 123 55 E
Tielt 11 51 0N 3 20 E
Tien Shan 31 42 0N 80 0 E
Tien-tsin = Tianjin 38 39 8N 117 10 E
T'ienching = Tianjin 38 39 8N 117 10 E
Tienen 11 50 48N 4 57 E
Tientsin = Tianjin 38 39 8N 117 10 E
Tierra Amarilla 73 36 42N 106 33W
Tierra de Campos 13 42 10N 4 50W
Tierra del Fuego, I. Gr. de 80 54 0S 69 0W
Tiétar → 13 39 50N 6 1W
Tieyon 45 26 12S 133 52 E
Tiffin 68 41 8N 83 10W
Tiflis = Tbilisi 23 41 43N 44 50 E
Tifrah 28 31 19N 34 42 E
Tifton 69 31 28N 83 32W
Tifu 35 3 39S 126 24 E
Tigil 25 57 49N 158 40 E
Tignish 63 46 58N 64 2W
Tigre → 78 4 30S 74 10W
Tigris = Dijlah, Nahr → 30 31 0N 47 25 E
Tigyaing 33 23 45N 96 10 E
Tîh, Gebel el 51 29 32N 33 26 E
Tijuana 74 32 30N 117 10W
Tikal 75 17 13N 89 24W
Tikamgarh 32 24 44N 78 50 E
Tikhoretsk 23 45 56N 40 5 E
Tiko 53 4 4N 9 20 E
Tikrīt 30 34 35N 43 37 E
Tiksi 25 71 40N 128 45 E
Tilamuta 35 0 32N 122 23 E
Tilburg 11 51 31N 5 6 E
Tilbury, Canada 62 42 17N 82 23W
Tilbury, U.K. 7 51 27N 0 24 E
Tilden, Nebr., U.S.A. 70 42 3N 97 45W
Tilden, Tex., U.S.A. 71 28 28N 98 33W
Tilichiki 25 60 27N 166 5 E
Till → 6 55 35N 2 3W
Tillabéri 53 14 28N 1 28 E
Tillamook 72 45 29N 123 55W
Tillsonburg 62 42 53N 80 44W
Tilos 19 36 27N 27 27 E
Tilpa 45 30 57S 144 24 E
Tilsit = Sovetsk 22 55 6N 21 50 E
Tilt → 8 56 50N 3 50W
Timagami L. 62 47 0N 80 10W
Timanskiy Kryazh 22 65 58N 50 5 E
Timaru 43 44 23S 171 14 E
Timau 52 0 4N 37 15 E
Timbedgha 50 16 17N 8 16W
Timber Lake 70 45 29N 101 6W
Timboon 45 38 30S 142 58 E
Timbuktu = Tombouctou 50 16 50N 3 0W
Timimoun 50 29 14N 0 16 E
Timişoara 15 45 43N 21 15 E
Timmins 62 48 28N 81 25W
Timok → 19 44 10N 22 40 E
Timon 79 5 8S 42 52W
Timor 35 9 0S 125 0 E
Timor □ 35 9 0S 125 0 E
Timor Sea 46 10 0S 127 0 E
Tinaca Pt. 35 5 30N 125 25 E
Tindouf 50 27 42N 8 10W
Tingo Maria 78 9 10S 75 54W
Tinjoub 50 29 45N 5 40W
Tinkurrin 47 32 59S 117 46 E
Tinnevelly = Tirunelveli 32 8 45N 77 45 E
Tinnoset 21 59 55N 9 3 E
Tinogasta 80 28 5S 67 32W
Tínos 19 37 33N 25 8 E
Tintinara 45 35 48S 140 2 E
Tioman, Pulau 34 2 50N 104 10 E
Tipongpani 33 27 20N 95 55 E
Tipperary 9 52 28N 8 10W
Tipperary □ 9 52 37N 7 55W
Tipton, U.K. 7 52 32N 2 4W
Tipton, Calif., U.S.A. 73 36 3N 119 19W
Tipton, Ind., U.S.A. 68 40 17N 86 0W
Tipton, Iowa, U.S.A. 70 41 45N 91 12W
Tiptonville 71 36 22N 89 30W
Tirān 31 32 45N 51 8 E
Tirana 19 41 18N 19 49 E
Tiranë = Tirana 19 41 18N 19 49 E
Tiraspol 23 46 55N 29 35 E
Tirat Karmel 28 32 46N 34 58 E
Tirat Yehuda 28 32 1N 34 56 E
Tirat Ẓevi 28 32 26N 35 31 E
Tire 30 38 5N 27 50 E
Tirebolu 30 40 58N 38 45 E
Tiree 8 56 31N 6 55W
Tîrgovişte 15 44 55N 25 27 E
Tîrgu-Jiu 15 45 5N 23 19 E
Tîrgu Mureş 15 46 31N 24 38 E
Tirich Mir 31 36 15N 71 55 E
Tirodi 32 21 40N 79 44 E
Tirol □ 14 47 3N 10 43 E
Tirso → 18 39 52N 8 33 E
Tiruchchirappalli 32 10 45N 78 45 E
Tirunelveli 32 8 45N 77 45 E
Tirupati 32 13 39N 79 25 E
Tiruppur 32 11 5N 77 22 E
Tiruvannamalai 32 12 15N 79 5 E
Tisa → 15 45 15N 20 17 E
Tisdale 65 52 50N 104 0W
Tishomingo 71 34 14N 96 38W
Tisza → 15 46 8N 20 2 E
Tit-Ary 25 71 55N 127 2 E
Titicaca, L. 78 15 30S 69 30W
Titiwa 53 12 14N 12 53 E
Titograd 19 42 30N 19 19 E
Titov Veles 19 41 46N 21 47 E
Titovo Užice 19 43 55N 19 50 E
Titule 54 3 15N 25 31 E
Titusville, Fla., U.S.A. 69 28 37N 80 49W
Titusville, Pa., U.S.A. 68 41 35N 79 39W
Tivaouane 50 14 56N 16 45W
Tiverton 7 50 54N 3 30W
Tívoli 18 41 58N 12 45 E
Tiwī 31 22 45N 59 12 E
Tizi-Ouzou 50 36 42N 4 3 E
Tizimín 74 21 0N 88 1W
Tiznit 50 29 48N 9 45W
Tjeggelvas 20 66 37N 17 45 E
Tjirebon = Cirebon 35 6 45S 108 32 E
Tlahualilo 74 26 20N 103 30W
Tlaxcala 74 19 20N 98 14W
Tlaxcala □ 74 19 30N 98 20W
Tlaxiaco 74 17 18N 97 40W
Tlell 64 53 34N 131 56W
Tlemcen 50 34 52N 1 21W
Tmassah 51 26 19N 15 51 E
Toad → 64 59 25N 124 57W
Toamasina 57 18 10S 49 25 E
Toamasina □ 57 18 0S 49 0 E
Toay 80 36 43S 64 38W
Toba 36 34 30N 136 51 E
Toba Kakar 32 31 30N 69 0 E
Tobago 75 11 10N 60 30W
Tobelo 35 1 45N 127 56 E
Tobermorey 44 22 12S 138 0 E
Tobermory, Canada 62 45 12N 81 40W
Tobermory, U.K. 8 56 37N 6 4W
Tobin, L. 46 21 45S 125 49 E
Tobin L. 65 53 35N 103 30W
Toboali 34 3 0S 106 25 E
Tobol 24 52 40N 62 39 E
Tobol → 24 58 10N 68 12 E
Toboli 35 0 38S 120 5 E
Tobolsk 24 58 15N 68 10 E
Tobruk = Tubruq 51 32 7N 23 55 E
Tocantinópolis 79 6 20S 47 25W
Tocantins → 79 1 45S 49 10W
Toccoa 69 34 32N 83 17W
Tochigi 36 36 25N 139 45 E
Tochigi □ 36 36 45N 139 45 E
Tocopilla 80 22 5S 70 10W
Tocumwal 45 35 51S 145 31 E
Tocuyo → 78 11 3N 68 23W
Todd → 44 24 52S 135 48 E
Todeli 35 1 38S 124 34 E
Todenyang 54 4 35N 35 56 E
Todos los Santos, B. de 79 12 48S 38 38W
Todos Santos 74 23 27N 110 13W
Tofield 64 53 25N 112 40W
Tofino 64 49 11N 125 55W
Tofua 43 19 45S 175 5W
Togba 50 17 26N 10 12W
Togian, Kepulauan 35 0 20S 121 50 E
Togliatti 22 53 32N 49 24 E
Togo ■ 53 8 30N 1 35 E
Togtoh 38 40 15N 111 10 E
Toinya 51 6 17N 29 46 E
Tojo 35 1 20S 121 15 E
Tokachi-Gawa → 36 42 44N 143 42 E
Tokaj 15 48 8N 21 27 E
Tokala 35 1 30S 121 40 E
Tōkamachi 36 37 8N 138 43 E
Tokanui 43 46 34S 168 56 E
Tokar 51 18 27N 37 56 E
Tokara Kaikyō 36 30 0N 130 0 E
Tokarahi 43 44 56S 170 39 E
Tokat 30 40 22N 36 35 E
Tokelau Is. 2 9 0S 171 45W
Tokmak 24 42 49N 75 15 E
Toko Ra. 44 23 5S 138 20 E
Tokushima 36 34 4N 134 34 E
Tokushima □ 36 34 15N 134 0 E
Tokuyama 36 34 3N 131 50 E
Tōkyō 36 35 45N 139 45 E
Tōkyō □ 36 35 40N 139 30 E
Tolbukhin 19 43 37N 27 49 E
Toledo, Spain 13 39 50N 4 2W
Toledo, Ohio, U.S.A. 68 41 37N 83 33W
Toledo, Oreg., U.S.A. 72 44 40N 123 59W
Toledo, Wash., U.S.A. 72 46 29N 122 51W
Toledo, Montes de 13 39 33N 4 20W
Tolga 50 34 40N 5 22 E
Toliara 57 23 21S 43 40 E
Toliara □ 57 21 0S 45 0 E
Tolima, Vol. 78 4 40N 75 19W
Tolitoli 35 1 5N 120 50 E
Tolleson 73 33 29N 112 10W
Tolo 54 2 55S 18 34 E
Tolo, Teluk 35 2 20S 122 10 E
Tolosa 13 43 8N 2 5W
Toluca 74 19 20N 99 40W
Tom Burke 57 23 5S 28 0 E
Tom Price 46 22 40S 117 48 E
Tomah 70 43 59N 90 30W
Tomahawk 70 45 28N 89 40W
Tomakomai 36 42 38N 141 36 E
Tomar 13 39 36N 8 25W
Tomaszów Mazowiecki 15 51 30N 19 57 E
Tombé 51 5 53N 31 40 E
Tombigbee → 69 31 4N 87 58W
Tombouctou 50 16 50N 3 0W
Tombstone 73 31 40N 110 4W
Tombua 56 15 55S 11 55 E
Tomelloso 13 39 10N 3 2W
Tomingley 45 32 6S 148 16 E
Tomini 35 0 30N 120 30 E
Tomini, Teluk 35 0 10S 122 0 E
Tomkinson Ranges 47 26 11S 129 5 E
Tommot 25 59 4N 126 20 E
Tomnavoulin 8 57 19N 3 18W
Tomsk 24 56 30N 85 5 E
Tonalá 74 16 8N 93 41W
Tonalea 73 36 17N 110 58W
Tonantins 78 2 45S 67 45W

Tonasket

Tonasket 72 48 45N 119 30W
Tonawanda 68 43 0N 78 54W
Tonbridge 7 51 12N 0 18 E
Tondano 35 1 35N 124 54 E
Tonekābon 31 36 45N 51 12 E
Tong Xian 38 39 55N 116 35 E
Tonga ■ 43 19 50S 174 30W
Tonga Trench 40 18 0S 175 0W
Tongaat 57 29 33S 31 9 E
Tongareva 41 9 0S 158 0W
Tongatapu 43 21 10S 174 0W
Tongcheng 39 31 4N 116 56 E
Tongchuan 39 35 6N 109 3 E
Tongdao 39 26 10N 109 42 E
Tongeren 11 50 47N 5 28 E
Tongguan 39 34 40N 110 25 E
Tonghua 38 41 42N 125 58 E
Tongjiang, Heilongjiang, China 38 47 40N 132 27 E
Tongjiang, Sichuan, China 39 31 58N 107 11 E
Tongking, G. of = Tonkin, G. of 39 20 0N 108 0 E
Tongliao 38 43 38N 122 18 E
Tongling 39 30 55N 117 48 E
Tonglu 39 29 45N 119 37 E
Tongnan 39 30 9N 105 50 E
Tongobory 57 23 32S 44 20 E
Tongoy 80 30 16S 71 31W
Tongren 39 27 43N 109 11 E
Tongres = Tongeren 11 50 47N 5 28 E
Tongsa Dzong 33 27 31N 90 31 E
Tongue 8 58 29N 4 25W
Tongue → 70 46 24N 105 52W
Tongyu 38 44 45N 123 4 E
Tongzi 39 28 9N 106 49 E
Tonk 32 26 6N 75 54 E
Tonkawa 71 36 44N 97 22W
Tonkin, G. of 39 20 0N 108 0 E
Tonlé Sap 34 13 0N 104 0 E
Tonopah 73 38 4N 117 12W
Tønsberg 21 59 19N 10 25 E
Tooele 72 40 30N 112 20W
Toompine 45 27 15S 144 19 E
Toonpan 44 19 28S 146 48 E
Toora 45 38 39S 146 23 E
Toora-Khem 25 52 28N 96 17 E
Toowoomba 45 27 32S 151 56 E
Top-ozero 22 65 35N 32 0 E
Topeka 70 39 3N 95 40W
Topki 24 55 20N 85 35 E
Topley 64 54 49N 126 18W
Topock 73 34 46N 114 29W
Topolobampo 74 25 40N 109 4W
Toppenish 72 46 27N 120 16W
Toraka Vestale 57 16 20S 43 58 E
Torata 78 17 23S 70 1W
Torbat-e Heydārīyeh 31 35 15N 59 12 E
Torbat-e Jām 31 35 16N 60 35 E
Torbay, Canada 63 47 40N 52 42W
Torbay, U.K. 7 50 26N 3 31W
Tordesillas 13 41 30N 5 0W
Torey 25 50 33N 104 50 E
Torfajökull 20 63 54N 19 0W
Torgau 14 51 32N 13 0 E
Torhout 11 51 5N 3 7 E
Torin 74 27 33N 110 15W
Torino 18 45 4N 7 40 E
Torit 51 4 27N 32 31 E
Tormes → 13 41 18N 6 29W
Tornado Mt. 64 49 55N 114 40W
Torne älv → 20 65 50N 24 12 E
Torneå = Tornio 20 65 50N 24 12 E
Torneträsk 20 68 24N 19 15 E
Tornio 20 65 50N 24 12 E
Tornionjoki → 20 65 50N 24 12 E
Tornquist 80 38 8S 62 15W
Toro, Cerro del 80 29 10S 69 50W
Toro, Pta. 74 9 22N 79 57W
Toroníos Kólpos 19 40 5N 23 30 E
Toronto, Australia 45 33 0S 151 30 E
Toronto, Canada 62 43 39N 79 20W
Toronto, U.S.A. 68 40 27N 80 36W
Toropets 22 56 30N 31 40 E
Tororo 54 0 45N 34 12 E
Toros Dağlari 30 37 0N 35 0 E
Torowie 45 33 8S 138 55 E
Torquay, Canada 65 49 9N 103 30W
Torquay, U.K. 7 50 27N 3 31W
Tôrre de Moncorvo 13 41 12N 7 8W
Torre del Greco 18 40 47N 14 22 E
Torrelavega 13 43 20N 4 5W
Torremolinos 13 36 38N 4 30W
Torrens, L. 45 31 0S 137 50 E
Torrens Cr. → 44 22 23S 145 9 E
Torrens Creek 44 20 48S 145 3 E
Torréon 74 25 33N 103 25W
Torres 74 28 46N 110 47W
Torres Strait 40 9 50S 142 20 E
Torres Vedras 13 39 5N 9 15W
Torrevieja 13 37 59N 0 42W
Torrey 73 38 18N 111 25W
Torridge → 7 50 51N 4 10W
Torridon, L. 8 57 35N 5 50W
Torrington, Conn., U.S.A. 68 41 50N 73 9W
Torrington, Wyo., U.S.A. 70 42 5N 104 8W
Tortola 75 18 19N 65 0W
Tortosa 13 40 49N 0 31 E
Tortosa, C. 13 40 41N 0 52 E
Tortue, I. de la 75 20 5N 72 57W
Tortuga, La 75 11 0N 65 22W
Ţorūd 31 35 25N 55 5 E
Toruń 15 53 0N 18 39 E
Tory I. 9 55 17N 8 12W
Tosa-Wan 36 33 15N 133 30 E
Toscana 18 43 30N 11 5 E
Tostado 80 29 15S 61 50W
Tosya 30 41 1N 34 2 E
Toteng 56 20 22S 22 58 E
Totma 22 60 0N 42 40 E
Totnes 7 50 26N 3 41W
Totonicapán 75 14 58N 91 12W
Tottenham 45 32 14S 147 21 E
Tottori 36 35 30N 134 15 E
Tottori □ 36 35 30N 134 12 E
Touba 50 8 22N 7 40W
Toubkal, Djebel 50 31 0N 8 0W
Tougan 50 13 11N 2 58W
Touggourt 50 33 10N 6 4 E
Tougué 50 11 25N 11 50W
Toul 12 48 40N 5 53 E
Toulepleu 50 6 32N 8 24W
Toulon 12 43 10N 5 55 E
Toulouse 12 43 37N 1 27 E
Toummo 51 22 45N 14 8 E
Toungoo 33 19 0N 96 30 E
Touraine 12 47 20N 0 30 E
Tourane = Da Nang 34 16 4N 108 13 E
Tourcoing 12 50 42N 3 10 E
Tournai 11 50 35N 3 25 E
Tournon 12 45 4N 4 50 E
Tours 12 47 22N 0 40 E
Touwsrivier 56 33 20S 20 2 E
Towamba 45 37 6S 149 43 E
Towanda 68 41 46N 76 30W
Towang 33 27 37N 91 50 E
Tower 70 47 49N 92 17W
Towerhill Cr. → 44 22 28S 144 35 E
Towner 70 48 25N 100 26W
Townsend 72 46 25N 111 32W
Townshend I. 44 22 10S 150 31 E
Townsville 44 19 15S 146 45 E
Towson 68 39 26N 76 34W
Toyah 71 31 20N 103 48W
Toyahvale 71 30 58N 103 45W
Toyama 36 36 40N 137 15 E
Toyama □ 36 36 45N 137 30 E
Toyama-Wan 36 37 0N 137 30 E
Toyohashi 36 34 45N 137 25 E
Toyokawa 36 34 48N 137 27 E
Toyonaka 36 34 50N 135 28 E
Toyooka 36 35 35N 134 48 E
Toyota 36 35 3N 137 7 E
Tozeur 50 33 56N 8 8 E
Trabzon 30 41 0N 39 45 E
Tracadie 63 47 30N 64 55W
Tracy, Calif., U.S.A. 73 37 46N 121 27W
Tracy, Minn., U.S.A. 70 44 12N 95 38W
Trafalgar, C. 13 36 10N 6 2W
Trail 64 49 5N 117 40W
Trainor L. 64 60 24N 120 17W
Tralee 9 52 16N 9 42W
Tralee B. 9 52 17N 9 55W
Tramore 9 52 10N 7 10W
Tranås 21 58 3N 14 59 E
Trancas 80 26 11S 65 20W
Trang 34 7 33N 99 38 E
Trangahy 57 19 7S 44 31 E
Trangan 35 6 40S 134 20 E
Trangie 45 32 4S 148 0 E
Trani 18 41 17N 16 24 E
Tranoroa 57 24 42S 45 4 E
Transcaucasia = Zakavkazye 23 42 0N 44 0 E
Transcona 65 49 55N 97 0W
Transilvania 15 46 19N 25 0 E
Transkei □ 57 32 15S 28 15 E
Transvaal □ 56 25 0S 29 0 E
Transylvania = Transilvania 15 46 19N 25 0 E
Transylvanian Alps 4 45 30N 25 0 E
Trápani 18 38 1N 12 30 E
Trapper Peak 72 45 56N 114 29W
Traralgon 45 38 12S 146 34 E
Tras os Montes e Alto Douro □ 13 41 25N 7 20W
Trasimeno, L. 18 43 10N 12 5 E
Traveller's L. 45 33 20S 142 0 E
Travers, Mt. 43 42 1S 172 45 E
Traverse City 68 44 45N 85 39W
Travnik 19 44 17N 17 39 E
Trayning 47 31 7S 117 16 E
Trébbia → 18 45 4N 9 41 E
Trebinje 19 42 44N 18 22 E
Třeboň 14 48 59N 14 48 E
Tredegar 7 51 47N 3 16W
Tregaron 7 52 14N 3 56W
Tregrosse Is. 44 17 41S 150 43 E
Tréguier 12 48 47N 3 16W
Treherne 65 49 38N 98 42W
Treinta y Tres 80 33 16S 54 17W
Trekveld 56 30 35S 19 45 E
Trelew 80 43 10S 65 20W
Trelleborg 21 55 20N 13 10 E
Tremonton 72 41 45N 112 10W
Tremp 13 42 10N 0 52 E
Trenche → 62 47 46N 72 53W
Trenggalek 35 8 3S 111 43 E
Trenque Lauquen 80 36 5S 62 45W
Trent → 6 53 33N 0 44W
Trentino-Alto Adige □ 18 46 30N 11 0 E
Trento 18 46 5N 11 8 E
Trenton, Canada 62 44 10N 77 34W
Trenton, Mo., U.S.A. 70 40 5N 93 37W
Trenton, N.J., U.S.A. 68 40 15N 74 41W
Trenton, Nebr., U.S.A. 70 40 14N 101 4W
Trenton, Tenn., U.S.A. 71 35 58N 88 57W
Trepassey 63 46 43N 53 25W
Tréport, Le 12 50 3N 1 20 E
Tres Arroyos 80 38 26S 60 20W
Três Corações 79 21 44S 45 15W
Três Lagoas 79 20 50S 51 43W
Tres Marías 74 21 25N 106 28W
Tres Montes, C. 80 46 50S 75 30W
Tres Puentes 80 27 50S 70 15W
Tres Puntas, C. 80 47 0S 66 0W
Três Rios 79 22 6S 43 15W
Treungen 21 59 1N 8 31 E
Treviso 18 45 40N 12 15 E
Triabunna 44 42 30S 147 55 E
Tribulation, C. 44 16 5S 145 29 E
Tribune 70 38 30N 101 45W
Trichinopoly = Tiruchchirappalli 32 10 45N 78 45 E
Trichur 32 10 30N 76 18 E
Trida 45 33 1S 145 1 E
Trier 14 49 45N 6 37 E
Trieste 18 45 39N 13 45 E
Triglav 18 46 21N 13 50 E
Tríkkala 19 39 34N 21 47 E
Trikora, Puncak 35 4 15S 138 45 E
Trim 9 53 34N 6 48W
Trincomalee 32 8 38N 81 15 E
Trindade, I. 2 20 20S 29 50W
Trinidad, Bolivia 78 14 46S 64 50W
Trinidad, Colombia 78 5 25N 71 40W
Trinidad, Cuba 75 21 48N 80 0W
Trinidad, Uruguay 80 33 30S 56 50W
Trinidad, U.S.A. 71 37 15N 104 30W
Trinidad, W. Indies 75 10 30N 61 15W
Trinidad → 74 17 49N 95 9W
Trinidad, I. 80 39 10S 62 0W
Trinidad & Tobago ■ 75 10 30N 61 20W
Trinity, Canada 63 48 59N 53 55W
Trinity, U.S.A. 71 30 59N 95 25W
Trinity →, Calif., U.S.A. 72 41 11N 123 42W
Trinity →, Tex., U.S.A. 71 30 30N 95 0W
Trinity B. 63 48 20N 53 10W
Trinity Mts. 72 40 20N 118 50W
Trinkitat 51 18 45N 37 51 E
Trion 69 34 35N 85 18W
Tripoli = Tarābulus, Lebanon 30 34 31N 35 50 E
Tripoli = Tarābulus, Libya 51 32 49N 13 7 E
Trípolis 19 37 31N 22 25 E
Tripp 70 43 16N 97 58W
Tripura □ 33 24 0N 92 0 E
Tristan da Cunha 2 37 6S 12 20W
Trivandrum 32 8 41N 77 0 E
Trnava 15 48 23N 17 35 E
Trochu 64 51 50N 113 13W
Trodely I. 62 52 15N 79 26W
Troglav 18 43 56N 16 36 E
Troilus, L. 62 50 50N 74 35W
Trois-Pistoles 63 48 5N 69 10W
Trois-Rivières 62 46 25N 72 34W
Troitsk 24 54 10N 61 35 E
Troitsko Pechorsk 22 62 40N 56 10 E
Trölladyngja 20 64 54N 17 16W
Trollhättan 21 58 17N 12 20 E
Tromelin I. 3 15 52S 54 25 E
Troms fylke □ 20 68 56N 19 0 E
Tromsø 20 69 40N 18 56 E
Tronador 80 41 10S 71 50W
Trondheim 20 63 36N 10 25 E
Trondheimsfjorden 20 63 35N 10 30 E
Troon 8 55 33N 4 40W
Tropic 73 37 36N 112 4W
Trossachs, The 8 56 14N 4 24W
Trostan 9 55 4N 6 10W
Trotternish 8 57 32N 6 15W
Troup 71 32 10N 95 3W
Trout → 64 61 19N 119 51W
Trout L., N.W.T., Canada 64 60 40N 121 14W
Trout L., Ont., Canada 65 51 20N 93 15W
Trout Lake 62 46 10N 85 2W
Trout River 63 49 29N 58 8W
Trouville-sur-Mer 12 49 21N 0 5 E
Trowbridge 7 51 18N 2 12W
Troy, Turkey 30 39 57N 26 12 E
Troy, Ala., U.S.A. 69 31 50N 85 58W
Troy, Idaho, U.S.A. 72 46 44N 116 46W
Troy, Kans., U.S.A. 70 39 47N 95 2W
Troy, Mo., U.S.A. 70 38 56N 90 59W
Troy, Mont., U.S.A. 72 48 30N 115 58W
Troy, N.Y., U.S.A. 68 42 45N 73 39W
Troy, Ohio, U.S.A. 68 40 0N 84 10W
Troyes 12 48 19N 4 3 E
Trucial States = United Arab Emirates ■ 31 23 50N 54 0 E
Truckee 72 39 20N 120 11W
Trujillo, Hond. 75 16 0N 86 0W
Trujillo, Peru 78 8 6S 79 0W
Trujillo, Spain 13 39 28N 5 55W
Trujillo, U.S.A. 71 35 34N 104 44W
Trujillo, Venezuela 78 9 22N 70 38W
Trumann 71 35 42N 90 32W
Trumbull, Mt. 73 36 25N 113 8W
Trundle 45 32 53S 147 35 E
Trung-Phan 34 16 0N 108 0 E
Truro, Canada 63 45 21N 63 14W
Truro, U.K. 7 50 17N 5 2W
Truslove 47 33 20S 121 45 E
Truth or Consequences 73 33 9N 107 16W
Trutnov 14 50 37N 15 54 E
Tryon 69 35 15N 82 16W
Tsaratanana 57 16 47S 47 39 E
Tsaratanana, Mt. de 57 14 0S 49 0 E
Tsau 56 20 8S 22 22 E
Tselinograd 24 51 10N 71 30 E
Tsetserleg 37 47 36N 101 32 E
Tshabong 56 26 2S 22 29 E
Tshane 56 24 5S 21 54 E
Tshela 54 4 57S 13 4 E
Tshesebe 57 21 51S 27 32 E
Tshikapa 54 6 28S 20 48 E
Tshofa 54 5 13S 25 16 E
Tshwane 56 22 24S 22 1 E
Tsigara 56 20 22S 25 54 E
Tsihombe, Madag. 55 25 10S 45 41 E
Tsihombe, Madag. 57 25 18S 45 29 E
Tsimlyanskoye Vdkhr. 23 48 0N 43 0 E
Tsinan = Jinan 38 36 38N 117 1 E
Tsineng 56 27 5S 23 5 E
Tsinghai = Qinghai □ 37 36 0N 98 0 E
Tsingtao = Qingdao 38 36 5N 120 20 E
Tsinjomitondraka 57 15 40S 47 8 E
Tsiroanomandidy 57 18 46S 46 2 E
Tsivory 57 24 4S 46 5 E
Tskhinvali 23 42 14N 44 1 E
Tsna → 22 54 55N 41 58 E
Tsodilo Hill 56 18 49S 21 43 E
Tsolo 57 31 18S 28 37 E
Tsomo 57 32 0S 27 42 E
Tsu 36 34 45N 136 25 E
Tsu L. 64 60 40N 111 52W
Tsuchiura 36 36 5N 140 15 E
Tsugaru-Kaikyō 36 41 35N 141 0 E
Tsumeb 56 19 9S 17 44 E
Tsumis 56 23 39S 17 29 E
Tsuruga 36 35 45N 136 2 E
Tsuruoka 36 38 44N 139 50 E
Tsushima 36 34 20N 129 20 E
Tual 35 5 38S 132 44 E
Tuam 9 53 30N 8 50W
Tuamotu Arch. 41 17 0S 144 0W
Tuamotu Ridge 41 20 0S 138 0W
Tuao 35 17 55N 122 22 E
Tuapse 23 44 5N 39 10 E
Tuatapere 43 46 8S 167 41 E
Tuba City 73 36 8N 111 18W
Tuban 35 6 54S 112 3 E
Tubarão 80 28 30S 49 0W
Tūbās 28 32 20N 35 22 E
Tubau 34 3 10N 113 40 E
Tübingen 14 48 31N 9 4 E
Tubruq 51 32 7N 23 55 E
Tubuaeran I. 41 3 51N 159 22W
Tubuai Is. 41 25 0S 150 0W
Tucacas 78 10 48N 68 19W
Tuchodi → 64 58 17N 123 42W
Tucson 73 32 14N 110 59W
Tucumcari 71 35 12N 103 45W
Tucupita 78 9 2N 62 3W
Tucuruí 79 3 42S 49 44W
Tudela 13 42 4N 1 39W
Tudmur 30 34 36N 38 15 E
Tudor, L. 63 55 50N 65 25W
Tuen 45 28 33S 145 37 E
Tugela → 57 29 14S 31 30 E
Tuguegarao 35 17 35N 121 42 E
Tugur 25 53 44N 136 45 E
Tukangbesi, Kepulauan 35 6 0S 124 0 E
Tukarak I. 62 56 15N 78 45W
Tūkrah 51 32 30N 20 37 E
Tuktoyaktuk 60 69 27N 133 2W
Tukuyu 54 9 17S 33 35 E
Tula, Hidalgo, Mexico 74 20 0N 99 20W
Tula, Tamaulipas, Mexico 74 23 0N 99 40W
Tula, U.S.S.R. 22 54 13N 37 38 E
Tulak 31 33 55N 63 40 E
Tulancingo 74 20 5N 99 22W
Tulare 73 36 15N 119 26W
Tulare Lake Bed 73 36 0N 119 48W
Tularosa 73 33 4N 106 1W
Tulbagh 56 33 16S 19 6 E
Tulcán 78 0 48N 77 43W
Tulcea 15 45 13N 28 46 E
Tulemalu L. 65 62 58N 99 25W
Tuli, Indonesia 35 1 24S 122 26 E
Tuli, Zimbabwe 55 21 58S 29 13 E
Tulia 71 34 35N 101 44W
Ţūlkarm 28 32 19N 35 2 E
Tullahoma 69 35 23N 86 12W
Tullamore, Australia 45 32 39S 147 36 E
Tullamore, Ireland 9 53 17N 7 30W
Tulle 12 45 16N 1 46 E
Tullibigeal 45 33 25S 146 44 E
Tullow 9 52 48N 6 45W
Tully 44 17 56S 145 55 E
Ţulmaythah 51 32 40N 20 55 E
Tulmur 44 22 40S 142 20 E
Tulsa 71 36 10N 96 0W
Tulsequah 64 58 39N 133 35W
Tulua 78 4 6N 76 11W
Tulun 25 54 32N 100 35 E
Tulungagung 34 8 5S 111 54 E
Tum 35 3 36S 130 21 E
Tuma → 75 13 6N 84 35W
Tumaco 78 1 50N 78 45W
Tumatumari 78 5 20N 58 55W
Tumba, L. 54 0 50S 18 0 E
Tumbarumba 45 35 44S 148 0 E
Túmbes 78 3 37S 80 27W
Tumby Bay 45 34 21S 136 8 E
Tumen 38 43 0N 129 50 E
Tumen Jiang → 38 42 20N 130 35 E
Tumeremo 78 7 18N 61 30W
Tumkur 32 13 18N 77 6 E
Tummel, L. 8 56 43N 3 55W
Tump 31 26 7N 62 16 E
Tumpat 34 6 11N 102 10 E
Tumu 50 10 56N 1 56W
Tumucumaque, Serra 79 2 0N 55 0W
Tumut 45 35 16S 148 13 E
Tumwater 72 47 0N 122 58W
Tunas de Zaza 75 21 39N 79 34W
Tunbridge Wells 7 51 7N 0 16 E
Tuncurry 45 32 17S 152 29 E
Tunduma 52 9 20S 32 48 E
Tunduru 54 11 8S 37 25 E
Tundzha → 19 41 40N 26 35 E
Tunga Pass 33 29 0N 94 14 E
Tungabhadra → 32 15 57N 78 15 E
Tungaru 51 10 9N 30 52 E
Tungla 75 13 24N 84 21W
Tungnafellsjökull 20 64 45N 17 55W
Tungsten 64 61 57N 128 16W
Tunguska, Nizhnyaya → 25 65 48N 88 4 E
Tunguska, Podkamennaya → 25 61 36N 90 18 E
Tunica 71 34 43N 90 23W
Tunis 50 36 50N 10 11 E
Tunisia ■ 50 33 30N 9 10 E
Tunja 78 5 33N 73 25W
Tunliu 38 36 13N 112 52 E
Tunnsjøen 20 64 45N 13 25 E
Tunungayualok I. 63 56 0N 61 0W
Tunuyán → 80 33 33S 67 30W
Tunxi 39 29 42N 118 25 E
Tuolumne 73 37 59N 120 16W
Tuoy-Khaya 25 62 32N 111 25 E
Tupelo 69 34 15N 88 42W
Tupik 25 54 26N 119 57 E
Tupinambaranas 78 3 0S 58 0W
Tupiza 80 21 30S 65 40W
Tupper 64 55 32N 120 1W
Tupper Lake 68 44 18N 74 30W
Tupungato, Cerro 80 33 15S 69 50W
Tuquan 38 45 18N 121 38 E
Tuque, La 62 47 30N 72 50W
Túquerres 78 1 5N 77 37W
Tura 25 64 20N 100 17 E

Wendell

Vulcan, U.S.A. 68 45 46N 87 51W
Vulcano 18 38 25N 14 58 E
Vung Tau 34 10 21N 107 4 E
Vyatka → 22 56 30N 51 0 E
Vyatskiye Polyany 22 56 5N 51 0 E
Vyazemskiy 25 47 32N 134 45 E
Vyazma 22 55 10N 34 15 E
Vyborg 22 60 43N 28 47 E
Vychegda → 22 61 18N 46 36 E
Vychodné Beskydy 15 49 30N 22 0 E
Vyg-ozero 22 63 30N 34 0 E
Vyrnwy, L. 6 52 48N 3 30W
Vyshniy Volochek 22 57 30N 34 30 E
Vyshzha = imeni 26 Bakinskikh Komissarov 23 39 22N 54 10 E
Vytegra 22 61 0N 36 27 E

W

W.A.C. Bennett Dam 64 56 2N 122 6W
Wa 50 10 7N 2 25W
Waal → 11 51 59N 4 30 E
Wabakimi L. 62 50 38N 89 45W
Wabana 63 47 40N 53 0W
Wabasca 64 55 57N 113 56W
Wabash 68 40 48N 85 46W
Wabash → 68 37 46N 88 2W
Wabeno 68 45 25N 88 40W
Wabigoon L. 65 49 44N 92 44W
Wabowden 65 54 55N 98 38W
Wąbrzeźno 15 53 16N 18 57 E
Wabuk Pt. 62 55 20N 85 5W
Wabush 63 52 55N 66 52W
Wabuska 72 39 9N 119 13W
Waco 71 31 33N 97 5W
Waconichi, L. 62 50 8N 74 0W
Wad Banda 51 13 10N 27 56 E
Wad Hamid 51 16 30N 32 45 E
Wâd Medanî 51 14 28N 33 30 E
Waddeneilanden 11 53 25N 5 10 E
Waddenzee 11 53 6N 5 10 E
Wadderin Hill 47 32 0S 118 25 E
Waddington, Mt. 64 51 23N 125 15W
Waddy Pt. 45 24 58S 153 21 E
Wadena, Canada 65 51 57N 103 47W
Wadena, U.S.A. 70 46 25N 95 8W
Wadesboro 69 35 2N 80 2W
Wadhams 64 51 30N 127 30W
Wadi Halfa 51 21 53N 31 19 E
Wadsworth 72 39 38N 119 22W
Wafrah 30 28 33N 47 56 E
Wageningen 11 51 58N 5 40 E
Wager B. 61 65 26N 88 40W
Wager Bay 61 65 56N 90 49W
Wagga Wagga 45 35 7S 147 24 E
Waghete 35 4 10S 135 50 E
Wagin 47 33 17S 117 25 E
Wagon Mound 71 36 1N 104 44W
Wagoner 71 36 0N 95 20W
Wah 32 33 45N 72 40 E
Wahai 35 2 48S 129 35 E
Wahiawa 66 21 30N 158 2W
Wahoo 70 41 15N 96 35W
Wahpeton 70 46 20N 96 35W
Waiau → 43 42 47S 173 22 E
Waibeem 35 0 30S 132 59 E
Waigeo 35 0 20S 130 40 E
Waihi 43 37 23S 175 52 E
Waihou → 43 37 15S 175 40 E
Waikabubak 35 9 45S 119 25 E
Waikaremoana 43 38 42S 177 12 E
Waikari 43 42 58S 172 41 E
Waikato → 43 37 23S 174 43 E
Waikerie 45 34 9S 140 0 E
Waikokopu 43 39 3S 177 52 E
Waikouaiti 43 45 36S 170 41 E
Waimate 43 44 45S 171 3 E
Wainganga → 32 18 50N 79 55 E
Waingapu 35 9 35S 120 11 E
Wainwright, Canada 65 52 50N 110 50W
Wainwright, U.S.A. 60 70 39N 160 1W
Waiouru 43 39 28S 175 41 E
Waipara 43 43 3S 172 46 E
Waipawa 43 39 56S 176 38 E
Waipiro 43 38 2S 178 22 E
Waipu 43 35 59S 174 29 E
Waipukurau 43 40 1S 176 33 E
Wairakei 43 38 37S 176 6 E
Wairarapa, L. 43 41 14S 175 15 E
Wairoa 43 39 3S 177 25 E
Waitaki → 43 44 56S 171 7 E
Waitara 43 38 59S 174 15 E
Waitsburg 72 46 15N 118 0W
Waiuku 43 37 15S 174 45 E
Wajima 36 37 30N 137 0 E
Wajir 54 1 42N 40 5 E
Wakasa-Wan 36 35 40N 135 30 E
Wakatipu, L. 43 45 5S 168 33 E
Wakaw 65 52 39N 105 44W
Wakayama 36 34 15N 135 15 E
Wakayama-ken □ 36 33 50N 135 30 E
Wake Forest 69 35 58N 78 30W
Wake I. 3 19 18N 166 36 E
Wakefield, N.Z. 43 41 24S 173 5 E
Wakefield, U.K. 6 53 41N 1 31W
Wakefield, U.S.A. 70 46 28N 89 53W
Wakema 33 16 30N 95 11 E
Wakkanai 36 45 28N 141 35 E
Wakkerstroom 57 27 24S 30 10 E
Wakool 45 35 28S 144 23 E
Wakool → 45 35 5S 143 33 E
Wakre 35 0 19S 131 5 E
Wakuach L. 63 55 34N 67 32W
Wałbrzych 14 50 45N 16 18 E
Walbury Hill 7 51 22N 1 28W
Walcha 45 30 55S 151 31 E
Walcheren 11 51 30N 3 35 E
Walcott 72 41 50N 106 55W
Waldburg Ra. 47 24 40S 117 35 E
Walden 72 40 47N 106 20W
Waldport 72 44 30N 124 2W
Waldron 71 34 52N 94 4W
Wales □ 7 52 30N 3 30W
Walgett 45 30 0S 148 5 E
Walhalla, Australia 45 37 56S 146 29 E
Walhalla, U.S.A. 65 48 55N 97 55W
Walkaway 47 28 59S 114 48 E
Walker 70 47 4N 94 35W
Walker L., Man., Canada 65 54 42N 95 57W
Walker L., Qué., Canada 63 50 20N 67 11W
Walker L., U.S.A. 72 38 56N 118 46W
Walkerston 44 21 11S 149 8 E
Wall 70 44 0N 102 14W
Walla Walla 72 46 3N 118 25W
Wallabadah 44 17 57S 142 15 E
Wallace, Idaho, U.S.A. 72 47 30N 116 0W
Wallace, N.C., U.S.A. 69 34 44N 77 59W
Wallace, Nebr., U.S.A. 70 40 51N 101 12W
Wallaceburg 62 42 34N 82 23W
Wallachia = Valahia 15 44 35N 25 0 E
Wallal 45 26 32S 146 7 E
Wallal Downs 46 19 47S 120 40 E
Wallambin, L. 47 30 57S 117 35 E
Wallaroo 45 33 56S 137 39 E
Wallasey 6 53 26N 3 2W
Wallerawang 45 33 25S 150 4 E
Wallhallow 44 17 50S 135 50 E
Wallingford 6 51 40N 1 15W
Wallis & Futuna 40 13 18S 176 10W
Wallowa 72 45 40N 117 35W
Wallowa, Mts. 72 45 20N 117 30W
Wallsend, Australia 45 32 55S 151 40 E
Wallsend, U.K. 6 54 59N 1 30W
Wallula 72 46 3N 118 59W
Wallumbilla 45 26 33S 149 9 E
Walmsley, L. 65 63 25N 108 36W
Walney, Isle of 6 54 5N 3 15W
Walnut Ridge 71 36 7N 90 58W
Walsall 7 52 36N 1 59W
Walsenburg 71 37 42N 104 45W
Walsh 71 37 28N 102 15W
Walsh → 44 16 31S 143 42 E
Walsh P.O. 44 16 40S 144 0 E
Walterboro 69 32 53N 80 40W
Walters 71 34 25N 98 20W
Waltham Sta. 62 45 57N 76 57W
Waltman 72 43 8N 107 15W
Walvisbaai 56 23 0S 14 28 E
Wamba 54 2 10N 27 57 E
Wamego 70 39 14N 96 22W
Wamena 35 4 4S 138 57 E
Wamsasi 35 3 27S 126 7 E
Wana 32 32 20N 69 32 E
Wanaaring 45 29 38S 144 9 E
Wanaka L. 43 44 33S 169 7 E
Wan'an 39 26 26N 114 49 E
Wanapiri 35 4 30S 135 59 E
Wanapitei L. 62 46 45N 80 40W
Wanbi 45 34 46S 140 17 E
Wanda Shan 38 46 0N 132 0 E
Wandoan 45 26 5S 149 55 E
Wangal 35 6 8S 134 9 E
Wanganella 45 35 6S 144 49 E
Wanganui 43 39 56S 175 3 E
Wangaratta 45 36 21S 146 19 E
Wangdu 38 38 40N 115 7 E
Wangerooge 14 53 47N 7 52 E
Wangiwangi 35 5 22S 123 37 E
Wangjiang 39 30 10N 116 42 E
Wangqing 38 43 12N 129 42 E
Wanless 65 54 11N 101 21W
Wanning 39 18 48N 110 22 E
Wanquan 38 40 50N 114 40 E
Wanxian 39 30 42N 108 20 E
Wanyuan 39 32 4N 108 3 E
Wanzai 39 28 7N 114 30 E
Wapakoneta 68 40 35N 84 10W
Wapato 72 46 30N 120 25W
Wapawekka L. 65 54 55N 104 40W
Wapikopa L. 62 52 56N 87 53W
Wapsipinicon → 70 41 44N 90 19W
Warangal 32 17 58N 79 35 E
Waratah 44 41 30S 145 30 E
Waratah B. 45 38 54S 146 5 E
Warburton, Vic., Australia 45 37 47S 145 42 E
Warburton, W. Austral., Australia 47 26 8S 126 35 E
Warburton Ra. 47 25 55S 126 28 E
Ward 43 41 49S 174 11 E
Ward → 45 26 28S 146 6 E
Ward Cove 64 55 25N 132 43W
Warden 57 27 50S 29 0 E
Wardha 32 20 45N 78 39 E
Wardha → 32 19 57N 79 11 E
Wardlow 64 50 56N 111 31W
Ware 64 57 26N 125 41W
Warialda 45 29 29S 150 33 E
Wariap 35 1 30S 134 5 E
Warkopi 35 1 12S 134 9 E
Warley 7 52 30N 2 0W
Warm Springs 73 38 16N 116 32W
Warman 65 52 19N 106 30W
Warmbad, Namibia 56 28 25S 18 42 E
Warmbad, S. Africa 57 24 51S 28 19 E
Warnambool Downs 44 22 48S 142 52 E
Warnemünde 14 54 9N 12 5 E
Warner 64 49 17N 112 12W
Warner Mts. 72 41 30N 120 20W
Warner Robins 69 32 41N 83 36W
Waroona 47 32 50S 115 58 E
Warragul 45 38 10S 145 58 E
Warrawagine 46 20 51S 120 42 E
Warrego → 45 30 24S 145 21 E
Warrego Ra. 44 24 58S 146 0 E
Warren, Australia 45 31 42S 147 51 E
Warren, Ark., U.S.A. 71 33 35N 92 3W
Warren, Mich., U.S.A. 68 42 31N 83 2W
Warren, Minn., U.S.A. 70 48 12N 96 46W
Warren, Ohio, U.S.A. 68 41 18N 80 52W
Warren, Pa., U.S.A. 68 41 52N 79 10W
Warrenpoint 9 54 7N 6 15W
Warrensburg 70 38 45N 93 45W
Warrenton, S. Africa 56 28 9S 24 47 E
Warrenton, U.S.A. 72 46 11N 123 59W
Warrenville 45 25 48S 147 22 E
Warri 53 5 30N 5 41 E
Warrina 45 28 12S 135 50 E
Warrington, U.K. 6 53 25N 2 38W
Warrington, U.S.A. 69 30 22N 87 16W
Warrnambool 45 38 25S 142 30 E
Warroad 70 48 54N 95 19W
Warsa 35 0 47S 135 55 E
Warsaw = Warszawa 15 52 13N 21 0 E
Warsaw 68 41 14N 85 50W
Warszawa 15 52 13N 21 0 E
Warta → 14 52 35N 14 39 E
Warthe = Warta → 14 52 35N 14 39 E
Waru 35 3 30S 130 36 E
Warwick, Australia 45 28 10S 152 1 E
Warwick, U.K. 7 52 17N 1 36W
Warwick, U.S.A. 68 41 43N 71 25W
Warwick □ 7 52 20N 1 30W
Wasatch Ra. 72 40 30N 111 15W
Wasbank 57 28 15S 30 9 E
Wasco, Calif., U.S.A. 73 35 37N 119 16W
Wasco, Oreg., U.S.A. 72 45 36N 120 46W
Waseca 70 44 3N 93 31W
Wasekamio L. 65 56 45N 108 45W
Wash, The 6 52 58N 0 20 E
Washburn, N. Dak., U.S.A. 70 47 17N 101 0W
Washburn, Wis., U.S.A. 70 46 38N 90 55W
Washim 32 20 3N 77 0 E
Washington, D.C., U.S.A. 68 38 52N 77 0W
Washington, Ga., U.S.A. 69 33 45N 82 45W
Washington, Ind., U.S.A. 68 38 40N 87 8W
Washington, Iowa, U.S.A. 70 41 20N 91 45W
Washington, Mo., U.S.A. 70 38 35N 91 1W
Washington, N.C., U.S.A. 69 35 35N 77 1W
Washington, Pa., U.S.A. 68 40 10N 80 20W
Washington, Utah, U.S.A. 73 37 10N 113 30W
Washington □ 72 47 45N 120 30W
Washington, Mt. 68 44 15N 71 18W
Washington I. 68 45 24N 86 54W
Wasian 35 1 47S 133 19 E
Wasior 35 2 43S 134 30 E
Waskaiowaka, L. 65 56 33N 96 23W
Waskesiu Lake 65 53 55N 106 5W
Wassenaar 11 52 8N 4 24 E
Waswanipi 62 49 40N 76 29W
Waswanipi, L. 62 49 35N 76 40W
Watangpone 35 4 29S 120 25 E
Water Park Pt. 44 22 56S 150 47 E
Water Valley 71 34 9N 89 38W
Waterberge 57 24 10S 28 0 E
Waterbury 68 41 32N 73 0W
Waterbury L. 65 58 10N 104 22W
Waterford 9 52 16N 7 8W
Waterford □ 9 52 10N 7 40W
Waterford Harb. 9 52 10N 6 58W
Waterhen L., Man., Canada 65 52 10N 99 40W
Waterhen L., Sask., Canada 65 54 28N 108 25W
Waterloo, Belgium 11 50 43N 4 25 E
Waterloo, Canada 62 43 30N 80 32W
Waterloo, S. Leone 50 8 26N 13 8W
Waterloo, Ill., U.S.A. 70 38 22N 90 6W
Waterloo, Iowa, U.S.A. 70 42 27N 92 20W
Watersmeet 70 46 15N 89 12W
Waterton Glacier Int. Peace Park 72 48 35N 113 40W
Watertown, N.Y., U.S.A. 68 43 58N 75 57W
Watertown, S. Dak., U.S.A. 70 44 57N 97 5W
Watertown, Wis., U.S.A. 70 43 15N 88 45W
Waterval-Boven 57 25 40S 30 18 E
Waterville, Maine, U.S.A. 63 44 35N 69 40W
Waterville, Wash., U.S.A. 72 47 38N 120 1W
Watervliet 68 42 46N 73 43W
Wates 35 7 51S 110 10 E
Watford 7 51 38N 0 23W
Watford City 70 47 50N 103 23W
Wathaman → 65 57 16N 102 59W
Watheroo 47 30 15S 116 0W
Watkins Glen 68 42 25N 76 55W
Watling I. = San Salvador 75 24 0N 74 40W
Watonga 71 35 51N 98 24W
Watrous, Canada 65 51 40N 105 25W
Watrous, U.S.A. 71 35 50N 104 55W
Watsa 54 3 4N 29 30 E
Watseka 68 40 45N 87 45W
Watson, Australia 47 30 29S 131 31 E
Watson, Canada 65 52 10N 104 30W
Watson Lake 60 60 6N 128 49W
Watsonville 73 36 55N 121 49W
Wattiwarriganna Cr. → 45 28 57S 136 10 E
Watuata = Batuata 35 6 12S 122 42 E
Watubela, Kepulauan 35 4 28S 131 35 E
Waubay 70 45 22N 97 17W
Waubra 45 37 21S 143 39 E
Wauchope 45 31 28S 152 45 E
Wauchula 69 27 35N 81 50W
Waugh 65 49 40N 95 11W
Waukegan 68 42 22N 87 54W
Waukesha 68 43 0N 88 15W
Waukon 70 43 14N 91 33W
Wauneta 70 40 27N 101 25W
Waupaca 70 44 22N 89 8W
Waupun 70 43 38N 88 44W
Waurika 71 34 12N 98 0W
Wausau 70 44 57N 89 40W
Wautoma 70 44 3N 89 20W
Wauwatosa 68 43 6N 87 59W
Wave Hill 46 17 32S 131 0 E
Waveney → 7 52 24N 1 20 E
Waverley 43 39 46S 174 37 E
Waverly, Iowa, U.S.A. 70 42 40N 92 30W
Waverly, N.Y., U.S.A. 68 42 0N 76 33W
Wavre 11 50 43N 4 38 E
Wâw 51 7 45N 28 1 E
Wâw al Kabîr 51 25 20N 16 43 E
Wawa 62 47 59N 84 47W
Wawanesa 65 49 36N 99 40W
Waxahachie 71 32 22N 96 53W
Way, L. 47 26 45S 120 16 E
Wayabula Rau 35 2 29N 128 17 E
Wayatinah 44 42 19S 146 27 E
Waycross 69 31 12N 82 25W
Wayne, Nebr., U.S.A. 70 42 16N 97 0W
Wayne, W. Va., U.S.A. 68 38 15N 82 27W
Waynesboro, Ga., U.S.A. 69 33 6N 82 1W
Waynesboro, Miss., U.S.A. 69 31 40N 88 39W
Waynesboro, Pa., U.S.A. 68 39 46N 77 32W
Waynesboro, Va., U.S.A. 68 38 4N 78 57W
Waynesburg 68 39 54N 80 12W
Waynesville 69 35 31N 83 0W
Waynoka 71 36 38N 98 53W
Wazirabad 32 32 30N 74 8 E
We 34 5 51N 95 18 E
Weald, The 7 51 7N 0 9 E
Wear → 6 54 55N 1 22W
Weatherford, Okla., U.S.A. 71 35 30N 98 45W
Weatherford, Tex., U.S.A. 71 32 45N 97 48W
Weaverville 72 40 44N 122 56W
Webb City 71 37 9N 94 30W
Webster, S. Dak., U.S.A. 70 45 24N 97 33W
Webster, Wis., U.S.A. 70 45 53N 92 25W
Webster City 70 42 30N 93 50W
Webster Green 70 38 38N 90 20W
Webster Springs 68 38 30N 80 25W
Weda 35 0 21N 127 50 E
Weda, Teluk 35 0 30N 127 50 E
Weddell I. 80 51 50S 61 0W
Wedderburn 45 36 26S 143 33 E
Wedgeport 63 43 44N 65 59W
Wee Waa 45 30 11S 149 26 E
Weed 72 41 29N 122 22W
Weemelah 45 29 2S 149 15 E
Weenen 57 28 48S 30 7 E
Weert 11 51 15N 5 43 E
Wei He →, Hebei, China 38 36 10N 115 45 E
Wei He →, Shaanxi, China 39 34 38N 110 15 E
Weifang 38 36 44N 119 7 E
Weihai 38 37 30N 122 6 E
Weimar 14 51 0N 11 20 E
Weinan 39 34 31N 109 29 E
Weipa 44 12 40S 141 50 E
Weir →, Australia 45 28 20S 149 50 E
Weir →, Canada 65 56 54N 93 21W
Weir River 65 56 49N 94 6W
Weiser 72 44 10N 117 0W
Weishan 39 34 47N 117 5 E
Weiyuan 38 35 7N 104 10 E
Weizhou Dao 39 21 0N 109 5 E
Wejherowo 15 54 35N 18 12 E
Wekusko L. 65 54 40N 99 50W
Welbourn Hill 45 27 21S 134 6 E
Welch 68 37 29N 81 36W
Welkom 56 28 0S 26 46 E
Welland 62 43 0N 79 15W
Welland → 6 52 43N 0 10W
Wellesley Is. 44 16 42S 139 30 E
Wellin 11 50 5N 5 6 E
Wellingborough 7 52 18N 0 41W
Wellington, Australia 45 32 35S 148 59 E
Wellington, Canada 62 43 57N 77 20W
Wellington, N.Z. 43 41 19S 174 46 E
Wellington, S. Africa 56 33 38S 19 1 E
Wellington, Salop, U.K. 6 52 42N 2 31W
Wellington, Somerset, U.K. 7 50 58N 3 13W
Wellington, Colo., U.S.A. 70 40 43N 105 0W
Wellington, Kans., U.S.A. 71 37 15N 97 25W
Wellington, Nev., U.S.A. 72 38 47N 119 28W
Wellington, Tex., U.S.A. 71 34 55N 100 13W
Wellington □ 43 40 8S 175 36 E
Wellington, I. 80 49 30S 75 0W
Wellington, L. 45 38 6S 147 20 E
Wells, Norfolk, U.K. 6 52 57N 0 51 E
Wells, Somerset, U.K. 7 51 12N 2 39W
Wells, Minn., U.S.A. 70 43 44N 93 45W
Wells, Nev., U.S.A. 72 41 8N 115 0W
Wells Gray Prov. Park 64 52 30N 120 15W
Wells L. 47 26 44S 123 15 E
Wellsboro 68 41 45N 77 20W
Wellsville, Mo., U.S.A. 70 39 4N 91 30W
Wellsville, N.Y., U.S.A. 68 42 9N 77 53W
Wellsville, Ohio, U.S.A. 68 40 36N 80 40W
Wellsville, Utah, U.S.A. 72 41 35N 111 59W
Wellton 73 32 39N 114 6W
Wels 14 48 9N 14 1 E
Welshpool 7 52 40N 3 9W
Wem 6 52 52N 2 45W
Wen Xian 39 32 43N 104 36 E
Wenatchee 72 47 30N 120 17W
Wenchang 39 19 38N 110 42 E
Wenchi 50 7 46N 2 8W
Wenchow = Wenzhou 39 28 0N 120 38 E
Wendell 72 42 50N 114 42W